An Engineering Approach to Computer Networking:

ATM Networks, the Internet, and the
Telephone Network

Addison-Wesley Professional Computing Series

Brian W. Kernighan, Consulting Editor

An Engineering Approach to Computer Networking:

ATM Networks, the Internet, and the Telephone Network

S. Keshav

ADDISON-WESLEY

An Imprint of Addison Wesley Longman, Inc.

Reading, Massachusetts • Harlow, England • Menlo Park, California
Berkeley, California • Don Mills, Ontario • Sydney
Bonn • Amsterdam • Tokyo • Mexico City

Many of the designations used by manufacturers and sellers to distinguish their products are claimed as trademarks. Where those designations appear in this book and Addison-Wesley was aware of a trademark claim, the designations have been printed in initial caps or all caps.

The authors and publishers have taken care in the preparation of this book, but make no expressed or implied warranty of any kind and assume no responsibility for errors or omissions. No liability is assumed for incidental or consequential damages in connection with or arising out of the use of the information or programs contained herein.

The publisher offers discounts on this book when ordered in quantity for special sales. For more information, please contact:

Corporate & Professional Publishing Group
Addison-Wesley Publishing Company
One Jacob Way
Reading, Massachusetts 01867

Library of Congress Cataloging-in-Publication Data

Keshav, Srinivasan.
    An engineering approach to computer networking : ATM networks, the internet, and the telephone network / S. Keshav.
        p.   cm.—(Addison-Wesley professional computing series)
    Includes bibliographical references and index.
    ISBN 0-201-63442-2
    1. Computer networks.   2. Asynchronous transfer mode.   3. Internet (Computer network)   4. Telephone systems.   I. Title.   II. Series.
TK5105.5.K48   1997
004.6—dc21   97–8249
                                                                      CIP

ISBN   0-201-63442-2

2 3 4 5 6 7   MA   00 99 98 97

2nd Printing   September, 1997

To
Appa and Amma,
Nicole and Maya

Contents

Preface

The world is surging toward a digital revolution where computer networks mediate every aspect of modern life, from paying bills to buying real estate, and from reading a book to watching a film. Computer networks are complex systems that almost magically link tens of millions of computers and more than a billion telephones around the world. A single mouse-click in a Web browser can download text, images, and animations from a computer hundreds or thousands of miles away. With a satellite or cellular telephone, even the most intrepid explorer in the remotest corner of the Earth can call home. How do we build these marvelous webs of interconnection? The goal of this book is to introduce readers to *what* lies at the basis of computer networks, and *why* they work the way they do.

This book is based on a course that I taught at the Indian Institute of Technology, Delhi, India, in the spring of 1993. My aim was to teach students why networks were built the way they were. I wanted them to question every design decision, and to understand how these decisions would change if we changed the assumptions. I call this an *engineering* approach to computer networking.

Perhaps it is easiest to appreciate this approach by comparing it with some other approaches. Suppose you wanted to route packets in a computer network. A *protocol* approach would describe the routing protocols in common use and their packet formats and algorithms, and perhaps compare several routing protocols. An *analytical* approach would model the network as a graph, assume a traffic distribution from every source to every destination, then compute optimal routing. In my opinion, both these approaches, though important, miss the point. A purely protocol approach tells the reader *how* routing works, but not *why* it was designed that way. The success of an analytical approach depends critically on the assumptions it makes. Unfortunately, because of the complexities of the real world, to make the problem tractable, the analyst must make many simplifying assumptions. In my experience, this simplification leads to "toy" models that do not explain what is really important, and what details we can ignore. In contrast, the engineering approach is to begin by identifying the fundamental constraints on the problem, make reasonable "real-world" assumptions, and then examine several alternative solutions, trading off their pros and cons. An engineer recognizes that no solution is perfect, but that every solution represents a particular trade-off between cost and benefit. This book focuses on identifying the fundamental problems and the trade-offs in solving them.

The second aspect of an engineering approach is to learn by doing. This book is meant to be used with implementation exercises on the Internet and on the REAL network simulator. These exercises, which are available on-line at http://www.aw.com/cp/keshav/engcom.html, allow students to learn protocol design and implementation hands-on.

Unlike other textbooks in the area, this book simultaneously studies the principles underlying the Internet, the telephone network, and *asynchronous transfer mode (ATM)* networks. The Internet is the most successful embodiment of a data network, and its study needs no further justification. The global telephone network is arguably the world's largest computer network, though it is specialized to carry voice. Unfortunately, few outside the telephone industry know much about how the telephone network operates, perhaps because of the layers of acronyms and arcana that surround its operations. This book is a small attempt to rectify the situation. Finally, many see ATM networks as the future of computer networking. Although this may not be true, ATM networks are interesting because they draw on experience with the telephone network and the Internet to build an integrated services network that provides end-to-end quality of service. This ambitious goal has led to a unique set of design decisions that have influenced both networking research and commercial networking products. Thus, ATM networks are well worth studying.

Target audience

I assume that readers will have some familiarity with data structures and algorithms, operating systems, elementary algebra, and computer architecture. Deeper material assumes knowledge of calculus and probability. However, most concepts do not require mathematical sophistication beyond a first undergraduate course. In particular, the book almost completely avoids use of queuing theory. Although an appreciation of queuing theory is important in engineering computer networks, I feel queuing theory is best studied as a separate course: to really understand its strengths and its domain of applicability, one needs a deep understanding of the topic that cannot be provided by a book such as this.

The bulk of this book is written at a level suitable for first-year graduate students in computer science or electrical engineering. It is also suitable for advanced undergraduate seniors. Students who intend to work in the area of computer networking or related areas should probably read through the entire text and attempt all the exercises.

A number of features make it easy to use for a first undergraduate course. First, every chapter is self-contained, so that instructors can skip entire chapters if necessary. Second, each topic is developed from first principles, with little assumption about the background of the reader, other than some familiarity with mathematics and operating systems. A more sophisticated development that follows from these first principles is marked with vertical sidebars and can be ignored in a first course. Third, most topics are presented at an intuitive level, with little mathematical or algorithmic formalism. Finally, complete solutions are provided to instructors for all numerical exercises.

The book is also targeted at professionals in the field, and at researchers in other areas who want an introduction to the current research frontiers in computer networking. A comprehensive index helps in locating a topic quickly. Moreover, the glossary is keyed to the section or subsection that describes the topic, so that one can rapidly look up the context for a technical term. For those interested in pursuing a topic further, an extensive annotated bibliography references key papers in the field.

Organization

The book has three sections. The first section is an overview of three important networking technologies: telephony (Chapter 2), Internet (Chapter 3), and ATM (Chapter 4). Each introductory chapter describes key elements in the technology, some history, and my perception of the important challenges for the technology.

The second section describes the pieces that come together to form a network. Most chapters in this section begin with an overview of a problem and a taxonomy of possible solutions. We then study a number of representative solutions, concentrating on the set of trade-offs they represent. We can apply most of these solutions to any protocol layer, so we study them independently of protocol layering.

The second section starts with an introductory chapter on protocol layering (Chapter 5) and an overview of the art and science of system design (Chapter 6). These chapters provide a "toolkit" of common system design techniques that we will use in subsequent chapters. Chapter 7 introduces the issue of multiple access, which arises in contexts as diverse as satellite networks, cellular telephony, and local area networks. Chapter 8 describes switching, which is fundamental to the operation of all nontrivial networks. In order to provide end-to-end quality of service, switches (and other multiplexing points) must implement a scheduling algorithm. We study scheduling algorithms in Chapter 9. The next two chapters cover naming, addressing, and routing. At this point, the reader knows enough about how to put together a wide-area network. But, for the network to work efficiently, we need to add two more functionalities: error control and flow control. We study these in Chapters 12 and 13. As we build larger and larger networks, the problem of network control becomes significant. We study this in Chapter 14.

The third section applies the tools and techniques discussed in the preceding chapters to understanding and implementing some common protocols. Chapter 15 presents a detailed description of protocol headers in the telephone network, Internet, and ATM networks, tying together the material in the previous chapters. Finally, Chapter 16 is a survey of protocol implementation techniques.

Style conventions

Textbooks, almost by definition, tend to be boring. A dry assemblage of facts does little to bring out the controversies, the intellectual fights, and the wide-eyed what-if questions that make networking such an interesting and challenging field. I have attempted to capture some of these in what I call *engineering boxes*. These boxes go off on a tangent from the text, question standard assumptions, and present viewpoints on the fringe of the mainstream. They offer a subjective commentary on the objective and dry material in the text.

I firmly believe in the use of numerical examples to explain concepts. Solved numerical examples throughout the book reinforce the use of back-of-the-envelope calculations in system design, and simultaneously introduce the student to "real-world" constants that engineers use in their calculations. I hope these examples will motivate readers to do their own rough calculations as they embark on a system design.

> Advanced material is in smaller font and set off with vertical sidebars as shown in this paragraph. Such material can be ignored in a first reading, or in an undergradute course, with no loss of continuity.

Usage guidelines

In a graduate class, I recommend that the instructor assign Chapters 1–5 as a single reading assignment at the end of the first class. The material here should serve primarily as a review. Subsequent chapters, starting with Chapter 6, can be covered in two or three one-hour lectures per chapter, except Chapter 11, which will require four lectures. In my courses, I used the first hour to cover principles, and the second (and, if necessary, third) to cover specific solutions. I also recommend choosing some exercises for homework and assigning one implementation exercise every two weeks.

In an undergraduate class, the instructor could spend the first several lectures on the first six chapters. The remaining chapters could be covered at the discretion of the instructor, perhaps skipping advanced material. In a first course, Chapters 13, 14, and 16 and advanced topics in Chapters 7, 8, 9, 11, and 12 can be left out entirely.

A reader unfamiliar with the field should probably first read Chapters 1–4. Subseqent chapters may be read as the occasion arises. Much of the material can also be accessed by way of the keyed glossary.

Acknowledgments

My sincere thanks to my management at AT&T Bell Laboratories and AT&T Labs, in particular Sandy Fraser, Chuck Kalmanek, Brian Kernighan, Ravi Sethi, Peter Weinberger, and Mihalis Yannakakis for allowing me to work on the book full time for over a year. I could not have undertaken this project without their generous support.

I have drawn upon many people in the course of writing this book. During my visit to the Indian Institute of Technology, Delhi, where work on this book began, I had the good fortune to interact with Professors B. N. Jain, S. N. Maheshwari, and Huzur Saran. Detailed class notes by Rajeev Leekha and V. N. Padmanabhan gave me the confidence to start writing this book and formed the core of the first draft. My thanks to them.

I gratefully acknowledge the support and good advice from my friends and colleagues at AT&T Bell Laboratories: Joe Condon, Sandy Fraser, Milan Jukl, Chuck Kalmanek, Hemant Kanakia, Alan Kaplan, Brian Kernighan, Rajiv Laroia, Bill Marshall, Partho Mishra, Sam Morgan, K. K. Ramakrishnan, Bob Restrick, Norm Schryer, Ravi Sethi, David Tse, John Venutolo, and Mihalis Yannakakis. In particular, Alan Kaplan's detailed review of the first two drafts cleared up many errors and inconsistencies, and added an insider's perspective on telephone networking. I also drew upon many colleagues to clear up specific questions. These include Tony Ballardie (UC London), Alan Berenbaum (Bell Labs), Jean Bolot (INRIA), Tony DeSimone (AT&T Research), Bharat Doshi (AT&T Research), Andrew Odlyzko (AT&T Research), Craig Partridge (BBN), K. K. Ramakrishnan (AT&T Research), Nambi Seshadri (AT&T Research), and Sandeep Sibal (AT&T Research). Special thanks to Pawan Goel at UT Austin for his detailed and perceptive comments on Chapter 9.

I received insightful comments from a number of reviewers on earlier drafts of the book. I received comments on the first draft from Rajeev Agrawal (U Wisconsin, Madison), Cagatay Buyukkoc (AT&T Research), Mark Clement (Brigham Young), Matthias Grossglauser (AT&T Research), Peter Haverlock (Bay Networks), Sugih Jamin (U Michigan, Ann Arbor), Alan Kaplan (AT&T Research), Brian Kernighan (Bell Labs), Doug McIlroy (Bell Labs), Sam Morgan (Bell Labs), Will Morse (BHP Petroleum), Badri Nathan (Andersen Consulting), Craig Partridge (BBN), Vern Paxson (Lawrence Berkeley Lab), Daniel Pitt (HP), Huzur Saran (IIT Delhi), Matthew Scott (Fore Systems), Rosen Sharma (Stanford), Harry Singh (Hitachi), David Tse (UC Berkeley), Roya Ulrich (ICSI), and Hui Zhang (Carnegie Mellon U). I received comments on the second draft from John Gulbenkian (Cerf Net), Alan Kaplan (AT&T Research), Brian Kernighan (Bell Labs), Sugih Jamin (U Michigan, Ann Arbor), Will Morse (BHP Petroleum), Daniel Pitt (HP), Ravi Prakash (FTP Software), Matthew Scott (Fore Systems), Huzur Saran (IIT Delhi), and Hui Zhang (Carnegie Mellon U). My thanks to them all.

I got valuable feedback, in the form of bug reports, from students in my courses at IIT Delhi in Spring 1993, Columbia University in Fall 1995, and Cornell in Fall 1996. My thanks to the students who took my course at IIT Delhi, in particular Surinder Singh Anand, Rahul Garg, Rajeev Leekha, R. N. Moorthy, V. N. Padmanabhan, R. P. Rustagi, Rosen Sharma, and Puneet Sharma. I received bug reports from Anwar Siddiqui and Kwok-Shing Cheng at Columbia University. From Cornell, I received feedback and bug reports from Chris Decenzo, Dan DiPasquo, Dan Gelb, Andrew Moore, Hoai Nguyen, Nikhil Shrikhande, Teerin Suwantaemee, Edward Wayt, James Yang, and Howard Yen. The second draft was used in Fall 1996 at U. Michigan Ann Arbor by Prof. Sugih Jamin. I received bug reports from Sunghyun Choi and David Nettleman at Ann Arbor.

This reprint incorporates bug reports I received from Efthymios Koutsianis (Sheffield University), Jose Landivar (University of Buffalo), Laurent Mathy (Lancaster University), and Subramaniam Vincent (ISI). Thanks to them all.

The production of the book was developed under the able guidance of John Fuller, Lana Langlois, and John Wait at Addison-Wesley. They kept the book on track, got numerous reviews, and helped me focus on the book. My thanks to them.

Last but not least, this book would not have been possible without the loving care of my wife Nicole. Thank you.

Online content

This book is accompanied by a World Wide Web site (http://www.aw.com/cp/keshav/ engcom.html) that contains a range of support materials:

- Microsoft PowerPoint slides covering the material in the book.
- A multithreaded, packet-level network simulator (called REAL) that allows users to simulate arbitrary protocols written in C.
- Simulation exercises, using REAL, on multiple access, error control, flow control, routing, and scheduling. The exercises come with a template for students and a full solution for instructors.
- A bibliography, with pointers to web sites referred to in the text.
- A searchable glossary.
- Solutions to all exercises (accessible only by instructors).
- Errata.

In closing

I believe that you cannot really learn something until you have used it to solve a problem. I urge you to attempt the review questions and exercises. Doing the exercises, or better yet, using the material to solve a real problem in a real network, will teach you more about networking than reading ten books about it. My aim is that you, after reading this book, will understand how to engineer computer networks. Perhaps it will entice you into a career in networking, or into doing research in the many open problems in this area. Whatever your purpose, I hope you will enjoy reading the book.

Please send all comments, suggestions, and errata to me at the following: skeshav@ cs.cornell.edu.

Good luck!

S. Keshav

Ithaca, NY
December 1996
http://www.cs.cornell.edu/home/skeshav

Section 1

Introduction

Chapter 1

Atoms, Bits, and Networks

1.1 Introduction

The world's economy today is devoted primarily to manufacturing, distributing, and retailing things you can see and touch, such as food, cars, and computers. Creating and distributing *information*, however, is playing an increasingly important economic role. One can argue that the primary activities of enormous industries such as publishing, banking, and film making are the creation and dissemination of information. These activities may well dominate the economy of the future.

We can represent information in either analog or digital form. Traditional representations are usually analog. For example, an invoice printed on a sheet of paper represents the information content of the invoice in analog (paper) form. Similarly, we can use celluloid film to create an analog representation of the information content of a motion picture. *Digitization* is the conversion of an analog representation to digital format using zeroes and ones, or *bits*. For example, optically scanning an invoice creates a digital bitmap that has almost exactly the same information content as the printed original (excepting quantization errors). Similarly, scanning each frame of a motion picture results in a digital representation of the information content of the film. Another way to view this dichotomy is to say that information stored in analog form uses *atoms*, but information stored in digital form uses *bits* [Negroponte 95].

Unlike analog representations, digital representations of information have three important properties. First, computers can easily manipulate information represented as bits. A printed photograph can be modified only by a trained touch-up artist. When represented as bits, the same photograph can be manipulated at will by a five-year-old!

The same holds true for films, text, or anything that can be digitized. Second, we can make as many copies of a digital representation as we wish, and every copy is *identical* to the original. Third, computer networks, such as the Internet, can be used to reliably and efficiently move bits. These three attributes make the representation of information using bits much more desirable than a corresponding analog representation, and they are the main motivations for the digital revolution.

Many objects in daily life are information represented as atoms instead of as bits. For example, a book is a collection of pages that carry picture or text information. A bill from the electric company carries information about how much electricity you consumed, and how much you must pay. Indeed, when you pay the bill with a check, you are sending some information to the electric company authorizing it to ask a bank to move some money from your account to theirs. Information in an analog form is pervasive in the modern world! However, we can make substantial gains in efficiency by moving information as bits instead. For example, if the electric company represented a bill as bits instead of a printed sheet of paper, it could send it to you as email so that it would reach you within minutes, instead of in the mail after many days. If you could pay your bills using bits in email, you could program your computer to pay your bills automatically when they became due. If everyone were to use computer networks to pay their bills, we would no longer need to cut down millions of trees for bills, envelopes, and stamps! It would also make life easier for the electric company, the bank, and you.

Consider an example closer to hand. You are reading a book printed on paper, though the same book also exists as a file on the computer I used to write it. It is more efficient to electronically mail this digital version to you than to print the file on paper, truck it to a warehouse, store it on a bookshelf, and wait for you to go to a bookstore and buy the book. If you could access the information content of a book as bits over a computer network, not only would it be far cheaper: books printed on paper might even become obsolete. The same holds true for music information sold as cassettes or CDs, for scholarly information published in journals, and so on.

Thus, computer networks, in conjunction with the digital representation of information, can radically alter entire industries, such as the music industry, the publishing industry, and the newspaper industry. The digitization of traditionally analog representations of information and the transmission and manipulation of digital information by computers are the driving forces behind the coming digital revolution [Negroponte 95]. After the revolution, we will no longer need to represent information in analog form. Instead, all information will be represented as infinitely manipulable, infinitely copyable bits. This revolution will likely reshape society, as did the agricultural and industrial revolutions in their day [BK 95, Penzias 89].

The digital revolution promises to lead to a strange new world, where vast torrents of bits will sweep across the face of the Earth, carrying conversations, electronic mail messages, music, films, art, photographs, lectures, scholarly journals, credit card verification messages, bills of lading, invoices, stock market quotations, medical consultations, and every kind of information under the sun. The success of the revolution, however, depends critically on the construction of computer networks that can move enormous quantities of bits reliably, and with the quality of service needed by each type of information. This then, is the topic of this book: how to engineer a computer network that can carry the information needs of the digital future, the network that some call the *Information Superhighway.*

1.2   Common network technologies

Before building the network of the future, we must first understand what exists. The two most successful computer networks at the present time are the telephone network and the Internet. Section 1 of the book, consisting of Chapters 1–4, is an overview of these networks presented at a level accessible to the interested layperson.

The telephone network interconnects more than a billion telephones worldwide. Though the interface provided to an end user is mostly analog voice, the bulk of the long-haul network carries digitized voice samples. Moreover, the network is controlled by a set of special purpose computers interconnected by an Internet-like computer network. Thus, we classify the telephone network as a digital computer network. **Chapter 2** is an introduction to the telephone network.

The Internet is the other major networking technology. It started as a research project in the late 1960s, but has since grown exponentially to interconnect tens of millions of computers around the world. At present the Internet carries computer data traffic almost exclusively, with little voice or video traffic. **Chapter 3** is an introduction to the Internet.

It is interesting to contrast the styles of the Internet and the telephone network. The Internet philosophy is to put intelligence at the endpoints, and to assume that the network may drop, mangle, and reorder data. It is up to the endpoints to maintain communication despite these impairments. Moreover, the network is not expected to maintain any information (or *state*) about the performance requirements of an endpoint. All packets are treated alike, no matter what bits they carry. Thus, an application cannot obtain a guarantee of performance, such as an assurance that the network will transfer information from end to end within a time bound. This makes it impossible, for example, to guarantee that a voice call placed on the Internet will sound "clean" with no drop-outs, echoes, unexpected call terminations, or prolonged delays. Experience shows that the Internet does a good job at carrying data, but a poor one at carrying anything that requires an end-to-end quality of service.

In contrast, the telephone network assumes that the endpoints are dumb, and that all the intelligence ought to be placed in the network. Moreover, the network is explicitly designed for a single application: digitized voice. Voice calls are guaranteed to receive sufficient bandwidth, a low delay, and zero loss. Unfortunately, as we will see in Chapter 4, the network achieves this at great expense. Specifically, even when a caller is not speaking, the network continues to reserve resources for the call. This wastes network resources that could otherwise be devoted to other callers. This is a fundamental reason why the telephone network is more expensive to operate than the Internet. Nevertheless, unlike the Internet, the telephone network can offer endpoints an end-to-end guarantee of quality of service.

The Holy Grail of computer networking is to design a network that has the flexibility and low cost of the Internet, yet offers the end-to-end quality-of-service guarantees of the telephone network. One approach to such a design is to add a quality-of-service mechanism to the Internet (we discuss this in Chapter 14). The other approach is to design a new network from scratch that has the desired properties. This is the stated goal of *asynchronous transfer mode* (*ATM*) networks, which we study in **Chapter 4.** Although it is too early to judge the extent to which ATM networks have achieved their goal, they are sure to play an important role in the future.

1.3   Networking concepts and techniques

Section 2 of the book, consisting of Chapters 5–14, is an introduction to some common networking concepts and techniques. These techniques are explained with examples from the three networks described in Section 1.

The section begins with **Chapter 5,** which introduces the concepts of a *protocol* and *protocol layering.* Protocols are the mortar that holds computer networks together. Much of network engineering lies in creating efficient, robust, and scalable protocols. In this chapter, we outline the services that network protocols must provide. This chapter also serves as an overview of the protocols used in the Internet.

A computer network is a complex system that brings together hardware and software to transport user information. A good designer can trade off cheaper hardware and software resources for more expensive ones to maximize system performance. In **Chapter 6,** we discuss some common system resources and techniques for trading them off. We use these techniques extensively in the rest of the book.

The remaining chapters in Section 2 focus on solutions to specific networking problems. **Chapter 7** discusses the multiple access problem, that is, how to share a medium where a transmission from one endpoint or *base station* can be heard by all the other endpoints. To avoid message garbling, if more than one station wants to transmit information simultaneously, we must somehow resolve the conflict. The chapter discusses several solutions to this problem.

We can avoid the multiple access problem by attaching each endpoint to a *switch* with a point-to-point link. A switch allows data arriving at any of its inputs to be transferred to any of its outputs. **Chapter 8** describes some common switching architectures and discusses how we can build switches that can handle hundreds or thousands of inputs.

Switching does not entirely avoid the multiple access problem. If two endpoints send data to the same switch for the same destination simultaneously, only one source can gain access to the destination. Data from the other source must be buffered and transmitted later. In general, a switch may receive data from several sources for the same destination, and, to avoid data loss, must buffer information. A *scheduling discipline* then decides the order in which the switch serves the buffered data. It turns out that the scheduling discipline has a critical role in providing end-to-end quality of service. We study scheduling and its role in providing quality-of-service guarantees in **Chapter 9.**

To allow an endpoint to send data to another endpoint, a network must allow endpoints to be associated with *names.* The source uses the destination's name to inform the network where to send the data. Names are typically human-readable, that is, variable length, with nearly arbitrary punctuation. Thus, they are hard for computers to parse. The network typically translates names to *addresses* which also refer to endpoints, but which are in a format more suitable for computer manipulation. We study naming and addressing in **Chapter 10.**

One of the hardest problems in building a network is to figure out how to route data from a source to an arbitrary destination that may well be halfway across the world. Worse, the source may want to send data to a set of destinations, and we may want to send as few copies of the data as possible. How can we determine the shortest path from a source to a destination, or the best tree along which to distribute data from a source to a set of destinations? This is the problem of *routing*, which we study in **Chapter 11.**

Data sent on a network may be corrupted, lost, or reordered. How can a source and destination cooperate in ensuring that they exchange bits reliably, and in order? We study this in **Chapter 12,** where we discuss *error control.* We study both *bit-level* and *packet-level* error detection and control. Bit-level error control is based on adding redundancy to messages to detect or correct bit inversions. Packet-level error control requires us to identify and retransmit lost packets.

Thus far, we have assumed that a network can carry all the traffic offered to it. This is a convenient fiction. In fact, sources must adjust their load so that they do not overload the network. To do so, they must either inform the network of their expected load and get clearance to begin transmission, or monitor the overall network load and reduce their flow rate when the network is overloaded. This is called *flow control,* and we study it in **Chapter 13.**

In **Chapter 14,** we study the problem of achieving end-to-end quality of service by managing traffic at multiple time scales. This is necessary to support the diverse applications that we expect will exploit the future networking infrastructure. This chapter brings together many of the techniques studied in the preceding chapters in a unified framework.

1.4   Engineering computer networks

Section 3 of the book, consisting of Chapters 15 and 16, applies the material in Section 2 to study some real protocols and their implementation. In **Chapter 15,** we dissect some common protocols used in the telephone network, the Internet, and ATM networks. The background material in Section 2 allows us to analyze these protocols in depth, albeit compactly.

Finally, **Chapter 16** is an introduction to protocol implementation techniques. We analyze several competing implementation techniques and their relative merits. We also study some rules of thumb for fast and efficient protocol implementations.

1.5   In closing

This chapter presents a bird's-eye view of the role of computer networking in the economy of the future. As more and more of the world turns to digital information, it will become increasingly economical to move bits instead of atoms representing bits. Computer networks, by moving bits efficiently, therefore provide critical infrastructure. The telephone network already is essential to the very survival of most industrial economies, and the Internet is fast taking its place alongside it. As computer networks increase in speed and geographical reach, we can expect them to play an even greater role in the future. This book presents a detailed description not only of current computer networks, but also of the principles and technologies that we expect will underlie the future Information Superhighway.

Chapter 2

The Telephone Network:
Concepts, History, and Challenges

Though the global telephone network is arguably the world's largest computer network, it is not recognized as such because it is specialized to carry voice. Besides voice, the network also carries video, facsimile, and telemetry data. It is enormous both in its reach and in the service it provides. More than a billion telephones interconnect a fourth of the world's population—from Argentina to Brunei, and from Yemen to Zambia. Though telephone service is more than a hundred years old, it is still growing rapidly because of innovations such as cellular telephones, pagers, and modems. In the United States alone, the largest telephone company, AT&T, carries nearly 200 million calls every day. In the intricacy of its interconnection, degree of organizational support, and economic importance, the telephone network far exceeds the Internet. Its size and success make it worthy of careful study.

2.1 Concepts

The telephone network offers a single basic service to its users: two-way, switched voice service with small end-to-end delays and a guarantee that a call, once accepted, will run to completion. It achieves this quality of service by setting up a *circuit* between the two endpoints. A circuit is a path from a source to a destination that is much like an electrical circuit, with signals flowing simultaneously in both directions (we also call this *full-duplex* communication). The network guarantees enough resources to each circuit to ensure that the service quality is met.

The telephone network consists of end-systems, usually ordinary telephones, but also fax machines and modems, connected by two levels of switches (Figure 2.1). A pair of wires connects each end-system to a *central office* (CO). This is called the *local loop*. The central office provides power for the operation of an end-system. It receives dialed digits and places calls on behalf of the end-system. It also digitizes incoming signals (typically voice), and sends them across the network to a remote end-system. From the perspective of the network, an end-system is a dumb device, and the network provides all the intelligence. Of course, with modem-equipped computers and microprocessor-controlled fax machines, end-systems are rapidly becoming more intelligent. This, however, has not significantly affected the architecture of the telephone network.

Figure 2.1 shows a highly simplified version of the U.S. telephone network, which typifies telephone networks around the world [Bellamy 91, BS 82]. End-systems connect to switches called *exchanges* in central offices, and exchanges connect to long-haul or *backbone* switches. The number of backbone switches is much smaller than the number of exchanges. For example, in the United States, there are about ten thousand exchanges, but fewer than five hundred backbone switches. The backbone network or *core* is nearly fully connected, that is, every switch on the backbone is logically one hop away from every other switch. When an exchange receives a call to an end-system attached to the same exchange (for example, a call from A to B in Figure 2.1), it creates a local path from the source to the destination end-system. If the call is not local (for example, from A to C or A to D), it forwards the call either to another exchange in the local area, or to the nearest switch in the backbone network. This switch in turn connects to the switch nearest to the destination exchange. Since backbone switches are one hop away from each other, choosing this path is easy. In some telephone networks, however, if the single-hop path is congested, the call is diverted to an alternate two-hop path. The destination exchange then connects the destination end-system to the originator.

Consider a call made from an end-system with telephone number 512-201-3212 to an end-system with number 613-555-1212. From the calling end-system's number, we know that it is in area code 512. When it dials the 613 number, its local exchange notices that

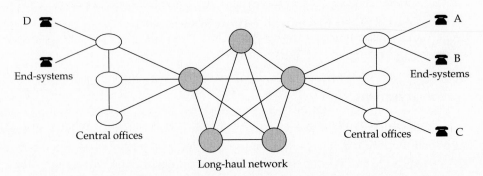

Figure 2.1: A simplified view of the U.S. telephone network. Circles represent long-haul (backbone) switches, which form a logically fully interconnected core. They are connected to central office switches, which, in turn, connect to end-systems such as telephones.

the area code (613) is different from its own (512). So, it forwards the call to the nearest backbone switch. At the backbone, the network establishes a one- or two-hop connection to the switch serving the 613 area, and from there to the exchange handling the 555 numbers. Finally, a connection is made to end-system 1212 in exchange 555. Thus, telephone numbers allow simple routing decisions that can be implemented with electromechanical switches, such as those used in early telephone networks. We will study telephone network routing in more detail in Chapter 11.

This picture of telephone network operation is highly simplified. In practice, a hundred years of evolution have substantially complicated the picture. For example, some central offices still forward analog voice to the backbone switches, so that backbone switches must be prepared to digitize incoming calls. Complexity also arises when the same backbone switch serves multiple area codes, or when an area code is spread over multiple exchanges. Moreover, multiple competing backbone networks may connect the local exchanges. Taken together, these details complicate what is, at its heart, a simple and robust technology.

Telephone numbers form a hierarchy, allowing distributed creation of new, globally unique telephone numbers. A central authority allocates each area or city a different *area code,* which is the first few digits of the telephone number, and each area assigns unique numbers to its exchanges. Each exchange in turn ensures that the end-systems within the exchange have unique numbers (except extensions). Thus, we can easily ensure that a telephone number is globally unique, which is essential for routing calls and billing.

A telephone number is a hint to its route. Although there may be more than one way to reach a particular end-system, the number identifies the components of the telephone network that the route *must* pass through. For example, the route to telephone number 512-224-3213 must pass through the backbone switch handling area code 512 and the 224 exchange, and it may also pass through other backbone switches and exchanges. For special area codes, such as 700, 800, 888, and 900 in the United States, the dialed number is used as an index to query a database that translates the number into a regular telephone number. Thus, for example, a call to 800-555-1212 may be translated to 512-643-4312. The service provider can change the translation depending on the source of the call, time of day, or other properties. This flexibility lets telephone customers access a wide variety of services using these special area codes.

We will study four components of the telephone network: *end-systems, transmission, switching,* and *signaling* [Noll 86, PN 90].

2.2   End-systems

The end-system attached to a telephone network is usually a telephone instrument that consists of five parts:

- A voice-to-electrical-signal transducer
- An electrical-signal-to-voice transducer
- A dialer

- A ringer
- A switchhook

We describe these in more detail next.

2.2.1   Signal transducers

Alexander Graham Bell invented the first voice-to-electrical-signal and electrical-signal-to-voice transducers in 1875–1876. One of his early voice-to-electrical-signal transducers (Figure 2.2) was a stretched membrane attached to a metal pin A which was dipped in a jar of conducting liquid B. The metal pin was connected to one terminal of a battery, and the other terminal was connected to the jar. Voice vibrations cause variable resistance in the path from A to B, which causes a variable voltage in the circuit. The electrical-signal-to-voice transducer (Figure 2.3) was an electromagnet D that vibrated a small metal reed E. The principles behind these transducers have changed little with time. Modern voice-to-electrical-signal transducers use either carbon granules or an *electret* microphone to create a variable resistance and thus a variable voltage. At the receiver, the electrical signal drives a small speaker in much the same way that Bell's receiver did more than a hundred years ago.

2.2.2   Sidetones and echoes

To allow two-way communication, the transmission and reception circuits of the communicating end-systems must be connected. Each circuit requires two wires, so the obvious way to connect a telephone to the central office is with four wires: one pair for each direction. A cheaper solution, however, is to let the two circuits share the same pair of wires, so that the transmitted and received signals are overlaid. This introduces two problems. First, at an end-system, the electrical signal from the voice-to-signal trans-

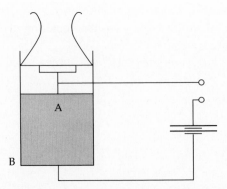

Figure 2.2: Bell's transmitter. Voice causes vibrations of a membrane, and thus a variable resistance in the circuit between A and B.

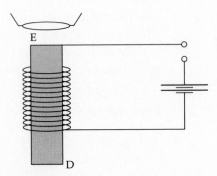

Figure 2.3: Bell's receiver. A variable current in coil D causes the reed E to vibrate, producing sound.

ducer flows directly to the reception circuit. So, whatever is spoken is heard loudly on the receiver. This is called *sidetone*. Although a certain amount of sidetone is required to let a speaker hear his or her own voice, some attenuation, using a *balance* circuit, is necessary to avoid deafening the speaker.

The second problem with using only two wires between an end-system and a central office is that this introduces an echo in the circuit. At each telephone, the received signal returns to the central office on the transmission circuit and is heard as an echo at the other end. For local calls, the presence of an echo is not a problem, because the human ear cannot distinguish between a sidetone and the echo. However, for long-distance calls, if the delay is more than about 20 ms, loud echoes can be annoying and must be attenuated or eliminated. This requires an expensive *echo cancellation* circuit that actively monitors the transmitted and received signal. Since the network must provide an echo canceller for each long-distance line, this can be a significant operating expense. To avoid the cost of echo cancellers, telephone companies try to reduce delay wherever possible. As we will see in Chapter 4, delay calculations were fundamental in deciding the essential parameters of ATM networks.

Most connections from an end-system to a central office are two-wire circuits, but connections between central offices are always four-wire (with separate transmission and reception). The central office does two-wire to four-wire conversion, and echo cancellation is done at backbone switches.

2.2.3   Dialing and ringing

Besides transducing from voice to electrical signal and vice versa, the end-system does the relatively simple operations of dialing and ringing. The dialer sends a series of tones or pulses to a central office. A special-purpose computer called a *switching system* interprets them to place a call or activate special features such as call forwarding. The switching system also sends a ring signal to the instrument when a call arrives. This rings a bell or activates a beeper. The central office supplies the power for ringing the bell.

The telephone network standard interface

The telephone network currently supports not only wired telephones, but also fax machines, cellular phones, cordless phones, answering machines, and modems. The key to managing this complexity is that the interface between the telephone network and the end-system is standardized. The telephone network expects either an analog signal that is bandlimited to 3.4 KHz (between 350 Hz and 3750 Hz), or a digital signal at 64 Kbps, and promises to replicate the signal at the far end. It makes no assumption about how the analog signal or bit-stream is generated, other than about its impedance and power limits. Thus, end-systems have evolved from analog telephones to digital handsets and cellular phones without changing the underlying architecture. This standard interface between the telephone network and the end-system allows each to evolve independently. The lesson is that we should be very careful when designing interfaces, since they are likely to outlast the technologies on either side of the interface.

2.3   Transmission

The telephone network carries signals generated by a telephone instrument over transmission links. In this section, we will discuss some metrics to describe these links. We will study how signals can be multiplexed to reduce the cost per bit. We will also look in detail at two transmission media: optical fiber and satellites.

2.3.1   Link characteristics

A transmission link can be characterized by its information-carrying capacity, the propagation delay it introduces, and how far it can carry a signal before the signal fades or is distorted beyond recognition (*link attenuation*).

The *bandwidth* of a link measures its information-carrying capacity [Blahut 90]. Using a plumbing analogy, it is the width of the "information pipe." A link carries information in the form of analog *symbols*, where a symbol may correspond to one or more bits. Thus, the *bit rate* of a line, measured in bits per second, is the product of its capacity measured in symbols per second and the mean number of bits each symbol represents. Computer network engineers tend to confuse bandwidth, capacity, and bit rate, using them interchangeably. In keeping with this tradition, and to maintain consistency with the literature, we will drop this distinction hereafter.

Link delay is determined by the time taken for a signal to propagate over the medium and is significant only for links longer than a few tens of kilometers. For example, light travels in optical fiber at 0.7 times the speed of light in vacuum, corresponding to a propagation delay of about 5 μs/km (~8 μs/mile). To get a sense of this, note that interactive voice conversation requires an end-to-end delay bound of 100 ms. The one-way propagation delay between New York and San Francisco, a distance of about 2500 miles, is about 20 ms. The delay between New York and London, a distance of about 3500 miles, is about 27 ms. Thus, on these links, a substantial fraction of the end-to-end delay budget is taken up by the speed-of-light propagation delay. Delay is a severe problem with geosynchronous satellite transmission, where the station-to-station propagation delay is around 250 ms. Conversations over a satellite link can be disjointed and exasperating!

As the length of a link increases, the quality of the carried signal degrades. To maintain link capacity, the signal must be regenerated after some distance. Regenerators are expensive and hard to maintain because they need a power supply, have active electronics that can fail, and are often in the middle of nowhere. We therefore prefer a link technology that requires the fewest regenerators. Recent advances in optical fiber technology have made it possible to build links that need regeneration only once every 5000 km or so. Moreover, with *optical amplification,* we can amplify an optical signal without converting it to electronic form. This makes it possible to use the same optical link to carry signals of various kinds without having to change all the regenerators along the path. In the future, these two technologies might make electronic regenerators obsolete.

2.3.2 Multiplexing

The pair of wires from a home to the central office carries one voice conversation. However, trunks between backbone switches need to carry hundreds of thousands of conversations. Laying hundreds of thousands of wire pairs between these switches is not economical. Instead, conversations are bundled or *multiplexed* together before transmission.

Telephone networks use both analog and digital multiplexors. Analog multiplexors work in the frequency domain: analog voice is bandlimited to 3.4 KHz and frequency shifted so that each conversation is in a noninterfering part of the spectrum. This technology is rapidly becoming obsolete, as the telephone network becomes all-digital.

Digital telephone networks digitize voice either in the telephone instrument or in a telephone exchange, and the rest of the network carries only digital signals. The key idea in voice digitization is to compare the amplitude of a voice signal with a small set of numbered amplitude thresholds, called *quantization levels.* We represent a voice amplitude digitally by the number of the quantization level closest to it. If quantization levels are properly chosen, the quantization error is small, and the regenerated analog signal is acceptable. The standard digitization scheme is to sample voice 8000 times a second, comparing the amplitude with 256 quantization levels, leading to 8-bit *samples.* This results in a standard voice bandwidth of 64 Kbps. Typically, quantization levels are logarithmically spaced, since this gives better resolution at low signal levels. Two choices of quantization levels are in common use, called *μ-law* (in the United States and Japan) and *A-law* (in the rest of the world). Unfortunately, this means that most international calls must be remapped.

Time division multiplexing (TDM) is used to combine 64-Kbps digital voice streams to form higher bandwidth streams. A synchronous time division multiplexor has *n* identical input links and one output link that is at least *n* times as fast. The multiplexor buffers incoming bits and places them, in turn, on the output line. Each set of *n* output samples, along with some additional overhead bits, constitutes a *frame.* A receiver at the other end of a multiplexed line can extract each constituent stream by synchronizing to frame boundaries.

Multiplexed links can be multiplexed further. The standard set of multiplexed line speeds is called the *Digital Signaling* or *DS* hierarchy in the United States and Japan (see Table 2.1). A similar hierarchy is an international standard (as in many other things, U.S. practice differs slightly from international standards). We will study the multiplexing hierarchy in more detail in Chapter 15.

Digital signal number	Number of previous level circuits	Number of voice circuits	Bandwidth
DS0	—	1	64 Kbps
DS1	24	24	1.544 Mbps
DS2	4	96	6.312 Mbps
DS3	7	672	44.736 Mbps

Table 2.1: U.S. digital transmission hierarchy. Each level in the hierarchy corresponds to a set of voice calls time-multiplexed together. Bandwidths are not exact multiples because of framing overheads.

2.3.3   Link technologies

Many link technologies are in common use today. These include unshielded twisted pair (UTP), coaxial cable, microwave, satellite links, and fiber optics. In this progression, the bandwidth increases, as does the cost per meter of the link. Table 2.2 summarizes typical capacities for these link technologies.

Link technology	Theoretical usable bandwidth
Twisted pair	200 Mbps over short distances
Coaxial cable	1 Gbps up to 1000 meters
Terrestrial microwave	2.4 Gbps
Satellite microwave	4–6 Gbps
Optical fiber	10–100 Gbps

Table 2.2: Typical capacity of some common link technologies.

The real cost of a link

The cost of a link has little to do with the cost per meter of the medium. In fact, the dominant cost of a link is in paying for the installation labor and rights-of-way. Thus, if a building or campus is to be wired anew, it makes sense to use the medium with the largest capacity, that is, optical fiber. These days, many builders install optical fiber, coaxial cable, and twisted pair to every room of a building as a matter of course. Even if only one of these is used, the money saved by not having to lay more wires makes the extra wires worthwhile. Installation costs are just as dominant in the wide area, where getting a right-of-way to lay a line is troublesome and expensive. In the wide area, it is common to install up to ten times the required capacity, just to be safe. Digging up a three-thousand-mile trench just to install an additional line is a bad idea!

Fiber optic links

Fiber optic links have revolutionized telecommunication networks. They have tremendous bandwidth (up to 100 Gbps in the lab and 19.2 Gbps in the field), are immune to electromagnetic interference, have very low signal attenuation even up to 100 km, and are hard to tap. These attractive characteristics have made fiber the technology of choice for wide-area trunks. As optical devices become cheaper, they are gradually penetrating into local area distribution as well. Because of their importance, it is worth understanding a little about how fiber optic systems work.

An optical fiber is a thin strand of extremely pure glass. When we introduce light into one end of the fiber, the fiber transmits it to the other end. To see why, let us first consider an interface between two media with differing refractive indices (Figure 2.4). When light beam A traveling in the medium with the higher index intersects the interface, beam B is *refracted* and beam C is *reflected* back. However, when a light beam such as D approaches the interface from an angle more than the *critical angle,* all the light is reflected (E). This is called *total internal reflection.* This phenomenon is quite common in real life: next time you are near an aquarium, bring your eyes to just below the water level and look up. You will see that the water surface looks like a mirror because of total internal reflection.

Optical fibers exploit the principle of total internal reflection to carry light. They consist of two concentric strands of glass (Figure 2.5). The inner *core* has a higher refractive index than the outer *cladding.* When light enters the fiber, it is nearly parallel to the layers and intersects their interface at an angle much greater than the critical angle. Thus, it is internally reflected, again at an angle greater than the critical angle. In this way, it is confined to the core of the fiber until it emerges from the far end. Of course, the light is attenuated in the glass, but with current technology, we can build fibers that lose as little

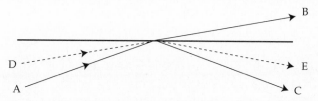

Figure 2.4: Total internal reflection. Ray A is partly refracted (B) and partly reflected (C). Ray D, incident at more than the critical angle, is totally internally reflected (E).

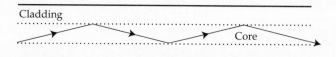

Figure 2.5: Optical fiber. Light entering at left is totally internally reflected inside the fiber and can be carried over long distances.

as 5.6% of their intensity per kilometer (in electrical engineering jargon, this is a drop of 0.25 dB/km).

We call the type of fiber just described a *step-index* fiber, since there is a step in the refractive index as one goes from the core to the cladding. In contrast, a *graded-index* fiber has a gradual decrease in the refractive index. Graded-index fibers have a lower attenuation and a higher bandwidth than step-index fibers, but are more expensive. It is also possible to build fibers where the core is so thin that only one mode of oscillation is possible for the signal traveling in the fiber. This reduces the attenuation and increases the bandwidth even further. We call this type of fiber *single-mode* fiber, and it is commonly used for wide-area communication. In contrast, step-index and graded-index fibers are called *multimode* fibers and are mostly popular for links shorter than a few kilometers. Multimode fibers have the added advantage that the transmitter is a cheap light-emitting diode, instead of an expensive laser. They are commonly used for in-building wiring.

Fiber optic links have three components: the fiber itself, the transmitter, and the receiver. Transmitters can either be light-emitting diodes (LEDs), used for multimode fibers, or lasers, for single-mode fibers. LEDs are cheaper, but are effective only over short distances. Lasers are much more expensive, but work over several hundred kilometers. Both LEDs and lasers are tuned to emit light at one of two wavelengths—1300 or 1550 nm. At these wavelengths, dispersion of light due to impurities in glass is the least.

Other link technologies

Other important link technologies are *coaxial cable* and satellites. Coaxial cable consists of a signal wire encased in an insulator and a wire mesh connected to ground. The mesh provides good protection against electromagnetic interference, allowing it to carry signals of a higher bandwidth than twisted pair. Typical unmodulated coaxial installations can carry 10 Mbps up to 8 km, or 1000 Mbps up to 1 km. Modulated coaxial cables, such as those used in cable television networks, can carry hundreds of Mbps over tens of kilometers.

Satellites provide links that traverse very long distances at high bandwidth. They use the 4- and 6-GHz bands, and their potential link bandwidth is in the order of Gbps. However, geosynchronous satellites must be placed in orbit about 36,000 km above the Earth. This introduces an up-and-down propagation delay of around 250 ms, which is unacceptable for most interactive services (though acceptable for television broadcast). Another problem with geosynchronous satellites is that to prevent interference between their uplinks, they must be spaced at least 4 degrees apart, so that the number of satellites that can be placed in this orbit is limited. This makes geosynchronous slots valuable commodities.

One way to get around the delay and slot congestion faced by geosynchronous satellites is to make the satellites nongeosynchronous. In other words, they would appear to move across the sky. To provide continuous coverage to an area, many such satellites need to be launched, only some of which would be used at a given time. A representative example is from Motorola Corporation, which is building a system called *Iridium* with 66 satellites in near-Earth orbits. Mobile telephones would be in touch with one or more of the satellites visible at any given time. A technically challenging aspect of the proposal is handing off calls between satellites as they appear and disappear from view.

2.4   Switching

The third important component of the telephone network is switching. Unlike the television network, which provides one-to-many communication, the telephone network mostly provides one-to-one communication.

How should a user be put in touch with every other user? A naive solution, infeasible in practice, is to physically link each user to every other user (imagine having a billion wires come into your home!). Instead, a pair of wires connects each user to a switch, which in turn is connected to other switches. When a call is placed to a user, the switches establish a temporary connection or circuit from the caller to the called user.

A telephone switch actually has two parts (Figure 2.6): The *switching* hardware carries voice and the *switch controller* handles requests to set up and tear down circuits. When a user dials a telephone number, the switch controllers set up a data transfer path from source to destination. During the call, voice samples travel through the switches without entering switch controllers. The controllers thus form an *overlay* network called the *signaling* network. We will study signaling in Section 2.5.

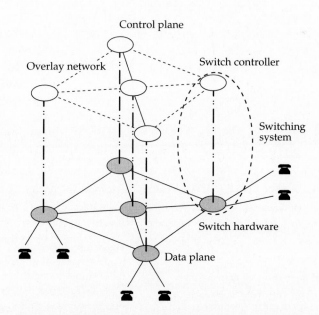

Figure 2.6: Switching fabric and switch controller. The switching fabric carries voice. The switch controllers form a logical network for setting up voice calls.

A switch transfers information from an input to an output. This can be complicated because a large central office switch can have more than 150,000 inputs and outputs. The two basic ways to connect inputs to outputs are *space division switching* and *time division switching*. In this chapter, we study simple space and time division switching elements. In Chapter 8, we will study large switches built from combinations of these elements.

The simplest space division switch is a *crossbar* (Figure 2.7). In a crossbar, inputs arrive along rows, and outputs are connected to columns. To connect any input to any output, the switch controller makes a connection at the point where the input row meets the output column. All other cross points are left unconnected. In this way, at a given time, the switch can connect any input to any output. For example, in the figure, input B has been connected to output 2, input C to output 3, and input E to output 4. If the lines entering a crossbar are multiplexed, then cross points must be rearranged once every sample time to switch a fresh set of samples. At the time of call setup, a switch controller determines a *schedule* that tells its associated switch how to set up crosspoints at each time slot of a frame.

We call a crossbar a space-division switch because the data paths are separated in space. Another way is to separate data paths in time, as in a *time division switch* (Figure 2.8). In this switch, the n inputs are stored in a temporary buffer. The switch reads from the buffer n times faster than the input and writes them to the outputs in the proper order. For example, to achieve the same connections as in Figure 2.7, the switch would read from buffer B and write to output 2, read from buffer C, write to output 3, and finally read from buffer E and write to output 4. Clearly, if the switch runs n times faster than the inputs, any input can be directed to any output. This type of switching element

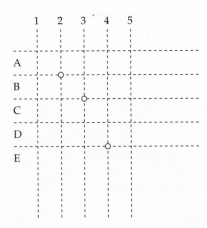

Figure 2.7: Crossbar switch. Inputs arrive along rows, outputs are connected to columns. Any input can be connected to any output by enabling the corresponding cross point.

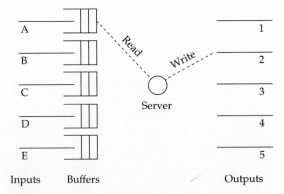

Figure 2.8: Time-division switch. Inputs are temporarily buffered while awaiting service. The server reads from input buffers in order, but writes to outputs according to a schedule. This allows any input to connect to any output. For example, the server could connect input A to output 2 by reading from input buffer A, then writing to output 2.

is also called a *time-slot interchange* or *TSI*. Note the close similarity between a time-division multiplexor (see Section 2.3.2) and a time-slot interchange.

Since all voice samples arrive synchronously, the only information a time-division switch needs is the order in which to write to outputs (the *schedule*). If an input is idle, however, the switch cannot use the slot for any other input—every idle slot must be wasted. This is inefficient if a conversation has long pauses. As we will see in Chapter 3, by adding a header to a voice sample, we can avoid this inefficiency.

2.5 Signaling

The last element of the telephone network we will study is signaling. Recall that a switching system consists of a switch, which carries data, and a switch controller, which is responsible for establishing a path from a calling telephone to a destination. When a subscriber dials a number, the pulses or tones representing the destination's number are sent to the exchange at the local central office. Here, the switch controller interprets the signals to decide the destination of the call. If the call is local, then the controller sets up a path in the local exchange from the input to the correct output. It then sends a signal on the wire connecting the central office to the telephone instrument to cause a bell to ring. When the handset is picked up, voice from either end is typically digitized and sent over the circuit. The controller also sets up billing records with the calling and called telephone numbers, the time of call, and the duration. When either party hangs up, the switch controller clears the circuit from the switch and marks the corresponding lines "idle."

If the call is to a remote destination, the switch controller sends a *setup* message to the switch controller managing the nearest backbone switch, requesting a circuit to the remote destination. This controller routes the call to a remote backbone switch by forwarding the setup message. If the line to the remote subscriber is free, then the message returns successfully and each switch on the return path is set up to complete the voice circuit. The remote central office rings the remote instrument's bell and the local central office generates a ringing tone for the caller's handset. When the remote subscriber picks up the handset, the switches along the path start forwarding voice samples.

Note that the switch controller is not in the path of the voice samples: it is only responsible for network control. Another way of putting it is to say that switches are in the *data plane,* whereas switch controllers are in the *control plane*. The data plane and the control plane were shown in Figure 2.6.

2.5.1 State transition diagrams

A switch controller's job is (a) to interpret actions from an end-system, (b) to set up calls for the end-system, and (c) to alert remote end-systems. The switch controller coordinates these actions by storing and interpreting the *state* of each connected end-system. When an end-system places a call, the switch controller goes through a series of state

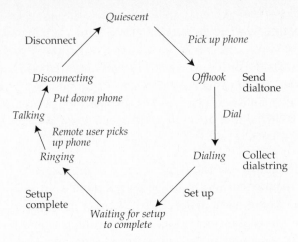

Figure 2.9: Simplified state diagram of a call at an originating switch. Actions by a user (in italics) or a switch controller (in regular font) cause the call to change state.

transitions initiated by actions of either the end-system or the switch controller. By examining the current state of the connection and signals representing the completion of an action, the switch controller knows the action to perform next.

Figure 2.9 is a typical state transition diagram at the originating switch's controller. Italics represent an end-system's actions and the regular font a switch controller's actions. As each action completes, the controller enters a new state and does the corresponding action. For example, if the call is in the *Talking* state and the disconnect button is pressed, the call enters the *Disconnecting* state and the switch controller initiates a disconnection.

Figure 2.9 is simplified—for example, it does not show actions if the called instrument is busy. What if the user wants a three-way conference call? What if the user places a credit card call? The switch controller must handle these, and other, situations. As a result, switch control software is complex—for example, the Lucent 5ESS switch control software for central office switches has more than 14 million lines of C code, with a large portion devoted to signaling! Unfortunately, complexity seems unavoidable when supporting the many features that telephone customers demand.

2.5.2   Common channel interoffice signaling

Switch controllers previously exchanged special tones to set up and tear down calls—for example, a "disconnect" tone would tear down a call. Other tones were used to disable billing or test switch features. Unfortunately, these tones attracted the attention of *phone phreaks*—people who discovered that special tone sequences permitted free long-distance calls. Telephone companies countered this attack by changing the mechanism for exchanging messages between switch controllers. Instead of using the same channel for both voice and signaling tones, a separate *Common Channel Interoffice Signaling* (*CCIS*) network interconnects switch controllers. This network is not directly accessible to subscribers. Because control information is separate from the voice channel, CCIS is called *out-of-band signaling.* CCIS is more flexible than in-band signaling because peer switch controllers can exchange arbitrarily complicated messages instead of just tone sequences. (Unfortunately, the CCIS network only shifted the attention of phone phreaks to cracking switch controllers.)

The messages sent on the common channel conform to an international signaling standard called CCITT 17, which is based on AT&T's *Signaling System 7* or SS7. We will study SS7 in more detail in Chapter 15. All international calls obey this standard, which is why international calling is possible. Incidentally, the CCIS network is based on *packet-switching,* a technique we will study in Chapter 3.

2.6   Cellular communications

Thus far, we have studied the wired portion of the telephone network. In the past few years, wireless (cellular) communication has grown rapidly to form a significant part of the infrastructure. Cellular communication replaces the two wires between an end-system and the central office with radio transmission over a pair of frequencies. Because radio frequencies are a scarce resource, they must be carefully allocated.

If each cellular phone had its own frequency, a central office serving ten thousand customers would need twenty thousand different frequencies to operate, although only a small fraction of them would be active at any given time. This number can be cut down by *spatial* and *temporal* reuse. Temporal reuse means using the same frequency for different calls at different times. When an end-system is turned on, it requests a frequency for the call, and when the call is set up, the phone is informed of the frequency to use for the call. The request is made over a common frequency that corresponds to the common signaling channel for CCIS.

Spatial reuse means using the same frequency in nonadjacent geographical areas. The provider divides the service area into small zones or *cells*. Each cell has a *base station* that is in wireless communication with cellular phones in its local area and is wired to a central office. Phones in adjacent cells are guaranteed to use different sets of frequencies. Nonadjacent cells may, however, use the same frequency, because their radio transmissions will not interfere. For example, in Figure 2.10, cells A and B are adjacent, so they cannot share a frequency. However, calls in cells A and C may use the same frequency.

Two important problems with cellular communication are (a) how to complete a call to a cellular phone (location tracking), and (b) how to deal with moving end-systems.

2.6.1   Location tracking

Each cellular phone is associated with a "home" central office, and all calls to the phone pass through a switch in this office. A unique number burned into a ROM in the phone

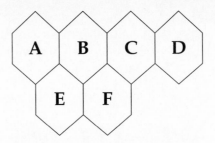

Figure 2.10: Cellular communication. Frequencies are assigned to each cell, and nonadjacent cells are allowed to share frequencies. This allows spatial reuse of frequencies.

identifies it, much like a telephone number. When a subscriber turns on the phone, it periodically broadcasts a message with this number on the signaling channel. A base station receiving this broadcast uses it to find the phone and enters this information into a database at the "home" central office. When someone calls the cellular phone, the switch controller at the "home" office uses this database to locate the phone and complete the call. Depending on the phone's location, the nearest base station assigns it a pair of available frequencies and instructs the phone to use these frequencies for communication. Thus, no matter where the phone is, the telephone network is still able to reach it to complete a call. We will study more about mobile phone routing in Chapter 11.

2.6.2   Hand-off

When a cellular phone crosses a cell boundary during a call, it must switch to a pair of frequencies available at the new cell. This is managed by a *hand-off* protocol. There are many hand-off protocols in common use, and we describe only a representative algorithm. In this scheme, all cellular phones in a cell monitor a signal (called a *beacon*) periodically broadcast by every base station. When a phone moves between cells, it passes through a transition zone where it receives beacons from more than one base station. The phone initiates a hand-off office if the strongest beacon is from a base station other than its own. When the hand-off completes, the phone is assigned to a new base station and a new frequency.

Cellular communication is convenient, but it introduces complexity in the end-system and in the central office. Moreover, bandwidth scarcity, a small market, and users' willingness to pay contribute to higher prices for cellular calls. With the recent rapid expansion of the cellular telephony market, however, economies of scale have made cellular telephony prices comparable to those of wired telephones. It may be the technology of choice in developing nations, where the wired infrastructure is sparse or subject to severe environmental conditions.

2.7   Historical sketch

In the late nineteenth century, telegraphy was well established and companies such as Western Union and Reuters were making fortunes carrying information over long distances. It was a natural next step to consider transmitting voice over the same wires. The telephone network started as an attempt to carry voice over long distances in the same way telegraph wires carried Morse code in dots and dashes.

The key breakthrough was the development, in 1875–1876 by Alexander Graham Bell, then a teacher in a school for the deaf, of transducers from voice to electrical signal and vice versa [Boettinger 77]. The possibility of carrying musical sounds over long distances by electrical currents rapidly turned on and off was realized in the 1860s by Helmholtz and others. Bell was the first to realize that carrying voice required *oscillating* currents, rather than *interrupted* currents. He also discovered that forced vibration of a diaphragm, rather than induced vibration of free reeds, was essential to carry voice. Putting these observations into practice with the help of Watson, Bell developed the first viable telephone instrument. Bell and Watson displayed the instrument in the Centennial Exposition of 1876 to the astonishment of the American public.

Bell quickly realized that the invention had tremendous potential and approached several industrialists for financing. Western Union, in a classic blunder, rejected the technology, claiming telephones had no future, since phone calls do not leave a written record the way letters and telegrams do. (Eventually, Bell's company, AT&T, bought out Western Union, and in 1992, the last telegraph offices in the United States were decommissioned.) Rebuffed by financiers, but funded in part by his father-in-law Gardiner Hubbard (better known as the founder of the National Geographic Society), Bell started the Bell Telephone Company to market his invention. In the early days, the company was financed mostly by Bell and Watson's public lectures! Soon, however, licensees all over the world supplied capital to keep the company going. Unfortunately, Bell's patents were infringed by many competitors (including Thomas Edison), and he spent the next twenty years taking them to court. Bell stopped working on telephony in 1877, just one year after his invention, when he was only 31. He left the management of his company to Hubbard and Watson, and went on to invent kites large enough to lift human beings and fast hydrofoil boats (he held the world water speed record at the age of 71).

Watson invented the ringer, the first switchboard, and many other things essential to transforming a laboratory toy into a commercial product. As the company grew, he hired a superintendent of the Post Office's Railway Mail Service, Theodore Vail, to manage the company. Vail had the vision to realize that the key to success was *seamless* provision of telephone *service* across wide areas. Selling service, rather than selling the instrument itself, insulated customers from changes in technology. Besides, it was better business to rent telephones than to sell them. By franchising telephone service to local businessmen in exchange for a share in their local stock, Vail ensured that the Bell Telephone Company controlled a substantial portion of the telephone service in the United States even after the expiration of Bell's patents in 1894. Vail proposed the notion of "universal access" and plowed back all profits into expanding telephone service. He also used the ever-increasing capital to buy out other telephone companies. By the time he was done, the American Telephone and Telegraph Company (AT&T) owned nearly every telephone instrument, every telephone switch, and every telephone pole in the country. Vail made sure that AT&T would survive the antimonopoly sentiments of the 1910s by investing in research, putting customer satisfaction first, and promising that every American would have access to the telephone network if AT&T were allowed to keep its monopoly. Such was the strength of his vision that AT&T retained almost complete control over the telephone network until 1984! Outside the United States, however, telephone service was viewed as a public utility and provided by government-run *Post, Telegraph and Telephone* companies (PTTs). The 1980s and 1990s have seen the gradual privatization of these PTTs.

Early telephones offered little more than point-to-point communication. The need for switching was quickly realized, and by the late 1880s manual switchboards were set up in many cities. To set up a call, subscribers picked up the phone and gave the operator the name of the subscriber to be called. The operator would then complete the circuit by hand. Human-powered switchboards could still be found till the mid-1980s, when they were finally replaced by switching systems.

One key development in telephony was the invention of the first practical automatic switch in the 1890s by Strowger, an undertaker who felt that business that was rightfully his was being diverted by spiteful operators. He hoped that his invention would put operators out of business and make the playing field level. At the heart of his step-by-step switch was an arc of ten electrical contact points, any one of which could be touched by a wiper mechanism. A pulse sequence rotated the wiper. For example, if four pulses were sent in, the wiper would rotate four steps. A second pulse sequence could move the wiper vertically up to nine steps, so that any of the rows in a half cylinder of vertically stacked arcs could be selected. Two other pulse sequences selected from one of a hundred banks of such cylinders. Thus, by electromechanically interpreting the pulse sequences, the step-by-step switch allowed an incoming call to connect to one of ten thousand possible outputs. This completely automated switching and enabled large switching offices to be built, making telephone service affordable by the public at large.

Fueled by Vail's vision, the telephone network was at the forefront of research and development, and the immense profits from telephone operation were used to improve the system continuously. This was reflected in the number of telephone instruments in service—3 in May 1876, 3000 in November 1876, and 240,000 in 1892. (Telephone service grew faster than even the Internet!) Step-by-step switches were replaced by more reliable crossbar switches, and PBX systems were invented for customer-premises switching. The vacuum tube amplifier, invented by DeForest in 1906, allowed voice signals to be amplified, permitting communication between the East and West Coasts of the United States. In 1925, AT&T engineers were organized into the Bell Telephone Laboratories. Soon, a slew of inventions such as talking pictures, videoconferencing (the first one-way videoconference was held in 1927 between the president of AT&T, W. S. Gifford, and then U.S. Secretary of Commerce Herbert Hoover), and radiotelephony poured out from the Labs.

Three key inventions just after the Second World War laid the foundation of modern telephony. First, Shannon at Bell Labs invented *information theory* (over lunch, two colleagues, Tukey and Hamming, suggested the term *bit*, or binary digit, as the unit of information). Second, Bardeen, Shockley, and Brattain, all at Bell Labs, invented the transistor. Finally, Eckert and Mauchly at the University of Pennsylvania built ENIAC, the first general-purpose electronic digital computer. (Though Zuse in Berlin built a similar machine in 1936, his results were lost during World War II, and he is often denied credit.) The transistor and the computer made it possible to easily manipulate digital information. Adding to this, Shannon and Nyquist's theoretical work showed that flexible and cheap transmission of voice calls could be accomplished if voice were digitized before transmission. These developments, therefore, played a key role in ushering in the digital revolution.

The invention of fiber optics by Corning Glass led to the next transmission revolution. Fiber optics enables much faster trunks, with greater reliability and cheaper cost-per-bit than twisted pair or microwave trunks. Telephone companies decided to upgrade all long-distance trunks to fiber optics. By the 1990s, this transition was essentially complete.

The latest revolution in the telephone network is the arrival of cellular telephony. Though prices for cellular phones are still relatively high, they hold the promise of making telephone service available to anyone, anytime, and anywhere.

The telephone network is still growing and evolving. Much of telephone network growth comes from developing nations. Compared to about 500 phones per thousand population in Japan and the United States, countries such as China and India have fewer than 10 phones per thousand population. With such countries' huge populations and recent economic liberalization, global telephone service is likely to continue growing for the next several decades.

2.8 Challenges

In this section, we discuss some challenges facing the global telephone network.

2.8.1 Multimedia

Multimedia communication, also called *integrated services* communication, is the simultaneous transmission of voice, video, and data traffic. An example of multimedia communication is a videoconference with a shared workspace.

The existing telephone network is inadequate for multimedia traffic in three ways. First, video requires between 0.35 and 3.5 Mbps of digital information per stream. Although the telephone network carries digital voice internally, regular telephone service from the local exchange to the home (the *local loop*) is analog over twisted-pair. The best current modems can achieve no more than 56 Kbps over this medium. Even if digital information is sent from the home using the ISDN (Integrated Service Digital Network) standard, only 128 Kbps is available. To carry switched video, at the high end, the network must increase the bit rate available to users by nearly two orders of magnitude. Moreover, switches must be capable of handling two orders of magnitude more bandwidth, adding to the difficulty.

Second, both compressed video traffic and data traffic are inherently bursty. In other words, the traffic rate over short periods (the peak rate) is higher than the rate over long periods (the average rate). For typical data traffic, the peak to average rate ratio can be as large as 1000. We saw earlier that time-slot interchanges (TSIs) are critical switching elements in the telephone network. For a TSI to work correctly, a source must send data to a TSI at or slower than the rate at which it is served. Otherwise, the buffer in the TSI will fill, leading to packet loss. A bursty traffic source has two choices. It must either ask the TSI to serve its traffic at the source's peak rate, or ask the TSI to reserve a buffer to store data arriving during a burst. If the TSI serves data at the source's peak rate, in the periods when the source sends slower than its peak rate, the TSI would be idle, wasting bandwidth. If the TSI serves slower than the peak rate, the buffer size at the TSI must be large enough to be able to absorb the largest burst, which can be expensive. We conclude that a TSI, and thus the telephone network, is inherently wasteful either of buffers or of bandwidth when carrying bursty data.

Third, network trunk capacities are decided based on the statistical behavior of large numbers of voice calls. For example, by observation over many decades, telephone engineers can accurately estimate the number of calls between New York and Chicago on a typical working day. This allows them to provision adequate capacity on a trunk between the corresponding backbone switches. With the arrival of multimedia communication, it is not clear whether voice call statistics are appropriate any longer. For example, modem (data) calls have much longer durations than voice calls—this means the network must provision larger bandwidth for trunks that carry more modem calls. How would holding times and aggregate bandwidth change if the sources were video-conferences? No one knows for sure.

2.8.2   Backward compatibility

Since telephone companies in developed nations have a huge investment in existing infrastructure, changes in the network have to be backward compatible. New equipment must interoperate with existing equipment, and services provided to customers must continue to be supported. This need for backward compatibility constrains the choices available when adding services to the network. Nevertheless, new services must be added to satisfy customer needs. Cellular communication, toll-free dialing services, and fax services are examples of new services that have been successfully integrated into the infrastructure. The challenge is to manage legacy hardware and systems while still being able to add new services rapidly. In this regard, developing countries probably have an advantage over developed countries, because they do not have a large investment in infrastructure.

2.8.3   Regulation

Most countries recognize that telephones provide an essential economic infrastructure and so telephone companies around the world are subject to strict regulation. In many countries, a government monopoly provides telephone service, and telephone service is often called a "natural monopoly." This tradition of regulation usually tends to stifle innovation, particularly when the telephone company is a monopoly (Bell Labs and AT&T are the exception rather than the rule!). For example, until recently, answering machines were illegal in Germany. Thus, German consumers were denied access to a convenient service because of out-of-date regulations. Technological innovations require rapid response, and the challenge is to do this within the regulatory environment.

2.8.4   Competition

Many countries have started to open their telephone services to competition. The idea is that free market forces will reduce prices and reward productivity. From a phone company's perspective, this means an end to good times, and an incentive to cut corners. The most prominent example of this is the breakup of AT&T in 1984. Until that time, within the United States, AT&T controlled not only long-distance lines, but also local telephone service and the instruments themselves (most subscribers leased instruments for a fee). The U.S. Justice Department ruled that this was monopolistic and not in the public interest. In 1984, AT&T was split into two parts—a long-distance company that retained the AT&T name, and a set of regional companies granted a monopoly on local service. Long-distance service was thrown open to competition, giving a free hand to companies such as MCI and Sprint—by 1995, more than a hundred long distance companies operated in the United States. Similar changes have happened or are in the works in Germany, Japan, Finland, and the United Kingdom. Competition has brought dramatic changes to former monopolies (the recent trivestiture of AT&T is a sign of the times). With the loss of a nearly guaranteed source of income, they have had to cut jobs, retrain their workforce, and be more responsive to technological innovations. This has sometimes come at the expense of the long-term thinking that characterized telephone company planning in the past.

The point is that although competition is good for society, the transition from a government-sanctioned monopoly to free competition has to be wisely managed. This may be the trickiest challenge facing telephone networks worldwide.

2.8.5   Inefficiencies within the system

One legacy of a long history is a proliferation of systems and formats that are similar, but incompatible. For example, the AT&T billing system processes more than two thousand types of billing records to generate a bill. Some formats date back several decades and must still be supported in the twenty-first century unless the billing system is completely overhauled—a daunting and expensive exercise. Unfortunately, this kind of inefficiency is more the norm than the exception. To take another example, switching systems are typically composed of many independently developed subsystems. Some subsystems were written in special-purpose languages or assembly language for special-purpose computers. This specialization was necessary when general-purpose machines were not powerful or reliable enough. With growth in computing power, many such systems can be moved to general-purpose systems, increasing maintainability. The challenge facing the system is to recognize and eliminate inefficiencies due to engineering decisions necessary in the past, but no longer relevant.

2.9   Summary

In this chapter, we have studied four essential components of the telephone system: (a) end-systems, (b) transmission, (c) switching, and (d) signaling. The telephone network has a long history and has evolved into a highly distributed, available, and reliable system. Nevertheless, it faces some important technical and social challenges. In later chapters, we will study more details about the telephone network, and how it is evolving to meet the challenges outlined in this chapter.

Chapter 3

The Internet: Concepts, History, and Challenges

The Internet connects tens of millions of computers around the world, allowing them to exchange messages and share resources. Users of the Internet can exchange electronic mail, read and post to electronic bulletin boards, access files anywhere in the network, and publish information for other users. The Internet, which started as a research project connecting four computers in 1969, had grown by late 1996 to a network of more than twenty million computers, linking an estimated sixty million people. It has consistently doubled in size almost every year since 1969. In 1996 alone, therefore, around ten million computers joined the Internet!

The Internet is a loose collection of networks organized into a multilevel hierarchy using a wide variety of interconnection technologies. At the lowest level, between ten and a hundred computers may be connected to each other, and to a *router*, by a local area network. (A router is a special-purpose computer that transfers data to and from the next higher level of the hierarchy.) Other computers at the lowest level may connect to a router over the telephone network using a modem or over a wireless link. A large business or university campus may have many routers. These routers are usually linked by a campus-wide network to a campus router that handles all traffic entering and leaving the campus. Campus routers are typically connected by leased lines to routers belonging to an Internet Service Provider. These, in turn connect to routers in a high-speed wide-area network called a *backbone*. A country usually has a handful of backbones linking all its Internet Service Providers. In the United States, the backbones are cross-connected at a small number of *Network Access Points* or *NAPs*. Finally, national backbones interconnect in a mesh using international trunk lines.[1]

EXAMPLE 3.1

Consider a packet sent from a computer in the Computer Science department at Cornell University to a computer at the Computer Science department at the Indian Institute of Technology, Delhi, India. The packet travels from the computer at Cornell over a local area network to a router, and from there to the Cornell campus router. The campus router forwards the packet to the Internet Service Provider's router (in this case, a router belonging to NYSERNET). This router, in turn, forwards the packet to a national backbone, say the one provided by MCI, which sends it to an international gateway router in Virginia. From here, the packet travels on a international line to Bombay, where it enters the Indian national educational and research backbone called ERNET. The ERNET backbone forwards the packet to its Delhi node, and from there the packet enters the Indian Institute of Technology campus router. Finally, the packet reaches the Computer Science department router, and uses a local area network to make the last hop to the remote computer. This path, which takes around 16 hops, is usually traversed in under a second.

Campuses are usually administered by a single authority, so that all computers within a campus trust each other (networks where all the computers trust each other are said to form an *intranet*). At higher levels, however, the network is heterogeneous, and individual administrative domains rarely trust each other.

3.1   Concepts

The Internet is bound together by *addressing, routing,* and the *Internet Protocol* (IP). Addressing provides a uniform way of identifying a destination in the network. Routing allows information to traverse the network from end to end. Finally, IP allows data to be interpreted consistently as they travel across the network. A common definition of the Internet is "the set of computers that are reachable with IP."

Perhaps the easiest way to understand these concepts is to look at the three steps involved in making a host "Internet-capable":

- First, people should be able to address data to you—that is, you need an Internet address. You can request an address from someone who already owns a part of

---

[1]For a more detailed description of Internet link technologies, see Section 15.3.

the Internet address space, such as the network manager of your organization, or an Internet Service Provider. If you intend to provide Internet service to others, you can request a chunk of Internet addresses from the Internet Addressing and Numbering Authority.

- Next, data originating from your computer must somehow travel to the destination. If you have only one connection to the Internet, all your data will be carried on the unique link. However, if you decide to get two Internet links (say, for reliability), then you will need to run a *routing protocol* to decide which link has a better path to each destination. This routing protocol must communicate with peer protocols running at neighboring computers to discover the nearby topology, so the protocol must be commonly known, at least in your local area. You must also have your routing protocol announce your presence to the rest of the network in a well-known way.

- Finally, when you do send data, you must have software on your computer that formats it using the *IP* format, so that routers along the path know what they are getting. If you insist on formatting data your own way, your data will meet a sure and untimely death.

Once you have completed these three steps, corresponding to addressing, routing, and IP, you can send data into the network, knowing that it will eventually arrive at its destination. You can also receive data from every other computer in the network.

One reason the Internet has spread so quickly is that the three basics, addressing, routing, and IP, are designed to scale. For example, the Internet does not have a centralized addressing authority, or routing coordinator. Any Internet service provider has the authority to give away part of the address space allocated to it without further reference to a higher authority. Similarly, the routing changes dynamically if hosts are added or removed or if transmission lines go up and down. This self-healing and distributed design of the net allows it to scale remarkably well. Nevertheless, as we will see in Section 3.7.2, there are some problems caused precisely by the decentralized nature of this design.

3.2   Basic Internet technology

Two key ideas in Internet technology are *packets* and *store-and-forward* transmission.

3.2.1   Packets

The Internet carries all information using *packets.* A packet has two parts: the information content, called the *payload,* and information *about* the payload, called the *meta-data* or *header.* The meta-data consists of fields such as the source and destination addresses, data length, sequence number, and data type. The introduction of meta-data is a fundamental innovation in networking technology. To appreciate this, recall that the telephone network carries voice using digital samples, which are not self-descriptive. Thus, the network cannot determine where samples originate, or where they are going, without additional context information. Meta-data makes information self-descriptive, allowing the network to interpret the data without additional context information. In particular, if the meta-data contains a source and destination address, no matter where in the network the packet is, the network knows where it came from and where it wants to go. The network can store the packet, for hours if necessary, then "unfreeze" it, and still know what has to be done to deliver the data. In contrast, in the telephone network, the destination of a sample is derived from the time slot in which it arrives at a switch. If a preceding switch stores the sample, this timing information is lost. Thus, unlike packet networks, telephone networks cannot store and then forward samples.

EXAMPLE 3.2

Packets are efficient for data transfer, but are not so attractive for real-time services such as voice. Suppose we digitize voice at 8000 samples/s, where each sample is 1 byte. (a) How long will it take to fill a 500-byte packet? (b) For interactive voice communication, a delay of 100 ms is considered the limit. What fraction of the 100 ms is spent in packetization?

Solution: (a) Each sample corresponds to 1/8000 seconds, so 500 samples take 500/8000 = 62.5 ms, (b) Thus, 62.5% of the delay budget is spent in packetization!

3.2.2   Store-and-forward

Meta-data allows a form of data forwarding, called *store-and-forward*, familiar to users of a postal system. In this method, a packet (letter with an address) is stored at a series of routers (post offices), and eventually delivered to the destination. The key point is that stored information can be released when convenient. For example, a local post office can forward letters to the main post office once a day, instead of sending a truck every time a patron mails a letter. Store-and-forward transmission in the postal network is cheaper than immediate (unbuffered) transmission, since the cost of the truck is amortized over many letters. Similarly, a store-and-forward packet network is allowed to store packets till they can be forwarded. By building up a backlog of stored packets before accessing an expensive transmission link, a packet network allows the cost of that link (such as an international telephone line) to be shared among many users. Moreover, if a link goes down, incoming packets can be stored and delivered when the link comes back up. Thus, the disruption of a single link need not cause a communication failure.

EXAMPLE 3.3

If the router comes back up, "unfreezes" its stored packets, and starts forwarding them again, what problems might arise? What might be your recommendation to a router manufacturer about "unfreezing" packets when recovering from a crash?

Solution: The receiver would see delayed and possibly reordered packets. If a source retransmits packets that reach the destination by another route, the destination may see duplicates. Recommendation: drop any undelivered packets—if they were important enough, the source would have retransmitted them anyway.

3.2.3 Problems with store-and-forward routing

A store-and-forward network is less expensive to operate than the telephone network, but users of the network suffer three problems. First, it is hard for users to control how long their packets will be delayed in the network. A stored packet might be forwarded only after a long delay. If it is important to avoid delays, as in a voice call, then a naive store-and-forward approach may not be sufficient. Second, since packets must be stored, switches need memory for buffers, which can be expensive. Finally, if many users decide to send packets to the same destination simultaneously, and there are not enough buffers to hold all the incoming data, then packets will be lost. Unless more controls are added, users of store-and-forward service have to assume that any of their packets could be dropped because of the arrival of bursts of packets from other users. In contrast, because all samples arrive at a telephone switch at a fixed rate, no samples are ever lost to buffer overflow.

Nevertheless, meta-data and store-and-forward packet switching are powerful ideas. They allow us to build systems where the cost of expensive links can be better shared among many users. By careful design, some of the shortcomings described earlier can be overcome. We will study some of these design techniques in Chapter 14.

3.3 Addressing

An Internet Protocol address, also called an IP address, corresponds to a *host-interface card*—the hardware device that connects a computer to a network. A computer with two host-interface cards needs two IP addresses, one for each interface. For hosts with only one network interface, which is the norm, an IP address assigned to a host-interface card can be viewed as the host's Internet address.

IP addresses are structured as a two-part hierarchy (Figure 3.1). The first part is the *network number* and the second part is the *interface number* (also called the *host number*). Since network numbers are globally unique, and interface numbers within a network are also unique, each interface in the Internet is uniquely identified. Once a central authority

Network number	Interface number
135.104.53	100

Figure 3.1: An Internet Protocol (IP) address. The address consists of a network number and an interface number.

assigns a network operator a unique network number, the operator can allocate a globally unique IP address with that prefix, allowing decentralized control of the address space. If IP addresses were "flat" or nonhierarchical, a central authority would need to check every new Internet address for uniqueness. We study Internet addressing in more detail in Chapter 10.

3.3.1   Address classes

An interesting problem is to decide how many bits of the IP address should correspond to the network number and how many to the interface number. If the Internet had many networks, but each network had only a few interfaces, it would be better to allocate more bits to the network number than to the interface number. If there were many interfaces per network and only a few networks, then we should reverse the assignment. IP version 4 addresses are 32 bits long. If we use 24 bits of the address for the network number and 8 bits for the interface number, we can address 2^{24} (16,772,216) networks, each with 256 interfaces. If we use 8 bits of the address for the network number and 24 bits for the interface number, we can address 256 networks, each with 2^{24} interfaces. Internet designers initially allowed only 8 bits for the network number, because they felt that the Internet would never have more than 256 networks! The current bit-assignment scheme allows greater flexibility.

We partition the address space into Class A, Class B, Class C, and Class D addresses with different numbers of bits assigned to the network and interface numbers in each class. Conceptually, a Class A address has 8 bits for the network number and 24 bits for the interface number. A single large component of the Internet would use a Class A address. In contrast, a Class C address has 24 bits of network number and only 8 bits for interface number. Only 256 hosts can be accommodated in a Class C network, which would still be sufficient for most LANs.

The network distinguishes among the four classes of addresses depending on the first few bits of the network number. If the first bit is a 0, then the address is a Class A address; if the first few bits are 10, it is a Class B address; if the bits are 110, it is a Class C address; if it is 1110, it is a Class D address. The use of network number bits to distinguish among address classes means that each class contains fewer networks than it might otherwise have. Thus, for example, Class A network numbers are only 7 bits long—there can be only 128 "large" networks—and Class B network numbers are only 14 bits long, allowing 16,384 "medium" networks.

EXAMPLE 3.4

How many Class C networks can there be?

Solution: Since 3 bits in the Class C network number are used for identification, we can have at most 2^{21} Class C networks.

Although class-based addressing allows some networks to be larger than others, it is not particularly flexible. For example, many campuses have more than 256 nodes and so need at least a Class B address. On the other hand, they have far fewer than the 65,536 hosts permitted in a Class B network. Thus, these campuses waste a substantial fraction of the IP address space. In an attempt to reduce this wastage, the Internet has recently adopted *Classless Inter Domain Routing addresses,* also called *CIDR addresses.* With this form of addressing, the network number can be an arbitrary number of bits long, so that a network's size can be bounded by any power of 2. More details about CIDR addresses can be found in Chapter 10.

3.3.2   Longer addresses

IP version 4 addresses are 32 bits long and can address 2^{32} (4,294,967,296) interfaces if the address space is completely used. In reality, once the central authority hands out a part of the address space, it cannot control how it is used. Even if an organization assigned part of the address space uses only a small fraction, the rest of the Internet must still respect the address space assignment.

In the early days of the Internet, when only a few organizations were connected, Class A and Class B addresses were given away freely to organizations that could not fully populate their share of the address space. Consequently, their address space is sparsely used, but cannot be reclaimed. Newer organizations on the Internet cannot get as large an address space as they need. It is estimated that by 1998, the address space will be exhausted. To solve this problem, IP version 6 is being defined with 128 bits of addressing. IPv6 designers expect that this large address space will solve the address-space congestion problem. We will study IPv6 in more detail in Chapter 10.

3.4   Routing

The Internet forwards IP packets from a source to a destination using the IP destination address field in the packet header. A *router* is defined as a host that has an interface on more than one network. Every router along the path has a routing table with at least two fields: a network number and the interface on which to send packets with that network number. The router reads the destination address from an incoming packet's header and uses the routing table to forward it on the appropriate interface. To understand this better, see Figure 3.2. Here, boxes represent host interfaces and the circle represents a router.

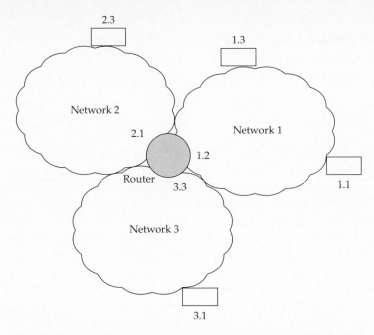

Figure 3.2: Internet routing. A router is a host with interfaces on more than one network. A routing table maps destination network numbers to interfaces. The router examines the destination address in a packet's header and uses the routing table to forward the packet on the appropriate interface.

There are three networks, labeled 1, 2, and 3, and the host interfaces are addressed with IP-style addresses. For example, a host interface with address 2.3 has network number 2 and interface number 3. In the figure, the router has an interface on all three networks.

Assume for the moment that an interface on a network can reach all other interfaces on that network. (This is easily accomplished on networks that share a broadcast physical medium, such as Ethernet.) Then, the router can reach all interfaces on all three networks because it has an interface on each network. By symmetry, every host interface can reach the router. Thus, when a host wants to send a packet to a remote host, it sends it to the router, which forwards it using its routing table. Since each host in each of the three networks in Figure 3.2 can reach every other host through the router, we can now consider the cluster of three networks to be fully connected in the same way as we assumed each individual network to be fully connected earlier. So, by introducing routers with interfaces on more than one cluster, we can connect clusters into larger ones. By induction, we can compose arbitrarily large networks in this fashion, as long as there are routers with interfaces on each subcomponent of the network. This is more or less how Internet routing works. We will study Internet routing in more detail in Chapter 11.

Note that the hierarchical IP address also contains a hint about the geographical location of the interface. For example, a host with an IP address of 3.1 suggests it is in network 3. If this is always true, the routing table in the router does not have to keep track of every address in network 3. It can simply say "If the destination address looks like 3.*, send it to interface 3." The geographical hint in the IP address allows *aggregation* of destination addresses and is essential to the scalability of Internet routing.

3.4.1 Default routes

Strictly speaking, a routing table must maintain the next hop for every network number in the Internet. The Internet in 1996 had as many as 60,000 networks, and asking every router to keep track of the next hop for all these networks is impractical. Thus, we only ask a router to keep track of detailed routes (that is, routes for fully qualified network addresses such as 135.104.53, instead of for aggregated addresses such as 135.*) for networks that are "nearby." All packets carrying a network address that is not "nearby" are forwarded to a *default address*, which is the address of a router that knows more about distant networks. For instance, a campus router would typically know the next hop only for on-campus LANs. If it receives an IP packet with an unknown destination address, it automatically forwards the packet on the default route to the next level in the Internet hierarchy, that is, a router in the regional network. Similarly, hosts on a single network typically keep only one route, which is the default route to their local router. Routers deeper in the network, such as those on the network backbone, must keep track of much more state—typically, the next hop to every network in the Internet.

3.4.2 Computing routing tables

We have looked at how routing is done when a routing table already exists. We now discuss how this table is computed. One way to do this would be for each host and router to report its presence and a list of neighbors to a central authority that would periodically compute optimal routing tables for all the routers. This solution is not desirable, because it does not scale. In other words, as the network size increases, the load on the central computer increases beyond the capacity of the largest available machines, limiting the scale of the network. Moreover, if this central computer were to crash, the entire network would be unusable.

Instead, peer routers exchange messages that indicate which networks they can reach, and the number of hops they need to get to that network. By examining its local state and combining it with the information received from its peers, each router can, in parallel, compute a consistent routing table. We will examine this process in detail in Chapter 11.

3.5 Endpoint control

Since the Internet design emphasizes decentralized control, endpoints cannot rely on the network for reliable or timely data transfer. An important part of the Internet philosophy is endpoint control, also called the "end-to-end argument" [SRC 84]. The idea is that reliable data transfer must be provided by protocols operating at the endpoints, not in the network. Thus, the network can be slow, "dumb," or broken, but intelligence in the endpoints should compensate for this. This is exactly the opposite of the design philosophy of the telephone network, where endpoints are assumed to be "dumb" and all the intelligence (with a few exceptions) is provided by telephone company equipment.

End-to-end reliability in the Internet is provided by a protocol layer that operates above the Internet Protocol (IP). IP provides end-to-end connectivity with no guaranty of reliability. A layer above IP, called the Transmission Control Protocol or TCP, usually provides error control and flow control to allow reliable and controlled data transfer over the unreliable network. We will study TCP in detail in Chapter 15.

Note that the philosophy of endpoint control allows the network to be built with few assumptions, making it easy to add new network types (such as packet-radio or satellite networks) into the Internet. Unfortunately, this also implies that a change in TCP involves changes to every endpoint, making it hard to upgrade. In contrast, in the telephone network, while adding new kinds of networks is harder, upgrading the technology of the existing network is easier because it does not need end-system cooperation. For example, the introduction of cellular telephones did not require existing telephones to be upgraded.

3.6   History

Though the Internet seemed to spring full-grown into public consciousness in the 1990s, the ideas behind the Internet date back to the early 1960s, and the earliest portion of the Internet dates to 1969. Perhaps future historians will call the Internet the third great contribution of the 1960s, along with space travel and the Beatles! In this section, we present an abbreviated history of the Internet. A more detailed history, with interesting anecdotes, can be found in *The Internet System Handbook*, by Lynch and Rose [LR 93].

The Internet owes its design to two basic needs: a need to share expensive computing resources among researchers, and the desire for the U.S. military to have a communications infrastructure that was robust against a large-scale nuclear attack by the former Soviet Union. These two needs mesh nicely in the decentralized design of the Internet.

The fundamental basis of the Internet, that is, store-and-forward packet switching, was invented in 1961 by Baran in the United States. He wrote a series of technical memos that laid out his ideas on packet switching, scalable routing, and survivable networks. He had three primary motivations. First, packet networks are cheaper to build and operate than telephone networks, since store-and-forward multiplexors could share expensive transmission facilities more efficiently than telephone switches. Second, they are more reliable, since retransmissions on each link could achieve reliability even on very noisy lines. Finally, a meshlike topology is less susceptible to nuclear annihilation than a telephone-network style star- or tree-shaped topology because it provides more alternative paths between end-systems.

3.6.1   ARPAnet

Baran's ideas lay dormant for some years (though independently discovered in France by Zimmerman, who worked on the CYCLADES packet-switched network) until the U.S. Department of Defense Advanced Research Project Agency sponsored a communication network called ARPAnet. The designers of ARPAnet, primarily interested in resource sharing among the few widely scattered time-sharing systems of the time, decided to use Baran's ideas to build the ARPAnet, because they wanted to share the cost of expensive long-distance telephone lines. ARPAnet was proposed in 1966 and built in late 1969 by researchers at a few universities and research labs. It pioneered the practical use of wide-area packet switching, decentralized routing, flow control, and many applications still in use today, such as telnet and FTP. The experience gained in building and operating ARPAnet was critical in the design of simple and effective protocols that would later be used in the Internet. ARPAnet was the first network in the Internet, fondly called "net ten" because of its network number.

The design of an "internet" or a network of networks was motivated by a packet radio network that was also sponsored by ARPA and built at the Stanford Research Institute (SRI) in Menlo Park, California [Clark 88]. Researchers using the packet-radio network wanted to communicate over the leased-line-based ARPAnet. This led to a shared packet format, routing, and addressing schemes. Nevertheless, care was taken to decentralize administration to allow independent expansion of the separate networks. The notion of a "gateway," a computer whose job was to route packets between networks, was developed. Also, it was necessary to decide that IP would not make any assumptions about the underlying transmission medium. These key decisions—*decentralization of administration, design for scaling,* and *bare-bones assumptions made by IP*—were the results of experiences with building this two-network Internet and have contributed greatly to the Internet's rapid growth. In many ways, these design decisions, made in the early 1970s, have not changed in the past twenty-five years.

Although ARPAnet was successful, it was restricted to sites that received funding from DARPA. However, many other universities were interested in obtaining a connection to a packet-switched network, even if they did not receive DARPA funding. This led to the construction of other ARPA-like networks, such as CSNET and NEARnet. By adopting the Internet standard addressing scheme and Internet standard routing, they could interoperate, leading gradually to an erasing of distinctions among these networks. By the early 1980s, ten of such networks joined to form the Internet.

3.6.2   DNA, SNA, and ISO

ARPAnet was not alone in the field of packet switching. Although it was unique in that it was designed explicitly for computers from multiple vendors, two other significant packet-switched networks were designed and built at the same time. International Business Machines (IBM) developed Systems Network Architecture (SNA) to interconnect its mainframes, and Digital Equipment Corporation (DEC) developed Digital Network Architecture (DNA, also called DECnet). Both of them were quite successful, and both networks are still around. However, they restricted endpoints to be IBM or DEC machines, and the key protocols and software were proprietary. In the face of competition from an open architecture, they have begun a long decline, because organizations committing to DNA or SNA are tied to DEC or IBM machines, but organizations choosing TCP/IP have their choice of vendors, including DEC and IBM. However, many ideas in SNA and DNA (such as in congestion and flow control) have had a strong influence on the evolution of the Internet. For example, the Internet's Open Shortest Path First (OSPF) routing protocol is based on DEC's Intermediate-System-Intermediate-System (IS-IS) protocol, and the Internet's Simple Network Management Protocol (SNMP) is derived from DEC's Network Control Protocol.

International standards bodies also played a role in the development of packet-switched networks. The International Organization for Standards (ISO) came up with a seven-layer architecture for packet switching, which we will study in Chapter 5 [Zimmerman 80]. It also promoted nonproprietary networking through its Open Systems Interconnect (OSI) standard. However, ISO/OSI protocols are far less popular in the marketplace than ARPAnet-like networks. Incidentally, the Internet has its own standardization body, called the Internet Engineering Task Force (IETF). The IETF recommends Internet-wide standards called *Requests for Comments (RFCs)*, which are typically determined by consensus among manufacturers and interested academics. See reference [LR 93] for more information on this process.

3.6.3   LANs and commercialization

One reason for the explosive growth of computer networking in the 1980s was the invention of Ethernet, a cheap Local Area Network (LAN) technology. Developed by researchers at Xerox's Palo Alto Research Center in the late 1970s (with support from Intel and DEC), Ethernet allowed computers within a small campus to be interconnected with little effort. Small switches called *bridges* allowed several Ethernets to talk to each other, expanding the scale of campus networks. Thus, colleges and universities could wire up their departments at a fairly low cost, creating a generation of students comfortable with using networks when they entered the workforce. Unfortunately, a critical barrier stood in their path.

From the early days of the Internet, DARPA policy was that although researchers could use ARPAnet facilities for personal uses, such as for email, this use was secondary to research in distributed computing. Commercial traffic was strictly forbidden; new users who posted advertisements received severe warnings from their peers. When funding from DARPA dried up in the late 1980s, new funding continued from the National Science Foundation (NSF) which continued the no-commercial-use policy. It made all participating institutions sign an "Acceptable Use Policy" which forbade commercial traffic on the Internet.

However, as the Internet grew to encompass nearly all of the higher educational institutions in the United States, the United Kingdom, and other developed countries, and as the U.S. federal government saw an opportunity to make the Internet a part of its National Information Infrastructure, there was considerable political backing to drop the Acceptable Use Policy. In 1992 the policy was withdrawn, allowing commercial organizations free access to the network. Simultaneously, a plan was made to withdraw U.S. federal funding of the national backbone gradually; federal funding stopped on May 1, 1995. The National Science Foundation still gives grants for Internet access to educational institutions, but the days of "free" Internet usage are gone. Moreover, advertising on the Internet has become common, perhaps even a dominant component of current Internet usage. This has also meant a decline in the influence of academics over the architecture of the Internet.

3.6.4   Growth

The Internet has continued to double almost every year for the last twenty-five years. The impetus for this growth comes from several sources. First, the U.S. government views the Internet as the first step to the "Information Superhighway." It has tried to encourage efforts to make Internet access universal, in the same way as telephone service in the United States is universal. Governments around the world have followed suit. Second, with commercial usage allowed, many companies view doing business on the Internet as a cost-effective way to reach customers to sell them goods and services, and to provide information and after-sales support. Companies also use the Internet to hook up their offices to form virtual private networks. Third, email on the Internet has become widespread and effective. Its asynchronous nature is perfectly suited to our increasingly busy lives.

3.6.5   The World Wide Web

The dominant application on the Internet today is the World Wide Web. Invented as a way for high-energy particle physicists to share experimental data and results, the Web has transformed the usage of the Internet. Before the availability of easy-to-use Web browsers, Internet users had to deal with complex and poorly documented command-line interfaces. With the current generation of browsers, using the Internet is literally as simple as pointing and clicking. Web browsers also support a rich palette of media types, such as pictures, audio, and video, instead of the text-only Internet of the past. Perhaps the most unexpected payoff is the ability of any user of the Web to become an information publisher. This role, formerly reserved for newspaper editors and film directors, is now possible for anyone who cares to put up a Web page.

A more detailed critique of the potential and problems facing the Internet can be found in reference [BK 95] and references therein.

3.7   Challenges

3.7.1   IP address space shortage

One of the most immediate technological challenges facing the Internet is the shortage of IP addresses. As we saw, IP addresses are hierarchically structured, with a network number and an interface number. Once a central authority gives an organization a network number, the organization can create addresses within that network whenever it wants. Unfortunately, if the organization chooses not to use the entire available address space, this space is not available to other organizations. In the early days of the Internet, Class A and B addresses were handed out freely, because no one anticipated the overwhelming success of the network. However, even the largest organizations cannot fully use the 2^{24} (approximately 16 million) addresses in a Class A address. Thus, the actual usage of the 32-bit address space is quite sparse.

The current solution is to assign newer organizations multiple Class C addresses instead of Class B or Class A addresses. However, each Class C address contributes an entry in the routing table of the backbone routers. Thus, their routing tables are large, making packet-forwarding inefficient.

Efforts are under way to increase the IP address space to 128 bits. This scheme has to be backward compatible with 32-bit addresses already in the Internet, and eventually the new scheme has to be adopted all over the network. Until this happens there will continue to be an IP address shortage.

3.7.2   Problems of decentralized control

The decentralization of control that was so essential to the Internet's scalability also threatens to turn it into an anarchy where *reliable* service can never be guaranteed. It only takes one router to drop or imperceptibly alter packets to cause problems everywhere in the network (for example, if corrupted routing packets cause routing tables to lose consistency). Because there is no control over adding routers to the network, this may be a disaster waiting to happen.

A more pernicious problem is security. Packets sent on the Internet are visible to anyone who wishes to examine them. Security was not a serious problem when the Internet was the preserve of academics. With commerce on the Internet, there is good reason to believe that packets sent into the Internet might be examined or spoofed by unscrupulous intermediates. End-to-end encryption partially solves this problem, but introduces complexity at the endpoints and requires a scalable and efficient key distribution scheme. These problems are less severe in an *intranet*, where all the computers and routers are administered by a single organization and therefore trust each other.

A third problem stemming from decentralized control is that there is no uniform way to do accounting on the Internet [MV 95]. Because neither academics nor soldiers cared much for accounting, mechanisms for billing and cost-sharing are nonexistent. This has led to flat-rate pricing based on the bandwidth of the access link. Although this system is simple and works reasonably well, as federal subsidies go away and the Internet begins to carry multimedia traffic, there is more need for accounting and billing. For example, consider a network provider who wants to bill users accessing a popular World Wide Web site on that network in the same way the telephone network bills calls to 900-series telephone numbers. Unlike the telephone network, the Internet does not provide a reliable way to identify users, so user authentication must be done with special passwords. This requires users either to remember a different password for every site, or to use the same one for all sites, leaving the door wide open if any one of the sites is successfully cracked. The point is that while accounting in the Internet is possible, it was never incorporated into the design and is complicated by decentralization.

Fourth, there is no equivalent of the white or yellow pages of a telephone directory. Discovering a user's email address reliably is impossible; even if one is obtained, there is no way to know whether the address is out-of-date or has been subverted by an unscrupulous user.

Finally, decentralized control means that routing can sometimes be nonoptimal. Since no single authority is responsible for globally optimal decisions, a series of locally optimal decisions can result in global chaos. As an extreme example, it was recently discovered that for several months, all traffic between France and the United Kingdom was being sent via the United States. Although this sort of suboptimal routing could occur in any network, the point is that this routing problem went undiscovered for many months because no single authority was in charge of routing.

3.7.3 Multimedia

"Multimedia" applications that need real-time performance guarantees such as bounded delay and a minimum throughput are not well supported in the current Internet. These performance parameters are often called "quality-of-service" parameters. A major challenge facing the Internet is integrating quality-of-service requirements into the existing architecture.

If a store-and-forward router stores traffic from all users in a shared buffer and serves them in the order received, a user who sends in a burst of packets and fills the shared buffer can cause higher delays and losses for other users. This is because packets belonging to other users are queued behind the burst of packets and get service only after the entire burst has been served. If the burst uses all available buffers, incoming packets from other users might be dropped. This is analogous to a post office where customers are served in the order they arrive. If twenty-five customers arrive simultaneously, new customers have to wait until all twenty-five are served. Someone who only wants to ask a question of an employee has to wait just as long as someone who wants to send a parcel. This is a natural consequence of the first-come-first-served (FCFS) service order. In a network, if one of the users competing with the burst is sending voice packets, the receiver will hear breakups, which can be annoying. Similarly, if a video is being transferred, the receiver may see jerkiness or gaps in the video.

A network can give users better quality of service if users share buffers fairly, and if it serves packets not in the order received, but round-robin among the sources. In our post office example, this would correspond to having separate lines for requesting information and sending parcels, so that users who need only a little service are not held up behind others. However, most routers in the Internet share buffers unfairly and provide FCFS service. Thus, to guarantee quality of service, all other existing routers need to change over to round-robin service. Given decentralized control, mandating this change is hard.

The other mechanism needed for providing quality of service is signaling to inform each router along the path about the quality of service needed by each *stream* of packets. Alternatively, this signaling mechanism has to set up quality-of-service parameters for each class of traffic, and each incoming packet has to be classified as belonging to an existing class. New streams, when they start, must be admitted (or denied admission) into the network. All this requires much more cooperation among routers than is provided for in the Internet or in its philosophy.

3.8　Summary

The Internet uses two key technologies: packets and store-and-forward switching. It is held together by addressing, routing, and the Internet Protocol (IP). The Internet has been wildly successful because of its decentralized control and store-and-forward architecture. Precisely these two features make it harder to introduce features such as billing, reliability, quality of service, and accounting. Only time will tell how successful the Internet will be in integrating these essential features.

Chapter 4

ATM Networks: Concepts, History, and Challenges

Asynchronous Transfer Mode (ATM) networks aim to combine the flexibility of the Internet with the per-user quality-of-service guarantees of the telephone network. They are designed for high bandwidth, scalability, and manageability. Thus, they have the potential to subsume both the Internet and the telephone network, creating a unified infrastructure that carries voice, video, and data. Although ATM networks are likely to play an important role in the future, the research community is still debating how best to build them. Moreover, we have neither consensus nor field experience for important components such as traffic specification, multicast, and fault tolerance. We must resolve these issues before ATM networks achieve their full potential.

Note that ATM refers not only to a network technology, but also to standards proposed by two standardization bodies, the *International Telecommunications Union—Telecommunications Standardization Sector (ITU-T)* and the *ATM Forum*. Unless otherwise stated, we will discuss ATM technology independent of these standards.

ATM networks are based on some important concepts: (1) virtual circuits, (2) fixed-size packets or *cells,* (3) small packet size, (4) statistical multiplexing, and (5) integrated services. Together, these ideas allow us to build networks that can carry multiple classes of traffic (unlike the telephone network) with quality-of-service guarantees provided to individual streams (unlike the Internet). They also enable large, parallel switches and provide a uniform framework for network management. We study these concepts next.

4.1   Virtual circuits

4.1.1   Synchronous Transfer Mode

ATM networks were initially designed in response to problems with the *Synchronous Transfer Mode (STM)* transmission used in telephone networks. We therefore first study how two time-division-multiplexed synchronous transfer mode circuits might share a physical link.

Consider a telephone trunk that connects two cities, say, Bangkok and Singapore. Imagine two users in Bangkok sharing the link to a common correspondent in Singapore as follows: from 1:00 A.M. to 2:00 A.M., user A has the link. From 2:00 A.M. to 3:00 A.M., user B has the link, and so on. Thus, if the transmitters and receiver agree on the time, to determine the transmitter, the receiver only has to know the current time. For example, if the time is 1:15 A.M., data arriving on the link must be coming from A. If the transmitters and the receiver agree on the time, that is, if they are in *synchrony*, data from the two users are never confused. We call this type of link-sharing synchronous transfer mode (STM). Notice that in STM, data arriving at the receiver do not need a descriptive header—the fact that data arrived at a particular time is sufficient to identify their source.

> In practice, achieving exact time synchrony between the transmitter and receiver is impossible, so a transmitter adds special synchronization bits in a well-known pattern. The receiver synchronizes itself to the transmitter by locking itself to the transmitted bit pattern. It can then extract the information from each multiplexed user, because this is present in a fixed order within a transmitted *frame*. The problems with STM described next remain even with these modifications to the operational details.

STM has two major problems. First, even if A does not have data to send—say, from 1:45 A.M. to 2:00 A.M.—B cannot use the link instead. In STM, unused time slots must be wasted, because the receiver distinguishes data from A and from B only from the current time (or, to be precise, the order of slots in a frame).

The second problem is more subtle. Synchronous transfer, in theory, does not prohibit two users, A and B, from sharing a link using an arbitrary schedule. For example, A could send for 21 seconds, then B for 18 minutes, then A for 12.43 minutes. This would allow A and B to share the link in arbitrary ways. The receiver must, however, know the entire schedule in advance, complicating its operation. To simplify matters, in practice, links are shared using a *fixed cyclical* schedule, where all slots in the schedule are equally long. Then, the only information the receiver needs is the length of a time slice and the schedule. For example, a time slice could be 10 milliseconds long, and the schedule might be ABAABB. If the schedule has N slots, and the shared link's bandwidth is B bps, then a user can get bandwidth *only* in chunks of B/N bps. In the telephone network, schedule slots are chosen to correspond to 64 Kbps (sufficient for one voice call) so that a user of the telephone network can get bandwidth only in 64-Kbps chunks. In other words, STM restricts the range of bandwidths available to a connection. This is a problem, for example, if an application wants 90 Kbps of bandwidth: it can receive only 64 or 128 Kbps.

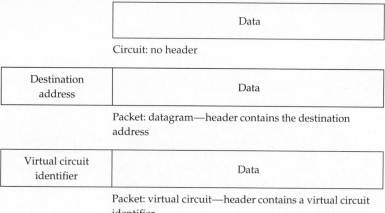

Figure 4.1: Fundamental differences among circuits, datagrams, and virtual circuits. Data in a circuit have no header. A datagram carries the full destination address. Packets in a virtual circuit network carry only an identifier instead of the full address. In the figure, the header is not to scale (virtual circuit identifiers are smaller than datagram headers).

4.1.2   Packet-switched networks

STM service is inflexible: circuits based on STM must have a bandwidth in multiples of a time slice, and a source wastes any portion of this bandwidth that it does not use. We solve these problems in a packet-switched network by introducing a *header* or *meta-data* to describe the data, in particular, its source and destination (Figure 4.1). The header allows intermediate switches to store packets, forwarding them when convenient. So, for example, if A is not using the link, B can use it, and the receiver can distinguish between the two from the meta-data. Moreover, more complicated link sharing is possible, since the receiver does not have to rely on a *fixed* frame format to decide the source of the data. In particular, a source can be allocated a bandwidth that is not necessarily a multiple of a fixed base rate, such as 64 Kbps. Thus, packet-switched networks are efficient and flexible.

4.1.3   Datagrams and virtual circuits

There are two ways to build a packet-switched network. The first is for each packet to carry a header with the full destination address (much like a postal address on an envelope). This is the *datagram* method, and each packet containing the full destination address is called a datagram. Addresses can be large, so if the average datagram length is small, this wastes bandwidth. For example, if the mean data length is 50 bytes, and the destination address is 4 bytes long, 8% of the bandwidth is wasted.

   In the second way to build a packet-switched network, packet headers carry identifiers instead of addresses, and each switch maintains a translation from the identifier to

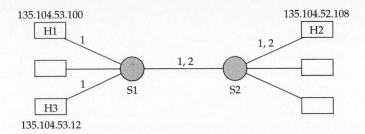

Figure 4.2: Virtual circuit concept. Host H1 sends data to host H2 using virtual circuit identifier 1. Switches S1 and S2 have been set up so that they know this mapping. Host 3 uses VCI 1 on link H3–S1 and VCI 2 on link S1–H2. S1 translates VCI 1 from H3 to VCI 2 on S1–S2.

a destination. This saves header space because identifiers are smaller than destination addresses (Figure 4.1). However, the mapping from an identifier to a destination must be set up at each switch along the path before data transmission begins. In other words, a *call setup phase* must precede a *data transmission phase*. We call this variant virtual circuit (VC) switching.

4.1.4   Virtual circuits

Consider a switch S1 connected to three endpoints as in Figure 4.2 (we will call the endpoints hosts, using IP terminology). Host H1 can send a message to host H2 in one of two ways. In the datagram method, it creates a header with H2's address and hands it to switch S1. The switch reads H2's address and a routing table directs it to pass on the packet to S2. S2 in turn forwards the packet to H2.

In the virtual circuit method, H1 sends a *setup* message to S1 requesting a connection to H2. Using the same routing table as before, S1 decides that the next switch along the path is S2. It forwards the setup message to S2 and returns an identifier called the Virtual Circuit Identifier or *VCI*[1] to the host (in the example, the VCI "1" is assigned to H1). It also creates a per-VC record that stores the output interface corresponding to the assigned VCI. After the setup completes, if H1 wants to send a message to H2, it only needs to put the VCI in the header instead of the full destination address. By examining the identifier, S1 knows that this message is destined to S2, and simply forwards it on the correct output interface.

Each header bit represents an unavoidable overhead because every packet must carry a header. Thus, we prefer to have as small a header as possible. Note that VCIs save header space, because identifiers are smaller than destination addresses. In this sense, virtual circuits are more efficient in their use of bandwidth than datagrams.

---

[1]The ATM Forum calls this a Virtual *Channel* Identifier.

Returning to our example, suppose host H3 also wants to communicate with H2. It must send a setup message to S1 and get a VCI in return. Consider the link from S1 to S2. Packets from H1 on this link have "1" in the header. If packets from H3 also have the same identifier on the link, then packets from H1 and H3 will be indistinguishable. Clearly, packets from H3 must use a different VCI. There are two ways to ensure this.

In one solution, any two virtual circuits sharing a link must be guaranteed to use different VCIs. A host that wants to set up a new connection must know which VCIs are being used by all other hosts sharing any link along its path. Although this solution is theoretically possible, it does not scale to large networks. A better solution is for switch S1 to resolve conflicts by *VCI swapping*. When S1 receives packets from H3, it modifies the VCI in the header from 1 to 2. Thus, packets on link S1–S2 have unique VCIs, as required. VCI swapping requires every switch to maintain a *translation table* mapping input VCIs to output VCIs. When a switch accepts a call, it chooses a unique VCI on the output trunk, and enters the translation from the input VCI to the output VCI in the translation table.

Virtual circuits are *connection-oriented*, that is, a source must establish a circuit or connection before it can transfer any data (for example, in the telephone network, you must dial and wait for the call to complete before you speak). In contrast, we call datagram networks *connectionless* networks, because a source does not need to establish a connection before communication (for example, you can post a letter without informing the recipient). We now make some observations about VC switching.

- Each switch has to maintain some information (state) about each virtual circuit for determining the output link and output VCI of an incoming packet. This information is kept in a table called the *translation table.* The translation table for switch S1 in Figure 4.2 is shown below.

In line	In VCI	Out line	Out VCI
H1–S1	1	S1–S2	1
H3–S1	1	S1–S2	2

- Since each packet carries an identifier and not the full destination address, and the identifier is known only to switches that have been set up, *all packets sent in the data transmission phase must follow the same route.* If any switch along the route fails, the virtual circuit also fails. Although a network can reroute a virtual circuit, this is complicated and tedious. In contrast, each datagram can choose the path to reach the destination independently. If a switch fails, datagrams stored in that switch would be lost, but the network can easily route other datagrams around the failure.

- Each switch stores per-VC state, that is, a per-VC entry in the translation table. This allows a switch to store other per-VC information, such as the relative priority of the VC and the amount of bandwidth reserved for that VC. By keeping this state information, *a switch can provide per-VC quality of service.* In contrast, datagram-oriented switches are not required to store per-stream state, or even distinguish between packets from different sources. Thus, it is harder to provide per-stream quality of service with datagram switches.

- The actions during the data transfer phase and call-setup (or *signaling*) phase are distinct. Switch controllers set up and tear down calls and are not involved during actual data transfer. This *separation of data and control* allows us to build the data transfer part of switches entirely in hardware, so that they are fast, cheap, and dumb. The complex signaling procedures needed for call setup, invoked only once per call, are performed by an intelligent switch controller that operates on a slower time scale. In contrast, in a datagram network a switch has to read the complete address and look up the route table for each incoming packet. This is harder to achieve in hardware.

- A virtual circuit does not automatically provide any guarantee of reliability. It is a myth that virtual circuits necessarily provide low loss rates and in-order delivery. A VC network is subject to the same kinds of loss behavior as a datagram network. The only obvious difference is that because all packets follow the same path, they are much more likely to be in order.

- Small identifiers for virtual circuits reduce header overhead. They also allow switches to store per-virtual-circuit state, such as the output on which packets should be forwarded, indexed by the VCI. When a cell arrives, the VCI in the header can be used to directly map to an array of per-VCI information, making switches easier to build in hardware.

- A source can transfer data on a virtual circuit only after it has been set up. Setup takes at least one round-trip time, because the setup message must propagate from the source to the destination and back. If the source and destination are far apart, this delay can be significant. For example, if a computer in New Jersey wants to send a 1-byte message to a computer in California 2500 miles away, it will take at least 39.6 ms for the circuit to be set up, and then another 19.8 ms for the byte to be transferred. In contrast, a datagram network needs no setup, and so the byte can arrive in as little as 19.8 ms, or three times as fast.

- A virtual circuit that is set up for a duration of a call, then torn down, is called a *switched virtual circuit* or *SVC*. Setting up an SVC requires signaling, which is complex, and takes time. To avoid signaling, a user can hard-wire an entry in the translation table at each switch along the path. A circuit created in this manner is called a *permanent virtual circuit* or *PVC*.

- One way to reduce the call setup latency is to preallocate a range of VCIs that go from a particular source to a particular destination. Then, by choosing a VCI in this range, a source avoids the need to perform call setup before data transfer. We call this range of preestablished VCIs a *virtual path*. Virtual paths not only require less signaling, but also need less table space at switches, because they aggregate information about many virtual circuits. On the other hand, resources allocated to a virtual path could lie unused even if no virtual circuit is using them.

- Another way to avoid call-setup latency is for a source to establish a call and send the first data packet immediately. The data packet is sent on a special VCI that has no translation table entry. When a switch sees a packet on this VCI, it holds in it a special buffer, awaiting further instructions from the switch controller. The switch controller uses the call-setup packet to determine the destination of the data packet, and when it installs the translation table entry, the data packet is released from the buffer and forwarded to the next switch. In this way, call establishment and data transfer occur in parallel. The disadvantage of this scheme is that it introduces additional complexity in the switch and the switch controller. Moreover, call establishment is typically much slower than data forwarding. Thus, the scheme avoids speed-of-light propagation delay, but is subject to call-establishment delays at every switch controller on the path.

- A third way to avoid call-setup latency is to dedicate a VCI to carry datagrams. A switch, therefore, simply hands packets arriving on this VCI to a co-located datagram router, which forwards the packet by examining its destination address.

- The distinction between datagrams and virtual circuits diminishes if a switch treats the source address/destination address pair like a large VCI. One can imagine a switch that hashes this address pair to a unique identifier and uses this to access state. When the first packet from a source to a destination arrives, the switch could determine the output interface and store this in a per-conversation table. Subsequent datagrams would not need route table lookups. This would give us the advantages of virtual circuits, such as per-VC state, but without the need for an explicit call setup or VCI swapping. If more than one flow of packets exists between a source and a destination, then the flows need to be further distinguished by a *flow identifier*. The IETF has proposed this scheme for IP version 6.

4.2   Fixed-size packets

ATM networks use fixed-sized packets called *cells* instead of variable-length packets for three reasons: (1) simpler buffer hardware, (2) simpler line scheduling, and (3) large parallel switches that are easier to build.

4.2.1   Buffer hardware

We saw in Chapter 3 that a packet switch must have buffers to store packets before they are forwarded. Dynamic storage allocation for variable-size packets is harder than for fixed-size cells. When laying out variable-size packets in memory, a switch must either find a contiguous space large enough to hold the packet, or link noncontiguous areas with pointers. When a packet is transmitted, a variable amount of buffer space is released, requiring housekeeping overhead to keep track of available memory. With fixed-sized cells, a switch can keep all buffers in a single free pool and easily find space for an incoming cell. Since all cells are the same size, no memory fragmentation will occur and compaction is unnecessary.

4.2.2   Line scheduling

Let us look more closely at Switch S1 in Figure 4.2, redrawn in Figure 4.3. Note that hosts H1 and H3 share link S1–S2. A link scheduler determines the nature of this sharing by deciding which packet goes next on the shared link. For example, if it decides to send three cells from H1 for every cell from H3, H1 will get up to three times the bandwidth of H3. If the scheduler decides to give cells from H1 priority over cells from H3, cells from H1 will get a lower queuing delay than cells from H3. Thus, the series of packet transmissions on an output link determine the bandwidth and delay received by a virtual circuit. By programming the link scheduler appropriately (with a *scheduling discipline*), a network operator can allocate different bandwidths and queuing delays to different virtual circuits. This allocation is simplified if packets are of fixed size. For example, a schedule that serves three cells from H1, then one from H3 guarantees a fourth of the link bandwidth to H3. If every packet could be a different size, bandwidth and delay allocations are harder to manage. For example, if H1 sends a 560-byte packet and H2 sends a 132-byte packet, to share the link bandwidth equally, the scheduler must remember to give a subsequent packet from H2 priority over a packet from H1, to even out their bandwidth share. Thus, it is harder to achieve simple ratios with variable-size packets. We will study scheduling in more detail in Chapter 9.

4.2.3   Large parallel packet switches

A straightforward way to build a switch is to buffer packets at each input, then have a processor poll inputs in turn, writing them to the appropriate output. Large telephone switches, which can have more than a hundred thousand inputs and outputs, cannot be built with a single processor; the switch must process packets in parallel. The usual way to build a parallel switch is to divide it into three parts—input buffers, *switch fabric*, and output buffers (Figure 4.3). The fabric is an interconnection of switching elements that transfers packets from any input to any output. To maximize parallelism, all switching elements must complete a partial packet transfer simultaneously. Since the packet transfer time depends on its length, the maximum parallelism is achieved when all packets are the same size. With variable-size packets, some switching elements will be idle, waiting for a previous element to complete its processing, thus decreasing the degree of parallelism. We will study switching in more detail in Chapter 8.

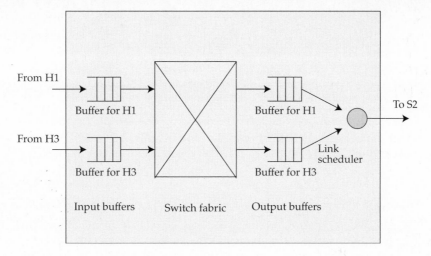

Figure 4.3: Output link scheduling. Packets from H1 and H3 are buffered at the output queue before transmission. The link scheduler decides which packet goes next on the link. Thus, it determines the delay and bandwidth received by H1 and H3.

4.2.4   Problems with fixed size

Fixed-size cells have some advantages over variable-size packets, but they also have some problems. A source that wants to send data larger than the chosen size must segment the data into fixed-size cells, and the destination may need to reassemble these packets. This processing can be computationally expensive, particularly if the chosen size is smaller than the mean application-level data unit, and if the network runs at high speeds. (Even in variable-sized-packet networks, endpoints must segment and reassemble data units larger than the maximum allowed packet size. This maximum size, however, is typically larger than the mean application data size.) Conversely, if a source wants to send less data than the chosen size, bandwidth is wasted. A second problem is that when fragmenting a long message into fixed-size cells, the last cell may not be fully filled. This wastes bandwidth. The designers of ATM technology felt that the advantages of a fixed cell size outweighed the problems.

4.3   Small packet size

ATM cells are small because of the way ATM networks carry voice traffic: the transmitter digitizes voice samples, puts them in a cell, adds a cell header, and hands the cell to the network for transmission. The receiver removes the samples, converts them to analog format, and plays them. The delay between speaking and hearing therefore depends on how many voice samples a transmitter collects in each cell. The smallest *packetization delay* occurs if a transmitter puts only one sample per cell. However, this also causes the

5 byte header	48 bytes of data

Figure 4.4: Standard ATM cell. The header portion is 5 bytes long, and the data portion is 48 bytes long, a compromise between 32 and 64 bytes.

largest cell header overhead, so sending only one sample per cell is inefficient. There is a trade-off between packetization delay and header overhead.

4.3.1   Standard cell size

When the CCITT (Consultative Committee on International Telephone and Telecommunications), the international standards body for telecommunications (now renamed ITU-T), was deciding the packet size for ATM in 1989, it debated the pros and cons of small and large cell size. Recall from Chapter 2 that telephone companies prefer small packetization delays, because this reduces the need for echo cancellation on long-distance trunks. Thus, there was a strong push from telephone company representatives for a packet size as small as possible, while still maintaining a tolerable header overhead. Because the United States is geographically spread out, with significant speed-of-light propagation delays, U.S. telephone companies had already invested in echo-cancellation equipment for long-distance service. Thus, they were keen to reduce header overhead as much as possible: they wanted a cell size of 64 bytes, corresponding to an 8-ms packetization delay. European and Japanese telephone companies did not have much investment in echo cancellation—because their countries are smaller—and to avoid adding echo cancellation to all their long-distance lines, wanted a cell size of 32 bytes, corresponding to a packetization delay of 4 ms. The two groups finally decided to split the difference, so that the ITU-T international standard for ATM cell size is 48 bytes (Figure 4.4). There is an additional 5-byte header, so that a full cell is 53 bytes long. Ironically, this decision fritters away one of the main motivations for virtual circuit switching, reduced header overhead. An ATM network is guaranteed to be at most 90.57% efficient because 5 bytes out of every 53 are overhead.

EXAMPLE 4.1

(a) Compute the packetization delay for an ATM cell and for a 1500-byte packet. (b) Assuming a service rate of 64 Kbps, and that voice calls can tolerate a round-trip delay of 100 ms, how many kilometers can a call span without using echo cancelers for 32- and 64-byte cells?

Solution: (a) The packetization delay for an ATM cell is 6 ms. For a 1500-byte packet, the delay is 187.5 ms. (b) With 32-byte cells, the transmission time is 4 ms, and the packetization time is 4 ms. Because this delay is seen in both directions, $100 - 2 * 8$ = 84 ms can be used by propagation delay. Light travels at 210,000 km/s in fiber, so this corresponds to a round trip of 17,640 km or a one-way span of 8820 km. With 64-byte cells, the transmission time is 8 ms, and the packetization time is also 8 ms, so that the propagation delay can be no more than $100 - 2 * 16 = 68$ ms, which corresponds to a round-trip distance of 14,280 km and a one-way span of 7140 km.

4.4 Statistical multiplexing

$T > La/R$

Consider a time-division multiplexor multiplexing ATM cells from four sources onto a shared output line (Figure 4.5). If exactly one cell arrives at each of the four inputs every second, the multiplexor must have an output rate of at least 4 cells/second, and each input buffers at most one cell. Because a cell has to wait for at most three other cells to be transmitted, a source would have a queuing delay of at most three cell service times. Now, assume that cells arrive in bursts, where each burst has 10 cells evenly spaced 1 second apart, corresponding to a peak rate of 1 cell/second. Let the mean interval between the end of a burst and the start of the next burst be 100 seconds, so that the average rate is 0.09 cells/second (10 cells arrive every 110 seconds). What should be the speed of the output line?

There is no single answer to this question. We could conservatively provision the output line at 4 cells/second. Then, even if all four bursts arrived simultaneously, they would not overload the multiplexor. It is likely, however, that only one burst would be active at any given time. Thus, we could optimistically set the output line speed at only 1 cell/second, at the expense of buffering cells if the output line is busy.

The trade-off between the output line speed and the mean delay of an input stream is shown in Figure 4.6. If the output line is faster than 4 cells/second, then the worst-case queuing delay waiting for service is three cell times at that speed—for example, when the line serves 4 cells/second, the delay is 0.75 seconds, because each cell service takes 0.25 seconds. If the output line serves less than the aggregated average rate of 0.36 cells/second, then the worst-case queuing delay is infinite, since input buffers will build up

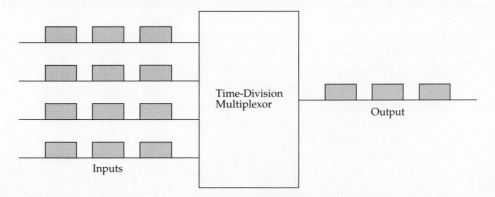

Figure 4.5: A time-division multiplexor. The output line must run faster than the sum of the inputs.

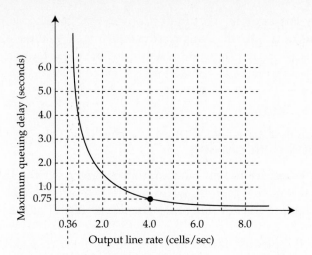

Figure 4.6: Trade-off between statistical multiplexing gain and worst-case delay. As the output line speed increases, the maximum queuing delay for a source decreases. When the output line is less than the sum of the average rates (0.36 cells/s), the maximum queuing delay is infinite. When it is more than the sum of the peak rates (4 cells/s), then the maximum queuing delay is the time to serve three cells at that rate.

without bound. Between these two rates, the worst-case delay is a decreasing function of the output line speed.

Suppose we choose an output line speed of 1.25 cells/second. Since we are not serving at the peak rate of 4 cells/second, we get a *statistical multiplexing gain* of 4 / 1.25 = 3.2. However, this also results in a worst-case queuing delay larger than 0.75 seconds. We can interpret the curve in Figure 4.6 as measuring the trade-off between the statistical multiplexing gain and the worst-case delay. For zero loss, the input buffer must be large enough to handle the worst-case delay. Thus, the curve also measures the trade-off between the statistical multiplexing gain and the buffer size for zero loss.

Thus far, we have considered statistical multiplexing in a simple time-division multiplexor. The same arguments also apply to a cell switch because the output link scheduler is identical to a time-division multiplexor. A cell switch can exploit statistical multiplexing gain in the same way as a time-division multiplexor.

We can generalize the notion of statistical multiplexing gain from our example. Suppose a resource is used by n bursty sources that have a peak rate of p and an average rate of a. In the worst case, requests from all sources could arrive simultaneously, so a conservative resource allocation scheme is to serve them at a rate of np. If this makes the server expensive, we can buffer some resource requests, and serve them at a rate r which is smaller than np, but larger than na. Then, the ratio np/r is the statistical multiplexing gain. To achieve this gain, resource requests must be buffered. If all bursts of requests last less than b seconds, the buffer needed to avoid losing requests is approximately

$nb(p - r)$. If the buffer is smaller, then some requests may be lost. The general principle is that whenever the long-term average rate differs from the peak rate, we can use statistical multiplexing to trade off service rate for mean delay.

EXAMPLE 4.2

Can different sources get different statistical multiplexing gains on the same output trunk?

Solution: Yes, if the link scheduler gives each source a different bandwidth allocation.

Statistical multiplexing gain is central to the design of ATM networks. Unlike STM networks, where voice samples cannot be buffered indefinitely awaiting an output line, ATM cells can be stored before they are forwarded, allowing ATM switches to trade off delay for a slower output line speed. Because, in the wide area, bandwidth is much more expensive than buffers, this gain makes an ATM network cheaper to operate than an equivalent STM network. Note that the statistical multiplexing gain depends greatly on the gap between the peak and average rate of a source. If ATM workloads turn out to have similar peak and average rates, then ATM networks cannot exploit statistical multiplexing gain.

4.5   Integrated service

4.5.1   Traditional service

Voice traffic has traditionally been carried in telephone networks, video traffic in broadcast television networks, and data traffic in data communication networks. Although the three networks often share the same physical link, they are different because they are switched by different switches, and managed by separate organizations, and even if the same link carries telephone voice, digital video, and computer data, this fact is hidden from the users of the three networks.

The three networks are separate because they carry different types of traffic, with different service requirements. Voice traffic sources need low end-to-end delays (around 100 ms for interactive conversations), and a nearly constant bandwidth of 10–64 Kbps. Broadcast video sources need up to a few tens of megabits per second of bandwidth (depending on the compression technology) and are insensitive to delays smaller than a few seconds. Data traffic sources want infinite bandwidth and zero end-to-end delay, but can tolerate far worse.

4.5.2   Integrated service

If we can carry all three media using a universal networking technology, and allow users to access one or more media simultaneously, we can build applications that exploit multiple media to provide new and interesting services. Obvious examples are videoconferencing—where a voice call is enhanced with video—and interactive game-playing, where two or more players share a single virtual environment and can communicate with voice or video. Moreover, the network becomes easier to manage and provision, since the artificial barriers between the networks disappear. From the consumer's perspective, a single plug in the home can provide voice, video, and data service. This unification of service is a powerful motivation for the design of ATM networks. Thus, a key requirement for ATM technology is that an ATM network should be able to support, and eventually replace, telephone, television, and data networking infrastructure. Let us see how the features of ATM we have studied earlier fulfill this requirement.

4.5.3   Bandwidth

ATM networks can provide enormous switched capacity because fixed-size ATM cells can be switched efficiently in hardware. With special-purpose integrated circuits, building an 8×8 ATM switch with an aggregate capacity of 1 Gbps for less than $100 is possible. Such speeds cannot be obtained at comparable costs with variable-sized packets. This bandwidth is necessary to support video sources that demand a sustained bandwidth of around 1.5 Mbps—with such a high data rate, even a 1 Gbps switch can only support 666 users.

4.5.4   Supporting different traffic types

An ATM network supports diverse performance requirements by allowing users to specify a desired quality of service during call setup, and by managing its resources to satisfy these requirements. During call setup, switches along the path from the source to a destination check if there are sufficient resources to support the call while maintaining the service quality of existing calls (*admission control*). An admitted call is guaranteed to meet its service requirement. The network can give performance guarantees to a source only if the source describes its behavior with a *traffic descriptor* at the time of call setup. The network must ensure that a source obeys its descriptor during the call (*traffic policing*). For example, a user may ask for a bandwidth of 1.4 Mbps during call setup. This resource request is made to every switch controller along the path. If a controller does not have the capacity to handle the call, it rejects the call. Otherwise, it guarantees the call this rate, and updates its per-call records to reflect the resource allocation. During the call, the switches ensure that the source does not transmit faster than 1.4 Mbps. The network can, similarly, provision a call to give it a delay bound. We study this in more detail in Chapters 9 and 14.

Besides admission control and policing, an ATM network must also do intelligent link scheduling to meet service requirements. Voice and video traffic are relatively continuous, unlike data, which is bursty. A voice call delivers data to a switch periodically, and a link scheduler must allow voice data to be transmitted periodically on the output link. In contrast, data arrives sporadically, and so data cells should be scheduled only when they arrive. Flexible scheduling is possible in ATM networks, unlike telephone networks, because meta-data in the cells (cell headers) allow a link scheduler to postpone service for lower priority calls (by buffering them) while it serves high-priority calls. We will study scheduling in Chapter 9.

Thus, we see that ATM technology allows integration of services traditionally considered separate. This can result in economies of scale, and the creation of new services that were previously infeasible or expensive.

4.6 History

Though ATM networks have been a topic of great interest since the late 1980s, the basic ideas in this field date back to the 1960s. In 1961, Kasahara, Tezuka, Nakanishi, and Hasegawa at Osaka University suggested that adding a header to each time slot could make a time-division multiplexor more efficient [KTNH 61, HTK 64]. As we saw in Chapter 3, at about the same time, Baran proposed a datagram approach to networking, recognizing that meta-data allows flexibility and efficiency.

These ideas lay dormant until the late 1960s. In 1968, Chu at Bell Labs independently discovered the idea of tagging TDM time slots with headers, a technique he called *asynchronous time division multiplexing (ATDM)*. His ideas strongly influenced Fraser, also at Bell Labs, who was on the lookout for techniques to build large, fast switches [Fraser 93]. Fraser realized that by swapping time-slot headers, he could generalize Chu's multiplexor to a network of ATDM switches. In 1968–1969, he proposed the concepts of virtual circuits and fixed-size packets for *Spider,* the first ATDM network (ATM refers to the international standard for ATDM) [Fraser 74]. The name "virtual circuit" was meant to suggest a similarity with virtual memory, since neither a virtual circuit nor virtual memory takes up resources until it is used. The Spider switch was based on a buffered crossbar STM switch designed at MIT by Marcus for his master's thesis [Marcus 69]. A whole generation of ATDM switches evolved from this early design.

In 1970, Fraser and Vollaro at Bell Labs started work on Spider, emulating the switch in software. The network was fully operational in 1972 and served as a research test bed for several years. Meanwhile, Fraser and Vollaro moved to the next generation of ATDM switches, called Datakit [Fraser 83]. Datakit was based on the idea that endpoints could plug into a network with the simplicity of Lego blocks if switch interfaces were specialized per-endpoint, and the switch backplane interface was fixed. For example, to plug a telephone into the network, the switch interface would provide conversion from voice samples to the backplane format. Once encapsulated, voice data could be carried in the network like any other data. In this way, Datakit switches could encapsulate SNA, TCP/IP, or any other protocol. Datakit later became an AT&T product and still serves many businesses all over the world.

Fraser's work laid the foundation of what later became standardized as ATM networking. His Spider and Datakit networks are very similar to today's ATM networks, with small, fixed-size cells, VC switching, and statistical multiplexing of bursty traffic. These ideas were independently invented in France by Coudreuse, who used them in the Prelude network.

By the mid-1980s, telephone companies around the world realized that customers wanted more than what telephone engineers call POTS (Plain Old Telephone Service). Many studies predicted that customers would soon want networks to carry not only voice, but also bursty video and data traffic, so that the existing telephone infrastructure would soon be inadequate. Telephone companies thus decided to build an integrated voice/data network that they called *ISDN (Integrated Services Digital Network)* [Stallings 88, Chapter 18]. An ISDN line contains two data lines, each at 64 Kbps, and one control line, at 16 Kbps. The two data lines can be merged to obtain an effective bandwidth of 128 Kbps. ISDN has not been very popular, at least in the United States, since the data bandwidth (64 or 128 Kbps) is too low for digital trunks or for delivering video to home consumers (in many European countries, government-controlled telephone companies provide ISDN service as a matter of course, but the data portion of the connection is not commonly used). In the mid-1980s, CCITT proposed what it called the *B-ISDN concept*, where the *B* stands for "broadband." This was to be similar to ISDN, except that the data channel would be wider.

At about this time, Stratacom (founded by Baran), AT&T, and others, who had experience with ATDM networks, proposed that the technology for B-ISDN ought to be ATDM. By the late 1980s, CCITT agreed in principle that the B-ISDN network would be built using ATDM, and the international standard was named ATM. Nevertheless, like all telephone company decisions, the time frame for converting to ATM was ponderous—adoption of ATM would be complete only around 2020! (Some wags still insist ATM stands for After The Millennium.)

When the news of ATM came to the attention of computer companies, they realized that ATM is another form of packet switching, a technology with which they had much experience. Moreover, ATM networks had an advantage over existing LANs because they offer *scalable bandwidth*. Traditional shared-medium LANs, such as Ethernet and *Fiber Distributed Data Interface (FDDI)*, are restricted to a single speed—10 Mbps for Ethernet and 100 Mbps for FDDI. A customer upgrading an Ethernet or FDDI network to a higher speed must therefore modify every endpoint in the network. In contrast, ATM switches can multiplex data received at different rates, so an endpoint can increase its network bandwidth independent of other endpoints. Thus, ATM networks allow scaling of the bandwidth available to an endpoint. (Note that a limited form of scaling is possible with switched Ethernet and FDDI, which we will study in Chapter 7.)

Nevertheless, the slow pace of the ITU-T was stifling, and computer companies wanted to create standards over a period of months instead of over decades. This motivated the companies to start a parallel standardization body called the ATM Forum. Unlike ITU-T, the Forum is not an international standards body in the strict legal sense. It is a body providing consensus and interoperability among manufacturers building ATM products. Eventually, ATM Forum standards are presented to the international standards organization by the country representatives of each manufacturer.

The ATM Forum has set the pace for ATM (though after an initial flurry of activity, this pace has slowed down considerably). It has brought out standards for signaling, physical level interconnection, and flow control that many manufacturers have implemented. The rapid pace at which standards are set has allowed the ATM industry to mature much more rapidly than envisioned by the telephone companies. In a reversal of roles, ATM technology, initially thought to be a preserve of telephone companies, is now driven in its standards and products mainly by computer companies.

Unlike the telephone network and the Internet, ATM technology is still under development. Researchers are still exploring the implication of design decisions and engineers have yet to determine the proper provisioning of ATM trunks. However, given the investment in the technology by computer and telephone companies, ATM networks will play an important role in the future.

4.7   Challenges

4.7.1   Quality of service

The key to providing integrated service is for connections of each service type to get a different quality of service. This quality must be provided by end-systems, switch controllers, and the switching fabric. A strong challenge to ATM networks is to come up with standards and systems that allow applications on end-systems to specify and receive quality of service from the network. Currently, standards exist only for networks, and providing quality of service in the end-system is an open research area.

4.7.2   Scaling

ATM networks are still small, but they are positioned to take over from some very large existing networks. Existing networks, for all their faults, do scale well: this is why they are large and successful. While designing and building ATM networks, it is important to ensure that the algorithms and protocols chosen for the network scale well. For example, the network should not have a single point of control, and globally unique identifiers must be hierarchically partitioned. Because large ATM networks have yet to be deployed as of the time of this writing, it is too soon to determine how well ATM protocols scale.

4.7.3   Competition from other LAN technologies

Computer communication companies position ATM as a "future-proof" technology for building LANs at speeds faster than 10 Mbps Ethernet. Problems with unreliable and expensive equipment, however, have made other high-speed LAN technologies, such as Gigabit Ethernet and FDDI, more credible. These other technologies do not scale to higher speeds and longer distances, but are reliable and widely available at a reasonable price. Given the confusion in the ATM ranks, these technologies might yet dominate the fast-LAN market. Although they cannot be used over wide areas, where ATM does not yet have any challengers, the migration of the LAN market to non-ATM technologies makes end-to-end quality of service harder to achieve.

4.7.4   Standards

In their infancy, the telephone and IP networks were guided by a handful of competent individuals who decided essential standards by consensus and based on technical merit. As these networks grew, and as more people have become involved, the standards process has necessarily slowed down, but the (technically sound) decisions made in the early days still guide network evolution. In contrast, ATM standards are being set in the ATM Forum by a large group of companies with mutually incompatible interests, not all of whom have experience with building and operating ATM networks. By attempting standardization before researchers have reached consensus, ATM Forum standards sometimes reflect outdated estimations of technical capabilities, such as how much buffering and processing is feasible at switches, and are open to purely political compromises. Experience with OSI, which attempted to standardize packet switching before the technology was mature, suggests that this process will probably lead to unnecessarily expensive networks. This may well delay the eventual adoption of ATM technology. The challenge for ATM networks is to allow enough leeway in the standards to permit innovative technology to take root.

4.7.5   ATM and IP

The worldwide Internet, which is based on IP, represents a vast and ever-growing non-ATM infrastructure. To make a dent in this market, and to protect the investment in Internet technology, ATM networks must interoperate with IP networks. Unfortunately, this interoperation is problematic, because ATM networks and IP networks have fundamentally differing design philosophies. For example, the Internet is connectionless, whereas ATM networks are connection-oriented. ATM networks emphasize resource reservation and quality of service, while the Internet emphasizes connectivity and best-effort service. Even the extensions to the Internet to enable quality-of-service guarantees are incompatible with ATM mechanisms. Finally, routing protocols in the Internet and in ATM networks differ significantly. In light of these differences, cobbling together an integrated IP/ATM network can be an exercise in frustration. Yet, if ATM networks are to be used by the ever-growing population of IP users, they must accommodate the wishes of those users. This is a challenge to designers of ATM protocols.

4.8   Summary

ATM networks try to combine the best ideas of the telephone network, such as connection-oriented service and end-to-end quality of service, and those of the Internet, such as packet switching. They are based on five important concepts: (1) virtual circuits, (2) fixed packet size, (3) small packet size, (4) statistical multiplexing, and (5) integrated service. Although still in their infancy, they have the potential to subsume both the Internet and the telephone network. However, before this can be achieved, several technical and social obstacles remain.

Section 2

Tools and Techniques

Chapter 5

Protocol Layering

The previous chapters have presented an overview of the telephone network, Internet, and ATM networks. This chapter describes *protocol layering*, a technique used in all three networks. We will study the notion of a protocol, protocol layering, and why layering is critical for building, operating, and maintaining networks. Finally, we will study the seven-layered protocol architecture for data communication developed by the International Organization for Standardization (ISO).

5.1 Protocols and protocol layering

Consider a customer who walks into a post office to send a letter to a friend abroad. A postal worker accepts the letter and forwards it to a postal worker in the foreign country, who eventually delivers it to the foreign customer. Notice that postal delivery involves an exchange of a letter between at least two sets of parties: first, the customer and her friend, who view the postal network as a black box that accepts letters at one end and delivers it at the other; and second, the two postal workers, who also handle the letter, though only on behalf of their customers (Figure 5.1). The two (or more) parties at the same level communicating with each other are called *peer entities*. In our example, the two customers are peers, as are the two postal workers. A *protocol* is a set of rules and formats that govern the communication between communicating peers [Zimmerman 80]. It allows the peers to agree on a set of valid messages and the meaning of each message. In general, protocols mediate *any* function that requires cooperation between peers.

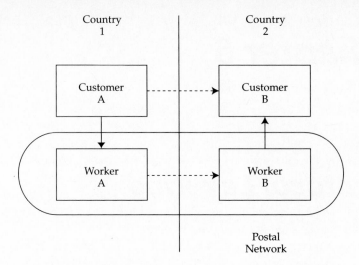

Figure 5.1: Peer entities in a postal network. Here, customer A in country 1 sends a letter to customer B in country 2 via postal workers A and B. Customer A and customer B are peers, as are worker A and worker B. Communication between peers is governed by a set of rules, called a protocol.

EXAMPLE 5.1

Consider two peers who want to exchange a file over a network that corrupts packets, but never loses or reorders them. To do so, they can use a file exchange protocol such as this: The sender sends the file as a series of packets, followed by a number computed by performing some function on each byte of the file. This function, called the *checksum*, can be as simple as the sum of all the bytes in the file. The receiver computes the checksum on the received file. If the checksums match, it sends an *OK* response; otherwise, it sends a *not-OK* response. If the sender gets an *OK* response, it stops; otherwise, it periodically retransmits all the packets in the file until it receives an *OK* response. This set of message exchanges informally describes the file exchange protocol. If the checksum is chosen to detect almost all packet corruptions, and at least one round of file exchange succeeds, this protocol, with high probability, will achieve its goal of reliable file transfer.

This protocol is simple but far from optimal. Even if one bit in one packet is corrupted, the checksum is likely to fail, and the sender must retransmit the entire file. It would be more efficient to retransmit only the corrupted packet. Moreover, we have left out many important details. For example, if the link to the sender and the receiver goes down, the sender will keep sending packets *ad infinitum*. A more insidious problem is that the *OK* and *not-OK* messages themselves are not protected from corruption. Thus, if the network corrupts both a packet and the *not-OK* response, the sender might incorrectly think that the network successfully transferred the file. If a protocol is to be robust, its designer must try to anticipate every eventuality!

An important role of a protocol is to describe the *semantics* of a message, that is, the meaning associated with the bits carried in a message. For example, the file exchange protocol in Example 5.1 must allow the sender and receiver to distinguish between file packets and checksum packets. Thus, the file and checksum packets must be in some agreed-upon format, as must be the values chosen to represent *OK* and *not-OK*. A protocol also specifies the *actions* taken on receipt of a message. For example, on receiving the checksum packet, the receiver must compute the checksum and match it with the one it receives. These agreements about message formats and actions to be taken when receiving a message are a detailed *specification* of the protocol.

Thus far, we have described a protocol as something that enables the solution of a shared problem. One may alternatively think of a protocol as providing a *service,* such as reliable file transfer. In other words, peer entities use a protocol to provide a service to a higher-level entity. The *service interface* to the peer entities hides the details of the protocols used in actually providing the service.

Each shared function (or service) in a communication network is achieved by an associated protocol. Thus, a network that provides many services must define many protocols. It turns out that some of these protocols are independent of each other, while others are dependent. A common form of dependency is where Protocol A uses Protocol B as a step in its execution. For example, one step in the execution of the file exchange protocol we discussed in Example 5.1 involves transferring a packet to the receiver. This transfer itself may be governed by, say, a data transfer protocol. We call this form of dependency *layering:* the file transfer protocol is layered above the data transfer protocol. The lower layer provides a service used by the higher layer in its execution. This is similar to the way a subroutine in a programming language provides a service to its calling program.

The interface between the lower and the upper layer is called a *service access point* or *SAP* [DZ 83]. The packets exchanged between peer entities in the same layer are called *protocol data units (PDUs).* The packets handed to a layer by an upper layer are called *service data units (SDUs).* A protocol data unit is typically a service data unit with an additional header or trailer that carries information needed by that layer's protocol.

EXAMPLE 5.2

Consider, again, the customer who hands a letter to a postal worker for delivery. The *service* provided by the postal service is mail delivery service. The *service access point* is the post office. Between customers, the *protocol data unit* is a letter. The *service data unit* for the post office is a letter, and the *protocol data unit* is a mailbag that contains letters to a common destination. Each service data unit or letter has a protocol header or envelope with a destination address, an optional source address, and a tamper-resistant stamp to indicate prepayment of service charges. Suppose the peer customers are using the mail service to negotiate a business deal. Then, the negotiation protocol is *layered* above the mail delivery protocol.

Continuing with the file exchange protocol in Example 5.1, the email protocol can utilize the service provided by the file exchange protocol, so we could layer the email protocol above the file transfer protocol. The three layers, email transfer, file transfer, and data transfer, thus constitute a *protocol stack*. Each layer in the stack uses the layer below it and provides services to the layer above it. A key observation is that once we define the service provided by a layer, we need know nothing further about the details of how the layer actually implements this service. The implementation of a layer in a protocol stack can therefore change without affecting the layers above (or below). This property is fundamental for designing networks that survive technological change. As we will see later in Section 5.3, the same information-hiding can also dramatically reduce system performance.

5.2   The importance of layering

Protocol layering provides three important advantages. First, it allows a complex problem to be broken into smaller, more manageable pieces. Second, because the specification of a layer says nothing about its implementation, the implementation details of a layer are hidden (*abstracted*) from other layers. This allows implementations to change without disturbing the rest of the stack. Third, many upper layers can share the services provided by a lower layer. We look at these three properties in more detail next.

A protocol stack allows a network to provide sophisticated services by composing simpler ones. For example, consider a World Wide Web user who clicks on some high-lighted text, thus setting into play activities such as determining the location of the server pointed to by that text, establishing a connection between the computer running the browser and the server, and reliable file transfer. Layering allows us to decompose this complicated task into simpler ones that we can solve independently and in parallel. Since each layer solves only a part of the problem, it is easier to write and debug than a mono-lithic approach to solving the whole problem.

The second advantage of layering is separation of implementation and specification. As we saw earlier, a layer is specified by the services it provides. If the service interface remains unchanged, we can therefore replace the implementation of a layer without affecting the other layers in the stack. For example, the long-distance component of the telephone network has migrated from copper wire to fiber optic cables at the physical layer without affecting customers' expectations of what telephone service means. This is because the layered telephone stack hides the physical medium used for carrying voice samples from the layers above. As technology improves, we can replace lower layers at will without risking the investment made at higher layers in the protocol stack, and vice versa.

Finally, layering allows us to reuse functionality. A lower layer implements common functionality once, which can then be shared by many upper layers. A good example of this is evident in the evolution of networking in the Microsoft Windows operating system. Early versions of the system had little networking support. Thus, every application program written provided its own protocol stack bundled into the application. Over time, application developers converged on the *Winsock* standard, which implements the Internet protocol stack in a shared library module, offering a standard interface to all application programs. Newer application programs layered over Winsock therefore do not need to bundle in networking.

5.3   **Problems with layering**

Layering is a form of *information hiding.* A lower layer presents only a service interface to an upper layer, hiding the details of how it provides the service. If the correct operation of a layer were to depend on knowing implementation details of another layer, changes in one layer could result in a change to every other layer, an expensive and complex proposition. Thus, network engineers are wary of *layering violations,* that is, a situation where a layer uses knowledge of the implementation details of another layer in its own operation.

Though information-hiding has its benefits, it can sometimes lead to poor performance [Clark 82]. To avoid this penalty, in situations where an upper layer can optimize its actions by knowing what a lower layer is doing, we can reveal information that would normally be hidden behind a layer boundary. For example, consider a flow control protocol that is responsible for throttling a source when it thinks that the network is overloaded. A widely used heuristic to discover an overload is to assume that overloads are correlated with packet loss. The protocol, therefore, could throttle the source sending rate when it detects a packet loss. (This is the heuristic used in the Internet's Transmission Control Protocol, which we study in Chapter 13.) Suppose, first, that the flow control protocol is layered above a protocol that is actually responsible for data transfer. Then, the flow control protocol does not know how packets are transferred across the network. Next, suppose that the end-system is connected to the network over a lossy wireless link so that packet losses happen mostly because of link errors, rather than network overload. Unfortunately, even in this situation, the flow control protocol thinks that the network is congested, and throttles a source even when there is no need to do so. The information that a packet is lost on the link, which is available to the lower (data transfer) layer, is hidden from the higher (flow control) layer, which results in inefficient flow control. If the lower layer were to inform the upper layer about packet loss on a link, the flow control layer could distinguish between the link and congestive losses and could do a better job. This, however, violates layering, because the flow control layer now knows about the details of data transfer over its local link. So, if the data transfer layer changes, perhaps because the end-system is using a different link technology, the flow control layer, which ought to be independent of the link technology, must also change. Here, we see a tension between information-hiding on one hand and performance on the other. The art of protocol stack design is to "leak" enough information between layers to allow efficient performance, but not so much that it is hard to change the implementation of a layer. Choosing this balance wisely is the hallmark of good design.

> A layered protocol model does not imply that each layer should be in a separate address space. Efficient implementations demand that layer-crossings be fast and cheap. We will study several implementation techniques in Chapter 15 where protocol layering is used only for information hiding, and all the layers are in the same address space.

5.4   ISO OSI reference model

All connected systems in a network must agree not only on what each layer does, but also on the protocols that are required to provide these services. We say that a set of protocols is *open* if protocol details are publicly available, and changes to the set are managed by an organization whose membership and transactions are open to the public. A system that implements open protocol standards is called an *open system.* The idea is that any vendor who has the specifications for an open standard can build a standards-compliant open system. This promotes competition, while still ensuring interoperability.

The Open System Interconnect (OSI) reference model developed by the International Organization for Standards (ISO) is the international standard that describes a particular choice of layering, and a particular choice of protocols that carry out the services at each layer [DZ 83]. Although OSI protocols are far from common in current networks, the OSI reference model is a good way to think of the functions provided by computer networks, and the model maps well to the protocol layering in common use. Thus, it is worthwhile to understand ISO's seven-layer OSI stack.

ISO distinguishes among three things that look identical at first glance: the *reference model,* the *service architecture,* and the *protocol architecture.*

- The reference model formally defines what is meant by a layer, a service, a service access point, name, etc. These concepts provide the building blocks for defining a seven-layer model for communication.

- The service architecture describes the services provided by each layer. As we saw earlier, each layer provides a service access point to the layer above and provides services using the services of a layer below. The service architecture tells us what services each layer provides and the details of its service access point interface. It does not, however, specify the protocols used to implement these services.

- Finally, the protocol architecture is the set of protocols that implement the service architecture. It is possible for a network to be OSI-service compliant without being interoperable with other OSI-service-compliant networks, since the two networks may implement the same service using different protocols.

Following popular usage, we will not distinguish among the reference model, the service architecture, and the protocol architecture. We will first look at the layering prescribed by the reference model, then look at the services provided by each layer. We will study some representative protocols implementing these layers in Chapter 15.

5.5 The seven layers

Figure 5.2 shows the seven layers of the ISO OSI reference model. Note that the end-systems contain all seven layers, but intermediate systems, such as switches and routers, implement only the lowest three layers. This is because the third (network) layer provides the abstraction of end-to-end data transfer to the layers above. Thus, at the transport layer and above, the peer layers at an endpoint can talk directly to their peers at the remote end-system without having to worry about intermediate systems. This is like the two postal customers in Example 5.1, who can mail each other letters without worrying about how the letters make their way through the postal system. At the level of the peer customers, protocol actions happen only at the endpoints. Intermediate systems, which provide only network-layer functionality (the equivalent of sorting and distributing mail), need not implement higher layers of the protocol stack (such as those between postal customers).

We will use two running examples to illustrate the operation of the seven-layer protocol stack. The first example continues with Example 5.1, which involves two customers using the postal network to exchange letters. In the second example, we discuss the Internet protocol stack. Taken together, these examples develop some intuitions about the function of each layer, and the reasoning behind ISO's service architecture.

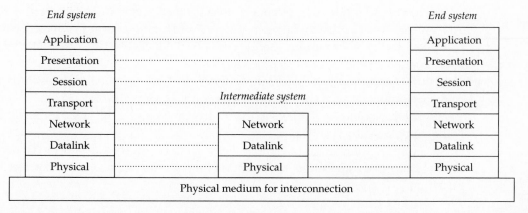

Figure 5.2: The ISO OSI seven-layer reference model. Each layer of the stack provides services to the layer above by using services from the layer below. Dotted lines represent peer-to-peer communication.

5.5.1   Physical layer

The physical layer is the lowest layer in the OSI stack. It is responsible for moving information between two systems connected by a single physical link. Physical-layer protocols describe such things as the coding scheme used to represent a bit on a communication link, connector shape and size, and bit-level synchronization. The physical layer provides the abstraction of bit transport, independent of the link technology. It is not aware of the notion of a packet or a multiplexing frame.

EXAMPLE 5.3

(a) In the postal network, the physical layer provides the technology for transporting letters. These include mail vans, bicycles, postal workers carrying mailbags, and airplanes. The datalink layer hands the physical layer a letter that it expects will eventually appear (with a certain probability) at the other end of a "link."

(b) In the Internet, the physical layer provides the technology for transporting bits. These include coaxial cable transmitters and receivers (in local area networks), satellite transponders and base stations, and optical fiber links with associated optical transmitters and receivers. The datalink layer hands the physical layer a bit that it expects will eventually appear (with a certain probability) at the other end of the link. With a broadcast medium, such as a coaxial cable or a radio link, the same bit appears at multiple endpoints.

5.5.2   Datalink layer

Consider a local area network (LAN) where a coaxial cable links several computers together. The physical layer ensures that a bit placed on the cable by any end-system can be received by all other end-systems. However, for a *packet* to be transferred over the LAN, an end-system must distinguish between an "idle" bit pattern, which occupies the cable when no one is transmitting, and "data" bits, which are parts of a packet. It can do so, for example, if every packet is preceded and followed by a special bit pattern, such as "01010101," which each end-system monitors. If these bit patterns or *markers* do not occur in the data stream, they frame the beginning and end of a packet.[1] We call the insertion of these types of markers in the bit stream *framing*. One of the important duties of a datalink layer is to frame packets.

For point-to-point communication over a broadcast LAN (such as the coaxial-cable link just described), all but the destination of a packet should refrain from receiving it.

---

[1] If these patterns do occur in the data stream, then the transmitting datalink layer replaces them with special markers that are converted to the original bit pattern at the receiver.

We can achieve this by associating each end-system with a unique *datalink-layer address* and requiring end-systems to only receive packets addressed to them. Moreover, because multiple end-systems share a common medium, we also need some way to arbitrate access to the medium. The datalink layer's *medium access control (MAC)* sublayer provides these two functions.

Some datalink layers provide not just framing and point-to-point communication, but also the ability to retransmit packets corrupted on the link (error control), and to pace the rate at which packets are placed on a link (flow control). These functions are considered part of the *logical link control* sublayer of the datalink layer, which is layered above the medium access control sublayer. We will study medium access in greater detail in Chapter 7, error control in Chapter 12, and flow control in Chapter 13.

Because the datalink layer is very dependent on the nature of the physical medium, each physical medium is usually associated with its own datalink layer protocol. In most systems, a single host-adaptor card provides both the datalink layer and the physical layer. For example, a commercially available Ethernet card provides not only the transmitter and receiver for placing and receiving bits on a coaxial cable, but also the ability to frame packets and the medium access control to arbitrate access to the medium. The network layer simply hands a packet with a particular destination address to the card, expecting that it will eventually appear at the other end of the link. The host-adaptor card may also flag errors in received packets.

EXAMPLE 5.4

(a) Consider the actions at a post office when it receives a letter. At the end of every collection period, a postal worker sorts mail according to whether it is local or remote. If it is local, it is distributed locally. Otherwise, all remote mail is placed in a mail bag and sent to the central post office. The mail bag "frames" the letters, so that the central post office can distinguish between incoming letters from each smaller post office. Moreover, the address on the mail bag allows it to be delivered to the correct central post office (if there is more than one in the area). Thus, a mail bag is the equivalent of a frame. The medium access control is the set of traffic rules and regulations a mail truck must obey in getting to its destination.

(b) The Internet supports a variety of datalink-layer protocols, of which the most common at the time of writing is Ethernet. Ethernet defines unique bit sequences to demarcate data bits in frames. Its MAC sublayer supports point-to-point communication with 6-byte globally unique datalink addresses to identify end-systems. Before placing a frame on the link, the MAC layer at the transmitter checks to see if the medium is already in use (we call this *carrier sensing*). Despite this check, two end-systems may still launch frames nearly simultaneously, and these *collisions* are resolved using the *carrier-sense multiple access/collision detect (CSMA/CD)* protocol. Besides Ethernet, other common data links in the Internet include *Fiber Distributed*

Data Interface (FDDI), Synchronous Optical Network (SONET), and *High-level Data Link Control (HDLC).* We will study them in more detail in Chapters 7 and 15.

5.5.3   Network layer

The main function of the network layer is to logically concatenate a set of links to form the abstraction of an end-to-end link. It allows an end-system to communicate with any other end-system by computing a route between them and using the services of the data-link layer to carry packets on this route. The network layer therefore allows a higher layer to communicate directly with its peer, though this peer may be reached only by travers-ing many intermediate systems. The network layer also hides idiosyncracies of the data-link layer from higher layers. For example, given a link that limits the largest allowed packet size, the network layer can fragment data handed to it by the transport layer when it enters such a link (*segmentation*) and reassemble it at the destination so that the next-higher (transport) layer is not aware of this limitation. Finally, to uniquely identify an end-system, the network layer provides unique network-wide addresses.

> Unlike datalink-layer addresses, network-layer addresses correspond to network topology, so that they can be *aggregated* in routing tables. We will study this point in more detail in Chapter 10.

The network layer is found both at end-systems and at intermediate systems. At an end-system, its task is limited primarily to hiding details of the datalink layer—for example, with segmentation and reassembly. It may also provide some error detection. At inter-mediate systems, and at end-systems connected to multiple routers, besides these func-tions, it participates in a routing protocol to discover the next hop for every possible destination in the network. In a datagram network, the network layer is responsible for forwarding packets, scheduling their transmission order, and, if necessary, dropping excess packets. Thus, it plays a critical role in providing end-to-end delay and loss-rate guarantees. We will study scheduling in Chapter 9, naming and addressing in Chapter 10, and routing in Chapter 11.

We organize the network layer differently in datagram and connection-oriented net-works. In datagram networks, the network layer provides both routing and data for-warding. In contrast, in a connection-oriented network, we distinguish between the *data plane* and the *control plane* (Figure 5.3). The data plane is the set of protocols involved in transferring data. The control plane contains protocols responsible for network and con-nection control. Thus, routing, call-establishment, and call-teardown protocols are in the control plane of a connection-oriented network, whereas data-forwarding protocols are in the data plane. In such networks, layers above the network layer may also be parti-tioned between the data and control planes. A good rule of thumb to distinguish between data and control plane actions is that if a function involves touching every packet, then it is in the data plane; otherwise, it is in the control plane.

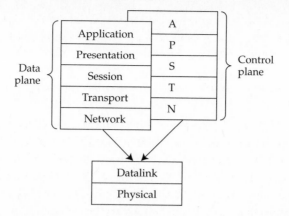

Figure 5.3: Data and control plane. In connection-oriented networks, protocols that transfer data are grouped in the data plane, whereas protocols that control the network and deal with connection management are in the control plane.

EXAMPLE 5.5

(a) The postal network's service interface to the outside world is at the network layer. This layer sets up internal routing tables so that postal workers can identify a source-to-destination path for every letter. Postal workers forward letters along this path, using the services of the datalink layer, to provide the abstraction of a single end-to-end logical link. Thus, like a datagram network, the postal network provides both routing and forwarding. Unlike data networks, however, postal network topology changes very slowly over time. Therefore, routing is essentially static. In contrast, a computer network uses dynamic routing to deal with rapid changes in network topology, for example, due to a power outage.

Interestingly, the postal network provides multiple qualities of service. Priority-mail letter services allow a customer to pay more to ensure speedy delivery. Similarly, bulk mailers pay less if they accept a "best-effort" delivery where they have to presort letters and put up with possibly large delays. These quality-of-service guarantees require *every* intermediate system in the postal network to be aware of customer requirements and act in according to these requirements.

(b) The Internet's *Internet Protocol (IP)* is found in all Internet-compatible routers and end-systems. It presents an end-system with the abstraction of an end-to-end logical link by providing routing, packet-forwarding, and segmentation and reassembly. End-systems that want to communicate with a remote destination need only format a packet with an IP header and the destination's IP address, and IP will carry it there, wherever in the world it may be!

The beauty of IP is that we can layer it over practically any datalink layer technology, because it makes very few assumptions about the datalink layer. This makes it easy to extend the Internet over new datalink technologies as they arise. The price to pay for this simplicity is that IP provides only a single "best-effort" quality of service. Although the IP header has a field that describes the type-of-service that a packet desires, in practice, this field is rarely heeded, since IP does not require the datalink layer to distinguish between different service qualities. For example, if a high-priority IP packet crosses a shared medium, such as Ethernet, the packet may still suffer long delays as it waits for lower-priority packets from other attached systems to use the medium. Since IP does not require Ethernet to provide different qualities of service, IP in turn cannot provide these to upper layers.

5.5.4   Transport layer

The transport layer is to the network layer as the datalink layer is to the physical layer. The network layer usually provides a "raw" end-to-end packet transport service. The transport layer uses this service to create the abstraction of an *error-controlled,* and *flow-controlled,* end-to-end link. By error-controlled, we mean that the transport layer guarantees that, with very high probability, a message will reach the destination despite packet loss, corruption, and duplication. Transport-layer protocols deal with loss by retransmitting lost packets; with corruption by detecting, discarding, and retransmitting corrupted packets; and with duplication by detecting and discarding duplicate packets. We study these mechanisms in more detail in Chapter 12.

Transport layers also provide *flow control,* that is, matching the transmission rate of a source to the rate currently sustainable on the path to the destination. For example, consider a personal computer (PC) communicating with a supercomputer. Usually, the supercomputer can pump out data far faster than the PC can absorb it. Flow control forces the supercomputer to pace its transmission to match the PC. It can do so either explicitly, where the PC informs the supercomputer of its maximum sustainable transfer rate, or implicitly, where the supercomputer uses some heuristics to estimate the PC's service rate. We will study explicit and implicit flow control in Chapter 13.

The third main function of a transport layer is to multiplex multiple applications to the same end-to-end connection. The network layer typically routes data to a particular end-system, without distinguishing among the applications supported at the end-system. The transport layer adds an application-specific identifier (usually called a *port number*) to a packet, so that the receiving end-system can hand an incoming packet to the correct application.

Not all transport layers implement the same set of services. Some lightweight transport layers provide a cursory (but easily computed) error-detection algorithm and multiplexing, but no flow control or retransmission. Others provide extensive error checking, sophisticated flow control, and retransmissions. An application must choose the transport mechanisms best suited to its needs.

EXAMPLE 5.6

(a) The postal system does not have a transport layer. This is implemented, if at all, by postal service customers. Suppose customers Alice and Bob want to achieve error-free service, with Alice sending a steady stream of letters to Bob, say, at the rate of a letter a day. The postal system does not corrupt letters, but it can reorder or drop them. To protect against these, Alice may write the date of posting on the letter (that is, in the letter's header). Bob can use these dates as *sequence numbers* to detect and correct letter reordering. Moreover, if Bob does not receive a letter posted on a particular day for a "long" time, he can assume that the letter is lost. He can then ask Alice to retransmit the lost letter. In this way, Alice and Bob can use sequence numbers, timeouts, and retransmissions to recover from letter loss and reordering. If Alice and Bob were clerks in a large firm, who carried out mail exchange on behalf of their bosses, then from the perspective of their bosses, the link between Alice and Bob is reliable and in-order.

(b) The two popular transport-layer protocols in the Internet are the *User Datagram Protocol (UDP)* and the *Transmission Control Protocol (TCP)*. UDP provides multiplexing, but not error recovery or flow control. It is typically used by applications that can either live with packet loss (such as audio or video applications), or those that provide their own retransmissions (such as the Network File System (NFS) protocol).

TCP provides error detection and correction, as well as multiplexing and flow control. It provides higher layers with the abstraction of an error-free, reliable, in-order stream of bits. Most Internet applications, such as the World Wide Web and file transfer, use TCP. TCP achieves error control using sequence numbers, timeouts, and retransmissions as outlined in part (a) of this example. It also does flow control by dynamically estimating the capacity available on the path from the source to the destination. We will study this in more detail in Chapter 13.

5.5.5   Session layer

The transport layer usually provides a degree of abstraction sufficient for most application programs. In some networks, however, an additional session layer adds the abstraction of full-duplex service (if the transport layer does not already provide this), expedited data delivery, and session synchronization [EC 83, Stallings 88, Chapter 16].

- Some transport layers provide only unidirectional or *simplex* transmission. In such networks, a session layer can manage two transport connections to provide the abstraction of bidirectional or *full-duplex* service.

- Expedited data delivery allows some messages to skip ahead of others in the session-layer message queue (using a separate, low-delay transport connection).

- Synchronization allows endpoints to place marks at specific points during data transfer and to roll back to a prespecified mark. This is useful for applications that need *atomic* data transfer, that is, either all or none of the data in a set should be transferred. Rollbacks allow a session layer to cleanly abort transfer of a data set.

EXAMPLE 5.7

(a) Consider a firm that has a clerk who handles only incoming mail ("receiving") and a clerk who handles only outgoing mail ("shipping"). Each clerk, therefore, implements one end of the transport layer. Suppose they report to a chief clerk who not only accepts letters for transmission from the firm's employees, but also delivers incoming mail to them. The chief clerk, therefore, plays the role of a session layer, managing two simplex connections to present the abstraction of a duplex connection. The chief clerk may also expedite some letters (using courier service instead of regular service). Finally, if the clerk is given a set of letters such that either all or none must be delivered (such as invitations to an important meeting), she can arrange with her peer to discard incomplete sets to provide this abstraction.

(b) The Internet does not have a standard session layer protocol. TCP already provides duplex and expedited data delivery, and session rollbacks are part of the application, if necessary.

5.5.6   Presentation layer

Unlike the other layers, which are concerned mostly with *meta-data* in headers, the presentation layer deals with *data*. The presentation layer hides data representation differences between applications. For example, one machine may store a word with high-order bytes first (*big-endian*), and another with the high-order bytes last (*little-endian*). The presentation layer converts the representations to a network standard so that this difference is hidden from the applications. The presentation layer may also encrypt data, both to authenticate it to the receiving application and to prevent unauthorized parties from accessing it. Like the session layer, the presentation layer is often ad hoc, if present at all.

EXAMPLE 5.8

(a) In the postal example, assume that the letters are being exchanged between firms in two countries that do not share a common language. The *contents* of the letter therefore must be translated before the recipient can understand it. This translation can be done either at the sending or receiving end. The person doing the translation plays the role of the presentation layer.

(b) The Internet does not support a standard presentation layer, and Internet applications usually incorporate appropriate presentation-layer functionality. The Internet, however, does support a standard byte-ordering for representing integers (but not floating-point numbers). In a Unix system, the macros `htons` and `htonl` convert a short or long number from host to network order. At the receiving host, the macros `ntohs` and `ntohl` convert them back to the byte order appropriate for the receiving host. Unfortunately, the wide variety in floating-point formats does not allow a similar simple conversion.

5.5.7   Application layer

The application layer is just another name for the set of applications running on an end-system. The application layer uses the complex services provided by the lower layers of the protocol stack, and does not provide services to any other layer. Although the ISO has described a standard set of applications, any program that uses the presentation layer's services can be considered a part of the application layer.

EXAMPLE 5.9

(a) In the postal example, the application layer is the entity in the firm that creates and mails letters. Suppose this were a department that does mass mailings for an automobile company. Let us trace the actions taken when the department is asked to send recall letters because of a defect in a product. The mail department, as part of application layer processing, collects the names and addresses of affected customers, then writes letters to each of them. The job of the presentation layer is to translate letters that are being mailed abroad. Letters, perhaps after translation, are handed to a session-layer mail clerk, who may send some by courier, some by priority mail, and others as bulk-rate mail. Each of these services corresponds to a particular transport clerk, who sends letters over the postal network and waits for an acknowledgment, retransmitting a letter if no acknowledgment is received in a reasonable time. The postal system, which supports the network layer interface, finds a route for each letter and transfers it to its destination. The datalink layer abstracts the details of whether the mail was transferred by truck, airplane, ship, or bicycle. Finally, the physical layer provides the actual transfer of mail.

We see that the protocol stack carefully coordinates many actions to provide a complex service interface to the end user (here, the person ordering the mass mailing). Each layer of the stack adds some services to the layer below it, so that, at the application layer, an application has a rich set of communication choices.

(b) The Internet supports many applications, some of which are so popular that they are sometimes mistaken for the Internet itself! The most widely used application at the time of the writing is the World Wide Web (WWW), which allows an application called a *browser* to retrieve specially formatted files from another application called a *server*. The formatting commands in the file not only allow a browser to display text, graphics, sound, and movies, but also allow the document to contain links to other formatted documents. A user can *navigate* from one document to another by following these links. The basic step in the World Wide Web, which is just file transfer, uses TCP for reliable communication. Some specialized services, such as real-time audio and video retrieval, use UDP. All services beyond those provided by TCP are made a part of the browser and server applications themselves.

The Internet's protocol layers, which we have studied in earlier examples, allow a browser to reliably access files from any end-system in the Internet. The files are transferred packet by packet over a route that dynamically compensates for failures, at a rate that automatically compensates for the activity of other users in the network. By building these services layer by layer, we can implement complex applications, such as a WWW browser, with relatively little added effort.

Examples 5.3–5.9 show how layering breaks up the complex task of reliable worldwide communication into several subproblems, and how each protocol layer tackles a different subproblem. The end user need not worry about how the packets got to the other end, possible traffic congestion, how files are fragmented into packets, or how to deal with physical links. Each layer of the stack provides a clean abstraction to the next higher layer so that the stack as a whole provides a complete service to the application. This is a key benefit of protocol layering.

Why seven layers?

Why are there seven layers in the OSI stack, and not eight, or five? In this box, we argue from first principles that there are good reasons to require at least five layers, and that no more are necessary.

For starters, we need at least the physical and application layers, which form the top and bottom of the protocol stack. Next, the datalink layer hides the details of the physical layer, and of the local link topology. Because each link technology is so different, it makes sense to bundle all the link-dependent details into the datalink layer, isolating upper layers from these irksome details. This argues for keeping the datalink layer. We are now up to three.

The task of communication involves both end-to-end and hop-by-hop actions. For example, routing *must* be done hop-by-hop, whereas flow control is best done end-to-end. This fundamental divide in function placement is why we need to partition the communication task into at least the transport and network layers, responsible for the end-to-end and hop-by-hop tasks, respectively. Since both need to be link-independent, this calls for at least two more layers. We are now up to five, as claimed.

The case for the session and presentation layers appears to be weak. Although they provide some useful features, these can be provided in the application with little extra work. This is why these layers are rarely found in current networks and have not yet been standardized.

So, to answer the question we started with, seven is not a magic number. It seems reasonable, however, to require at least five layers, and, in fact, we find these five layers in all data communication networks.

Note that the principles outlined here are not sufficient to prescribe which functions ought to be in which layer. For example, error control can be either end-to-end or hop-by-hop, so it can be placed at the application, transport, network, or datalink layers. Similarly, flow control can be done in either the network or transport layer. Different networks partition functionalities differently. In this book, therefore, we study network functionality while purposely ignoring layering.

Why did the ISO OSI protocol stack fail?

By now, it is commonly accepted that the Internet protocol stack has decisively won over the OSI stack both in usage and industry support. Even in the late 1980s, however, the OSI stack was a serious contender as a worldwide networking standard. Why this sudden demise?

As with any complex situation, there are many answers to this question. One clear problem with OSI was that the standardization process was slow, cumbersome, and tended to stifle innovation through endless, politically motivated bickering. In contrast, the Internet's free-and-easy attitude toward standardization encourages innovation. Thus, for example, multicast service spread across the Internet through the efforts of a handful of people. In contrast, the OSI stack does not yet support multicast and may never do so.

A second problem with OSI is that it was specified before there was much experience in designing and building large-scale OSI networks. Thus, several design choices were made in the absence of concrete evidence of their effectiveness. In contrast, the Internet philosophy is to standardize only after implementation. This guarantees robust standards.

In sum, the success of protocol depends on a game of numbers. With two competing standards, application developers are drawn to a stack that has a larger user base, which results in making a popular standard even more popular. By the time OSI proponents got their act together, the Internet was too large to be successfully challenged, and the OSI stack is now just a historical footnote.

5.6   Summary

Protocols allow networks to provide services that need the cooperation of more than one end-system. We can sometimes layer protocols, so that a protocol is a step in the execution of another, higher protocol. Layering allows us to break up a complex task into smaller ones, and to separate layer implementation from its specification. However, this separation, unless carefully implemented, can lead to degraded performance.

The International Organization for Standards prescribes a seven-layer protocol architecture for data communication that has strongly influenced protocols in the field. In this chapter, we studied the functions of each layer, and some example protocols at each layer.

Chapter 6

System Design

6.1 Introduction

A computer network is a distributed system built from hardware, such as switches and transmission links, and many layers of software, as described in Chapter 5. The software and hardware in a computer network provide computational, storage, and transmission *resources* that are used to provide network services. System design is the art and science of putting together these resources into a harmonious whole. In this chapter we will study some techniques for system design, in particular as they apply to computer networks. More general treatments can be found in books on operating systems, such as references [SG 94] and [Tanenbaum 92], and books on computer architecture, such as reference [PH 95].

6.1.1 Performance metrics and resource constraints

In any system, some resources are more freely available than others. For example, consider a high-end personal computer connected to the Internet with a 28.8-Kbps modem. In this system, for tasks that require only a moderate amount of processing, such as reading email, the rate at which the computer can process information far exceeds the capacity of the transmission link.[1] We call a freely available resource an *unconstrained* resource, and a resource whose availability determines overall system performance a *constrained* resource. In this system, the link's bandwidth constrains the overall performance, as measured by the effective throughput of the link. This, therefore, is the constrained resource. In this example, the computer's processing speed and memory size are unconstrained resources.

A system designer must typically optimize one or more performance metrics given a set of resource constraints. A *performance metric* measures some aspect of a system's performance, such as throughput, response time, cost, development time, or mean time between failures (we will define these metrics more formally in Section 6.2). A *resource constraint* is a limitation on a resource, such as time, bandwidth, or computing power, that the design must obey. By explicitly identifying performance metrics and resource constraints, a system designer ensures that the design space is well defined, the solution is feasible, and the design is efficient. She can then trade unconstrained resources for constrained ones to maximize the design's utility at the least cost. Continuing with our example, a system designer might use the PC's surplus computational power to compress data as much as possible, to best exploit the limited capacity of the transmission link. A well-designed system maximizes achievable performance while still satisfying the resource constraints.

EXAMPLE 6.1

System design is important not only in computer systems, but also in other areas, such as automobile design. For example, a car designer might try to maximize the reliability of a car (measured in the mean time between equipment failures) that costs less than $10,000 to build. In this example, the mean time between failures measures performance, and the resource constraint is money. In real life, of course, designs must try to simultaneously optimize many, possibly conflicting metrics (such as reliability, performance, and recyclability) while satisfying many constraints (such as the price of the car and the time allowed for the design).

6.1.2   System design in real life

If we could quantify and control every aspect of a system, then system design would be a relatively simple matter. Unfortunately, there are several practical reasons why system design is both an art and a science. First, although we can quantitatively measure some aspects of system performance, such as throughput or response time, we cannot mea-

---

[1]How do we know that? Assume that the computer processes 30 million instructions per second. At 28.8 Kbps, it can expend more than 32,000 machine instructions for each incoming byte (ignoring operating system overheads). This is more than enough to handle most per-byte computational tasks.

sure others, such as simplicity, scalability, modularity, extensibility, and elegance. Yet a designer must make a series of trade-offs among these intangible quantities, appealing as much to good sense and personal choice as performance measurements. Second, rapid technological change can make constraint assumptions obsolete. A designer must not only meet the current set of design constraints, but also anticipate how future changes in technology might affect the design. The future is hard to predict, and a designer must appeal to instinct and intuition to make a design "future-proof." Third, market conditions may dictate that design requirements change when part of the design is already complete. Finally, international standards, which themselves change over time, may impose irksome and arbitrary constraints. These factors imply that, in real life, a designer is usually confronted with a complex, underspecified, multifactor optimization problem. In the face of these uncertainties, prescribing the one true path to system design is impossible.

Nevertheless, it is still possible to identify some principles of good design that have withstood the test of time and are applicable in a variety of situations. In Section 6.2, we will study some common resources, so that the reader can get some intuition in identifying them in real systems. We will then build up, in Section 6.3, a set of tools to help us trade freely available (unconstrained) resources for scarce (constrained) ones. Properly applied, these tools allow us to match the design to the constraints at hand. Finally, in Section 6.4, we will outline a methodology for performance analysis and tuning. This methodology helps pinpoint problems in a design and build a more efficient and robust system.

6.2   Common resources and their metrics

We can describe most computer system resources as a combination of five common resources: *time, space, computation, money,* and *labor.* We now study these resources in more detail, with examples of how they arise in real-world problems, and a description of associated performance metrics. Our definitions of these resources are purposely vague, since the exact definition varies with the problem.

6.2.1   Time

Time can constrain a design in many ways. For example, a user may require a task to complete before a given time, or may want to limit the time taken for a packet to travel from a source to a destination. At a different level, there may be a time constraint on how long it can take to design and build a system (time-to-market). Or, we may want to maximize the mean time between failures. We now study some standard ways to measure the use of time in a system.

We call the mean time to complete a task its *response time* and the mean number of tasks that can be completed in a unit time the *throughput*. There is an important relationship between throughput and response time that we will use often in this book: the mean number of concurrent activities in a system, also called its *degree of parallelism,* is the product of the throughput and the response time. Let

R = response time (seconds/task)
T = throughput (tasks/second)
D = degree of parallelism

$$D = R * T \qquad\qquad (6.1)$$

EXAMPLE 6.2

Consider a building that has two floors, with an escalator to carry people from one floor to the other. Ignoring queuing delays, the response time for a passenger is the mean time taken by the escalator to ascend or descend one floor. The throughput (bandwidth) is the mean number of passengers that can be loaded or unloaded per second. Suppose that an average of five people step on the escalator in one second, and that the escalator takes an average of 10 seconds to go up one floor. The response time for a passenger, therefore, is 10 seconds, and the throughput of the escalator is 5 passengers/second. Thus, the degree of parallelism, which is the mean number of passengers carried simultaneously, is $5 * 10 = 50$. To see this, mark a passenger with a daub of red paint as she steps on the escalator. In the ten seconds that she takes to reach the top, we expect that fifty more passengers boarded the escalator. Thus, when she steps off, the escalator carries an average of fifty passengers, which is its degree of parallelism.

EXAMPLE 6.3

If, in a system, on an average, 20 tasks complete in 10 seconds, and each task takes 3 seconds, what is the degree of parallelism?

Solution: The throughput is 20/10 tasks/second, and the response time is 3 seconds. Thus, the degree of parallelism = 20 / 10 * 3 = 6. In other words, an average of six tasks execute in parallel in the system.

6.2.2 Space

Like time, space is a resource that can constrain a design in many ways. Space constraints in computer networks are usually expressed as a limit on the memory available to hold packets in switches and routers. For example, a host-adaptor card may have 2 Kbytes of RAM for packet storage, or an ATM switch may have 10,000 cells of buffering at each output port.

A stream of packets on a connection uses a fraction of link capacity in the same way as a set of packets uses a fraction of a switch's buffers. In this sense, we can view bandwidth also as a space resource. For example, a T3 link has a bandwidth of 44.768 Mbps. If we use it to carry compressed video streams, each with a mean bit rate of 1.5 Mbps, we can fit at most 29 streams on the link.

> **Megabit versus megabyte**
>
> We measure space in kilobytes (KB) or megabytes (MB), and bandwidth in kilobits/second (Kbps) or megabits/second (Mbps). Unfortunately, while a kilobit/second means 1000 bits/second, a kilobyte is not 1000 bytes, but 1024 bytes. Similarly, 1 Mbps is 1,000,000 bps, but 1 megabyte is 1,048,576 bytes. For back-of-the-envelope calculations, we can assume that an 8-Mbps link carries 1 megabyte in 1 second. However, for more precise calculations, a careful engineer must make the necessary conversions. In this book, we will always do so.

6.2.3   Computation

Computation refers to the processing that can be done in a unit time. Using processors in parallel can increase computational power (as can waiting for a year or two—a reasonable rule of thumb is that computational speed doubles every 18 months!). We measure computation in millions of instructions per second (MIPS). We assume here that every instruction takes the same time to execute, which is more or less true for reduced-instruction-set (RISC) processors.[2] In mid-1996, even low-end Intel 80486-class microprocessors processed about 30 million instructions per second. At the high end, Alpha processors from Digital Equipment processed more than 500 million instructions per second. With operating-system overheads, however, only about 80% of this rate is available to applications.

6.2.4   Money

A successful design cannot cost more than what the market can bear. This affects the choice of components used in building the system, the number of engineers assigned to the task, and the time available. Moreover, to achieve economies of scale, the design must be manufacturable at a reasonable cost. All these considerations affect the design.

---

[2] Actually, load and store instructions take longer (two or sometimes more cycles) if they refer to a memory location not in the on-chip cache. Thus, the effective instruction rate depends on the cache hit rate, which, in turn, depends on the workload. To a first approximation, assuming reasonably effective on-chip caches, we can think of all instructions as taking the same time.

6.2.5   Labor

Labor is the human effort required to design and build a system. No amount of money can compensate for the lack of trained labor. Given a labor constraint, a designer must decide which parts of the design need the most work, and which can be ignored. Unfortunately, the labor constraint is one of the least understood and most ignored constraints on engineering design.

6.2.6   Social constraints

Besides constraints on these five resources, two major constraints are purely social: standards and market requirements.

- *Standards* force the design to conform to some widely agreed-upon requirements that may or may not be appropriate for that particular design. Though standards are essential to allow interoperability and can reduce costs by promoting competition, poorly designed standards severely restrict the design space. Worse yet, an underspecified standard may lead to faulty implementations that are not even interoperable. A good example of a bad standard is the Q.2931 standard for signaling in ATM networks. The standard is unnecessarily complex, and therefore hard to implement and hard to modify. Yet, to succeed in the marketplace, switch manufacturers have to obey it, thus slowing the rate at which ATM networks spread.

- *Market requirements,* like poorly designed standards, are unfortunate realities. A company may decide that products being designed must be backward-compatible with a previous product, or that they must use a particular operating system, or that they must support some set of standards. These essentially political decisions set the framework for a design. Market requirements may also determine the amount of human effort that can be expended on a design project. It is remarkable how much time is spent on building graphical user interfaces, sometimes at the expense of the system underlying the interface!

6.2.7   Scaling

The last constraint, *scaling*, is different from the others in that it constrains, not resources, but design elements. A centralized design, that is, a design that incorporates a single point of storage or control, is limited to the storage or processing capacity of the central point. Thus, an arbitrarily scalable design must minimize its use of centralized elements. This forces such designs to use distributed algorithms for control and coordination. Of course, a distributed system has its own problems, such as communication overhead and complex interconnection. Scaling is hard to measure, and arguments about whether a design can scale verge on the religious. Nevertheless, history shows that a system must scale well if it is to succeed.

EXAMPLE 6.4

Consider an airline reservation system, where agents from any part of the world can make a reservation for seats on any flight on any airline. One design for this system is to send all reservation requests to a single central computer. This design is simple, but has two problems. First, if the central computer crashes, every agent is affected. Second, as the number of agents increases, we need to expand the capacity of the central computer. However, the number of reservation requests, particularly during peak travel periods, may increase beyond the capacity of the largest computer that we can build or buy. Then, the response time suffers, and system performance degrades. We can solve this problem by replacing the central computer with a set of regional reservation centers that coordinate among themselves to maintain a consistent view of the system state (such as whether a flight is full or not). Then, as the number of reservation requests increases, we can just add another reservation center. We must, however, pay for this with a communication overhead for coordination, and a complex network to interconnect the regional reservation centers.

6.3   Common design techniques

In any system, some resources are less constrained than others. We call the most constrained resource in a system (or the *binding* constraint) its *bottleneck*. System performance improves if and only if we devote additional resources to a bottlenecked resource. Conversely, decreasing the amount of an unconstrained resource does not adversely affect performance. When we relieve one bottleneck, however, it is possible for another resource to become a bottleneck. Thus, we must remove the bottlenecks one by one until all the resources are equally constrained. We call such a system a *balanced* system.

   A balanced system is optimal, in that we fully utilize every component. However, in practice, we rarely achieve balanced systems. Rapid changes in technology, market constraints, and customer expectations mean that a system's components are almost constantly in flux, with the bottleneck moving from place to place in the system.

EXAMPLE 6.5

Henry Ford's Model T car is an interesting example of a balanced system. As a frugal capitalist and early practitioner of performance analysis, Ford wanted to make sure that he manufactured no part of the Model T to a quality greater than necessary. He hired a team of inspectors to tour automobile junkyards, determining which parts did not wear out. Whenever he found a part that consistently outlived the rest, he reduced its quality (and its cost), without affecting the longevity of the car. Thus, a Model T was as cheap as possible (though a proud owner might some-day wake up to find that every component of the car had failed simultaneously!).

EXAMPLE 6.6

Assume that we want to increase the speed with which we can store data on a tape drive attached to a computer through an I/O bus. The three components affecting the speed are the CPU, the I/O bus, and the tape-drive write mechanism. Measurements may show that the slowest component in the system is the tape drive. Then, no matter how fast the CPU or the I/O bus, system performance will not improve unless the tape drive's performance improves. Suppose we now replace the drive with a faster one. Then, we may find that the I/O bus is too slow to match the tape drive. The bottleneck resource, therefore, is now the I/O bus. We must improve the I/O bus to match the drive speed, perhaps by using a different I/O bus technology (of course, this might require us to change the tape drive to be compatible with the new bus!). This process continues until we meet the performance target or run out of time or money. Ideally, the I/O bus, drive, and CPU will simultaneously reach their maximum performance, so that the system is balanced.

A design that uses more of an unconstrained resource to reduce the load on a constrained resource will increase the system's performance. For example, if a task is time-sensitive and computational power is freely available, we should try to parallelize the task. This allows us to trade off computation for time to meet the time constraint and maximize performance. A good design methodology is to start with a set of resource constraints and performance metrics, then trade off one resource for another to maximize utility.

We will now look at some standard optimization techniques that are the "Swiss army knife" of system design. Whenever you run into a resource crunch or want to improve performance, you can try one of these techniques to help.

6.3.1   Multiplexing: Trading time and space for money

Multiplexing means sharing a single resource among many users (Figure 6.1). Because each user must wait for its turn to use a multiplexed resource, the user's response time increases. Moreover, waiting users take up space. Thus, multiplexing trades a reduction in the number of resources for time and space. Economies of scale typically make a single large resource cheaper than multiple unshared and smaller resources. Thus, multiplexing ultimately trades money for time and space.

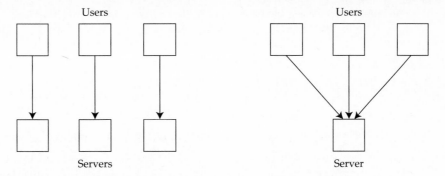

Figure 6.1: Multiplexing. Multiplexing allows money to be traded off for time and space. Without multiplexing, each user has its own server. With multiplexing, a single server serves users in turn. This saves money, but each user must wait, and occupies space while waiting.

EXAMPLE 6.7

Imagine a bank where each arriving customer had his or her own teller, and never had to wait in line. This would be terribly expensive and the bank might go out of business. Instead, the bank saves money by sharing (multiplexing) a single teller among multiple customers, at the expense of building a waiting area (space) and the time its customers waste by waiting in line.

Multiplexing a link is useful when data from many users share the same path. Along the shared portion, economies of scale make it cheaper to run a single link at a higher bandwidth than multiple per-user links at a lower bandwidth. As we saw in Section 4.4, while this reduces the per-user cost of a link, data from a user may be delayed if data from another user is occupying the link.

EXAMPLE 6.8

Consider the set of simultaneous phone calls between New York and Chicago. Suppose we know that the peak usage on this route is 10,000 simultaneous calls. We can run 10,000 wires between the two cities, where each wire carries a single call. This is expensive. Instead, we can run a single line between the cities, with a capacity of 10,000 calls, time-shared among the active calls. By multiplexing this line, we save money, because we have to lay fewer cables. However, we have to pay for a multiplexor that stores a voice sample while it waits for its turn on the wire. Moreover, each sample experiences a queuing delay (though this is at most one sample time, 125 μs). Thus, we trade time and space for money.

An interesting view of multiplexing is to think of a multiplexed shared resource as an *unshared virtual* resource. Consider a customer using the services of a bank teller, as in Example 6.7. While the teller is helping the customer, the fact that other customers are waiting in line is of no consequence. If we magically put a customer in suspended animation when she is waiting in line, and wake her up when the teller becomes available, then from her perspective, the teller is never unavailable. From this perspective, the bank teller is, therefore, an unshared virtual resource.

EXAMPLE 6.9

When you make a telephone call, your voice travels over the telephone network to the destination. The network allocates resources along the shared portions of the route for the duration of the call. When you put the phone down, these shared resources are available to others. From your perspective, the entire telephone network is devoted only to serving you (unless the network refuses you a connection because a trunk is full or the destination is busy). In other words, the telephone network is really a shared (multiplexed) network, but appears to be an unshared network to its customers.

A *server* typically controls access to a shared resource. Whenever the shared resource has more than one task contending for access, the server decides the service order according to a *schedule.* For example, the server may schedule tasks in order of their arrival (first-come-first-served). A schedule determines each user's relative delay and resource share. Intelligent scheduling plays an important role in managing shared resources; we will study it in Chapter 9.

EXAMPLE 6.10

An airplane is a multiplexed resource, and a member of the flight crew typically controls access to it. At the time of boarding, the crew member uses priority to minimize the waiting time for people who pay more (first class), fly more (frequent-flyer club members), or are most in need (elderly people and families with small children). This prioritized schedule increases the delay of the rest of the passengers, while decreasing the waiting time for some. The key point is that the schedulers directly control service quality.

A particularly interesting form of multiplexing is possible if the tasks sharing the resource have *elastic* resource requirements, that is, they can adapt their resource usage to prevailing conditions. Then, a resource can signal its current utilization to the contending tasks and they can scale their request size to use their currently available share. For example, an elastic file-transfer task may be willing to reduce its share of link bandwidth if there are other competing file-transfer tasks at a shared link. Then, the link could efficiently multiplex its bandwidth among the contending transfers by implicitly or explicitly informing each competing task of its current resource share, thus allowing it to use all the available capacity without overload or underload. This general technique is used in most feedback flow-control schemes, including that in TCP.

Statistical multiplexing

Suppose a resource has a capacity C and is shared by N identical tasks, where each task has a capacity requirement of c. If $Nc \leq C$, then the resource always has sufficient capacity to handle incoming tasks. Now, suppose that tasks can be either active or inactive, and that at any time, we know that at most 10% of the tasks are active. Then, we could size the resource to be as small as $Nc/10$ without degrading performance. In other words, by making use of statistical knowledge about the system, we can reduce resource requirements at a shared resource. We call this statistical multiplexing.

   The two important types of statistical multiplexing are *spatial* and *temporal*. In spatial statistical multiplexing, which we discussed in the preceding paragraph, we can decrease resource sizing because we expect only a small fraction of tasks to be active. In temporal statistical multiplexing, all tasks may be simultaneously active, but we expect a task's *average* resource consumption to be less than its *peak*. More precisely, let the Ith task have a peak resource consumption of $P(I)$, and an average resource consumption (measured asymptotically over increasingly longer periods of time), of $A(I)$. Then, a conservative sizing of the resource is $Cmax = \Sigma P(I)$, that is, when the resource can handle a simultaneous set of requests at the peak rate from all active tasks. The minimum sizing is $Cmin = \Sigma A(I)$, when there is just enough resource to handle the average rate, and traffic arriving during the peak load must wait in a buffer for access. Of course, we can choose any C in the range [$Cmin, Cmax$], depending on how conservative we want to be. The point is that by using knowledge about the temporal behavior of the tasks, we can reduce the size of the shared resource.

EXAMPLE 6.11

A 100-room hotel needs to obtain external telephone connections to allow its guests access to the telephone network. Assume that the hotel manager must inform the telephone company how many lines he needs, and must pay dearly for the installation of each line. A conservative manager may ask for 100 connections, so that, even if every guest simultaneously made an outside call (perhaps when the hotel catches fire!), they will all have a line available. A less conservative manager may expect no more than 10 guests to be simultaneously active. So, she may reduce the number of connections to 10, reducing her installation cost by 90%, but introducing the possibility that an external call is blocked. This is the trade-off with *spatial* statistical multiplexing.

Even when a telephone line is in use, pauses in conversation mean that a typical line is used only 40% of the time. Thus, if we were to place voice samples from each user in ATM cells, the hotel manager could ask for an external ATM link that had a capacity of only four voice calls, and could multiplex this line with cells from ten simultaneous connections. This reduces the size of the external link even further. This reduction is possible because the manager has statistical information about the average fraction of activity within a conversation, and is an example of *temporal* statistical multiplexing gain.

Note that we can obtain gains from spatial and temporal statistical multiplexing simultaneously. Moreover, a circuit-switched network can only obtain spatial statistical multiplexing gain. To obtain temporal gain, we must employ packet switching.[3]

To obtain statistical multiplexing gain, a designer must have good statistical information about the expected number of users and their usage patterns. Without such information, or if these statistics change over time, an attempt to obtain statistical multiplexing gain can lead to severe congestion. A clear example of this danger can be found in the current road system, which was designed for a smaller population. As population has grown in metropolitan areas, the load on the system has increased beyond its capacity, leading to chronic congestion.

6.3.2   Pipelining and parallelism: Trading computation for time

In some situations, we may want to decrease the time to complete a task, and have the freedom to use multiple processors to do so. The solution is simple if we can divide a task into N *independent* subtasks. Then, N processors can execute the independent subtasks in parallel to decrease time taken to complete the task by a factor of N. For example, if we can divide a task T into two independent subtasks T_1 and T_2, then executing the two tasks in parallel reduces the completion time to the larger of the execution times of the subtasks. The decomposition is optimal when the two subtasks have the same exe-

---

[3]This is not strictly true. A technique called *Time Assignment Speech Interpolation*, or *TASI*, allows a circuit to be shared among many voice calls. A monitoring circuit dynamically assigns a circuit to a call when it detects speech, and releases the circuit during a silence period. This is a coarse-grained sharing of channels (the time to acquire and release a channel is on the order of 250 ms), and user activity is implicitly detected. In contrast, with packet switching, the sharing is fine-grained, and user activity is explicitly known from the packet header.

cution time, so that the execution time for the task halves and the task throughput doubles.

We say that a task has a *linear speedup* if we can divide it into N subtasks such that executing the subtasks in parallel increases task throughput by a factor of N. A non-optimal decomposition will reduce the speedup to a factor smaller than N, specifically to the ratio of the task's execution time to the slowest subtask's execution time. Thus, the improvement in performance, when decomposing a problem into parallel subtasks, is determined by the speed of the slowest subtask. If we want to improve overall performance, we should improve the performance of this subtask.

EXAMPLE 6.12

Consider a page on the World Wide Web that contains several images. A browser that downloads this site either can download the images one by one, or can try to download all the images in parallel. Assume that we can allocate a separate processor for downloading each image. Each download is independent of the others, so the completion time of the parallel version is the time it takes for the slowest download to complete. If a site has three images, with download times of 3, 5, and 10 seconds, the unparallelized (serial) version takes 18 seconds to download, whereas the parallel version takes 10 seconds. The speedup is 18 / 10 = 1.8, which is determined by the time taken for the slowest image to download. If each image took the same time to download, that is, 6 seconds, then the speed up would be 18/6 = 3. This is the optimal decomposition of the task.

If we can divide a task T into subtasks T_1 and T_2 such that T_2 can begin only after T_1 completes, then the two tasks are *serially dependent*. If we can divide a task into N equal serially dependent subtasks, then a *pipeline* of N processors can achieve a throughput N times greater than a single processor (Figure 6.2). We call each processor in a pipeline a *stage*. The first stage of the pipeline completes the first subtask and hands the remaining computation to the next stage. This executes the next subtask and passes the remaining work downstream. If each stage of the pipeline takes unit time, a pipeline with N stages takes N time units to load up. In every subsequent time unit, if the pipe remains full, it outputs a task requiring N time units.

EXAMPLE 6.13

An automobile assembly line is an excellent example of a pipeline. Assume that at the start of a day, the assembly line is empty, and that the line has 10 stations, each requiring 10 minutes of work. The line completes the first job 100 minutes after the start of work. Every 10 minutes thereafter, if there are no glitches, the line com-

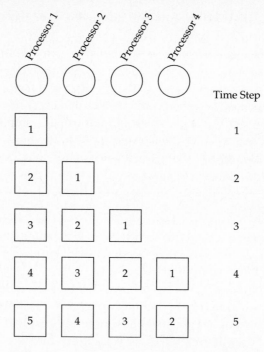

Figure 6.2: A pipeline of four processors. Numbers in squares refer to the sequence number of the task performed at that time step. For example, at time step 1, processor 1 performs part of task 1, and at time step 2, processor 1 performs part of task 2. Each processor (or stage) executes part of a task, then hands the rest of the task to the next stage.

pletes another job. Each job spends 100 minutes in the assembly line, 10 minutes at each station. Thus, the delay of a job does not decrease, but the overall throughput, measured in the number of jobs per hour, increases by a factor of 10.

EXAMPLE 6.14

Suppose we wanted to parallelize a protocol stack, allocating one processor to the datalink layer, one to the network layer, one to the transport layer, and one to the application layer. Assume that each layer takes the same amount of time, say 10 ms, to process a packet (a rather unrealistic assumption!). In the unparallelized (serial) version of the stack, the stack takes 40 ms to process a packet. In the parallelized (pipelined) version, each packet has a processing delay of 40 ms, as in the serial version, but the pipeline processes a packet every 10 ms, instead of a packet every 40 ms.

What happens if different stages of a pipeline can take different amounts of time? We will use the relationship *throughput * response time = degree of parallelism* (Equation 6.1) to analyze the problem. Let the sum of the times taken at all the stages be R, and let the slowest stage take time S. By definition, the response time of the pipeline is R. Since the slowest stage takes time S, the pipeline outputs a packet once every S seconds, giving a throughput of $1/S$. Thus, the degree of parallelism is R/S.

EXAMPLE 6.15

Continuing with Example 6.14, assume that the datalink layer takes 6 ms, the network layer 3 ms, the transport layer 10 ms, and the application 4 ms. The response time is 23 ms. The throughput is one job every 10 ms. The degree of parallelism is, therefore, $23/10 = 2.3$. In other words, at a given time, only 2.3 of the four processors are active; the others are stalled waiting for an earlier stage to complete.

Because the slowest stage in a pipeline controls its throughput, we maximize the throughput and the degree of parallelism when every stage takes the same time. We call such a pipeline a *balanced* pipeline. In a balanced pipeline with N stages, the response time is $N * S$, the throughput is S, and the degree of parallelism is N. A balanced pipeline achieves a linear speedup, although its subtasks are serially dependent.

6.3.3   Batching: Trading response time for throughput

EXAMPLE 6.16

Suppose you lived a 20-minute drive away from a grocery store. One way to manage your grocery purchasing would be to go to the store when you needed something. This would reduce the time you spent in a dissatisfied state where you knew you needed something, but did not have it. However, if you thought of something to buy just after you returned from a trip, you would have to make the trip again, taking at least 40 minutes more. In the worst case, you would purchase one item every 40 minutes, and spend all your time driving to and from the grocery store! You could, instead, make a grocery list and buy everything on the list once a day, thus incurring the overhead of driving to the store only once every day. However, you may have to wait as long as one day to obtain something. By *batching* your purchases, you have increased your throughput at the expense of a longer worst-case response time.

Batching is effective when (a) a task's overhead increases less than linearly with the number of tasks, and (b) the time taken to accumulate a batch is not too long. Then, by batching tasks, we reduce the aggregate overhead at the cost of degrading the worst-case response time. Stated more precisely, let a task take S time units to execute, and let it have an overhead of O time units. If we do a task immediately on its arrival into the system, if the system is idle when the task arrives, we have:

$$\text{Worst-case response time for the task} = S + O \tag{6.2}$$

$$\text{Worst-case throughput} = 1/(S + O) \tag{6.3}$$

Let us batch N tasks that take a time A to arrive into the system. Assume that the overhead for N tasks is P, such that $P < N * O$. Now, if the batched tasks are served in first-come-first-served order:

$$\text{Worst-case response time} = A + N * S + P \tag{6.4}$$

$$\text{Worst-case throughput} = N/(N * S + A + P) = 1/(S + (A + P)/N) \tag{6.5}$$

The proportional increase in throughput when batching is thus $(S + O) / (S + (A + P)/N)$. This is greater than 1 when $A < (N * O - P)$, that is, the time wasted in accumulating N packets is less than the time gained in the decreased overhead.

Note that during time A, the system is free to do other tasks. Thus, if we measure throughput only during the time the system devotes to this task, we get

$$\text{Throughput} = 1/(S + P/N) \tag{6.6}$$

which is always greater than the throughput obtained without batching.

EXAMPLE 6.17

Continuing with Example 6.16, we have $O = 40$ minutes. Assume that S, the time taken to shop for one item, is 1 minute, and that we accumulate an average of $N = 10$ items over $A = 4$ hours $= 240$ minutes. The overhead for shopping for 10 items is 40 minutes, so that $P = 40$. Without batching, the throughput is $1/(40 + 1) = 0.0243$ items/minute. With batching, substituting into Equation 6.5, the throughput is $1/(1 + (240 + 40)/10) = 1/29 = 0.034$ items/minute. The throughput, therefore, improves by a factor of 1.4. However, the worst-case response time degrades from 41 minutes to 281 minutes.

EXAMPLE 6.18

On receiving a packet, a host-adaptor usually raises an interrupt to inform the CPU that it has some work to do. The time taken in fielding an interrupt can be a significant overhead in packet processing, thus motivating batching. A common strategy while batching interrupts is to raise an interrupt a fixed delay after receiving a packet. This constrains the worst-case response time, while increasing the throughput if several packets arrive back-to-back.

Suppose the host-adaptor interrupts the CPU 10 ms after the arrival of a packet, whether or not it has another packet in the batch. Let the packet processing time per packet be $S = 2$ ms, and the interrupt-fielding overhead $O = 5$ ms. Then, the worst-case response time without batching is $5 + 2 = 7$ ms, and with batching is $10 + 5 + 2 = 17$ ms. Without batching, the best achievable throughput is 1 packet every 7 ms $= 0.143$ packets/ms. However, if the mean packet arrival rate $\lambda = 1$ packet/ms, we expect to have $\lambda A = 10$ packets in a batch, improving the throughput to 10 packets every $(10 + 2 * 10 + 5) = 35$ ms $= 0.285$ packets/ms. If we ignore the time spent waiting for packets when computing throughput, this improves to 10 packets every 25 ms $= 0.4$ packets/ms.

EXAMPLE 6.19

A remote terminal (telnet) session sends a packet for every character typed, which can be inefficient. Suppose you had to design a telnet application that batched characters. Assume that users type characters at a peak rate of 5 characters/second, and at an average rate of 1 character/second. (a) If we can delay characters no more than 500 milliseconds before we must send them out, what is the largest and average batch size? (b) If the batch size is fixed at 20 characters, what are the best and average case application-level delays? (c) What does this tell us about batching for telnet?

Solution: (a) The largest batch size is when characters arrive at the peak rate of 5 characters/s $= 200$ ms/character. Thus, the largest batch size is $\lceil 500/200 \rceil = 3$ characters. The average batch size is $\lceil 500/1000 \rceil = 1$ character. (b) If the batch size is 20 characters, the best response time is 20 characters/5 characters/s $= 4$ seconds. The average response time is $20/1 = 20$ seconds. (c) If our assumptions about normal typing speeds and response time requirements are correct, it does not pay to design a batched telnet!

6.3.4   Exploiting locality: Trading space for time

Locality means that if the system accessed some data at a given time, it is likely that it will access the same or "nearby" data "soon." Locality is a general principle that we see in many systems. For example, a user who accesses a particular file is likely to touch the file again in the near future. Similarly, a program that refers to a memory address to retrieve data or program instructions is likely to refer to contiguous addresses in the near future.

Locality can be *spatial, temporal,* or both. Spatial locality means that data items *close* to a currently used data unit are more likely to be used in the future than others. Temporal locality means that if the system refers to a data unit now, it is likely to refer to the same data unit *soon.* Of course, both kinds of locality may coexist. We can exploit locality to optimize system operation, as the next two examples illustrate.

EXAMPLE 6.20

Locality motivates the powerful tool of *caching,* that is, storing a recently accessed data unit "closer" to the accessor. We typically organize computer storage as a hierarchy, where higher levels have small capacity but fast access times and lower levels have larger capacity and correspondingly lower access times. For example, using 1996 numbers, a RAM has an access time of around 60 ns, and a hard disk has an access time of around 10 ms. However, typical RAM capacity is about 16 Mbytes, but a typical disk stores around 1 Gbyte. With caching, if an application refers to a part of a file, then the operating system reads other parts of the same file from the disk into the RAM, so that, because of spatial locality, most accesses are to the fast RAM rather than the slower disk. Thus, with caching, the storage system has the capacity of a disk, but appears to have only slightly more than the access time of a RAM.

EXAMPLE 6.21

During file transfer, the sending protocol stack typically segments files into several packets that it then sends closely spaced in time. Thus, a receiver who receives the beginning of a file from a sender is likely to get more file transfer packets from the sender in the near future. If the receiver caches the housekeeping records associated with that file transfer in fast memory, it can retrieve them rapidly, thus increasing system throughput.

6.3.5 Optimizing the common case

Many systems obey the 80/20 rule: 80% of the time is spent in 20% of the code and 20% of the time is spent in 80% of the code. Thus, optimizing the 20% that really counts can improve overall system efficiency. Unfortunately, it is not always clear which 20% of the system we should optimize. We can usually determine this only by instrumenting a running system and measuring its usage. Once this is done, however, the improvements can be dramatic.

EXAMPLE 6.22

An excellent example of optimizing for the common case is in the design of Reduced Instruction Set Computers (RISC). These were motivated by instruction traces that showed that a few instructions dominate the CPU usage of common programs. RISC processors minimize the time taken to perform these common tasks at the cost of increasing the time taken to perform less common instructions. Nevertheless, this still improves the overall processor performance, because the chip area devoted to complex, less commonly used instructions is devoted to performance boosters such as on-chip caches, additional registers, and better translation lookaside buffers.

EXAMPLE 6.23

In a typical protocol stack, packet processing for most packets traverses the same path in the code, which is the path taken when the packet is in-sequence and error-free. We can improve protocol performance by minimizing the time taken to execute this path. At the start of packet processing, we test to see if the packet falls into the common case. If so, we process it using highly optimized code. If not, we process it using the usual code.

How much does improving the common case help? We can answer this using *Amdahl's law* [PH 95, p. 71]. The law states that the execution time after improving a system is given by:

> Execution time after improvement =
>   (Execution time affected by improvement / Amount of improvement)
>   + Execution time unaffected (6.7)

EXAMPLE 6.24

Suppose 80% of packets fall into the common case, and 20% need special handling. Initially, we assume that the common case takes 3 units of time, and the special case takes 5 units of time. Then, initially, the expected time to process a packet is $0.8 * 3 + 0.2 * 5 = 3.4$ time units. Note that the common case contributes 2.4 time units to this total. If we speed up the common case by a factor of 3, then the expected execution time drops to $0.8 * 3/3 + 0.2 * 5 = 1.8$ time units, where the common case contributes only 0.8 time units to the total of 1.8. A further speedup by a factor of 4 gives us an expected execution time of $0.8 * 1/4 + 0.2 * 5 = 1.2$, where the contribution of the common case drops further to 0.25. However, the overall processing time does not improve much because the time taken by the specially handled packets now dominates. We see, therefore, that beyond a point, speeding up the common case results in diminishing returns. This is the key intuition behind Amdahl's law.

6.3.6   Hierarchy

A hierarchy is a structure composed of smaller hierarchies, where the base level is a *parent* with one or more *children*. We can build a system as a hierarchy if it is possible to recursively decompose it into subsystems that depend only on their parent for correct execution. Hierarchies scale well because the only communication is between children and their parents and there is no single point of control. Like any distributed system, a hierarchy has a communication overhead when compared with a functionally equivalent monolithic system. Moreover, if we do not allow peer subsystems to communicate except through a shared ancestor, the hierarchy may behave suboptimally. Hierarchies are common in the natural world because they are simple and scale well. Blood vessels, tree branches, and commodity distribution systems are all examples of hierarchies.

Strict hierarchies do not permit child nodes to interconnect, which may sometimes introduce inefficiency. Loose hierarchies, such as the telephone and road networks, allow child nodes to interconnect, so that local traffic can use local routes.

EXAMPLE 6.25

Hierarchies are particularly useful in managing a *name space,* that is, the set of names of objects in a network. Consider a network of a million computers which requires the name of every computer to be globally unique. With a single, monolithic name space, the owner of a new computer must check that its name does not clash with any of the million existing names, which is impractical. Instead, we could use hierarchy to partition the computers into several domains, and identify a computer as ⟨domain-name, local-name⟩ tuple. Then, if we choose globally unique domain addresses, a new owner has to check for uniqueness only in her local domain, which takes less computation and less time. This technique is applied recursively in the Internet Domain Name System, which we will study in Chapter 10.

6.3.7   Binding and indirection

EXAMPLE 6.26

Suppose you have a friend, John Doe, who frequently changes email addresses as he moves from one Internet provider to another. You could save yourself some trouble if you had an alias for John, say "jdoe," and you updated an alias file every time John's address changed. Then, you could always send mail to "jdoe," and the alias file allows the system to translate this alias to the current email address. We say that you are *indirecting* through the alias file to *bind* the alias "jdoe" to John's current email address.

We can describe a system at many levels of abstraction. The greater the level of abstraction, the more the generality of description. However, at some point, we need to go from the general to the specific. We call this *binding* an instance to an abstraction. In Example 6.26, we bound an alias to the current email address for John Doe.

If we store the translation from an abstraction to its current instance in a well-known location, the system can use this information to automatically dereference the abstraction. We call this *indirection.* In Example 6.26, indirection allows the user to always send mail to "jdoe," and the system translates this automatically to the current email address. Indirection allows us to delay binding until the last possible moment, at the expense of an extra lookup. Generally speaking, indirection allows us to dynamically associate instances with abstractions by modifying the translation stored in a well-known location.

EXAMPLE 6.27

Indirection is essential in cellular telephony. As a cellular subscriber moves, the information needed to reach her keeps changing. However, callers always use the same telephone number to access the subscriber. The telephone network dynamically binds the number to a particular cell and communication frequency, and telephone switches use indirection to determine the latest binding.

EXAMPLE 6.28

Indirection is used to provide *virtual memory* in operating systems. Programs use *virtual* addresses to address memory locations. The operating system maintains a translation from a virtual address to a physical address in a *page table.* On a reference to a virtual address, the processor uses the page table to determine the current physical address bound to this virtual address. This allows a physical page to be moved anywhere in memory without affecting a program referring to data or instructions in that page.

6.3.8   Virtualization

Recall that multiplexing allows us to convert a physical resource to multiple virtual resources (see Section 6.3.1). Indirection allows us to refer to a virtual resource with an abstract reference that is resolved (bound) dynamically. *Virtualization* combines multiplexing with indirection to allow us to refer to a virtual resource exactly as if we were referring to the physical resource itself. This allows the system to reallocate the physical resources without affecting the behavior of entities using the abstraction.

EXAMPLE 6.29

You might have seen advertisements that say at the end, "For more information, call Chris at 1-800-555-1212." Presumably, Chris is the person answering the telephone at that number. Now, suppose Chris resigns from the company, and someone else takes his or her place. A customer calling that number after reading the ad would still want to talk to "Chris." This is a problem, because Chris is no longer there. The mistake the company made was to bind the abstraction "person answering phone" to "Chris" too early. One way to fix the problem is to run ads saying, "For more information, call Technical Support at 1-800-555-1212." Unfortunately, this sounds less personal. Instead, we can *virtualize* Chris. In the first step, whoever answers the telephone is, for the purposes of the call, Chris. This is just indirection: the caller calls the abstraction "Chris" that automatically binds to "person answering phone."

We can go one step further. Suppose many people simultaneously call the number, so that some of them have to wait in line. To reduce queuing, we can split incoming calls among several people, and all of them answer the phone as "Chris." (Note our cunning use of a unisex name.) In this way, everyone calling the number thinks he is talking to the "Chris" in the ad. Behind the scenes, the company can change the number of "Chris"es in the system to dynamically adapt to customer demand. We have thus virtualized Chris, in the same way American malls have virtualized Santa Claus.

EXAMPLE 6.30

Let us consider virtualization in a networking context. First, consider the design of an automatic teller machine that runs a single special-purpose program to communicate to a bank using a modem. Since only a single program accesses the modem, the program can treat the modem as a physical resource. Now, suppose we want to run many separate programs on the teller machine that may all want to communicate using the modem. We must, therefore, multiplex access to the modem. One way to do this is to control access to the modem by a scheduler that accepts device requests and carries out data transfer on behalf of an application. Another approach is to virtualize the modem using multiplexing and indirection. Specifically, each application accesses what it thinks is its own modem. Behind the scenes, read and write requests to the virtual modem are mapped to accesses on the actual modem. The application programmer need never know that other applications are also sharing the modem. If we add more modems to the machine, we can schedule read and write requests to modems in the pool, thus improving performance without having to change any existing applications.

6.3.9   Randomization

Randomization is a powerful tool in building robust systems. For example, it allows us to break a tie without knowing the number of contending parties or systematically discriminating against one of the contending parties. We can apply randomization in different ways in system design, and the examples that follow give some contexts for its use.

EXAMPLE 6.31

Consider a system where many stations share a single *broadcast* medium. That is, a transmission from any station can be heard at all the others. Thus, if two stations transmit simultaneously, their transmissions collide and garble, and they must both try again. A simple algorithm to share the medium is for a station to sense if the medium is idle, and, if so, transmit a packet. Suppose stations A and B have packets to send, and they simultaneously realize that the medium is idle. They will both transmit a packet, which will get garbled. What should they do next? If we use a deterministic algorithm to pick the time of the next transmission, then the retransmission will also collide! A good solution is for A and B to pick a random timeout interval, so that their retransmissions are unlikely to collide (this solution is used in the Ethernet local area network). Thus, randomization allows us to break ties cleanly.

EXAMPLE 6.32

Surprisingly, randomization can be used in routing packets from a source to a destination. Suppose each router knew the best path to a given destination (we will study how this is chosen in Chapter 11). It then forwards incoming packets on the output interface corresponding to the best path. If the output trunk is busy, incoming packets must be queued, and if the queue is full, dropped. To prevent packet loss, the router could forward a packet that would otherwise be dropped to a random idle output. That router can then forward the packet to the destination.

How well does this work? Suppose that the network is idle, except for traffic from endpoint A to endpoint B. As the load on the path increases, some routers along the path will start "spreading" the load to nearby routers, "widening" the path from A to B. The heavier the load on the path, the wider the set of paths automatically coopted in carrying the traffic. Thus, randomized routing helps to distribute load away from heavily loaded paths. Under some assumptions in topology, we can show that this form is optimal.

EXAMPLE 6.33
Consider the situation where a source wants to transfer a packet to a set of recipients reliably. Assume that the source and recipients are members of a *multipoint multicast* group, so that packets transmitted by any group member are distributed to all other members (though some recipients may not get a copy of the packet because of packet loss on a link). One way to assure reliability is for each recipient to acknowledge the receipt of each packet. This causes an *acknowledgment implosion* at the source, so it is not feasible for large multicast groups with thousands of receivers. Instead, each receiver could send a *negative acknowledgment* (nack) when it detected a packet loss (we will discuss how to detect packet loss in Chapter 12). Unfortunately, if many recipients simultaneously detect a packet loss, this leads to an implosion of nacks. We can get around this problem by asking recipients to choose a random time interval before sending a nack. Moreover, on hearing a nack, the sender multicasts the retransmission to the entire group, and other receivers cancel their nack timer. We can show that with carefully chosen ranges for random timeout generation, packet loss is repaired with a single nack [FJMZL 95].

6.3.10 Soft state

"State" refers to memory in the system used to influence future behavior. For example, in a virtual-circuit network, per-circuit state allows a switch to route a packet based on its VCI. In the telephone network, per-call state allows the network to log each call and bill a subscriber based on its duration. State is usually created during connection establishment and updated during the lifetime of the connection. The more state stored in the network for a call, the less needs to be sent in each packet header. Thus, for example, a datagram header needs to carry the entire destination address, but an ATM cell needs only a VCI.

A big problem with storing state in the network is that we need to explicitly create and remove it. If state is not correctly removed, system performance may degrade, or the system may even fail. For example, each ATM switch stores per-VCI information such as the amount of resources reserved for that VCI. If the network reroutes the connection (or abnormally terminates it), unless we explicitly inform the switch, the state persists, and other connections cannot access the reserved resources. Thus, persistent or *hard* state can lead to complicated designs to detect and remove "garbage." An interesting alternative to hard state is *soft* state, where the state associated with a connection has a predefined time interval during which it is valid. At the end of this time, the state is automatically removed. To maintain its state, a connection must periodically refresh its state. Soft state allows us to retain the benefits of state in the network (such as small packet headers) without having to deal with the problems of persistent state. Soft state trades bandwidth and computation for robustness and simpler system design.

EXAMPLE 6.34

University computer system administrators have to create new accounts on their system each semester. The account and associated password constitute system state. With hard state, students must explicitly request account creation and deletion (when they join and leave school). If a student does not explicitly request account deletion, his or her account persists for months or, sometimes, years! With soft state, when an account is created, it is automatically set to expire at the end of the year. Unless a student requests that an account be retained, it vanishes at that time. Thus, the administrator does not need to remind students to cancel their accounts before they leave. Of course, long-term students have to deal with the hassle of renewing their accounts once a year, but that is the trade-off we make with soft state.

When using soft state, care should be taken to choose fairly long deletion times. Otherwise, bandwidth is wasted on repeated refreshes. A more insidious problem is that if the deletion time is small and chosen independent of the refresh interval, users may see inconsistent state. Continuing with Example 6.34, this is like a system administrator who decides to start timing out accounts every month, instead of every year. This introduces unnecessary overhead, and, in the case of a student who does not hear about the change in the deletion time, an unpleasant surprise.

6.3.11 Exchanging state explicitly

In every system design, the designer has to make a careful choice about which parts of the system state should be explicitly exchanged, and which implicitly determined.

EXAMPLE 6.35

Consider a sender who sends a sequence of packets to the receiver, where some packets could be lost. How should the receiver detect packet loss? One technique is to have the receiving transport layer peek into the contents of the packet. With sufficient knowledge of application semantics, it can *implicitly* detect packet loss. An easier solution is to have the sending transport layer explicitly number packets with a sequence number. This allows the receiving transport layer to immediately detect a packet loss (or reordering) when a packet arrives out of sequence. Thus, in this case, explicit state determination is preferable to implicit state determination.

Explicit state determination is usually better than implicit determination because the entity receiving the information does not need to guess about the state of the sender. A good rule of thumb is to prefer explicit state determination, resorting to implicit state determination only when exchanging state information is too bandwidth-intensive.

6.3.12   Hysteresis

Consider a system that changes state depending on the range in which the value of some variable falls. Unfortunately, this can lead to problems if the variable happens to be near the endpoint of a range. Then, even small changes in the variable lead to frequent changes in system state. For example, assume that the system is in state A or state B, depending on whether a variable is positive or negative. If the value of the variable is slightly positive, say 0.005, then even small oscillations in the value of the variable can lead to rapid changes in system state. We can avoid this problem by choosing different thresholds depending on the current state (that is, a *state-dependent* threshold). For example, the threshold could be 0.1 if state is currently B, and −0.1 if it is A. Then, the variable must change by at least 0.2 for the system to change from state A to B and back again.

EXAMPLE 6.36

In some techniques for cellular telephony, a mobile station measures the signal intensity from two base stations and picks the one that has the higher signal strength as its current base station. If the mobile is near a cell boundary, it may receive roughly equal signals from two base stations, so that one or the other base station has a stronger signal for short times. Because handing off from one base station to another is expensive, we use hysteresis to *damp* the system. A mobile requests a handoff only if the increase in signal strength would be above some threshold. This reduces the chance that a mobile would rapidly change its preferred base station when it is near a cell boundary.

6.3.13   Separating data and control

We can often divide actions involved in data transfer among those that happen once per connection and those that happen per-packet. Per-packet actions are part of the *data path*, that is, the path taken by the data as it makes its way from a source, through intermediate switches or routers, to the destination. If we want to achieve a high throughput, we must restrict the work done in the data path. Actions not in the data path are part of the *control* path. It is usually a good idea to minimize work in the data path, moving as much work as possible to the control path. We call this "separating data and control."

EXAMPLE 6.37

A good example of separating data and control is in virtual circuit networks. Here, each packet carries only a virtual circuit identifier (VCI). During call establishment, we set up a routing entry and reserve resources for that VCI. This means that no control information need be carried with a data packet other than the VCI itself. Moreover, any changes in the connection state (such as resource renegotiation or call termination) are carried in a separate signaling channel. Thus, we can build fast switching hardware that does not need to be aware of anything other than the data path. In contrast, in a datagram network, control information, such as the desired type of service, may be present in any packet. Thus, the switching engine needs enough intelligence to also process control information, limiting its speed. However, most datagrams do not carry control information, so modern datagram routers process the common case in a hardware fast path. An adjunct processor handles datagrams carrying control information. This separation allows datagram routers to achieve high speed.

The advantage of keeping some control information along with the data is that it makes the packet self-contained. The greater the separation of data and control, the more the state we need to install in the network to allow us to interpret the data packet correctly.

EXAMPLE 6.38

Every router in the network knows what to do with a datagram: look at the destination address field and forward it to the next hop toward that destination. Thus, if a link goes down, a router can simply pass a packet headed for that link onto any link (other than the one it came on) and expect it to reach its destination. In contrast, a VCI has only local significance. If a link goes down in a virtual-circuit network, we need to reestablish connections before packet forwarding can resume.

EXAMPLE 6.39

Each IP packet carries a "type-of-service" field that describes the service quality it would like to receive. This field is universally ignored in the current Internet. However, if this were not so, the field allows a source to ask for per-packet service quality. One could think of different packets in the same stream having different service quality: some may be more important than others, for instance. In contrast, with a virtual circuit network, all packets in a stream must have the same service quality; we can determine this quality only by referring to state in the network.

6.3.14 Extensibility

As user needs and technology change, systems must evolve to meet new needs and constraints. It is always a good idea to allow the design to be extensible. We can do so by putting in "hooks" that allow for future growth.

EXAMPLE 6.40

The IP header has a version field that indicates the format of the rest of the header. In principle, to extend IP, we simply need to add a new version number, then make everyone in the Internet aware of how to handle the new header type. The version number field makes IP extensible, so that we can dynamically introduce new versions, and both the old and new versions of the protocol can coexist.

EXAMPLE 6.41

When two modems first contact each other, they exchange messages at 1200 bps. If this message exchange succeeds, they try exchanging messages at 2400 bps; otherwise, they return to 1200 bps. This process continues until both modems agree on the highest speed they can both sustain. This simple protocol allows modems at higher and higher speeds to be gracefully introduced into a network. At first, a higher-speed modem is forced to talk at slower speeds. As more high-speed modems become available, the protocol allows them to take over from existing modems gradually. This is an excellent example of extensibility in protocol design.

6.3.15 Summary

Table 6.1 summarizes the techniques covered in this section.

Technique	When to use it	What it buys you
Multiplexing	When a resource is scarce or expensive	Allows resource sharing; with an explicit scheduler, each user can be guaranteed a quality of service
Pipelining and parallelism	When processing power is cheap and throughput must be maximized	Increases throughput by using processors in parallel
Batching	When the overhead for a task increases sublinearly with the number of tasks	Decreases the effective overhead per task and increases the throughput, at the expense of a larger worst-case response time
Exploiting locality	When access patterns show spatial or temporal locality	Depending on the situation, decreased response time or increased throughput
Optimizing the common case	Always	Reduces execution time
Hierarchy	When a task can be recursively decomposed into subtasks	Allows the system to scale arbitrarily
Indirection	To delay the binding between an abstraction and an instance	Allows the system to use an abstraction independent of the current instance
Virtualization	When a resource is scarce or expensive	Allows users to access a shared resource as if it were an unshared resource
Randomization	When a deterministic order of execution can make a system vulnerable to unfairness or failure	Makes a system more robust
Soft state	When the loss of hard state is possible and disastrous, or the overhead in creating and deleting hard state is high	Trades off bandwidth for the ability to automatically delete state when it is no longer needed
Exchanging state explicitly	Always, unless exchanging state requires too much bandwidth	Allows the receiver to use reliable knowledge of the sender's state to make intelligent decisions
Hysteresis	When the system is sensitive to small perturbations in the value of a variable	Dampens the system by making it less sensitive to perturbations
Separating data and control	Always	Allows the data path to be fast, while the control path is slower, but sophisticated
Extensibility	Always	Allows the system to evolve gracefully as resource constraints change

Table 6.1: Some common techniques for system design.

6.4   Performance analysis and tuning

A design is successful only if it meets its performance targets. Performance analysis is the art and science of examining a system's resource usage and trading off unconstrained resources for constrained ones to improve system performance. Although performance analysis is an important discipline in its own right and uses many techniques beyond the scope of this book, this section gives a bird's-eye view of how to tune the performance of an existing system. The key observation is that we can apply the optimization techniques described earlier not only to system design, but also to improve the performance of existing systems. More details can be found in references [Ferrari 78], and [Jain 91]. An interesting discussion of tuning a single system using some of these principles can be found in reference [Kaplan 92].

6.4.1   Measurement

The first step in performance analysis is to measure how the existing system uses each of the five basic resources: time, space, computation, money, and labor. We must decide upon resource consumption metrics for that particular system and instrument the system to collect these measurements. This step is critical, because imprecise metrics and measurements lead to bad optimization choices.

6.4.2   Workload characterization

The next step is to collect measurements for "typical" system usage (its *workload*). Characterizing a system's workload is not an easy task. We have to guess whether a measured usage is typical or just a random fluctuation. Although a long sample may represent true "average" behavior, the real problem is that the workload changes with time. Predicting which components of the workload will change, and by how much, is hard.

6.4.3   System model

The third step is to use the measurements to build a system model that eliminates all but the essential details. Building accurate models is a challenge, because experience is often the only guide for picking out the essential aspects of a system. System models are usually expressed in terms of entities, their performance, and their relationships. For example, a CPU, a memory, an I/O bus, and peripherals can represent a computer system. We can construct models at several levels of detail, where a higher-level model omits more details, but has a broader scope.

6.4.4   Analysis

The fourth step is to either simulate the model on a simulator or analyze it using mathematical techniques such as queuing theory. Mathematical modeling is usually intractable without many simplifying assumptions, so we must ensure that the assumptions do not deviate too far from reality. Analysis and simulations aid in determining the bottleneck resource in the system. We can then use some techniques in Section 6.3 to trade off cheaper resources for the bottlenecked resource. As we ease each bottleneck, another part of the system will become the bottleneck. We must remove each bottleneck in succession till we meet the performance goals. The result of performance tuning is a set of recommendations for modifying the system.

6.4.5 Implementation

The final step is to carry out these modifications and measure the modified system to quantify the performance gain. The modified system may meet its performance target, or it may still fail. Failure is usually due to an inadequate system model. We have to judge what the model lacks and go back to the simulation or analysis to retune the system. We must repeat the retuning step until we meet the system performance target.

Performance analysis is a necessary component of system design. By following the steps outlined earlier, a designer can ensure that the system does what it was supposed to—provide the users of the system with an acceptable performance at an acceptable cost.

6.5 Summary

Five basic resources constrain system design: time, space, computation, labor, and money. A designer must identify resource constraints and performance metrics and trade off nonbinding constraints for binding constraints. Table 6.1 summarizes some techniques to help make this trade-off and to improve overall system performance. These techniques can also be used for performance-tuning an existing system.

Chapter 7

Multiple Access

7.1 Introduction

Imagine an audioconference where voices get garbled if two or more participants speak simultaneously. How should the participants coordinate their actions so that people are not always talking over each other? A simple *centralized* solution is for a moderator to poll each participant in turn, asking whether he or she wants to speak. Unfortunately, with this solution, a participant who wants to speak must wait for the moderator's poll, even if nobody else has anything to say. Moreover, if the moderator's connection fails, no one can speak until the problem is detected and corrected. A better *distributed* solution is for a participant to start speaking as soon as someone else stops, hoping that no one else is about to do the same. This avoids the time wasted in polling and is robust against failed connections, but two speakers waiting for a third speaker to stop speaking are guaranteed to *collide* with each other. If collisions are not carefully resolved, the meeting will make no progress, because the two speakers could repeatedly collide. Thus, both solutions have their faults. Designing coordination schemes that simultaneously minimize collisions and a speaker's expected waiting time is surprisingly hard. In the literature, this is called the *multiple-access* problem.

The multiple-access problem arises when a transmission medium is *broadcast*, so that messages from one endpoint (usually called a *station* in the literature) can be heard by every other station in its listening area. Thus, if two stations in each other's listening area send a message simultaneously, both messages are garbled and lost. Our goal is to devise a scheme (or *protocol*) that maximizes the number of messages that can be carried per second, simultaneously minimizing a station's waiting time. This abstract problem mani-

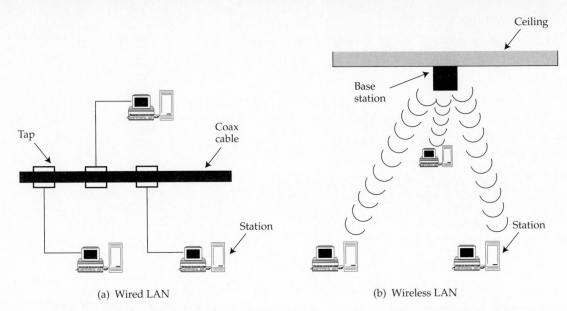

Figure 7.1: Contexts for multiple access. The multiple access problem arises in five main contexts: (a) wired local area network, (b) wireless local area network, (c) packet radio, (d) cellular telephony, and (e) satellite communication. In each network, the medium is broadcast, so stations in the same listening area must coordinate with each other to share access to the medium.

fests itself in many systems that outwardly appear different. Thus, before we study the abstract multiple-access problem, it is worth looking at some physical contexts in which it arises (Figure 7.1).

7.1.1   Contexts for the multiple-access problem

The multiple-access problem appears in five main contexts:

- *Wired local area networks:* The most common context for multiple access is in a local area network, where multiple stations share the "ether" in a coaxial cable or a copper wire. Two common solutions to the problem are *Ethernet* [MB 76] and *Fiber Distributed Data Interface* (FDDI) [Jain 94].

- *Wireless local area networks:* These are increasingly popular replacements for wired LANs, where we replace the coaxial cable with an infrared or radio-frequency link. As with a coaxial cable, a radio link is inherently broadcast, thus requiring a multiple-access protocol. A good example of a wireless LAN is the one described in the IEEE 802.11 standard.

- *Packet radio:* Packet-radio networks replace one or more links in a traditional wired network with radio links. They are the wide-area analogs of a wireless

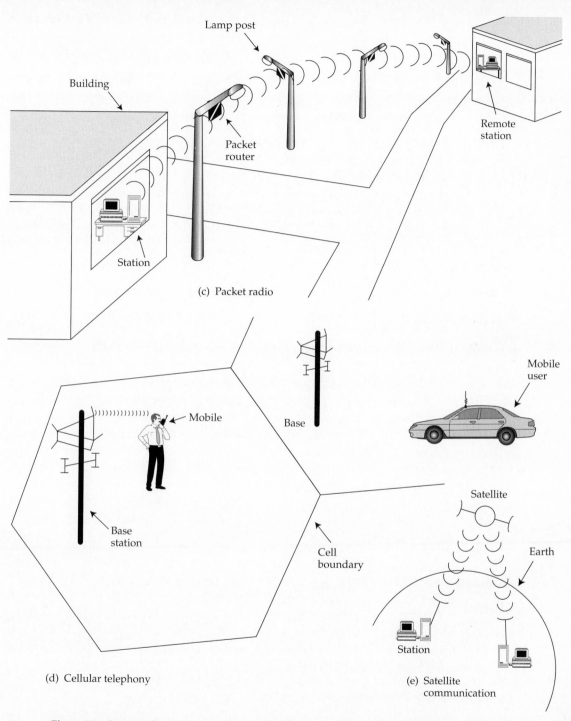

(c) Packet radio

(d) Cellular telephony

(e) Satellite communication

Figure 7.1: Continued.

LAN. Metricom's Ricochet service is an example of an operational packet-radio network [Metricom 96].

- *Cellular telephony:* Cellular telephones share the radio spectrum when transmitting to a base station and, therefore, must coordinate access with other cellular telephones in the same service area. Analog and digital cellular telephony service is provided by most major telephone companies around the world.

- *Satellite communication:* Low-earth and geostationary satellites typically rebroadcast messages that they receive from any of the earth stations. Data rates of up to 500 Mbps are possible, though the station-to-station propagation delay for geosynchronous satellites is at least 240 ms. Satellite data service and telephony is provided by networks such as INMARSAT. A good overview of satellite communication technology can be found in Chapter 10 of reference [Stallings 88].

In this chapter, we will study both the abstract multiple-access problem and its instantiation in the five networks just described.

7.1.2   Rest of the chapter

We usually solve the multiple-access problem in two steps. The first step is to choose a "base technology" to isolate traffic from different stations. This isolation can be in the time domain (stations go one after another), or in the frequency domain (different stations use different frequencies), or in both. Unfortunately, we rarely have enough time slots or enough frequencies to be able to exclusively dedicate one or the other to each station. Thus, in the second step, the multiple access-scheme determines the allocation of transmission resources (in the time or frequency domain) to individual stations. We will study base technologies for multiple access in Section 7.3 and multiple access schemes in Sections 7.4 and 7.5. Section 7.6 summarizes the chapter.

Before we study base technologies, we make a small diversion, in Section 7.2, to discuss the fundamental choices in designing multiple-access schemes, and some constraints that might affect the design.

7.2   Choices and constraints

7.2.1   Choices

The designer of a multiple-access scheme has two fundamental design choices. These are between a centralized and a distributed design, and between a circuit-mode and a packet-mode design. We discuss these choices next.

Centralized versus distributed communication

In many situations, one station is a "master" station, and all others are "slaves" in the sense that the master decides when a slave is allowed to send data. This is also called a *centralized* design. The master-to-slave *downlink* may have different physical properties than the slave-to-master *uplink*. An example is in cellular telephony, where the base station acts as a master to coordinate the actions of the cellular mobile telephones.

With a *distributed* design, no station is a master, and every station is free to talk to every other station. An example is in wired LANs such as Ethernet, where all stations are peers. Multiple-access algorithms are usually optimized to exploit one or the other situation.

Circuit-mode versus packet-mode transfer

The second choice in the design depends on the workload being carried. Note that the multiple-access problem occurs both in the telephone network and in local area networks that carry data traffic. Thus, solutions to the problem must deal not only with smooth, continuous traffic streams, characteristic of voice, but also with *bursty* data traffic streams, where the transmission rate in some time intervals is much higher than in others. If stations generate a steady stream of packets, then it makes sense to allocate part of the link to the source for its exclusive use, thus avoiding the need to negotiate link access for every packet in the stream. If, on the other hand, sources generate bursty traffic, negotiating link access on a packet-by-packet basis is more efficient. We call the first mode of link operation *circuit-mode* and the second *packet-mode*. Circuit and packet-mode access are linked in an interesting way: packets containing circuit reservation requests contend for link access using packet mode. Once this packet-mode access succeeds, subsequent data transmission on the circuit uses circuit mode.

In a meeting, circuit mode corresponds to the situation where each participant makes a long speech. Thus, it makes sense to spend some time determining the order and duration of each speech. Packet mode is more like a free-for-all brainstorming session, where participants have only a one- or two-sentence thought to share. It therefore does not make sense to choose any particular order in which participants speak.

We can use these two choices to categorize multiple-access schemes as shown in Table 7.1. We will study centralized schemes in Section 7.4 and distributed-access schemes in Section 7.5.

7.2.2   Constraints

The design of a multiple-access scheme is often highly constrained by its implementation environment. In this subsection, we discuss three common constraints: spectrum scar-

Access schemes	Centralized (Section 7.4)	Circuit mode
		Packet mode
	Distributed (Section 7.5)	—
		Packet mode

Table 7.1: Classification of multiple-access schemes.

city, radio link impairments, and the parameter "*a*." The first two are important for radio links, which are used in wireless LANs, packet radio, and cellular telephony. The third plays an important role in packet-mode networks.

Spectrum scarcity

The electromagnetic spectrum, which is used for all radio-frequency wireless communication, is a scarce resource. National and international laws allow only a few frequencies to be used for radio links that span 1 to 10 miles.[1] For example, in the United States, the FCC allows unlicensed data communication in this range only in the 902–928 MHz and 2.40–2.48 GHz bands (also called the Industrial, Scientific, and Medical or *ISM* bands).[2] Thus, multiple-access schemes using radio-frequency links are tightly constrained by the available spectrum.

Radio link properties

A radio link is subject to many impairments. *Fading* is a spatial phenomenon that refers to the degradation of a received signal because of the environment, such as a hill, dense foliage, or a passing truck. *Multipath interference* occurs when a receiver's antenna receives the same signal along multiple paths, which mutually interfere. These two effects cause long periods of bit errors, which must be compensated for using error-control schemes, such as those discussed in Chapter 12.

Besides these two common impairments, two other properties of a radio link affect multiple-access protocols. The first problem, called the *hidden-terminal* problem, occurs when a station can be heard only by a subset of receivers in the listening area. For example, in a master–slave configuration, the master may hear all the slaves, but transmissions from some slaves may not be heard by other slaves. Thus, a slave sensing the transmission medium may think that the medium is idle, while, in fact, the medium is occupied by another slave. Multiple-access schemes must deal with the hidden-terminal problem.

The second problem with radio links, called the *capture* or the *near–far* problem, occurs when a station receives messages simultaneously from two other stations, but the signal from one of them drowns out the other, so that no collision occurs. The station with the higher received power is said to have captured the receiver. Capture is good in that it reduces the time wasted on resolving collisions. On the other hand, a transmitter whose signals happen to be received weakly at other stations may be completely shut out of the medium. To prevent starvation, a multiple-access scheme should give such transmitters a chance to transmit by somehow shutting off competing sources.

---

[1] Low-power transmitters, such as those used by remote-control toys, can operate in a wider range of frequencies. However, because of their limited range (around 20–200 feet, depending on the environment), they are not commonly used for data communications.

[2] In the United States, the FCC has recently made 350 MHz of spectrum available at 5.15–5.35 GHz and 5.725–5.875 GHz for use by a new category of unlicensed equipment called National Information Infrastructure/SUPERNet devices.

The parameter "*a*"

The performance of a packet-mode multiple-access scheme is heavily influenced by a parameter known in the literature as "*a*" and defined as follows. Let:

D = maximum propagation delay between any two stations (in seconds)

T = time taken to transmit an average size packet (in seconds)

Then,

$$a = \frac{D}{T} \tag{7.1}$$

Intuitively, *a* is the number of packets (or fraction of a single packet) that a transmitting station can place on the medium before the station farthest away receives the first bit. When *a* is small ($\ll 1$), propagation delay is a small fraction of the packet transmission time. Thus, every station in the network receives at least part of a packet *before* the transmitting station finishes its transmission. *a* is usually small (around 0.01) for wired and wireless LANs, cellular telephony, and packet radio. However, as the speed of a link increases, T decreases, increasing *a*. Thus, with faster LANs, *a* can be on the order of 1 (in other words, a sender may send a whole packet before some receiver sees the first bit of the packet). When *a* is large, a source may have sent several packets before a receiver sees the first bit. This is true mostly for satellite links, where *a* can be as large as 100.

The value of *a* determines what happens when two stations send a message simultaneously. When *a* is small, their messages *collide* soon and get garbled. Thus, if both sources listen to the medium, they soon realize that the other is active. If they pause, somehow resolve who goes first, then try again, they will not waste much time. When *a* is large, a collision affecting a packet from a station happens substantially *after* its transmission (Figure 7.2). Thus, a station does not know for a fairly long time if its transmission was successful. In this case, just sensing the medium is not sufficient to recover from collisions. It makes sense to impose some more structure on the problem, so that the stations *avoid* collisions. We will see the influence of *a* on the design of multiple-access solutions throughout this chapter.

7.2.3   Performance metrics

We measure the performance of a multiple-access scheme in several ways.

- *Normalized throughput or goodput:* This is the fraction of a link's capacity devoted to carrying non-retransmitted packets. *Goodput* excludes time lost to protocol overhead, collisions, and retransmissions. For example, consider a link with a capacity of 1 Mbps. If the mean packet length is 125 bytes, the link can ideally carry 1000 packets/s. However, because of collisions and protocol overheads, a

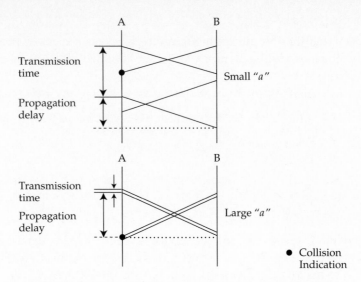

Transmission time

Propagation delay

Small "a"

Transmission time

Propagation delay

Large "a"

● Collision Indication

Figure 7.2: The parameter "a." In the figure, time increases going down the vertical axis, and each vertical line corresponds to a station. Pairs of parallel slanted lines represent packets, where the distance between a pair is the transmission time, and the vertical drop represents the propagation delay.

The upper portion of the figure shows a network where "a" is small, so that the transmission time is larger than the propagation delay. We see that a collision between packets from A and B happens after each has transmitted only a part of a packet.

The lower portion of the figure shows the situation when "a" is large. The stations detect that their transmissions interfered only several transmission times after sending the packets.

particular multiple-access scheme may allow a peak throughput of only 250 packets/s. The goodput of this scheme, therefore, is 0.25. An ideal multiple-access protocol allows a goodput of 1.0, which means that no time is lost to collisions, idle time, and retransmissions. Real-life protocols have goodputs between 0.1 and 0.95.

- *Mean delay:* This is the mean time that a packet at a station waits before it is successfully transmitted (including the transmission time). The delay depends not only on the multiple access scheme, but also on the load generated by the stations and characteristics of the medium.

- *Stability:* When a shared link is underloaded, it can carry all the traffic offered to it. As the offered load increases, the chances of a collision increase, and each collision results in wasted time on at least two retransmissions. These retransmissions may, in turn, collide with newly generated packets, causing further retransmissions. When the load increases beyond a threshold, a poorly designed multiple-access scheme becomes unstable, so that practically every access causes a collision, and stations make slow progress. Thus, we define *stability* to mean that the throughput does not decrease as we increase the offered load. We can show that if an infinite number of *uncontrolled* stations share a link, no multiple-access scheme is stable [Kleinrock 75]. However, if control schemes are carefully chosen that reduce the load when an overload is detected, a finite population can stably share a link even under heavy load.

- *Fairness:* It is intuitively appealing to require a multiple-access scheme to be "fair." There are many definitions for fairness. A minimal definition, also called *no-starvation*, is that every station should have an opportunity to transmit within a finite time of wanting to do so. A stricter metric is that each contending station should receive an equal share of the transmission bandwidth.

These performance metrics must be balanced by the cost of implementing the scheme. This depends on the hardware and software costs, which depend on the scheme's complexity.

The limitation of analytical modeling

The goodput and mean delay of various multiple access schemes have been thoroughly studied in the queuing theory literature [Kleinrock 75]. Unfortunately, to make any sort of analysis feasible, it is necessary to assume that all sources generate "well-behaved" traffic of a mathematically tractable sort. These assumptions rarely hold in real life [PF 94]. Thus, it is best to take these measures of a scheme's performance as only *indicative* of performance, rather than an absolute metric. It is likely that, in practice, factors such as battery strength at a mobile transmitter, the presence or absence of foliage, weather conditions, and the workload have a greater impact than what is predicted by mathematical analysis. We will therefore concentrate on a qualitative description of multiple-access schemes, rather than a queuing-theoretic analysis of their performance.

7.3 Base technologies

A "base technology" serves to isolate data from different stations on a shared medium. The three common base technologies are *frequency division multiple access* (FDMA), *time division multiple access* (*TDMA*), and *code division multiple access* (*CDMA*). We study these in subsections 7.3.1, 7.3.2, and 7.3.3, respectively.

7.3.1   FDMA

The simplest base technology, and the one best suited for analog links, is *frequency division multiple access*, or *FDMA*. In FDMA, each station is allocated its own frequency band, and these bands are separated by *guard* bands. Continuing with the meeting metaphor, assume that each participant speaks in a different frequency or pitch, such as basso, contralto, or alto. Thus, tuning to a frequency band corresponds to tuning to a sentence spoken at a particular pitch. With FDMA, a participant is assigned a speaking pitch. Receivers who want to listen to a particular participant "tune in" to sentences spoken at the corresponding pitch.

FDMA is common in the radio and television broadcast industry, where each radio or TV station has its own channel. FDMA is adequate for these purposes because a listening area, such as a large city, has at most a few hundred transmitters. With cellular telephony, however, a single listening area may contain hundreds of thousands of simultaneously active transmitters. If we were to assign each transmitter a separate frequency, we would need hundreds of thousands of frequency bands, which is infeasible because the electromagnetic spectrum is a scarce resource. Thus, a naive implementation of FDMA cannot support a large user population. To work around the problem, we must reduce transmitter power and spatially reuse frequencies in different geographical zones called *cells* (see Example 7.1 and Exercise 7.3). A direct consequence is that mobile stations that cross cell boundaries must change their transmission frequency, thus requiring a *handoff*. Handoffs are complicated because they require synchronization between a mobile station and two geographically separated base stations. Thus, cellular telephony trades off an increase in system complexity for the ability to support many more users.

EXAMPLE 7.1

A voice channel takes 30 KHz, including a *guard* band that provides protection against small drifts in transmission frequency. How many one-way channels can we fit in a 25-MHz band? If we divide the listening area into square cells, so that no two adjacent cells that share a side use the same frequency bands, how many calls can the 25-MHz spectrum support in a city with 250 cells?

Solution: A 25-MHz band can support 833 channels. To ensure that no two adjacent cells use the same frequencies, we must partition this into five sets of channels, so that each cell can support only 166 calls. In a city with 250 cells, this allows 41,500 simultaneous calls. This is a factor of nearly 50 better than with a single city-wide cell!

7.3.2 TDMA

In *time division multiple access* or *TDMA*, all stations transmit data on the same frequency, but their transmissions are separated in time. Continuing with our meeting metaphor, a TDMA meeting is where all participants speak at the same pitch, but take turns to speak. In TDMA, we divide time into fixed-length or variable-length *slots*, and each station limits its transmission to a single slot. If all stations are time-synchronized, and stations somehow resolve contention for access to a time slot, the single frequency can be shared among many users. TDMA is universally used in computer communication networks, where a slot duration corresponds to the transmission time required for a single packet. Time synchronization is usually achieved by having one of the stations emit a periodic synchronization signal.

Advantages

Compared with an FDMA system, where we partition a single, large frequency band among many stations, a TDMA station uses the *entire* frequency band, but only for a fraction of the time. Thus, given the same frequency band, a TDMA system and an FDMA system can be shared by roughly the same number of stations. It can be shown, however, that the mean delay to transmit an N-bit packet over a TDMA system is lower than in an FDMA system [Sklar 88]. Besides this, TDMA has several advantages over FDMA. First, unlike FDMA, users can be dynamically allocated different bandwidth shares by giving them fewer or more time slots. Second, a mobile station can use the time slots in which it is not transmitting to measure the received power from multiple base stations, allowing it to request a handoff to the base station with the most received power. Finally, TDMA mobile stations typically require less power than with FDMA, because they can switch their transmitters off except during their time slot [PGH 95]. For these reasons, TDMA is a better solution for multiple access than FDMA.

Problems

TDMA, however, is not without its problems. Every station must synchronize to the same time base. Thus, we must devote a significant portion of the bandwidth to transmitting synchronization signals, and even so, we must surround each time slot by guard times to deal with out-of-synch stations. It has been estimated that 20–30% of the bandwidth in a TDMA system is wasted on synchronization and guard bit overhead [FAG 95]. TDMA does not do away with the need for handoffs, since battery-powered mobiles have limited transmission power. Thus, as a mobile moves away from a base station, its transmitted signal weakens, and the mobile must be handed off to a nearer base station. Finally, since a station transmits data in a wider frequency band, the duration of the transmission is smaller than in FDMA. This leads to greater problems with multipath interference, which must be countered with an adaptive equalization circuit in each receiver.

A more detailed comparison of TDMA and FDMA, with a greater emphasis on the radio engineering aspects of the tradeoffs, can be found in reference [PL 95].

7.3.3 | CDMA

Frequency-hopping CDMA

The easiest way to understand *code division multiple access* or *CDMA* is to first consider a variant of CDMA called *frequency-hopping CDMA* or *FH/CDMA*. An FH/CDMA station transmits at a particular frequency for a short duration, then hops to another frequency, where it transmits for a fixed duration, and then it hops again. If the receiver and the transmitter synchronize hop schedules, the receiver can decipher the transmitter's signal. Continuing with the meeting metaphor, with FH/CDMA, each speaker speaks each sentence in a different pitch. The first sentence may be in a low pitch, the second in a high pitch, and the third in a medium pitch. If a receiver knows the sequence of pitches that the speaker plans to use, he or she can decode the transmission.

With FH/CDMA, two stations can share the same large frequency band if they agree to use a different bandlimited portion of the spectrum each time they hop. A receiver can choose to receive data from one or the other station by choosing the appropriate hopping sequence. Thus, unlike FDMA or TDMA systems, where stations are separated either in time or in frequency, in CDMA, stations can be distinguished only by simultaneously considering *both* time and frequency.

Direct-sequence CDMA

A second technique for CDMA is more complicated, but uses the same general principle of taking the user signal and spreading it over a wider frequency spectrum. In this technique, called *direct sequence CDMA* or *DS/CDMA*, each bit of the transmitter is replaced by a *sequence* of bits that occupy the same time duration. For example, if the transmitter wants to send the bit "1," it may normally send a signal corresponding to "1" for 1 second, thus requiring a bandwidth of 1 Hz. With DS/CDMA, the transmitter might send the *codeword* "10110110" during the same second instead, thus requiring a bandwidth of at least 8 Hz. We call each bit in the codeword a *chip*, and measure the bit-rate of the codeword in *chips/second*. We can view this replacement of the single bit by a codeword as "smearing" or spreading the single bit over a wider frequency spectrum. The receiver receives the eight bits at the higher frequency, and retrieves the original information using a *decorrelator* that "unsmears" according to the given codeword. Thus, if a narrowband noise signal corrupts some part of the 8 Hz spectrum, enough information is carried in the rest of the spectrum that the original signal ("1") can still be correctly retrieved.

If a second user wanted to use the same 8 Hz spectrum, it could do so by spreading its bits with a different codeword. For example, it might represent a "1" by the code "00101101." We can show that even if both stations sent their codewords simultaneously, a decorrelator tuned to one of the codewords (and time-synchronized with the transmitter) can extract the signal corresponding to that codeword even in the presence of the other codeword. If the transmitters' phases are uncorrelated, a receiver can extract a particular transmitter's signal even if all the transmitters use the same codeword [Abramson 94]. Of course, the codewords must be chosen in a special way to prevent too much confusion at a receiver. These sets of compatible codewords are said to be *orthogonal*, and a great deal of research has gone into creating optimal orthogonal codewords [Viterbi 95].

As we mentioned before, both FH/CDMA and DS/CDMA systems spread a transmitter's signal over a larger frequency spectrum. In some sense they use a wider spectrum than is strictly necessary for carrying the transmitter's signal. Thus, we also call them *spread-spectrum* communication techniques [Abramson 94].

Advantages

Why would a transmitter want to hop from frequency to frequency or use an entire codeword when a single bit will do? An obvious answer, for those in the spy business, is that it is very hard to eavesdrop on a frequency-hopping transmitter. If the receiver does not know the exact sequence of hops that the transmitter intends to make, or the codeword it uses to spread its bits, it cannot decipher the transmitter's message. Indeed, the first use for CDMA was in the military, presumably for use in the battlefield. However, spread-spectrum communication has other interesting properties that make it attractive for civilians.

First, if the spectrum is subjected to narrowband noise, such as a jamming signal from an enemy, then it does not greatly affect the transmitted signal, since only part of the transmission is in any given frequency band. A transmitter can make its signal immune to narrowband noise by using sufficiently long interleaved error-correcting codes that span over multiple narrowband frequencies (see Chapter 12 for more details on interleaving and error-correcting codes). Moreover, it can be shown that a CDMA receiver is less susceptible to errors due to multipath interference than FDMA or TDMA.

Second, unlike TDMA, where all stations must share the same time base, in CDMA, stations can use different time bases. It is sufficient for the receiver and the sender to agree on a time base: because other stations see the effect of the transmission only as noise, they do not need to synchronize with the sender.

Third, CDMA allows adjacent base stations to communicate with the same mobile station if they share a CDMA code or FH sequence. Thus, handoffs between cells can be made "soft" by asking more than one base station to transmit (or receive) using the same CDMA FH sequence or the same CDMA code. This reduces the interruption during a handoff. We cannot do this using FDMA, where adjacent cells are not allowed to use the same frequency, or TDMA, where soft handoff would require time synchronization between cells.

Fourth, unlike a TDMA or FDMA system, a CDMA system has no hard limit on capacity. Each station appears as a source of noise for every other station. Thus, the number of stations can be increased without limit, at the expense of decreasing the effective bit-rate per station.

Fifth, frequency planning in a CDMA system is much easier than in FDMA. Recall that in FDMA, adjacent cells may not use the same set of frequencies. In CDMA, the same frequency band is used in all cells; thus, no frequency planning is needed. This feature is often called *universal frequency reuse*.

Sixth, unlike FDMA and TDMA, higher-powered CDMA transmitters can be used in the unlicensed ISM bands in the United States. Thus, all products operating in the ISM bands (other than low-power devices) use CDMA.

Finally, in an FDMA or TDMA system, if a station is inactive, the signal-to-noise ratio of the other stations does not increase. In CDMA, a station's silence directly benefits other stations. Thus, a transmitter can increase overall system performance (and decreases its own power consumption) by switching itself off when it has nothing to send. CDMA allows us to take advantage of this common situation.

Problems

CDMA's benefits come at a price. The three major problems with CDMA are (a) its implementation complexity, (b) its need for *power management* (also called *power control*), and (c) its need for a large, contiguous frequency band. We discuss these in more detail next.

First, CDMA requires receivers to be perfectly synchronized with transmitters, and introduces substantial computational complexity either for tracking hops (with FH/CDMA) or for decorrelation (with DS/CDMA). This increases the cost of receivers (though this cost is dropping rapidly).

A more insidious problem is power management. If a CDMA receiver receives a low-power signal from an intended, but remote, transmitter, and a higher-power noise signal from a nearer transmitter, it has a hard time recovering the intended signal. Unless nearby transmitters reduce their transmission power, they can completely shut out distant transmitters. The solution is to require each transmitter to vary its power in inverse proportion to its distance from its intended receiver. If each cell has only a single CDMA receiver (as is the case in telephony), and if the path from the transmitter to the receiver is symmetric, then a simple power management technique is for the transmitter to ensure that the sum of its transmission and reception power is constant. This automatically ensures that when a receiver is far away (so that its transmissions are faint), the transmit power is increased (so that the receiver can hear). Conversely, when the receiver is near (so that its transmissions are loud) the transmit power is reduced. If the system has multiple rapidly moving CDMA receivers, the power management problem is much more complicated [Viterbi 95].

Finally, introducing DS/CDMA into the existing infrastructure is hard because it needs a large, contiguous frequency band. In contrast, FDMA, TDMA, and FH/CDMA can use multiple, noncontiguous frequency bands.

On balance, CDMA seems to have more advantages than disadvantages. As we will see in Section 7.4, many commercial systems are moving from FDMA to TDMA and CDMA.

CDMA Performance

Although CDMA has many advantages over TDMA and FDMA, at least in theory, field trials of the technology in cellular telephone networks have produced disappointing results. As of the time of this writing (1996), no service provider in the United States is using CDMA for cellular access, though extensive field trials are in progress in some major cities. Engineers estimate that changing from FDMA to TDMA allows a provider to increase channel capacity by a factor of 7.5 [Cox 96]. To be competitive, CDMA must give an improvement of at least 7.5, and preferably around 10, to offset the greater cost of equipment. Unfortunately, while early, controlled trials reported improvement factors of 25 to 40, trials in less controlled environments have shown improvements of only around 6 to 8 [Cox 96]. Unless the technology improves dramatically, CDMA may not be successful for cellular telephony.

7.3.4   FDD and TDD

In many situations a pair of stations must simultaneously communicate with each other. For example, a person speaking on a cellular phone may simultaneously want to hear a signal from the other end. Two standard techniques to establish two-way communication between a pair of stations are called *frequency division duplex* (FDD) and *time division duplex* (TDD). FDD is analogous to FDMA, in that the two directions use different frequencies. In TDD, we slice a single frequency band into time slots, and each end takes turns in using the time slots.

TDD, FDD, TDMA, FDMA, and CDMA can be simultaneously used to create several interesting combinations. For example, combining FDD with TDMA, one frequency band is time shared between multiple stations that want to transmit *to* a base station, and another frequency band is time shared for communication *from* a base station to several other stations. If the system is master–slave, FDD is very common, with the master-to-slave channel using TDMA (since synchronizing time bases with a single master is easy), and the slave-to-master channel shared using either TDMA or CDMA.

Second-generation cordless phones use a TDD/FDMA scheme, where different phone/base-station pairs use different frequencies, but in a given frequency band, the base station and the phone share time slots for communication. Digital cellular phones use FDD/TDMA/FDMA, where each cell has some number of frequency bands, each frequency band is time-shared using TDMA, and phone-to-base and base-to-phone communications use different frequencies. Digital cordless phones (often advertised as 900-MHz phones) use a TDMA/TDD/FDMA scheme, where each phone/base-station pair is assigned not only a particular frequency band, but also a time slot in the frequency band, and the base station and phone take turns in sharing time slots in a single frequency band.

7.4 Centralized access schemes

We now turn our attention to multiple-access schemes that build on the base technologies described in Section 7.2. We will first study schemes where one of the stations is a *master*, and the others are *slaves*. By this, we mean that the master can prevent a slave from transmitting until told to do so. This mode of operation makes multiple access straightforward, since the master provides a single point of coordination. On the other hand, a master–slave system can be less robust because the master is also a single point of failure. Moreover, since the master is involved in every transmission, it adds delay to every message exchange. The reliability issue can be solved by allowing slaves to reelect a master in case the master goes down. However, this complicates the system, something we wanted to avoid with a master–slave arrangement in the first place!

Physical constraints often lead naturally to a master–slave configuration. For example, in a wireless LAN, the base station is the only station guaranteed to be in direct communication with every other station (since it is usually mounted on a ceiling, where it has a clear infrared or radio path to every station). Similarly, in a cellular phone network, the base station is the only one with a wired connection to the network, and it can have a transmission power much greater than any mobile. In these situations, it often makes sense to have the base station also act as the master for a multiple-access scheme.

In this section, we will study three centralized schemes. In Section 7.4.1, we study circuit-mode schemes, primarily for cellular telephony. In Sections 7.4.2 and 7.4.3, we study two packet-mode schemes: polling and reservation.

Access schemes	Centralized (Section 7.4)	Circuit mode	Cellular telephony (7.4.1)
		Packet mode	Polling (7.4.2)
			Reservation (7.4.3)
	Distributed (Section 7.5)	—	
		Packet mode	

Table 7.2: Classification of multiple-access schemes—centralized schemes.

7.4.1   Circuit mode

The most common centralized multiple-access scheme for circuit-mode communication is cellular telephony. As we saw in Section 7.2, partitioning a service area into cells allows a provider to increase the number of simultaneous voice calls it can support. Each geographically separated cell has a *base station* that provides access to the wired telephone infrastructure and manages access to the broadcast medium (as was shown in Figure 7.1).

When a cellular phone is turned on, it sends a registration message to the base station on a control channel. This message contends for access with other phones accessing the control channel using the ALOHA packet-mode multiple access protocol described in Section 7.5.5. Once the base station correctly receives the registration message, it allocates the cellular phone either a frequency (FDMA), time slot (TDMA), or code (CDMA) that the phone uses for subsequent voice transfer. Since the voice call is carried in circuit mode, once the cellular phone acquires its channel, it never has to contend for access again.

We now outline three common cellular telephone standards, which combine centralized control and circuit-mode operation with one of the base technologies described in Section 7.2. These are EAMPS, the analog telephone technology common in the United States; GSM, a digital cellular technology common in Europe; and IS-95, a proposal for CDMA cellular telephony.

EAMPS

The earliest cellular telephones, and the ones most common in the United States at the time of this writing (1996), use *analog* FDD/FDMA. In the United States, this is called the Extended Advanced Mobile Phone Service or EAMPS (other parts of the world use similar systems, but with different acronyms—for example, TACS in Europe and JTACS in Japan [PGH 95]). In EAMPS, mobiles use a 25-MHz band from 824 to 849 MHz, and the base station uses a 25-MHz band from 869 to 894 MHz. The large difference in frequency bands (45 MHz) minimizes interference between the transmitter and the receivers. The base station uses the higher of the two bands, since higher-frequency bands are subject to higher propagation losses, and the base station has more transmission power than the mobiles. Both 25-MHz bands are divided into 832 channels, each 30 KHz wide. EAMPS uses a hexagonal cell structure, so each cell can support at most $832/7 = 118$ simultaneous voice calls (see Example 7.1).

GSM

The second generation of cellular phones, currently very popular in Europe, use *digital* TDMA with FDD. The standard system in Europe is the *Global System for Mobile Communication* or *GSM*. In GSM, the uplink occupies the 935–960 MHz band, and the downlink the 890–915 MHz band. Each band is divided into a number of 200-KHz-wide channels, and each channel is shared among eight users using TDMA. GSM has several advantages over EAMPS, as described in Section 7.2.2. Thus, it is being adopted around the world, as usual, under a variety of names and frequency allocations. In the United States, a variant of GSM with six-slot 20-ms frames and 30-KHz channels is called IS-54, and it occupies the same frequency bands as EAMPS. In Japan, the GSM variant is called Personal Digital Cellular. A second system currently being introduced in Europe has the same technology as GSM, but is centered around the 1800-MHz band and is, therefore, called DCS-1800 (except in the United Kingdom, where it is called Personal Communications Network).

IS-95

The latest technology for digital cellular telephony is CDMA, which has the advantages outlined in Section 7.3.3. The U.S. standard for CDMA is called *Interim Standard-95* or *IS-95*. In IS-95, each user channel at 9.6 Kbps is spread to a rate of 1.2288 Mchips/s (a spreading factor of 128). On the downlink, user data is encoded using a rate $\frac{1}{2}$ convolutional code (see Chapter 12 for a description), interleaved, and spread with one of 64 orthogonal spreading codes called the Walsh spreading codes. Adjacent base stations coordinate their use of the codes to minimize interference. On the uplink, the data stream is encoded with a rate $\frac{1}{3}$ convolutional coder and six-way interleaved. The interleaved bits are then spread using a Walsh code. The power of the uplink is tightly controlled (to within 1dB) to avoid the near–far problem. To ensure compatibility, IS-95 mobile stations can also interoperate with EAMPS base stations, and the IS-95 frequency bands are the same as the EAMPS frequency bands. IS-54, IS-95, GSM, and other digital cellular telephony services are also called *Personal Communication Services* or *PCS*.

Cellular Digital Packet Data (CDPD)

Cellular telephony providers have realized that to make inroads into the data communication market, they ought to somehow provide packet-mode access. The *Cellular Digital Packet Data (CDPD)* standard provides an overlay network over the existing circuit-mode cellular network to provide packet access [DN 96]. CDPD uses "channel-sniffing" to detect currently unused voice channels, and acquires them for packet data. Thus, the total bandwidth available through CDPD fluctuates with the voice load and is around 12 Kbps per available voice channel. CDPD packets contend for channel access using the BTMA access scheme described in Section 7.5.3.

7.4.2 Polling and probing

In Section 7.4.1, we studied centralized control for *circuit-mode* communication for cellular telephony (similar schemes are also used for cordless telephones). In this and the next section, we will study two classes of schemes with centralized control of *packet-mode* communication. Recall that in packet mode, stations generate bursts of traffic that cannot be predicted in advance. Thus, a station must contend for medium access for each packet. A central controller mediates this contention.

One of the simplest schemes for central control in packet-mode is *roll-call polling*. In this scheme, the master asks each station in turn whether it has data to send. If the station has data, it sends it to the master (or directly to another station). Otherwise, the master continues polling. The main advantage of roll-call polling is that it is simple to implement. It is inefficient if (a) the time taken to query a station is long (due to station or propagation delays), (b) the overhead of polling messages is high, or (c) the system has many terminals. Roll-call polling can lead to high mean message delays. In the worst case, each station has data to send just after it has been passed over during a poll, so that it has to wait for every other station to send data before it has a chance to send anything. A detailed analysis of polling under some simple mathematical assumptions of source behavior can be found in Chapter 7 of reference [Hayes 84] (also see Exercise 7.6).

A variant of roll-call polling that is more intelligent in its polling order is called *probing*. In this scheme, stations are given consecutive addresses. We assume that each station can program its host interface to be able to receive data addressed not only to itself, but also to multicast addresses (this will become clear in Example 7.2).

EXAMPLE 7.2

Suppose a network has eight stations numbered 0–7 (000 to 111 in binary). In the first time slot, the master sends a message to the multicast address 0*, asking for data. This query is received by all stations that have a 0 in the first bit of their address (that is, stations 000, 001, 010, and 011). If one of them has data to send, it replies and is given permission to send data in the next time slot. If more than one station in this range has data to send, then both reply, and their replies collide. On seeing the collision, the master restricts the query to 00* and polls again. This time, only stations 000 and 001 may answer. If there is another collision, stations 000 and 001 are polled in turn, followed by a poll to the multicast address 01*. Continuing in this manner, the master can skip over large chunks of the address space that have no active stations, at the expense of repeated polls in sections of the address space that have more than one active station. In the worst case, when all stations are active, this results in doubling the number of poll messages. However, if many stations share the medium, of which only a few are active, probing is quite efficient [Hayes 84].

7.4.3   Reservation-based schemes

A different approach to centralized control becomes necessary for packet-mode transmission when a is large, so that collisions are expensive, and the overhead for polling is too high. This is common in satellite-based networks, where the round-trip propagation delay between stations varies between 240 and 270 ms (depending on whether the satellite is near the zenith or the horizon, respectively), and the packet transmission time is roughly a few milliseconds, leading to an a value of around 100. Then, it is more efficient for a master (which can be located at either the satellite or a ground station) to coordinate access to the medium using a reservation-based scheme.

The essential idea in a reservation-based scheme is to set aside some time slots for carrying reservation messages. Since these messages are usually smaller than data packets, reservation time slots are smaller than data time slots and are called *reservation minislots*. When a station has data to send, it requests a data slot by sending a reservation message to the master in a reservation minislot. In some schemes, such as in *fixed priority-oriented demand assignment* or *FPODA*, each station is assigned its own minislot. In other schemes, such as in *packet-demand assignment multiple access* or *PDAMA*, slaves contend for access to a minislot using one of the distributed packet-based contention schemes described in Section 7.5.5 (such as slotted ALOHA). When the master receives the reservation request, it computes a transmission schedule and announces the schedule to the slaves.

In a reservation-based scheme, if each slave station has its own reservation minislot, collision can be completely avoided. Moreover, if reservation requests have a priority field, the master can schedule slaves with urgent data before slaves with delay-insensitive data. Packet collisions can happen only when stations contend for a minislot. Therefore, the performance degradation due to collisions is restricted to the minislots, which use only a small fraction of the total bandwidth. Thus, the bulk of the bandwidth, devoted to data packets, is efficiently used. Further details about reservation-based schemes can be found in reference [Stallings 88] and in the references therein.

7.5   Distributed schemes

In Section 7.4, we studied several multiple-access schemes where one of the stations plays the role of a master. As we saw, the presence of a master simplifies a multiple-access scheme since it provides a single point of coordination. However, we are often interested in a distributed access scheme, because these are more reliable, have lower message delays, and often allow higher network utilization. The price for these benefits is increased system complexity, for example, to synchronize stations to the same time base.

Most distributed multiple access schemes support only packet-mode access. The reason for this, perhaps, is that with circuit-mode transfer, the overhead of negotiating medium access for each packet in a stream is unacceptable. It makes more sense to use a master–slave configuration for circuit-mode access, since the one-time coordination overhead is amortized over many packets. Circuit-mode access is not ruled out with a distributed scheme, but it is rare.

Access schemes	Centralized (Section 7.4)	Circuit-mode (7.4.1)	
		Packet-mode (7.4.2 and 7.4.3)	
	Distributed (Section 7.5)	Packet-mode	Decentralized polling (7.5.1)
			CSMA (7.5.2)
			BTMA and MACA (7.5.3)
			Token passing (7.5.4)
			ALOHA (7.5.5)

Table 7.3: Classification of multiple-access schemes—distributed schemes.

7.5.1 Decentralized polling and probing

Perhaps the simplest distributed access schemes are variants of the centralized *polling* and *probing* schemes described in Section 7.3.2. Both schemes can work without a master, if all the stations agree on a single time base. In the centralized version of polling, the master polls each slave in turn. In the distributed version, a station sends data in its time slot, or else is idle (this is just TDMA). For this to work correctly, we assume that a station is statically associated with its own private time slot, and that there are at least as many time slots as possible stations.

We will study the decentralized version of probing, also called *tree-based multiple access*, continuing with the example introduced in Section 7.3.2.

EXAMPLE 7.3

Recall that in Example 7.2, we have eight stations, addressed 000–111, trying to access the shared medium. In the tree-based scheme, in the first time slot, every station with a 0 in its high-order address bit places a packet on the medium. If there is a collision, in the second time slot the stations with an address of the form 01* become idle, and the two stations with the address 00* try again. If another collision happens, station 000 goes first, followed by station 001. The two stations with address 01* now contend for access, and so on. Thus, if stations have the same time base, they can carry out what looks like centralized probing, but without a master.

This approach works well when the parameter *a* is small, so that stations can detect collisions quickly and can easily establish a common time base. When *a* is large, a station detects a collision only several time slots *after* it has transmitted a packet. This requires the station either to introduce an idle time after each transmission while it waits for a possible collision, making the scheme inefficient, or to roll back its state if a collision is detected, making the scheme complex. Thus, tree-based multiple access is best suited only for networks with small *a*.

7.5.2 CSMA and its variants

The problem with polling and tree-based algorithms is that they waste time when the number of stations is large, but the number of simultaneously *active* stations is small. Consider a system with 1024 stations, of which at most two are simultaneously active. With polling, in the worst case, a station may need to wait 1023 slots before it has a chance to send a packet. Even with a tree-based algorithm, the station may need to wait up to ten slots while the medium lies unused. A clever idea that makes better use of the medium is to introduce a *carrier-sensing* circuit in each base station. This allows the station to detect whether the medium is currently being used. This is like a participant in a meeting keeping one ear open to find out if another participant is speaking. Schemes that

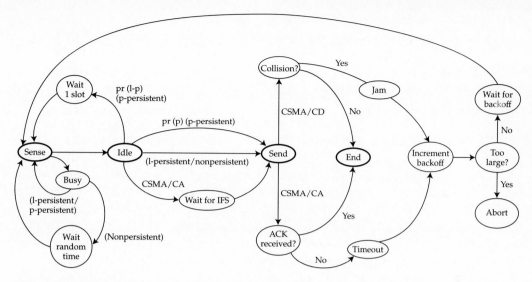

Figure 7.3: CSMA schemes. The various CSMA schemes differ in their persistence and how they detect a collision. These options are shown in a unified state diagram. Details are in the text.

use a carrier-sense circuit are classed together as *carrier-sense multiple access* or *CSMA* schemes. In this subsection we will study CSMA and two of its variants, *CSMA/CD* and *CSMA/CA*.

An important parameter in all CSMA schemes is the time taken for a message sent from one station to be heard by the station furthest away. This is just the maximum propagation delay in the system. CSMA schemes assume that this value is small compared with a packet transmission time, that is, the parameter a is small. Usually, a is assumed to be 0.1 or smaller. In slotted versions of CSMA, where packet transmissions are aligned to a slot boundary, the slot time is chosen to be the maximum propagation delay.

The simplest CSMA scheme is for a station to sense the medium, sending a packet immediately if the medium is idle. If the station waits for the medium to become idle, we call it *persistent*; otherwise we call it *nonpersistent*. With nonpersistent CSMA, when a station detects that the medium is busy, it sets a timer for a random interval, then tries again. Thus, a nonpersistent CSMA source probes the medium at random intervals, transmitting a packet immediately after detecting that the medium is free (Figure 7.3).

With persistent CSMA, what happens if two stations become active when a third station is busy? Both wait for the active station to finish, then simultaneously launch a packet, guaranteeing a collision! There are two ways to handle this problem: *p-persistent CSMA* and *exponential backoff*.

P-persistent CSMA

The first technique is for a waiting station not to launch a packet immediately when the channel becomes idle, but first toss a coin, and send a packet only if the coin comes up heads. If the coin comes up tails, the station waits for some time (one slot for slotted

CSMA), then repeats the process (Figure 7.3). The idea is that if two stations are both waiting for the medium, this reduces the chance of a collision from 100% to 25%. A simple generalization of the scheme is to use a biased coin, so that the probability of sending a packet when the medium becomes idle is not 0.5, but p, where $0 < p \le 1$. We call such a scheme p-persistent CSMA. The original scheme, where $p = 1$, is thus called 1-persistent CSMA.

The choice of p represents a trade-off between performance under heavy load and mean message delay. Note that if n stations are waiting for the end of a packet transmission, then the mean number of stations that will send a packet at the end of the transmission is just np. If $np > 1$, then a collision is likely, so we must choose $p < 1/n$. Since n increases with system load, a smaller p leads to good behavior for higher offered loads. On the other hand, as p decreases, a station is more likely to wait instead of sending a packet, though the medium is idle. Thus, the smaller the value of p, the greater the mean message delay. In a given system design, p must be chosen to balance the message delay with the required performance under heavy offered loads.

Exponential backoff

The second technique to deal with collisions between CSMA stations is to use *exponential backoff*. The key idea is that each station, after transmitting a packet, checks whether the packet transmission was successful. Successful transmission is indicated either by an explicit acknowledgment from the receiver or by the absence of a signal from a *collision detection* circuit (this circuit is similar to the carrier-sensing circuit, and detects a collision by noticing that the signal energy in the medium is greater than the energy placed on the medium by the local station). If the transmission is successful, the station is done. Otherwise, the station retransmits the packet, simultaneously realizing that at least one other station is also contending for the medium. To prevent its retransmission from colliding with the other station's retransmission, each station *backs off* (that is, idles) for a random time chosen from the interval [0, 2* max_propagation_delay] before retransmitting its packet. If the retransmission also fails, then the station backs off for a random time in the interval [0, 4* max_propagation_delay], and tries again. Each subsequent collision doubles the backoff interval length, until the retransmission finally succeeds (thus, the expected duration of a backoff interval increases exponentially fast).[3] On a successful transmission, the backoff interval is reset to the initial value. Intuitively, sources rapidly back off in the presence of repeated collisions, thus drastically reducing the load on the medium, and ideally averting future collisions. We call this type of backoff *exponential backoff*. With exponential backoff, even 1-persistent CSMA is stable, thus freeing network designers from the onerous task of choosing an optimal p.

We mentioned earlier that a station determines that its transmission is successful either using an explicit acknowledgment or using a collision detection circuit. CSMA

---

[3]Most real systems give up after backing off a certain number of times, typically 16.

with collision detection is common enough to merit its own acronym, CSMA/CD. It is the scheme used in Ethernet, to which we now turn our attention.

Ethernet

Ethernet is undoubtedly the most widely used local-area networking technology. Actually, "Ethernet" is a trademark that refers loosely to a variety of products from many manufacturers. Network cognoscenti prefer to use the term IEEE 802.3, which is the international standard describing the physical and datalink-layer protocols used in Ethernet-like LANs. In this book, for the sake of convenience, we use "Ethernet" when we mean IEEE 802.3.

Ethernet uses a variant of 1-persistent CSMA/CD with exponential backoff on a wired LAN. Moreover, if a station detects a collision, it immediately places a "jam" signal (a sequence of 512 bits) on the medium, ensuring that every active station on the network knows that a collision happened and increments its backoff counter. Since Ethernet is used for networks where a is small, collisions can be detected within a few bit-transmission times. Thus, the time wasted in each collision is small (about 50 microseconds), which increases the effective throughput of the system. To keep things simple, the Ethernet standard requires a packet to be large enough that a collision is detected before the packet transmission completes. Given the largest allowed Ethernet segment length and speed-of-light propagation times, the minimum packet length in Ethernet turns out to be 64 bytes. If the largest distance between any pair of stations is longer, the minimum packet size is correspondingly higher.

The first version of Ethernet ran at 3 Mbps and used "thick" coaxial cable for the physical medium. Subsequent versions have increased the speed to 10 Mbps and, more recently, to 100 Mbps. The physical medium has also diversified to include "thin" coaxial cable, twisted-pair copper, and optical fiber. In an attempt to keep things straight, the IEEE classifies Ethernet using a code of the form *<Speed> <Baseband or Broadband> <Physical medium>*. The first part, speed, is 3, 10, or 100 Mbps. The second part describes the infrastructure over which the network is run. Ethernet can be used not only within a building between computers, but also within a frequency band allocated to it in the cable-television infrastructure. The former is called *baseband*, and the latter *broadband*. The third part, the physical medium, is either a number, which refers to the longest allowed segment, in hundreds of meters, that the medium supports, or a letter, which represents a particular medium type. For example, 10Base2 is a 10 Mbps Ethernet that uses the baseband, and therefore is confined to a single building or campus. The "2" means that this physical medium can run at most 185 meters before a repeater must be installed. "2" usually refers to cheap, "thin" 50-ohm cable that is a poor substitute for the "thick" coaxial cable used in 10Base5 Ethernet. 10BaseT is 10 Mbps Ethernet over unshielded twisted-pair copper. Finally, 10Broad36 is Ethernet over the cable TV plant, with at most 3600 meters between repeaters. This is the technology used for some so-called "cable modems" (and has turned out to be a commercial failure). A wealth of practical details on Ethernet can be found in reference [Ethernet-FAQ 96].

The problem with Ethernet

Ethernet has several features that endear it to network administrators. It is easy to set up, requires no configuration, and is robust to noise. However, Ethernet suffers from four significant problems. First, as the load on an Ethernet increases, collisions become common. Thus, stations may back off several times, increasing their mean delay and an application's response time. In the extreme, as the system load tends to infinity, the throughput available to an individual source drops nearly to zero. In practice, Ethernet loads rarely exceed 30%, so this is not a severe problem.

Second, Ethernet gives users a *nondeterministic* service: it is possible for a packet to suffer indefinite delay because of repeated collisions. Thus, Ethernet is not suitable for situations where a station needs a deterministic bound on worst-case delay, or even a guarantee of reliable delivery. This rules out a whole class of "real-time" applications (discussed in more detail in Chapter 14).

A third problem with CSMA in general, and Ethernet in particular, is that it does not support priorities. Every station has an equal chance to transmit data. This is not necessarily a good idea in LANs that support client–server applications, where we would like to give a server greater access to the LAN than a client.

Finally, Ethernet requires a minimum packet length of 64 bytes. This imposes a heavy overhead on applications that would like to exchange small (1–5 byte) packets.

Ethernet is wildly successful despite these problems, because the problems become serious only with high offered loads. At low loads, only one or two stations are ever active, so that collisions are rare, and almost every packet is delivered immediately after it is presented to the medium. Thus, if a network administrator keeps an Ethernet network lightly loaded, users are happy.

Fortunately, Ethernet allows network administrators to distribute the load on a heavily loaded cable by breaking it into *segments*, separated by a relatively cheap datalink-layer bridge. A bridge passes on only those packets destined to segments other than the ones from which they originated. If administrators place stations that frequently communicate with each other on the same segment, with bridges to eliminate cross-segment traffic, they can reduce the load on each segment. Thus, network administrators can work around Ethernet's deficiencies and give users good service with a combination of overprovisioning and careful bridge placement.

Three recent developments give LAN administrators even more options in managing their infrastructure. The first of these, *switched* Ethernet, continues to use 10-Mbps links, but each station is connected to a hub (also called an *Ethernet switch*) by a separate wire, as in 10BaseT [Switched Ethernet FAQ 96] . However, unlike 10BaseT, each line card in the hub has a buffer to hold an incoming frame. A fast backplane allows packets to be transferred from one line card to another. Since packets arriving to the hub simultaneously do not collide, switched Ethernet has a higher intrinsic capacity than 10BaseT. This comes at the expense of memory in the line card.

The other two developments increase Ethernet speed from 10 to 100 Mbps. The first variant, called IEEE 802.3u or *Fast Ethernet*, is conceptually identical to 10BaseT, except that the line speed is increased to 100 Mbps [Johnson 96]. Like 10BaseT, it requires a point-to-point connection from a station to a hub. Fast Ethernet is not supported on bus-based Ethernets such as 10Base5 and 10Base2. It is rapidly gaining popularity because it can reuse telephone wiring, just like 10BaseT. The other alternative in the 100-Mbps Ethernet market is IEEE 802.12 or *100VG AnyLAN* [AnyLAN 96, AnyLAN FAQ 96]. In this system, a station makes explicit service requests to a master, which is also a repeater, and these requests can be scheduled by the master using one of the scheduling disciplines to be discussed in Chapter 9. By eliminating collisions and prioritizing packet transmission, AnyLAN can provide deterministic delay guarantees, which are important for multimedia applications. However, it has not been a commercial success.

Commercially available hubs are rapidly erasing the distinctions among 10BaseT, switched Ethernet, Fast Ethernet, and switched Fast Ethernet. These hubs support line cards in all four formats interchangeably, allowing customers to upgrade their line cards one at a time.

CSMA/CA

Unlike wired LANs, where a transmitter can simultaneously monitor the medium for a collision, in many wireless LANS the transmitter's power overwhelms a colocated receiver. Thus, when a station transmits a packet, it has no idea whether the packet collided with another packet or not until it receives an acknowledgment from the receiver. In this situation, collisions have a greater effect on performance than with CSMA/CD, where colliding packets can be quickly detected and aborted. Thus, it makes sense to try to avoid collisions, if possible. A popular scheme in this situation is *CSMA/Collision Avoidance*, or *CSMA/CA*. The IEEE has standardized CSMA/CA as the IEEE 802.11 standard. CSMA/CA is basically *p*-persistence, with the twist that when the medium becomes idle, a station must wait for a time called the *interframe spacing* or *IFS* before contending for a slot. A station gets a higher priority if it is allocated a smaller interframe spacing.

When a station wants to transmit data, it first checks if the medium is busy (Figure 7.3). If it is, it continuously senses the medium, waiting for it to become idle. When the medium becomes idle, the station first waits for an interframe spacing corresponding to its priority level, then sets a *contention timer* to a time interval randomly selected in the range [0, *CW*], where *CW* is a predefined contention window length. When this timer expires, it transmits a packet and waits for the receiver to send an ack. If no ack is received, the packet is assumed lost to collision, and the source tries again, choosing a contention timer at random from an interval twice as long as the one before (binary exponential backoff). If the station senses that another station has begun transmission while it was waiting for the expiration of the contention timer, it does not reset its timer, but merely freezes it, and restarts the countdown when the packet completes transmission. In this way, stations that happen to choose a longer timer value get higher priority in the next round of contention.

7.5.3   Dealing with hidden terminals: BTMA and MACA

CSMA/CA works well in environments where every station can hear the transmission of every other station. Unfortunately, many environments suffer from the *hidden terminal* and *exposed terminal* problems [PL 95, Karn 90]. In the hidden terminal problem, station A can hear transmissions from stations B and C, but B and C cannot hear each other (Figure 7.4). Thus, when C sends data to A, B cannot sense this, and thinks that the medium is idle. B's transmission after an IFS, therefore, causes a collision at A. Continuing with the meeting metaphor, a hidden terminal situation occurs when a participant can hear speakers on either side, but these speakers cannot hear each other speak.

The exposed terminal problem is shown in Figure 7.5. Here, we have two local areas, with station B talking to station A in its local area, and station C with a packet destined to D in its own local area. C is "exposed," perhaps because it is on a hilltop, or mounted on the ceiling of a large hall. Thus, unlike D, it can hear B when B is transmitting to A. Since C can hear B, C defers to B when B is active, though B and C can be simultaneously active. Thus, because of C's exposed location, it defers to faraway transmitters even when it need not. Karn reports, "Sometimes there can be so much traffic in the remote area that the well-sited station seldom transmits. This is a common problem with hilltop [stations]" [Karn 90]. Again, CSMA/CA does not work, because the exposed station senses

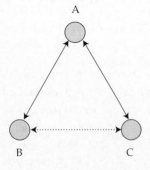

Figure 7.4: The hidden terminal problem. Station A can hear stations B and C, but they cannot hear each other. So, when C is transmitting to A, B may attempt a transmission, causing a collision at A.

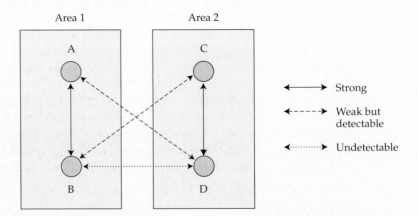

Figure 7.5: Exposed terminal problem. Assuming radio propagation along links is symmetrical, C ought to be able to transmit to D the same time B transmits to A. But C hears B, so it defers to B, even when it need not. C is, therefore, an exposed terminal.

more than it ought to. We now study two solutions to these problems, *busy tone multiple access* and *multiple access collision avoidance*.

Busy tone multiple access

In *busy tone multiple access* (*BTMA*), we assume that for any two stations A and B, if station A can hear station B, then station B can hear station A (that is, the wireless links are symmetrical) [TK 75]. We divide the available frequency band into a message channel and a smaller "busy-tone" channel. While a station is receiving a message, it places a tone on the busy-tone channel. Other stations that want to send a message to this receiver (or, any other receiver that is in range of the receiver) thus know to avoid placing a message on the channel. When sending a message, a transmitter ignores its carrier-sense circuit, and sends a message if and only if the busy-tone channel is idle. BTMA provides protection against the hidden terminal and exposed terminal problems. For example, in Figure 7.4, when A receives data from B, it places a busy tone on the busy-tone channel. Since A can hear C, C can hear A's busy tone, and it does not send data to A. In the exposed terminal situation (Figure 7.5), if C does not interfere with A, C does not hear A's busy tone, so it goes ahead with its transmission to D (even if it senses carrier from B). BTMA is used in CDPD.

Multiple access collision avoidance

The problem with BTMA is that it requires us to split the frequency band into two parts, making receivers more complex (because they need two separate tuners). The two bands need to be well separated to prevent crosstalk. Unfortunately, the propagation characteristics of a radio link depend on the frequency. Thus, a station may hear another station's busy tone even if it cannot hear that station's data, or vice versa, causing a problem for the BTMA protocol [Karn 90]. We can avoid these problems by using a single frequency band for all messages, and replacing the busy tone with an explicit message that informs all stations in the area that the receiver is busy. This is done in the *multiple access collision avoidance* or *MACA* scheme.

In MACA, before a station sends data, it sends a *request to send* (*RTS*) message to its intended receiver. If the RTS succeeds, the receiver returns a *clear to send* (*CTS*) reply. The sender then sends a packet to the receiver. If a station overhears an RTS, it waits long enough for a CTS message to be sent by a receiver before it tries to send any data. If a station hears a CTS (which carries the length of the data packet in its body), it waits long enough for the data packet to be transmitted before it tries sending a packet.

The RTS and CTS messages allow intended receivers and transmitters to overcome the hidden terminal and exposed terminal problems. Consider, first, the hidden terminal problem (Figure 7.4). Suppose B wants to transmit data to A, but C cannot hear B. When A sends a CTS to B, C hears the CTS, and realizes that A is busy. It, therefore, defers its RTS until B's transmission completes. This solves the hidden terminal problem. In the exposed terminal scenario (Figure 7.5), C hears B's RTS, but not A's CTS. Thus, it assumes that D cannot hear it either, and sends D an RTS after waiting for A's CTS to reach B. If D cannot hear A, it replies immediately with a CTS. If A were a hidden terminal, so that

D could hear it, but not C, D would reply with a CTS only when A finished. In either case, the C–D transmission is not unnecessarily affected by the B–A transmission. Thus, the RTS/CTS messages solve the hidden and exposed terminal problems.

Although MACA has several advantages over BTMA because it uses a single frequency band, it is found to suffer from many problems when implemented on a real test bed. Some of these are overcome in a variant of MACA called *MACAW* [BDSZ 94].

7.5.4   Token passing and its variants

Recall that in the distributed polling network (Section 7.5.1), all stations share the same time base, and each station uses its time slot to place a message on the medium. Ensuring that all stations acquire and maintain time synchronization is nontrivial and requires some bandwidth for training and synchronization signals. If a station could inform the "next" station in the polling sequence when it was done with its transmission, stations no longer need precise time synchronization. This is the basic idea used in *token-ring* networks.

In a token-ring network, stations are placed in a fixed order along a ring. This does not necessarily correspond to actual physical connectivity: the key idea is that each station has a well-defined predecessor and successor. A special packet called a *token* gives a station the right to place data on the shared medium. If a station has data to send, it waits till it receives the token from its predecessor, then holds on to the token when it transmits one or more packets. After packet transmission, it passes the token to its successor. The token mechanism allows the medium to be shared fairly among all the stations (no station will ever starve, as might happen with Ethernet). The obvious analogy in a meeting context is to require a participant to obtain a "right-to-speak" marker before speaking, which is passed on to a successor when she or he is done.

We mentioned earlier that a token ring does not necessarily require stations to be connected in a ring. To stress this point, we show four topologies in Figure 7.6 that all form logical rings. The first topology connects stations in a single physical ring (Figure 7.6a). Each station needs only one transmitter and one receiver. During normal operation, a station copies packets from its receive buffer to its transmit buffer, additionally copying the packet to a local buffer if the packet is addressed to it. Thus, packets eventually return to the sender, who removes them from the ring. The returning packets are an implicit acknowledgment that the receiver has seen them (or, the receiver may explicitly mark a packet when it copies it into its local buffers). A variant of this scheme requires a busy/idle flag in the token. When a station that has data to send sees an idle token, it changes the flag to busy and then starts sending data. When it is done, it waits for the token to return, then resets the flag to idle.

The major problem with a single-ring configuration is that if one link, transmitter, or receiver fails, the entire ring fails. We can mitigate this problem by using a second topology, which is the dual counterrotating ring shown in Figure 7.6b. In normal operation, only one ring is used, and the other serves as a backup. A single failure causes the ring to go into "wrap" mode, where the two rings are collapsed to form a single ring,

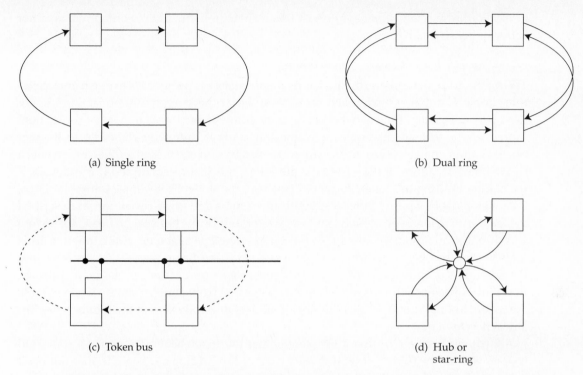

(a) Single ring

(b) Dual ring

(c) Token bus

(d) Hub or
star-ring

Figure 7.6: Four logically equivalent token-ring topologies. The property of the ring is that each node has a distinct logical predecessor and successor. The nodes themselves may or may not form a physical ring.

thus allowing traffic to be carried without pause while the fault is corrected. However, each node requires two transmitters and receivers, and stations must constantly monitor their neighbors, checking to see if the network should change from regular mode to "wrap" mode and vice versa. A good example of this topology is *FDDI*, which is described at the end of this subsection.

The third topology, also called a *token bus*, dispenses with the ring altogether and stations are connected to a single bus, as in Ethernet (Figure 7.6c). A station gets to speak when it gets a token from its predecessor that is explicitly addressed to it. Having spoken, it passes the token to its logical successor. Thus, a token bus forms a single logical ring.

The fourth topology, shown in Figure 7.6d, is called a *star-ring* or *hub* topology. A *passive* hub acts only as a wiring concentrator and does not participate in the token-ring protocols. It simplifies wiring because, to add a new station, we need only run a pair of wires from the station to the hub, instead of between the new station, its predecessor, and its successor. Thus, this is identical to the single ring shown in Figure 7.6a. With an *active* hub, also called a *bridge*, the hub is both a predecessor and successor to every station, thus fully participating in the token-ring protocol. An active hub can monitor the ring for link and station failures, eliminating failed components from the ring. This is very important in practice, when machines, interfaces, and links fail with tedious regularity. For these practical reasons, most token rings in the field are configured as either active or passive star-rings.

Advantages and problems with token rings

The main virtue of a token ring is that its medium access protocol is explicit, and therefore simple. If a station has a token, it can send data, otherwise, it cannot. Stations do not need carrier sensing, time synchronization, or complex protocols to resolve contention. Moreover, the scheme guarantees zero collisions and can give some stations priority over others. Unfortunately, these virtues are tempered by a major vice: the token represents a single point of failure in the system. If the token gets lost or corrupted (for example, if the station holding the token suddenly crashes), the network becomes unusable. Thus, the token must be carefully protected with checksums and error-correction, as described in Chapter 12. Moreover, stations must actively monitor the network to detect token loss and duplication. Usually, one of the stations is elected as a *monitor*. If the monitor finds that the ring has been idle for some time and no token has passed by, it assumes that the token has been lost or corrupted and generates a new token. A station can decide that a token has been duplicated if it receives a packet from another station when it holds the token. In this case, it purges the ring of all data and tokens, and the monitor eventually generates a new token.

A second problem with a token ring is that the token scheme requires a station to cooperate with the others, at least to the extent of forwarding a token if it does not need it. If a station crashes, refusing to accept or forward the token, it can hold up every other station. Thus, the network must monitor and exclude stations that do not cooperate in token passing. These two requirements (to monitor tokens and stations) reintroduce complexity back into the system. Indeed, a major reason for the initial unpopularity of token rings was the cost and added complexity of the *station management* functions, which are responsible for monitoring the health of the token and the stations.[4]

Fiber distributed data interface (FDDI)

Currently, the most popular token ring is FDDI, which uses a dual counterrotating token-ring LAN. Each link in FDDI runs at 100 Mbps over an optical fiber medium. Cheaper variants over copper wires are called *copper-DDI* or *CDDI*.

An FDDI network uses the token-passing mechanism discussed earlier. In addition, it supports real-time applications by ensuring that a station I can send data for at least *Synchronous Allocation(I)* seconds once every *target token rotation time* (TTRT). To guarantee this, each station maintains a timer called the *Token Rotation Timer* or *TRT*. This timer roughly measures the time since the station last forwarded the token. Thus, if a station receives the token when *TRT* is smaller than *TTRT*, it has $TTRT - TRT$ seconds to send data without violating the target rotation time.

---

[4]It did not help that token rings were trying to compete with Ethernet at a time when Ethernet was already very popular. Thus, not only was token ring competing against a technology with a large user base, putting it at a serious disadvantage, but also economies of scale made Ethernet interfaces substantially cheaper.

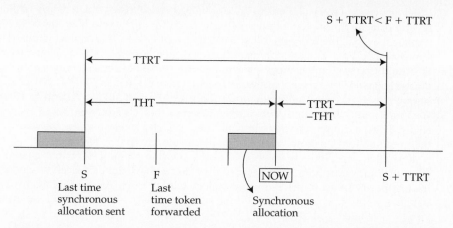

Figure 7.7: Why the FDDI algorithm works. Note that THT is the time since S, which is the last time the source sent a synchronous packet. Since S is smaller than F, the last time the source forwarded the packet, the time the station forwards the packet = S + THT + (TTRT − THT) = S + TTRT < F + TTRT, which guarantees that the rotation target is met.

What actually happens is that when a station receives a token, it sends synchronous packets up to its allocation, regardless of the value of TRT (we must somehow ensure that the sum of the synchronous allocations is smaller than the target token rotation time). It then resets TRT to zero, saving the previous value of TRT in the *Token Holding Time* (*THT*). If $THT < TTRT$, the station can send $TTRT - THT$ worth of non-real-time packets without violating the $TTRT$. To see this, let F denote the time when the station last forwarded the token and S the time since the station last sent a synchronous packet (Figure 7.7). Note that $S < F$. So, THT, which is the time since S, must be larger than the time since F. Thus, if a station sends asynchronous data for $TTRT - THT$ time, it will forward the token at a time at most $TTRT$ seconds after S, which is smaller than $TTRT$ seconds after F, which means that the rotation target certainly will be met. If the station does not have enough time to send a non-real-time packet, it immediately forwards the token, waiting for the next opportunity to transmit. In this way, a real-time application that *must* receive the token within a bounded time period can be guaranteed access.

EXAMPLE 7.4

Suppose a station receives a token when the TRT is 100 ms, and the $TTRT$ is 200 ms. Suppose its synchronous allocation is 20 ms. Then, it sends 20 ms of real-time traffic, by which time the THT increases to 120 ms. The station can then send $TTRT - THT = 200 - 120 = 80$ ms worth of traffic before forwarding the token.

FDDI also allows some stations to have a higher priority than others. Each station is allocated several priority thresholds for non-real-time data. To understand how this works, note that the smaller the *THT*, the more the *slack*, measured as *TTRT* − *THT*, that a station has to fill with non-real-time data. So, after transmitting real-time packets, if *THT* is smaller than a given threshold (the station has more slack than some threshold), the station is allowed to transmit data at that priority level. For example, an FDDI network with a *TTRT* of 100 ms may have three stations, with priority thresholds of 20, 30, and 40 ms at station A, and 5, 10, and 30 ms at stations B and C. If station A gets a token when its token holding time is 15 ms, it has a slack of 85 ms. Thus, it can send packets from all three priority levels, because the slack is greater than that required for transmitting data from all three levels (100 − 20 = 80, 100 − 30 = 70, and 100 − 40 = 60 ms, respectively). Stations B and C, with the same *THT*, may transmit only packets from the highest priority level because they do not have enough slack to send data from the lower-priority levels, which require a slack of at least 90 ms (corresponding to a *THT* of 10 ms).

FDDI port types

A standard FDDI station has two ports, called *A* and *B*, where a port refers to a transmitter–receiver pair (Figure 7.8). A station's B port is connected to a neighbor's

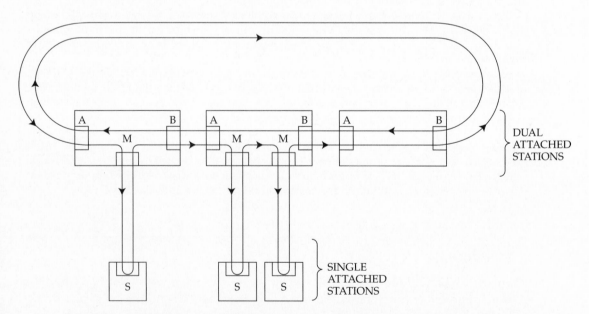

Figure 7.8: Typical FDDI ring. An FDDI ring supports dual-attached stations, which are a part of both the primary and the backup ring, and single-attached slave stations, which are attached to a master port on a concentrator.

A port, and its A port is connected to the other neighbor's B port. Stations that have both an A and a B port are members of both rings and are said to be *dual attached*.

To reduce costs for station management, the FDDI standard allows special dual-attached stations to act as proxies for other stations (in Figure 7.8, these are the two stations on the left). These special stations, called *concentrators*, have ports called *master* or M ports, attached, using a pair of bidirectional links, to *slave* or S ports. Stations with a slave port are attached to only one ring, so we also call them *single attached*. These stations have less reliable connectivity than dual-attached stations, but are cheaper to hook up. Moreover, if a slave station fails, the concentrator can bypass it using an *optical bypass*. Note that FDDI also allows concentrators to connect to other concentrators with an M–A connection to create a tree-of-rings topology. More details on FDDI can be found in references [Jain 94, FDDI FAQ 96].

Bus or ring?

Early Ethernets were truly buslike: a long coaxial cable was laid along corridors in a building, and computers in each room were attached through a *tap*. Some early FDDI rings were laid as a topological ring, with a pair of wires between adjacent computers. Both topologies turned out to be unmanageable, because a break in the wire needed an administrator to walk the entire building, looking for a fault. The only topology that seems to be manageable in practice is a star, where a central *hub* is connected by a cable to several computers. With a hub, though more wire is used, if a wire does break it can be tested and isolated from a single point. Moreover, if rooms are wired with multiple pairs of wires, on a failure it is easy to cut over to another pair.

With a hub-based topology, some of the distinctions between buses and rings disappear. In particular, if the hub provides some buffering, so that packets launched simultaneously by two computers do not collide, then the problems associated with Ethernet during overload are mitigated. Ethernet still has the advantage that it is simpler to install, since it only requires passive taps and has no overhead for station management. On the other hand, a ring allows a wider geographical spread and greater bandwidth, and it is more easily upgraded to fiber-optic links. Moreover, it allows priorities, prevents starvation, and has monotonically increasing throughput with increasing load. Thus, there is no clear overall winner.

In the real world, the choice between Ethernet and FDDI is constrained more by economics and wiring infrastructure than strictly by technical merits! High-speed fiber-optic token rings (such as FDDI) need optical interfaces and complex station management, making host-adaptors expensive (in 1996, most Ethernet cards for PCS cost less than $100, whereas FDDI cards cost around $1200 for fiber and around $700 for copper links). Most buildings are not wired for optical fiber; thus, network administrators have to take the wiring cost into account when choosing a fiber-optic token-ring (though this is not a factor with copper-FDDI). Moreover, token-ring manufacturers do not have sufficient economies of scale to bring prices to the rock-bottom levels achieved by Ethernet manufacturers. Thus, token rings are usually viewed as the technology of choice for high-speed backbones, rather than for access to the desktop. Desktop access is usually through cheap, ubiquitous Ethernet. A common topology, therefore, is to link several hubs with FDDI, and provide Ethernet access from a hub to the desktop. A hub provides a common point of access from several Ethernet buses to the high-speed token-ring-based backbone, thus distributing the cost of an expensive FDDI adaptor over many endpoints.

7.5.5 ALOHA and its variants

The ALOHA multiple access protocol is one of the simplest multiple access protocols and was the earliest to be developed and analyzed [Abramson 70, Kleinrock 75]. In ALOHA, when a station wants to send data, it just sends it, without checking to see if any other station is active. After sending the packet, the station waits for an implicit or explicit acknowledgment. If the station receives no acknowledgment, it assumes that the packet got lost, and tries again after a random waiting time. ALOHA is useful when the parameter a is large, so that carrier-sensing and probing techniques are impractical.

Unlike the schemes we studied earlier in the chapter, stations implementing ALOHA do not need carrier sensing, time-base synchronization, token passing, or any other contention-resolution mechanism. Moreover, ALOHA's performance is independent of the

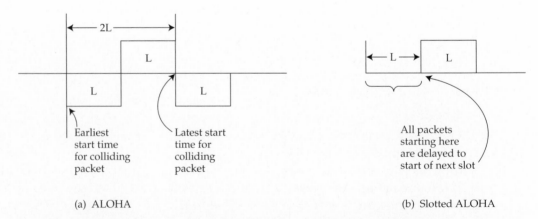

(a) ALOHA   (b) Slotted ALOHA

Figure 7.9: Vulnerability period in ALOHA and S-ALOHA. In ALOHA, a packet of duration L collides with every other packet generated (and transmitted) in a time period 2L, but in S-ALOHA, it collides with packets generated in time period L. Thus, S-ALOHA can achieve twice the peak goodput of ALOHA.

value of *a*. Thus, ALOHA has the clear advantage of simplicity. On the other hand, its performance, compared with the more sophisticated schemes, is quite poor. Under some simplifying mathematical assumptions, we can show that the peak achievable goodput of the scheme is only 18%. This figure has often been used to "prove" that ALOHA is an unusable multiple-access scheme. In fact, if the workload does not obey the simplistic assumptions, much higher goodput is achievable (consider, for example, the case of a single user accessing the medium, who can achieve a goodput of 100%). Moreover, if channel capacity is sufficiently high, so that the normalized offered load is low, the sheer simplicity of ALOHA makes it very attractive. Thus, ALOHA can still be found as a component in many multiple-access schemes. For example, in the cellular telephone network, when a cellular telephone is turned on, it must contact the base station and request a frequency (or time slot) on which to carry a voice call eventually. It uses ALOHA to send this initial request. Since the offered load from frequency-allocation requests is small, ALOHA is sufficient for this purpose. Several variants of ALOHA, such as *slotted ALOHA* and *reservation ALOHA*, are widely used, and we study them next.

Slotted ALOHA

In ALOHA a newly emitted packet can collide with a packet already in progress. If all packets are the same length and take *L* time units to transmit, then it is easy to see that a packet collides with any other packet transmitted in a time window of length 2*L* (Figure 7.9). We call this the *window of vulnerability*. If we somehow reduce this window, then the number of collisions decreases, and throughput increases. One way to achieve this is for stations to share the same time base by synchronizing with a master that periodically broadcasts a synchronization pulse. We divide time into equal *slots* of length *L*. When a station wants to send a packet, it waits till the beginning of the next slot. This reduces the window of vulnerability by a factor of two, doubling the peak achievable throughput, under the same set of mathematical assumptions as with ALOHA, to 36% (Figure 7.9b). This version of ALOHA is called *slotted ALOHA* or *S-ALOHA*. This scheme has a clear advantage in throughput, but introduces complexity in the stations and bandwidth overhead because of the need for time synchronization. It is best suited in an environment where time synchronization is already needed for another purpose. For example, in the TDMA GSM cellular telephone system, stations use slotted ALOHA to request a TDMA time slot. Since stations need to synchronize for TDMA anyway, slotted ALOHA poses little additional overhead.

Loss detection

We remarked earlier that a station in a multiple-access scheme can detect packet loss either implicitly or explicitly. Satellite ALOHA networks use an implicit loss-detection scheme. Usually, a satellite simply broadcasts whatever signal it receives from any station. Thus, a station knows that it should receive whatever it sent to the satellite one round-trip time later. If what it receives at this time is garbled, its packet suffered from a collision and must be retransmitted (Figure 7.10). Cellular ALOHA networks use an explicit acknowledgment scheme. When the base station successfully receives a channel-request message on an uplink, it places an acknowledgment on the downlink (this

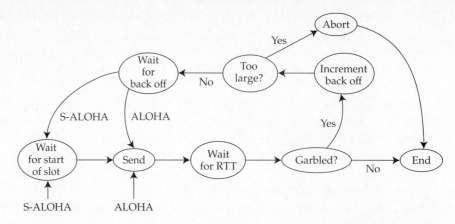

Figure 7.10: State diagram for ALOHA and S-ALOHA. A station sends a packet immediately in ALOHA, and on a slot boundary in S-ALOHA. In both mechanisms, a collision causes a random backoff. After too many failures, the link is declared down and transmission is aborted.

acknowledgment can be a busy tone on an acknowledgment channel, or setting a busy/idle bit on a downlink frame to "busy"). If a station does not see an acknowledgment in a reasonable amount of time, it times out, waits for a random time, and retransmits the packet.

Problems with stability

Besides the low achievable goodput, a second major problem with ALOHA and slotted ALOHA is that of stability. Since ALOHA is essentially uncontrolled, a sudden burst of traffic leads to numerous collisions. Each lost packet is retransmitted, and may, in turn, collide with newly generated packets that also require access to the medium. If the offered load is sufficiently high, the network can be put in an unstable state where every packet is a retransmission, and the goodput drops to zero. Luckily, this grisly fate can be avoided by using a sufficiently aggressive backoff policy, such as *binary exponential backoff*, described in Section 7.5.2. Designers of all ALOHA-like multiple access systems must include reasonable backoff mechanisms to assure system stability.

Reservation ALOHA

Reservation ALOHA or *R-ALOHA* combines the notion of slot reservation in schemes such as FPODA, described in Section 7.4.3, with the slotted ALOHA multiple-access scheme. Unlike a centralized reservation-oriented scheme (such as FPODA), R-ALOHA and its variants do not have a master that can resolve channel access priorities. Instead, stations independently examine reservation requests and come to consistent conclusions about which station owns which transmission slot. Thus, in R-ALOHA, all stations have the same priority (though streams within a station can get different priorities).

In the simplest version of R-ALOHA, we divide time into *frames*, where each frame consists of a fixed number of time slots [CRWOH 73]. A station that wins access to a slot using S-ALOHA is automatically assured ownership of the same slot in the next frame. A station that has data to send keeps track of which slots are idle in the current frame:

these slots are fair game for contention in the next frame. Thus, a station that has a steady stream of packets to send (as in circuit mode) needs to contend for access only once, while stations that want to access the medium in packet-mode are not shut out. Since a station does not suffer from collisions once it has acquired a slot, we can show that the performance of R-ALOHA is usually better than that of S-ALOHA.

In R-ALOHA, a station determines which data slots in a frame are available to it by using information from a previous frame. Thus, the previous frame must be long enough so that a station receives at least the start of the previous frame before the frame's transmission ends. In other words, the frame length must be at least as long as a. For example, in a network where $a = 200$, a station may send 200 packets before another station sees the first one. If the first of these contained the reservation minislots, for example, the station ought not start the next frame till at least 200 slot times have passed. Thus, the smallest possible frame length is 200 slots. This restriction on the size of a frame also bounds the delay performance of a reservation scheme. Since a packet that arrives to a previously idle station must wait for a reservation before it can be sent, the packet will see a delay of at least a slots.

Besides this, R-ALOHA suffers from two other problems. First, a station that gains access to the medium, and always has something to send, cannot be preempted. Thus, a station that initiates a low-priority bulk transfer cannot be evicted in favor of a high-priority transfer. Second, if all stations want to use packet mode, the automatic reservation of a slot in the next frame means that packets that need only one slot still use two. This doubles the packet-mode bandwidth overhead. We can avoid this overhead if a station appends an "end-of-transmission" flag to its last packet, which signals that its slot in the next frame is up for grabs [Lam 80]. Variants of R-ALOHA that allow a certain amount of preemption are described in references [Binder 75, Roberts 75].

7.6   Summary

This chapter discusses multiple-access schemes that arise in five main contexts: wired LANs, wireless LANs, packet radio, cellular telephony, and satellite communications. Despite their differences, they all face a similar problem, which is to coordinate access to a shared medium. In solving this problem, we can choose to build a centralized or a distributed system and use circuit-mode or packet-mode transfer. Designers must try to maximize the throughput and minimize the mean delay; they must also try to achieve stability, at least at low loads. It is useful to divide the multiple-access problem into providing base technologies and multiple-access schemes.

The three main base technologies are FDMA, TDMA, and CDMA. Each has its own problems, and all three are used in real-life systems. TDMA represents a compromise between FDMA and CDMA in terms of complexity and flexibility, and is popular for both circuit-mode and packet-mode transmission.

Centralized schemes use a master station to coordinate the actions of the slave stations. Circuit-mode centralized schemes, which are used in cellular telephony, can be categorized according to the base technology they use. In the United States, the most popular cellular technology is EAMPS, which uses FDMA, and in Europe, the most common scheme is GSM, which uses TDMA. Other, centralized packet-mode schemes are polling, for wired LANs, and reservation schemes, which are used primarily for satellites.

Distributed schemes are usually packet mode and are common in wired and wireless LANs. The simplest of these schemes is distributed polling, which is similar to the centralized version. For networks where the propagation delay is small compared with the packet transmission time, carrier sensing is effective and is used in the CSMA scheme. CSMA's variants, particularly CSMA/CD, which is used for Ethernet, dominate multiple access for wired local-area networks. Token-ring schemes, such as the double counter-rotating ring design used for FDDI, are also popular choices for these networks. Wireless LANs use either CSMA/CA, or, when hidden and exposed terminals are common, BTMA or MACA. Finally, the ALOHA scheme and its variants, S-ALOHA and R-ALOHA, are common in satellite networks.

Table 7.4 summarizes the schemes we studied in this chapter. A network designer should choose a scheme that best satisfies the requirements posed by link characteristics, station complexity, and achievable performance.

Quality of service with multiple access

Most current multiple access schemes do not provide good support for per-connection, or even per-station, quality of service. In other words, it is usually not possible for a connection or station to ask for, and get, a particular bandwidth or delay bound allocated to them. For example, with Ethernet, a station is not even guaranteed that its packet will ever get through, let alone given a delay bound! The only exceptions we have studied are FPODA, where a master regulates accesses, and FDDI, where the TTRT allows stations to bound the worst-case delay in accessing the ring. FDDI also allows stations to request a *synchronous allocation*, which corresponds to a bandwidth bound. However, this is only a crude technique for guaranteeing quality of service, since the granularity of the TTRT can be quite high (around a hundred milliseconds).

Since multiple-access LANs are usually the first and last hops in any wide-area connection, the lack of quality of service in these LANs makes the QoS guarantees in the wide-area network (described in more detail in Chapter 14) moot. Therefore, there has been much interest in non-broadcast media for local area networks. A prime example is local-area ATM networks, which place wide-area ATM technology in the local area. Since an ATM switch can provide per-VC QoS, and ATM links are not shared, a local-area ATM network can provide end-to-end QoS, at least at the datalink layer.

Other technologies that can provide the same service guarantees as ATM, but do not do so currently, are switched Ethernet and 100VG AnyLAN. If there is sufficient demand for QoS-aware applications, we can expect to see better support for QoS in both multiple-access and non-shared local area networks of the future.

Base technologies	FDMA				
	TDMA				
	CDMA				
	FDD				
	TDD				
Access schemes	Centralized	Circuit mode	EAMPS		Cellular telephony
			GSM		
			IS-95		
		Packet mode	Polling and probing		Wired LAN
			Reservation-based schemes	FPODA	Satellite
				PDAMA	
	Distributed	Packet mode	Polling and probing		Wired LAN
			CSMA	CSMA/CD	
				CSMA/CA	Wireless LAN
			BTMA	MACA	
				MACAW	
			Token ring	FDDI	Wired LAN
			ALOHA	Pure ALOHA	Satellite
				S-ALOHA	
				R-ALOHA	

Table 7.4: Classification of multiple access schemes. The table shows the relationship among the schemes we studied in this chapter. We classified schemes according to whether they are centralized or distributed. Alternative ways of classification are circuit mode versus packet mode, and by the type of LAN in which the access method is used. These alternative classifications are shown on the right.

Review questions

1. How could you eliminate the multiple-access problem for local-area networks?
2. What is the parameter a?
3. When is circuit-mode access justified?
4. What are the ISM bands?
5. What is the hidden-terminal problem?

6. What is goodput?

7. What are the three metrics of a multiple-access scheme's performance?

8. Why do FDMA networks need cells?

9. If you wanted to give some station twice the bandwidth of another, would you prefer to use FDMA or TDMA? Why?

10. Why do FH/CDMA receivers need to take both time and frequency into consideration?

11. What is a *chip* in the context of CDMA?

12. How is "soft" handoff done in a CDMA network?

13. Why is it hard to introduce DS/CDMA into existing infrastructure?

14. What is the multiple-access technology used in the EAMPS standard?

15. What is the multiple-access technology used in GSM?

16. Why does the bandwidth available from CDPD vary?

17. What is the difference between polling and probing?

18. Why do reservations use minislots instead of regular data slots in reservation-based schemes?

19. What is the common feature of CSMA schemes?

20. What is the difference between nonpersistent CSMA and *p*-persistent CSMA?

21. What is binary exponential backoff?

22. What is the purpose of a "jam" signal in Ethernet?

23. What is the motivation for CSMA/CA?

24. If stations A and B in CSMA/CA have interframe spacings of 3 and 5 slots, which has the higher priority?

25. What is an exposed terminal?

26. What is the purpose of a busy tone in BTMA?

27. What is a station's action when it hears an RTS in MACA?

28. In MACA, what happens if two stations send an RTS at the same time?

29. What is "wrap" mode in FDDI?

30. What happens if a token gets corrupted in a token ring?

31. What is the ALOHA protocol?

32. What is the difference between S-ALOHA and ALOHA? What overhead does S-ALOHA incur?

33. What are the disadvantages of R-ALOHA?

Exercises

7.1. Compute *a* for a network where the mean packet size is 500 bytes, and (a) link bandwidth is 10 Mbps and link delay is 5 μs; (b) link bandwidth is 500 Kbps and link delay is 250 ms.

7.2. Can a multiple-access scheme support both packet and circuit mode? If so, describe how such a scheme might work.

7.3. Suppose a cellular telephony company bought two 7-MHz TV channels for its FDD/FDMA system. How many EAMPS voice channels could it provide assuming a single cell per city? How many if the city were divided into 60 hexagonal cells, and no two adjacent cells used the same frequencies? What is the increase in the number of available channels using cellular telephony? Recompute the increase factor if the city were divided into 600 hexagonal cells.

7.4. Use the audioconference metaphor to describe DS/CDMA.

7.5. If a 14.4-Kbps bit stream is spread using an 8-bit codeword, what is the spread-spectrum rate in chips/second?

7.6. Derive an expression for the normalized throughput of roll-call polling if a station has a packet to send with probability p, the number of stations is N, the mean round-trip delay in accessing a station is R, the medium has a bandwidth b, a poll/poll reply message is of length l bytes, and the mean message length is L bytes. Compute the peak achievable goodput for $p = 0.01, N = 1000, R = 0.1$ s, $b = 10$ Mbps, $l = 10$ bytes, and $L = 500$ bytes. Recompute the goodput for $p = 0.9$. Why is polling not a good multiple-access scheme in this environment?

7.7. Suppose a local area network has 25 stations, of which stations with addresses 14, 17, and 23 have something to send. Trace the sequence of poll requests and data transfers when using probing.

7.8. Repeat Exercise 7.7 assuming a decentralized tree-based scheme.

7.9. What is the trade-off made in the design of a backoff scheme?

7.10. What is the design technique used in moving from BTMA to MACA?

7.11. Suppose two stations are both sending to the same destination in MACA, and suppose both have a steady stream of packets to send. If each has an initial time-out of 1 second, describe a possible sequence of actions that leads to one of the stations being shut out.

7.12. Use the audioconference metaphor to explain the exposed terminal problem.

7.13. What conditions must synchronous allocations obey in FDDI for the token to meet its $TTRT$? What happens if a station with $THT = 0$ sends a burst of non-real-time data for time $TTRT$? (Hint: Consider what happens in the next rotation time.)

7.14. If you were the hardware designer for an FDDI host-adaptor card, to maximize network performance, what design parameter should you minimize? Why?

7.15. At low loads, would you use R-ALOHA, S-ALOHA, or ALOHA? Why? Can you suggest a hybrid scheme that combines the best properties of each scheme? Outline how it would work.

Chapter 8

Switching

8.1 Introduction

Every day, hundreds of millions of people use the telephone network to get in touch with a billion or so telephone customers around the world. These calls travel through a vast maze of switches and transmission lines to reach across the globe. How do telephone switches handle so many simultaneous calls?

Every day, millions of people use the World Wide Web to reach tens of millions of Web sites. With a click of a mouse, a user's request for data snakes its way across the Internet and contacts a remote site. The response works its way back through a vast interconnection of routers and returns to the user. How do the routers in the Internet handle this flood of packets, forwarding each packet to its destination?

In this chapter, we will study *switching*, the process by which a network element forwards data arriving at one of its inputs to one of its outputs. We will study three kinds of switching elements: (a) telephone switches, which support the telephone network, (b) datagram switches (also called *routers*), which tie the Internet together, and (c) ATM switches, optimized to deal with small, fixed-size packets called *cells*.

8.1.1 Classification

We categorize switching elements in two ways (Table 8.1). Routers and ATM switches are both *packet* switches, that is, they switch packets that contain both data and descriptive meta-data. In contrast, telephone switches are *circuit* switches that switch voice samples that contain no meta-data.

	Connectionless (datagram)	Connection-oriented (switching system = switch + switch controller)
Packet switch	Internet router	ATM switching system
Circuit switch		Telephone switching system

Table 8.1: Classification of switching elements.

We also categorize switching elements as *connectionless* or *connection-oriented*. A connectionless switching element or router reads the destination address in an incoming packet's header and looks up a routing table to determine its output interface. Each packet is *self-contained* in that it contains sufficient information to be routed to its destination. In contrast, a connection-oriented *switching system* consists of a switch and a switch controller. During connection setup, the *switch controller* uses the destination address to associate a data forwarding path in the *switch* with either a particular time slot or a virtual circuit identifier. During the data transfer phase, the switch moves cells or samples from an input to an output using this association. Note that in a connection-oriented switching element, correct switching requires preestablishment of a data forwarding association. In this sense, neither voice samples nor ATM cells are self-contained.

Besides switching packets, switching elements perform three other important functions. First, they participate in routing algorithms to build *routing tables,* which map a destination address to an output trunk. A connectionless switch consults the routing table for every incoming packet, and a connection-oriented switch controller consults this table during connection establishment.[1] We will study how routing tables are built in Chapter 11. Second, switching elements resolve contention for access to an output trunk. By intelligently *scheduling* access, a switching element can give different connections (or packets) different qualities of service. We will study scheduling in more detail in Chapter 9. Third, a switching system in a connection-oriented network participates in *admission control* to decide whether to accept an incoming call. We will study this in Chapter 14.

In this chapter, we focus on routers and the switch portion of a switching system. Unless otherwise specified, we will use the term "switch" to refer to them both.

8.1.2 Requirements

The *capacity* of a switch is the maximum rate at which it can move information, assuming all data paths are simultaneously active. The primary requirement of a switch is to maxi-

---

[1]During data transfer, an ATM switch looks up a translation table for each incoming cell to determine its output interface.

mize capacity for a given cost and a given reliability. In practice, only a fraction of paths are simultaneously active, so switches rarely achieve their rated capacity.

A circuit switch must reject a call if it does not have a path from an input to an output to carry the call, since it cannot buffer data. This is called *call blocking*. In a packet switch, data can be stored in a buffer, so call blocking is not a concern. Instead, the analog of call blocking is *packet loss*, that is, the loss of one or more packets because of a buffer overflowing when a burst of packets arrives at the switch. The second requirement for a switch is that it should minimize call blocking and packet loss.

Finally, a switch should not reorder packets. With reordering, receivers must buffer out-of-order packets, increasing both their cost for memory and the end-to-end packet delay. Consequently, ATM switches are prohibited from reordering cells. Routers are more lax in maintaining packet order, and packet reordering is common in the Internet.

8.1.3 A generic switch

A generic switch has four parts: input buffers, a port mapper, a switch fabric, and output buffers (Figure 8.1).

- Input buffers store packets or samples as they arrive on the input lines. Some switches have tiny input buffers that hold data only while it is contending for the switch fabric. Other switches have almost all their buffers at the inputs.

- The port mapper is found only on packet switches. It reads either the destination address or a virtual circuit identifier from an incoming packet's header and uses

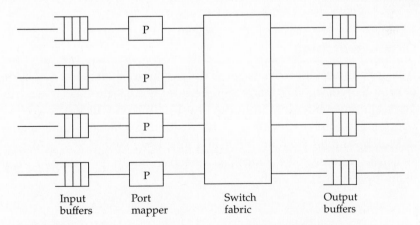

Figure 8.1: A generic switch. Data arrive on multiple trunks and are stored in an input buffer. In a packet switch, a port mapper assigns each packet to one or more outputs. A circuit switch does not need a port mapper, since the destination of a sample is known from its arrival time on a multiplexed input. A switching fabric moves data from input buffers to output buffers, which then transmit data to output trunks.

a table to decide the packet's output port. A circuit switch does not need a port mapper because each time slot is automatically associated with a path from an input to an output.

- The switch fabric routes data from an input to an output. The simplest switch fabric is a processor that reads data from an input port and writes it to an output port. Switch fabrics can also be complex multiprocessor systems that simultaneously transfer thousands of packets along many parallel data paths.

- Output buffers store data as they wait for a turn on the output line. At each output port, a scheduler manages the output buffers and arbitrates access to the output line. As with input buffers, these can be small or large.

Some switches distribute, combine, or omit one or more of these functions. For example, a switch may combine the input and output buffers, distribute the port mapper among the input ports, or omit the input buffers. We will see examples of these later in the chapter.

8.1.4 Rest of the chapter

We will first study circuit switching in Section 8.2, then study packet switching, which encompasses both datagram and virtual circuit switches, in Sections 8.3–8.6. Section 8.3 is an introduction to packet switching and discusses three types of packet switches. Section 8.4 concentrates on switch fabrics for packet switches. Section 8.5 deals with the placement of buffers in packet switches, and Section 8.6 is devoted to multicast switches.

8.2 Circuit switching

A telephone circuit carries voice samples that are 8 bits long and correspond to 125 μs of sampled voice. Note that a sample does not have a header describing its source or destination: we infer this from the physical line on which it is present and the time at which it is placed on the line (i.e., its position in a *frame*). In this section, we study how to switch samples from an input of a telephone switch to an output. Before we study switches, we first make a small diversion to study the essentials of multiplexing and demultiplexing.

8.2.1 Multiplexors and demultiplexors

Most telephone trunks carry more than one voice circuit, sharing (or *multiplexing*) the trunk among samples from these circuits. At a central office, calls arriving from active local loops are combined before being placed on a shared long-distance trunk, and calls to active local loops are removed (or *demultiplexed*) from incoming trunks. Multi-

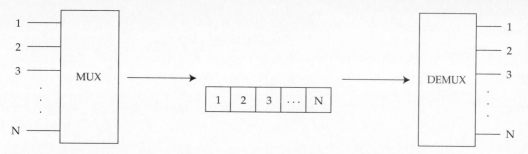

Figure 8.2: Multiplexing and demultiplexing. A multiplexer takes samples from N inputs and places them one by one on an output that is N times faster. A demultiplexer distributes data from a fast input onto N outputs, each N times faster than the input. Neither requires header information to do its task.

plexors and demultiplexors are, therefore, fundamental to the operation of the telephone network.

A synchronous multiplexor consists of N input lines and an output line that runs N times as fast (Figure 8.2). Each input line is associated with a buffer that can store at least one sample. The multiplexor visits each input buffer in turn, placing the sample on the output line. If the input lines are 64 Kbps, then a sample lasts 125 μs on the input line, but slightly less than 125/N μs on the output line (because framing bits take some time).

We can cascade multiplexors to carry more voice circuits on a single physical line. The T hierarchy, described in Chapter 2, is the set of rates allowed on a multiplexed line in the telephone network. For example, a T1 line carries 24 voice circuits at 1.544 Mbps, and a T3 line carries 28 T1s at 44.736 Mbps.

A demultiplexor has one input line and N output lines that run N times slower than the input line. Each output line is associated with at least 8 bits of buffering. Incoming samples are placed in an output buffer in round-robin order. From there they are transmitted on the corresponding output lines. Note that neither a multiplexor nor a demultiplexor needs addressing information. Their operation requires only accurate timing information.

Inverse multiplexing

Inverse multiplexing is the aggregation of multiple independent information channels across a network to create a single higher-rate information channel [Duncanson 95]. For example, with inverse multiplexing, we can combine three 1.5-Mbps T1 channels to create a single 4.5-Mbps channel. The incoming data stream is partitioned into multiple data streams and sent on separate connections. At the receiver, misordered data is reordered, and the separate streams are combined to form a single higher-rate stream. An *inverse multiplexor* establishes the separate channels and makes sure they stay up, establishing alternate connections if performance on an existing connection degrades. It can also dynamically change the number of streams to match the incoming data rate. Thus, from the perspective of the endpoints, an inverse multiplexor provides a single higher-rate stream, with a capacity that can dynamically adapt to the rate of the incoming data stream.

Inverse multiplexing is very useful in networks that are unable to provide individual higher-rate streams. For example, inverse multiplexors can be used to aggregate multiple telephone channels to provide a higher-speed link between datagram routers. They are commonly used to link corporate LANs over wide-area telephone circuits [Duncanson 95].

Add–drop multiplexing

A common use for multiplexors and demultiplexors is in adding or removing some calls from a trunk. Consider a DS3 trunk from New York to Chicago that passes through Harrisburg, PA. At Harrisburg, we may want to remove calls destined locally, and insert other calls that originate from Harrisburg and go to Chicago. Instead of installing a switch at Harrisburg, which is expensive, we can accomplish this task with an *add–drop multiplexor*. This demultiplexes the DS3 to DS0s, allowing some calls to be diverted, while new calls are remultiplexed and put back on the trunk.

> Add–drop multiplexors for DS trunks are expensive (though less expensive than switches) because DS framing requires complete demultiplexing before calls can be added or removed. One motivation to migrate from the DS hierarchy to Synchronous Optical (SONET) links is that we can add or remove calls from a SONET trunk without demultiplexing it into DS0s, because the SONET frame header carries enough information to locate a single call. This allows us to build cheaper add–drop multiplexors for SONET [Bellamy 91] (also see Section 15.2.3).

8.2.2   Circuit switching

A circuit switch handling N voice circuits conceptually consists of N inputs and N outputs (in practice, N can be as large as 120,000). This corresponds to far fewer physical input and output lines if these lines are time-multiplexed. For example, if the inputs are DS3s that each carry 672 voice calls, the number of physical lines is reduced by a factor of 672. In this chapter, if the inputs are multiplexed, we will assume that all inputs are at the same level in the multiplexing hierarchy, and that voice samples on all inputs arrive synchronously. (In reality, small jitters in the arrival times of samples must be smoothed out by an input buffer.) The goal of a circuit switch is to get an incoming sample to the right output line and to the right slot in the output frame.

Before we study switching strategies, we distinguish between switches that connect individual telephone lines, called *line* switches, and switches that interconnect multiplexed trunks, called *transit* switches [Bellamy 91]. A line switch must connect a specific input to a specific output. In contrast, a transit switch need only connect an input to *one* of the outputs going in the right direction. For example, a transit switch in Chicago may switch some calls from a 672-call DS3 from New Jersey to another DS3 going to California. In this case, the switch need only connect an input line to one of the outputs going to California.

The difference between line switching and transit switching becomes important when considering the possibility of *blocking* in a switch. A call is blocked if no path can take it from an input to an output. At the time of call admission, the switch controller rejects blocked calls. There are two types of blocking: *internal* blocking and *output* blocking. Internal blocking occurs if the output is available, but there is no path through the switch. Output blocking occurs if two inputs compete for the same output, in which case one of them is output blocked. To return to line and transit switching, note that if an input can choose to go to any one of a set of outputs, then both internal and output blocking are reduced. Thus, a transit switch can achieve the same blocking probability as a line switch with less hardware.

The two basic strategies in circuit switching are time-division and space-division switching. We will study them next, then consider multistage switches that combine time and space switching. These topics are covered in greater detail in reference [Bellamy 91].

8.2.3 Time-division switching

A *time-slot interchanger* or *TSI* used in time-division switching has only one input and one output line, but these lines carry samples from N multiplexed voice circuits. A TSI writes incoming samples in an N-byte buffer, one byte per incoming circuit, and reads them out in a different order. The different order on the output line, when passed through a demultiplexor, results in samples being placed on different output lines. In other words, a TSI switches samples by rearranging the order of samples on a multiplexed line.

EXAMPLE 8.1

Consider a company that has two branch offices A and B, each with 24 lines. We want any telephone in A to be able to connect over a T1 line to any telephone in B. We do this by installing small switches, called *private branch exchanges* (PBXs), at sites A and B. Each PBX has 24 lines connecting it to 24 telephones and a T1 connecting it to the other PBXs (Figure 8.3a). Samples from each telephone are multiplexed in some fixed order and placed on the T1 line. Samples arriving on the T1 connection are given to a TSI, which has 24 1-byte buffers into which it cyclically writes these samples. The TSI interchanges samples before handing them to a demultiplexer.

Suppose the second telephone in A, corresponding to the second sample in the frame leaving A, wants to connect to the third telephone in B. To make this connec-

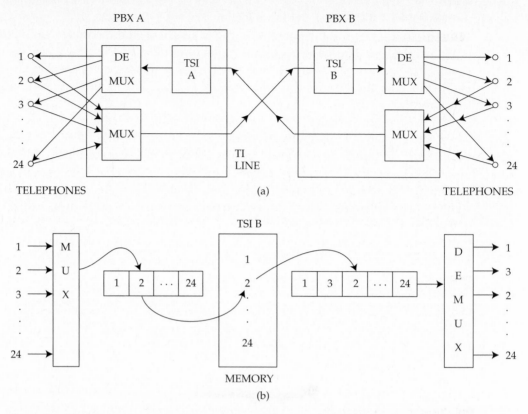

Figure 8.3: Time-division switching. A time slot interchange reorders samples on a trunk. This has the effect of switching when the trunk is demultiplexed. See Example 8.1 for details.

tion, the TSI at B places the second input sample in the third time slot on its output line (Figure 8.3b). When the output line of the TSI is demultiplexed, A's second sample is thus placed on B's third line, as desired.

If we wanted to build a large switch from a single TSI, how large a switch can we build? The limit to scaling a TSI is the time taken to read and write a sample from memory. Suppose we wanted to build a switch as large as the largest switches currently in the field, which handle around 120,000 calls. To build a TSI that can switch 120,000 circuits, we need to read and write samples from a memory 120,000 times every 125 μs. This would require each read and write operation to take on the order of half a nanosecond, which is unattainable at any price with present technology. Thus, building a switch this size with a single TSI is not practical. These days, typical DRAM access times are around 80 ns, and 40-ns memories can be bought quite cheaply. If we use a 40-ns memory, the access time is 80 times as slow as what we need for a 120,000-line switch, so the switch capacity is at most 120,000/80 = 1500 circuits, which is quite small! Thus, to build large switches, we need to turn to other techniques. *good pt*

8.2.4   Space-division switching

In space-division multiplexing, each sample takes a different path through the switch, depending on its destination. We illustrate this using an example.

EXAMPLE 8.2

Suppose we wanted to use space-division switching in the PBXs of Example 8.1. We can do so by first demultiplexing the T1 line onto 24 different lines, then connecting the demultiplexor's output to the correct telephone (Figure 8.4). The sample from the second telephone in A appears at the second output line of the demultiplexor. This is connected, using the space-division switch, to the third telephone in B. Other samples can be simultaneously switched along other paths in the space-division switch.

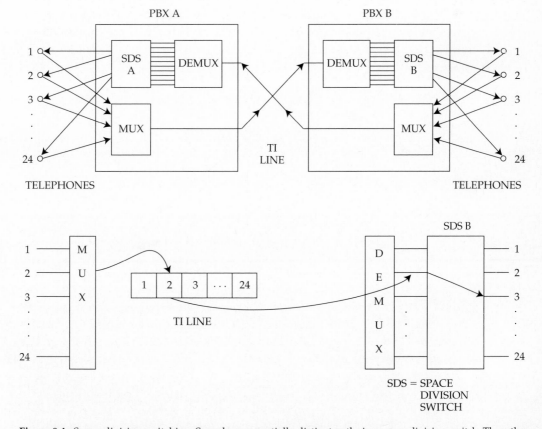

Figure 8.4: Space-division switching. Samples use spatially distinct paths in a space division switch. Thus, the space division switch in PBX B distributes the demultiplexed samples to the appropriate output ports over separate physical paths.

Crossbar

The simplest space-division switch is a crossbar (Figure 8.5). Samples arrive on rows and are output along columns. Active elements called *crosspoints* are placed between input and output lines. If the crosspoint is active, data flows from the input to the output line; otherwise, the two are disconnected. (Note that a crossbar need not have the same number of input lines and output lines. An $n \times k$ crossbar has n input and k output lines.) If the input lines are not multiplexed, a crossbar always connects the same inputs to the same outputs, much like a static patch panel. However, if the input lines carry multiplexed samples, and different samples have different destinations, a crossbar requires a *schedule* that tells it which crosspoints to activate during each sample time. Depending on this schedule, samples are transferred from the selected input to the selected output.

A crossbar is *internally nonblocking* (i.e., no sample is blocked in the switch waiting for an output line). Unfortunately, an $N \times N$ crossbar uses N^2 elements and therefore is expensive for large N, such as $N = 100,000$ (also see the next box). A second problem with building large crossbars is that the signal distribution time; that is, the time taken for a controller to inform each crosspoint whether it should be on or off, grows large for large N. Third, a single crosspoint failure isolates an input from an output line, making a crossbar less robust to faults than the multistage crossbars we discuss next. However, crossbars are an excellent solution for building smaller (say, 8×8 or 64×64) switches.

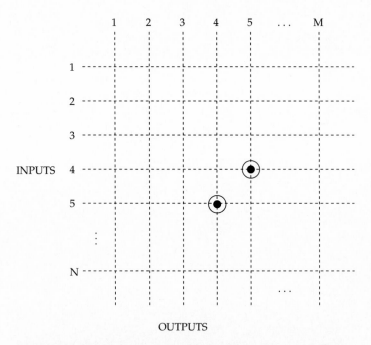

Figure 8.5: Simple crossbar. Inputs arrive along rows and are placed on columns if the corresponding crosspoint is active. A schedule sets each crosspoint for each incoming sample.

As we will see, more complex switch designs are composed from smaller switching blocks, which can be built as crossbars.

Multistage crossbar

A simple generalization of a crossbar allows us to save many crosspoints. Notice that during each switching time (the time taken to transfer one sample across the crossbar) only one crosspoint in each row or column is active. If we can somehow get an internal element to receive samples from multiple input lines, we can get rid of this inefficiency. This is done with multistage switching (Figure 8.6). Here, the inputs are broken into groups, which are internally switched by a crossbar. We allow multiple paths between input and output groups to share a center stage, thus reducing the number of crosspoints. However, at each time slot, each array in the multistage switch has to be rearranged. In a typical multistage switch, the first stage consists of N/n arrays of size $n \times k$, the second stage consists of k arrays of size $N/n \times N/n$, and the third stage consists of N/n arrays of size $k \times n$. In Figure 8.6, $N = 20$, $n = 10$, and $k = 3$.

Notice that we now have k disjoint paths from any input array to any output array. If k is small, as in Figure 8.6, it is possible that an input and output are both idle, but no path to connect the two exists (i.e., the switch can be internally blocking). How large should k be for the switch to be internally nonblocking? Clos showed that if a switch controller is willing to rearrange existing connections when a new call arrives, the condition is [Clos 53]:

$$k > 2n - 2 \tag{8.1}$$

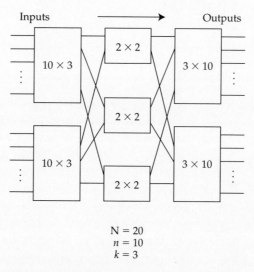

$$N = 20$$
$$n = 10$$
$$k = 3$$

Figure 8.6: Multistage switch. The key idea is that each element in the center stage can be accessed by multiple elements in the first stage. This reduces the wasted crosspoints in a single-stage crossbar.

Thus, a switch using a Clos network is also called a *rearrangably nonblocking* switch. In practice, circuit switches rarely rearrange existing connections, so this result is primarily of theoretical interest.

A Clos network of size $N \times N$ has:

$$\text{number of crosspoints} = 2N(2n - 1) + (2n - 1) * (N/n)^2 \qquad (8.2)$$

which is smaller than N^2, as is the case with a crossbar. This number is minimized when $n = O(\sqrt{(N)})$.

In a single-stage switch, finding a path from an input to an output is trivial. In a multistage switch, the switch controller must find a valid path from an input to an output at the time of call admission. The controller keeps track of the inputs and outputs that are free during each time slot, and uses a search algorithm, such as depth-first-search, to find a path. This path is then stored in a switch schedule and handed to the switch for execution during actual data transfer.

Even a Clos network does not scale very well with N. For example, if we let $N = 120,000$, the optimal $n = 346$; then we need $k > 690$, say $k = 691$. Then, the corresponding Clos network needs 248.8 million crosspoints! To reduce this number to reasonable values, we need to combine time and space switching. Alternatively, we can choose to build a blocking switch, and accept the risk of a call being rejected due to internal blocking. A telephone company has to make the trade-off between the call blocking probability and the cost of the switch. In practice, most telephone switches do have a nonzero, but small, blocking probability. We will study how to compute these blocking probabilities in Section 14.11.2.

Are crosspoints really expensive?

Crosspoints used to be electromechanical devices that were expensive and prone to failure, and so minimizing the number of crosspoints made sense. With current VLSI designs routinely placing millions of reliable gates on a single chip, do we really need to worry about the number of crosspoints?

A typical VLSI implementation uses a set of N input buses, each attached to N output multiplexors. Each output multiplexor is programmed to select one of the N inputs. The complexity in building a VLSI crossbar is the chip area for N multiplexors. Since a multiplexor that selects one of the N inputs takes area proportional to N, an $N \times N$ crossbar requires a chip area proportional to N^2.

For large N, a crossbar's cost increases not only because of the large chip area, but also because the crossbar needs to be split across multiple packages. Moreover, the scheduler must program each of the output multiplexors individually, which takes time. For example, for a 64×64 crossbar, the scheduler must address and individually set up 64 output multiplexors. Setting one multiplexor requires six addressing pins and one data pin. Even if a crossbar chip allocates fifty-six pins for scheduling so that a scheduler can address eight multiplexors simultaneously, setting up the crossbar takes eight clock cycles. For these reasons, a crossbar is useful only when N is small (64×64 or smaller). We need to look to other switching fabrics to reduce the number of switching elements when building large switches.

8.2.5   Time–space switching

Recall that a time-slot interchange (TSI) has a single input and a single output, and can be thought of as rearranging samples on the input line. In time-space (TS) switching, the outputs of many TSIs are fed into a space-division switch (Figure 8.7). There are two ways to view a TS switch. From one perspective, the TSI delays samples so that they arrive at the right time for the space division switch's schedule. If the time or T stage were missing, then, at a given time, we might have many inputs of the space or S stage destined for the same output, which would cause blocking. By rearranging the order in which the S stage receives samples, we gain a degree of freedom in picking the S stage schedule. This allows us to build a space-division switch with fewer crosspoints than a Clos switch, but still make it nonblocking.

EXAMPLE 8.3

Consider a 4×4 crossbar shown in Figure 8.7 that has four time-multiplexed inputs, each carrying four circuits. Thus, the switch switches 16 circuits, four at a time. Note that in the first time slot, samples from both circuit 1 and 13 arrive. If both want to use output trunk 1, one of them will be blocked. We call this output blocking. Now, suppose we insert TSIs at each input. We can rearrange the sample from 1 so that it arrives at time slot 2 instead, so that 1 and 13 no longer conflict. This is the key advantage of the TS switch: it can reduce blocking by rearranging inputs.

A second way to view TS switching is to think of the space-division switch as allowing us to swap samples between two TSI output lines. A TSI allows us to interchange the order of samples within a line, but does not allow us to place a sample on a different output line. By tying together a set of TSIs with a space-division switch, we can take a sample arriving on, say, input line 1, and transmit it on, say, line 3.

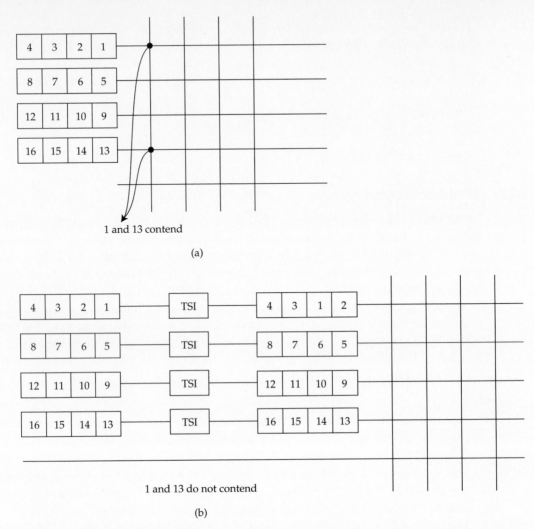

Figure 8.7: Time–space switching. Note that in (a) the samples in time slots 1 and 13 contend for output 1, so that one of them has to be buffered or dropped. With a TSI interchanging samples 1 and 2 (b), the contention disappears. Thus, the TSI allows reduced blocking in the crossbar.

8.2.6 Time–space–time switching

A time–space–time (TST) switch is similar to a three-stage crossbar, except that we replace the input and output crossbar stages with TSIs (Figure 8.8). The easiest way to understand the functioning of a TST switch is to compare it with a TS switch. A TS switch can reorder samples within an input line, and switch them to a different output line. Suppose two input lines want to send a sample to the same output line simultaneously, leading to output blocking. We could then use the TSIs at the input to rearrange the samples so that they did not suffer from output blocking. However, this rearrangement may result in samples arriving at the outputs out of sequence. By placing a second TSI at

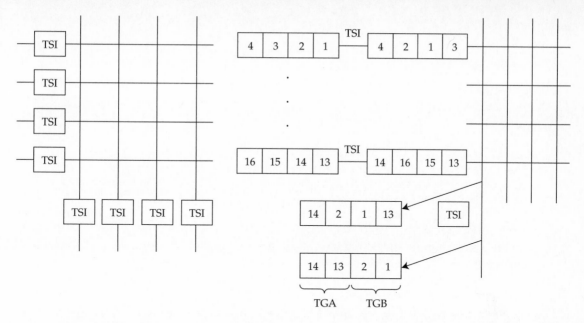

Figure 8.8: Time–space–time switching. A TST switch is similar to a TS switch, except that TSIs at the output allow samples to be rearranged at the output as well as the input. Thus, rearranging samples at inputs as well as outputs lets any free slot in the space-division switch be used for switching.

every output, we can achieve any desired sequencing on each output line. Thus, we can use any available time slot of the space-division switch to exchange samples between lines, reducing the chances of call blocking in the space-division switch.

EXAMPLE 8.4

In Figure 8.8, assume that samples 1 and 2 from input line 1 and samples 13 and 14 from input line 4 should be switched to output line 1. Further, assume that the first two samples on output 1's frame are sent on trunk group A, and the second two samples on trunk group B. We want samples 13 and 14 to be sent on trunk group A, and 1 and 2 on trunk group B. To achieve this, note first that samples 1 and 13 and samples 2 and 14 are output blocked. At the input TSIs, we rearrange them as shown to avoid output blocking. However, the order at the output line, 14, 2, 1, 13 is wrong. The TSI on the output line allows us to rearrange the order appropriately.

Many generalizations of TST switching are used in practice. For example, we can replace the S stage by a three-stage space-division switch, thus reducing the number of cross-points. This leads to a TSSST fabric, used in the EWSD switch from Siemens. The 4ESS switch from Lucent Technologies, which uses a similar principle, is a TSSSST switch with

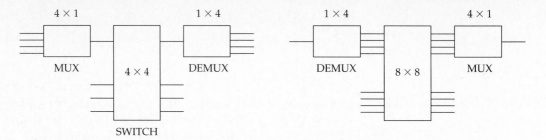

Figure 8.9: Dealing with line speed heterogeneity. If some incoming trunks are slower than others, they can be multiplexed to the standard line speed. Conversely, if some trunks are faster than others their load can be spread among multiple input ports.

four internal space-division stages and two TSIs at the ends. These complex multistage switches can handle 100,000 to 200,000 circuits and are widely deployed in the telephone network.

Dealing with line heterogeneity

Most circuit-switch designs assume that all incoming and outgoing trunks have the same rate. If this is not the case, we can use multiplexors to work around the problem. If some incoming trunks are too slow, we can multiplex them before they enter the switch. Conversely, if an input is too fast, it can be demultiplexed before being switched. Figure 8.9 illustrates multiplexor and demultiplexor placement for these solutions. In the rest of the section, we will assume that all input and output trunks have the same speed.

The true cost of telephone switching

Though space and time division switches lie at the heart of telephone switching, the real cost of a switching system is usually not in the switch, but in the associated line cards. A line card converts analog voice from the customer into digital samples. A central office needs only one switch for a hundred thousand customers, but one line card for each customer![2] Thus, even with cheap line cards, their costs dominate the cost of a central office.

Stepping back a bit further, the cost of line cards, in turn, is dwarfed by the cost of laying copper wire from a central office to customer premises. This "local loop" is responsible for nearly 80% of the cost of telephone infrastructure. Similarly, at long-distance switching centers, switching costs are dwarfed by the cost of laying long-distance transmission lines, acquiring rights of way, and the cost of writing, updating, and maintaining complex switch-control software. Thus, although clever optimizations in switching are of academic interest, in the larger scheme of

---

[2]To be precise, we need one analog-to-digital conversion circuit per customer. In practice, typical line cards contain 16 of these circuits.

things, saving a few thousand crosspoints is not likely to make the overall cost of providing telephone service much lower.

8.3 Packet switching

In a circuit switch, the output port of a sample is completely decided by the time at which it arrives at an input port. At every time slot, we can trace the path taken by an incoming sample to a particular output port. Thus, a circuit switch does not need a sample to carry a header to switch it. In contrast, with a packet switch, incoming packets carry a destination field that allows them to be stored and transmitted later. Consequently, unlike in a circuit switch, the destination of an incoming packet is no longer a function of its arrival time. Thus, we cannot statically allocate a path through the switch at each time slot. Instead, a port mapper examines packet headers to determine the output port for incoming packets.

In this section, we will study two types of packet switches: virtual circuit ATM switches and datagram routers. The difference between them is that ATM switches handle fixed-size packets and the port mapper decides a destination based on the packet's VCI. In contrast, a router handles variable-size packets, and the port mapper has to parse the entire destination address to decide a packet's destination. These are small enough differences that we will treat both the same, calling them both "switches." We discuss the effects of packet size on performance toward the end of this section.

Repeaters, bridges, routers, and application-level gateways

Datagram switches are given different names depending on their position in the protocol stack. *Repeaters* operate at the physical level and repeat the input signal on one or more outputs, amplifying the signal strength. They allow a link to span a longer distance. *Bridges* operate at the datalink layer to partition a shared LAN medium (such as Ethernet) into segments. A bridge forwards incoming packets by buffering them, then contending as any other station would on the destination segment. Bridges discover the end-systems on each segment by snooping on the source datalink-layer address on packets arriving on that segment. Incoming packets whose source and destination are in the same segment do not leave the segment. Carefully partitioned segments, therefore, allow network administrators to build large shared-medium LANs that still have good performance.

Routers operate at the network layer. They examine a packet's network-level address (such as an IP address) to forward it on one of their output links. Unlike bridges, which discover the network topology mainly by observing their inputs, routers do so by participating in elaborate routing protocols (described in Chapter 11). Routers allow LANs or smaller networks to be interconnected, to form *inter-networks*. A good reference on bridges and routers is reference [Perlman 92].

An *application-level gateway* is a datagram switch that operates at the application layer. Unlike peer routers or bridges, which communicate with each other over single hops, peer application-level gateways may be separated by the diameter of the network. Application-level gateways usually translate among data representations or protocols. For example, exchanging electronic mail between the Internet and a commercial online service which has its own mail protocol requires the intervention of an application-level gateway. Such gateways typically operate on entire messages, with full knowledge of application semantics, instead of at the packet level. Common examples of application-level gateways are mail gateways; Web proxy gateways, which cache Web traffic to reduce access time to popular Web sites; and *transcoders*, which convert multimedia data from one format to another.

As we progress from repeaters to bridges, routers, and application-level gateways, we gain functionality, but lose forwarding speed. To obtain the best performance, forwarding functionality should be pushed to as low a level in the protocol stack as possible.

Port mappers in datagram routers

Before studying packet switching, we briefly examine the design of port mappers for routers. Routers examine an incoming packet's destination address and match it with a routing table to decide its destination interface number. This matching is nontrivial because the router must *efficiently* find the *best* match between the destination and all the entries in the routing table. For example, assume that packets are addressed using IP addresses (described in Section 3.3.1), and the incoming packet has a destination of 128.32.1.20. If the routing table has entries for 128.32.*, 128.32.1.*, and 128.32.1.20, the router should match only the third entry. This best-match problem is hard because a routing table may have tens of thousands of entries.

A *trie* data structure is commonly used to find the best match [Perlman 92]. We define an *alphabet* to be a finite set of elements used to form address strings. A trie is a tree where each node corresponds to a string that is defined by the path to that node from the root. The children of each node correspond to every element of the alphabet. In practice, to keep things simple and maximize access speed, each node is represented by an array that is as long as the alphabet size. An entry in the array can have one of three values:

(a) a pointer to another array, indicating that better matches exist
(b) a special symbol indicating that no better matches are known
(c) a null pointer, indicating that the longest match is to the parent of this node

In cases (a) and (b), the element is also annotated with the output interface for route to the destination associated with that node. Incoming packets are forwarded on the interface number corresponding to the best match. The operation of a trie is illustrated in the next example.

EXAMPLE 8.5

Consider the trie in Figure 8.10. In the figure, the alphabet consists of the natural numbers {0, 1, 2, . . . , 255}. The root is associated with the null string and has the default route for the router (the next hop for packets whose destination is unknown). The root has 256 possible children, of which children 128, 32, and 10, corresponding to IP addresses 128.*, 32.*, and 10.*, have known routes. Thus, at the top level array, the tenth and thirty-second entries contain a special symbol annotated with the interface number for the next hop toward that destination, and the 128th entry contains a pointer to the next level of the trie. All other entries are null, corresponding to the default route. The second level of the trie, below 128, corresponds to a better match for certain addresses. Here, the trie stores pointers to lower levels at the thirty-second and fifty-fourth entries, corresponding to IP addresses 128.32.* and 128.54.*. All other entries are null. Similarly, the 128.32 level is expanded to form more detailed routes.

When an IP packet with a destination, say, 128.32.1.2, arrives at the router, it follows the trie links as far down as possible. The router first parses the incoming address into its fields, which are letters in the alphabet. Here, the string is "128, 32, 1, 2." At each level, if the corresponding element has a pointer to the next

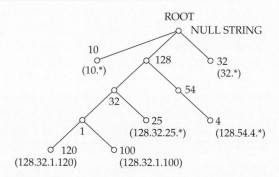

Figure 8.10: A trie. The trie data structure allows efficient search for the best match of a given string. Each node represents a partial string (and an associated output interface) and each child represents one possible single-letter extension. The leaves represent the strings stored in the trie. In this example, we show some of the strings stored by this trie, such as 128.32.1.120 and 128.54.4.*. For an incoming packet with a destination 128.32.1.2, the best match is the node 128.32.1.*, and the router forwards the packet to the destination interface associated with that node.

level, we follow the pointer down. If the corresponding element has the special symbol, we know the correct interface from its annotation. If the element has a null pointer, we use the interface associated with the parent level. In this case, we follow the trie using the pointer for 128 at the top level, to 32 at the next level, and to 1 at the third level. The pointer to 2 is null, so the route is the one associated with 128.32.1.*. This algorithm results in determining the best possible match for a string with four elements with at most four matching operations. Thus, a trie efficiently solves the best-match problem.

We can improve a trie's performance in two ways. First, using the principle of locality (see Section 6.3.4), we expect that if we see a packet for a particular destination, we are likely to see packets for the same destination again soon. Thus, we store the translation from a destination to its output port for recently seen destinations in a cache, checking the cache before traversing the trie. The second trick is to optimize for the common case. It is likely that certain addresses will be looked up more often than others (for example, addresses corresponding to local destinations). We can make these addresses part of the first level of the trie, trying them before traversing the trie. This is essentially a permanent cache based on previous knowledge of the system. Depending on the workload, these two tricks can dramatically improve trie performance.

8.3.1   Blocking in packet switches

In a packet switch, as with a circuit switch, we can have both *internal* blocking and *output* blocking. A blocked packet is either dropped or buffered. In a circuit switch, if two circuits block each other, they interfere with each other once every frame time, and therefore the switch must reject one of them. In contrast, in a packet switch, even if packets *a* and *b* on connections *A* and *B* block each other, subsequent packets on *A* and *B* may not block each other. Thus, in a circuit switch, either a path from an input to an output is available at call-setup time and therefore is always available, or a path is not available at call-setup time and the call is rejected. In contrast, in a packet switch, it is nearly impossible to predict whether individual packets on a connection will be blocked. To minimize blocking loss, we can use one or more of the following techniques:

- *Overprovisioning:* By making internal links faster than inputs, the switch fabric can forward packets from more than one input in the time it takes for a single packet to arrive. Thus, for example, if the internal links are twice as fast as input links, when two packets collide, *both* contending packets can be carried, one after the other, in the switch fabric, before subsequent arrivals on those inputs.

- *Buffers:* By placing buffers at the input or in the switch fabric, we can delay packets that do not enter the switch fabric until a link is available. Of course, persistent blocking, due to overcommitment of the switch fabric, leads to packet loss. The switch controller must ensure, at the time of call admission, that the switch fabric can handle all admitted calls.

- *Backpressure:* Backpressure allows a stage in a multistage switching fabric to prevent the previous stage from sending it any more data. If an output is blocked, backpressure signals quickly propagate back to the input, forcing packet buffering and packet loss to happen only at the inputs. Thus, with backpressure, the switch fabric needs only a minimal amount of buffering.

- *Sorting and randomization:* As we will see in Section 8.4, for certain types of switch fabrics, preceding the switch fabric by a sorting or randomization stage reduces internal blocking in the fabric.

- *Parallel fabrics:* By connecting input ports to output ports with multiple parallel switching fabrics, packets can be carried from inputs to outputs in parallel. This reduces contention for the fabric, but requires faster access to output buffers. This is the spatial analog of running the fabric faster.

8.3.2 Three generations of packet switches

It is convenient to categorize packet switches into three types, which make different trade-offs between cost and performance. These are also called three switching generations, though they reflect an evolution in switching capacity rather than in technology. Thus, a first-generation switch might use more sophisticated technology than a second-generation switch. Given the same technology, however, a second-generation switch achieves a higher capacity (but only at a higher cost). Table 8.2 summarizes the characteristics of switches from the three generations.

Generation	Description	Bottleneck	Example
1	CPU transfers packets among adaptor cards	I/O bus, CPU, main memory, or host adaptor	Low-end Internet routers
2	Controllers on adaptor cards transfer packets among each other over a shared bus	Shared bus	High-end routers, low-end ATM switches
3	Switch fabric allows parallel transfers over multiple buses	Output queue controller or input-queue arbiter	High-end ATM switches

Table 8.2: The three generations of packet switches.

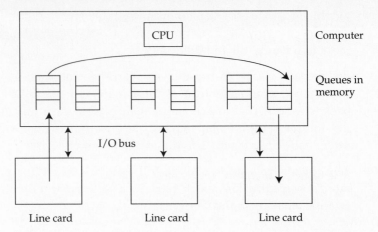

Figure 8.11: First-generation packet switch. The CPU stores packets received on line cards in its main memory, and routes them to output queues. These, in turn, contend for access to an output line card and are scheduled by a software packet scheduler.

8.3.3 First-generation switches

A first-generation packet switch is just a computer with multiple line cards (Figure 8.11). The processor periodically polls each input line card or is interrupted on packet arrival. When a packet is available, the processor reads the packet's header, determines the proper output port from a routing table, and deposits it in the appropriate output buffer. The processor also arbitrates access to the output lines. The switch buffers packets in the computer's main memory. Thus, the main cost of this switch is typically for the computer itself, followed by the cost of adaptors. Most Ethernet bridges and low-cost packet routers in the Internet are first-generation switches.

The advantage of a first-generation switch is that it is simple to build. Unfortunately, a first-generation switch usually has lower performance than a second- or third-generation switch built with the same technology (although it also costs less). The bottleneck in such a switch may be the processor, the main memory, the I/O bus, or the host-adaptor card. With recent advances in processor technology, fast processors far outstrip the I/O bus, which is usually the bottleneck. With newer I/O buses, however, in some recent designs, host-adaptors have become the bottleneck. Thus, in a first-generation switch, the bottleneck resource changes with changes in technology. A careful designer can overcome bottleneck resource limitations by employing some of the techniques discussed in Chapter 6.

EXAMPLE 8.6

Consider a first-generation packet switch built with an Intel Pentium 133-MHz processor. Assume that the mean packet size is 500 bytes, and that an interrupt takes

10 microseconds to process. Also assume that the packet-forwarding code takes 200 machine cycles independent of the packet size, and that it takes 50 ns to read or write a 4-byte word from memory.[3] (a) How fast can it switch packets if the processor is involved in data copies? (b) How fast can it switch packets if the processor only copies a 20-byte header, and the data is transferred directly from one host adaptor to another?

Solution: A data copy loop looks something like this:

```
register ← memory (read_ptr)
memory(write_ptr) ← register
read_ptr ←read_ptr + 4
write_ptr ←write_ptr + 4
counter ←counter − 1
if (counter is not 0) jump to top of loop
```

The counter is initialized to the size of the copy and read and write pointers are appropriately initialized. The loop has two memory accesses, three register operations, a test, and a branch. We assume that the register operations and test take one machine cycle each. Since the processor is a 133-MHz processor, each cycle is 7.52 ns, and so these four operations take 30.08 ns. Added to the 100 ns for the two memory accesses, the time to copy a 4-byte word is 130.08 ns.

(a) The 500-byte packet corresponds to 125 4-byte words. If the entire packet is copied, the copy takes $125 * 130.08$ ns $= 16.26$ μs. The packet-forwarding code takes $200 * 7.52 = 1.504$ μs. Thus, the total processing time is 17.764 μs. Added to the interrupt time, this gives us 27.764 μs per 500-byte packet, or an effective data rate of 144.1 Mbps.

(b) If the processor only copies the header, it takes $20/4 * 130.08 = 650.4$ ns to copy the header. Processing the packet takes an addition $200 * 7.52$ ns $= 1.504$ μs. Added to the interrupt time, this gives us a total of 12.15 μs per 500-byte packet, or an effective rate of 329.21 Mbps.

These back-of-the-envelope calculations make some strong assumptions. First, we assume that the bottleneck in the system is the processor. If the host adaptors or the I/O bus cannot keep up with the processor, the performance of the switch is dictated by their capacities. Second, we assume that each packet requires an interrupt. In reality, packets arrive as bursts, so a processor pays the interrupt overhead only once for two or three packets. This increases its switching capacity. On the other hand, we assume that the processor is doing no other work. Taking into account the overhead for doing route-table computation and other processing, the rate should be lower than what we computed. With any luck, this overhead cancels

---

[3]We are ignoring cache effects, which can reduce the costs of accessing memory words, depending on complex parameters such as the cache line size, the read-ahead policy, and the overall system workload.

the gain from amortizing interrupts over many packets, so that the calculations are likely to be at least approximately correct. This sort of back-of-the-envelope calculation, with a "fudge factor" to account for unknown effects, is how systems are built in real life.

8.3.4 Second-generation switches

In a second-generation switch, line cards have some intelligence, so that they are able to decide a packet's output port without help from a central processor (Figure 8.12). In other words, the port mapping functionality is distributed among the line cards. When a packet arrives at a line card, it matches the destination address (or VCI) with entries in a routing cache. In an ATM switch, the cache is guaranteed to contain an entry for the VCI, because it is put there by the switch controller at the time of call establishment. If a route is found, the card sends the packet over a bus to an output port. If no route is found, the card sends the packet to a control computer, which forwards the packet and installs a route in the line card. Note that if a packet is sent to a control computer (which might happen in a router, but not in an ATM switch), packets can be reordered, because packets forwarded on the fast path may be sent before packets that arrived earlier, but were forced to go through the slower path. High-end packet switches, such as the 7500 series of routers from Cisco Systems, are examples of second-generation switches. Another example is FORE Systems' ASX-200 series ATM switch.

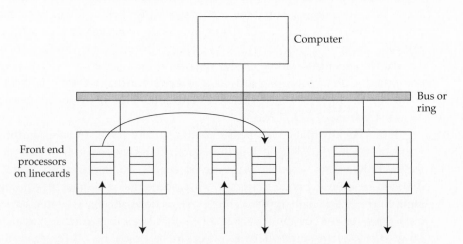

Figure 8.12: Second-generation switch. In a second-generation switch, the routing functions migrate to the front-end processors, which also provide input and output queues. The processors contend for access to a shared bus or ring, which is therefore the bottleneck in the system. If routes cannot be found, packets are handed to the control computer, which routes packets and installs a new route in the front-end processor.

An interesting variation of the slow-path/fast-path approach is used in switches from Ipsilon Networks Inc., which introduced the concept of *IP switching*, also called *cell-switched routing* [NL 96]. Given an underlying ATM network that carries IP traffic, the idea is to build an IP router by adding an adjunct processor to an ATM switch. Normally, IP datagrams arriving to the router as cells on an ATM virtual circuit are reassembled into datagrams and routed by the adjunct processor as in a first-generation datagram switch. When the adjunct detects a sequence of packets to the same destination interface on a given virtual circuit, it requests the previous router along the path (the upstream router) to send these packets on a particular VCI. If the upstream router complies, the router installs a route to that destination interface for that virtual circuit in the ATM switch. Subsequent cells arriving to the router on that virtual circuit are switched as ATM cells without intermediate reassembly. One way to view this is that packets on the slow path that place a heavy demand on switching resources are allocated a VCI in the fast path, so that subsequent packets need not use the slow path. In this sense, the incoming stream of packets constitutes implicit ATM signaling.

The line cards in a second-generation switch communicate with each other using a shared bus or a ring. The bus (or ring, as in the *Paris* switch [GCM 87]) is usually the bottleneck in the system, since it carries data from all the ports. If each input line card has bandwidth b, and there are N line cards, then the bus must have a bandwidth of Nb. Second-generation switches with 10-Gbps aggregate capacity are commercially available today.

If the network is connection oriented, we can reduce a switch's cost by placing port-mapping logic on a shared port-mapper card, instead of on every line card. At the time of call setup, the switch controller updates a routing table in the port mapper. Line cards forward all incoming packets to the port mapper, which examines the header, reads the routing table, and forwards the packet to its output line card. Since every call must be set up, every incoming packet is guaranteed an entry in the table, so there are no cache misses, and we can make the port mapper very fast. Detecting routing inconsistencies is also easier, because there is only a single copy of the routing table in the switch (besides the one in the switch controller). In this approach, every packet makes its way to the port mapper and then back to another line card, doubling the contention for the bus. We can avoid this by using two unidirectional buses, as in Datakit switches [Fraser 83].

8.3.5   Third-generation switches

In a third-generation switch, the shared bus of a second-generation switch is replaced by a *switch fabric*, which, in its most general form, is an interconnection of buses and switching elements that provides multiple parallel paths from any input to any output (Figure 8.13). When packets arrive at an input port, a port mapper module or a shared control processor tags them with the destination port ID and hands them to the switch fabric. The switch elements automatically route it to the correct output port, where the packet is queued. Thus, the switching fabric is *self-routing*. Although switch fabrics can carry variable-length packets, we will assume, unless otherwise specified, that all packets are the same size, such as, for example, ATM cells.

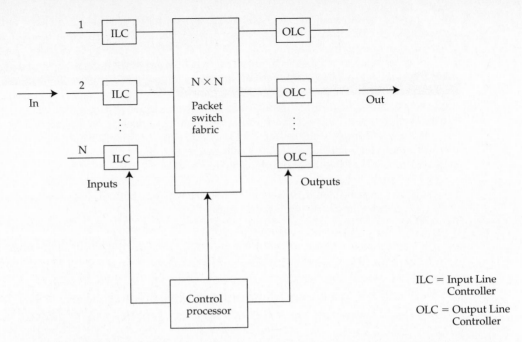

Figure 8.13: Third-generation switch. In a third-generation switch, the shared bus of a second-generation switch is replaced by a switch fabric. Packets arriving at the input ports are simultaneously introduced into the switch fabric, where they are routed in parallel to output ports.

The position of the bottleneck in a third-generation switch depends on whether it has buffers mainly at the input, or mainly at the output. If buffers are at the output, packets arriving at multiple inputs must be loaded into the output buffers rapidly to prevent packet loss. Thus, the bottleneck in the switch is the speed at which we can write packets into the output buffer. If packets are mainly at the input, the bottleneck is the speed at which an arbiter can decide which inputs should be allowed access to the switch fabric and the output line. We will study the effect of these bottlenecks on performance in more detail in Section 8.5. We now turn our attention to switch fabric designs, primarily for third-generation switches.

8.4   Switch fabrics

A switch fabric is a set of links and switching elements that transfers a packet from any input port to any output port. Many switch fabric designs have been proposed in the literature, of which we will study only a few important representatives. Variations and extensions of these designs can be found in some excellent surveys and the references therein [AD 89, DLV 89, Jacob 90, OSMKM 90, Tobagi 90]. Table 8.3 summarizes the fabrics studied in this section.

Name	Subsection
Crossbar	8.4.1
Broadcast	8.4.2
Switching element	8.4.3
Banyan	8.4.4
Sorting and merging fabrics	8.4.5
Batcher–Banyan	8.4.6

Table 8.3: Selected switch fabrics.

Why are third-generation switches rare?

Though many proposals for complicated switch fabrics have been studied on paper, few have been implemented, and fewer yet used in commercial products. There are two reasons why this happened. First, building a switch is much harder than designing it on paper. Many academic designs ignore important practical considerations such as switch cost, robustness to hardware defects and failures, need for clock synchronization, and manufacturability. These designs are doomed to failure right from the start. Even the designs that are practical and implementable have not been commercially successful because the switching capacity of second-generation switches has proven sufficient for most purposes. Only in the mid-1990s, as the demand for network bandwidth skyrocketed, have manufacturers turned to third-generation switch fabric designs. Thus, we are likely to see more switches using these designs in the years to come. In any case, though much research effort has gone into switch fabric design, many researchers now believe that the hard part in designing a switch is not the switch fabric, but deciding where to place buffers and how to schedule access to the buffers and bandwidth. We study these problems in Chapter 9.

8.4.1   Crossbar

The simplest switch fabric is a crossbar (Figure 8.5). An $N \times N$ crossbar has N input buses, N output buses, and N^2 crosspoints, which are either on or off. If the (i, j) crosspoint is on, then the ith input is connected to the jth output. A crossbar is internally nonblocking.

A crossbar needs a *switching schedule* that tells it which inputs to connect to which outputs at a given time. If packets arrive at fixed intervals, for example, if all the connections are constant bit rate, then the schedule can be computed in advance. Otherwise, the switch has to compute the schedule on-the-fly.

If a switch has N inputs and outputs, a perfectly used crossbar is N times faster than a bus-based (second-generation) switch. However, if two packets at the inputs want to

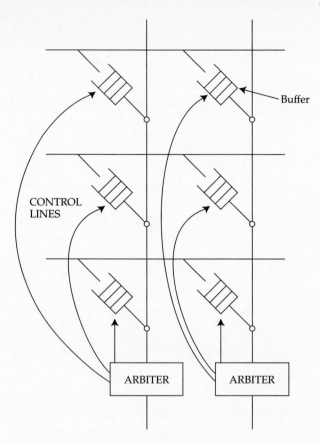

Figure 8.14: A buffered crossbar. In this variation of a crossbar, each crosspoint is associated with a buffer. Incoming packets are buffered at the crosspoint, and a per-output arbiter schedules a packet from one of the crosspoint buffers for transmission on the output trunk.

go to the same output, then they suffer from output blocking and the crossbar is not fully used. We can avoid output blocking by either running the crossbar N times faster than the inputs (which is hard to do, and expensive), or placing buffers inside the crossbar. One interesting variation is to put a buffer at every crosspoint (Figure 8.14) [Marcus 69]. An arbiter per output line then decides which of the buffered packets to serve. This is used in the Scorpio 10-Gbps ATM switch [Scorpio 95].

As with circuit-switched crossbars, packet-switched crossbars do not scale well. They are suitable for small switches, or as building blocks for larger switches.

8.4.2   Broadcast

Another simple switching fabric is based on broadcast (Figure 8.15). The switch tags a packet arriving at any input with the output port number and broadcasts it to all outputs.

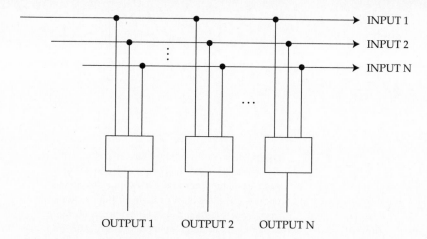

Figure 8.15: A broadcast switch. Each input is broadcast on a bus. Line cards at output ports load packets that match their port address. This configuration makes it easy to implement multicast in hardware.

Each output port stores incoming packets that match its own port address in an output queue. A scheduler resolves contention for the output trunk. In contrast to a crossbar, a broadcast switch does not have to be scheduled for each packet transmission. This comes at the expense of address matching logic at each output.

Since the switch broadcasts all packets to all output ports, a small change makes it easy to implement hardware multicast. Instead of matching port addresses, each output port matches a packet's VCI. At the time of call setup, each port is informed of the VCIs it must match, and at the time of data transfer, each port matches a packet's VCI with its list of eligible VCIs.

The problem with a broadcast switch, as with a crossbar, is that it does not scale. In an $N \times N$ switch, each output must be connected to N buses, and it needs to do an address match on packets arriving at all the inputs. For a thousand-port switch, each output needs to be connected to a thousand inputs, which becomes a physical routing problem. Moreover, address matching must be done N times faster than the speed of an input line, which becomes hard at high speeds and for large N. For example, typical input line speeds are 155-Mbps, which corresponds to 2.73 microseconds per ATM cell. For a 1000×1000 switch, the output port must do one address match every 2.73 nanoseconds! However, we can cheaply build the equivalent of an 8×8 crossbar using broadcast, then use the techniques described next to compose these 8×8 stages to build larger switches.

8.4.3   Switch fabric element

We can build a variety of complex switch fabrics using a basic fabric element consisting of two inputs, two outputs, and an optional buffer (Figure 8.16). Packets arrive simultaneously at both inputs. The element examines the packet header and uses a switching

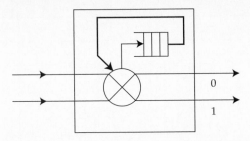

Figure 8.16: A switching-fabric element. This element is repeated many times in a switch fabric. It has two inputs and two outputs. Incoming packets are either sent to their output of choice (usually determined from a bit in the routing tag) or stored in a buffer. Stored packets contend with incoming packets at subsequent times.

rule to direct incoming packets to one or both outputs. For example, if the packet has a 1-bit header, the rule might be: forward on the upper output if the bit is 0, and on the lower output if the bit is 1. If both packets at the inputs want to go to the same output, then one of them is forwarded, and the other is either buffered (if there is space in the buffer) or dropped. We can generalize an element to N inputs and outputs, where the distribution inside an element uses a broadcast or a crossbar switch.

Switching fabrics based on switching-fabric elements share some attributes:

- For an $N \times N$ switch, if each element switches $b \times b$ lines, then the switch has $\lceil \log_b N \rceil$ stages, with $\lceil N/b \rceil$ elements per stage. For example, a 4096×4096 switch built with 8×8 blocks has four stages, with 512 elements in each stage.

- Once a packet has been labeled with the correct output port, it will automatically make its way from any input to its correct output. This is called *self-routing*.

- The fabric is recursively composed from smaller components that resemble the larger network. In other words, the topology of a fabric with bN elements is similar to that of a fabric with N elements and is built from b fabrics with N elements each.

- The fabric can be synchronous or asynchronous. In a synchronous fabric, all elements forward packets simultaneously. In an asynchronous fabric, elements forward packets as they arrive. An asynchronous fabric must have per-element buffering, but it permits variable-length packets.

- The fabrics are regular and suitable for VLSI implementation.

8.4.4   Banyan

The simplest self-routing switch fabric is the *Banyan* (Figure 8.17) [GL 73]. In a Banyan switching fabric, incoming packets are tagged with the output port expressed in binary.

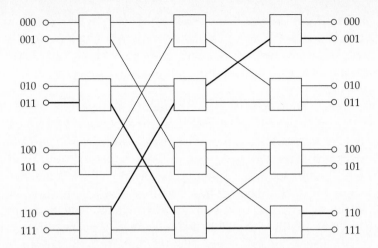

Figure 8.17: A Banyan switch fabric. A Banyan switch fabric consists of switch elements that route packets either to port 0 (their upper output) or port 1 (their lower output), depending on a specific position in the routing tag. In the figure, we see the route followed by two packets with tags 110 and 001 as they enter from ports 011 and 110 respectively. Verify that the packets would be routed to the proper output irrespective of their input port.

Each switching element at the ith layer looks at the ith bit in the header to make its decision: if the bit is 1, the packet is forwarded to the lower output, and otherwise to the upper output. A Banyan fabric with 2^n outputs needs n stages, with 2^{n-1} elements in each stage. Thus, the total number of elements is $n2^{n-1}$.

Let us see how a Banyan switch works. Number the input and output ports in binary, starting from 0, so that the uppermost input port and the uppermost output port are labeled 0. We would like a packet with a binary label to reach the corresponding output port. Note that a single switching fabric element correctly routes packets based on a single bit of their routing tag. In other words, it is a 2×2 switch. We now take two 2×2 switches and label them 0 and 1. We take two other 2×2 switches and place them before the ones labeled 0 and 1. When a packet enters a switching element in the first stage, it is sent to the 2×2 switch labeled 0 if the first bit in its routing tag is 0; otherwise, it is sent to the switch labeled 1. This combination forwards packets labeled 00, 01, 10, or 11 correctly and is a 4×4 Banyan network. We can extend this to the third stage, by labeling two 4×4 switches as 0 and 1, and preceding them with switching elements that forward packets to one of them based on the first bit of the routing tag. Note that this gives us several equivalent 8×8 Banyans, only one of which is shown in Figure 8.17.

If two incoming packets both want to go to the same output port, they collide and *block* at some internal switching element. For example, in Figure 8.17, if the top two inputs have packets destined to outputs 010 and 011, they collide at the first stage. To prevent packet loss, we can introduce packet buffers in each switching element [DJ 81, TW 83, Turner 85, Turner 88]. Thus, blocking results only in packet delay, rather than packet loss. If the same switching element repeatedly blocks, because of the packet arrival pattern (that is, it is a *hot spot*), then packet loss will eventually occur. If we want to avoid packet loss completely, the buffer size must be large enough to hold the worst-case input traffic pattern. This is a problem in traffic management, which we will discuss in Chapter 14.

A buffered banyan switch has two significant problems. First, introducing buffers in each switching element makes each element expensive. Since the elements are repeated hundreds or thousands of times, this increases the overall cost of the switch. Second, if the switch is to have zero loss, it can be shown that the utilization of a buffered switch, even with uniform random traffic, is limited to 45% when each switch element has a single buffer [Jenq 83]. Though this increases to 60% with a buffer size of 4, it is still low.

Instead of installing buffers in each switching element, an alternate proposal is to *check* whether a path is available before launching packets from the inputs [HA 87]. In this three-phase scheme, input ports send requests to the outputs during the first phase. Some requests are lost to blocking, and in the second phase, the output ports inform the winners that they can now send packets. These are then sent in the third phase. The three-phase scheme thus avoids packet loss, but require buffers at the inputs. As we will see in Section 8.5.1, if these input buffers are organized as FIFOs, then the throughput of the switch is restricted to 58%. A small variation reduces the number of phases. In this scheme, input ports send the entire packet in the first phase, but also store a copy. In the second phase, the output ports inform the winners, who then purge their copies. The losers try again in the next round.

A third way to improve Banyan performance is to use several Banyans in tandem [TKC 91]. In this design, when two packets collide in a switching element, one of them is misrouted and marked with a tag. The switch diverts untagged packets to the output port at the end of the first stage, and reintroduces misrouted packets into a second Banyan stage, where they have a second chance to reach a given destination. This process continues for several stages, until, at the end of the last stage, misrouted packets are dropped. It can be shown that for a 32×32 switch, with uniform random traffic, a tandem of nine Banyans is sufficient to reduce the packet drop probability to 10^{-9}. Of course, this performance comes at a price. First, since the switch uses several Banyans instead of just one, the hardware is much more expensive. Second, the switch can reorder packets. Finally, since outputs have to be prepared to accept packets simultaneously from any one of k stages, they have to be run k times faster than the inputs.

Finally, we can avoid the problems associated with blocking in Banyan networks by choosing the order in which packets appear at the input ports. Consider the ordered set of output port numbers of packets waiting for service at the input of a Banyan switch. For example, if input port 001 has a packet destined for output port 011, input port 010 has a packet for 010, input port 011 has no packet awaiting service, and input port 100 has a packet for output port 011, the set is {X, 011, 010, X, 011, X, X, X}, where X marks a gap. It can be shown that if this set is sorted, with gaps and duplicates removed, then a Banyan network preceded by a *perfect-shuffle* network is internally nonblocking

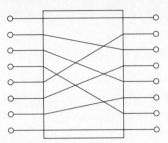

Figure 8.18: A shuffle-exchange network. If sorted inputs pass through a shuffle network and enter a Banyan network, the Banyan network suffers no collisions.

(so switch elements do not need buffers) [Lee 88] (Figure 8.18). Continuing with our example, we first sort the inputs to be {010, 011, 011, X, X, X, X, X}, then remove duplicates to form {010, 011, X, X, X, X, X, X}, then shuffle them using the network in Figure 8.18, to form {010, X, 011, X, X, X, X, X}. When this is presented to the Banyan network, it is nonblocking (which can be verified from Figure 8.17). Operationally, we achieve this by placing a *sorting, trap,* and *shuffle* network before a Banyan fabric. The sort network sorts the inputs in order of their output ports, the trap network removes duplicates, and the shuffle network implements a perfect shuffle. Since these networks are typically cheaper than having per-element buffering, this reduces the overall cost of the switch fabric.

8.4.5 Sorting and merging networks

Sorting networks can be built from *merging* networks, that is, networks that take two sorted lists and merge them to make a larger sorted list [Batcher 68]. We call such a sorter network a *Batcher network* after its inventor. A Batcher network that sorts N inputs needs $\lceil \log N \rceil \lceil \log N + 1/2 \rceil$ stages.

How does a sorter work? For the moment, assume we know how to merge two sorted lists to form a longer sorted list. Then a strategy to sort by merging is as follows: we divide the list of N elements into pairs, and sort each pair. This gives us $N/2$ lists, each of which is sorted. Since we assume we know how to merge sorted lists, we can combine these to form $N/4$ sorted lists, with four elements each. We repeat to form $N/8$ sorted lists, with eight elements each, and so on. In the end, we get one fully sorted list. All we need, therefore, is a way to sort two elements, and a way to merge sorted lists. The first requirement is easily met using a comparator. The second requires a merging network, which we study next.

EXAMPLE 8.7

Sort the list 5, 7, 2, 3, 6, 2, 4, 5 by merging.

Solution: In the first step, we sort elements two-by-two to get four sorted lists, {5, 7}, {2, 3}, {2, 6}, and {4, 5}. In the second step, we merge adjacent lists to get two four-element lists: {2, 3, 5, 7} and {2, 4, 5, 6}. In the third step, we merge the two lists to create a fully sorted list: {2, 2, 3, 4, 5, 5, 6, 7}.

Merging networks

A merging network of size $2N$ takes two sorted lists of size N as inputs, and creates a merged list of size $2N$ (Figure 8.19). It consists of two N-sized merging networks. One of them merges all the even elements of the two inputs and the other merges all the odd elements. The outputs of the mergers are handed to a set of 2×2 comparators. It can be proved that this structure correctly implements merging [Batcher 68].

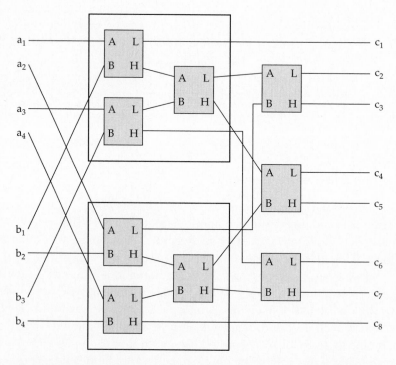

Figure 8.19: A merging network. This network takes two sorted lists and merges them to form a sorted list twice as long. The network is based on the idea that to merge two sorted lists, we need to merge their even and odd elements separately, then combine the outputs with a set of carefully placed comparators.

EXAMPLE 8.8

Merge the two lists {2, 3, 4, 7} and {2, 4, 5, 6}.

Solution: In the first stage, we merge even elements from the two lists, i.e., merge {2, 4} with {2, 5}. Recursing, we need to merge {2} with {2} and {4} with {5}, then compare them. The results of the two merges are {2, 2} and {4, 5}. Comparing the higher element of the first list with the lower element of the second list, we determine that the merged list is {2, 2, 4, 5}. We next merge {3, 7} with {4, 6}. This requires merging {3, 4} and {7, 6}. The results are {3, 4} and {6, 7}. Comparing the high and low elements, respectively, we get a merged list {3, 4, 6, 7}. Carrying out the comparisons shown in Figure 8.19, we get the final merged list {2, 2, 3, 4, 4, 5, 6, 7}.

8.4.6   Batcher–Banyan

A Batcher–Banyan network is composed from a Batcher network that sorts packets according to their output port numbers, followed by a trap network to remove duplicates, a shuffle network, and a Banyan network (Figure 8.20) [HK 84]. Since all the inputs are sorted, the Banyan is internally nonblocking. However, we still have to deal with trapped duplicates. One solution is to recirculate duplicates back to the entrance of the Batcher, so that in the next cycle they can compete with incoming packets. This is the technique used in the Starlite switch [HK 84]. The problem with this approach is that it requires at least half the Batcher's inputs to be devoted to recirculated packets. Moreover,

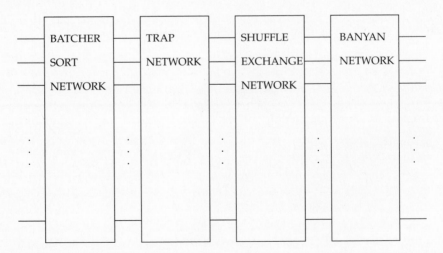

Figure 8.20: A Batcher–Banyan switch. By sorting the inputs to a Banyan switch, we avoid internal blocking. Thus, we precede the Banyan stage by a Batcher sorting stage, then use a trap network and a shuffle-exchange network to remove duplicates and gaps.

the recirculated packets have to be synchronized with fresh arrivals, which is hard to do at high clock speeds [CT 92]. An alternative is to take the output of the Batcher and pass them through multiple Banyan networks in parallel, where each packet that wants to go to the same output is put on a separate Banyan (this is also called *dilation*). This way, we remove the internal blocking in the Banyan at the expense of faster output buffers. This technique is used in the Sunshine switch [GHMSL 91].

Packet size and switch performance

One motivation for small, fixed-size cells in ATM is the claim that cells make it easier to build packet switches. Is this really true? It seems that although smaller packets make it easier to provide real-time delay guarantees in large switches, a small packet size may not help in building switches. Fixed-size packets may be similarly overrated. Let us see why.

In a first-generation switch, packet size is more important than whether the packets are fixed size. If the packets are small, then the interrupt overhead is large, so we prefer large packets to small ones. Moreover, fixed-size packets do not particularly improve performance either, because the switch deals with packets individually, independent of their size.

In a second-generation switch, packets contend for bus access, and the longer the packet, the more that can be sent after a single bus contention and setup cycle. Thus, larger packets are again more efficient for second-generation switches. Besides, because packets are handled serially on the bus, fixed-size packets do not help.

In a third-generation switch, having a small packet size neither helps nor hurts, because a self-routing switch fabric is oblivious to packet size. If anything, for an input-queued switch, a small packet size makes it harder to arbitrate among packets. So, even for a third-generation switch, larger packet sizes may be better. Fixed-size packets allow a switch fabric to forward packets in synchrony. However, the switch could easily fragment packets at the entrance to the fabric and reassemble them at the exit. Or, switch elements could have sufficient intelligence to deal with variable-size packets. Or, the fabric may only switch fixed-size headers, allowing the output port to transmit data from a shared-memory buffer. It is not clear that these, or other alternatives, are too expensive.

Thus, variable-size packet switches do not seem infeasible or overly expensive. It seems fair to say that the jury is still out on whether ATM cells are necessary for fast packet switching.

8.5   Buffering

Unlike circuit switches, packet switches need buffers because their inputs are unpredictable. Even if sources agree to regulate their behavior, they can still transmit bursts at any time. Moreover, contention for a shared output line means that even smooth inputs entering a packet network may become bursty. These bursts must then be forwarded through the switch fabric (or the shared bus) and the output trunk. If either is busy, packets from the bursts must either be buffered or dropped. Thus, to reduce packet loss, packet switches need buffers to hold packets as they wait for access to the switch fabric or the output trunk. We can place these buffers at the input port, at the output port, in the switch fabric, or in a common location shared by the input and output ports. Various combinations of these schemes are possible. In this section, we focus on the pros and cons of each choice. Note that though our discussion assumes that the switch is a third-generation switch, it applies equally to second-generation switches, where a single bus or ring replaces the switch fabric.

8.5.1 Input queuing

In a purely input-queued switch, packets are buffered at the input and released when they win access to both the switch fabric and the output trunk (Figure 8.21). An arbiter schedules access to the fabric depending on the status of the fabric and the output lines. Since packets leaving the input queue are guaranteed access to the fabric and the trunk, there is no need for an output queue.

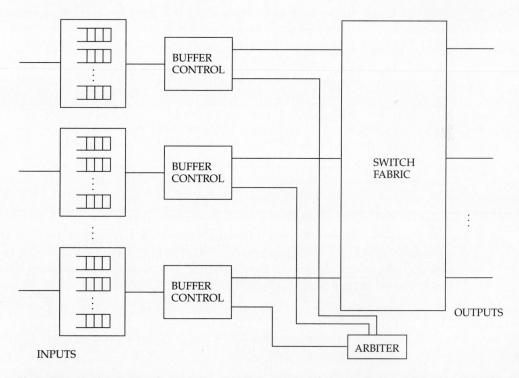

Figure 8.21: An input-queued switch. In a purely input-queued switch, all the buffering is done at the input ports. An arbiter releases packets from the input queue when a path through the switch fabric and the output trunk is available.

The main advantage of an input-queued switch is that links in the switch fabric (and the input queues themselves) need to run only as fast as the input lines. For an $N \times N$ switch, the only element that needs to run N times faster than the inputs is the arbiter. We can, however, easily build fast arbiters, since they typically require only combinational logic. As we will see, with output-queued switches, the output queues need to run faster than the inputs. Thus, for a given level of technology, we can build a faster input-queued switch than an output-queued switch.

The problem with an input-queued switch is that if the input queues are served in FIFO order, and the packet at the head of the queue is blocked, it blocks others in the queue, though they might have an open path to their output. We call this *head-of-line* blocking. If packets at each input arrive randomly distributed to all outputs (uniform random traffic), then it can be shown that an input-queued switch can achieve at most ~58.6% utilization [KHM 87, HK 88]. The performance is even worse if some outputs are favored over others.

EXAMPLE 8.9

Consider a 2 × 2 switch serving virtual circuits A, B, and C. Cells from A and B arrive at input 1, and cells from C arrive at input 2. Suppose A and C want to go to output port 1, and B wants to go to output port 2. The accompanying table shows a particular arrival pattern.

Time	Input	Virtual circuit	Sequence number	Destined for port
0	1	A	1	1
	2	C	1	1
1	1	B	1	2
	2	C	2	1

At time 0, the arbiter must choose a cell from either A or C for output port 1. Suppose the arbiter chooses the cell from C. Then, at time 1, the input queue at port 1 has cells from A and B awaiting service, and input port 2 has a cell from C awaiting service. If the arbiter decides to choose the cell from C again, the cell from B suffers from head-of-line blocking, because it has a path to 2, but cannot use it.

We can overcome head-of-line blocking by separating the queues for each output port at each input, and selecting one packet from each queue for each output port. More precisely, let the switch have N ports. Then, at each input, we maintain N queues, one per output. At each time step, the arbiter must select at most one packet from each input port so that, of all the packets selected from all the inputs, no two packets are destined to the same output port. The problem is hard because of the interdependencies when making this selection (this is explained at greater depth in Example 8.10).

An interesting algorithm for making this selection is a three-phase algorithm, similar to the one described in Section 8.4.4 in the context of Batcher–Banyan switch fabrics, called *Parallel Iterated Matching* [AOST 93]. In the first phase, each input port requests permission to transmit a packet from the set of destinations corresponding to packets queued at that input. The second phase (consisting of several *matching rounds*) selects a set of input ports for packet transmission in the third phase. In each matching round, an output grants permission to a randomly selected member of its set of requesting inputs. This may result in some input port getting more than one grant. In this case, the input randomly selects an output and withdraws its requests from the other output ports. The losing input ports and the losing output ports then repeat this process. It has been shown that three or more rounds of matching are usually adequate to find the best possible match, that is, a match that selects the most packets. The DEC Autonet2 switch carries out four rounds of matching in hardware before each packet transmission [AOST 93].

EXAMPLE 8.10

Consider a 4×4 switch that has input queues as shown in the table.

Input port #	Packets for output port #	Output port #	Requests from input port #
1	1, 2, 3	1	1, 2, 3
2	1, 3, 4	2	1, 4
3	1, 3	3	1, 2, 3
4	2, 4	4	2, 4

In the first round, input 1 sends requests to output ports 1, 2, and 3, input port 2 sends requests to output ports 1, 3, and 4, and so on. Each output port grants requests randomly. Suppose output ports 1, 2, and 3 all pick 1, and output port 4 picks 2. Now, input port 1 has three grants, so it may pick output port 1. Thus, output ports 2 and 3 and input ports 3 and 4 lose. In the second round, input port 3 sends a request to output port 3 (since 1 is already taken), and input port 4 sends a request to output port 2 (since 4 is already taken). These are automatically granted. Thus, in two rounds, the parallel iterated match has found the best possible match. The scheme does not guarantee fairness, since the same input may win repeatedly. This is unlikely, because of the randomness in the selection, but still possible.

Note that the arbiter, by choosing a packet for transmission, effectively allocates each connection with bandwidths and delays. It would, therefore, be useful to have the arbiter emulate a discipline such as weighted fair queuing, described in more detail in Section 9.4.4. A variation of the parallel iterated match scheme, called *fair arbitrated round robin*, can achieve nearly the same performance as a multipriority weighted fair queuing output-queue scheduler [LPR 96]. Other schemes for iterated matching are also described in reference [McKeown 95].

Arbitration schemes for input-queued switches are still on the research frontier. Since the arbiter is the bottleneck component in an input-queued switch, coming up with efficient and fair arbitration algorithms is an interesting open challenge [MAW 96].

8.5.2   Output queuing

A pure output queued switch buffers data only at its outputs (Figure 8.22). It serves packets from the output queue using one of the scheduling disciplines described in Chapter 9. Since output queues do not suffer from head-of-line blocking, we prefer output-queued switches to input-queued switches. However, in the worst case, packets at all the input ports may be destined to the same output port. If the switch has no input buffers and we want to avoid packet loss, the switch fabric must deliver N packets to a single output, and that output queue must store N packets in the time it takes for one packet to arrive at an input. This makes the switch fabric and queues more expensive than with input-queued switching. Given the same technology, building an input-queued switch is cheaper than building an output-queued switch. Alternatively, for the same cost, we can build a faster input-queued switch than we can an output-queued switch.

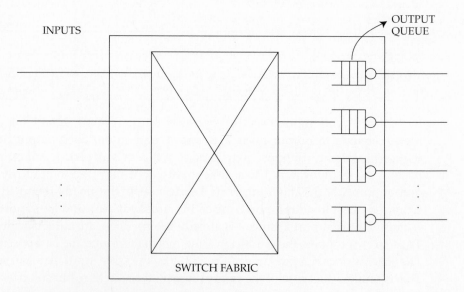

Figure 8.22: An output-queued switch. In a purely output-queued switch, buffers are found only at the output. The output buffers and the switch fabric have to run N times faster than the input trunks in order to avoid packet loss. This makes output-queued switches expensive. However, they allow fine-grained control on output scheduling.

EXAMPLE 8.11

Consider a 2×2 switch that has virtual circuits A and B arriving at input ports 1 and 2, both destined to output port 1. Suppose that cells from both A and B arrive at each time interval, and that the switch has no input queues. If the switch fabric does not serve the cells arriving at time 0 before the second set of cells arrive, then some cells will be lost. Similarly, the output queue at port 1 must be fast enough to store two cells in one cell arrival time. Otherwise, one of the two cells will be lost.

One way to reduce the cost of an output-queued switch is to use the *knockout* principle [YHA 87]. This principle states that if a switch has N inputs, it is very unlikely that *all N* packets will simultaneously arrive at the same output. Therefore, the output queue is run only S times faster, where $S < N$. It can be shown that for a variety of input distributions, $S = 8$ reduces the loss probability to less than 1 in 10^6. The knockout principle has been used in the *Knockout* switch (Figure 8.23) [YHA 87] and the *Gauss* switch [Vries 90]. The difficulty in designing the knockout circuit is to ensure that packet losses are fairly distributed among the incoming virtual circuits.

8.5.3 Shared memory

In a shared-memory switch, input and output ports share a common memory (Figure 8.24). Packets are stored in the common memory as they arrive, and the packet header is extracted and routed to the output port. When the output port scheduler schedules a packet for transmission, it removes the packet from the shared memory. Since the switch fabric only switches headers, it is easier to build. However, an $N \times N$ switch must read and write N packets in one packet arrival time. Because memory bandwidth is usually a highly constrained resource, this restricts the size of the switch.

EXAMPLE 8.12

What should be the read cycle time for a 64×64 shared-memory ATM switch, where each input runs at 155 Mbps and the memory is accessed as 4-byte words? As 53-byte words?

Solution: On a 155-Mbps trunk, a 53-byte ATM cell arrives once every 2.73 microseconds. Thus, the shared memory should be able to read 64 cells in 2.73 microseconds, or one 4-byte word every 3.05 nanoseconds. Typical dynamic RAM access times in 1996 using *Extended Data Out (EDO)* technology are 60 ns for the first word, and ~20 ns for subsequent words in the same memory line. Thus, we cannot build a 64×64 shared-memory switch with 4-byte-word accessed DRAM. Comparable static RAM access times are 2.5 to 50 ns, with the cost increasing very rapidly for

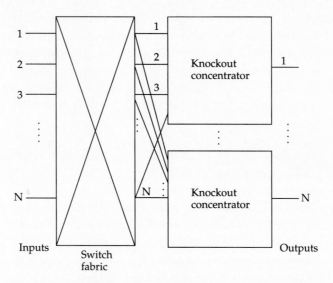

Figure 8.23: A knockout switch. The knockout principle states that an output is likely to receive packets simultaneously from only a few inputs. Thus, the output trunk runs only S times faster than the inputs, where $S < N$. If, however, more than S packets do arrive at the output, the knockout circuit eliminated some of the excess packets, fairly distributing the losses among the inputs.

shorter access times (moreover, with access times shorter than 5 ns or so, the length of the lead also adds delay, since an electromagnetic signal travels at most 30 cm in 1 ns). Therefore, while a 64×64 word-accessed shared memory switch is feasible with fast SRAM technology, it would be prohibitively expensive. An easier way to get fast memory access speed without paying for SRAMs is to access memory a cell at a time, instead of a word at a time. If we access 53 8-bit-wide memories simultaneously, we only need to read and write one cell every 42.9 nanoseconds. This is feasible with low-end SRAMs.

An interesting example of a shared memory switch is IDTI Inc.'s *Datapath* switch (Figure 8.25) [Kanakia 94]. The key idea in this switch is to integrate eight input and

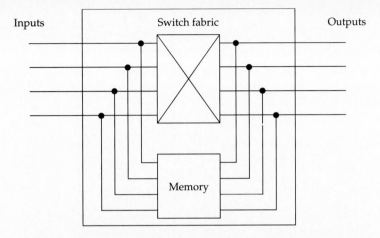

Figure 8.24: A shared memory switch. Incoming packets are stored in the memory and the packet header is routed to the output. When a packet is scheduled for transmission, the output port removes the packet from the shared memory. Note that only the header needs to be routed. Thus, packets can be variable size as long as the header size is fixed.

output port controllers and a shared memory module on a single VLSI chip. Serial inputs are parallelized in a shift register, and the entire shift register, containing an ATM cell, is read into the memory in parallel. This greatly reduces the read/write performance required from the memory (using the figures from Example 8.12, a read cycle for an 8×8 switch can take as long as 341.9 ns). A separate fabric-controller chip reads the packet header and assigns the packet to an output port. When the output port scheduler decides to serve a packet, it reads the entire packet in parallel into a shift register; the packet is converted to serial and transmitted. The VLSI packaging makes the chip economical: a 1.2 Gbps switch-on-a-chip costs only around $50. Datapath chips can be interconnected in various ways to form larger, buffered switch fabrics.

8.5.4 Buffered fabric

In a buffered-fabric switch, data buffers are associated with each switching element, with no input or output queues. Incoming packets are stored in the first stage's data buffers and propagate through the switch fabric, buffered in per-element buffers when a path to

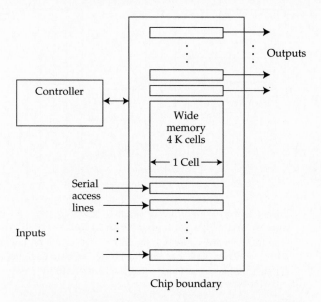

Figure 8.25: Datapath switch. A Datapath switch has eight input shift registers that shift in data from eight input lines and eight output registers that shift data out to eight output lines. An incoming ATM cell is buffered in a shift register, then written into the wide memory in a single write cycle. An adjacent controller decides the order in which cells in the memory are written to one of the output shift registers. Thus, Datapath is an 8×8 switch-on-a-chip.

the next element is unavailable. The output link scheduler schedules access to the output trunk from the last stage's buffers.

The advantage of a buffered-fabric switch is that buffers need to run only as fast as a switching element's fan-in ratio. Moreover, hardware backpressure between switching elements can be used to minimize the probability of buffer overflow. During overload, the resulting queue is distributed among several switching elements, so no queue gets too large. On the other hand, a switch that has many switching elements needs a lot of memory. Moreover, it is nearly impossible to achieve the equivalent of per-output per-VC weighted fair queuing, which is desirable for switches that provide per-connection quality of service guarantees (see Chapter 9 for details). Thus, a purely buffered-fabric switch does not seem practical. It seems more suitable when each switching element itself is a smaller switch, such as a shared-memory switch.

8.5.5 Hybrid schemes

So far, we have studied pure buffering schemes, where buffering is present only at one point in the switch. In reality, these schemes are easily combined. For example, a switch may have a few input buffers to deal with output blocking, with much larger output buffers that are scheduled according to a more sophisticated scheduling discipline. Many commercial switches use a shared bus, with each interface card providing both input and output buffering. The performance of a hybrid scheme depends on the degree to which it models one of the buffering schemes described earlier.

Transmission cost versus buffer cost

Many switch designers try to cut down on the number of switch buffers. Looking at the current (1996) cost of memory and transmission costs, this makes no sense: 80-ns DRAM memory costs about $20 a Mbyte, and long-haul transmission costs about $1000 a mile a year for DS3 trunks. If 10 Mbytes of memory increase link utilization for a 100-mile link by even 1%, the $200 it costs for memory is more than recovered in the $1000 saved per year. Thus, it is always better to have as large a memory as possible, if this results in better link utilization.

8.6 Multicasting

Thus far, we have assumed that at a switch, each incoming packet is destined for a single output. This is the case when the connection is a unicast connection. All connections in the telephone network are unicast. In the Internet and ATM networks, however, some connections are point-to-multipoint, or multipoint-to-multipoint. When a packet on a non-unicast connection arrives at a switch, it must be copied and transmitted to multiple outputs. In this section, we will study some strategies for multicast at the packet level. We will study multicast routing in Chapter 11.

We will assume that when a multicast packet arrives at a switch, the port mapper retrieves a list of output ports associated with that packet instead. The problem, then, is to copy the packet and distribute the copies to several outputs, and, for an ATM network, potentially assigning a different VCI for the packet at each output. We will study two separate problems: generating and distributing the copies, and VCI translation for the copies.

8.6.1 Generating and distributing copies

Packet copies can be generated and distributed either implicitly or explicitly. The implicit approach is suited to second-generation switches, and to broadcast-based or crossbar-based third-generation switches. An incoming multicast packet is placed on a bus and multiple output ports are simultaneously enabled. Thus, a copy of the packet is available at each output port. This approach is used in the *Paris* and *Datapath* switches, among others [GCM 87, Kanakia 94].

With a Banyan-like switch fabric, a switch must explicitly create packet copies. This is done by a *copy* network [Turner 85]. The input port attaches a header to a packet containing the number of copies needed, and this modified packet is introduced into the copy network. A copy network is similar to a Banyan network, except that each switching element places a copy of the packet on *both* outputs, decrementing the packet's copy count as it does so. At the exit of the copy network, therefore, several outputs receive copies of the packet. These can then be placed into a standard switching fabric. With both the explicit and the implicit approach, multicasting increases the output blocking probability.

8.6.2   Header translation

With a unicast connection, header translation from an incoming VCI to an output VCI can be done either at the input port or the output port. With a non-unicast connection, this translation is more easily done at the output port. The translation table is identical to a unicast translation table. With this approach, multicasting requires a switch to separate the port mapping and header translation table. The first table is at the input and maps an incoming VCI to a set of output ports. The second table translates a given VCI and input port to an outgoing VCI on the current output port. Thus, a switch must perform at least two table lookups per packet.

8.7   Summary

This chapter describes techniques for building circuit and packet switches (summarized in Table 8.4). We studied techniques for switching samples within a trunk (time-slot

Circuit switching (telephone switches)	Time division (8.2.3)	
	Space division (8.2.4)	
	Combined	Time–space (8.2.5)
		Time–space–time (8.2.6)
Packet switching (routers and ATM switches)	First generation (8.3.3)	
	Second generation (8.3.4)	
	Third generation (8.3.5)	Switch fabrics
		Crossbar (8.4.1)
		Broadcast (8.4.2)
		Banyan (8.4.5)
		Batcher–Banyan (8.4.6)

Table 8.4: Summary of switching techniques.

interchanging) and among trunks (space-division switching). We also saw how to combine time and space stages to build large circuit switches.

Packet switches fall into three generations. The first generation is just a computer with multiple link interfaces, with all the switching done by the processor. These can achieve speeds up to 300 Mbps with current processors. These speeds can be multiplied by a factor of eight or more with second-generation switches, where line cards are connected by a high-speed bus. Third-generation switches give even higher performance by using multiple parallel buses. We studied switching fabrics such as the Banyan interconnection network, and several variations that increase its performance. Finally, we studied the several alternatives for buffer placement: at the input, at the output, shared, or in the switch fabric. Input-queued switches might be best suited for building fast switches, although algorithms to arbitrate contention for an output port are still an active research area.

Review questions

1. What is the primary function of a switch?
2. What does a port mapper do?
3. Why is blocking reduced in transit switches?
4. How many inputs and outputs does a TSI have?
5. How does a TSI switch?
6. What is meant by internal blocking?
7. Does a crossbar suffer from internal blocking?
8. Can a multistage network have internal blocking?
9. Can a crossbar suffer from output blocking?
10. Can a multistage network have output blocking?
11. How many TSIs does a 64×64 TST switch have?
12. Why does a TS fabric have a smaller blocking rate than an S fabric?
13. Why does a TST fabric have a smaller blocking rate than a TS fabric?
14. What is a first-generation packet switch?
15. What is usually the bottleneck in a first-generation switch?
16. What is a trie used for?
17. What is the bottleneck in a second-generation switch?
18. Where is the queuing in a second-generation switch?
19. Why does a third-generation switch provide more bandwidth than a second-generation switch?
20. Can a crossbar used a precomputed schedule with VBR connections?
21. Does a broadcast switch need a switching schedule? Why or why not?
22. Do packets destined for output ports 000 and 001 at input ports 1 and 2 of a Banyan collide?
23. Do packets destined for output ports 001 and 000 at input ports 1 and 7 of a Banyan collide?
24. How does a tandem Banyan fabric work?

25. What is head-of-line blocking? What is a simple way to prevent it?
26. What problem does parallel iterated matching solve?
27. What is the fastest component in an input-queued switch?
28. What is the fastest component in an output-queued switch?
29. What is the bottleneck in a shared-memory switch?
30. Where is header translation done in a multicast ATM switch?

Exercises

8.1. Suppose the telephone network had no switches, and every user had a point-to-point link to every other user. How many lines are required for five users? Fifty users?

8.2. Assume that a router reorders packets so that a packet with sequence s may arrive after a packet with seqence $s + 2$ (but no later). If the maximum packet size is 500 bytes, how much buffering is needed at the receiver to guarantee zero loss?

8.3. How long does a 8-bit voice sample last on a T1? On a T3?

8.4. How many bytes of storage does a T3 TSI need?

8.5. (a) How would you use a TSI to build a switch that can handle 1024 individual T1 trunks? (b) How fast must the TSI read samples into its memory? Suppose you built it as a TS switch, with a 16×16 crossbar. (c) How fast do samples need to be read? (d) Describe an algorithm for a controller to find a path for a particular call from an input to an output trunk. (e) Suppose the output trunk is immediately demultiplexed to a set of DSOs. How does a TST switch help over a TS design in this situation?

8.6. Using the numbers from Example 8.5, compute the increase or decrease in packet-switching bandwidth if (a) the interrupt time is reduced from 10 μs to 5 μs, (b) the number of non-data-touching cycles is reduced from 200 to 100, (c) and the mean packet size is 53 bytes instead of 1500 bytes. (d) What conclusions can you draw about the relative effects of these perturbations?

8.7. Does the time taken to match an incoming string depend on the number of elements stored in a trie? What is the smallest and greatest number of operations taken to match an incoming string of length 4 in a trie that stores (a) 10 distinct strings, (b) 1000 distinct strings?

8.8. Suppose the Pentium packet routers in Example 8.5 were attached to a 1-Gbps bus. (a) Describe the data path from an input to an output of this second-generation switch. (b) How many processors can be attached to the bus before it is fully loaded? (c) What would happen if more processors were attached to the bus? (d) If the processors queue data FIFO, what is the data rate achievable assuming uniform random traffic?

8.9. Assume that the port-mapping information is distributed among the processors of a third-generation switch. (a) How is this state set up? (b) What happens if the switch controller reboots? (c) Propose a protocol for reestablishing state on a reboot.

8.10. Suppose you were to use the processors in Example 8.11 as input and output port controllers in a third-generation switch, built as a 64 × 64 crossbar. What is the best achievable throughput? What is the throughput achievable with uniform random traffic and FIFO input queuing? What is the throughput achievable in the worst case?

8.11. Draw a 16 × 16 Banyan switching fabric.

8.12. How many equivalent 8 × 8 Banyan fabrics are there?

8.13. Sort 3, 1, 9, 2, 0, 1, 3, 7 by merging.

8.14. What is the largest number of rounds that parallel iterated matching may take for a 16 × 16 switch?

8.15. What is the largest purely output-queued ATM switch we can build if we use 80-ns 4-byte-wide DRAM with a zero cell loss requirement? Assume input lines are 155 Mbps. How large can the switch be with cell-wide access? If we decide to run the outputs at only $0.4\,N$ times the input lines (instead of N times faster than the input lines), how big a switch can we build?

Chapter 9

Scheduling

9.1 Introduction

Computer networks allow users to share (or *multiplex*) resources such as printers, file systems, long-distance trunks, and sites on the World Wide Web. Sharing, however, automatically introduces the problem of *contention* for the shared resource.

EXAMPLE 9.1

Consider the set of queries made to a server hosting a World Wide Web search engine. Each query represents a service request from a user contending for access to the shared resource, that is, the search engine. Assume that the server can serve only one request at a time, so that requests that arrive when a server is busy must wait. A busy server holds an incoming search request in a *service queue* and eventually selects it for service. We define the *queuing delay* of a request as the time between its arrival and eventual service. The server allocates different mean queuing delays to different requests by its choice of service order. For example, if the server always serves requests from a particular user A as soon as they arrive, then A's requests receive a lower mean queuing delay than requests from other users.

Given a set of resource requests in the service queue, a server uses a *scheduling discipline* to decide which request to serve next. Scheduling disciplines are important because they are the key to fairly sharing network resources and to providing performance-critical applications, such as telephony and interactive multiparticipant games, with performance guarantees. In this chapter we will study several scheduling techniques, comparing their relative merits in providing fairness and performance guarantees.

A scheduling discipline actually has two orthogonal components. First, it decides the order in which requests are serviced. Second, it manages the service queue of requests awaiting service. To understand this further, let us return to the situation in Example 9.1. If, because of a statistical fluctuation, requests arrive at the search engine faster than it can serve them, some requests must wait in the service queue, taking up storage space. If storage is limited, and requests keep coming in faster than they can be served, then the server must eventually drop some requests. Which ones should the server drop? In the same way as a scheduling discipline allocates different *delays* to different users by its choice of service order, it allocates different *loss rates* to different users by its choice of which requests to drop. Continuing with Example 9.1, if the server preferentially drops service requests from user B whenever the service queue overflows, B has a higher loss rate than A. Thus, a scheduling discipline allocates different service qualities to different users by its choice of service order and by its choice of which requests to drop.

Though a network must schedule access to *every* multiplexed resource, in this chapter we will restrict our attention to the two most commonly scheduled resources: the bandwidth on a link, and buffers at a multiplexing point. Techniques for scheduling these resources are applicable, with little change, to other multiplexed resources.

Scheduling, like error control and flow control, can be done at one of several layers of a protocol stack. In the literature, scheduling disciplines are usually studied for the output queue of a switch and are placed in the network layer. However, as we saw in the Web server application, we also need scheduling at the application layer. In general, any layer dealing with a multiplexed resource must deal with scheduling.

We note in passing that scheduling is important only when statistical fluctuations in the input traffic result in queuing at a multiplexing point. In circuit-switched networks, source traffic is smooth and without significant fluctuations. Therefore, scheduling is not an important problem in such networks, and we will study only packet-switched networks (such as the Internet and ATM networks) in the rest of the chapter.

9.1.1   Why do we need a scheduling discipline?

Before we study scheduling disciplines in detail, we make a small detour to understand why we need a nontrivial scheduling discipline in the first place. Ultimately, the motivation comes down to our guesses about the performance requirements of future networked applications, a topic we study in greater detail in Section 14.4, and summarize here.

Most experts agree that future networks will carry at least two types of applications. Some applications (which are already common on the Internet) are relatively insensitive to the performance they receive from the network. They are happy to accept whatever performance the network gives them. For example, a file transfer application would prefer to have an infinite bandwidth and zero end-to-end delay. On the other hand, it works correctly, though with degraded performance, as the available bandwidth decreases and the available end-to-end delay increases. In other words, the performance requirements of such applications are *elastic*: they can *adapt* to the resources available. Such applications are called *best-effort applications*, because the network promises them only to attempt to deliver their packets, without guaranteeing them any particular performance bound. Note that *best-effort service*, which is the service provided for best-effort applications, does not require the network to reserve resources for a connection.

Besides best-effort applications, we expect future networks to carry traffic from applications that *do* require a bound on performance. For example, an application that carries voice as a 64-Kbps stream becomes nearly unusable if the network provides less than 64 Kbps on the end-to-end path. Moreover, if the application is two-way and interactive, human ergonomic constraints require the round-trip delay to be smaller than around 150 ms. If the network wants to support a perceptually "good" two-way voice application, it must guarantee, besides a bandwidth of 64 kbps, a round-trip delay of around 150 ms. Thus, this application, and other applications of its kind, demand a *guarantee* of service quality from the network. We call these applications *guaranteed-service* applications. Guaranteed-service applications require the network to reserve resources on their behalf.

The reason these application characteristics affect scheduling is that the performance received by a connection depends principally on the scheduling discipline present at each multiplexed server along the connection's path from a source to a destination.[1] These servers are typically the ones scheduling packets at each output link at a switch or router. Recall that a switch queues resource requests, represented by packets ready for transmission, in a per-link output queue. At each output queue, a server uses a scheduling discipline to choose which ready packet to transmit next,[2] and to control access to output queue buffers. The server can allocate different *mean delays* to different connections by its choice of service order. It can allocate different *bandwidths* to connections by serving at least a certain number of packets from a particular connection in a given time interval. Finally, it can allocate different *loss rates* to connections by giving them more or fewer buffers. Thus, to build a network that gives guaranteed-service applications performance guarantees, we require scheduling disciplines that can support per-connection delay, bandwidth, and loss bounds.

Although best-effort applications do not require performance bounds, the partitioning of available bandwidth and buffers to best-effort connections, which is the role of a scheduling discipline, determines how *fair* the network is. Fair resource allocation is an intuitively desirable property of a computer network (see also Section 9.2.2). To build a

---

[1]We assume that the path does not include broadcast links, as such links typically do not provide quality-of-service guarantees (see Section 7.6). Alternatively, we can assume that these links, if present, are lightly loaded, and therefore do not significantly affect the overall performance received by a connection.

[2]In this chapter, we will assume that the switch fabric (see Section 8.1) is fast enough that all the queuing happens at the output queue. Otherwise, we must schedule access to the switch fabric in much the same way as scheduling access to the link.

network that allocates resources fairly among best-effort connections, we must implement scheduling disciplines that support fair resource allocation among best-effort connections at each switch.

In this chapter, we will study the requirements of a scheduling discipline (Section 9.2) and the degrees of freedom available in designing a scheduling discipline (Section 9.3). We then examine some link scheduling disciplines that are suitable for best-effort connections (Section 9.4), and others that are suitable for guaranteed-service connections (Section 9.5). A comprehensive table in Section 9.6 summarizes all the disciplines studied in Section 9.4 and 9.5 and serves as a road map. Finally, in Section 9.7, we will study how to schedule buffers.

The Conservation Law

The simplest possible scheduling discipline is *first-come-first-served* (FCFS). In this discipline, the scheduler transmits incoming packets in the order they arrive at the output queue, and drops packets that arrive at a full queue. The disadvantage with strict FCFS scheduling is that the scheduler cannot differentiate among connections. Thus, it cannot explicitly allocate some connections (which may pay the network operator for this privilege) lower mean delays than others. Although a more sophisticated scheduling discipline can achieve this objective, an important theorem states that the *sum* of the mean queuing delays received by the set of multiplexed connections, weighted by their share of the link's load, is *independent* of the scheduling discipline. In other words, a scheduling discipline can reduce a particular connection's mean delay, compared with FCFS, only at the expense of another connection. We state this result more formally as follows [Kleinrock 75, p. 117].

Consider a set of N connections at a scheduler, such that traffic arrives from connection i at a mean rate λ_i and the mean service time for a packet from connection i is x_i. Let $\rho_i = \lambda_i x_i$ be the mean utilization of a link due to connection i (this expression holds because requests arrive from connection i at rate λ_i, and each request has a mean service time x_i). Let connection i's mean waiting time at the scheduler be q_i. Then, the *Conservation Law* states that if the scheduler is *work-conserving* (i.e., it is idle only if its queue is empty),

$$\sum_{i=1}^{N} \rho_i q_i = Constant \qquad (9.1)$$

Since the right-hand side of the equation is independent of the scheduling discipline, a work-conserving scheduling discipline can only reallocate delays among the connections. So, if, with a particular scheduling discipline, a particular connection receives a lower delay than with FCFS, this must be at the expense of another connection. Note that a non-work-conserving discipline, which may be idle even when the service queue is nonempty, can only result in mean queuing delays *larger* than with FCFS scheduling. Thus, the sum of delays with FCFS service is a tight lower bound whether or not the server is work conserving.

EXAMPLE 9.2

Consider ATM virtual circuits A and B with arrival rates 10 and 25 Mbps that share an OC3 link. Suppose that with FCFS, both their mean queuing delays are 0.5 ms, and that with a new discipline, A's mean delay is reduced to 0.1 ms. What is B's new mean queuing delay?

Solution: Since both connections are ATM, the mean service time for a packet from each connection is the same, and can be ignored. From the Conservation Law, we get:

$$10/155 * 0.5 + 25/155 * 0.5 = 10/155 * 0.1 + 25/155 * B's\ queuing\ delay$$

Solving, we get B's new mean queuing delay to be 0.66 ms, which is higher than its earlier delay of 0.5 ms.

9.2 Requirements

A scheduling discipline must satisfy four sometimes contradictory requirements:

- Ease of implementation (for both guaranteed-service and best-effort connections) (Section 9.2.1)
- Fairness and protection (for best-effort connections) (Section 9.2.2)
- Performance bounds (for guaranteed-service connections) (Section 9.2.3)
- Ease and efficiency of admission control (for guaranteed-service connections) (Section 9.2.4)

Each scheduling discipline makes a different trade-off among these requirements. Depending on the situation, some of these requirements may be more important than others. The "best" choice, therefore, depends on the applicable binding constraints. In this section, we study the requirements in more detail.

9.2.1 Ease of implementation

In a high-speed network, a server may need to pick the next packet for transmission every time a packet departs, which can be once every few microseconds. Thus, it has very little time to make a decision. A scheduling discipline for a high-speed network should require only a few simple operations; preferably, it should be implementable inexpensively in terms of hardware. In particular, the number of operations to implement a discipline should be as independent of the number of scheduled connections as possible. If a switch is serving N simultaneous connections, a scheduler that takes $O(N)$ time does not scale, and we prefer a scheduler that takes $O(1)$ time. Local-area switches typically serve 50–100 simultaneous connections, whereas wide-area switches can serve up to 100,000 simultaneous connections. Thus, scaling is particularly important for wide-area switches.

If we want to implement a scheduler in hardware, the scheduling discipline must be amenable to easy hardware implementation. Surprisingly enough, with modern VLSI technology, it is nearly as easy to implement the logic of a complicated scheduling algorithm as that of a simple one. The binding constraint, instead, is mainly in the memory required to maintain *scheduling state* (such as pointers to packet queues, and memory about the service already received by a connection) and the time required to access this state. The smaller the scheduling state associated with scheduling discipline, the easier it is to implement in VLSI. For example, implementing a scheduler that keeps all packets in a single shared buffer is easy, because the only state the scheduler requires is pointers to the head and tail of the shared queue, and these pointers can be rapidly accessed. In contrast, a scheduler that keeps a per-connection service queue needs a pointer to the head and tail of every queue. The state needed scales linearly with the number of connections, raising questions about its feasibility in a large wide-area switch.

9.2.2   Fairness and protection

A scheduling discipline allocates a share of the link capacity and output queue buffers to each connection it serves. We call an allocation at a switch *fair* if the allocation satisfies the max–min allocation criterion discussed in the next box. Fairness is an intuitively desirable property of a scheduling discipline serving best-effort connections. For guaranteed-service connections, which should pay the network operator a fee in proportion to their resource usage, fairness is not a concern.

Fair resource allocation to a set of connections is a *global* objective, whereas a scheduling discipline takes only *local* resource allocation decisions. To translate from a local decision to a global one, each connection should limit its resource usage to the *smallest* locally fair allocation along its path. It can be shown that this results in a globally fair allocation [BG 92]. Note that a sudden decrease in the resource usage by one connection can potentially increase the fair allocations of other connections who share part of their path with that connection. However, sources can increase their resource usage to the new globally fair allocation only after a propagation delay. Thus, in a network where usage patterns change rapidly with time, even if every switch locally allocates resources fairly, users may not receive globally fair allocations, because by the time a source adapts to the current allocation, its allocation may have changed! This topic is discussed in more detail in reference [CR 96].

Protection means that misbehavior by one connection (by sending packets at a rate faster than its fair share) should not affect the performance received by other connections. For example, FCFS does not provide protection, because the mean delay of a source may increase if the sum of the arrival rates over all sources increases. Thus, a misbehaving source, by sending too fast, increases the mean delay of all other connections. In contrast, with round-robin scheduling, a misbehaving source overflows its own queue, and the other sources are unaffected [Nagle 87]. If a scheduler provides protection, then it also guarantees a minimum bandwidth to every connection, whatever the behavior of other connections.

The relationship between fairness and protection is that a fair scheduler automatically provides protection, because it limits a misbehaving connection to its fair share. However, the converse need not be true. For example, if connections are *policed* at the entrance to the network (that is, the network forces them to conform to a predeclared traffic pattern; see Section 13.3 for details) they are protected from each other, but their resource shares may not be fair. We study scheduling disciplines that provide fair service in Section 9.4.

Max–min fair share

We often run into the problem of dividing a scarce resource among a set of users, each of whom has an equal right to the resource, but some of whom intrinsically demand fewer resources than others. How, then, should we divide the resource? A sharing technique widely used in practice is called *max–min fair share*. Intuitively, a fair share allocates a user with a "small" demand what it wants, and evenly distributes unused resources to the "big" users. Formally, we define the max–min fair share allocation to be as follows:

- Resources are allocated in order of increasing demand
- No source gets a resource share larger than its demand
- Sources with unsatisfied demands get an equal share of the resource

This formal definition corresponds to the following operational definition. Consider a set of sources $1, \ldots, n$ that have resource demands $x_1, x_2, \ldots, x_n$. Without loss of generality, order the source demands so that $x_1 \leq x_2 \ldots \leq x_n$. Let the server have a capacity C. Then, we initially give C/n of the resource to the source with the smallest demand, x_1. This may be more than what source 1 wants, so that $C/n - x_1$ of the resource is still available as unused excess. We distribute this excess evenly to the remaining $n - 1$ sources, so that each of them gets $C/n + (C/n - x_1)/(n - 1)$. This may be larger than what x_2 wants, perhaps, so we can continue the process. The process ends when each source gets no more than what it asks for, and, if its demand was not satisfied, no less than what any other source with a higher index got. We call such an allocation a *max−min fair* allocation, because it maximizes the minimum share of a source whose demand is not fully satisfied.

EXAMPLE 9.3

Compute the max−min fair allocation for a set of four sources with demands 2, 2.6, 4, 5 when the resource has a capacity of 10.

Solution: We compute the fair share in several rounds of computation. In the first round, we tentatively divide the resource into four portions of size 2.5. Since this is larger than source 1's demand, this leaves 0.5 left over for the remaining three sources, which we divide evenly among the rest, giving them 2.66 . . . each. This is larger than what source 2 wants, so we have an excess of 0.066 . . . , which we divide evenly among the remaining two sources, giving them $2.5 + 0.66 . . . + 0.033 . . . = 2.7$ each. Thus, the fair allocation is: source 1 gets 2, source 2 gets 2.6, sources 3 and 4 get 2.7.

Thus far, we have assumed that all sources have the same right to the resources. Sometimes, we may want to give some sources a bigger share than others. In particular, we may want to associate *weights* $w_1, w_2, w_3, . . . , w_n$ with sources 1, 2, 3, . . . , n, which reflect their relative resource share. We extend the concept of max−min fair share to include such weights by defining the *max−min weighted fair share allocation* as follows:

- Resources are allocated in order of increasing demand, normalized by the weight
- No source gets a resource share larger than its demand
- Sources with unsatisfied demands get resource shares in proportion to their weights

The following example shows how to achieve this in practice.

EXAMPLE 9.4

Compute the max−min fair allocation for a set of four sources with demands 4, 2, 10, 4 and weights 2.5, 4, 0.5, 1 when the resource has a capacity of 16.

Solution: The first step is to normalize the weights so that the smallest weight is 1. This gives us the set of weights as 5, 8, 1, 2. We can now pretend that the number of sources, instead of being 4, is $5 + 8 + 1 + 2 = 16$. We therefore divide the resource into 16 shares. In each round of resource allocation, we give a source a share proportional to its weight. Thus, in the first round, we compute C/n as $16/16 = 1$. In this round, the sources receive 5, 8, 1, 2 units of the resource, respectively. Source 1 gets 5, and only needs 4, so we have 1 unit extra. Similarly, source 2 has 6 units extra. Sources 3 and 4 are backlogged, since their share is less than their demand. We now have 7 units of resources which have to be distributed to sources 3 and 4. Their weights are 1 and 2, and the smallest weight is 1, so there is no need to normalize the weights. We give source 3 an additional $7 * 1/3$ units (since its weight is 1), and source 4 an additional $7 * 2/3$ units (since its weight is 2). This increases source 4's share to $2 + 7 * 2/3 = 6.666$ units, which is more than it needs. So, we give the excess 2.666 units to source 3, which finally gets $1 + 7/3 + 2.666 = 6$ units. The final shares are, therefore, 4, 2, 6, 4. This is the max–min weighted fair share allocation.

9.2.3 Performance bounds

The third major requirement of a scheduling discipline is that it should allow a network operator to guarantee *arbitrary* per-connection performance bounds, restricted only by the Conservation Law (for example, we cannot give *all* connections a delay lower than they would receive with FCFS). An operator can guarantee performance bounds for a connection only by reserving some network resources, either on-the-fly, during the call-establishment phase of the connection, or in advance. Since the amount of resources reserved for a connection depends on its traffic intensity, guaranteed-performance connections must agree to limit their usage. We can view the relationship between the network operator and the user as a legal contract: the user agrees that its traffic will remain within certain bounds, and, in turn, the operator guarantees that the network will meet the connection's performance requirements [FV 90]. In this chapter, we assume that a user somehow communicates the performance requirements for a connection to the operator, deferring the details to Section 14.4.1. Note that to meet its contract, an operator must control a connection's performance not only when served by a single scheduler, but also when the connection passes through many schedulers in tandem. In a heterogeneous network, where different parts of the network may employ different scheduling disciplines, guaranteeing end-to-end performance bounds is a hard problem, and an area of active research [GLV 95].

To specify and guarantee performance requirements, we have to be more precise about how to measure a connection's performance. We now take an extended diversion to study this problem.

Deterministic and statistical bounds

We start by noting that performance bounds can be expressed either *deterministically* or *statistically*. A deterministic bound holds for every packet sent on a connection. A statistical bound is a probabilistic bound on performance. For example, a deterministic delay bound of 10 s means that every packet sent on a connection has an end-to-end delay smaller than 10 s. On the other hand, a statistical bound of 10 s with a parameter of 0.99 means that the probability that a packet has a delay greater than 10 seconds is smaller than 0.01.[3] In general, deterministic bounds require a larger fraction of the network resources to be reserved than statistical bounds.

Another way to express statistical bounds is as a *one-in-N* bound. In the latter form, the guarantee is that no more than one packet in N consecutive packets will violate the bound. For example, the statistical bound just discussed could be expressed as follows: no more than one packet in 100 will have a delay larger than 10 seconds. Statistical bounds of the second sort are easier to verify at the endpoint but harder to implement, because intermediate network elements need to keep track of the state of every connection. Continuing with the example, if a network element drops a packet from a connection, it must remember not to drop packets from that connection for at least a hundred more packets (the situation is even more complex when multiple switches must cooperate to meet a one-in-N bound).

Common performance parameters

Four common performance parameters are widely used in the literature: *bandwidth, delay, delay-jitter,* and *loss.* We study these in turn.

A *bandwidth* bound requires that a connection receive at least a minimum bandwidth (measured over a prespecified interval) from the network. Guaranteed-service connections usually require at least a bandwidth bound. In practice, most current integrated-service networks provide only a bandwidth bound.

A *delay* bound is a deterministic or statistical bound on some parameter of the delay distribution, such as the worst-case delay, the mean delay, or the 99-percentile delay (Figure 9.1).

- The *worst-case* delay is the largest delay suffered by a packet from a connection. To compute the worst-case delay, we assume that every other connection at every scheduler along the path behaves in the worst possible manner. Computing it is easy if we can clearly identify the worst case.

- Strictly speaking, we must measure the *average* delay over all possible traffic arrival patterns of every other connection in the system, because these may influence the delay of a packet in the connection under study. Thus, the *true* average delay is impossible to measure, or even to define precisely. In practice, when we refer to a connection's average delay, we are talking about the mean delay *measured* over the packets sent on that connection. If the connection lasts long enough, and the other traffic sources are independent, then this approximates the true average delay.

---

[3]The probability has to be measured in an appropriate space, for example, over all packets from all connections with that requirement.

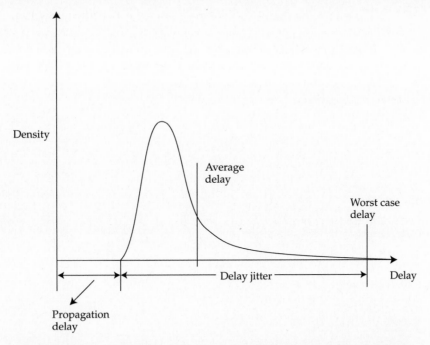

Figure 9.1: Delay and delay jitter. The figure shows the end-to-end delay distribution for a typical connection. The delay is always more than the propagation delay and is bounded by the worst-case delay bound. The support of the density function is the delay-jitter bound. Note that the average delay is typically much smaller than the worst-case delay.

- Ninety-nine percent of the packets on a connection are guaranteed to suffer a delay smaller than the *99-percentile* delay. As with the mean delay, the true 99-percentile delay is impossible to measure, and we usually settle for the measured 99-percentile delay.

   Though the worst-case delay is usually substantially larger than the measured mean delay, because it is impossible for a network to compute or guarantee the true average-case delay, guaranteed-service networks are expected to specify and guarantee only the deterministic or statistical worst-case delay.

   Some disciplines couple bandwidth and delay bounds such that to obtain a lower worst-case delay, a connection needs to reserve a larger bandwidth at a scheduler. This is inefficient for connections that would like to obtain a smaller worst-case delay while still reserving only a small bandwidth (see Example 9.11). We therefore prefer disciplines that decouple performance bounds over disciplines that couple them.

- A *delay-jitter* bound requires that the network bound the difference between the largest and smallest delays received by packets on that connection (this is equivalent to bounding the width of the end-to-end delay histogram—see Figure 9.1). Note that the delay-jitter bound is trivially as large as the delay bound less the propagation delay, since a packet's queuing delay could be as small as zero and as large as the delay bound less the propagation delay.

Playback applications

A delay-jitter bound is useful mainly in the context of a *playback application.* In such an application, the sender digitizes a continuous information stream, such as an audio or video stream, and sends it to the receiver, which plays back the stream. Many important applications, such as two-way interactive voice calls, videoconferencing, and TV distribution, fall into this class. A playback receiver should choose playback instants so that when it is ready to output the information contained in a packet, the packet has already arrived. Ensuring this is not trivial because a long-delayed packet may arrive at the receiver well after the receiver wanted to play the information contained in that packet.

If the delay jitter over a connection is bounded, the receiver can eliminate delay variations in the network by delaying the first packet on that connection by the delay-jitter bound in an *elasticity buffer,* then playing packets out from the connection a constant time after they were transmitted (Figure 9.2). Thus, the larger the delay-jitter bound, the larger the elasticity buffer required at the receiver. Interactive applications may become unusable if the delay jitter is too large.

If a receiver delays packets to eliminate jitter, packets that arrive before their delay bound serve no useful purpose and only occupy buffers at the receiver. It is better to delay such packets in the network, so that packets from other delay-sensitive connections can get lower queuing delays.

Finally, a *loss bound* requires that the fraction of packets lost on a connection be smaller than some bound. As with the average delay, the true loss rate is impossible to measure, and we usually settle for the loss rate measured over a certain number of packets, over a certain time interval, or over the lifetime of the connection. In this chapter, we will only consider the simple case of a zero loss bound. We will consider nonzero loss bounds in Chapter 14 when studying admission control.

9.2.4   Ease and efficiency of admission control

A scheduling discipline should permit easy admission control. A switch controller should be able to decide, given the current set of connections and the descriptor for a new connection, whether it is possible to meet the new connection's performance bounds without jeopardizing the performance of existing connections. Moreover, the scheduling discipline should not lead to network underutilization (subjectively measured by the

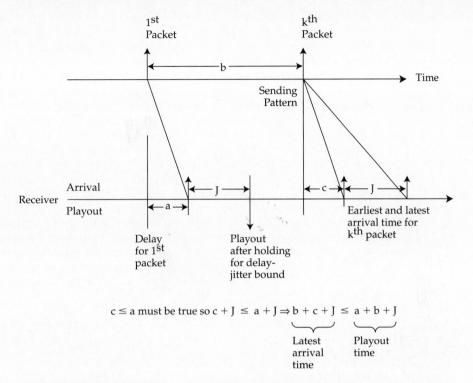

$c \leq a$ must be true so $c + J \leq a + J \Rightarrow b + c + J \leq a + b + J$

$\underbrace{\qquad}$ Latest arrival time $\underbrace{\qquad}$ Playout time

Figure 9.2: Removing delay jitter. The receiver delays the first packet it receives by the delay-jitter bound, and then plays out packets with the same spacing as they are generated. Suppose the first packet has a delay a, and let the delay-jitter bound be J. The kth packet from the source, sent b seconds after the first packet, has a delay of at least c, where c is the propagation delay, and a delay at most $c + J$. Since $a \geq c$, $a + b + J$, which is the time at which the kth packet is played out, is guaranteed to be larger than $c + b + J$, which is the latest time it could arrive. Thus, by delaying packets in a buffer for time J, the receiver can eliminate jitter in the arrival stream, and guarantee that a packet has always arrived by the time the receiver is ready to play it.

network operator). For example, with FCFS scheduling, we can give all connections a worst-case delay bound by restricting the number of connections and the largest burst size that each connection may send. However, this typically results in an underutilized network.

Schedulable region

The *schedulable region* is both a technique for efficient admission control and a way to measure the efficiency of a scheduling discipline. To understand this concept, recall that a scheduler must reserve resources to provide performance bounds to guaranteed-service connections. Since resources are finite, this implies that a scheduler that provides performance bounds can only serve a finite number of connections. We call the set of all possible combinations of performance bounds that a scheduler can simultaneously meet its *schedulable region* [HLP 91b]. Given a schedulable region, admission control is simple, because we only need to check whether the resulting combination of connection parameters lies within the schedulable region or not. Moreover, all else being equal, the larger the schedulable region, the more efficient a scheduling discipline, because it can support a wider range of connection requirements.

The schedulable region for a scheduler is hard to determine analytically; it can only be approximated experimentally. However, in the special case where we can assign connections to a few performance classes, the schedulable region is more easily computed (Figure 9.3). For example, assume that all Class I connections require a queuing delay of no more than 100 ms per scheduler, and a bandwidth of at least 1 Mbps. Similarly, we might assume that Class 2 connections require a delay of at most 10 ms per scheduler, and a bandwidth of at least 64 kbps (these correspond, roughly, to video and voice calls). Then, the schedulable region is the set of all tuples (a, b), where a and b are the number of simultaneous Class I and Class II calls that can be supported at any time while still meeting the delay and bandwidth constraints. We can represent these tuples in a schedulable region diagram, as shown in Figure 9.3.

The difficulty with this approach, however, is coming up with a set of classes that adequately cover user requirements. Users must choose their performance requirements from a fixed menu, so to keep customers happy, the network operator must anticipate all possible application requirements! Thus, it is not clear whether such an approach will make it out of research papers into the real world.

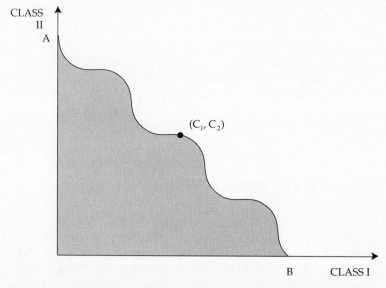

Figure 9.3: Schedulable region. The schedulable region describes the set of calls that can be admitted while still meeting their performance bounds. This figure shows a hypothetical schedulable region when the performance bounds fall into one of two classes. The scheduler can simultaneously admit:

A Class II calls and zero Class I calls, or
B Class I calls and zero Class II calls, or
C_1 Class I and C_2 Class II calls.

9.3 Fundamental choices

There are four principal degrees of freedom in designing a scheduling discipline:

- The number of priority levels (Section 9.3.1)
- Whether each level is work-conserving or non-work-conserving (Section 9.3.2)
- The degree of aggregation of connections within a level (Section 9.3.3)
- Service order within a level (Section 9.3.4)

In this section, we will examine these four choices.

9.3.1 Priority

In a priority scheduling scheme, each connection is associated with a priority level. If there are n priority levels, and a higher-numbered priority level corresponds to a connection with higher priority, the scheduler serves a packet from priority level k only if there are no packets awaiting service in levels $k + 1, k + 2, \ldots n$ (we also call this *multilevel priority with exhaustive service*). Priority allows a scheduler to give packets at a higher priority level a lower mean queuing delay at the expense of packets at lower priority levels.

A scheduler can have an arbitrary number of priority levels. In practice, the number of levels depends on the number of delay classes that the network operator wants to support. In an integrated services network, at least three priority levels are desirable: a high priority level for urgent messages, usually for network control; a medium priority level for guaranteed service traffic; and a low priority level for best-effort traffic.

A priority scheme allows a misbehaving user at a higher priority level to increase the delay and decrease the available bandwidth of connections at all lower priority levels. An extreme case of this is *starvation*, where the scheduler never serves a packet at a lower priority level, because there is always something to send from a higher priority level. Thus, in a priority scheduler, it is critical that appropriate admission control and policing restrict the service rates from all but the lowest priority level.

Implementation

Priorities are simple to implement in both software and hardware because, to make a scheduling decision, a scheduler needs to determine only the highest priority nonempty service queue. It also requires only a small amount of scheduling state for buffer management: two pointers at each priority level that point to the head and tail of the service queue at that level.

Analysis

If a combination of admission control and policing (see Section 13.3) restricts the rate at which data enters a priority scheduler, the performance of connections at a lower level can be computed by modeling service at that level by a *vacationing server*. The idea is that the server is on vacation when it is serving higher priority levels. The worst-case arrival pattern at the higher priority levels bounds vacation durations, and thus the worst-case delay for the packet at the head of the per-level service queue (subsequent packets could have larger worst-case delays). Moreover, the mean rate at which level k is served is just the link rate minus the rate at which vacations are taken at all higher priority levels (also see Exercise 9.3).

9.3.2   Work-conserving versus non-work-conserving disciplines

A work-conserving scheduler is idle only when there is no packet awaiting service. In contrast, a non-work-conserving scheduler may be idle even if it has packets to serve. At first glance, non-work-conserving schedulers make little sense: why would network operators want to leave a line idle, wasting bandwidth, if they could use the time to carry traffic? The reason is that a non-work-conserving scheduler, by idling away time, makes the traffic arriving at downstream switches more predictable, thus reducing both the buffer size necessary at output queues, and the delay jitter experienced by a connection. Let us see how this works with an example.

EXAMPLE 9.5

Consider two switches S1 and S2 in tandem, with connections A and B sharing the link S1–S2, but going to different output queues at switch S2 (Figure 9.4). Now, focus on the pattern of packet arrivals from A at S2. Since A and B share link S1–S2, this arrival pattern may depend not only on the way A is served at S1, but also on B's traffic arrival pattern at S1. For example, if S1 serves packets in FCFS order, and many packets from A pile up behind a burst from B at the head of the queue, when B's packets finally depart, packets from A will arrive at S2's output

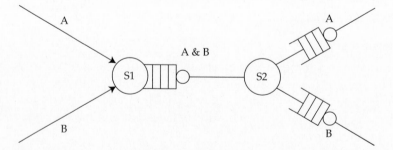

Figure 9.4: An example showing the need for non-work-conserving disciplines. Connections A and B share a common link, so the burstiness of Connection A traffic at S2's output port depends on B's behavior. If B is bursty, and S1 is work-conserving, even if A is smooth when it enters S1, it can be bursty when it enters S2. However, if S1 is non-work-conserving, the traffic entering S2 is smooth, even if B is bursty.

queue in a burst, even if they entered S1 evenly spaced. Observe that if S1 is free to transmit an entire burst from A at the link rate, then, to prevent packet loss, S2's output queue must be large enough to absorb the burst. Moreover, if this burst is buffered at S2 awaiting service, and more packets arrive on connection A before S2 can serve the burst, then the burst grows even larger as it exits S2. It is possible to come up with pathological scenarios where each switch adds a little to an initial burst, so that as the traffic from A leaves the network, it does so as a series of fast bursts. This potentially bursty behavior leads to a large delay jitter (because the first packet of a burst has a smaller queuing delay than the last) and the need for larger buffers at switches (because they must accommodate large bursts). With a non-work-conserving discipline, a connection needs the same number of buffers, no matter how deep in the network it is [ZK 91, GGPS 96, Zhang 95].

We can reduce both the delay jitter and the number of buffers needed to prevent packet loss if we allow a switch to send a packet only when the packet is *eligible*. If a packet is not eligible for service, the switch leaves its output queue idle until the packet becomes eligible. By choosing eligibility times carefully, we can ensure that the output from a switch is predictable, so that bursts do not build up within a network. For example, if the $(k + 1)$st packet on connection A becomes eligible for service only i seconds after the service of the kth packet, we ensure that the downstream switch receives packets on A no faster than one every i seconds. If the downstream switch serves the connection at a rate faster than one every i seconds, it needs to buffer at most one packet from A, limiting the size of the buffer at the switch. Moreover, since the queuing delay at each switch is bounded, the end-to-end delay jitter for packets from A is also bounded. Thus, a scheduler that delays packets until they are eligible, while potentially wasting bandwidth, makes the traffic in the network more predictable and easier to manage.

Besides reducing the need for switch buffers and the delay-jitter bound, non-work-conserving disciplines have two other advantages [Zhang 95]. First, with non-work-conserving schedulers, the sum of the per-hop bounds can tightly bound the end-to-end delay and delay-jitter bounds. This makes the end-to-end performance bounds relatively simple to compute. Second, since the regulator reshapes traffic at each hop, it is easy to bound the performance of heterogeneous networks, where each switch may implement a different non-work-conserving scheduling discipline. This becomes particularly important when it is necessary to compute performance bounds over paths that span multiple administrative domains.

Choosing eligibility times

There are two well-understood ways for a scheduler to choose eligibility times [KKK 90, Golestani 90a, ZF 94]. With *rate-jitter* regulation, the scheduler guarantees that source traffic leaving the scheduler conforms to a given *rate descriptor*. For example, assume that all packets are the same size, and the scheduler wants to guarantee a particular peak rate. Then, the eligibility time for a packet is the sum of the eligibility time of the previous packet on that connection and the inverse of the peak rate (that is, the time taken to serve a fixed-size packet at the peak rate). More precisely, if $E(k)$ represents the eligibility time for the kth packet, and $A(k)$ its arrival time at the scheduler, then

$$E(1) = A(1)$$

$$E(k + 1) = \max(E(k) + Xmin, A(k + 1)), \tag{9.2}$$

where $Xmin$ is the inverse of the peak rate, measured in seconds/packet. This is similar to the peak-rate regulator described in Section 13.3.2.

Another way to choose eligibility times is with a *delay-jitter regulator*. A scheduler implementing this regulator guarantees that the sum of the *queuing* delay in the previous switch and the *regulation* delay in the current switch is constant. This removes the effect of queuing-delay variability in the previous switch. In other words, the output stream from the regulator is a time-shifted and *fully reconstructed* version of the traffic that entered the previous switch. By composing a series of such regulators, the network assures a source that at every switch the input arrival pattern is fully reconstructed, so that burstiness does not build up within the network. More precisely, if $E(i, k)$ is the eligibility time for the kth packet at the ith switch, then

$$E(0,k) = A(0,k)$$

$$E(i + 1, k) = E(i, k) + D + L \tag{9.3}$$

where D is the delay bound at the previous switch, and L is the largest possible delay on the transmission link between switch i and switch $i + 1$. The kth packet is eligible for service at the 0th switch the moment it arrives. However, at subsequent switches, it becomes eligible for service only after a fixed time interval of length $D + L$, which is the longest possible delay in the previous switch and in the previous link. So, if a packet is served before its delay bound at the previous switch, or receives a delay smaller than L on the link, the delay-jitter regulator at the downstream switch adds sufficient delay to convert this to the longest possible delay. When the packet leaves the regulator, it is as if it received exactly D seconds of queuing delay at the previous switch and L seconds of propagation delay at the previous link. Thus, the output of the regulator is a $(D + L)$-second time-shifted version of the traffic that left the previous regulator along the path. If a source is policed at the input to obey a certain traffic descriptor, the delay-jitter regulator automatically assures us that the source's traffic obeys this descriptor at the output of every regulator in the network. Note that a delay-jitter regulator, by itself, cannot provide protection between sources, because misbehaving traffic at the entrance to the network is simply replicated at every hop.

A delay-jitter regulator is harder to implement than a rate-jitter regulator. Not only does it require the network operator to know a bound on the propagation delay on each link, it also requires the network to maintain clock synchrony at adjacent switches at all times. Since, in the real world, clocks drift out of synchrony unless corrected, delay-jitter regulation implicitly assumes the presence of a mechanism for maintaining clock synchrony. Because of its complexity, it seems unlikely that delay-jitter regulation will make the transition from a research paper to the real world. Nevertheless, it is worth studying, because it introduces the notion of perfect traffic reconstruction. We can judge the effectiveness of other regulators by the extent to which they can reconstruct the input traffic stream.

Do we need non-work-conserving disciplines?

Non-work-conserving disciplines were introduced as a research idea, and, as of early 1996, have not been implemented in commercial products. One reason for this is their implementation complexity, since we need to store per-connection state to hold their traffic descriptors. Ignoring this for the moment, is there still a case for non-work-conserving disciplines in future networks? In this box, we will go over some arguments in the debate over non-work-conserving disciplines.

The first argument against non-work-conserving disciplines is that, from the perspective of a user, their only purpose is to reduce the delay jitter in a connection. However, endpoints can remove delay jitter with an elasticity buffer. With the rapidly dropping cost of memory, perhaps we do not need to bound delay jitter in the first place [Partridge 91]. The rebuttal to this is that non-work-conserving disciplines also reduce the number of buffers needed at each switch. These buffers are expensive because they need to be accessed at much higher speeds than buffers at endpoints (see the discussion in Section 8.5.3). Thus, it may make sense to use non-work-conserving disciplines even if endpoints can remove the effect of delay jitter.

Second, non-work-conserving disciplines reduce the delay jitter at the expense of *increasing* the mean delay of a connection. Is this not a problem? The answer is that, for playback applications, which delay packets until the delay-jitter bound, increasing the mean delay does not affect the perceived performance. The receiver buffers packets that arrive early anyway, so all that matters is the worst or 99-percentile delay, rather than the mean delay.

A third argument against non-work-conserving schedulers is that they waste bandwidth. Note, however, that a non-work-conserving scheduler does not necessarily have to waste bandwidth when it has no eligible packets to serve. It can simply serve best-effort packets to use up the otherwise idle link. This traffic does not typically expect any loss-rate guarantees, so these packets may be dropped if the downstream switch does not have sufficient space to buffer a burst without violating any performance guarantees.

Finally, critics argue that non-work-conserving schedulers *always* punish a source that does not obey its descriptor, even if bandwidth is available [Zhang 95]. A source that sends data at a rate faster than allowed is regulated to obey its stated descriptor. In contrast, with a work-conserving discipline, connections can automatically use excess capacity even if they do not obey their descriptor (of course, their delay bounds are not valid if they send excess traffic). Therefore, with non-work-conserving disciplines, there is a greater need for sources to characterize themselves accurately. This is hard to do for online and interactive sources. Proponents have yet to rebut this argument.

To sum up, there are arguments both for and against non-work-conserving disciplines. Ultimately, their eventual success or failure depends on whether their benefits outweigh their costs.

Implementation

The standard way to implement a non-work-conserving scheduler is by means of a *calendar queue* [Brown 88]. A calendar queue consists of a clock and an array of pointers to lists of eligible packets (Figure 9.5). Each pointer corresponds to a "day," and the list of packets pointed to by the "today" pointer are the packets to be served "today." Every time the clock ticks, we move the "today" pointer to the next day and serve the packets eligible on that day (if any). The length of a day multiplied by the number of days is the length of a "year." If a packet becomes eligible more than a year in the future, we insert it into the corresponding day, but with a tag implicitly indicating its future service time. When serving packets from a day, the regulator ignores packets that are not in the current year. For example, in Figure 9.5, events B and D belong to future years, and the regulator ignores them when serving packets in the current year.

A calendar queue allows a scheduler to serve packets only after they become eligible for service, where the eligibility time is rounded off to the size of a clock tick. If a "year" is long enough, most eligibility times are within a year of the current time, and insertion

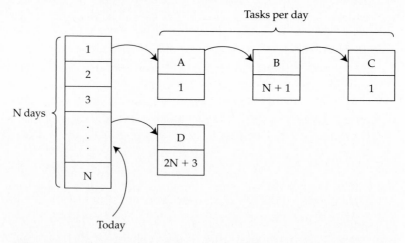

Figure 9.5: A calendar queue. A calendar queue consists of an array of pointers to lists of tasks; each pointer corresponds to a day, and the array corresponds to one year. The "today" pointer points to the set of tasks to be executed that day. Each task is implicitly tagged with its year of execution: each day, the scheduler marks all tasks for that day that belong to the current year as eligible for service. For example, in the figure, tasks A and C can be served in the current year. Task B is served in year 2, and task D in year 3.

and deletion times from the queue take only a constant number of steps. Thus, a calendar queue can be efficiently implemented in both hardware and software. (If the year is too short, each "day" contains events from many "year"'s, so that the scheduler may need to sort through many events at each step. Also, see Exercise 9.5.)

9.3.3   Degree of aggregation

The third degree of freedom in the design of scheduling disciplines is the degree to which individual connections are aggregated in deciding their service order. At one extreme, the scheduler uses a single state variable to describe all connections, which must all, therefore, share the same quality of service. At the other extreme, the scheduler maintains per-connection state, and can give different connections different bandwidth and delay bounds. With an intermediate degree of aggregation, the scheduler treats all packets from connections in the same *class* the same way (that is, maintains per-class state). In this scheme, the scheduler provides different qualities of service to different classes, while connections within a class share the same service quality. Classes of service, therefore, allow us to bridge the spectrum between per-connection service guarantees and a single shared service quality.

EXAMPLE 9.6

Assume that each connection that requires a worst-case delay bound from an FCFS scheduler can bound the size of its largest burst. We denote the largest burst from connection i by b_i, measured in bits. For simplicity, we assume that the link speed is 1 bit per second, and that we are interested only in a single-switch delay bound.

- If the scheduler aggregates all connections, then it cannot distinguish between packets from individual connections. The worst-case delay is achieved when bursts from all the sources arrive simultaneously, leading to a queue of length Σb_i. Thus, even if one connection requires a delay bound d_i, we require the admission control algorithm to ensure that

$$\Sigma b_i \leq d_i,$$

where we take the sum over all connections at the switch. On the other hand, the scheduler requires very little state space.

- If the scheduler aggregates connections in classes corresponding to their delay bounds, we can use a multilevel priority scheduler where increasing priority levels correspond to increasing delay bounds. At the highest priority level, we ensure that

$$\Sigma b_{i \; \epsilon \; highest \; priority \; class} \leq delay \; bound \; of \; highest \; priority \; class$$

At lower priority levels, the sum has to be taken over connections belonging either to the delay class assigned to that level or to a class assigned to a higher priority levels. Moreover, we have to account for all packets that arrive at a higher priority level before a packet from a lower level gets service, a tedious but straightforward task. Note that this scheme requires per-class scheduler state, which is more than in the previous case.

- With no aggregation, we can assign a connection to a priority level that corresponds exactly to its delay bound: the smaller the delay bound, the higher the priority level. This allows us to give a connection a small delay bound without requiring other, lower-priority connections to constrain their burst size. However, this flexibility comes at the cost of increased per-scheduler state.

Aggregation trades off a smaller amount of scheduler state for a coarser-grained differentiation in quality of service. Moreover, as the preceding example shows, for some disciplines, the greater the degree of aggregation, the fewer connections can be admitted. Why, then, should we aggregate connections? The main advantage is in reducing the state in the scheduler, which is important for two reasons. First, as discussed in Section 9.2.1, scheduler state is the critical resource in implementing a scheduler. Thus, the smaller the amount of scheduler state required for a particular scheduling discipline, the easier it is to implement. Second, when establishing a connection, a source needs to know if schedulers along the route can support its performance requirements. Instead of blindly trying all possible paths, switches could advertise their current state to the rest of the network, allowing a source to select a path that is likely to have sufficient resources. However, the more state there is in the scheduler, the more there is to advertise, which costs bandwidth. Thus, reducing the amount of scheduler state is a good idea.

A second advantage of aggregation is that it evenly distributes the jitter induced by bursts due to members of the class [CSZ 92]. Consider a set of ten connections sharing a non-work-conserving scheduler that regulates each of them to the same service rate. Assume that nine of them send packets evenly spaced, while a tenth one sends them in bursts of five packets at a time. If connections are not aggregated, the tenth connection would have a large delay jitter, because the fifth packet from every burst would have a much larger delay than the first. The other connections would be unaffected by this burstiness. In contrast, if the connections are aggregated, the burst from the tenth connection would be served consecutively, so that all other connections would see an increased jitter. However, the jitter for the tenth connection would be smaller because all other members in its aggregation class share its jitter. Thus, aggregation allows connections to obtain a smaller jitter when they send a burst, at the expense of being willing to absorb jitter when other connections sharing the class send a burst.

The main problem with aggregation is that connections within the same class are not protected from each other. Because the scheduler cannot distinguish between connections in the same class, the misbehavior of one connection in the class affects the whole. For example, if the class is served by a non-work-conserving scheduler with a peak-rate rate-jitter regulator, even if one connection of the class sends data too fast, all other connections will experience packet delays and may suffer from packet loss. Thus, the degree of aggregation is inversely proportional to the degree of protection. When designing a network, we have to balance these pros and cons to choose the appropriate degree of aggregation.

> A second problem with aggregation is that if a scheduler gives aggregated congestion feedback signals to an ensemble of feedback flow-controlled connections (described in Chapter 13), a well-behaved connection may perceive congestion signals caused by the bad behavior of other connections as misbehavior on its own part. Therefore, if any one of the aggregated connections sends at a rate fast enough to build up queues at bottleneck, all the other connections receiving a shared feedback signal will be affected. We can show that in a network of schedulers that provide aggregate feedback to an ensemble of feedback flow-controlled connections, even if individual connections are well-behaved, the ensemble could still be unstable (that is, the vector of transmission rates from each source never converges to an equilibrium value) [Shenker 90]. Moreover, if any one of the connections chooses to ignore congestion signals, it can hog the entire capacity available to the aggregate. For example, if we have an ensemble of TCP-style feedback flow-control connections sharing a single FCFS queue, where the aggregated feedback signal is packet loss, the misbehavior of one connection will cause all other connections to lower their window size, and thus their transmission rate. In contrast, under the same assumptions, non-aggregated service and non-aggregated feedback results in guaranteed fair allocations [Shenker 90]. Thus, whenever it is feasible, we prefer per-connection queuing to aggregated queuing. However, if the traffic sharing a class is well behaved, and if all the connections sharing a class have approximately the same behavior, then aggregating them into a class does not significantly affect the degree of protection. (If they are well behaved, they do not need to be protected from each other in the first place!)

9.3.4 Service order within a priority level and aggregation class

The fourth and final degree of freedom in designing scheduling disciplines is the order in which the scheduler serves packets from connections (or aggregates of connections) at the same priority level. There are two fundamental choices: serving packets in the order they arrive, or serving them out of order, according to a per-packet *service tag*. With the second option, the properties of the scheduler depend heavily upon how the scheduler computes the tag. Nevertheless, all scheduling disciplines that serve packets in non-FCFS order need to sort packets implicitly or explicitly, which results in an implementation overhead.

The main problem with FCFS is that it does not allow packets that want a lower delay to skip to the head of the queue. In contrast, if we serve in order of service tags, we can give packets that want a low delay a lower tag value than others in the queue, which allows them to jump to the head of the queue. A second problem with FCFS service is that the allocation of bandwidth to individual connections is not max–min fair (see Section 9.2). Connections receive service roughly in proportion to the speed at which they send data into the network. During overload, when bandwidth is scarce, this rewards bandwidth "hogs," at the expense of connections obeying a cooperative closed-loop flow control scheme, such as the TCP dynamic window scheme. Thus, FCFS service is an incentive for an endpoint to behave greedily, because greediness is rewarded!

With service in order of service tags, it is possible to achieve allocations that are "close" to max–min fair. We discuss this in more detail in Section 9.4.

Implementation

FCFS service is simple to implement, because packets can be placed in a queue as they arrive and removed from the queue when the trunk becomes free. To implement a discipline that serves packets according to explicit service tags, we need several mechanisms. First, on packet arrival, we need to compute its tag. This may require looking up the state associated with its connection, or with the aggregate that contains its connection. We must then insert the tagged packet in a data structure that allows us to determine the packet with the smallest service tag (since this is the next packet to serve) and the largest service tag (since this is the next packet to drop, if the scheduler runs out of buffers).

There are several choices for such a data structure [Keshav 91]. The simplest is a sorted linked list. Unfortunately, although finding the largest and smallest elements in such a list is easy, inserting a packet in a list of M packets can take as much as $O(M)$ time. If, however, packets within a connection are guaranteed to have monotonically increasing tag values, we can do the insertion in only $O(\log N)$ time, where N is the number of connections and typically is much smaller than M.

A second choice is to use two (partly sorted) heaps for storing the smallest and largest service tags in each connection (Figure 9.6). This data structure requires $O(\log N)$ time to insert a packet, and $O(\log N)$ time to remove the smallest or largest packet [Keshav 91].

If we can tolerate a certain amount of misordering in service tags, then we can use a calendar queue to enqueue and dequeue packets in constant time. All packets with service tags that lie within the range of a "day" are treated equally and served in an arbitrary order. After serving these packets, the scheduler searches for the next "day" with packets to serve. However, we still need a heap on the largest service tag in each connection, since a calendar queue does not allow us to extract the packet with the largest service tag easily.

9.3.5   Summary

In this section, we have examined the four degrees of freedom in designing scheduling disciplines: (1) priority, (2) work-conserving or non-work-conserving service, (3) degree of aggregation, and (4) service order within a priority level. By appropriately combining elements along each axis, we can come up with new disciplines that provide a trade-off between implementation complexity and desirable features. The important message, as always, is that each feature comes at some cost. Depending on the situation, a designer must match the need for a feature with its implementation cost. For example, for a small LAN switch, where traffic loads are likely to be much smaller than the available capacity,

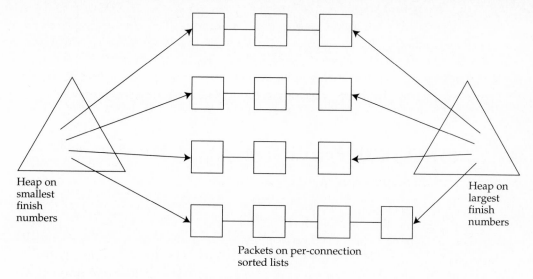

Heap on
smallest
finish
numbers

Heap on
largest
finish
numbers

Packets on per-connection
sorted lists

Figure 9.6: An efficient data structure to implement per-packet service tags. Packets are stored in per-connection lists, and since packets on a connection have monotonically increasing service tags, these lists are automatically sorted. A heap holds the smallest service tag in each list, so the packet with the smallest service tag in the priority queue, which will be served next, can be determined in $O(\log \# \text{ connections})$. Another heap holds the largest service tag in each list; thus the first packet to discard, which has the largest service tag, can also be determined in time $O(\log \# \text{ connections})$.

service queues are usually small, and users are cooperative. In such a system, a single-priority FCFS scheduler, or, at most, a two-priority scheduler, with the higher level devoted to guaranteed-service traffic, is sufficient. For a heavily loaded wide-area public switch with possibly noncooperative users, a scheduler must provide protection with the ability to sustain high trunk utilization. This may require a more sophisticated scheduling discipline, which may involve the use of multiple priority levels, non-work-conserving service at some priority levels, aggregation within some priority levels, and non-FCFS service order.

What is actually "out there"?

Although this section presents a number of choices for scheduling disciplines, the range of choices available in commercial switches (as of early 1996) is very limited. Most schedulers are first-come-first-served, with a single level of priority (this is true of the vast majority of routers in the Internet). Some switches and routers allow multiple levels of priority, but even this is rarely used. We are only beginning to see the sale of switches and routers that provide more interesting alternatives, such as weighted round-robin (which we will study in Section 9.4.2). No commercial switches provide non-work-conserving service, and it is debatable whether this idea will make it to the marketplace before the turn of the century! Although this may sound disheartening, the good news is that manufacturers are slowly beginning to realize the need for good scheduling disciplines, and this has resulted in some excellent research in this area. With any luck, we will see the results of this research appear in switches and routers over the next decade.

9.4   Scheduling best-effort connections

9.4.1   Generalized processor sharing

Section 9.2 makes the case that the scheduling objectives for best-effort and guaranteed-service connections are different. For best-effort connections, we would like the scheduling discipline to provide a *max−min fair* allocation, as described in Section 9.2. We can achieve a max−min fair allocation with an *ideal* (and unimplementable) work-conserving scheduling discipline called *Generalized Processor Sharing (GPS)*. Intuitively, GPS serves packets as if they are in separate logical queues, visiting each nonempty queue in turn and serving an infinitesimally small amount of data from each queue, so that, in any finite time interval, it can visit every logical queue at least once. Connections can be associated with service weights, and they receive service in proportion to this weight whenever they have data in the queue. If they do not have data, the scheduler skips to the next nonempty queue. We claim that this service order results in a max−min fair share bandwidth allocation.

To see this, consider a switch where N connections with equal weights send data to the scheduler infinitely fast. The server should allocate each of them a $1/N$th share of the bandwidth, which is their max−min fair share. Because the scheduler serves an infinitesimal from each connection in turn, it achieves this goal. Now, if one source, say, source A, sends data more slowly than this share, its queue at the scheduler is occasionally empty. When this is so, the scheduler skips A's queue, and, because of its round-robin service, the time thus saved is *equally* distributed to the other connections. Now, if another connection, say, B, has an incoming rate that is *larger* than $1/N$, but *smaller* than the new service rate it receives because A's queue is occasionally empty, B's queue will also be occasionally empty. Thus, the remaining connections (other than A and B) will receive a little more service, which may, in turn, cause still other connections' queues to be occasionally empty. Continuing in this fashion, we see that every connection that has a demand smaller than its fair share gets allocated its demand, whereas every connection that has a greater demand gets an equal share. Thus, by definition, GPS service achieves the max−min fair share.

If we allow a connection to specify a weight, then in each round of service, a GPS server serves data from each nonempty connection queue in proportion to the connection's weight. An extension of the previous argument shows that the GPS server also achieves the max−min *weighted* fair share. Note that, because GPS is fair, from the arguments in Section 9.2.2, it also offers protection.

While GPS is ideal in that it exactly achieves a max–min fair allocation, it is also unimplementable. We now study some scheduling disciplines that are implementable, and try to approximate GPS.

Here is a more precise definition of GPS. In GPS, we call a connection *backlogged* whenever it has data in its queue. If the N connections being served by a GPS server have positive real weights $\phi(1), \phi(2), \ldots, \phi(N)$, then the server serves $S(i, \tau, t)$ amount of data from the ith connection in the interval $[\tau, t]$, so that for any connection i backlogged in $[\tau, t]$, and for any other connection j, we have:

$$\frac{S(i, \tau, t)}{S(j, \tau, t)} \geq \frac{\phi(i)}{\phi(j)} \tag{9.4}$$

Intuitively, a non-backlogged connection is already getting as much service as it could possibly use. A GPS server ensures that backlogged connections (which receive less service than they could use) share the remaining bandwidth in proportion to their weights. Thus, by definition, it achieves a max–min fair bandwidth allocation.

Relative and absolute fairness bounds

GPS is an ideal scheduling discipline in that it provides an exact max–min weighted fair share allocation. Thus, we measure the effectiveness of a fair scheduler by how closely it approximates GPS. Golestani has proposed two fairness metrics for this purpose [Golestani 94]. Both metrics use the variable $g(i, k)$, which is the service rate allocated to connection i at the kth switch on its path from its source to its destination. Let the service rate of the kth switch along the path be $r(k)$. We define $g(i, k)$ as:

$$g(i, k) = \phi(i, k)\, r(k)/\Sigma\, \phi(j, k) \tag{9.5}$$

where $\phi(i, k)$ is the weight of the ith connection at the kth switch, and the sum is taken over all the connections at switch k. We also define $g(i)$ to be the smallest of the $g(i, k)$s over all k. Then:

(a) Given that sessions i and j, which always have packets to send, are assigned service rates $g(i)$ and $g(j)$, actually receive $S(i, \tau, t)$ and $S(j, \tau, t)$ amount of service in time $[\tau, t]$, we define the *relative fairness bound (RFB)* to be:

$$RFB = |S(i, \tau, t)/g(i) - S(j, \tau, t)/g(j)| \tag{9.6}$$

(b) Given that session i receives $S(i, \tau, t)$ amount of service in time $[\tau, t]$ under an emulation of GPS, and $G(i, \tau, t)$ under GPS, we define the *absolute fairness bound (AFB)* to be:

$$AFB = |S(i, \tau, t)/g(i) - G(i, \tau, t)/g(i)| \tag{9.7}$$

If a scheduling discipline has an AFB of x, then it automatically has an RFB of $2x$, because one session could receive x more service than GPS, and the other could serve x less. Also, GPS has both an RFB and an AFB of zero. For most scheduling disciplines, obtaining an AFB is usually much harder than obtaining an RFB.

9.4.2 Weighted round-robin

The simplest emulation of GPS is *round-robin*, which serves a packet from each nonempty connection queue, instead of an infinitesimal amount. Round-robin approximates GPS reasonably well when all connections have equal weights and all packets have the same size. If connections have different weights, then *weighted round-robin (WRR)* serves a connection in proportion to its weight.

EXAMPLE 9.7

Suppose connections A, B, and C have the same packet size, and weights 0.5, 0.75, and 1.0. How many packets from each connection should a round-robin server serve in each round?

Solution: We normalize the weights so that they are all integers, giving us weights 2, 3, and 4. Then in each round of service, the server serves two packets from A, three from B, and four from C.

If packets from different connections have different sizes, a weighted round-robin server divides each connection's weight by its mean packet size to obtain a normalized set of weights.

EXAMPLE 9.8

Suppose connections A, B, and C have mean packet sizes of 50, 500, and 1500 bytes, and weights 0.5, 0.75, and 1.0. How many packets from each connection should a round-robin server serve in each round?

Solution: We divide the weights by the mean packet size to obtain normalized weights 0.01, 0.0015, and 0.000666. Normalizing again to obtain integer weights, we get weights 60, 9, and 4. Thus, the scheduler serves 60 packets from A, 9 from B, and 4 from C in each round of service. This results in 3000 bytes from A, 4500 bytes from B, and 6000 from C served in each round, which is exactly according to their weights of 0.5, 0.75, and 1.0.

To emulate GPS correctly when packets can be of different sizes, a weighted round-robin server must know a source's mean packet size in advance. However, in practice, a source's packet size may be unpredictable. For example, if a source is sending compressed video images, packet size may depend on the degree of motion in a scene. If a source cannot predict its mean packet size, a weighted round-robin server cannot allocate bandwidth fairly.

A second problem with weighted round-robin service is that it is fair only over time scales longer than a round time. At a shorter time scale, some connections may get more service than others. If a connection has a small weight, or the number of connections is large, this may lead to long periods of unfairness. This is illustrated by Example 9.9.

EXAMPLE 9.9

Consider a wide-area T3 trunk that serves 500 ATM virtual circuits with weight 1 and 500 virtual circuits with weight 10. If no connection is ever idle, what is the length of one round?

Solution: A 53-byte cell takes 9.422 μ on a 45 Mbps T3 trunk. A round takes 500 + 500 * 10 = 5500 service times = 51.82 ms. Thus, over a time smaller than 51.82 ms, some connections get more service than others (that is, the service can be unfair).

More sophisticated scheduling disciplines, which we study next, eliminate these two problems. These sophisticated schemes are desirable mainly in the context of a variable-packet size or slower-speed network. In high-speed ATM networks, with fixed-size packets and short round times, GPS emulation using weighted round-robin is usually good enough.

9.4.3 Deficit round-robin

Deficit round-robin modifies weighted round-robin scheduling to allow it to handle variable packet sizes without knowing the mean packet size of each connection in advance [SV 95b]. A DRR scheduler associates each connection with a *deficit counter* initialized to 0. The scheduler visits each connection in turn and tries to serve one *quantum* worth of bits from each visited connection. The packet at the head of the queue is served if it is no larger than the quantum size. If it is larger, the quantum is added to the connection's deficit counter. If the scheduler visits a connection such that the sum of the connection's deficit counter and the quantum is larger than or equal to the size of the packet at the head of the queue, then the packet at the head of the queue is served, and the deficit counter is reduced by the packet size. For example, let the quantum size be 1000 bytes, and let connections A, B, and C have packets of size 1500, 800, and 1200 bytes queued at a DRR scheduler (Figure 9.7). In the first round, A's counter increases to 1000, B's first packet is served, and its deficit counter becomes 200 (= 1000 − 800). C's counter is 1000, and no packet from C is served. In the second round, A's packet is served, and its counter is set to 1000 + 1000 − 1500 = 500. Similarly, C's counter is set to 800. Since there is no packet at B, its counter is reset to 0 (otherwise, B builds up credits indefinitely, eventu-

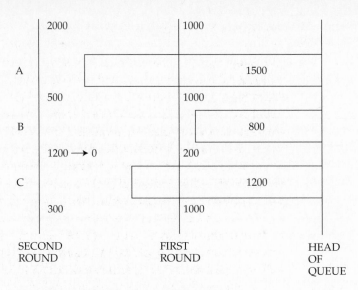

Figure 9.7: Example to illustrate DRR. One packet each from connections A, B, and C is queued at the DRR scheduler. The quantum size is 1000 units. In the first round, B's packet is served, and deficit counters for A and C increase to 1000. In the second round, A's packet is served, and its deficit counter is set to 500. C's packet is also served and its deficit counter is set to 800. B's counter is cleared, because it has no packets to send.

ally leading to unfairness). In the weighted version of DRR, the scheduler serves the quantum size times $\phi(i)$ bits from connection i.

To assure that the DRR scheduler always serves at least one packet from each connection, the quantum size is recommended to be at least *Pmax*, the largest possible packet size in the network. A DRR scheduler does only a constant amount of work per step in its execution. Thus, implementing in hardware is easy.

Let the frame time, *F*, be the largest possible time taken by the scheduler to serve each of the backlogged connections (taking into account their relative weights). We can also show that the relative fairness bound for DRR is $3F/r$ [SV 96]. Thus, the fairness is linked to the frame size.

The main attraction of DRR is its ease of implementation. However, like weighted round robin, it is unfair at time scales smaller than a frame time. For example, consider a 45 Mbps link shared by 500 connections, where the packet size can be as large 8 Kbytes. Then, the frame time can be as large as 725 ms. DRR, therefore, is unfair on time scales smaller than 725 ms. Things are much better if the packet size is 48 bytes, as with ATM networks, but with fixed-size packets DRR reduces to weighted round-robin. Thus, DRR is suitable when fairness requirements are loose or when the packet sizes are small.

9.4.4 Weighted fair queuing and packet-by-packet generalized processor sharing

Weighted fair queuing (WFQ) and *packet-by-packet generalized processor sharing (PGPS)* are approximations of GPS scheduling that do not make GPS's infinitesimal packet size assumption, and, with variable-size packets, do not need to know a connection's mean packet size in advance [DKS 89, Parekh 92, PG 93, PG 94]. Since PGPS and WFQ, though independently invented, are identical, we will only study WFQ.

The intuition behind WFQ is to compute the time a packet would complete service had we been serving packets with a GPS server, then serve packets in order of these finishing times. In other words, WFQ simulates GPS "on the side" and uses the results of this simulation to determine service order. We call a packet's finishing time under GPS a *finish number*, rather than a finish time, to emphasize that it is only a service tag that indicates the relative order in which the packet is to be served, and has nothing to do with the actual time at which the packet is served.

Finish number computation

The computation of the finish number depends on a variable called the *round number*. We will first study how to compute the round number when all weights are equal. For the moment, model a GPS server as doing *bit-by-bit* service, rather than infinitesimal-by-infinitesimal service. With this simplification, we define the round number to be the number of rounds of service a bit-by-bit round-robin scheduler has completed at a given time. A noninteger round number represent a partial round of service, so that, for example, a round number of 3.5 indicates that we are halfway through the fourth round of service. Note that each round of service takes a variable amount of time: the more connections served in a round, the longer the round takes. We call a connection *active* if the largest finish number of a packet either in its queue or last served from its queue is larger than the current round number. Thus, the length of a round, that is, the time taken to serve one bit from each active connection, is proportional to the number of active connections.

If we know the round number, we calculate the finish number as follows. The finish number of a packet arriving at an *inactive* connection is the sum of the current round number and the packet size in bits, because this is the round number when a bit-by-bit round-robin server would have completed service of that packet. For example, if a packet of size 10 bits arrives when the round number is 3, then the packet completes service ten rounds later, in the thirteenth round, when the round number is 13. If a packet arrives on an *active* connection, the arriving packet's finish number is the sum of the largest finish number of a packet in its queue (or last served from its queue) and the arriving packet's size (in bits). For example, if a packet of size 10 bits arrives to a queue that already contains a packet with a finish number of 20, we know that the packet in the queue completes service when the round number is 20. Thus, the incoming packet completes service when the round number reaches $20 + 10 = 30$. Combining these statements, if $P(i, k, t)$ is the size of the kth packet that arrives on connection i at time t, when $R(t)$ is the round number, and $F(i, k - 1, t)$ is the finish number for the $(k - 1)$th packet on that connection, then

$$F(i, k, t) = \max\{F(i, k - 1, t), R(t)\} + P(i, k, t) \tag{9.8}$$

We define the largest finish number of a packet in a connection's queue, or served from that connection's queue, to be the *connection's* finish number.

We mentioned earlier that the round number increases at a rate inversely proportional to the number of active connections. Instead of viewing the round number as the number of service rounds completed by a bit-by-bit round-robin server, we can redefine the round number to be a real-valued variable that increases at a rate inversely proportional to the number of currently active connections. From this perspective, the round number no longer has a physical meaning: it is just a convenient abstraction useful in computing finish numbers. With this modification, WFQ emulates GPS, instead of bit-by-bit round-robin scheduling.

WFQ also prescribes a buffer-drop policy. If a packet arrives to a scheduler with a full queue, the scheduler drops enough packets, in decreasing order of their finish numbers, to make room for the incoming packet. It is easy to show that this results in a min–max fair allocation of buffers at the switch (see Section 9.7.2).

We now make some observations about the relationship between WFQ and GPS.

- In GPS, a packet completes service when the round number increases beyond the packet's finish number.

- The finish time for a packet in WFQ is not the same as its finish number.

- Once assigned, the finish number does not depend on future packet arrivals and departures.

- The finish number of a packet is independent of the other connections awaiting service, because the rate of increase of the round number varies with the number of active connections.

We illustrate these with the next example.

EXAMPLE 9.10

Suppose packets of size 1, 2, and 2 units arrive at a WFQ scheduler at time 0 on equally weighted connections A, B, and C. Also, assume that a packet of size 2 arrives at connection A at time 4. (a) If the link service rate is 1 unit/s, compute the finish number of all the packets. (b) What is the round number when the system becomes idle, and (c) when does this happen?

Solution: We show the computation graphically in Figure 9.8. Notice that the round-number variable has a slope inversely proportional to the number of active connections.

(a) At time 0, the finish number for all three connections, as well as the round number, is initialized to 0. Consider the first packet arriving to the first

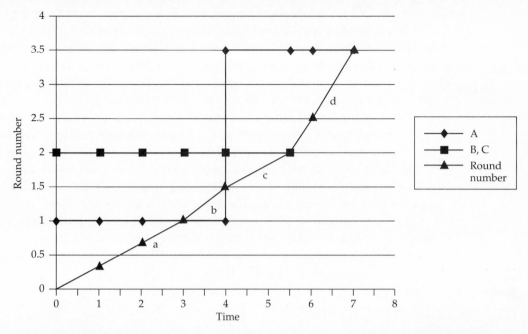

Figure 9.8: Illustration for Example 9.10. In time [0, 3] (segment "a") the round number line has a slope $\frac{1}{3}$, because the server has three backlogged connections. At time 3, connection A becomes inactive, and the slope increases to $\frac{1}{2}$ (segment "b"). At time 4, a second packet from A arrives and gets a finish number of 2 + 1.5 = 3.5. The slope decreases to $\frac{1}{3}$ again (segment "c"). At time 5.5, the round number increases to 2, and connections B and C become inactive. Thus, the slope of the round number line increases to 1 (segment "d"). At time 7, the round number increases to 3.5, and the second packet from A completes service. Since the line has a service rate of 1 unit/s, and a total of seven units are served, the line becomes idle at time 7.

connection. Since the connection's finish number is 0, from Equation 9.8, the first packet's finish number is max (0,0) + 1 = 1. Similarly, the finish numbers for the packets arriving at connections B and C are both 2. Note that the finish numbers are not the times when the packets complete service. Indeed, the first packet to be served is packet 1 from source 1, which completes at time 1. The second packet to be served is either the packet from connection B or the packet from connection C. Breaking the tie at random, say, by choosing B, the packet from B completes at time 3. Finally, the packet from C completes service at time 5.

To compute the finish number for the second packet on connection A, we need to know the round number at time 4. Note that at time 0, we have three active connections, so that the round number increases at the rate of $\frac{1}{3}$ units/s. Thus, the round number at time 3 is 1.The first packet from A completes service in the GPS emulation when the round number is 1 (this is when the round number line intersects the finish number line for the first packet from source A). Thus, connection A becomes inactive at time 3. In the time from 3 to 4, only connections B and C are active, and thus the round number has a slope of $\frac{1}{2}$. So, at time 4, the round number is 1.5. Because a packet of size 2 arrives to connection A's empty queue at time 4, its finish number is $1.5 + 2 = 3.5$. The arrival of this packet does not change the finish numbers of the packets already in B's and C's queues.

(b) The server becomes idle when the second packet from A completes service. Because this packet has a finish number of 3.5, the round number at that time must be 3.5. To understand this better, note that in GPS, the packets from B and C *simultaneously* complete service when the round number becomes 2, which happens at time 5.5. In the remaining 1.5 time units, the GPS round number increases with slope 1, so that it increases to 3.5 at time 7, when the second packet from source A completes service. The actual service order is A, B, C, A, in increasing order of the finish numbers.

(c) To compute the time when the server becomes idle, note that a total of seven units arrived for service, and the system serves one unit per second. So, the system becomes idle at time 7.

Iterated deletion

The main problem in computing a packet's finish number is determining the current round number of the simulated GPS server. Computing the exact round number is hard because of the *iterated deletion* problem [Keshav 91]. An example best explains the problem. Suppose the round number at time 0 is 0 and has a slope $\frac{1}{5}$. Then, we might incorrectly suppose that at time 5, it would have a value of $0 + \frac{1}{5} * 5 = 1$. However, our computation might be wrong because one of the five connections active at time 0 might become inactive before time 5. For example, say connection 1 becomes inactive at time 4, so that at time 4, the slope of the round number line increases from $\frac{1}{5}$ to $\frac{1}{4}$. Thus, at time 5, the round number would actually be $4 * \frac{1}{5} + 1 * \frac{1}{4} = 1.05$, which is greater than 1.0. The problem does not stop here. Suppose another connection, say connection 2, has a finish number smaller than 1.05. Then, connection 2 would also become inactive before time 5, so that the slope of the round number would further increase beyond 1.05 at time 5. Thus, if the increase in the slope of the round number causes a conversation to become inactive, the round number's slope further increases, so that more conversations might become inactive, and so on. In other words, if a conversation becomes inactive and is *deleted* from the list of active connections, it might cause other conversations also to become inactive, causing an *iterated deletion*. Computing the list of deletions at any given time is therefore hard. A fair queuing server updates its notion of the round number on every packet arrival and departure. Thus, it has to do a fairly complex computation once every few microseconds. This is a major problem with implementing fair queuing in high-speed networks. In Section 9.4.5, we study some techniques for overcoming this problem.

Thus far, we have studied the unweighted version of fair queuing. In the weighted version, connection i's finish number is updated by $P(i, k, t)/\phi(i)$, instead of by $P(i, k, t)$, where $\phi(i)$ is the weight of the ith connection:

$$F(i, k, t) = \max\{F(i, k - 1, t), R(t)\} + P(i, k, t)/\phi(i) \qquad (9.9)$$

In addition, the round number increases with a slope $1/\Sigma\phi(i)$, where we take the sum over all active sessions. It can be shown that this modification emulates GPS while allowing for weights [Parekh 92].

Implementation

When a packet arrives to a fair queuing scheduler, the scheduler updates its notion of the current round number, if necessary performing an iterated deletion. The scheduler then computes the finish number of the packet and places it in a priority queue, so that it is served in order of its finish number. Note that within a connection, finish numbers increase monotonically with time. The key to implementing fair queuing is in devising a fast and efficient priority queue, as discussed in Section 9.3.4.

Analysis

Let $Pmax(i)$ be the size of the largest possible packet sent on connection i, and let $Pmax$ be the size of the largest possible packet in the network. Recall that we define $G(i, \tau, t)$ to be the service received by connection i, using GPS, in the interval $[\tau, t]$, and $g(i)$ to be the smallest of the rates allocated to a connection along its path. It can be shown that WFQ can lag GPS by at most $Pmax/g(i)$, that is [GM 92, Parekh 92],

$$S(i, \tau, t)/g(i) \geq G(i, \tau, t)/g(i) - Pmax / g(i) \qquad (9.10)$$

However, under WFQ, a connection can receive substantially *more* service than with GPS, in other words, its *absolute fairness bound* is larger than $Pmax/g(i)$. This can result in bursty service over short time scales [BZ 96]. We can avoid this problem by changing the WFQ service rule. Instead of choosing the packet with the smallest finish time among all packets awaiting service, the scheduler should serve the packet with the smallest finish time among all the packets that have started service (and possibly finished) in the corresponding GPS system at that time [BZ 96]. We call this variant worst-case-fair-WFQ (WF²Q), and it can be proved to have an absolute fairness bound of $Pmax/g(i)$.

Evaluation

Weighted fair queuing (or PGPS) has three desirable properties. First, because it approximates GPS, it protects connections from each other. This *firewalling property* is important for public data networks. Second, under certain assumptions, a connection can obtain a worst-case end-to-end queuing delay that is independent of the number of hops it traverses and of the behavior of other connections. (We will study this in Section 9.5.) This allows networks of fair queuing schedulers to provide real-time performance guarantees, which is important for guaranteed-service connections. Finally, WFQ gives users an incentive to implement intelligent flow control mechanisms at the end-systems. With WFQ, a source is not required to send at a rate smaller than its currently allocated rate. However, a source that consistently sends more than its fair share is likely to lose packets from its own buffers, so it has an incentive to match its flow to the currently available service rate.

On the other hand, a WFQ scheduler requires per-connection (or per-aggregate) scheduler state, which leads to implementation complexity and can be expensive for schedulers that serve large numbers of connections. It requires an expensive iterated deletion algorithm to update its round number. Moreover, it requires explicit sorting of the output queue on the service tag, which requires time and complex hardware or software.

Despite these problems, increasing numbers of manufacturers are implementing weighted fair queuing in their router and switch products. As of early 1996, both the leading line of routers from Cisco, Inc., and ATM switches from FORE Systems, Inc., provide some form of WFQ scheduling. In the next subsection, we will examine some variants of WFQ that alleviate some problems faced with WFQ.

9.4.5 | Some variants of WFQ

Self-clocked fair queuing

One of the biggest problems with WFQ is implementing the algorithm for updating the round number on packet arrival, since this may lead to iterated deletion of connections. *Self-clocked fair queuing (SCFQ)* is a way to speed up round-number computation [DH 90, Golestani 94]. In SCFQ, when a packet arrives to an empty queue, instead of using the round number to compute its finish number, it uses the finish number of the packet *currently in service*. Using the same notation as in Equation 9.8, the new round number update rule is:

$$F(i, k, t) = \max(F(i, k - 1, t), CF) + P(i, k, t)/\phi(i) \qquad (9.11)$$

where CF is the finish number of the packet currently being served.

Golestani has shown that the *relative fairness bound* for SCFQ is:

$$RFB = Pmax(i)/g(i) + Pmax(j)/g(j), \qquad (9.12)$$

where $Pmax(i)$ and $Pmax(j)$ are the sizes of the packets that can be sent by connections i and j. The absolute fairness bound for SCFQ is currently unknown.

Although the SCFQ round number update rule is easy to implement, it can be unfair over short time scales. Consider a scheduler that is serving a connection with a weight of 50, and fifty connections with a weight of 1. Let unit-size packets from each of the fifty connections arrive at time 0; they will all get a finish number of 1. Let a packet from the connection with weight 50 arrive just after time 0. Since the packet in service has a finish number of 1, this packet will get a finish number of $1 + 1/50 = 1.02$. Therefore, it will be served after one packet from all the other connections, i.e., at time 50, incurring a delay of 50 time units. If the scheduler were WFQ, the packet would have received a finish number of 0.02, incurring a delay of only 1 time unit (for the current packet to finish service). Thus, SCFQ leads to larger worst-case latencies than WFQ, and, consequently, greater unfairness at shorter time scales. To be more precise, if the largest packet allowed in the network has a packet size $Pmax$, the scheduler is serving N connections, and the service rate of the scheduler is r, then the worst-case latency for SCFQ is $Pmax/g(i) + (N - 1)\, Pmax/r$ for SCFQ, compared to $Pmax/g(i) + Pmax/r$ for WFQ [GLV 95, SV 96].

Start-time fair queuing

The computational benefits of SCFQ, but without the penalty of a large worst-case delay and short-term unfairness, can be obtained with a variant of SCFQ called start-time fair queuing [GVC 96]. In this scheme, we compute both the finish number and the *start number* of each arriving packet. The start number of a packet arriving at an inactive connection is set to the current round number. Otherwise, it is set to the finish number of its previous packet. A packet's finish number is the sum of its start number and its packet size divided by its weight. The round number is set to the start number of the packet currently in service. If there are no more packets to send, the round number is set to the largest of the finish numbers of any packet sent until that time. Service is in order of increasing start numbers. It can be shown that start-time fair queuing has the same low implementation complexity as SCFQ. Moreover, its worst-case delay is much lower than with SCFQ. Other properties of the discipline are described in reference [GVC 96].

9.4.6   Summary

The ideal discipline for best-effort connections is generalized processor sharing (GPS) (Section 9.4.1), but it is unimplementable because it serves an infinitesimal amount from each nonempty connection queue. An obvious emulation of GPS uses weighted round-robin (Section 9.4.2), but this does not work well if packets can be of different sizes, or if we want a fair allocation of bandwidth at small time scales. The deficit round-robin discipline is similar to weighted round-robin, but works well even with variable-size packets (Section 9.4.3). However, it, too, does not allocate bandwidth fairly at short time scales. We overcome this with the weighted fair queuing (WFQ) algorithm, where packets are served in order of service tags, which are computed by simulating GPS in parallel (Section 9.4.4). Although WFQ compares favorably with GPS in fairness, it is complex because of its simulation of GPS. Variants of WFQ, such as self-clocked fair queuing and start-time fair queuing, have almost the same fairness properties as WFQ, but are easier to implement (Section 9.4.5).

9.5   Scheduling guaranteed-service connections

9.5.1   Weighted fair queuing

It turns out that the weighted fair queuing (WFQ) discipline can also be used to give connections performance guarantees. First, note that WFQ gives a bandwidth bound to each connection, since connection i is guaranteed $\phi(i, k) / \Sigma\, \phi(j, k)$ share of the link capacity at its kth hop. Parekh and Gallager proved an important bound on the worst-case end-to-end delay suffered by a connection traversing a series of WFQ schedulers; we now state this bound [Parekh 92, PG 93, PG 94].

Let a leaky-bucket-constrained[4] source i with parameters $(\sigma(i), \rho(i))$ pass through K schedulers, where the kth scheduler, $1 \le k \le K$, has a link rate $r(k)$. Let $g(i, k)$ be the service rate assigned to the connection at the kth scheduler, where:

$$g(i, k) = \phi(i, k) \, r(k)/\Sigma \, \phi(j, k) \tag{9.13}$$

and we take the sum over all connections sharing the kth scheduler. Let $g(i)$ be the smallest of the $g(i, k)$s over all k. We assume that $g(i) \ge \rho(i)$; otherwise, the queue at one of the schedulers will build up without bound. If the largest packet allowed on that connection is of size $Pmax(i)$, and the largest packet allowed in the network is of size $Pmax$, then, independent of the number of schedulers the connection traverses, and independent of the behavior of the other connections (even if they are not leaky-bucket bounded), the worst-case end-to-end queuing and transmission delay $D^*(i)$ is bounded by [GV 95]:

$$D^*(i) \le \frac{\sigma(i)}{g(i)} + \sum_{k=1}^{K-1} \frac{Pmax(i)}{g(i, k)} + \sum_{k=1}^{K} \frac{Pmax}{r(k)} \tag{9.14}$$

To understand this result, note that when $Pmax \approx 0$, that is, when all packets are infinitesimally small, the delay is bounded by $\sigma(i)/g(i)$. Intuitively, this means that though the connection actually traverses a series of schedulers, it behaves as if it were served by a single scheduler with rate $g(i)$, so that when the source sends a burst of length $\sigma(i)$, it experiences a worst-case delay $\sigma(i)/g(i)$. A correction term, $Pmax(i)/g(i, k)$ at each scheduler, models the situation where a packet from source i arrives just after it would have received service under GPS. It can be shown that this packet is delayed by at most $Pmax(i)/g(i, k)$. The third term, which is independent of $g(i)$, reflects the fact that if a packet from i arrives at a busy scheduler, the packet may have to wait up to $Pmax/r(k)$ time before it is served.

Parekh and Gallager's theorem shows that, with a suitable choice of parameters, a network of WFQ servers can provide worst-case end-to-end delay guarantees. A source needing a particular worst-case end-to-end delay bound need only pick an appropriate value for g.

EXAMPLE 9.11

Consider a connection with leaky bucket parameters (16,384 bytes, 150 Kbps) that traverses 10 hops on a network where all the links have a bandwidth of 45 Mbps. If the largest allowed packet in the network is 8192 bytes long, what g value will guarantee an end-to-end delay of 100 ms? Assume a propagation delay of 30 ms.

Solution: The queuing delay must be bounded by $100 - 30 = 70$ ms. Plugging this into Equation 9.14, we get $70 * 10^{-3} = \{(16384 * 8) + (9 * 8192 * 8)\} / g + (10 * 8192$

---

[4]We will study leaky-bucket regulation in more detail in Section 13.3.4. For the moment, note that a source is leaky-bucket constrained with parameters (σ, ρ) if, in any interval of length t, it can transmit at most $\sigma + \rho t$ bits.

* 8)/(45 * 10^6), so that g = 12.87 Mbps. Notice that this is more than 85 times larger than the source's average rate of 150 Kbps. This is because the $(K-1)Pmax/g$ term contributes to nearly 46 ms of the 70 ms delay bound, and the $K * Pmax/r$ term contributes another 14 ms. The σ/g term contributes only 10.8 ms to the end-to-end delay! The lesson is that with large packets, packet delays can be quite substantial.

WFQ does not provide a nontrivial delay-jitter bound (i.e., a delay-jitter bound smaller than the delay bound itself). Moreover, as shown in Example 9.11, to obtain a lower delay bound, a connection must make a large reservation, even if it cannot use the entire reserved bandwidth. Finally, WFQ has the problems with implementation complexity that we discussed in Section 9.3.4.

Although variance of WFQ, such as self-clocked fair queuing, have lower implementation complexities, they also have similar end-to-end delay bounds. However, start-time fair queuing, under some conditions, has been shown to have a lower end-to-end delay bound than WFQ [GVC 96]. It is therefore better than WFQ, both for guaranteed-service and for best-effort connections.

9.5.2 Virtual clock

The virtual clock scheduling discipline is similar to weighted fair queuing and was independently proposed by Zhang [Zhang 90]. A virtual clock scheduler stamps packets with a tag, and packets are served in order of their tags, as in WFQ. However, the tag values are not computed to emulate GPS scheduling. Instead, a virtual clock scheduler emulates time-division multiplexing in the same way that a fair queuing scheduler emulates GPS. Specifically, using the same notation as in Equation 9.8, the finish number is computed as:

$$F(i, k, t) = \max(F(i, k-1, t), \text{real time}) + P(i, k, t)/\phi(i) \tag{9.15}$$

Comparing with Equation 9.9, we have replaced the round number with the real time. Because the round number in WFQ is hard to compute, this simplifies the calculation of the virtual clock finish number. When all connections are backlogged, virtual clock and fair queuing provide identical service and identical worst-case end-to-end delay bounds [GLV 95]. Thus, we can substitute it for WFQ when serving guaranteed-service connections. However, when used for best-effort connections, the relative fairness bound for virtual clock is infinity [SV 96]. In other words, when two connections are backlogged, one of them may obtain a throughput infinitely more than another. If we only want to implement one scheduler in a switch, we may be better off with implementing WFQ.

9.5.3 Delay-earliest-due-date and jitter-earliest-due-date

In classic earliest-due-date (EDD) scheduling, we assign each packet a deadline, and the scheduler serves packets in order of their deadlines. If the scheduler is overcommitted, then some packets miss their deadlines. With EDD, packets assigned deadlines closer to their arrival times receive a lower delay than packets assigned deadlines farther away from their arrival times.

Delay-EDD is an extension of EDD that specifies the process by which the scheduler assigns deadlines to packets [FV 90]. During call setup, each source negotiates a service contract with the scheduler. The contract states that if a source obeys a peak rate descriptor, then every packet on that connection receives a worst-case delay smaller than some bound. During call admission, the scheduler ensures not only that the sum of the peak rates of the admitted calls is smaller than the link capacity, but also that even in the worst case, when every connection sends traffic at its peak rate, it meets its delay bound (the *schedulability* test) [FV 90].

The key to delay-EDD lies in the way the scheduler assigns deadlines to packets. The scheduler sets a packet's deadline to the time at which it should be sent had it been received according to the connection's contract, that is, slower than its peak rate. By reserving bandwidth at a connection's peak rate, a delay-EDD scheduler can ensure that it has served the previous packet from that connection before the next packet arrives, so that every packet from that connection obeying the peak rate constraint receives a hard delay bound. Note that the delay bound for a connection is independent of its bandwidth reservation, in that a connection reserving a small bandwidth can still obtain a small delay bound. Therefore, unlike GPS-emulation schedulers, delay-EDD separates the bandwidth and delay bounds, but at the cost of reserving bandwidth at the peak rate, giving up temporal statistical multiplexing gain [GV 95, Zhang 95].

Since a delay-EDD scheduler serves packets in order of their deadlines, it needs to place them in a priority queue as in WFQ. The scheduler also needs to store per-connection finish numbers as in WFQ. Thus, its implementation is as complex as a WFQ implementation, except that it does not need round-number computation. Delay-EDD's main advantage over WFQ-like schedulers is that it provides end-to-end delay bounds independent of the bandwidth guaranteed to a connection. On the other hand, it requires every connection to reserve bandwidth at its peak rate, whereas a WFQ-like server need only reserve bandwidth at the connection's average rate. Moreover, it cannot provide a nontrivial end-to-end delay-jitter bound.

In a jitter-EDD (J-EDD) scheduler, a delay-jitter regulator (described in Section 9.3.2) precedes the EDD scheduler [VZF 91]. With a delay-jitter regulator, all packets receive the same delay at every hop (except at the last hop), so the difference between the largest and the smallest delays, which is the delay jitter along the connection, is reduced to the delay jitter on the last hop. Thus, a network of J-EDD schedulers can give connections end-to-end bandwidth, delay, and delay-jitter bounds. The J-EDD scheduler incorporates a delay-EDD scheduler, so to obtain a worst-case delay bound, a connection must reserve bandwidth at its peak rate. The call admission control algorithm is identical to that of delay-EDD.

9.5.4   Rate-controlled scheduling

Rate-controlled scheduling disciplines are a class of scheduling disciplines that can give connections bandwidth, delay, and delay-jitter bounds. A rate-controlled scheduler has two components: a *regulator* and a *scheduler* (Figure 9.9). Incoming packets are placed in

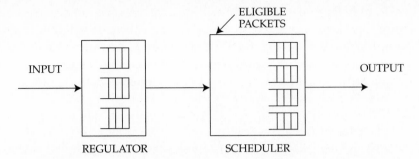

Figure 9.9: Rate-controlled scheduler. A rate-controlled scheduler consists of a regulator and a scheduler. The regulator delays packets until they are eligible, and the scheduler arbitrates among eligible packets. By choosing different regulators and schedulers, a rate-controlled discipline can provide a variety of bandwidth, delay, and delay-jitter guarantees.

the regulator, which uses one of many algorithms to determine the packet's *eligibility* time. When a packet becomes eligible, it is placed in the scheduler, which arbitrates among eligible packets. By delaying packets in the regulator, we can shape the flow of incoming packets to obey any constraint. Two examples of constraints are (1) packets should arrive to the scheduler at a rate less than a peak rate (a rate-jitter regulator) and (2) packets should arrive to the scheduler a constant delay after leaving the scheduler at the previous switch (a delay-jitter regulator). The scheduler can serve packets first-come-first-served, place them in a multilevel priority queue (thus giving some of them lower delays), or serve them using WFQ (thus giving them a weighted fair share of the link bandwidth). The service properties of a rate-controlled scheduler therefore depend on the choices of the regulator and scheduler.

It can be shown that a rate-controlled scheduler can emulate a wide range of work-conserving and non-work-conserving scheduling disciplines [ZF 94]. For example, if the regulator ensures that for each connection, over a specified time period, no more than a specified number of cells are marked eligible, then the rate-controlled discipline emulates the *hierarchical round-robin* discipline described in reference [KKK 90]. Similarly, if we use a delay-jitter regulator and an earliest-due-date scheduler, then the rate-controlled discipline emulates jitter-earliest-due-date (Section 9.5.3). It can also emulate other disciplines in the literature (but not described here), such as *rate-controlled static priority* [ZF 93] and *stop-and-go* [Golestani 90a, Golestani 90b].

Implementation

Implementing a rate-controlled discipline requires us to implement a regulator and a scheduler. We discussed implementation issues for regulators in Section 9.3.2 and for schedulers in Section 9.3.4. To recapitulate, if we can tolerate some granularity in time stamps, we can implement a regulator using a calendar queue, which allows us to build efficient and simple regulators in either hardware or software. However, for delay-jitter regulation, we need clock synchronization in the network, as well as time stamps in the header of every packet, which might prove expensive in practice. The implementation complexity of the scheduler depends on the choice of scheduler. If the scheduler is a multipriority FCFS queue, then it only requires a head and tail pointer to point to a queue of packets at each priority level. If we use an earliest-due-date scheduler, we need to implement a sorted priority queue, as discussed in Section 9.3.4.

Analysis

With a rate-controlled discipline, a connection's rate is monitored and shaped at each regulator. So, if a connection sends traffic faster than the rate it agreed to at the time of admission control, its packets are delayed at the queue at the first regulator. Thus, by protecting a connection from other connections, a rate-controlled discipline assures each connection a guaranteed bandwidth.

It is relatively simple to compute end-to-end delay bounds for rate-controlled disciplines because they partially or completely reconstruct input traffic at each switch. One can think of each scheduler along the path as introducing distortion in a connection's traffic, which is partially or completely removed by the regulator at the next switch. With a *delay-jitter* regulator, the traffic arriving at the kth scheduler along the path has the same characterization as the traffic arriving at the first scheduler, which is known to obey the source traffic description. Thus, if an individual scheduler can bound the delay for a traffic source obeying a particular descriptor, the end-to-end delay is just the sum of the individual delay bounds. Even with a *rate-jitter* regulator, we can show that the end-to-end queuing delay is bounded from above by the sum of the individual delay bounds [ZF 94]. More precisely, for a rate-jitter regulator, if the delay bound at the kth hop is $d(k)$, and the *smoothing delay*, that is, the delay in converting the input traffic descriptor to the descriptor enforced by the first regulator, is D, then the end-to-end delay is bounded by $D + \Sigma\, d(i)$, where we take the sum over the schedulers along the connection's path [Zhang 95]. Thus, for both sorts of regulators, we need only compute the worst-case delay bound for traffic arriving at a single scheduler, greatly simplifying the problem. Moreover, with both regulators, by using a multipriority scheduler we can decouple bandwidth and delay bounds. That is, we can give a connection a small bandwidth assignment as well as a small delay bound. This is not possible with WFQ.

EXAMPLE 9.12

Consider a rate-controlled scheduler composed from a rate-jitter regulator and a multilevel priority FCFS scheduler (this is also called a *rate-controlled static priority* or *RCSP* scheduler [ZF 94]). Suppose we allocate connections A and B rates of 64 Kbps and 1.5 Mbps. This means that after serving a packet of size l bits from A, the next packet from A is eligible for service only after a time interval t, where $t = l/64$ Kbps. Once it is eligible, however, it is immediately placed in one of the priority classes of the scheduler. Suppose we want to give connection A a small delay bound, and connection B a large delay bound. We assign A to a higher priority level, and B to a lower priority level. Even if packets from both A and B become eligible simultaneously, A's packet gets a lower queuing delay because it has higher priority than B at the scheduler. Thus, we can give A's packet a lower delay bound, though it has a smaller bandwidth allocation than B. This is possible because the scheduler decouples bandwidth and delay allocations. With WFQ, to get a smaller delay bound, A would have to reserve a large bandwidth, reducing the potential for temporal statistical multiplexing gain.

With a delay-jitter regulator, the end-to-end delay jitter is the delay bound at the last scheduler. No nontrivial delay-jitter bound can be obtained with rate-jitter regulation. When using regulators that emulate other disciplines, the end-to-end delay and delay-jitter bounds are the same as the ones presented for these disciplines in the literature.

> One might assume that, for a given source descriptor, and a given bandwidth reservation at each hop, a rate-controlled discipline would have an end-to-end delay bound that is larger than the delay bound from a GPS-emulation scheduler, because a rate-controlled discipline may be non-work-conserving, thus increasing the sum of the mean delays over all connections. However, it has been shown that if each regulator limits a connection's traffic to its prespecified leaky-bucket bound, a rate-controlled server achieves the same end-to-end delay bound as WFQ [GGPS 96]. Moreover, if the scheduler at each node is EDD, then there are some delay assignments that are feasible with these types of rate-controlled schedulers that are infeasible with WFQ. In other words, the set of calls that can be admitted with these specially designed rate-controlled schedulers is larger than the class of calls that can be admitted with WFQ schedulers [GGPS 96]. This is particularly interesting because neither EDD nor the regulator requires the complicated round-number-updating algorithm needed for WFQ. Therefore, this form of rate-controlled service is a replacement for WFQ that not only provides the same end-to-end delay bound as WFQ, but may also be easier to implement. (As of the time of this writing, we have little experience with actually implementing rate-controlled disciplines, so it is still too early to declare it a clear winner.) Unfortunately, since its delay bound is identical to WFQ, like WFQ, this variant of rate-controlled scheduling links the bandwidth and delay bounds.

Evaluation

Rate-controlled disciplines have several advantages over other disciplines:

- They are flexible, in that they can emulate a variety of other disciplines.

- With some choices of regulators and schedulers, they can decouple bandwidth and delay assignment.

- With both delay-jitter and rate-jitter regulators, end-to-end delay bounds can be easily computed.

- They do not require complicated schedulers to guarantee protection (the scheduler can just be multilevel static priority or even FCFS).

- With properly chosen regulators, they can achieve WFQ delay bounds without the complexity of updating the wrong number.

On the other hand, they require a per-scheduler calendar queue, and they achieve a delay-jitter bound only at the expense of increasing the mean delay. Besides, if the scheduler uses a delay-jitter regulator, it must, in addition, police all connections, because a delay-jitter regulator does not automatically restrict a connection's bandwidth share. Nevertheless, in view of their advantages and flexibility, rate-controlled disciplines may be the best available disciplines for serving connections that require bandwidth, delay, and delay-jitter bounds in high-speed networks.

> **Interoperability**
>
> In our discussion thus far, we have assumed that all the schedulers along the path implement the same scheduling discipline. In reality, because equipment can come from different manufacturers, and because connections can span networks administered by different domains, we may want to provide performance guarantees for connections served by heterogeneous scheduling disciplines. This area is still an open research area, though some progress has been made recently [GLV 95, SV 96]. Specifically, if all the schedulers along the path provide some form of protection, that is, a connection is guaranteed a minimum bandwidth independent of the behavior of the other sources, then we can extend Parekh and Gallager's result to provide end-to-end delay bounds over a tandem of such schedulers. Details can be found in references [GLV 95, SV 96].

9.5.5   Summary

In this section, we studied some scheduling disciplines that allow guaranteed-service connections to obtain bandwidth, delay, and delay-jitter bounds. We first showed that weighted fair queuing (WFQ) allows us to obtain bandwidth and worst-case end-to-end delay bounds (Section 9.5.1). However, to obtain a low end-to-end worst-case delay, a connection must reserve a large bandwidth, reducing the potential for temporal statistical multiplexing gain and making the network more expensive to operate. WFQ's variants, such as virtual clock, also provide a similar bound, and have a similar problem (Section 9.5.2). We then studied delay-earliest-due-date and jitter-earliest-due-date, two disciplines that provide bandwidth and delay bounds and do not couple them, at the expense of a reservation for the peak rate of a connection (Section 9.5.3). We generalized the jitter-earliest-due-date discipline to obtain the class of rate-controlled disciplines (Section 9.5.4). Disciplines in this class are composed from a rate regulator and a scheduler. They can provide a variety of performance bounds by appropriate choice of these components.

9.6   Comparison

The tables in this section summarize the disciplines described in Sections 9.4 and 9.5.

A second way to summarize the disciplines is to look at the mechanisms they use for providing protection and performance bounds, and for decoupling bandwidth from delay allocations. Table 9.2 extends the one presented in reference [ZF 93].

	W/N		Work-conserving or non-work-conserving
B		Bandwidth bound	
D		Delay bound	
J		Nontrival delay-jitter bound	

Name	W/N	Summary	B	D	J	Advantages	Disadvantages
First-come-first-served (FCFS)	W	Packets are served in the order they arrive at the scheduler.	—	—	—	Easy to implement. Requires very little scheduler state.	No protection between well-behaved and misbehaved connections. Cannot provide per-connection quality-of-service guarantees. Can increase connection burstiness.
Weighted fair queuing (WFQ)	W	Emulates GPS. Scheduler tags packets with completion times under GPS, then serves packets in order of tags.	✔	✔	—	Provides both protection and some degree of fairness. Can provide per-connection bandwidth and delay bounds. Smooths bursts in the network. No need to police traffic.	Computing round number can be complicated. Needs per-connection state. Packets have to be at least partially sorted before being served. Small delay bound requires large bandwidth reservation.
Self-clocked fair queuing (SCFQ)	W	Same as WFQ, except that round number is set to finish number of packet in service.	✔	✔	—	Same as WFQ. Does not require complicated round-number computation.	Same as WFQ, except round-number computation. Worst-case end-to-end delay is much larger than with WFQ.
Worst-case fair weighted fair queuing (WF²Q)	W	Same as WFQ, except that scheduler chooses the packet with the smallest finish time among all the packets that have already started service in the corresponding GPS emulation.	✔	✔	—	Same as WFQ. Has a smaller absolute fairness bound, so has better fairness than WFQ (it can be shown that no packet-by-packet discipline can be fairer).	Same as WFQ. Requires an additional regulator to hold back ineligible packets (i.e., those that have not yet started service in the corresponding GPS emulation).

Table 9.1: Comparison of scheduling disciplines.

Name	W/N	Summary	B	D	J	Advantages	Disadvantages
Start-time fair queuing (SFQ)	W	Same as WFQ, except that round number is set to start number of packet in service.	✔	✔	—	Same as WFQ. Does not require complicated round-number computation. Low-throughput flows have a smaller delay than with WFQ. Can be used with variable-rate servers.	Same as WFQ, except round-number computation. Worst-case end-to-end delay is similar to that of WFQ.
Virtual clock	W	Emulates time-division multiplexing. Scheduler tags packets with completion times under TDM, then serves packets in order of tags.	✔	✔	—	Provides protection. Can provide per-connection bandwidth and delay bounds. Does not require complicated round-number computation.	Potentially unlimited relative unfairness between two connections. Needs per-connection state. Packets have to be at least partially sorted before being served.
Delay-earliest-due-date	W	Scheduler tags packets with a deadline, which is the sum of the expected arrival time and the delay bound. Packets are served in order of their deadline. Admission control guarantees that all deadlines can always be met.	✔	✔	—	Can provide end-to-end delay and bandwidth bounds. End-to-end delay bound trivial to compute. No need for complicated round-number computation. Separates allocation of bandwidth and delay.	Bandwidth must be reserved at peak rate instead of at the average rate. Needs per-connection state and sorted priority queue. More buffers are needed deeper along a connection's path.
Jitter-earliest-due-date	N	Consists of a regulator and scheduler. Regulator reconstructs traffic to original form. EDD-scheduler is as above.	✔	✔	✔	Can provide delay-jitter bounds as well as bandwidth and delay bounds. End-to-end delay and delay-jitter bounds are trival to compute. Requires a fixed-size buffer reservation along its path.	Same as delay-EDD. Separate regulator makes implementation complex. To reduce delay jitter, all packets receive a large delay.

Table 9.1: Continued.

Name	W / N	Summary	B	D	J	Advantages	Disadvantages
Rate-controlled disciplines	W / N	Generalize RCSP to allow arbitrary regulators and schedulers. With appropriately chosen regulators and schedulers, can emulate other disciplines.	✔	✔	✔	Can provide bandwidth, delay, and delay-jitter bounds. Decouples bandwidth and delay bounds. Easy to implement in hardware. Sources need not reserve bandwidth at the peak rate to receive delay bounds. With specially chosen regulators, can provide same delay bounds as WFQ.	With delay-jitter regulation, sources must be policed. Separate regulator complicates implementation. In order to satisfy delay-jitter bound, all packets receive a large delay.

Table 9.1: Continued.

		GPS emulations	Delay-EDD	Jitter-EDD	Rate-controlled
Protection and bandwidth allocation	Policing at entrance to network				DJ
	Logical or physical per-VC queue	✔	✔	✔	RJ
Bounded delay	Multilevel priority				✔
	Sorted priority queue	✔	✔	✔	✔
Bounded delay jitter	Traffic reconstruction in a regulator			✔	✔
Decoupled delay and bandwidth allocation	Separate regulator and scheduler			✔	✔
	Service order based on real-time delay bounds		✔		

Table 9.2: Comparison of scheduling disciplines.

9.7   Packet dropping

A scheduler buffers packets awaiting service, and if the buffer fills, drops them according to the *packet-drop strategy* component of the scheduling discipline. In the same way as the scheduler decides which packet to *serve* next, during overload it also decides which packet to *drop* next.

A scheduler should not drop packets unless absolutely necessary. Dropping a packet that has already used bandwidth to reach the loss point wastes network resources. Unfortunately, if the network is overloaded, losses from best-effort connections are inevitable (losses from guaranteed-service connections ought to be rare, because admission control ensures that they have sufficient resources). In such a situation, the scheduler must carefully choose which packets to drop, because a naive drop policy can lead to unfair service. For example, consider the analog of the FCFS policy, which is to drop the incoming packet when the single shared queue is full. This policy is trivial to implement. However, a misbehaving source that keeps the buffer always full would cause losses even for well-behaved connections. The packet-drop strategy should *protect* well-behaved connections from misbehaving ones.

We can classify packet-drop policies along four lines, which roughly parallel the classification of scheduling disciplines: (a) degree of aggregation, (b) choice of drop priorities, (c) early or overloaded drop, and (d) drop position.

9.7.1   Degree of aggregation

As with scheduling, the drop algorithm may maintain per-connection state, or may aggregate connections into classes. With per-connection state, the drop policy provides more protection, at the expense of more state. At the other extreme, with a single class, the state information is minimal, but during overload, connections are not protected from each other. The greater the aggregation, the greater the loss of protection.

If packets are queued per-connection (or per-class) and share buffers from a common pool, the drop algorithm can achieve a min–max fair allocation of buffers by always dropping packets from the longest queue. To see this, note that when the buffers are not full, connections are allocated whatever buffers they need. However, when a packet arrives to a full buffer, the scheduler drops one or more packets from the longest queue, creating space for the incoming packet. This automatically ensures that backlogged connections get equal shares, while non-backlogged connections are fully satisfied, which is the criterion for min–max fairness. If the scheduler implements WFQ-like service, then the longest queue is the one that contains a packet with the largest finish number. Therefore, a WFQ-like server can emulate dropping a packet from the longest queue by dropping the packet with the largest finish number, even if packets are not queued per-connection.

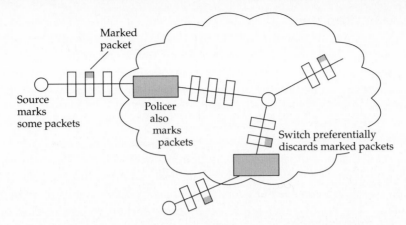

Figure 9.10: Priority packet dropping. Either the source or a policer marks lower-priority packets. The switch preferentially drops lower-priority packets when buffers are full. Thus, when the network is unloaded, excess capacity can be absorbed. When the network is loaded, unmarked packets are unaffected.

9.7.2   Drop priorities

A network operator can increase network efficiency by allowing some packets to be marked as lower-priority packets. When the network is underloaded, these packets soak up available bandwidth, but during overload, because marked packets have lower priority, regular traffic is unaffected (Figure 9.10). For example, consider a source that encodes audio or video data with a layered encoder that produces two packet streams: an *essential* layer, and an *enhancement* layer. The essential layer is sufficient to give a coarse rendering of the media stream, and the enhancement layer improves its quality. The source can then mark packets in the enhancement layer with a *congestion loss priority bit*. Switches are expected to drop lower-priority packets when they have a choice. Thus, when the network is underutilized, a receiver obtains a higher-quality media stream, but as the load increases and schedulers must drop packets, the quality automatically decreases.

This approach has several problems. First, a layered encoder is much harder to build than a standard encoder. Second, it is hard for the source to decide what traffic descriptor to choose for the layered streams. If it chooses a descriptor sufficient only for the essential layer, it risks delivering a poor-quality stream to the receiver. On the other hand, if it chooses a descriptor that covers both streams, there is not much point in marking the enhancement stream. Finally, to reconstruct the media stream, the receiver must deal with jitter and lost packets in multiple streams. This makes its job more complex. It is not clear that the additional complexity is worth the price.

Besides the source, a *policer* can also set the congestion loss priority bit for packets that exceed the source traffic descriptor. This approach suffers from the same problems as when the source sets a bit.

A second form of loss priority concerns packet versus cell loss. As shown in Chapter 12, when AAL5 frames are carried in an ATM network, the loss of a single cell causes the entire frame to be lost. Thus, the loss of a burst of cells could cause multiple frames to be lost, resulting in error multiplication [RF 94]. To avoid this problem, when a switch drops a cell, it declares the corresponding connection to be in the "drop" state, and drops all subsequent cells that arrive on that connection until it receives the last cell of the frame. This strategy, called *packet discard* (as opposed to *cell discard*), works best in combination with early drop, which we discuss in Section 9.7.3.

A third form of drop priority is to prefer to drop packets from connections that originate nearby, rather than those that originate farther away. The idea is that dropping a packet that has already used a lot of network resources is a waste, so dropping packets that have only recently entered the network is better. In practice, each packet carries a hop count, incremented at every hop. The scheduler then prefers to drop packets with smaller hop counts. This approach requires packets to be sorted in order of increasing hop counts, which increases the drop algorithm's implementation complexity. Moreover, commonly implemented hop counts, such as IP's time-to-live field, *decrease* from a nearly arbitrary initial value, instead of increasing. Thus, we cannot implement this form of drop priority on the Internet.

9.7.3   Early or overloaded drop

Early-drop schedulers drop packets even if the buffer is not full. This is suitable for networks where endpoints are sensitive to packet loss and reduce their flow rate in response to a loss (such as sources implementing TCP on the Internet). Thus, an early-drop scheduler implicitly signals endpoints to reduce their rate by dropping their packets. Of course, if an endpoint does not reduce its rate, the switch will become overloaded and drop packets anyway. Thus, with early drop, cooperative sources get lower overall delays, while uncooperative sources are likely to see severe packet loss.

Two forms of early drop have been studied in the literature, both in the context of a single aggregated queue: *early random drop* [Hashem 89] and *random early detection* [FJ 93]. In early random drop, whenever the aggregate queue length exceeds a certain *drop level*, the switch drops each arriving packet with a fixed drop probability. The intuition is that misbehaving sources send more packets, so dropping an arriving packet at random is more likely to drop a packet from a misbehaving source than one from a well-behaved source. Thus, the scheme tries to target misbehaving sources without unduly affecting the bandwidth received by well-behaved sources. However, it has been shown that this drop policy is not successful in controlling misbehaving users [Zhang 89].

Random early detection (RED) improves on early random drop in three ways. First, packets are dropped based on an exponential average of the queue length, rather than the instantaneous queue length. This allows small bursts to pass through unharmed, dropping packets only during sustained overloads. Second, the packet drop probability is a linear function of the average queue length. As the mean queue length increases, the probability of packet loss increases. This prevents a severe reaction to mild overload (as with early random drop). Finally, RED switches can not only drop packets, but mark offending packets. With suitably modified endpoints, RED switches allow congestion avoidance similar to the DECbit scheme described in Chapter 13.

It has been shown that RED substantially improves the performance of a network of cooperating TCP sources, and that the probability that a connection loses packets is roughly proportional to its actual throughput share (so that ill-behaved connections are more likely to lose packets) [FJ 93]. Moreover, RED does not have a bias against bursty sources. That is, it does not preferentially drop packets from bursty sources. This is important for TCP connections that send packets in bursts when they start (Section 13.4.5). If RED were biased against bursts, newly opened connections might never open their flow-control window fully before shutting the window down again in response to a packet loss. Finally, like all drop policies, RED can control the queue length irrespective of endpoint cooperation.

9.7.4 Drop position

Packets can be dropped from the head or tail of a per-connection (or aggregated) queue, or from a random position, or the entire queue can be dropped. Each option has some advantages and disadvantages.

Dropping from the *tail* of the queue is the default approach and is easy to implement, because the scheduler can simply drop the incoming packet without touching the queue head and tail pointers. Dropping from the head of the queue is somewhat harder to implement, because the scheduler must modify the queue pointers. However, it has an important side effect. Consider a source that detects lost packets using duplicate acks, as discussed in Section 12.4.7 (in this approach, when the sender receives duplicate cumulative acks, it guesses that a packet has been lost). If the packet is dropped from the tail, the sender discovers the fact that packets have been lost only after the entire queue has been served, because the "hole" in the sequence number space is at the tail of the queue. If packets are dropped from the head, instead, this information reaches the source sooner, and it can take corrective action sooner (Figure 9.11) [LNO 95]. Thus, drop from head, although somewhat more expensive to implement, improves the performance of sources that implement fast retransmission, such as TCP.

Dropping packets from a random position[5] in the queue distributes losses fairly among connections. One can think of the buffer at a scheduler as a sample of the traffic arriving to the scheduler. Connections that send data at a faster rate are more likely to have packets in the buffer than connections that send data at a slower rate, so dropping a packet from a random position punishes sources in proportion to their sending rate. This punishes bandwidth hogs, sparing well-behaved connections that try to keep only a few packets in the bottleneck buffer. Dropping packets from a random position is fairly complex, since the scheduler not only needs to compute a random number, but also must

---

[5]Which is not the same as early random drop or random early drop, which drop a packet randomly in time, but from the tail of the queue.

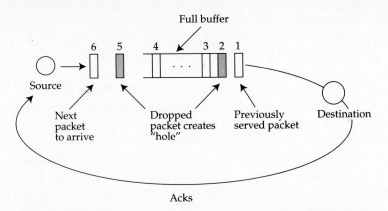

Figure 9.11: Drop from head versus drop from tail. With drop from head, when a packet is lost, the "hole" in the sequence space (sequence number 2) is known to the source earlier than with drop from tail, where the hole occurs at sequence number 5.

remove a packet from an arbitrary position in the queue. Thus, it is not implementable in real systems.

Finally, a recent and novel (but unpublished) proposal is to drop the entire longest per-connection queue when it is full [Restrick 94]. The idea is that the longest queue belongs to the worst-behaved connection, so dropping its queue reclaims the most buffer space while still protecting well-behaved connections. This policy is trivial to implement at high speeds. Moreover, in cell-based networks, it at least partly avoids the error-multiplication problem, since the longest queue is likely to contain some number of full frames and one partial frame. For these reasons, this rather extreme policy makes good sense. Simulations show that with an intelligent retransmission policy, the effective throughput with the drop-longest-queue policy is not much smaller than with drop-tail-from-longest-queue policy.

9.7.5   Combinations

The four strategies outlined earlier are mostly orthogonal and can be combined as needed. For example, one might choose to drop a packet from the longest queue, but then look at the congestion loss priority bit to pick a packet from that queue. Or, having chosen the longest queue, the scheduler could choose to drop an entire frame from the head of the queue. Depending on the situation, we can combine the elements described earlier to create drop policies tailor-made to the situation at hand.

9.8   Summary

In this chapter we have studied the basic issues in scheduling access to a shared resource. We first examined the requirements of a scheduling discipline: fairness, ability to provide performance bounds, ease of implementation, and ease of admission control. We then studied four mechanisms that can be combined to create a scheduling discipline: the degree of aggregation, priority, work-conserving or non-work-conserving service, and service order within a priority level. We then studied several scheduling disciplines that combine these elements in various ways for best-effort and guaranteed-service connections. Each discipline trades off implementation complexity with the ability to provide good performance or fairness bounds. We also looked at the complementary problem of packet dropping. Here, too, we can combine four elements to create customized drop policies: degree of aggregation, drop position, early or overloaded drop, and drop priorities. Ultimately, the best scheduling discipline and drop policy for a given situation depends on the binding constraints.

Review questions

1. What is the function of a scheduler?
2. Where is the scheduler located in a switch?
3. What does the Conservation Law imply?
4. Why must a scheduling discipline be easy to implement?
5. What is meant by protection?
6. What is the difference between fairness and protection?
7. What is delay jitter? Why is it important?
8. What is the advantage of a statistical performance bound over a deterministic bound?
9. What is the schedulable region of a scheduler?
10. What are the four degrees of freedom in designing a scheduling discipline?
11. What is the danger with a priority scheme?
12. What is the main purpose of a non-work-conserving discipline?
13. What is the difference between a delay-jitter and a rate-jitter regulator?
14. What is the purpose of a calendar queue?
15. What is the error introduced by a calendar queue?
16. When is aggregation useful?
17. What are the two fundamental choices for service order within a level?
18. Can a calendar queue be used for implementing a sorted priority queue?
19. What is the main problem when emulating GPS with (unweighted) round-robin?
20. Why do we prefer WFQ to WRR even in networks with fixed-size packets?
21. When a connection considered active in WFQ?
22. What is the iterated deletion problem in WFQ?
23. What is the end-to-end delay bound for a connection over a network of GPS servers?
24. What is the relative fairness bound of a GPS-emulation discipline?
25. How is the round number computed in SCFQ?
26. What is the quantum size in DRR, and how large should it be?

27. Why can delay-EDD separate delay and bandwidth bounds?
28. How does a J-EDD regulator provide jitter bounds?
29. Can a rate-controlled server achieve the same end-to-end delay bound as a GPS-emulation server?
30. What are the four degrees of freedom with packet drop policies?
31. What are the problems with using a congestion loss priority bit?
32. What is the point of doing early drop?
33. What is the advantage of the drop-from-head strategy?

Exercises

9.1. Consider two connections with loads 0.2 and 0.4 that have mean waiting times of 0.3 and 0.4 s at an FCFS scheduler. If a new scheduler gives the first connection a mean delay of 0.1, what must the mean delay of the other connection increase to?

9.2. A connection has a mean rate of 1 Mbps, a peak rate of 10 Mbps (both measured over 100-ms intervals), and a delay jitter of 500 ms. What is the amount of buffer needed at the receiver to remove the delay jitter?

9.3. Compute the worst-case queuing delay suffered by connections A and B, described by leaky buckets with parameters (10 pkts, 5 pkt/s) and (10 pkts, 2 pkt/s), respectively, when connection A is assigned to the higher level, and B to the lower level, of a two-priority scheduler serving a link with capacity 10 packets/s.

9.4. A connection with a declared peak rate of 16 Mbps is being regulated by a peak-rate jitter regulator. If all packets on the connection are 2 Kbytes long, and the fourth packet arrives at the regulator at time 5.0 s, when is the earliest time that the fifth packet can become eligible?

9.5. If the day length in a calendar queue is too short, then the queue may contain many events from future years. Thus, each day, a scheduler may need to search through many events before locating the next eligible event. Can you suggest a scheme to reduce this overhead?

9.6. Compute the max−min fair allocation for sources A, B, C, D, and E, when their demands are 2, 3, 4, 4, 5, and the resource size is 15.

9.7. Connections A and B are continuously backlogged during time [0,1] and have weights 1 and 4. A receives 4 Kbits of service in [0,1]. What service is B guaranteed to receive with FCFS and GPS disciplines?

9.8. Packets of length 100 and 200 bits from connections A and B arrive at an empty FQ scheduler at time 0. If the line rate is 100 bits/s, (a) at what real time do the packets complete service? (b) What is the corresponding round number (virtual time) when each packet completes service? (c) If a packet of length 10 arrives on connection A at real time 1.5 s, what would be its finish number?

9.9. If connections A and B in Exercise 9.8 have weights of 2 and 5, respectively, recompute parts (a), (b), and (c) above.

9.10. Consider a connection with leaky bucket parameters (2000 bytes, 20 Kbps) that traverses 10 hops on a network where all the links have a bandwidth of 45 Mbps. If the largest allowed packet is 8192 bytes long, what g value will guarantee an end-to-end delay of 500 ms? Assume a propagation delay of 60 ms.

9.11. Packets of length 10 and 15 arrive at connections A and B at a scheduler serving a link of unit rate at time 0. Packets of length 5 and 10 arrive at connection A at times 9 and 17. What are their finish numbers under SCFQ?

9.12. If the quantum size for a DRR scheduler is 8192 bytes, and the server can serve as many as 500 connections on a 45-Mbps link, what is the worst-case delay for a packet?

9.13. A source negotiates a transmission rate of 1 Mbps from an EDD scheduler, but sends a burst of 100 packets at a rate of 2 Mbps instead. What are the possible outcomes of this action?

9.14. A source negotiates a rate of 1 Mbps and a delay bound of 15 ms at a J-EDD scheduler. What is the buffering needed at the next regulator?

Chapter 10

Naming and Addressing

10.1 Introduction

Consider a user who walks up to a computer connected to the Internet and types *ftp research.att.com*, thus asking for a file transfer session to be initiated between the local computer and a computer with the name *research.att.com*. The local computer must first translate from a human-understandable *name* (research.att.com) to a numerical identifier called the destination's *address* (here, 135.104.117.5). Understandably, both names and addresses must be globally unique. *Naming* is the process of assigning unique names to endpoints, and *addressing* is the process of assigning unique addresses. We call the process of translating from a name to an address *resolution*.

After figuring out the address, the network must find a *route*, that is, a way to get from the source to the destination. A route may be found before data transfer, as in a connection-oriented network, or may be found on-the-fly, when a packet arrives at a router, as in a datagram network. In either case, given a destination address, switches or routers need a way to find the next hop on which to forward a call-setup packet or a datagram. This is the function of *routing*. In this chapter, we will study naming and addressing. We will study routing in Chapter 11.

10.2 Naming and addressing

If names and addresses both serve to identify a destination uniquely, why do we need them both? There are two reasons. First, names are usually human-understandable, therefore variable-length, and potentially rather long. For example, you could name your computer *very_long_name_and_I_dare_you_to_change_it*, and that would be perfectly acceptable. However, every packet in a datagram network must carry an indication of its destination. If we use names in packet headers, the source and destination fields in the packet header must be variable-length, and possibly quite long. Not only does this waste bandwidth, but also it would be more complicated for a router receiving the packet to look up the name in a routing table. Using fixed-length identifiers (that is, addresses) in packet headers is more efficient. (This restriction is less applicable in connection-oriented networks, where the destination identification is carried only once during connection establishment.)

The second reason to separate names and addresses is that this separation provides a level of indirection, giving network administrators some leeway in independently reorganizing names and addresses. For example, if a computer moves from one location to another within the same building or campus, an administrator can change its address without changing its name. If we inform the name-to-address translation mechanism about the change, users of the computer's name are not affected.[1]

10.3   Hierarchical naming

Suppose you were given the job of uniquely naming every computer in the Internet. One way to do this would be to give each machine a name from a dictionary, choosing names in some order, and crossing off names as you assign them. This is easy enough when only a single naming authority (that is, you) is allowed to choose names. However, if many authorities were to choose names in parallel, conflicts are likely. For example, you may choose to name a computer *rosebud* exactly at the same time as another authority. You could come up with a protocol where you circulate a proposed name to every other naming authority before finalizing it. This would ensure global uniqueness, but can be somewhat time-consuming, especially if there are many widely separated naming authorities (see Exercise 10.2). A better solution is possible if we invoke a higher authority that assigns each naming authority a unique prefix. For example, you may be allowed to name machines with names starting with *a*, and another authority may be allowed to name machines with names starting with *b*. If both of you obey this rule, you can choose any name you wish, and conflicts will never arise.

Partitioning the set of all possible names (the *name space*) into mutually exclusive portions (or *domains*) based on a unique prefix simplifies distributed naming. The unique prefix introduces a *hierarchy* in the name space, as shown in Figure 10.1. Here, we use the rule that names starting with *a* are written in the form *a.name*, where the "." is a special character showing the domain boundary. We can generalize the name assignment rule to multiple levels of hierarchy. For example, you may choose to give your subordinates portions of the name space prefixed by *a.a, a.b, a.c*, etc. If they start their names with these prefixes, the names they generate are guaranteed to be universally unique.

---

[1]If the administrator wants to retain consistency with hierarchical naming semantics, as described in Section 10.3, the computer should not be moved out of the naming domain without changing its name.

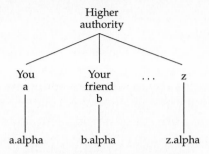

Figure 10.1: Hierarchical name space. If an authority distributes unique prefixes, naming authorities at the next level can freely assign names while still guaranteeing uniqueness.

We call the first level in the hierarchy the *top-level domain*. The rule for naming is, therefore, that a global authority assures uniqueness of names in the top level. Authorities in a given domain can give away part of the name space to lower-level naming authorities, if the prefixes handed to these authorities are unique within that domain. This rule applies recursively at all levels, and therefore we can make the naming hierarchy arbitrarily deep.

A hierarchically organized name space scales without bound, yet allows names to be chosen without consulting every other naming authority on the planet. Because of these wonderful properties, it is used in every large network, including the Internet, the telephone network, and ATM networks.

- Names on the Internet follow the conventions established by the *domain name system*, or DNS [Mockapetris 87, MD 88]. A global authority assigns top-level domains with unique names, such as *edu, com, cz, in,* or *net*. Naming authorities in charge of each domain then parcel out names within that domain to lower-level authorities.

EXAMPLE 10.1

The name administrator at UC Berkeley might be given the authority to give names in the domain *berkeley.edu*. (Note that Domain Name System uses a unique *suffix* rule, instead of a unique prefix rule. This is an equally valid way to create a hierarchy.) The campus naming administrator, might, in turn, give the naming authority in the Mechanical Engineering Department fiefdom over the domain *mech.berkeley.edu*. A lowly graduate student lording it over a roomful of PCs might receive the domain *pclab.mech.berkeley.edu*, and may name the machines, prosaically, *pc1.pclab.mech*.

berkeley.edu, pc2.pclab.mech.berkeley.edu, etc. By construction, these names are unique.

- The telephone network identifies endpoints with hierarchical telephone numbers. Since these are not understandable by normal human beings, the telephone network, arguably, has no naming, only addressing.

- Current ATM networks typically use the Domain Name System to name endpoints. However, as we will see in Section 10.7, these names are translated to different addresses than those used by the Internet.

10.4   Addressing

Addresses are numerical identifiers that, like names, are globally unique. Therefore, just like names, we usually organize them as a hierarchy. Another important reason for hierarchical addresses is that they allow *aggregation* in routing tables, as shown in Figure 10.2. We now study the relationship between hierarchical addressing and aggregation.

EXAMPLE 10.2

In Figure 10.2a, we see a 10-node network where the addresses have been chosen from a nonhierarchical (or *flat*) name space. Suppose computer 3 wanted to send a message to computer 5. Since 3 and 5 are not directly connected, 3 must choose to send the message to either 2 or 4, which, in turn will forward it to 5. It turns out that if 3 sends it to 2, the packet will take at least four hops, but if it sends it to 4, it can take as few as two hops. Thus, 3 should send it to 4. Usually, 3 needs to maintain a *routing table* that shows the next hop for every destination in the network.

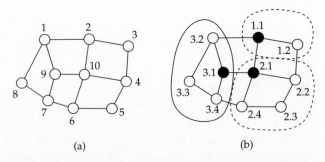

(a)   (b)

Figure 10.2: Aggregating addresses. Hierarchical addresses allow us to aggregate them in routing tables. This allows us to create smaller routing tables, at the cost of possibly longer routes.

Here, because 3 has nine possible destinations, the routing table will have nine entries.

Although having one entry per destination is reasonable for networks with hundreds, or even thousands of destinations, it is impractical for networks with tens of millions of destinations, such as the Internet. To work around this problem we must aggregate addresses into clusters by using a hierarchical address space.

EXAMPLE 10.3

In Figure 10.2b, we have renamed each node with a two-part address. We now call node 5 node 2.3, which we interpret as computer 3 in subnetwork 2. Certain nodes in each subnetwork are shaded, to mark them as special nodes. We call these *border routers*, and they carry all the traffic into and out of the subnetwork. Now, when node 3 in Figure 10.2a (now called 1.2) wants to contact 2.3, it simply sends the packet to its border router, 1.1. The routing table in 1.1 shows that the shortest path to subnetwork 2 is via computer 2.1, which, in turn, routes the packet through either 2.4 or 2.2 to 2.3. Router 1.1 only stores a route to *subnetwork* 2, instead of to every router in subnetwork 2. Thus the router *aggregates* routes to subnetwork 2, making its routing table smaller.

Note that the route from 1.2 to 2.3 is four hops long, which is longer than the two-hop shortest path. On the other hand, every nonborder router has only one entry in its routing table, the address of its border router. Each border router has an entry for every computer in its subnetwork, but only one entry for every other subnetwork. Thus, we have traded off some inefficiency in routing for a dramatic reduction in the number of routing entries. This reduction is possible because the addresses are hierarchical, and the network is partitioned along the same lines as the addresses. If computers in subnetwork 3 could have arbitrary addresses, border routers in other subnetworks would need to have one routing entry for each computer in 3. We can reduce the number of entries in a border router only because every node in subnetwork 3 has a prefix of 3. We refer to addresses in subnetwork 3, and the subnetwork itself, as 3.*.

Hierarchy without aggregation

It is possible to assign addresses hierarchically without requiring addresses in the same subnetwork to share the same address prefix (or suffix). This allows the addresses to be globally unique, but prevents aggregation. A good example is the

Ethernet datalink-layer address, which is a globally unique address allocated to an Ethernet host-adaptor card. An Ethernet address has two parts: a 3-byte manufacturer code, and a 3-byte adaptor number. A global authority assigns each manufacturer a unique code, and each manufacturer gives an adaptor a unique number. Thus, the 6-byte Ethernet address is unique. However, each Ethernet adaptor on a subnetwork may have a different manufacturer, and noncontiguous subnetworks may have adaptors from the same manufacturer. Therefore, we cannot aggregate Ethernet addresses in routing tables, and large-scale networks cannot use Ethernet addresses to identify destinations.

10.5 Addressing in the telephone network

Telephone addresses (telephone numbers) follow the E.164 specification of the International Telecommunications Union [ITU-E.164]. The ITU has assigned each country a unique *country code*. A country's naming authority is allowed to choose arbitrary-length *area codes*. In each area, a naming authority gives each central office an *exchange number*. The last four digits of the telephone number are assigned to a particular local loop from the central office to a subscriber. This defines a global hierarchy that uniquely addresses every telephone in the world. Note that telephone numbers are of variable length, and, therefore, potentially difficult to parse. However, the number is carried only in the call-setup packet, not in every voice sample. Thus, we incur the complexity in parsing the number only once per call.

A fully specified telephone number is globally unambiguous, but dialing it is hard. An optimization in using telephone numbers is to allow users to specify a destination using only a subset of the address. For example, if the user dials 555-0902, it is understood that the destination and source share the same country and area codes. To disambiguate between full and partial E.164 addresses, we usually give the root of the name space a special code that cannot be used for any country. In the United States, the code 011 identifies the rest of the address as a full address, and therefore able to address any telephone in the world. Telephone naming authorities in the United States ensure that no area or exchange code begins with 011. Similarly, if the address begins with a 1, then it is assumed to refer to a nonlocal area. No exchange number is allowed to start with a 1.

10.6 Addressing on the Internet

The Internet addresses host interfaces instead of endpoints. Thus, a computer with multiple interfaces on the Internet has an address for each interface. Internet addresses are used by the Internet Protocol (IP), so they are usually called IP addresses. There are two versions of IP addresses: version 4, also called IPv4 addresses, and version 6, called IPv6.

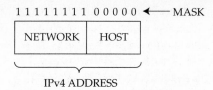

Figure 10.3: IPv4 address. The address is 4 bytes long and is hierarchically partitioned. The subnet mask indicates the portions corresponding to the network and host numbers.

IPv4 addresses are 4 bytes long and are divided in a two-part hierarchy. The first part is called the *network* number, and the second part is a *host* number (although it addresses an interface). A *subnet mask* describes the partition between the two (Figure 10.3). The logical AND of the IP address and the associated subnet mask is the network number, and the remaining portion is the host number. The subnet mask allows arbitrary partitioning of the address into the network and host number. The Internet Numbers Authority guarantees that subnet numbers are globally unique, and within each subnet, individual network administrators guarantee that IP addresses are unique.

Since IP addresses are partitioned, they can be aggregated, and routing tables in the core of the network need only store a specific route to the router responsible for a particular network. For example, routers in the core of the Internet store a route only to the network number 135.104.*. The router in charge of this network routes the packet to the final destination within 135.104, such as 135.104.53.100.

10.6.1   Address classes

The first cut at IP addresses had a fixed network–host partition with only 8 bits of network number.[2] The designers did not envisage more than 256 networks ever joining the Internet "experiment"! They soon generalized this to allow the address to be partitioned in one of three ways:

- Class A addresses have 8 bits of network number and 24 bits of host number
- Class B addresses have 16 bits of network and host number
- Class C addresses have 24 bits of network number and 8 bits of host number

The classes are distinguished by the leading bits of the address. If the address starts with a 0, it is a Class A address. It has 7 bits for a network number, and 24 bits for a host number. Thus, there can be 128 Class A networks, each with 2^{24} hosts (actually, there can

---

[2]Initially, 16 bits were allocated to the host number, but this was later increased to 24 bits, to make the address 4-byte aligned.

be only 126 networks, since network numbers 0 and 127 have special significance[3]). If the address starts with a 10, it is a Class B address; if it starts with a 110, it is a Class C address. Two special classes of addresses are those that start with 1110 (Class D), which are used for multicast (which we will study in Section 11.11), and those that start with 1111 (Class E), which are reserved for future use.

This solution proved adequate until 1984, when the growth of the Internet forced the first of three changes: subnetting, described in Section 10.6.2; *CIDR*, described in Section 10.6.3; and *dynamic host configuration,* described in Section 10.6.4.

10.6.2 Subnetting

Owners of Class B addresses had always wanted to further partition their set of host numbers into many smaller *subnets.* Then, routing tables within the network need only store routes to subnets, instead of to individual hosts. The class structure is too coarse to deal with this, because the Class B address administrator cannot use the class structure to further partition its address space. The solution is to introduce the subnet mask that we studied at the beginning of this section (Figure 10.3). Note that the subnet mask chosen within a network is not visible outside the network. Core routers route packets to the border router responsible for the network, where the incoming packet's IP address is interpreted according to the subnet mask valid in that particular network.

EXAMPLE 10.4

Suppose you are the administrator for the Class B address 135.104.*. If you do not partition the address, every router in your network has to know the route to every host, because you have no way to describe aggregates of hosts within your network. For instance, hosts 135.104.5.0, 135.105.5.6, and 135.105.5.24 may lie in the same physical LAN segment and may all be reachable from router 135.105.4.1. There is no way to express this using the class notation, because these computers all have the same Class B address. You need some extra information to describe this aggregation, which is the subnet mask. Suppose you decide that no subnet is likely to contain more than 256 hosts. Then, you could partition the 65,536 addresses in your domain into 256 subnets, each with 256 addresses. This is expressed by the subnet mask 255.255.255.0 (1111 1111 1111 1111 1111 1111 0000 0000), as shown in Figure 10.4. Addresses within your local Class B network would then be treated as if the network number were the first 24 bits (instead of the first 16 bits), and the host number were the last 8 bits (instead of the last 16 bits). Because the

---

[3]Network 0 when used in a source network number means "this network" and is used by a host that does not know its network number, usually when it is booting. Network 127 is a "loopback" network number. All packets sent to this network number are supposed to be looped back to the sender. It is meant for debugging and maintenance.

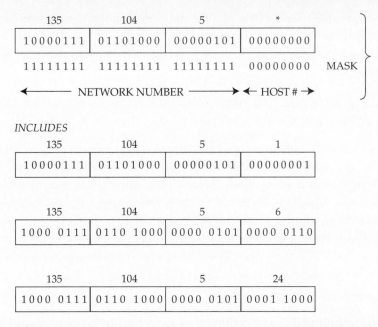

Figure 10.4: Subnetting in the Internet. The subnet mask allows us to arbitrarily partition an IP address into a network part and a host part, thus overcoming the limitation of a fixed partition enforced by the class structure.

hosts 135.104.5.0, 135.104.5.1, and 135.104.5.2 all lie in the same subnet, that is, 135.104.5.*, routing tables within your Class B network need only have an entry for 135.104.5.* (expressed as 135.104.5.* plus the subnet mask 255.255.255.0) pointing to 135.105.4.1 (the next hop), instead of entries to each of the individual computers. This saves routing table space and route table computation time.

10.6.3   CIDR

As the Internet grew, most networks were assigned Class B addresses, because their networks were too large for a Class C address, which can hold only 256 hosts, but not large enough for a Class A address, which can hold more than 4 million hosts. In 1991, it became clear that the 16,382 Class B addresses would soon run out, which resulted in a crisis in the Internet community. Some network engineers noted that addresses from the enormous Class C space were rarely allocated, since most networks have more than 256 hosts. Their solution was to allocate new networks contiguous subsets of Class C addresses instead of a single Class B address (the allocated set of Class C addresses usually spans a smaller portion of the address space than a single Class B address). To aggregate routes to sets of Class C addresses, routers in the core of the network must now carry a *prefix indication*, just as routers within a network carry subnet masks. The prefix indication is the number of bits of the network address that should be considered part of the network number. Routing protocols that substitute multiple Class C addresses for a Class B address are said to obey *classless interdomain routing* or *CIDR* (pronounced "cider").

EXAMPLE 10.5

With CIDR, a network could be allocated eight Class C networks, spanning the 2048 addresses from 201.10.0.0 to 201.10.7.255, instead of a single Class B network, with 65,536 addresses. Since the network administrator is allocated eight Class C networks, which use three bits of the Class C space, the remaining 21 bits must be the network number. The address and prefix describing the network are, therefore, 201.10.0.0 and 21, usually written 201.10.0.0/21 (Figure 10.5).

10.6.4 Dynamic host configuration

A third technique to extend the life of the v4 address space is to dynamically allocate hosts with IP addresses. In many situations, a computer, such as a laptop, may access the Internet only once in a while. These hosts need an IP address only when they are active.

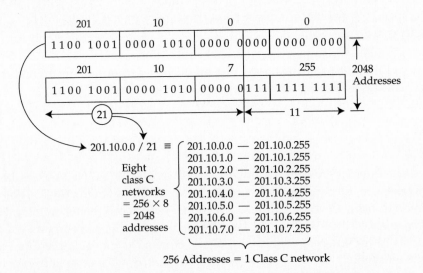

Figure 10.5: CIDR example. With CIDR, a host can aggregate multiple Class C addresses to get an address space larger than that of a Class C network, but smaller than that of a Class B network. In this example, the 2048 addresses in the range 201.10.0.0 to 201.10.7.255, which belong to eight Class C networks, are aggregated to form a single CIDR class, described by the notation 201.10.0.0/21. This means that the first 21 bits of the address should be interpreted as the network number.

Thus, a clever network operator can share the same IP address among different computers, as long as they are not simultaneously active. The protocol to do so is called the *Dynamic Host Configuration Protocol,* or *DHCP* [Droms 93].

In DHCP, a newly booted computer broadcasts a *DHCP discover* packet on its local LAN. This packet contains host-specific information, such as its hardware address. DHCP servers that receive this packet reply with a *DHCP offer* packet that contains an offered IP address and other configuration parameters. A host that receives one or more replies selects a server and IP address, and confirms its selection by broadcasting a *DHCP request* packet that contains the name of the selected server. The server confirms receipt of this message and confirms its offer with a *DHCP ack.* Other servers, on hearing a DHCP request, automatically withdraw their offers. When a host is done, it sends a *DHCP release* message to its selected server, which releases its IP address for use by other hosts.

DHCP has the notion of a *lease,* which is the time for which a host's IP address is valid. A host can guess the time for which it wants an address and put this request in its request packet, can ask for an infinitely long lease, or can periodically renew its lease. When a lease expires, the DHCP server is free to reassign the IP address to other hosts. (This is an example of *soft state,* which we studied in Section 6.3.10.) A wise server should reuse least-recently-used addresses first, to deal with forgetful hosts that may retain their IP addresses past their lease.

A similar technique is used to dynamically allocate IP addresses to computers that access the Internet on a dial-up line. The widely-used *Point-to-Point Procotol* (PPP) allocates a temporary IP address to a host when it dials in. Since only a fraction of dial-up hosts are simultaneously active, an Internet Service Provider can share a pool of IP addresses among a larger set of dial-up hosts.

10.6.5   IPv6

Although CIDR bought the Internet Numbering Authority some breathing space, the 32-bit IP address space will eventually run out. This problem is being rectified in IP version 6, which uses 128-bit addresses [DH 96]. It has been calculated that, even in the most pessimistic scenario, this will result in more than 1500 IP addresses available for each square meter of surface area on the planet [Huitema 94]! Like v4, v6 distinguishes between multicast and unicast addresses based on a well-known prefix. Version 6 has address prefixes, as in CIDR, to allow aggregation without reference to classes. Subnetting with subnet masks is also allowed.

IP version 6 distinguishes among three types of addresses: *provider-oriented unicast, anycast,* and *multicast.* Provider-oriented unicast addresses, the vanilla variety, address individual host interfaces and start with the prefix "010" (Figure 10.6). The next field

0 1 0	REGISTRY ID	PROVIDER ID	SUBSCRIBER ID	SUBNET ID	INTERFACE ID

Figure 10.6: IP Version 6 unicast address format.

(*registry id*) identifies an *address registry*, which is an authority that assigns provider identifiers (*provider id*) to Internet service providers. Providers (commercial companies such as AT&T or MCI) can then assign portions of the address space to their subscribers, distinguished by their *subscriber id*. The *subnet id* identifies a specific subnet belonging to a particular subscriber. The *interface id* identifies a single interface among the group of interfaces identified by the subnet prefix. The lengths of these fields has not yet been specified, but are likely to be chosen according to the guidelines in reference [LR 95].

Anycast addresses correspond to more than one interface. The idea is that a packet sent to an anycast address is sent to *one* of the interfaces sharing the address. Anycast is useful when a source would like to send a packet to a destination using a specific provider (we will study *provider selection* in more detail in Section 11.12.2). The source formats the packet header with the anycast address for the provider (which addresses all the routers owned by the provider) and the final destination. The network uses the partial route specified in the header to route the packet to the nearest router owned by the provider, which can then use the destination address to continue packet forwarding. The format of an anycast address is identical to a provider-oriented address.

Multicast addresses correspond to multicast groups. They start with the bit sequence FF. A packet sent to a multicast address is routed to every member of the corresponding multicast group. Multicast addresses contain a flag to show whether the group is well known and therefore permanent, or whether it is transient. We will study multicast routing in Section 11.11.

To ease the transition from IPv4 to IPv6 addresses, a special form of the v6 address allows v4 addresses to be encapsulated. In these v6 addresses, the first 80 bits are zero and the next 16 bits are all ones. A complicated set of rules allows interoperation between v6 and v4 hosts through intermediate routers that may or may not understand v6 addresses.

How expensive are IPv6 addresses?

The cost of v6 addresses is that they require larger IP headers than do v4 addresses, and thus more bandwidth. Because IPv6 headers are 40 bytes long, compared with 20-byte v4 headers, the overhead per packet is doubled. This is a problem if the future Internet will mostly carry small packets.

Detractors argue that the 16-byte v6 address is wasteful, and that an 8-byte address would have been sufficient. Proponents argue that this is the only way to end the address size problem forever. Moreover, the mean packet size in the Internet is increasing, since newer local-area networks, such as FDDI, allow larger packets than Ethernet. With a 1500-byte mean packet size, for example, the additional 20-byte overhead is not objectionable. Only time will tell if the v6 address size was a sound choice.

10.7   NSAPs: Addressing in ATM networks

ATM endpoints are addressed using the *Network Service Access Point* (NSAP) format specified by the International Standards Organization, originally for the ISO OSI protocol stack [ISO 93]. An NSAP is variable-length—between 7 and 20 bytes long—and is potentially longer than even IPv6 addresses (Figure 10.7). A bewildering set of acronyms describes an NSAP, which we show in Table 10.1.

An NSAP is designed to devolve the authority in creating unique addresses as much as possible. Moreover, it allows address formats to be endlessly customized, almost beyond reason! The general idea is that the International Standards Organization (ISO) hands a naming authority a unique ID (call the *Authority and Format Indicator* or *AFI*) and washes its hands of the whole business. For example, the U.S. government is given the AFI of 47. The authority's ID indicates not only the name of the authority, but also the format of the rest of the NSAP. Each naming authority, in turn, hands off a part of the address space to an *addressing domain*. The domain is given a range of values for the *Initial Domain Identifier* or *IDI* field. The AFI and the IDI together uniquely identify an addressing domain and are called the *Initial Domain Part*, which should not be confused with the Initial Domain Identifier.

Three combinations of the AFI and IDI are well known:

- In the *E.164 NSAP* format, the IDI is an E.164 address (that is, like a telephone number). In this format, one can think of the IDI as belonging to an organization that runs an ATM network. It is meant for use by providers of *public* ATM networks, that is, ATM networks that anyone can connect to, much like the public telephone networks around the world. The other two combinations are used for *private* ATM networks, which may restrict access.

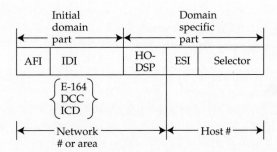

Figure 10.7: NSAP address. The address has a globally unique Initial Domain Part and a locally assigned Domain Specific Part. Subnetting can be done using the High-Order DSP field. All fields except the one-byte Selector field are variable-length.

Acronym	Expansion	Comment
NSAP	Network Service Access Point	This is the format for an ATM endpoint's address.
AFI	Authority and Format Indicator	A unique number allocated to each addressing authority by the International Standards Organization.
IDI	Initial Domain Identifier	The identifier of a domain within the purview of a given addressing authority.
ICD	International Code Designator	An IDI code allocated to domains by the British Standards Institute that uniquely identifies international organizations.
DCC	Data Country Code	An IDI code allocated to domains by the ISO National Member in each country.
IDP	Initial Domain Part	The concatenation of the AFI and the IDI.
DSP	Domain Specific Part	An address allocated to an end-system by a domain's addressing authority.
HO-DSP	High-Order bits of the Domain Specific Part	The part of the Domain Specific Part that corresponds to a network number in IP.
ESI	End-System Identifier	The part of the Domain Specific part that identifies an end-system, corresponding to a host number in IP.
SEL	Selector	A field that selects a protocol within an end-system.

Table 10.1: Acronyms used in describing Network Service Access Point addresses.

- In the *ICD NSAP* format, the AFI identifies the British Standards Institution, and the IDI field is a code given to international organizations, such as the International Red Cross, by the institute.

- In the *DCC NSAP* format, the AFI identifies a country, and the IDI is a code administered by the ISO National Member in each country.

Owners of private ATM networks, can therefore, approach an organization approved by the British Standards Institution, or the ISO National Member in their country, to get one or more IDI codes assigned to their private network. Each owner of a private network is guaranteed a unique slice of the global address space by virtue of the uniqueness of the Initial Domain Part. Incidentally, the IDI field can be variable-length, but within an organization's network, since the Initial Domain Part is fixed, all the addresses have a unique, fixed-length prefix.

Once the owner of a set of ATM networks obtains an IDP, it can start numbering networks and hosts in its networks. These numbers constitute the lower-order parts of the NSAP and are called the *Domain Specific Part* (*DSP*). The high-order part of the DSP, called the *HO-DSP*, corresponds to the low-order part of the network number in IP. The HO-DSP field allows subnetting in the Domain Specific Part. Just as the subnet mask allows a fine-grained partition between the network number and the host number, the HO-DSP field allows NSAPs to be aggregated at a level lower than the DSP. Within each network, each end-system is identified with an *End-System Identifier* (*ESI*). Finally, the 1-byte Selector field allows multiple logical network interfaces to share the same physical interface. For example, an interface may receive cells meant either for IP or for a native-mode ATM network layer. By choosing different Selector values, a source can inform the datalink layer hardware which protocol stack should receive the incoming cell.

From the perspective of routing, an NSAP can be thought to consist of the *Area, ESI,* and *Selector* fields (Figure 10.7). Routers ignore the last byte of the address, which is Selector field, since it has significance only at the host. The Area field is treated like an IP network number. Thus, route tables store routes to an Area, and endpoints send packets to the nearest router that handles that Area.

10.8   Name resolution

Users typically supply applications with a destination's name. Applications use *name servers* to resolve a name to an address. A name server is like a telephone directory that stores name-to-address translations. An application resolves a name by sending a query to the name server, which responds with the translation.

The simplest design for a name server is to have a single name server for the entire network. This has the advantage that the resolution is always guaranteed to be consistent, because only one copy of the translation exists. On the other hand, the central name server is not only a single point of failure, but also a choke point, since every endpoint directs its name-resolution queries to it. Thus, we usually compose name servers from a set of distributed agents that coordinate their actions to provide the illusion of a single translation table. Perhaps the most successful distributed name service is the Internet's *Domain Name System* (*DNS*), which we will use as an example of good name server design [MD 88].

Recall that DNS partitions names, such as *pc1.pclab.mech.berkeley.edu,* into several hierarchically organized domains, such as *mech, berkeley,* and *edu.* The hierarchy can span arbitrarily many levels. The DNS consists of many name servers, each responsible for a subtree of the name space corresponding to a domain boundary (Figure 10.8). Each server may delegate part of the name space to other servers. For example, the name server responsible for the *berkeley.edu* domain gives responsibility for names ending with **.mech.berkeley.edu* to the *mech.berkeley.edu* name server. This delegation of authority allows domains to match administrative boundaries, considerably simplifying name-space management. DNS administrators arrange things so that every DNS name is guaranteed to be correctly translated by at least one *Authoritative Server* for that name.

When an endpoint wants to translate a name, it sends a query to the server serving the root of the name space. The root parses the name right-to-left, determines the server

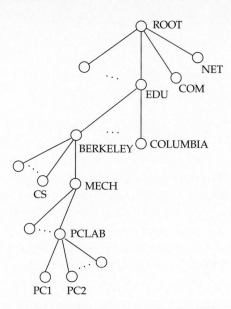

Figure 10.8: Name domains. The Domain Name System partitions the name space into domains. Each domain is served by an associated name server. The domain structure can be arbitrarily deep, allowing distributed management of the name space.

responsible for the name (the name after the last "."), and forwards the query to that server. For example, if the query is for the name *pc1.pclab.mech.berkeley.edu*, the root server forwards the query to the server responsible for the *edu* domain. This server, in turn, hands off the query to the *berkeley* name server, and so on.

Although the scheme described so far allows each authoritative server to independently update its translation table, it still places a heavy load on the root name server. Moreover, if the root server fails, the entire name resolution process will come to a halt. DNS uses two techniques to combat these problems: *replication* and *caching*.

- *Replication:* DNS allows more than one server to handle requests for a domain, since these servers coordinate among themselves to maintain consistency. In particular, the root name server itself is highly replicated, so that a single failure will not cause any problems. A name resolution query can be made to any of the replicated servers, and an end-system typically chooses the nearest or least loaded one.

- *Caching:* When an endpoint (or an agent acting on its behalf) resolves a name, it stores the result in a cache. Thus, if the query is repeated, it is answered without recourse to the root name server (this is an example of exploiting locality, as described in Section 6.3.4). Endpoints can cache not only the results of a query, but also the addresses of the Authoritative Servers for commonly queried domains. Thus, future queries need not go through the root server. This has been found to reduce name-resolution traffic dramatically [MD 88]. Cached entries are flushed after a time specified in the name-translation table at authorized servers, so that changes in the table are eventually reflected in the entire Internet.

Mail exchange using DNS (MX records)

Each name server in the DNS stores translations as *Resource records*. Resource records correspond not only to a translation from a DNS name to an IP address, but many other kinds of translations. One of the more useful translations is provided by MX or mail exchange records [Partridge 86].

The Internet carries mail addressed in many different formats, such as Lotus Notes, the Internet's Simple Mail Transfer Protocol, and ISO's X.400. When a user sends electronic mail, the local mail application must determine, from the destination address, the server to which the mail should be forwarded. If the destination is accessible over IP (that is, is part of the Internet), then the local mail application simply opens a TCP/IP connection to the remote destination and forwards the mail. However, the destination addressed by the mail header may not be accessible over IP. Then, the local mail application forwards the mail to an *application-level gateway* that accepts mail for other systems. The mail gateway corresponding to a given destination can be found from an MX record in the DNS. For example, a user may send mail to *remote_user@aol.com*. Now, *aol.com* corresponds to the commercial America Online service provider, which may not run IP internally, or may not want arbitrary users to open TCP/IP connections to their internal machines. Instead, AOL delegates one of its machines, *a.mx.aol.com*, which is on the Internet, to accept mail for AOL's users. The local mailer opens a connection to this machine, which accepts the mail, and then forwards it within AOL using a proprietary protocol. In this way, DNS allows email to span mutually incompatible networks gracefully. DNS MX records are, therefore, one reason the Internet is so popular: Internet mail can go everywhere, even where the Internet itself does not.

To protect machines inside a domain described by MX records, mail transfer protocols are required first to query DNS for MX records to a destination. If an MX record is found, it *must* be used, instead of connecting directly to the destination. This allows a form of *firewalling*, that is, protecting hosts inside a particular administrative domain from interference from untrusted outside hosts.

10.9   Datalink-layer addressing

Although the bulk of our discussion of routing deals with network-layer addresses, we will delve briefly into datalink-layer addressing for two common datalink layers—Eth-

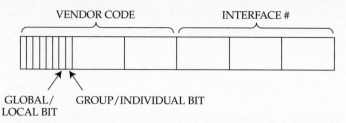

Figure 10.9: IEEE 802 address. The address is 6 bytes long. The last two bits of the high-order byte are used as flags. If the local bit is on, the address has only local significance. If the group bit is on, the address is a multicast address.

ernet and FDDI— because they are commonly used for routing and bridging within a local-area network (LAN).

Both FDDI and Ethernet follow an addressing specification laid down by the 802 committee of the Institute of Electrical and Electronics Engineers (IEEE). This committee is responsible for most LAN standards, and every IEEE 802 LAN obeys the 802 addressing scheme (FDDI is not an IEEE 802 standard, but it uses 802 style addressing anyway).

An 802 address is 6 bytes long (Figure 10.9). The IEEE globally assigns the first 3 bytes, and host-adaptor manufacturers uniquely assign the next 3 bytes, imprinting the resulting address on a ROM on the host-adaptor card. The last two bits of the first byte of the address are used for the *global/local* and *group/individual* flags. If the global flag bit is set, then the address is guaranteed to be globally unique; otherwise, it has only local significance. Thus, an experimental prototype card can be assigned a temporary (but still valid) 802 address, if the local bit is set. The *group* bit marks the address as a datalink-layer broadcast or multicast address. Packets with this bit set can be received by more than one destination (but they must be previously configured to accept packets from this address). The group bit allows efficient datalink-level multicast and broadcast, since an 802 host adaptor needs to match the address on an incoming packet with a set of active multicast addresses only when the bit is set. We will study LAN multicast in more detail in Section 11.11.5.

10.10 Finding datalink-layer addresses

As we saw in Section 10.8, distributed name servers allow us to translate from a name to a network-level address. This network-level address is used to locate a unique destination in the network. However, the destination's host-interface card may only recognize and accept packets labeled with its datalink-layer address (this problem only arises in broadcast LANs; in point-to-point LANs, a destination does not require a datalink-layer address). Thus, the last router along the path to the destination must encapsulate an incoming IP packet in a datalink-layer header that contains a datalink-layer address corresponding to the final destination (Figure 10.10). Symmetrically, if a source connects to

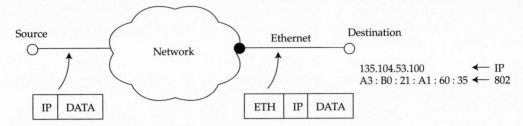

Figure 10.10: IP and Ethernet addresses. If a host is on an 802 LAN, the last IP router has to translate from an IP address to the 802 (MAC) address using the Address Resolution Protocol.

a router within an 802 LAN, it must encapsulate the outgoing packet with a datalink-layer header containing the datalink layer address of the router's host-interface. We usually call the datalink-layer address the *Medium Access Control* or *MAC* address.

If both the source and destination of a packet are on the same broadcast LAN, we can easily translate from an IP address to a MAC. This is because the authoritative translation from a network-layer (IP) address to a MAC address is always available from at least one of the hosts on the LAN. When a source wants a translation, it broadcasts a query on the LAN, and the computer that owns the network-layer address replies with its MAC address. The Internet protocol that carries out this operation is called the *Address Resolution Protocol* or *ARP* [Plummer 82].

An ARP packet contains the MAC address of the sender and the IP address that the sender wants to resolve. The packet is addressed with the LAN's broadcast address. Every host on the LAN is required to listen to ARP broadcasts and respond to an ARP query containing its own IP address with its MAC address. The reply is sent to the querier's MAC address, available from the ARP request. The originator of an ARP reply saves the reply in an *ARP cache* so that future translation will not require a broadcast. Cache entries are discarded after a while, so that if the MAC address of a host changes, this will eventually be noticed by every other host on the LAN.

ARP works well only on broadcast LANs. In point-to-point LANs, ARP queries are replied to by an *ARP server,* which is essentially a name server. When a host boots up, it registers its MAC address with the ARP server. When a host wants to find out a destination's address, it asks the ARP server, instead of initiating a broadcast. This technique is used when carrying IP over ATM LANs [Laubach 94] (also see Section 15.5).

10.11 Summary

Naming and addressing are essential to the operation of any network. Although names can be arbitrarily long and are (usually) human understandable, addresses are usually fixed-length and are meant to be easily parsed by routers. Both names and addresses must be unique, yet should not require a naming authority to consult with every other naming authority in the network. For these reasons, both names and addresses are organized hierarchically. Moreover, hierarchical addressing allows us to aggregate sets of computers when describing routes to them in a routing table. Naming and addressing are closely tied to routing, which we study in Chapter 11.

The telephone network uses the E.164 standard to address endpoints. Though E.164 addresses can be variable-length, they are used only at the time of call setup, so the parsing overhead is paid only once.

The Internet uses IP addresses, which come in two flavors, version 4 and version 6. Version 4, which is the current standard, divides the address into two parts, called the network number and the host number. A variable number of bits can be assigned to each portion by using a subnet mask. Sets of addresses can also be grouped together to form a larger address space by specifying an address prefix. Moreover, a host can be dynamically assigned an IP address when it joins the Internet. These three innovations allow us to manage the v4 address space more effectively, but it is still running out of addresses. Version 6 addresses, which are four times the size of version 4 addresses, promise to solve the address scarcity problem once and for all.

ATM endpoints are addressed with one of several variants of the NSAP format. These addresses are also variable-length and have many levels of hierarchy to allow decentralized administration of the address space.

Name resolution is the process by which names are associated with addresses. A common solution is to distribute this functionality among a set of name servers. Replicating servers and caching replies are two techniques to increase reliability and to avoid excessive name-resolution traffic.

In broadcast LANs, we need to translate a network-layer address to a datalink-layer address. This is done in the Internet with the Address Resolution Protocol. A host broadcasts a resolution request on its LAN and receives a reply from any system that knows the answer. The telephone and ATM networks do not need address resolution because they are carried over point-to-point networks that do not need a datalink-layer address.

Review Questions

1. What are the differences and similarities between a name and an address?
2. When do virtual-circuit switches look up a routing table? When do datagram routers look up a routing table?
3. What is a top-level domain? Why should the name server for the top-level domain be replicated?
4. What are the two purposes of an address hierarchy?
5. How many levels of hierarchy does a telephone number have?
6. Is a subnet mask visible outside an IP network?
7. Is a CIDR network prefix visible outside an IP network?
8. How long is an IPv6 address?
9. What does the Area field of an NSAP correspond to in an IP address?
10. How long is an 802 address? How many bytes are globally assigned?

11. Why does DNS replicate the root server?
12. What does ARP do? What is an ARP-cache?

Exercises

10.1 (a) What changes to the name-resolution service and routing reachability advertisements must a network administrator make to change an endpoint's address without changing its name? (b) What changes must it make to change the name without changing the address? (c) What changes are necessary if the endpoint moves permanently to a new location (describe the changes depending on whether the endpoint retains its name, address, neither, or both identifiers)?

10.2 Here is a simple protocol that allows global uniqueness of names without hierarchical naming: Each naming authority (NA) multicasts a proposed name to all other NAs. A name is finalized only if no other NA disagrees. This protocol works when everything is up and running. What happens if (a) the multicast packet fails to reach some of the NAs, or (b) if one of the NAs goes down?

10.3 What are the network number, subnet number, and host number for address 135.104.192.100, mask 255.255.128.0?

10.4 How many addresses are spanned by the CIDR address 205.12.192.0/20, and what range do they span?

10.5 Suppose DNS restricted domain names to only two levels, in the same way as the original IP addresses. How might the *edu* top-level domain be organized? What coordination mechanisms are needed in each university? How does permitting an arbitrary number of levels eliminate the coordination problem?

10.6 What is the trade-off accomplished by aging out DNS records?

10.7 Why does the telephone network not require ARP?

Chapter 11

Routing

11.1 Introduction

Routing is the process of finding a path from a source to every destination in the network. It allows users in the remotest part of the world to get to information and services provided by computers anywhere in the world. Routing is what makes networking magical: allowing telephone conversations between Botswana and Buenos Aires, and video clips from the space shuttle to be multicast to hundreds of receivers around the world! How does a network choose a path that spans the world? How does the routing system scale to describe paths to many millions of endpoints? How should the system adapt to a failed link? What if the user wants to choose a path that has the least delay, or the least cost, or the most available capacity? What if the users are themselves mobile, attaching to the network from different wired access points? These are the sorts of questions we will study in this chapter.

Routing is accomplished by means of *routing protocols* that establish mutually consistent *routing tables* in every router (or switch controller) in the network (Figure 11.1). A routing table contains at least two columns: the first is the address of a destination endpoint or a destination network, and the second is the address of the network element that is the next hop in the "best" path to this destination. When a packet arrives at a router (or when a call-setup packet arrives at a switch controller), the router or switch controller consults the routing table to decide the next hop for the packet.

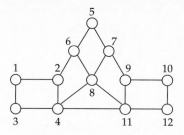

ROUTING TABLE AT 1

Destination	Next hop	Destination	Next hop
1	—	7	2
2	2	8	2
3	3	9	2
4	3	10	2
5	2	11	3
6	2	12	3

Figure 11.1: Routing table. The figure shows the routing table at node 1. The table shows the next hop for each destination (which corresponds to a specific interface at host 1).

EXAMPLE 11.1

An example of a routing table for a toy network is shown in Figure 11.1. We see that the routing table for node 1 has one entry for every other node in the network. This allows it to choose the next hop for every possible destination. For example, packets that arrive at node 1 destined for node 10 are forwarded to node 2.

Notice that node 1 has only two choices: to forward a packet to 2 or to forward it to 3. This is a *local* routing choice. Yet this choice depends on the *global* topology, because the destination address by itself does not contain enough information to make a correct decision. For example, the shortest path from node 1 to node 6 is through 2, and the shortest path to 11 is through 3. Node 1, just by looking at the destination address "6," cannot decide that node 2 should be the next hop to that destination. *We conclude that any routing protocol must communicate global topological information to each routing element to allow it to make local routing decisions.* Yet global information, by its very nature, is hard to collect, subject to frequent change, and voluminous. How can we summarize this information to extract only the portions relevant to each node? This lies at the heart of routing protocols.

A routing protocol asynchronously updates routing tables at every router or switch controller. For ease of exposition, in the remainder of the chapter, we will refer to both routers and switch controllers as "routers." Recall that switch controllers are called upon to route packets only at the time of call setup, so that they route connections, instead of packets (Section 8.1.1).

11.2   Routing protocol requirements

A routing protocol must try to satisfy several mutually opposing requirements:

- *Minimizing routing table space:* We would like routing tables to be as small as possible, so that we can build cheaper routers with smaller memories that are more easily looked up. Moreover, routers must periodically exchange routing tables to ensure that they have a consistent view of the network's topology: the larger the routing table, the greater the overhead in exchanging routing tables. We usually require a routing table to grow more slowly than the number of destinations in the network.

- *Minimizing control messages:* Routing protocols require control message exchange. These represent an overhead on system operation and should be minimized.

- *Robustness:* The worst thing that a router can do is to misroute packets, so that they never reach their destination. (They are said to enter a *black hole.*) Routers in error may also cause *loops* and *oscillations* in the network.

EXAMPLE 11.2

If routing tables are inconsistent, loops can easily be formed. For example, router A may think that the shortest path to C is through B, and B may think that the shortest path to C is through A. Then, a packet to C loops back and forth between A and B until some other procedure (such as a *hop count* reaching zero, as described in Section 12.4.2) detects the loop and terminates the packet.

Oscillations can be caused if the routing protocol chooses paths based on the current load. Consider routers A and B connected by paths P1 and P2. Suppose P1 is heavily loaded and P2 is idle. The routing protocol may divert all traffic from P1 to P2, thus loading P2. This makes P1 more desirable, and traffic moves back to P1! If we are not careful, traffic oscillates from P1 to P2, and the network is always congested.

Black holes, loops, and oscillations are rare under normal conditions, but can show up if routing tables are corrupted, users specify incorrect information, links break or are restored, or routing control packets are corrupted. A robust routing protocol should protect itself from these types of problems by periodically running consistency tests, and by careful use of checksums and sequence numbers as described in Chapter 12.

- *Using optimal paths:* To the extent possible, a packet should follow the "best" path from a source to its destination. The "best" path may not necessarily be the shortest path: it may be a path that has the least delay, the most secure links, or the lowest monetary cost, or one that balances the load across the available paths. Routers along the entire path must collaborate to ensure that packets use the best possible route to maximize overall network performance.

As always, these requirements represent trade-offs in routing protocol design. For example, a protocol may trade off robustness for a decrease in the number of control messages and routing-table space. Many common protocols trade off a dramatic reduction in routing-table space for slightly longer paths.

11.3   Choices

Designers of routing protocols have many mechanisms available to them. In this section, we will describe some commonly available choices for routing [ME 90]. These choices also represent a rough taxonomy to categorize routing protocols.

- *Centralized versus distributed routing:* In centralized routing, a central processor collects information about the status of each link (up or down, utilization, and capacity) and processes this information to compute a routing table for every node. It then distributes these tables to all the routers. In distributed routing, routers cooperate using a distributed routing protocol to create mutually consistent routing tables. Centralized routing is reasonable when the network is centrally administered and the network is not too large, as in the core of the telephone network. However, it suffers from the same problems as a centralized name server: creating a single point of failure, and the concentration of routing traffic to a single point.

- *Source-based versus hop-by-hop:* A packet header can carry the entire route (that is, the addresses of every router on the path from the source to the destination), or the packet can carry just the destination address, and each router along the path can choose the next hop. These alternatives represent extremes in the degree to which a source can influence the path of a packet. A source route allows a sender to specify a packet's path precisely, but requires the source to be aware of the entire network topology. If a link or a router along the path goes down, a source-routed packet will not reach its destination. Moreover, if the path is long, the packet header can be fairly large. Thus, source routing trades off specificity in routing for packet-header size and extra overhead for control messages.

    An intermediate solution is to use a *loose source route*. With loose source routes, the sender chooses a subset of routers that the packet should pass through, and the path may include routers not included in the source route. Loose source routes are supported in the IP version 4 and 6 headers.

- *Stochastic versus deterministic:* With a deterministic route, each router forwards packets toward a destination along exactly one path. In stochastic routing, each router maintains more than one next hop for each possible destination. It randomly picks one of these hops when forwarding a packet. The advantage of stochastic routing is that it spreads the load among many paths, so that the load oscillations characteristic of deterministic routing are eliminated. On the other hand, a destination may receive packets along the same connection out of order, and with varying delays. Consequently, modern networks usually use deterministic routing.

- *Single versus multiple path:* In single-path routing, a router maintains only one path to each destination. In multiple-path routing, a router maintains a *primary* path to a destination, along with *alternative* paths. If the primary path is unavailable for some reason, routers may send packets on the alternative path (with stochastic routing, routers may send packets on alternative paths even if the primary path is available). Single-path routing is used on the Internet, because maintaining alternative paths requires more routing table space. Telephone networks usually use multiple-path routing, because this reduces the call blocking probability, which is very important for customer satisfaction.

- *State-dependent versus state-independent:* With state-dependent or *dynamic* routing, the choice of a route depends on the current (measured) network state. For example, if some links are heavily loaded, routers may try to route packets around that link. With state-independent or *static* routing, the route ignores the network state. For example, a shortest-path route (where we measure the path length as the number of hops) is state independent. State-dependent routing usually finds better routes than state-independent routing, but can suffer from problems caused by network dynamics (such as the routing oscillations described earlier). It also requires more overhead for monitoring the network load. The Internet uses both state-dependent and state-independent routing. Telephone network routing used to be state independent, but state-dependent routing with multiple paths is now the norm.

Having broadly considered the choices in routing protocol design, the rest of the chapter deals with specific routing protocols that make a selection from the choices described earlier. The literature on routing (both in the telephone network and in the Internet) is vast. We can only touch upon the essential ideas in this book. We first study routing in the telephone network, then in the Internet. At the time of this writing, routing in ATM networks was still being discussed, but the outcome is likely to closely resemble routing in the Internet. We therefore do not discuss ATM routing in any detail.

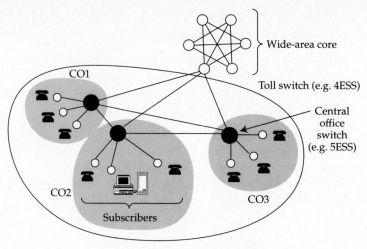

Figure 11.2: Simplified view of the telephone network. Subscribers are connected to a local exchange carrier (LEC). Central offices owned by LECs connect to a toll (wide-area) switch. Toll switches are connected to each other using single-hop paths.

11.4   Routing in the telephone network

In this section, we will focus on concepts and techniques for routing in the telephone network. A good reference that covers this material in greater depth is [Girard 90].

A national telephone network is structured as a fairly rigid three-level hierarchy, where the levels represent subscriber telephone instruments or modems, central offices, and long-distance or *toll* switching offices (Figure 11.2). We will refer to the set of toll switches as the network *core*. A *local exchange carrier,* such as Bell Atlantic in the eastern United States, provides local telephone service and manages many central offices interconnected with one-hop links. Every central office in each local exchange carrier's domain logically connects to one node (or, rarely, two nodes) in the core.[1] Each element in the core, such as the Lucent 4ESS switch we mentioned in Chapter 8, can switch up to 120,000 simultaneous calls and costs several million dollars.

The core is structured as a fully connected mesh or *clique,* with every toll switch connected to every other toll switch by a logical one-hop path. The number of interconnections is truly enormous. For example, the AT&T wide-area network core has around

---

[1]This is a simplification. Many local exchange carriers use *tandem* switches to provide an intermediate level in the hierarchy, and core switches connect to tandems instead of to central offices. Moreover, in some countries, such as the United States and Finland, several long-distance companies compete to provide network cores. Subscribers can choose one of several cores to complete their call, and local exchange carriers connect to multiple cores from their central offices.

135 switches interconnected by nearly 5 million *trunks*. [2] This dense connectivity simplifies routing. The routing algorithm is as follows:

(a) If a call's source and destination are within a central office, directly connect them.
(b) If the call is between central offices within a local exchange carrier, use a one-hop path between central offices.
(c) Otherwise send the call to (one of) the core(s).

The only major decision is at a toll switch, which chooses either a one-hop or a two-hop path to a destination switching system. It is not necessary to consider longer paths because the core is a logical clique. Thus, for an m-element core, each direct path corresponds to $m - 1$ alternative two-hop paths. The essence of telephone-network routing is in determining which one-hop path to choose in the core, and if this is fully used, the order in which to try two-hop paths.

Over the past hundred years, many different routing policies have been used in the telephone network. The computational limitations of electromechanical relays highly constrained the earliest policies. As computerized switching systems have replaced these, the routing policies have become increasingly sophisticated. However, all telephone routing policies have the same features, which we discuss next.

11.4.1 Features of telephone network routing and a comparison with Internet routing

All telephone routing policies draw upon the fact that aggregated telephone traffic is very predictable. Thus, it is possible to compute the approximate load between every pair of toll switches in advance, for every interval of every day. This allows routes to be chosen in advance. Second, telephone switches and links are extremely reliable. Switches go down no more than an average of a few minutes per year, and links are out of commission no more than a few hours every year. Therefore, unlike the Internet, where we can rarely count upon links to stay up, in the telephone network, the normal situation is that nearly all trunks and switches are up. This allows the routing protocol to be highly optimized: instead of just trying to maintain connectivity, network administrators can use sophisticated load-balancing strategies.

The third feature of a long-distance telephone network is that a single organization controls the entire network. Thus, traffic measurement and management policies can be universally implemented. Moreover, upgrades to routing policies can be carried out uniformly. In contrast, in the Internet, network administrators in different domains may choose differing policies, or worse, run out-of-date and inconsistent routing protocols.

Fourth, the network is very highly connected, with many equal-length alternative paths. In contrast, the Internet is rather sparse, so there are few choices for alternative

---

[2] A trunk corresponds to a pair of time slots carrying duplex 64-Kbps voice traffic. A single optical fiber can carry as many as 50,000 trunks. A collection of trunks between the same source destination pair form a *trunk group*.

paths in the core. (If this changes, some techniques used in the telephone network might become applicable to the Internet.)

Finally, routes in the telephone network are associated with a quality of service guarantee. Therefore, unlike the Internet, mere connectivity is not sufficient to complete a call: the path must also have sufficient resources available. Note, however, that all voice calls require the same, simple quality of service, so the admission control decision is trivial.

The cost of telephone network routing

Telephone network routing is simple because, historically, the electromechanical relays used for network control could not execute sophisticated programs. This simplicity, however, comes at a cost. For example, if a switch in the core crashes, the telephone network routing protocol cannot find an alternative path to an end-system reached through that switch. We conclude that to make the system reliable, *every* switch must be reliable. Similarly, the routing protocol requires every pair of switches to be connected by a one-hop logical trunk group. Although the physical connectivity is much sparser, creating and maintaining this logically fully connected clique is expensive. Would it not be cheaper to build a network where sophisticated routing algorithms lower the requirements for connectivity and component reliability? This is a hundred-billion dollar question!

If we could build a network that has all the features of the telephone network (low blocking probability, very high reliability, global coverage) using newer switching systems, the new network need not require a fully interconnected and reliable core, thus reducing costs. However, the switching, billing, signaling, and operations support systems that currently sit on top of this relatively simple core are so extensive, and so coupled to the existing architecture, that making a sudden change is too expensive.

Eventually, the telephone network core will run over ATM, allowing greater flexibility in routing and network topology. However, a complete cut over to ATM is likely to take at least a decade, if not longer. So, the short answer is, yes, current telephone network routing leads to increased cost, but, in the near term, the topology of the core is too ingrained to change.

In any case, note that a good rule of thumb is that about 80% of the cost of the entire telephone network is in the local loop, and about 90% of the local loop cost is in the labor of installation. The expense of nonoptimal routing in the core pales in comparison with these costs!

11.4.2 Dynamic nonhierarchical routing

The simplest possible routing algorithm in the network core is for it to accept a call if and only if the one-hop path is available. This algorithm is nonoptimal, in that a call may be rejected though a two-hop path was available. A major advance in telephone routing was the introduction of *dynamic nonhierarchical routing (DNHR)*. DNHR divides the day into approximately ten periods. In each period, each toll switch is assigned a primary (one-hop) path to another toll switch, and an ordered set of alternative (two-hop) paths. Incoming call-setup packets are first forwarded on the primary path. If sufficient resources are not available on the primary path, then the switch tries each of the allocated two-hop paths in turn (we call this *spilling* or *overflow*). The switch rejects the call if all the alternative paths are busy. The process in which a call rejected on a primary path is retried on an alternative path is called *crankback*. Crankback is necessary in any routing policy that supports quality-of-service constraints and wants to achieve a low call rejection rate.

DNHR draws upon the predictability of aggregated telephone traffic, and the fact that switches and links are usually available, to select optimal alternative two-hop paths. DNHR performance suffers when traffic changes unexpectedly, so that the list of alternative paths ought to change, but does not. This might increase load on trunk groups that are already heavily loaded while leaving other trunks underutilized. These problems are corrected with more sophisticated routing algorithms, which we discuss in Sections 11.4.3 and 11.4.4. We now make a small diversion to study the dynamics of routing with DNHR.

The Erlang map

An important idea associated with routing in general, and with telephone routing in particular, is the *Erlang map* [Girard 90, p. 159]. The *Erlang blocking formula*, described in Section 14.11.2, allows us to compute the blocking probability of a trunk group if we know the load on the group and its capacity. Given a fixed external call load on the network core, a routing strategy determines the load on each trunk group, and therefore the blocking probability for that trunk group. DNHR assigns a set of alternative paths to toll switches so that the expected blocking probability for an incoming call is minimized. Thus, the path of a new call depends on the expected load on each trunk group, which depends, in turn, on the routing! This circular dependency between routing and blocking probability leads to a system of equations called the *Erlang map*. We can show that the Erlang map has a *unique* fixed-point solution called the *Erlang fixed point*.

More precisely, we define $B(k)$ to be the blocking probability on trunk k, where $B(k) = E(L(k), C(k))$, $E(...)$ is the Erlang formula, $L(k)$ is the load on link k, and $C(k)$ is its capacity. Now, if a route r is denoted by a set of links, and $\nu(r)$ represents the external load on r, then we can approximate $L(k)$ by [Kelly 91]:

$$L(k) = \sum_{r:k\in r} \nu(r) \prod_{j\in r-\{k\}} (1 - B(j)) \qquad (11.1)$$

To see this, note that $\nu(r)$ is the intrinsic load on route r. Each factor of $(1 - B(j))$ represents a "thinning" of the load, so that the load on trunk k is just the thinned sum of the loads on all the routes that share trunk k. $B(k)$ clearly depends on some number of other $B(j)$s, through $B(k) = E(L(k), C(k))$ and Equation 11.1. Thus, each of the $B(k)$s is implicitly defined by the others and forms the Erlang map.

Metastability in DNHR

Though the Erlang map has a unique solution, which represents a long-term mean blocking rate on each link, this solution is often the time-average of two distinct values, one high and the other low [Kelly 91]. In other words, given a blocking probability for a particular link, b, as the solution to Equation 11.1, we achieve b as the mean of two other values b_{high} and b_{low}. The underlying physical mechanism is that given a particular traffic load, the network periodically changes from a state where most blocking probabilities are low (b_{low}) to a state where most blocking probabilities are high (b_{high}). The *mean* blocking probability, b, is their average, and, in practice, the network may never achieve it. Let us see why.

Consider a network where a sudden burst of activity between toll switches A and B forces traffic to be off-loaded (spilled) onto paths ACB and ADB, adding extra load to links AC, CB, AD, and DB (Figure 11.3). If more traffic now appears on any one of these links, this traffic may, in turn, be diverted to other two-hop paths, making the situation worse. The key point is that every time a toll switch spills traffic to a two-hop alternative path, it increases the blocking probability for *two* other one-hop paths that use these links. We can show that the network, under a heavy load, can reach a *metastable* state where almost every call takes a two-hop path. Moreover, even with no change in mean offered load, the network can suddenly return to a "normal" state, where most paths are single hop. This is the physical mechanism underlying the multiple blocking probabili-

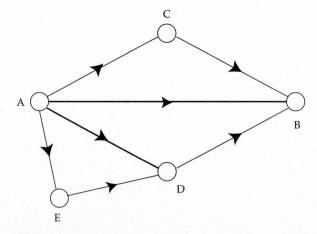

Figure 11.3: Metastability in telephone networks. Suppose the one-hop path from A to B is full (indicated by the heavy line), so that calls spill to two-hop paths A–C–B and A–D–B. This increases the load on trunks AC, AD, CB, and CB. The additional load may cause trunk AD to fill, causing calls from A to D to further spill to trunks AE and ED. If this continues, all calls take only two-hop paths through the core, although by rearranging calls, most or all of them can be diverted to one-hop paths. This is called metastability.

ties we mentioned in the previous paragraph. Metastability is undesirable because it can lead to a high call blocking rate even with moderate loads.

The existence of metastability in the telephone network is a cause of much concern. However, we can prevent it by simply reserving some part of the capacity on each trunk for one-hop calls [Akinpelu 84]. Continuing with our example, when the trunk AB is busy, AC and CB are allowed to carry no more than a given fraction of two-hop calls. Thus, new calls requiring, say, the CB trunk, would always have a good chance of being carried on a one-hop path. It can be shown that this technique (called *trunk reservation*) prevents the network from entering a metastable state [Girard 90, pp. 182–186]. The cost of trunk reservation is that the network may block a call even when it has sufficient capacity, thus increasing call blocking probability. However, because the network never reaches the metastable state, the *overall* blocking probability drops.

Shadow prices

How should the network allocate the set of alternative paths to a toll switch? The key theoretical result here is the computation of a *shadow price* to carry a call on a trunk [Kelly 88]. The idea is that if a call is carried on a trunk, it increases the blocking probability for future calls on that trunk. We quantify this increase in blocking probability as a shadow price. When a call comes in, we can compute the sum of the shadow prices for every alternate path. If the sum is larger than the revenue gained from a single call on every path, then the network should drop the call. Otherwise, the network should route it on the trunk that has the least cost. Given past traffic history, a network administrator can compute the expected least cost trunks for each period. These, then, form the set of alternative paths allocated to each toll switch by DNHR. If we can measure trunk loads dynamically, the shadow price approach allows a toll switch to compute optimal alternative paths for each call, instead of once every time period, as in DNHR.

11.4.3   TSMR

In DNHR, a central computer gives each toll switch a set of alternative paths based on past measurements, which are updated once a week. If a sudden surge of calls arrives on a trunk, the only adaptability in the network is to start trying the previously prescribed alternate paths. Although this was suitable for earlier toll switches that had very limited computational power, modern switch controllers can do much better. One step in this direction is *trunk status map routing,* or TSMR. In this scheme, each switch controller measures the load on each of its outgoing links and tells this to a central computer. The central computer periodically computes optimal alternative paths for each toll switch (based, for example, on the current load and the corresponding shadow prices) and loads these into all the toll switches. Thus, the central computer updates the choice of alternative paths more often than with DNHR. To dampen routing changes, a toll switch updates its load measurement only if this load changes "significantly," meaning, typically, 12.5%.

11.4.4   RTNR

The latest in the series of telephone routing algorithms is *real-time network routing* (telephone routing algorithms seem to require four-letter acronyms, and this is called RTNR).

RTNR, which typifies the current generation of telephone routing algorithms, replaced DNHR in AT&T's long-distance network in 1991. Unlike DNHR and TSMR, RTNR does not use centralized control. Instead, each toll switch monitors the loading of every outgoing trunk and computes a list of lightly loaded trunks. If the primary path for a call is busy, the originating toll switch asks the destination for the destination's list. Since calls are symmetric, the logical AND of the two lists is the set of lightly loaded alternative paths from the originating switch to the destination. For example, toll switch A may have light loads on links AB, AC, and AE. If the destination is D, D may report light loads on DC, DE, and DG. If DC is lightly loaded, from symmetry, so is CD. So, A knows that AC and CD are both lightly loaded, and discovers that A–C–D is a good alternative path.

RTNR allows a trunk to be partitioned among multiple traffic classes. Each class has its own blocking probability goal and trunk reservation level. When the network is lightly loaded, we give a class as much bandwidth as it can use, but under heavy loads, admission control ensures that the network meets the class's reservation level. Note that the traffic class here is used in a rather restricted sense to mean a voice call, a data call, or a multiplexed ($N*$ 64 kbps) call.

RTNR is very effective in practice (see Exercise 11.1). For example, AT&T's long-distance network carries up to 260 million call attempts on busy days. Of these attempts, only about one or two are blocked in the core! Other telephone companies, with similarly engineered network cores, have similar call-blocking statistics.

11.5   Distance-vector routing

Telephone network routing is specialized to take advantage of the unique features of the telephone network, such as a predictable traffic flow, and a relatively small network core. Large packet networks, such as the Internet, present a very different environment. In the Internet, links and routers are unreliable, alternative paths are scarce, and traffic patterns can change unpredictably within minutes. It is not surprising that routing in the Internet, and in ATM networks, which are likely to have Internet-like characteristics, follows a different path. The two fundamental routing algorithms in packet-switched networks are *distance-vector* and *link-state.*

Both algorithms assume that a router knows (a) the address of each neighbor, and (b) the cost of reaching each neighbor (where the cost measures quantities like the link's capacity, the current queuing delay, or a per-packet charge). Both algorithms allow a router to find *global* routing information, that is, the next hop to reach every destination in the network by the shortest path, by exchanging routing information with only its neighbors. Roughly speaking, in a distance-vector algorithm, a node tells its *neighbors* its distance to *every* other node in the network, and in a link-state algorithm, a node tells *every* other node in the network its distance to its *neighbors.* Thus, both routing protocols are *distributed* and are suitable for large internetworks controlled by multiple administrative entities. In this section, we will focus on distance-vector algorithms. We will study link-state algorithms in Section 11.6.

11.5.1   Distance-Vector Algorithm

In distance-vector routing, we assume that each router knows the identity of every other router in the network (but not necessarily the shortest path to it). Each router maintains a *distance vector*, that is, a list of ⟨*destination, cost*⟩ tuples, one tuple per destination, where *cost* is the current estimate for the sum of the link costs on the shortest path to that destination. Each router initializes the cost to reach all nonneighbor nodes to a value higher than the expected cost of any route in the network (commonly referred to in the routing literature as *infinity*). A router periodically sends a copy of its distance vector to all its neighbors. When a router receives a distance vector from a neighbor, it determines whether its cost to reach any destination would decrease if it routed packets to that destination through that neighbor (Figure 11.4). It can easily do so by comparing its current cost to reach a destination with the sum of the cost to reach its neighbor and its neighbor's cost to reach that destination.

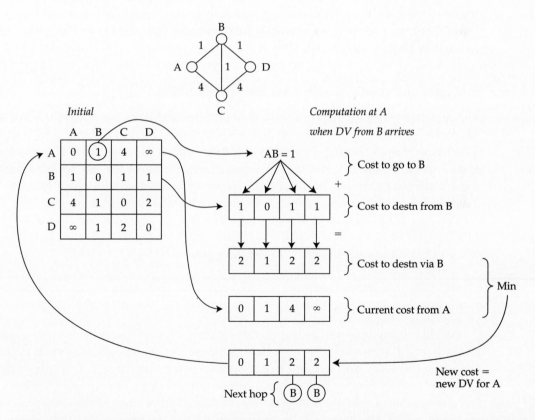

Figure 11.4: Distance-vector algorithm at node A. In the figure, A receives a distance vector from its neighbor B. It uses this information to find that it can reach nodes C and D at a lower cost. It therefore updates its own distance vector and chooses B as its next hop to nodes C and D.

EXAMPLE 11.3

In Figure 11.4, if router A has an initial distance vector of $(\langle A, 0\rangle, \langle B, 1\rangle, \langle C, 4\rangle,$ $\langle D, \infty\rangle)$, we see that the arrival of a distance vector from B results in A updating its costs to C and D. If a neighbor's distance vector results in a decrease in a cost to a destination, that neighbor is chosen to be the next hop to get to that destination. For example, in Figure 11.4, the distance vector from B reduced A's cost to D. Therefore, B is the next hop for packets destined for D. A router is expected to advertise its distance vector to all its neighbors every time it changes.

We can show that even if nodes asynchronously update their distance vectors, the routing tables will eventually converge. The intuition behind the proof is that each router knows the true cost to its neighbors. This information is spread one hop with the first exchange of distance vectors, and one hop further on each subsequent exchange. With the continued exchange of distance vectors, the cost of every link is eventually known throughout the network. We also call the distance-vector algorithm *Bellman–Ford* after its creators [Bellman 57, FF 62].

11.5.2 Problems and solutions with distance-vector routing

The distance-vector algorithm works well if nodes and links are always up, but it runs into many problems when links go down or come up. The root cause of problems is that when a node updates and distributes a distance vector, it hides the sequence of operations it used to compute the vector. Thus, downstream routers do not have sufficient information to figure out whether their choice of a next hop will cause loops to form. This will become clear when we look at the *count-to-infinity* problem.

Count-to-infinity

We illustrate this problem with the next example.

EXAMPLE 11.4

Consider the simple network shown in Figure 11.5. Initially, A routes packets to C via B, and B uses its direct path. Now, suppose the BC link goes down. B updates its cost to infinity, and tells this to A. Suppose, in the meantime, A sends its distance vector to B. B notices that A has a two-hop path to C. Therefore, it updates its routing table to reflect this information, and tells A that it has a three-hop path to C. In the previous exchange, A discovered that B did not have a path to C any more, and had updated its table to reflect that. When B joyfully announces that it does indeed have a path, A updates its routing table to show a four-hop path to C. This process of increasing the hop count to C continues until the hop count reaches

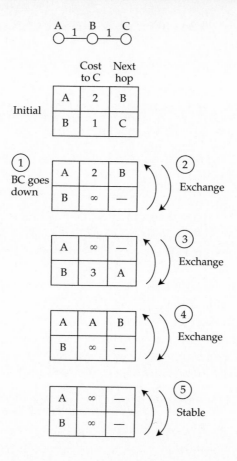

Figure 11.5: Count-to-infinity. The figure illustrates a possible problem with the distance-vector algorithm. When BC goes down, B thinks that it can reach C through A. When A learns that BC is down, it thinks it can reach C through B, and so on. Both nodes ultimately realize that C is unreachable, but in the meantime, packets may loop.

infinity, when both nodes realize that no route to C exists after all. Note that during the process of counting-to-infinity, packets from A or B destined to C are likely to loop back and forth between A and B. Thus, if the counting process takes a while, many packets may wander aimlessly in the network, making no progress, and causing congestion for everyone else. It makes sense to try to avoid counting to infinity.

Path vector

The reason for count-to-infinity is that when B updated its path to C to go through A, it did not realize that A's path to C was through B. In other words, the distance vector that

A sent B hid the fact that B was on A's route to C. There are several ways to add information to the distance vector to solve this problem. One solution is to annotate each entry in the distance vector with the path used to obtain this cost. For example, in Step 2 of Figure 11.5, A can tell B that its cost to C is 2, and the path to C was C–B. When B sees this, it realizes that no route to C exists, and the count-to-infinity problem goes away. This solution is also called the *path-vector* solution, since routers annotate the distance vector with a path. The path-vector approach is used in the *border gateway protocol (BGP)* in the Internet core. Note that path vectors trade off a larger routing table and extra control overhead for robustness.

Split horizon

The problem with path vectors is that the vectors require large table sizes, which can prove expensive. Several other solutions to the count-to-infinity problem avoid this overhead. In one solution, called *split-horizon routing,* a router never advertises the cost of a destination to its neighbor N, if N is the next hop to that destination. For example, in Figure 11.5, this means that A does not advertise a cost for C to B because it uses B as its next hop to C. This trivially solves the count-to-infinity problem in Figure 11.5. However, it can be shown (see Exercise 11.5) that split horizon works only when two adjacent routers count to infinity: it is ineffective when three routers mutually do so.

A variant of split-horizon, called *split horizon with poisonous reverse,* is used in the *Routing Information Protocol (RIP)* on the Internet [Hedrick 88]. When A routes to C via B, it tells B that it has an *infinite* cost to reach C (with normal split horizon, A would not tell B of a path to C at all). Though this sometimes accelerates convergence, it does not prevent three-way counting to infinity.

Triggered updates

While the classical distance-vector algorithm prescribes that a router should advertise its distance vector every time it changes, this can lead to a flurry of updates every time a link cost changes. If, for example, the cost measures link delay, a router may update its distance vector quite often. To prevent this, most distance vector algorithms prescribe that distance vectors be advertised only once in about 30 seconds. This adversely affects the time taken to recover from a count-to-infinity situation. Consider the situation in Figure 11.5, where each node must count from 1 to infinity. If we define infinity to be 16, then it will converge only $15 * 30$ seconds later = 7.5 minutes. The network will be in an unstable situation during this entire interval. To avoid this, we can trigger distance vector changes immediately after a link is marked down. This rapid propagation removes some race conditions required for count-to-infinity and is adopted in the Internet RIP protocol.

Source tracing

Source tracing was independently and simultaneously proposed in references [CRKG 89, RF 89]. The key idea is to augment a distance vector so that it carries not only the cost to a destination, but the router *immediately preceding* the destination. We can show that this information is sufficient for a source to construct the entire path to the destination.

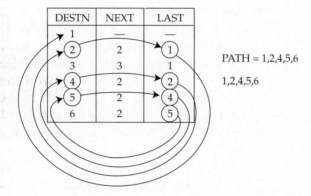

Figure 11.6: Source tracing. The source-tracing approach adds an additional field to the distance vector: the router immediately preceding a destination. This information can be used to discover the path from a source to any destination in the network, thus allowing a source to check for loops.

EXAMPLE 11.5

Consider Figure 11.6, which shows the routing table for router 1. Suppose we want to trace the path to router 6. First, we locate 6 in the routing table and see that the preceding router on the path to 6 is 5. We now look for 5, and find 4 as the preceding router. Continuing in this fashion, it is easy to compute the path as $1-2-4-5-6$. This allows us to get the same information as a path vector, but with very little additional table space.

When a router updates its distance vector, if its cost to a destination decreases, it replaces the preceding-router field for that destination in its routing table with the corresponding value in the incoming distance vector. Distance vector with source tracing is guaranteed to be loop free if routers follow the rule that if a router changes its notion of the next hop for a destination D, then it should use the same neighbor for all destinations for which D lies along the shortest path.

DUAL

The *distributed update algorithm (DUAL)* is a technique to assure loop-free routing tables even in the presence of rapid changes in network topology. With DUAL, a router maintains a pared-

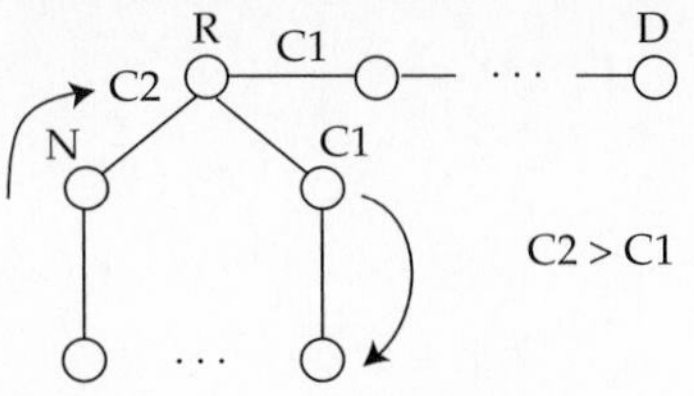

Figure 11.7: If a node updates its next hop because of a decrease in the distance to some node, then a loop cannot be formed. This is because if a loop forms, the reported cost must include the cost of the loop, which is larger than the direct cost.

down version of the network topology by storing the distance reported by each of its neighbors to each destination (this is just the union of their distance vectors). If the cost from a particular router R to a destination D *decreases* because of the receipt of a distance vector from a neighbor N, then it is impossible for a loop to form if R updates its tables based on that distance vector (Figure 11.7). The reason is that if a loop forms, the reported cost to D from N in the incoming distance vector C2 must *include* the previously reported cost from R to D, C1. Thus, C2 must be larger than C1. If R updates its tables only for distance vectors such that C2 < C1, then loops will not form.

Now, suppose R receives an update such that the distance to a destination increases because of an increase in a link's cost or because of a link failure. Then, R first checks if it can find a shorter path to this destination through another neighbor using its topology table. If not, it *freezes* its routing table and distributes the new distance vector to all its neighbors. The neighbors check whether this increases their cost to D. If so, they freeze their tables in turn and spread the vector to their neighbors. The computation *expands* in this manner until all the routers affected by the change (that is, all routers whose distance to any endpoint increases because of this change) know of it. If all the neighbors of a router already know of the change or are unaffected, they inform the router that they are done. The router unfreezes its state and informs the router that previously informed it of the change, which, in turn, propagates this information. Thus, the computation *contracts* until the router that first detected the change knows that the effect of the change has propagated to every router that ought to know of it. This is called a *diffusion computation*. It can be shown that the DUAL algorithm results in loop-free routing [Garcia–Luna–Aceves 89]. DUAL is implemented in the Extended Interior Gateway Routing Protocol (EIGRP), a proprietary routing protocol from Cisco Systems.

How often should distance vectors be exchanged?

The interval between exchanges of distance vectors represents a trade-off between sensitivity to link loads and failures (finding the "best" path) and the overhead in exchanging and processing routing information. Moreover, if loops are possible, the update frequency determines the rate at which the nodes in the loop count to infinity. Finally, some protocols, such as RIP, infer that a peer router is unreachable when they receive no updates from it for some time. The longer the update interval, the longer it takes for a router to detect a failed peer. Thus, choosing a good update interval is nontrivial.

RIP suggests that vectors be exchanged once every 30 s, and if a router does not hear from its neighbor for six consecutive intervals, the neighbor is assumed to be down. Thus, a node can be down for 3 minutes before anyone notices. This information will then take its time to be propagated throughout the network. However, if the routing protocol uses triggered updates, convergence after a failure can be made much more rapid. Thus, a good compromise may be to use a slow update interval (around 30 s) in the common case, but to trigger rapid distribution of distance vectors in the case of link or router failure. Besides, we can eliminate dependency on the update interval for detecting router and link failures by using explicit HELLO messages between peers, and a finer-grained timeout on HELLO messages.

11.6   Link-state routing

In distance-vector routing, a router knows only the cost to each destination or, sometimes, the path to the destination. This cost or path is partly determined on its behalf by other routers in the network. This hiding of information is the cause of many problems with distance-vector algorithms.

In contrast, the philosophy in link-state routing is to distribute the topology of the network and the cost of each link to all the routers. Each router independently computes optimal paths to every destination. If each router sees the same cost for each link and uses the same algorithm to compute the best path, the routes are guaranteed to be loop free. Thus, the key elements in link-state routing are a way to distribute knowledge of network topology to every router in the network, and a way to compute shortest paths given the topology. We will study these in turn.

11.6.1   Topology dissemination

Each router participating in the link-state algorithm creates a set of *link-state packets* (*LSPs*) that describe its links. An LSP contains the router's ID, the neighbor's ID, and the cost of the link to the neighbor. The next step is to distribute a copy of every LSP to every router using *controlled flooding*. The idea is that when a router receives a new LSP, it stores a copy of the LSP in an *LSP database,* and forwards the LSP to every interface other than the one on which it arrived. It can be shown that an LSP is never transferred over the same link twice in the same direction. Thus, if a network has E edges, flooding requires at most $2E$ transfers.

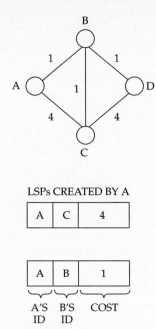

LSPs CREATED BY A

A	C	4

A	B	1

A'S   B'S   COST
ID   ID

Figure 11.8: Link-state packets. Each router participating in link-state routing creates and distributes a set of link-state packets that contain the router's cost to reach each neighbor.

EXAMPLE 11.6

In Figure 11.8, A creates two LSPs, ⟨A, B, 1⟩ and ⟨A, C, 4⟩. The other nodes in the network create similar LSPs. Let us trace the path taken by the LSP ⟨A, B, 1⟩ that originates from A. In the first step, the LSP reaches B, which in turn forwards it to C and D, but not to A, because it arrived from A. When C gets the LSP, it forwards it to A and D. A does not forward the LSP further, because its database already contains the LSP. If D got the LSP from B before it got it from C, D detects that the LSP is a duplicate and does nothing. Otherwise, it forwards it to B, who does nothing. Thus, in a few short steps, the LSP reaches every router in the network.

Sequence numbers

Although flooding is easy to understand when links and nodes stay up, as with distance-vector algorithms, complexity creeps in when links or routers can go down. For example, in Figure 11.8, suppose link AB goes down. We would like the LSP corresponding to AB to be removed from all the other routers. Router B detects that link AB is down and sends an LSP with an infinite cost for AB to all the other routers. The other routers must somehow determine that this LSP overrides the information already existing in their databases. Therefore, every LSP must have a sequence number, and LSPs with newer sequence numbers override LSPs with older sequence numbers. This allows us to purge the old LSPs from each router's database.

Wrapped sequence numbers

Unfortunately, every sequence number has finite length and therefore is subject to wrap-around. We have to ensure that a new LSP that has a numerically lower (but wrapped-around) sequence number still overrides an old LSP that has a numerically higher sequence number. For example, if sequence numbers are three bits long, thus spanning the space from 0 to 7, we would like a newer LSP with sequence number 0 to override an older LSP with sequence number 7. We can solve this problem by using very large sequence numbers. Then it is almost certain that if the difference between the sequence numbers of an existing and an incoming LSP is large, so that the numerically smaller LSP is actually newer. For example, if sequence numbers are 32 bits long, then they span the space from 0 to 4,294,967,295. If an old LSP in the database has a sequence number toward the end of the space, say, 4,294,967,200, and a new LSP has a sequence number toward the beginning of the space, say, 20, then the difference is 4,294,967,180. We therefore declare the LSP with sequence number 20 to be the newer one. More precisely, if the LSP sequence number space spans N sequence numbers, sequence number a is older than sequence number b if:

$$a < b \quad \text{and} \quad |b - a| < N/2,$$
$$\text{or} \quad a > b \quad \text{and} \quad |b - a| > N/2. \tag{11.2}$$

Initial sequence number

When a router starts, it must choose a sequence number such that its LSPs in other routers' databases are overridden. If the router does not know what LSPs it used in the past, it may risk flooding new LSPs that are always ignored. For example, with the $0-2^{32} - 1$ sequence space, the LSPs in the databases may have a sequence number 5. If the router comes back up and chooses to start numbering LSPs with sequence number 0, other routers ignore the new LSPs. There are two ways to solve this problem: *aging* and a *lollipop sequence space* [Perlman 83].

Aging

With *aging*, the creator of an LSP sets a field in the LSP header to a maxiumum age (MAX_AGE). A router receiving this LSP copies the current age to a per-LSP counter in its database and periodically decrements it. If decrementing an LSP counter makes it zero, the router purges the LSP from its database. To preserve a consistent view of the network topology, the router should quickly request the rest of the network to discard this LSP. It does so by initiating flooding with the zero-age LSP. When a router gets an LSP with zero age and the latest sequence number, it purges the LSP and floods the zero-age LSP to its neighbors. This quickly restores consistency. After a purge of an LSP from a particular router, any subsequent LSP from that router will automatically enter the LSP database. Thus, if a newly booted router waits for a while before sending new LSPs, it

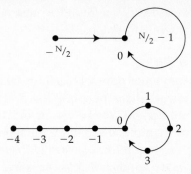

Figure 11.9: Lollipop sequence space. This space has a unique "smallest" sequence number, which allows rebooted routers to flush old LSPs from the LSP databases of other routers. It also deals correctly with sequence number wrap-around.

knows that its old LSPs will be purged, and its new LSPs will override all LSPs from its previous incarnation.

Although this scheme does work, the choice of initial LSP age is problematic. We would like the latest LSP from a router to be flooded throughout the network before its previous one times out. Otherwise, some routers may purge the LSP from their databases before the new LSP reaches them, leading to inconsistent routes. To minimize the overhead of sending LSPs frequently, we should use a fairly large initial LSP age, on the order of an hour or so.[3] However, to allow purging of old LSPs, after rebooting, a router must wait for a time on the order of the initial LSP age before it can start sending new LSPs. So, we cannot simultaneously minimize control overhead and the dead time after a router reboots.

Lollipop sequence space

A better solution is for newly booted routers to use a sequence number that uniquely differentiates it from every other sequence number that it could have used in the past. Although this is impossible with a circular sequence space, we can achieve this using a *lollipop sequence space* [Perlman 83] (Figure 11.9). Here, we have partitioned the sequence space of size N into three parts: a negative space from $-N/2$ to 0, the sequence number 0, and a positive space of size $N/2 - 1$. When a router comes up, it uses the sequence number $-N/2$ for its LSPs, and subsequent LSPs use $-N/2 + 1$, $-N/2 + 2$, etc. When the sequence number becomes positive, subsequent sequence numbers wrap around in

---

[3]If the initial LSP age is small, then the time interval between the creation of two LSPs must be small; otherwise, a distant router may time out an LSP before the next LSP reaches it. This increases routing overhead.

the circular part of the space. An LSP with sequence number a is older than an LSP with sequence number b if:

- $a < 0$ and $a < b$, or
- $a > 0, a < b$, and $b - a < N/4$, or
- $a > 0, b > 0, a > b$, and $a - b > N/4$

Note that $-N/2$ is therefore the oldest sequence number.

We add the rule that if a router gets an LSP from another router that has an older sequence number than the one in its database, it informs the other router of its sequence number. Because a newly booted router always generates a packet with the oldest sequence number, it is guaranteed to be told by its neighbors of the sequence number it had used before it crashed. It then jumps to a sequence number 1 larger than this, so that subsequent LSPs override its past LSPs. For example, as shown in Figure 11.9, a newly booted router starts with sequence number -4. If existing routers have an LSP from this router with a sequence number 2, they inform the newly booted router of this. The newly booted router then uses 3 for its newer LSPs and continues to number packets as 3, 0, 1, 2, 3, 0, etc., until it boots again. This solution does not require the newly booted router to wait for its LSPs to require. Intuitively, the neighbors of a router act as a distributed memory recording its actions. By sending a unique packet (with sequence number $-N/2$), a newly booted router can access this memory to regain its past state.

Recovering from a partition

LSP databases remain coherent if the network does not partition into two or more fragments. However, when recovering from a partition, databases may become inconsistent. We illustrate this with the next example.

EXAMPLE 11.7

Consider the network shown in Figure 11.10. Assume that at the start of time, all routers have consistent LSP databases. Now, suppose link 4–5 breaks. This partitions the network into two independent fragments. If links 7–8 and 1–2 break later, the databases in each fragment evolve independently of each other. For example, node 2 is unaware of the break in link 7–8. This does not pose a problem if 4–5 stays down. However, when it comes up, routers on each side of the partition must update their view of the other side; otherwise, routing loops are possible (for example, 2 may route packets to 8 via 7, not knowing that link 7–8 is down).

Routers on each side of the newly restored link cooperate to restore LSP databases. Each LSP in the database is associated with a link ID and a version number. Routers increment the version number each time the LSP value changes. A set of *database descriptor records*,

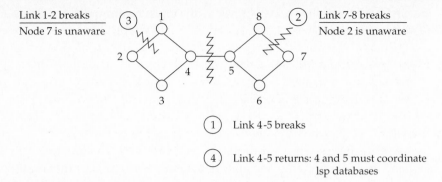

Figure 11.10: LSP database recovery after network partition. When the network partitions, each side independently updates its databases. When the partition heals, routers on both sides must resynchronize, using database description records.

also maintained in the database, describe the link IDs and version numbers in the database. Database descriptor records are like link-state packets, except that they store far less information, so that exchanging these records is less expensive than exchanging LSPs. When a link comes up, routers at each end exchange a complete set of database descriptor records. By comparing them, each determines the set of records that are either nonexistent or out-of-date in their database. They request their peer router to send them these LSPs, which they then flood into their respective fragments. This restores a uniform view of the topology to the entire network.

Link or router failure

When a link fails, the routers on either side notice this and can flood the network with this information. Thus, link failures are relatively easy to recover from. However, when a router fails, there is no direct way to detect this. Most link-state protocols require routers to exchange HELLO packets with their neighbors. If a router does not respond to a series of HELLOs, it is likely to be down. The neighbors should immediately flood this information.

It is possible to construct scenarios where, because of a series of failures, the HELLO protocol does not detect a dead router (for example, an undetectable corruption in the source address may make a HELLO packet from a router that is alive look like a HELLO from a dead router). To prevent databases from becoming corrupted without explicit failure detection, LSP records are usually aged (even with lollipop-space sequence numbers). When an LSP times out at some router, the router immediately floods the network with a special packet that informs every other router that the LSP timed out, and that they should delete this (stale) LSP from their LSP database. This allows the network eventually to recover from almost every possible sequence of failures [Perlman 83].

Securing LSP databases

Loop-freeness in link-state routing requires that all routers share a consistent view of the network. If a malicious agent injects spurious LSP packets into a router, routing becomes unstable. Thus, routers must actively protect their LSP database not only from corruption, but also from malicious interference. Several techniques for securing LSP databases are well known. First, link-state packets are protected by a checksum, not only when sent over a transmission link, but also when stored in the database. This detects corruption on the link or on a disk. Second, the receiver acknowledges LSP exchanges, so that a sender can recover from link losses using timeouts and retransmissions. Third, LSP exchanges are authenticated by a password known only to routing administrators. This makes it harder for malicious users to inject LSPs into a database. Several other techniques to ensure security in LSP exchange are described in reference [Perlman 83].

11.6.2   Computing shortest paths

Thus far, we have seen how every router in the network obtains a consistent copy of the LSP database. We now study how a router can use this database to compute optimal routes in the network. A router typically uses *Dijkstra's shortest-path algorithm* [Dijkstra 59] to do so.

Dijkstra's algorithm

Dijkstra's algorithm computes the shortest path from a *root* node (corresponding to the router where the algorithm is being run) to every other node in the network. The key idea is to maintain a set of nodes, P, for which the shortest path has already been found. Every node outside P must be reached by a path from a node already in P. We find out every way in which an "outside" node o can be reached by a one-hop path from a node already in P, and choose the shortest of these as the path to o. Node o can now be added to P, and we continue in this fashion until we have the shortest path to all the nodes in the network.

More precisely, we define two sets P and T (standing for permanent and temporary). Set P is the set of nodes to which shortest paths have been found, and set T is the set of nodes to which we are considering shortest paths. We start by initializing P to the current node, and T to null. The algorithm repeats the following steps:

1. For the node p just added to P, add each of its neighbors n to T such that (a) if n is not in T, add it, annotating it with the cost to reach it through p and p's ID, and (b) if n is already in T and the path to n through p has a lower cost, then remove the earlier instance of n and add the new instance annotated with the cost to reach it through p and p's ID.
2. Pick the node n that has the smallest cost in T and, if it is not already in P, add it to P. Use its annotation to determine the router p to use to reach n. If T is empty, we are done.

When the algorithm stops, we have, for each router, the router on the shortest path used to reach it. As we did with source tracing for distance-vector routing, this allows us

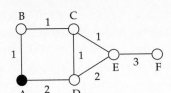

B(A,1) means B was
reached by A, cost 1

Permanent	Temporary	Comments
A	B(A,1), D(A,2)	Root and its neighbors
A, B(A 1)	D(A,2), C(B,2)	Add C(B,2)
A, B(A,1) D(A,2)	E(D,4), C(B,2)	C(D,3) didn't make it
A, B(A,1) D(A,2), C(B,2)	E(C,3)	E(D,4) too long
A, B(A,1) D(A,2), C(B,2) E(C,3)	F(E,6)	
A, B(A,1) C(B,2), D(A,2) E(C,3), F(E,6)	Null	Stop

A •

A •——1——•
         B

D
2 •
  ╱
A • ——1——• B

D
2 •
  ╱
A • ——1—— • ——1—— •
   B   C

D
2 •
  ╱
A •
   1 • ——1—— • ——1—— •
      B   C   E

D
2 •
  ╱
A •
   1 • ——1—— • ——1—— • ——3—— F
      B   C   E

Figure 11.11: Dijkstra's algorithm. We show the computation at router A. At each step, A adds the closest router in its temporary set to its permanent set, then updates the temporary set with the newly added router's neighbors. This is guaranteed to compute shortest paths from A to all routers in the network.

to compute the next hop on the shortest path for every destination in the network. Figure 11.11 shows an example of Dijkstra's algorithm.

11.6.3 Link state versus distance vector

Given a choice between link-state and distance-vector routing, which style should we prefer? Arguments on this issue among experts often parallel the medieval discussion of how many angels could dance on the head of a pin! Conventional wisdom is that link-state algorithms are more stable because each router knows the entire network topology. On the other hand, transient routing loops can form while the new topology is being flooded. If the network is so dynamic that links are always coming up or going down, then these transients can last for a long time, and the loop-free property is lost. Moreover, as we have seen, simple modifications to the vanilla distance-vector algorithm can prevent routing loops. Thus, one should not prefer link-state protocols for loop-freeness alone.

A second argument in favor of link-state algorithms is that they allow multiple routing metrics. The idea is that each LSP can carry more than one cost. Thus, each router can compute multiple shortest-path trees, one corresponding to each metric. Packets can then be forwarded on one of the shortest-path trees, which they can select with a flag in the header. For example, an LSP may carry a delay cost and a monetary cost. This would allow every router to compute a shortest-delay tree and a lowest-monetary-cost tree. Incoming packets that prefer lower delays (and, perhaps, are willing to pay for it) would be routed according to the shortest-delay path.

Although this sounds attractive at first, it assumes that every router will agree to report the same set of metrics. If some routers do not report some metrics, this is not a disaster if all the other routers assign it a consistent default. However, the benefits from multiple metrics seem more tenuous if a considerable fraction of the routers along the path choose not to report one or more metrics of interest. Moreover, the benefits of multiple metrics can be realized by path-vector-type distance-vector algorithms.

Third, we prefer link-state algorithms because, after a change, they usually converge faster than distance-vector algorithms. It is not clear that this holds if we use a distance-vector algorithm with triggered updates and one of the several algorithms to ensure loop-freeness (and therefore, absence of counting to infinity). Convergence depends strongly on the network topology, the load on the routing protocol, and the exact sequence of link failure and recovery. Thus, it is impossible to argue convincingly for either link state or distance vector.

Distance-vector algorithms do seem to have two advantages over link-state algorithms. First, much of the overhead in link-state routing is in the elaborate precautions necessary to prevent corruption of the LSP database. We can avoid these in distance-vector algorithms because we do not require that nodes independently compute consistent routes. Second, distance-vector algorithms typically require less memory for routing tables than do link-state protocols. Again, this is because they do not need to maintain an LSP database. On the other hand, this advantage disappears when we use path-vector-type distance-vector algorithms.

Because there is no clear winner, both distance-vector and link-state algorithms are commonly used in packet-switched networks. For example, in the Internet, the two "modern" routing protocols are *Open Shortest Path First* (*OSPF*), which is a link-state protocol, and *Border Gateway Protocol* (*BGP*), which is a path-vector protocol (more about these in Section 11.9). Examples of both algorithms will probably exist in datagram networks for many years to come.

11.7   Choosing link costs

Thus far, we have assumed that network administrators somehow assign a reasonable cost to each link in the network, which they then distribute to other routers in the network. We have not really considered how the choice of a link cost affects the flow of traffic in the network. As we see next, the cost of a link and the load on it are coupled in a manner reminiscent of the Erlang map, which couples routing strategies and blocking probabilities in the telephone network. The key idea is that the choice of link costs implicitly defines the way in which traffic load is distributed in the network. The lower the cost of a given link, the higher the probability that it is a part of a shortest path to some destination, and the higher the expected load on it. Therefore, if link costs depend on the current load on the link (which is usually a good idea), a high cost lowers the load on the link, which, in turn, lowers its cost. Our goal is to choose an appropriate cost function so that the load and cost converge on a desirable fixed point. A poor cost function leads to routing oscillations, which are highly undesirable.

11.7.1   Static metrics

For the moment, let us ignore the dynamics of routing and focus on the simplest possible way to assign weights, the *hop-count* metric. Here, we give every link a unit weight, so that the shortest-cost path is also the path with the smallest hop count. Allocating all links a unit weight is reasonable when the links are homogeneous. However, it makes little sense if some links run at DS3 speeds (45 Mbps), while others are DS1 (1.5 Mbps). Here, we should probably give links with lower bandwidth a higher cost, so that the load is mostly carried on high-capacity links. This is illustrated in the next example.

EXAMPLE 11.8

Consider the network in Figure 11.12. Here, links AB, AC, and BD are T3 links, and BC and CD are T1 links. If we assign all links a unit cost, then traffic from B to C will go over the BC link. All other things being equal, it is a better idea to route B–C traffic on the path B–A–C, because it has nearly thirty times the capacity.

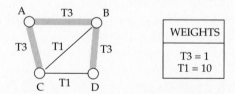

Figure 11.12: Problem with static weights. If the weights are as shown, the BC path is never used, even if the AC or AB path is heavily loaded.

Therefore, we could assign T1 links a weight of 10, and T3 links a weight of 1. Then, links BC and CD are never used (unless one or more of the T3 links goes down). Unfortunately, even if link AB is highly congested and BC is idle, traffic will *still* take the BAC path instead of the BC path. This points out the inherent problems of *statically* assigning weights to links. It may be a better idea to assign link costs dynamically, based on the current load on the link.

11.7.2 Original ARPAnet dynamic metrics

One of the earliest dynamic cost allocation techniques was used in the original ARPAnet [KZ 89]. In this scheme, the cost of a link is directly proportional to the length of a router's output queue at the entrance to that link. If a link has a long queue, no matter the link's capacity, it is considered overloaded and given a higher cost. Continuing with Example 11.8 and Figure 11.12, assume that link A–B was heavily loaded in the A-to-B direction. Then, the queue at router A for that link would be long. If A therefore advertises a higher cost for A–B, this would divert the C-to-B traffic to the path C–B from C–A–B, reducing the load on A–B.

Although the idea of a dynamic link cost is a good one, the original ARPAnet implementation is a case study in the unintended consequences of a complex design [KZ 89]. In its defense, the scheme did work well when the network was lightly loaded. However, many problems appeared under a heavy load. First, the link cost depended on the queue length averaged over 10 seconds. Since the backbone ran at only 56 Kbps, this represented too small a time granularity at which to measure queue lengths. Thus, transient spikes in the queue length could trigger major rerouting in the network. Second, link costs had a wide dynamic range (that is, they could be very low or very high). Consequently, it turned out that the network completely ignored paths with high costs. Although we should avoid high-delay links, they should not be unused! Third, the queue length was assumed to be a predictor for future loads on the link. In other words, if the queue length was long, the link cost was increased in the expectation that the link would continue to be overloaded in the future. In fact, the opposite was true. When a link's cost was large, it was avoided, so that when routes were recomputed, the link's load dramatically decreased. Fourth, there was no restriction on the difference between successively reported costs for a link. This allowed link costs to oscillate rapidly. Finally, all the routers tended to recompute routing tables simultaneously. Thus, links with low costs would be chosen to be on the shortest path simultaneously by many routers, flooding the link.

11.7.3 Modified ARPAnet metrics

The modified version of the ARPAnet link-cost function avoided many errors made in the first version and was much more successful. In this scheme, link costs are a function not only of the measured mean queue length, but also of the link's capacity. When the link's load is low, its cost depends entirely on the link's capacity, and the queue length comes into play only at higher loads. Thus, at low loads, network routing essentially uses static costs, making it stable. Moreover, link costs are *hop normalized,* that is, the weight of a link is measured in "hops." Traversing a link with a weight c is as expensive as traversing c links with unit weight. The higher the advertised hop-normalized cost, the greater the barrier to using the link, but the barrier is not overwhelmingly high.

Two schemes were also added to dampen the oscillation in link costs. First, the dynamic range of link costs was reduced from a range of $127:1$ to $3:1$ (the worst cost a link can advertise is that it equals 3 hops). Second, a router was allowed to change the link cost by only half a hop in successive advertisements. With these changes, and a few others described in reference [KZ 89], routing oscillations were nearly eliminated even under heavy load.

11.7.4 Routing dynamics

We mentioned earlier that the load on a link and the probability of its use in shortest-path routes are tightly coupled. We illustrate this by using two functions called the *metric map* and the *network response map* [KZ 89]. The metric map translates the load on a link to its link-cost metric and is the link-cost function we described in the previous paragraph. The network response map translates from a given link metric to the expected load on that link, given the current topology and traffic load. Although the metric map is precisely defined, the network response map is empirically determined by modifying the cost of one link at a time and measuring the additional traffic due to that change, then averaging this over all links. We show the general form of these maps in Figure 11.13. In Figure 11.13a we see that as the load increases, the link cost first is flat (as explained

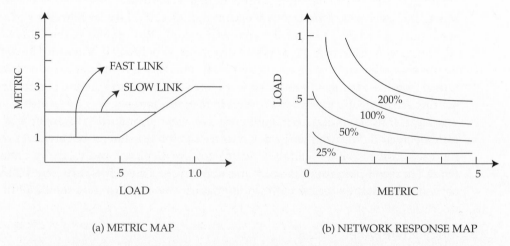

(a) METRIC MAP   (b) NETWORK RESPONSE MAP

Figure 11.13: Metric map and network response map. The metric map describes how to compute a link metric depending on the network load. At low loads, the metric depends entirely on the link type (a static weight). As the load increases beyond a threshold, the metric increases. The network response map shows the decrease in network load as a link's metric increases. The figure shows a family of curves, each corresponding to a particular overall network load.

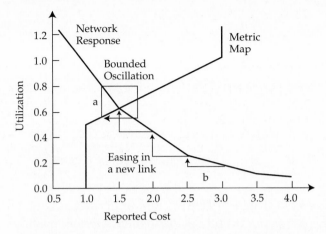

Figure 11.14: Routing dynamics (from [KZ 89]). We can compute routing dynamics by overlaying the metric and network response maps (the abscissa and ordinates of the metric map have been interchanged). For example, path (a) shows the stable state, where a reported link cost of 1.25 leads to a utilization of around 0.8, which leads to a metric of 1.75, which leads to a utilization of around 0.6, which leads to a metric of around 1.25, and so on. Path (b) shows how a new link starts at a high metric and decreases it gradually to enter the steady state.

earlier), and then rises linearly to 3, where it saturates. In Figure 11.13b, we show a family of curves, each corresponding to an overall network load, which plot the load on an "average" link as a function of the cost of that link. We see that as the link cost increases, the mean load on a link decreases from 1.2, when the cost is 0, to nearly 0, when the cost is 5.

We can envision the dynamics of routing in the network by putting these two maps together, as shown in Figure 11.14. Paths in this map show the evolution of the system. We choose an arbitrary initial load in the system, and compute the corresponding cost metric by drawing a horizontal line and choosing its intercept on the metric curve. The corresponding load in the next time step can now be obtained by drawing a vertical line through that metric and noting the intercept on the load curve. By repeating these steps, we can determine the dynamics of the system starting from an arbitrary initial load.

For example, consider the path marked *a* in the figure. This represents a link at equilibrium, where the link load and its cost metric suffer from a bounded oscillation. Note that the link cost is allowed to change by only half a hop in successive advertisements, which tightly bounds the range of oscillations. This fact is dramatically illustrated by the path marked *b*. Here, we see the effect of introducing a new link into the system. We artificially start the link off with a high cost, reducing the cost by half a hop each time step. Because of the high initial cost metric, the initial load on the link is low. Each subsequent advertisement therefore reduces the metric by half a hop, gradually increasing the load. The network eventually stabilizes with a small, bounded oscillation. If link costs

# nodes	Table space	Computation
1	1	O(0)
1,000	1,000	O(3,000)
1,000,000	1,000,000	O(6,000,000)
100,000,000	100,000,000	O(800,000,000)
10,000,000,000	10,000,000,000	O(100,000,000,000)

Table 11.1: Scaling properties of routing protocols.

were allowed to change by larger amounts in successive advertisements, link loads and metrics would suffer from large oscillations. System evolution diagrams such as these are very useful in evaluating heuristics for link-cost metrics.

11.8   Hierarchical routing

If a network with N nodes and E edges uses link-state routing, it can be shown that computing shortest paths takes $O(E \log E)$ computation at each router, and the routing table requires $O(N)$ storage. E is at least the same size as N, because even for a tree-shaped graph, which requires the smallest number of edges for a given number of nodes, $E = N - 1$. Assuming, conservatively, that $E = N$, and that computation for a network with one node takes unit time, Table 11.1 shows the approximate computation and space requirements as a function of N.

Clearly, the computation and space requirements for a routing protocol become excessive when N is large. Because both the Internet and the telephone network are expected to grow to several billion endpoints, we must use *hierarchical routing* to rein in routing costs.

We alluded to hierarchical routing when we discussed hierarchical addressing and address aggregation in Section 10.3. The idea is to partition the network into multiple hierarchical levels. A handful of routers in each level are responsible for communication between adjacent levels. Thus, at each level, only a few hundred routers need to maintain shortest-path routes to each other. A router that spans a hierarchy boundary agrees to route packets from the rest of the network to every router in its "area," and from every router in its area to the rest of the network.

11.8.1   Features of hierarchical routing

Figure 11.15 shows a detailed view of how a nationwide Internet Service Provider might put together a hierarchically routed network. First, note that we have partitioned the network into four routing levels. Each level contains only a few routers, thus making it easy to compute routing tables.

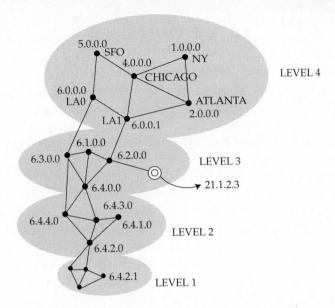

Figure 11.15: Example of a hierarchically routed network. The network is hierarchically partitioned into four levels. Routers at each level cooperate to find shortest paths, as explained in the text.

Second, the network is not a strict hierarchy, because more than one router may advertise reachability to the same part of the address space. For example, both routers in Los Angeles, named LA0 and LA1, advertise that they can carry traffic for addresses of the form 6.*. When a packet with an address in 6.* arrives at San Francisco, it should forward the packet to LA0, but the router at Atlanta should forward it to LA1. Making the hierarchy looser lets the network survive faults more easily. For example, if LA0 went down, traffic for destination in 6.* could be routed via LA1.

Third, routers that span levels, such as 6.0.0.0 and 6.4.0.0, participate in routing protocols at both levels. For example, router 6.4.0.0 discovers, using a level-3 routing protocol, that the shortest path to networks advertised by router 6.3.0.0 is its direct link to 6.3.0.0. If the link goes down, level-3 routing informs 6.4.0.0 that it should use router 6.1.0.0 instead. 6.4.0.0 also participates in level-2 routing to find, for instance, that the shortest path to 6.4.2.0 is through 6.4.3.0. The routing protocols at the two levels may be completely different (one may be link-state, and the other distance-vector). Therefore, routers that route between levels must be prepared to speak multiple protocols.

Finally, note that we have a router in level 3 marked 21.1.2.3. Why would a router with address 21.* be placed under a router with address 6.*? This might be because of address-space exhaustion in the 6.* space. Or, a company that had obtained the address space 21.1.2.* for its computers from a service provider with authority over 21.*, then moved to a new location, might want to retain its old addresses (because renumbering computers on the Internet requires manual reconfiguration of every end-system and router). In any case, router 6.2.0.0 must advertise reachability to 21.1.2.3. Moreover, routers 6.0.0.1 and 6.0.0.2 at the network core must also advertise that they can route to 21.1.2.3, and every other router in the core must know that packets for 21.1.2.3 must be forwarded to one of these two routers. The lesson is that if we introduce a router at a lower level whose address cannot be aggregated into an existing address space, then each router in the core of the network must contain a routing table entry for it.

In the current Internet, addresses obey a three-level hierarchy (network number, subnet number, and host number). Because the highest possible degree of aggregation of addresses is at the network level, routers in the network core, which benefit most from aggregation, advertise routes to networks. For example, routers at the core will usually advertise routes to network 135.104.*, instead of to 135.104.53, 135.104.52, etc., which are subnets within 135.104. This approach to aggregation works well when the number of networks is small and routers at a lower level can handle routing within a network. Unfortunately, because of exhaustion of Class B addresses, many networks received multiple Class C network addresses instead. Consequently, routers in the core need to store table entries for routes to thousands of Class C networks. By 1996, each core router carried routes to more than 80,000 networks. Thus, even if addresses are hierarchical, they must be carefully managed, or routing tables and route computation can still be expensive. The CIDR scheme for addressing, discussed in Section 10.6.3, alleviates some of these problems.

11.8.2 External and summary records

Consider the four level-3 routers in Figure 11.15 with addresses 6.1.0.0, 6.2.0.0, 6.3.0.0, and 6.4.0.0. Suppose they use link-state routing to compute routes. What should be the next hop for a packet arriving at 6.4.0.0 that is destined to an address in 5.*? From the topology of the network, note that if the network uses a least-hop cost metric, then the next hop should be 6.3.0.0. Thus, we want router 6.4.0.0 to discover that there is a 3-hop path through router 6.3.0.0 to 5.0.0.0, whereas the path through 6.2.0.0 is at least 4 hops long. Unfortunately, since router 5.0.0.0 is not part of the level-3 network, 6.4.0.0 would not ordinarily be aware of its existence. We need a mechanism that allows routers that participate in level-4 routing to advertise paths to routers that are external to the level-3 network. This is done by using *external records* in the LSP database.

For example, router 6.0.0.0, which knows that it has a 1-hop path to 5.0.0.0 using level-4 routing, creates an *external LSP* that advertises a link to 5.0.0.0 with a link cost of 1 and floods this within the level-3 network. Similarly, 6.0.0.1 uses level-4 routing to learn that its least-cost path to 5.0.0.0 is 2 hops and floods this information in the level-3 network. Thus, routers 6.0.0.1 and 6.0.0.2 pretend that 5.0.0.0 is a level-3 router that happens to be connected to them with a 1- and 2-hop path, respectively. When this information is propagated within the level-3 network, 6.4.0.0 automatically discovers that its shortest path to 5.0.0.0 is through 6.3.0.0, as we wanted. External LSPs, therefore, allow optimal routes to be computed despite the information-hiding inherent in hierarchical routing.

Summary records

An external record allows routers within level 3 to discover shortest paths to external networks. The symmetrical problem is for external networks to discover shortest paths to level-3 networks that are not visible at level 4. This is done using *summary* records. For example, 6.0.0.0 advertises to level-4 routers that it has a path to 6.1.0.0 that is of length 2, to 6.2.0.0 of length 3, to 6.3.0.0 of length 1, and to 6.4.0.0 of length 2. It is as if these are *single* links with higher costs. Level-4 routers do not need to know the exact topology within the level-3 network, just the costs. Note that cost information in a summary record is functionally equivalent to a distance vector, because it summarizes the distance from a level-4 router to every level-3 router connected to it.

The network uses summary records to compute optimal paths. For example, the Atlanta router knows from 6.0.0.1's summary records that it has a 1-hop path to 6.2.0.0. It also knows (from level-4 routing) that it has a 1-hop path to 6.0.0.1. Therefore, its cost to reach 6.2.0.0 through 6.0.0.1 is 2 hops. In contrast, its path to 6.2.0.0 via 6.0.0.0 is (from these same sources of information) 5 hops. Therefore, it routes packets destined to 6.2.0.0 through 6.0.0.1, as we wanted.

Continuing with our example, the LSP database at router 6.0.0.0 therefore contains the following:

- LSP records for every link in its level-3 network
- LSP records for every link in its level-4 network
- External records that summarize its cost to reach every router in the level-4 network
- Summary records for virtual links that connect it to every level-3 router in its area
- Summary records received from other level-4 routers for virtual links to their level-3 routers

These records allow it to compute optimal paths not only to other level-4 routers, but also to level-3 routers within other level-4 networks.

11.8.3   Interior and exterior protocols

In the Internet, we distinguish between three levels of routing (corresponding roughly to the three-level address hierarchy), where we allow each level to use a different routing protocol. The highest level is the Internet backbone, which interconnects multiple *autonomous systems* (*AS*s) (Figure 11.16). Routing between autonomous systems uses the *exterior gateway protocol*. The name reflects the history of the Internet, when a *gateway* connected university networks to the ARPAnet. The protocol that gateways spoke to each other therefore was the *exterior* gateway protocol. Symmetrically, the protocol that the gateway spoke to routers within a campus (and now, within an AS) is called the *interior gateway protocol*. At the lowest level, we have routing within a single broadcast LAN, such as Ethernet or FDDI. In this section, we will discuss the requirements for interior and exterior protocols, and problems with their interconnection.

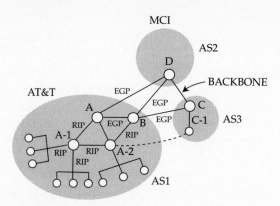

Figure 11.16: Example of exterior and interior gateway protocols. Routers within the AT&T and MCI domains speak interior gateway protocols, while their border gateways speak both. Exterior gateway protocols have to ensure that their network is not used for transit (unless authorized), that backdoors remain hidden, and that their own packets do not traverse unauthorized or insecure domains.

Exterior protocols

Although all the routers within an AS are mutually cooperative, routers interconnecting two ASs may not necessarily trust each other. Exterior protocols determine routing between entities that can be owned by mutually suspicious domains. An important part of exterior protocols, therefore, is configuring *border gateways* (that is, gateways that mediate between interior and exterior routing) to recognize a set of valid neighbors and valid paths. This is illustrated in Figure 11.16.

EXAMPLE 11.9

In Figure 11.16, assume that border routers A and B belong to AT&T, and router D belongs to MCI. Say that the AB link goes down. A can still reach B through D, and a generic link-state routing protocol will easily find this path. However, the thought that internal AT&T packets traverse MCI's router may upset both MCI's and AT&T's managements! Therefore, the exterior protocol must allow A and B to state that if the A–B link goes down, the A–D–B path is unacceptable. Of course, for packets destined to D, the A–D link is perfectly valid, and, similarly, the D–B link may also be independently valid. It is only their combination, A–D–B, that is prohibited. Accounting for administrative issues such as these complicates the design of exterior routing protocols, and these protocols often require manual configuration and intervention.

A related problem is that of *transit.* Suppose autonomous system A and autonomous system C set up a backdoor link between A.2 and C.1 for their own purposes. Since B knows from its interior routing protocol that C.1 is reachable through the backdoor link, it might advertise this to the rest of the Internet. This might cause A's facility to be used for packets destined for neither A nor C, which might annoy their administrators. Therefore, B should know that some links advertised by an interior protocol are special and should not be advertised (summarized) externally. This is another problem that usually requires manual intervention.

Exterior gateway protocols must be suspicious of routing updates. It should not be possible for malicious users to bring down the Internet by sending spurious routing messages to backbone gateways. Typically, every routing exchange is protected by a link password. Routing updates that fail the password check are rejected.

Interior protocols

Interior protocols are largely free of the administrative problems that exterior protocols face. Just as autonomous systems hierarchically partition the Internet at the top level, interior routing protocols typically hierarchically partition each AS into *areas.* However, the same interior protocol routes packets both within and among areas. The issues in generating external and summary records, which we studied in Section 11.8.2, apply to routing among areas, in the same way as they do to routing between autonomous systems.

Issues in interconnecting exterior and interior routing protocols

The key problem in interconnecting exterior and interior protocols is that they may use different routing techniques and different ways to decide link costs. For example, the exterior protocol may advertise a 5-hop count to another AS. However, each of these hops may span a continent and cannot be compared with a 5-hop path in the interior of the AS. How is a router to decide which is the shortest path when routers use link costs that cannot be compared? The solution is to use the least common denominator, usually a hop-count metric, when computing routes outside the AS. This is not necessarily the optimal path, but at least it is a path that works!

A similar problem arises if the interior and exterior routing protocols use different routing schemes. For example, the exterior protocol may use path-vector routing, and the interior may use link-state routing. Thus, the border gateway must convert from an LSP database to a set of distance vectors that summarize paths to its interior. In the other direction, it must convert from distance-vector advertisements to external records for the interior routing protocol. Things are easier if both the interior and exterior routing protocols use the same basic routing scheme.

The bottom line is that interconnecting a given interior and exterior protocol requires a fair amount of manual intervention, and frequent monitoring to ensure that the network stays up. This is a direct consequence of the heterogeneity in the administration of the Internet, and of its decentralized control. Of course, many of these issues are relevant to ATM networks as well. As ATM networks scale to span the globe, they, too, will need to resolve these issues. ATM network routing is still a topic of intense research.

11.9   Common routing protocols

This section presents a highly abbreviated introduction to Internet and ATM routing protocols. Details on Internet routing can be found in references [Huitema 95, Perlman 92], and details on ATM routing are available from the ATM Forum.

The Internet distinguishes between interior and exterior routing protocols because of the different demands that they pose on the routing system. Two protocols are commonly used as interior protocols. These are the *Routing Information Protocol* (*RIP*) and the *Open Shortest Path First* protocol (*OSPF*). The protocols commonly used for exterior routing are the *Exterior Gateway Protocol* (*EGP*) and the *Border Gateway Protocol* (*BGP*).

The protocol recommended for ATM routing is part of the *Private Network–Network Interface* (PNNI) and is usually called PNNI routing.

11.9.1   RIP

RIP, a distance-vector protocol, was the original routing protocol in the ARPAnet [Hedrick 88]. It uses a hop-count metric, where infinity is defined to be 16. Peer routers exchange distance vectors every 30 s, and a router is declared dead if a peer does not hear from it for 180 s. The protocol uses split horizon with poisonous reverse to avoid the count-to-infinity problem. RIP is useful for small subnets where its simplicity of implementation and configuration more than compensates for its inadequacies in dealing with link failures and providing multiple metrics.

11.9.2   OSPF

OSPF, a link-state protocol, is the preferred interior routing protocol on the Internet [Moy 91]. It uses the notion of *areas* to route packets hierarchically within an AS. It also uses all the techniques for achieving LSP database consistency described in Section 11.6. Consequently, it is rather complex to describe and implement.

OSPF uses two tricks for dealing with broadcast LANS that substantially reduce the number of LSPs needed to advertise routes through broadcast LANs. First, if a router routes packets to a set of hosts that are all on the same broadcast LAN (Figure 11.17a), OSPF allows routers to advertise single-hop access to a *set* of hosts on that LAN, instead of advertising a separate LSP for each host on the LAN. Second, if a set of routers are all part of the same broadcast LAN (Figure 11.17b), instead of generating an LSP for every pair of routers on the LAN, one of the routers is elected as a *designated* router, and it pretends to have a single link to each of the other routers on the LAN. If a designated

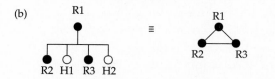

CLASSIC LINK STATE: LSPs FOR R-H1, R-H2, R-H3, R-H4

OSPF: LSP FOR R-SUBNET

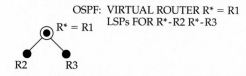

CLASSIC LINK STATE: LSPs FOR R1-R2, R1-R3, R2-R3

OSPF: VIRTUAL ROUTER R* = R1
LSPs FOR R*-R2 R*-R3

Figure 11.17: OSPF techniques to reduce routing tables in the context of broadcast LANs. (a) A router connected to several hosts on a LAN advertises the entire subnet, instead of a link to every host. (b) Peer routers within a LAN elect a designated router (in this case, router RI), and the designated router reports links to all other routers on that LAN.

router goes down, a backup designated router takes over until a new router can be elected.

11.9.3   EGP

The original exterior protocol in the Internet was the distance-vector-based *Exterior Gateway Protocol* or EGP [Rosen 82]. EGP allows administrators to pick their neighbors in order to enforce inter-AS routing policies. To allow scaling, EGP allows address aggregation in routing tables.

EGP routers propagate distance vectors that reflect a combination of preferences and policies. For example, in the NSFnet backbone, a router advertises the distance to another AS as 128 if the AS is reachable, and 255 otherwise. This reduces EGP to a reachability protocol rather than a shortest-path protocol. Therefore, unless we structure the network backbone as a tree, EGP leads to routing loops! The reason for choosing 128 as the standard inter-AS distance is that it enables *backdoors*. Backdoors between autonomous systems are always given a cost smaller than 128, so that the two ASs sharing the backdoor will use it while keeping the backdoor invisible to outside systems. EGP is no longer widely used because of many deficiencies, particularly its need for loop-free topologies.

11.9.4   BGP

The preferred replacement for EGP is the *Border Gateway Protocol, version 4,* commonly referred to as BGP4 [RL 95]. BGP4 is a path-vector protocol, where distance vectors are annotated not only with the entire path used to compute each distance, but also with certain policy attributes. An exterior gateway can usually compute much better paths with BGP than with EGP by examining these attributes. Since BGP uses true costs, unlike EGP, it can be used in non-tree topologies. Its use of a path-vector guarantees loop-freeness, at the expense of much larger routing tables. BGP routers use TCP to communicate with each other, instead of layering the routing message directly over IP, as is done in every other Internet routing protocol. This simplifies the error management in the routing protocol. However, routing updates are subject to TCP flow control, which can lead to fairly complicated and poorly understood network dynamics. For example, routing updates might be delayed waiting for TCP to time out. Thus, the choice of TCP is still controversial.

If an AS has more than one BGP-speaking border gateway, path vectors arriving at a gateway must somehow make their way to all the other gateways in the AS. Thus, BGP requires each gateway in an AS to talk to every other gateway in that AS (also called *internal peering*). BGP4 is hard to maintain because of the need to choose consistent path attributes from all the border routers, and to maintain clique connectivity among internal peers.

11.9.5   PNNI routing

PNNI routing (usually called just PNNI) is the recommended standard for routing in ATM networks [Halpern 96]. PNNI is a link-state protocol that supports many levels of hierarchical routing. Switch controllers at each level form a *peer group*. A group is expected to have between ten and a hundred switch controllers. Each peer group selects a *peer-group leader* as a member of the next-higher-level peer group. Communication between peer groups proceeds only through peer-group leaders. Peer-group leaders summarize information about their lower-level peer group (corresponding to summary records) when sending link-state information to members of the higher-level peer group, thus allowing aggregation of routing state. As of this writing, there is no aggregation in the other direction: all infomation received by a peer-group leader is flooded to all members of the group. Techniques for aggregation in this direction, corresponding to external records, are still under development.

To allow switch controllers to choose paths according to quality of service requirements, LSPs can be annotated with a variety of per-link quality-of-service metrics. Thus, each switch controller obtains a view of network topology that includes information about the available service quality on each link. It uses these to construct source routes for signaling messages. The use of source routing eliminates routing loops and speeds convergence in case of a link or switch-controller failure. Because only signaling messages need full source routes, the header overhead in source routing is not a concern.

PNNI's proponents claim that it can scale well because of its support of deep hierarchies. Moreover, it explicitly allows routing based on quality of service. However, at the time of this writing, there is little experience with running large ATM networks with PNNI, and it is too early to comment about its performance.

11.10   Routing within a broadcast LAN

Thus far we have looked at the routing problem for the network as a whole. In this section, we view the routing problem from the perspective of an endpoint—that is, how should the routing module at an endpoint decide where to forward a packet that it receives from an application?

An endpoint connected to a router by a point-to-point link (as in an ATM network) simply forwards every packet to that router. However, if the endpoint is part of a broadcast LAN, we can exploit the LAN's inherent routing capacity to reduce the load on routers. Specifically, the routing module must make four decisions:

- Is the packet meant for a destination on the same LAN?
- If so, what is the datalink-layer (MAC) address of the destination?
- If not, to which of the several routers on the LAN should the packet be sent?
- What is the router's MAC address?

EXAMPLE 11.10

Consider host H1 shown in Figure 11.18. If it wants to send a packet to H2, it should determine that H2 is local, then figure out H2's MAC address. If it wants to send a

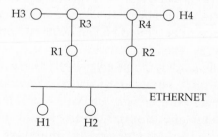

Figure 11.18: Routing within a broadcast LAN. As explained in the text, hosts H1 and H2 need to find each other's MAC address, the existence of routers R1 and R2, and the correct router to use to reach remote hosts H3 and H4.

packet to H3, it should find out that the next hop should be R1. If R1 goes down, it should send the packet to R2. Similarly, packets for H4 should go to R2, unless it is down, in which case it should be sent to R1.

These decisions typically require a combination of addressing conventions, explicit information, and exploiting the broadcast nature of the LAN. In the Internet, the first problem is solved by agreeing that all hosts that have the same network number must belong to the same broadcast LAN. (Although a single physical LAN may carry more than one IP subnet, hosts on different subnets on the same LAN communicate only through a router.) Thus, a host can determine whether the destination is local simply by using its subnet mask to extract the network number of the destination and comparing this with its own network number. For example, if host 135.104.53.100, with a subnet mask of 255.255.255.0, wants to send a packet to 135.104.53.12, it uses the subnet mask to determine that the destination's network number is 135.104.53. Since this matches its own network number, the destination must be on the local LAN (see Exercise 11.13).

The sending host must next determine the MAC address of the host to which it wants to send. It does so using the Address Resolution Protocol described in Section 10.10. It installs the MAC address in a local ARP cache and uses it for further transmission.

11.10.1 Router discovery

If a packet's destination address is nonlocal, then the host must send the packet to one of the routers on the LAN. A host can discover all the routers on the local LAN by means of *router advertisement* packets that each router periodically broadcasts on the LAN [Deering 91b]. A router advertisement has a *preference level* and a *time-to-live*. Hosts first check that the router corresponds to their own subnet by masking the router's IP address with their subnet mask and comparing with their subnet number. They then install a *default* route to the router with the highest preference. All nonlocal packets are sent to the default router, if necessary, resolving the router's MAC address with an ARP request.

A router advertisement is placed in a cache and flushed when its time-to-live expires. The time-to-live is typically around half an hour, and routers send advertisements about once every 10 minutes. The idea is that if a router dies, the host deletes old state information automatically (a form of *soft state*; see Section 6.3.10). If a newly booted host does not want to wait several minutes for a router advertisement, it can force all routers to send an advertisement using a *router solicitation* packet.

If a default router goes down, then the host must somehow determine this and switch to an alternative router, if one exists. Otherwise, all packets from the host will be lost without trace (the *black hole* problem). The Internet protocol suite does not specify any single algorithm to cover black hole detection, though several heuristics are proposed in reference [Braden 89, p. 52]. The general idea is that if a host does not hear anything from a router (such as a reply to an ARP request) for some time, it should assume that the router is down, and it can force routers to identify themselves with a router solicitation message. To prevent network load, hosts are required to send no more than three solicitation messages before they give up and assume that no router is available.

11.10.2 Redirection

With a default route, a host sends all nonlocal packets to only one of possibly many routers that share its subnet on the LAN. It may happen that, for a particular destination, it ought to use another router. To solve this problem, if a host's default router is not the right choice for a given destination, the default router sends a control message (using the *Internet Control Message Protocol* or ICMP) back to the host, informing it of a better choice. This *redirect* message is stored in the host's routing table for future use.

EXAMPLE 11.11

In Figure 11.18, host H1 may have selected R1 as its default router. It may then send a packet for H4 to R1. R1 can reach R4 either through the broadcast LAN and R2, or through R3. Assume, for the moment, that R1's next hop to R4 is through R2. When R1 gets a packet for H4, it can detect that R2 is a better routing choice for H1, because R1's next hop for H4 is R2, which has the same network address as R1 and H1. It therefore sends an ICMP redirect message to H1, asking it to use R2 in the future, and hands the packet to R2 for transmission. In this way, hosts automatically discover the best path to remote destinations.

11.11 Multicast routing

In our discussion of routing, we have implicitly assumed that a packet sent from a source is meant for a single destination. We call this *unicast*. However, several new applications are made possible (or more efficient) if a packet from a source can be received by multiple receivers, that is, if packets can be *multicast*. Examples of such applications are multiparticipant videoconferences, distance learning (where a teacher communicates with a geographically dispersed class), and resource location (where a host multicasts a query to a set of servers, and one or more send a reply). Therefore, it is useful to study how to implement multicast efficiently in a wide-area network. Our discussion is based on IP multicast in the Internet, which is the source of all the major ideas in the field. Multicast in ATM networks, when it is developed, is likely to draw heavily on these ideas.

11.11.1 Multicast groups

A key concept in Internet multicast is the notion of a *multicast group.* A multicast group associates a set of senders and receivers with each other, but conceptually exists indepen-

MULTICAST GROUP

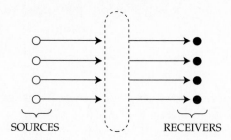

Figure 11.19: Concept of a multicast group. The group exists independent of the senders and receivers. Packets from any sender are delivered to all receivers.

dently of them (Figure 11.19). More precisely, a multicast group is created either when a sender starts sending to the group (even if no receivers are present) or when a receiver expresses its interest in receiving packets from the group (even if no senders are currently active). The group continues to exist if at least one receiver or one sender is active. Every receiver in the group receives packets from every sender. We call this *multipoint-to-multipoint* multicast. (If we limit each multicast group to a single sender, we call this *point-to-multipoint* multicast.)

A multicast group is associated with a unique IP multicast (Class D) address. Senders send IP packets with the destination field set to this address, and receivers request routers to forward packets with this address to them. The "magic" of Internet multicast is in linking senders and receivers who have only the address of a multicast group in common. We will assume that potential group members find out about the existence of the group using some higher-level protocol (for instance, advertisements in a well-known location). Thus, we separate the problems of (a) discovering the set of current multicast groups, (b) expressing interest in receiving packets from a group, (c) discovering the set of receivers in a group, and (d) delivering data to every member of the group.

Note that a multicast group, by decoupling senders and receivers, makes it possible for a sender to locate a set of receivers without knowing their identity. For example, a sender may want to know of all printers that can process a color image. If each printer that can satisfy this request registers to receive packets from a well-known group address, a sender can find one of them simply by sending a query to that address. The multicast address, therefore, serves as a logical *rendezvous point* between senders and receivers. We can view receivers as waiting at the rendezvous for some sender to send them information, and the network takes care of distributing every packet that arrives at the rendezvous point to every registered receiver. In this sense, a multicast group provides a dynamic directory service, where a sender can resolve the multicast address to the set of receivers associated with the group, and this set can dynamically change. By separating the set of receivers from the multicast address, a multicast group allows great flexibility in resource location and management.

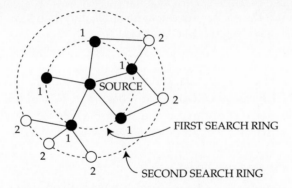

Figure 11.20: Expanding-ring search. The source sets the first query packet's time-to-live (TTL) to 1 and multicasts it. If no reply is received, the source increases the TTL by 1 and tries again. This technique systematically locates increasingly distant resource providers.

11.11.2 Expanding-ring search

A clever technique that exploits multicast for resource discovery is *expanding-ring search* (Figure 11.20). This technique exploits the fact that the IP header has a "time-to-live" field that is decremented at every hop. Thus, if the sender sets the field to 1 and sends the packet to a multicast group address, it will reach all receivers at most 1 hop away. To perform an expanding-ring search, all resource providers (in our example, all color printers) register themselves with a well-known multicast group address. A sender sends the first query in an IP packet with a time-to-live field set to 1. This finds the nearest resource provider that is willing to provide the desired service. If the sender receives no reply for some time, it increases the time-to-live field by 1, and tries again. This sends the query to all resource providers at most 2 hops away. By systematically increasing the time-to-live field, a sender can find the "nearest" provider, in the sense of lowest hop count, without knowing the set of resource providers or their locations. Since resource providers have the option not to reply if their load is high, this can also achieve the effect of load balancing.

11.11.3 Multicasting versus multiple unicast

If each sender knows the identity of every receiver in the group, multicast can be trivially simulated by sending a packet over multiple unicast routes, but this approach is inefficient if the unicast routes substantially overlap.

EXAMPLE 11.12

In Figure 11.21, if A wanted to send a packet to hosts B, G, H, and I using multiple unicasts, link AC would carry three copies of the same packet. It is more efficient (particularly if AC is a low-bandwidth or congested link) to have router C make two copies of the packet, send it to D and E, and then have D make two more copies of the packet and send it to G and H.

Ideally, we send a multicast packet exactly once on every link. Note that the dashed lines in Figure 11.21 form a tree with A at the source. We call this the *multicast tree* rooted at A. A multicast tree is optimal if multicast packets follow the shortest path from A to every destination, and we call this the *shortest-path tree* rooted at A.

11.11.4 Issues in wide-area multicast

Wide-area multicast is made more complex by the fact that sources may join or leave a multicast group while a multicast is in progress. Therefore, the shortest-path tree has to be dynamically updated. A second source of complexity is that the leaves of a multicast tree are often members of a broadcast-type LAN (such as Ethernet or FDDI). We can greatly improve multicast performance if we can exploit a LAN's multicast capability. Finally, we would like a receiver to be able to join or leave a multicast group without explicitly notifying the senders. Otherwise, multicast cannot scale to accommodate hundreds or thousands of possible recipients.

We will first focus on multicast within a broadcast LAN, then move up to a WAN environment.

EXAMPLE 11.13

In Figure 11.22, hosts G, H, and I are attached to the same broadcast LAN as router D. Instead of making three copies of a packet at D, D can simply multicast the

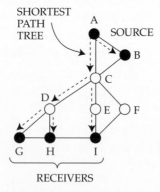

Figure 11.21: Shortest-path tree. Dotted lines show the shortest-path tree rooted at A. Packets that follow this tree to a destination are guaranteed to take the shortest path from A to the destination.

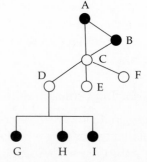

Figure 11.22: Integrating LAN and WAN multicast. We would like to exploit LAN multicast so that D sends only one copy of a packet from A to G, H, and I, instead of three separate copies.

packet on the LAN, where it can be picked up by these hosts. We want the multi-cast-routing protocol to somehow integrate LAN multicast into the WAN multicast over point-to-point links.

11.11.5 Multicast in a broadcast LAN

Broadcast LANs reserve part of the MAC address space for multicast addresses. For example, in an IEEE 802 address (used in Ethernet and FDDI), if the multicast bit is set in the high-order byte, the address is a multicast address. Hosts on an IEEE 802 LAN can configure their host-adaptor hardware to recognize and capture packets from a limited number of multicast addresses (usually 16 or 32). We assume that senders and receivers can determine the IP address of a multicast group through some unspecified higher-layer protocol. The problem, therefore, is how to translate from a well-known IP multicast address to a MAC multicast address. Once this is known, senders send to this address, and receivers configure their host adaptors to receive from this address.

Recall that the IEEE 802 address is 6 bytes long, of which the lower 3 bytes are locally assigned. IP multicast convention is to use the lower 23 bits of the IP multicast address as the lower 23 bits of the 802 address (Figure 11.23). Thus, the translation from IP multicast to a LAN multicast address is trivial. Note that an IP address is 32 bits long, of which only 23 are used to distinguish between MAC multicast addresses. The hope is that IP multicast is rare enough that it is very unlikely that the same LAN will carry packets from two multicast groups with the same 23 lower-order bits.

IGMP

Although the IP to MAC translation is straightforward, another important problem at the LAN level is for a router to detect whether its local LAN contains any receivers for a

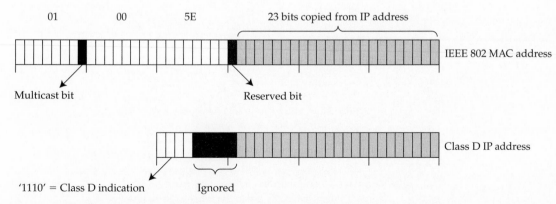

Figure 11.23: Translating from an IP address to an IEEE 802 address. The lower 23 bits of the IP addresses form the lower 23 bits of the 802 address, and the 802 multicast (group) address bit is set.

particular multicast group. If a LAN has no receivers for the group, then the router should tell its parent in the shortest-path multicast tree not to send it any more packets for that group (we call this *pruning*). Routers determine whether a LAN has any members for a particular multicast group using the *Internet Group Management Protocol* (*IGMP*). IGMP is used *only* on broadcast LANs. It consists of a *query* and a *report* message. The router periodically broadcasts a query on the LAN requesting membership information. Each host on the LAN that wants to receive multicast messages sends back a report with a list of groups in which it is interested.

If a LAN has hundreds of hosts and all of them simultaneously reply to an IGMP query, the LAN will become congested. Thus, IGMP specifies that when a query arrives, each host sets a timer to a random value and replies when the timer expires (Figure 11.24). The reply is broadcast to the entire LAN. When a host sees that another host has replied for a group in which it is interested, it cancels its query reply timer, since the router needs only one reply to agree to multicast incoming packets for that group on that LAN.

When a host wants to receive multicast packets from a particular multicast group, it configures its host adaptor to receive packets on the corresponding multicast MAC address. If another host on the LAN has already informed the router of its desire to receive packets from that group, the packets will automatically be received at the new receiver. Otherwise, the new receiver must wait for the next query message from the router before it can report its interest in the group. This design decision reduces LAN traffic at the cost of a few additional seconds of start-up delay for the first host to receive packets from a particular group on a LAN.

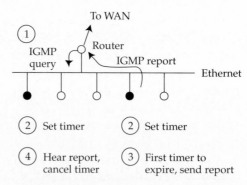

Figure 11.24: Internet Group Management Protocol (IGMP). IGMP allows a router to discover whether any host on its LAN is interested in listening to an active multicast group. The router periodically posts an IGMP query for every active group. Hosts interested in a group choose random timers and reply when the timer expires. A host cancels its own reply if it hears a reply from some other host.

11.11.6 Wide-area multicast: Flooding and reverse-path forwarding

Having studied how packets are multicast within a LAN, we now turn our attention to a WAN, where we assume that each endpoint is a router that has a list of current group members, determined using IGMP. Our goal is to distribute packets coming from any sender directed to a particular group to all routers lying on the path to any receiver.

The simplest possible solution to this problem is to flood all multicast packets to all routers. The flooding protocol is the same as the one used for LSP flooding: if the router has not seen the packet before, it is forwarded on all interfaces except the incoming one. Flooding is simple, but has two major problems. First, flooding results in routers receiving duplicate packets. Consider the situation in Figure 11.25. Suppose packets from A are flooded to B and C. B has not seen the packet before, so it sends it to C and E. Meanwhile, C may have forwarded the packet to E and F. If the CE link is slow and the CF and FE links are fast, it is quite likely that E will receive the same packet on C–F–E as well. Thus, E receives three copies of the same packet! This is inefficient.

The second problem with flooding is that every node has to store an identifier for every packet it received in the past, so that it can identify duplicates. In a long-lasting multicast session, this overhead is unacceptable (see Exercise 11.18).

A simple technique that avoids the overhead of storing packet identifiers is called *reverse-path forwarding* [DM 78]. The reverse-path-forwarding rule is that a router forwards a packet from a source S to all its interfaces if and only if the packet arrives on the interface that corresponds to the router's shortest path to S. This is illustrated in Example 11.14.

EXAMPLE 11.14

Consider the situation in Figure 11.25, where C receives a packet from A through B. With flooding, C has to recognize that it has already received the packet from A, so it has to store a unique identification for that packet. With reverse-path forwarding, C realizes that its shortest path to A is link CA. Therefore, the packet from B

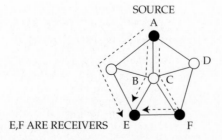

Figure 11.25: Problem with flooding for multicast. With simple flooding, E receives three copies of the same packet from A.

need not be forwarded. This has the same effect of flooding without requiring any storage at C.

Although reverse-path forwarding saves storage at a router, it does not eliminate duplicates. We can partly avoid duplication by further exploiting the unicast routing table. For example, in Figure 11.26, note that the shortest path from D to A is the link D–A. C should not forward a multicast packet to D because the shortest path from D to A does not include C, and so D will simply discard C's packet. The rule, therefore, is that every router R should send a packet to a downstream router only if the shortest path from the downstream router to the source includes R. This rule avoids some duplication associated with flooding, but runs into problems when a downstream router has multiple equal-length paths to a source. For example, returning to Figure 11.25, E has a 2-hop path to A through both B and C. B may think that the shortest path is through C and may not forward a packet. C may think similarly, and no packet reaches E (F will not forward to E because F is not on E's shortest path to A). We need a way to break ties in this situation, and heuristics to uniquely break such ties are specified in all Internet multicast protocols.

11.11.7 Pruning

Although the extension to reverse-path forwarding described in the previous paragraph eliminates most duplicates, it still does not avoid the problem that a source's packets are received by every other router in the network. For example, in Figure 11.26, multicast packets from A are sent to B, C, and D, though B and C do not need the packet. Neither reverse-path forwarding nor its extension is sufficient to prevent A from forwarding packets to B. We therefore introduce the notion of *pruning* to deal with this problem.

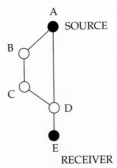

Figure 11.26: Extended reverse-path forwarding. Since E's shortest path to A is not through C, C should not forward a multicast packet to E.

The principal idea in pruning is for a router to inform its parent in the shortest-path tree that it is no longer interested in receiving multicast packets from a particular source sending to a particular group. This is shown in the next example.

EXAMPLE 11.15

Continuing with Figure 11.26, C can find, using IGMP, that no hosts on its LAN are interested in receiving any multicast packets from A. C therefore sends a prune message to B saying that it no longer wants to receive multicast messages from A (though it may still be interested in hearing from other sources sending to that group). B marks its link with this information and does not forward any more packets from A to C. If B also has no hosts interested in hearing from A, it forwards a prune message to A, which marks the AB link as being pruned. Then, packets from A follow only the A–D–E path, which is optimal.

Prunes can be associated either with a multicast group, or with a particular source *and* a group. In the first case, routers need to store only one prune indication per output interface per group, but receivers that prune messages from one source cannot receive messages from any other source in that group. In the second case, receivers can be more selective, but routers must store a prune indication per-group and per-sender for each interface. Thus, the two alternatives trade off selectivity for space.

What happens if a host attached to C's LAN decides to join the multicast group and listen to A? Recall that C periodically broadcasts an IGMP query on its LAN. The IGMP report will let C know that it should rejoin the multicast group. But B has already pruned the BC link! One solution is for C to explicitly send a *graft* message to B, which forwards it to A. A then grafts AB back to its tree, and B does likewise. This reconnects C to the multicast tree. An alternative solution is for A (and B) to periodically flood packets from A using the extended version of reverse-path forwarding. In this solution, C simply waits for the flood message and desists from sending a prune message to B. This automatically joins C in the multicast tree. We often call the second solution the *flood-and-prune* approach to multicast tree management. It was used in the first implementation of multicast in the Internet [Deering 91a].

11.11.8 DVMRP and MOSPF

Reverse-path forwarding and its extension require each router to know its shortest path to every source, and the shortest path from each neighbor to every source. This information is available from the unicast routing table, such as that maintained by RIP, OSPF, or BGP. If every router in the Internet uniformly supported multicast, then the multicast packet forwarding agent could simply look up the unicast routing table for shortest-path information. Unfortunately, many routers in the Internet do not support multicast, because the host and router extensions for multicast are only now being standardized. To gain experience with Internet multicast, its designers decided to *overlay* the Internet with another network, the *Multicast Backbone* or *MBONE.*

Tunneling

The main idea in constructing an overlay network is to build *virtual links* between multicast-capable routers. This is illustrated in Example 11.16.

EXAMPLE 11.16

In Figure 11.27, A, E, and F are in the MBONE, and the other routers are not. There is no direct link from A to F. Consider a packet for a particular multicast group that arrives at A. Suppose A decides that it should forward it to F. What should be the destination address on the packet's IP header? If this is the multicast group's IP address, then D discards the packet, since it is not multicast capable and it cannot recognize the packet's destination address. If the packet's destination is changed to that of F, F loses information about the multicast group address! The solution is to make the packet's destination F, but put the multicast group address in the data portion of the packet (thus encapsulating the packet with another header that contains F's IP address). This allows the packet to *tunnel* to F, which strips the header and uses the multicast address to forward the packet. Tunneling allows us to establish a virtual link from A to F (which can be deleted when D becomes multicast capable).

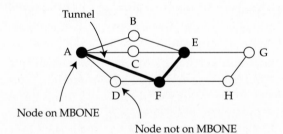

Figure 11.27: Tunnels and the need for multicast routing. Shaded nodes, such as E, are on the MBONE, and other nodes, such as C, are not. Since D is not multicast capable, A must tunnel its packets to F by encapsulating the multicast packet (with a Class D address) in a regular IP packet with a destination set to F. We need a separate multicast routing protocol because, for the tunneled case, the shortest path between A and E using tunnels (F) is not the shortest path according to unicast routing (C).

Multicast routing protocols

Routers on the MBONE need to know the shortest path to a source using only other routers on the MBONE. Therefore, MBONE routers must run their own routing protocol, where shortest paths to a source may be different from the shortest path in the regular unicast protocol. For example, in Figure 11.27, according to the unicast routing protocol, the shortest path from A to E is through C, which is therefore the next hop. However, if we configure the MBONE with virtual links from A to F and F to E, but not A to E, the next hop from A to E is F, not C. Therefore, if some routers in the Internet are not multicast capable (are not on the MBONE), routers on the MBONE must run their own routing protocol to decide shortest paths. The first such protocol was the *Distance Vector Multicast Routing Protocol,* or DVMRP [WPD 88, Deering 91a]. DVMRP is a classical distance-vector protocol that uses the hop-count metric. It provides the "unicast" routes that are used for reverse-path forwarding. DVMRP uses the flood-and-prune approach to determine multicast trees, with per-source and per-group information at each router interface. Unlike vanilla flood-and-prune, explicit join messages reduce the latency in joining a group.

DVMRP is an experimental protocol that suffers from the problems of distance-vector protocols that we saw earlier. Given the advantages of the link-state approach, a natural next step is to replace it with a link-state protocol. This is the motivation for *Multicast OSPF (MOSPF)*, which is an extension of OSPF to handle multicast [Moy 94]. MOSPF adds LSP database records to indicate which routers want to listen to which groups, thus allowing a router to compute a pruned tree without explicit flooding and pruning. Routers store per-group prune information. When a host wants to listen to a particular multicast group, it uses IGMP to inform its local router, which then floods the network with an LSP containing this information. This automatically ensures that when the shortest-path tree is recomputed, the router will start receiving packets for that group. Thus, hosts can join and leave groups without flood-and-prune, but at the expense of a much larger LSP database, since the database must contain one record for every group on every link in the network. Moreover, the shortest-path computation must be done separately for every potential source, which is computationally expensive. Recall that OSPF allows external and summary records to reduce the size of the LSP database. MOSPF is rather complex because it must correctly propagate group-membership information when computing these records.

11.11.9 Core-based trees

As we have seen, DVMRP suffers from two problems: (a) periodic flooding and pruning to compute the shortest-path pruned tree for a source, and (b) the need to store per-source, per-group prune records at each router. Though MOSPF does not require flooding, it substantially adds to the LSP database size and the computation required at each router. The *core-based trees* (*CBT*) approach addresses these deficiencies of DVMRP and MOSPF [BFC 93].

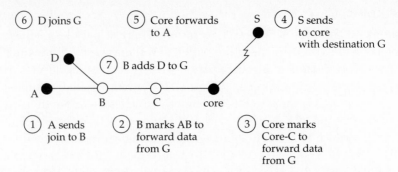

Figure 11.28: Core-based tree (CBT). CBT defines a core, to which a host sends join and leave requests. Intermediate routers use unicast routing to forward the packet to the core, noting the interface on which the join request arrived for forwarding multicast packets in the future.

The key idea in CBT is to explicitly define *core* routers that coordinate multicasts. When a router discovers that a host attached to its LAN wants to receive packets from a group, it forwards a special packet, the *join request*, toward the core (Figure 11.28). Each router along the path to the core, on seeing this request, marks the interface on which the request arrived as the interface on which to forward packets for that group. This is illustrated in Example 11.17.

EXAMPLE 11.17

For example, in Figure 11.28, when A sends a join message for group G to the core, routers B and C, which are on its path, mark the appropriate interfaces as the ones on which to forward packets on G. When D similarly joins the group, its join packet only goes as far as B, because B already knows about the group. B adds D to the list of interfaces on which to forward the packet for group G, and does not forward the join packet to C. When source S wants to send a packet to G, it simply sends it to the core router, which forwards it to all the interfaces on which it has received join requests so far. Leave requests are similarly coordinated. Join requests make it easy for a router to know the interfaces on which it should forward a packet without using prune messages.

A core-based tree has several advantages over flood-and-prune when the multicast group is sparse. First, routers that are not members of the multicast group never know of its existence. Thus, we avoid the expense of flooding. Second, join and leave messages are explicit. Thus, a host can join or leave the group without waiting for the next flooded packet. Third, each router needs to store only one record per group (the interfaces on which to forward packets for that group). It does not need to compute a shortest path tree explicitly (as in MOSPF), or store per-source prune information (as in DVMRP). On the other hand, all traffic for the group must pass through the core router, which can become a choke point. Moreover, if the core router goes down, every multicast group that goes through it also goes down. This can make the system unreliable.

11.11.10 Protocol-independent multicast

The key idea in *protocol-independent multicast* (*PIM*) is to use different multicast routing strategies depending on whether a multicast group is *dense* or *sparse* [DEFJLW 94]. A dense group is one where most of the routers in the network are likely to be members, whereas a sparse group has only a few, widely scattered members. Flood-and-prune and CBT are suited to different environments. When a group is dense, flood-and-prune is efficient, since only a few prune messages are necessary, but CBT is inefficient, since every router has to send an explicit join message to the core. Moreover, all the traffic and routing messages are concentrated at the core. In contrast, when a group is sparse, CBT has the upper hand, as described in Section 11.11.9. With PIM, a multicast group can declare itself as dense or sparse. Dense-mode PIM is nearly identical to flood-and-prune, the major difference being the introduction of an explicit join message to reduce the join latency.

Sparse-mode PIM is similar to CBT, with two major differences. The first difference is that routers can choose to receive data from either the core or a shortest-path tree. Consider, for example, router A in Figure 11.29, which wants to receive data from source router E. In CBT, E must send data to the core, which forwards it along A through C and B. However, a shorter path from E to A is directly through B. In sparse-mode PIM, a core is renamed a *rendezvous point*, and it explicitly provides the rendezvous functionality of a multicast group. Receivers initially send join messages to the rendezvous point, and, as in CBT, intermediate routers process the join message to set up routing tables.

Once a source starts sending data, intermediate routers can determine whether they have a shorter path to the source by comparing the interface on which they receive data from the core with the interface corresponding to the shortest path *to* the source. In Figure 11.29, B knows that its shortest path to E is on link BE, but it receives multicast

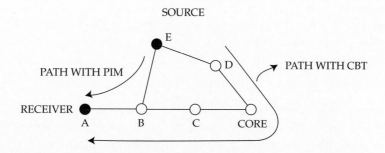

Figure 11.29: PIM versus CBT. CBT requires that multicast packets traverse the core, which can be inefficient. PIM allows a source to join a shortest-path tree instead, which is optimal.

packets from E on link BC. It therefore sends a join message to E, requesting it to send data for the multicast group on link BE. When this succeeds, B sends a prune message toward the core, which prunes multicast transfer on the core–C and C–B links. This avoids the inefficiency in CBT, where all the data must pass through the core. Moreover, even if the core goes down, at least the routers that have moved away from it can continue to receive packets from the source. On the other hand, PIM requires a complex protocol to ensure that A does not receive duplicate packets, or lose connectivity, when the handoff is in progress.

The second major difference between CBT and PIM is that in PIM, rendezvous points periodically send a message downstream announcing that they are alive. Leaf routers (those attached to LANs) set a timer every time they receive an advertisement. If a router does not receive an advertisement before the timer expires, it assumes that the rendezvous point is no longer reachable and initiates a join message toward a (preconfigured) alternative rendezvous point. Of course, if a router has already switched to a shortest-path tree, it no longer needs to worry about a rendezvous point going down. This mechanism is intended for routers that receive packets only from the core and would like to avoid disruption due to a single point of failure.

Work on PIM is still in progress. For example, PIM does not describe how a multicast group decides whether it is dense or sparse, or how a router determines the rendezvous point associated with a particular multicast group. However, because of its efficiency, it is likely to become a future Internet standard.

11.12 Routing with policy constraints

Our discussion of routing has assumed that all paths from a source to a destination (or a set of destinations) are equally good. Although this assumption is valid when the network is administered by a single authority or a set of closely cooperating authorities (such as in the telephone network or in the early days of the Internet), it rarely applies to internetworks that span multiple, mutually suspicious autonomous systems. *Policy routing* refers to computing routes that satisfy not just strictly topological metrics such as a shortest hop count, but complex policy directives such as the following: [Clark 89, Estrin 89]

- *Source and destination of the packet:* An autonomous system (AS) may not accept packets from some other AS.

- *Constraints on the ASs used for transit:* Communication between two autonomous systems may be constrained not to pass through some other AS.

- *Quality of service:* Every packet from an AS to some other AS may need to have a minimal resource commitment from intermediate routers or switches.

- *Time of day:* Certain paths may not be available at certain times of day to certain classes of traffic.

- *Charging and accounting policies:* Routes may be required to go only through routers that support accounting, or to smallest-monetary-cost paths, where the cost is a complex function of usage and the resources consumed by a packet.

The general problem of computing routes subject to a large set of (perhaps mutually conflicting) policy requirements is still an open research problem. In this section, we will consider some preliminary approaches to solving this problem.

11.12.1 Multiple metrics

Perhaps the simplest approach to policy routing is to advertise multiple metrics per link. For example, with link-state routing, every router could advertise the cost of a link based on current delay, available bandwidth, and the cost per packet. Each router can then independently compute shortest-cost trees for each metric. Packets could have a type-of-service field in their header that expresses their preference for a particular metric. Routers can use this field to decide the next hop.

EXAMPLE 11.18

In Figure 11.30, router A can reach router B using one of two paths. One of them has a higher monetary cost, but a lower delay. If a packet with a type-of-service

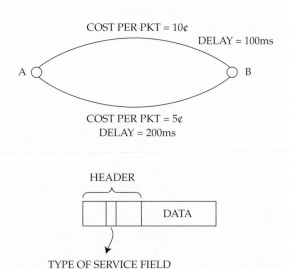

Figure 11.30: Routing with multiple metrics. The shortest path from A to B depends on the metric: cost or delay. Packets specify a type-of-service in the header, which routers examine to select a path.

field set to "minimize-delay" arrives at A, it is sent on the upper path. Packets with the field set to "minimize-cost" are sent on the lower path. We implicitly assume that packets cannot have both fields set. If such a packet arrives, the routing protocol must specify a tie-breaking rule.

Policy routing with multiple metrics is rather unsatisfactory. Unless all routers use the same rule in computing paths and forwarding packets, loops can easily be formed. Moreover, once a host sends a packet into the network, the packet's route is controlled entirely by the routers along the path, who may misinterpret a host's policy wishes [BE 90]. Therefore, a better solution for policy routing is *source routing,* where a packet's header carries either the entire path, or at least a set of autonomous systems that it wishes to traverse in reaching the destination. Routers can examine this list to decide the next AS along the path, routing the packet within the autonomous system in the same way as other packets.

11.12.2 Provider selection

A form of source routing that is easy and effective is called *provider selection.* The idea is that more than one network provider may provide all, or almost all, of the transmission facilities used in reaching a destination. Thus, a source can express policy objectives (in a coarse sense) by choosing a provider. For example, in the United States, customers can dial a long-distance access code to select one of more than four hundred long-distance telephone service companies. Each company then interprets the rest of the telephone number to provide a route to the same destination. In the same way, a source may select one of several IP service providers by means of a loose source route to the service provider's access point. A more detailed explanation of this idea can be found in reference [Tsuchiya 91].

11.12.3 Crankback

Routing becomes even more complex when packets require a quality-of-service guarantee [LHH 95]. Then, routers must compute a path based not only on reachability and number of hops, but also on whether the path has sufficient capacity. Some techniques used in telephone network routing, such as *crankback,* are being explored for routing in large ATM networks. Recall that in crankback, a router tries a path to a destination, but if this path does not have sufficient resources, the call "cranks back" to the previous router, which tries an alternative path. The call fails only if no path with sufficient resources exists between the source and the destination. Crankback has been suggested for adoption in the proposed ATM routing standard called *Private Network–Network Interface* (*PNNI*).

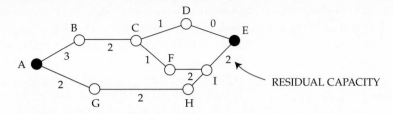

Figure 11.31: Crankback. When a path must satisfy QoS constraints, a cell-establishment packet may need to backtrack or "crank back." A initially tries to find a path with a residual capacity of at least 2 through B, and fails. A then tries through G, finding a satisfactory path.

EXAMPLE 11.19

In Figure 11.31, router A wants to connect to router E so that the call has at least two resource units on every hop. The weights on each link show the remaining resource on the link. Suppose the call originates from A and goes to B and C, where it is tentatively accepted. C cannot forward it to D or F because the path does not have sufficient resources. So C cranks back the call to B, and then A, which tries again with G. This time the path A–G–H–I–E succeeds, and the call completes. Note that this path is not the shortest path from A to E, but is the shortest path with sufficient capacity.

11.13 Routing for mobile hosts

What happens if a destination is not attached by a wire to a router, but instead can move about? Packets destined to that host somehow have to be forwarded to its new location, wherever it may be. The problem naturally resolves itself into two parts: finding out where a host is, and getting packets or calls to it. We will study these two problems in this section. Research in host mobility is continuing apace, and we will present only an outline of some basic techniques.

11.13.1 Mobile routing in the telephone network

Cellular telephones use radio frequencies to communicate with a *base station*—usually located on a tall tower with a triangular platform on top, which you can see along major highways or in city centers—that relays their call to a *mobile telephone switching office* (*MTSO*). (To prevent unfair advantage to the local telephone company, the Federal Communications Commission in the United States requires that MTSOs be separated from central offices, though they serve nearly the same purpose.) In this section, we will focus on routing calls to and from a cellular telephone that may be associated with any MTSO in the cellular-service provider's service area.

Each cellular phone is statically assigned a globally unique ID and a *home* MTSO that does billing and provides access to the long-distance (toll) telephone network. The phone is also assigned a telephone number from the address space assigned to the home MTSO. When a cellular phone is switched on, it uses ALOHA contention on a common signaling channel to identify itself to the local MTSO. The MTSO, in turn, contacts the home MTSO and informs it of the phone's location.

When someone makes a call *to* the phone, the telephone network delivers it automatically to the home MTSO, which sets up a connection to the phone through the remote MTSO, using *Signaling System 7* (SS7) signaling (Figure 11.32). The remote MTSO contacts the nearest base station, which rings the cellular phone. The identity of the nearest base station is dynamically updated using the cellular handoff described in Section 2.6.2.

To keep billing and accounting simple, all calls *from* the phone are always routed back to the home MTSO before they enter the toll network. Thus, the remote MTSO acts like a dumb switch to route calls to and from the home MTSO. If the phone moves from one MTSO to another, this information is sent back to the home MTSO, which updates its local database. Calls in progress are rerouted from the remote MTSO to the home MTSO, again using SS7 signaling.

This architecture allows cellular phones to roam within the entire service area freely, but has the overhead that calls are always routed to the home MTSO, requiring addi-

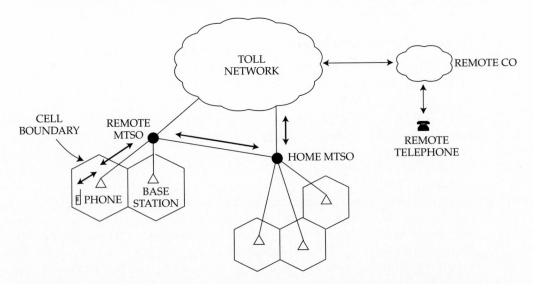

Figure 11.32: Routing for cellular phones. Each cellular phone is assigned to a mobile telephone switching office (MTSO). Calls to the phone are routed through the home MTSO to the nearest base station via a remote MTSO. As the phone moves, the home MTSO is updated with the location of the MTSO nearest the phone.

Acronym	Expansion	Comment
MH	Mobile host	The host that moves.
CH	Corresponding host	The host that the mobile is talking to.
HAA	Home address agent	The "home" base assigned to the mobile host.
COA	Care-of agent	The base closest to the mobile host that forwards packets to it.

Table 11.2: Acronymns used in mobile routing on the Internet.

tional hops in the network. It scales well, because new MTSOs can be added dynamically as service demands increase. Moreover, heavily loaded MTSOs can be split to share the load. The cellular phone solution to mobility is simple and robust and has been modified for solving the mobility problem on the Internet.

11.13.2 Mobile routing in the Internet

In this section, we will study the basic model for mobile routing in the Internet and a simple solution. Extensions to the standard solution that add robustness, efficiency, and security are still areas of active research. The field has evolved its own set of acronyms, which are presented in Table 11.2.

The basic model for mobile routing, which is similar to the cellular telephone model, is shown in Figure 11.33. Mobile hosts (MHs), which are mobile computers with a fixed IP address (much like a cellular phone with a fixed telephone number) communicate with the nearest base station, which is attached to a *care-of agent* (*COA*). The care-of agent, which corresponds to a remote MTSO in cellular telephony, receives messages on behalf of the MH. We statically assign each MH to a *home address agent* (*HAA*), which corresponds to a local MTSO. We call the machine that the MH is communicating with the *corresponding host*, or CH.

When a corresponding host wants to send a datagram to a mobile host, it puts the mobile host's IP address in the packet destination and hands it to the wide-area network. Using normal network routing, this packet eventually reaches the home address agent. The home address agent is always kept informed of the current care-of agent (we will shortly see how this is done). It encapsulates the incoming packet with a new header that has its destination set to that of the care-of agent (this is identical to the tunneling used in the MBONE). The care-of agent retrieves the packet and hands it to the base station, which sends it through a wireless link to the mobile host. When the mobile host wants to send a datagram to the corresponding host, it simply puts the corresponding host's IP address in the packet destination, and it is delivered to the corresponding host using normal routing. This solution is nearly identical to the cellular network solution, except

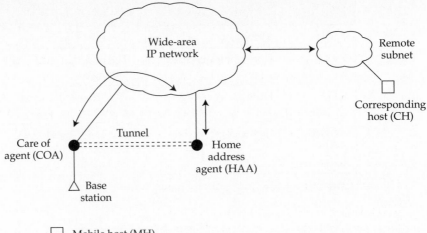

Figure 11.33: Mobile routing on the Internet. Packets to a mobile host (MH) are always routed through a home address agent (HAA), which tunnels packets for the MH to a care-of agent (COA). When the MH moves, it listens to beacons to detect that it has a new COA. It then updates both the HAA and the old COA. Packets from the MH use normal routing.

that we gain some efficiency in the path from the mobile host to the corresponding host, which does not need to go through the home address agent.

We still need to solve two problems: first, how does a base station know that it has a mobile host in its area, and second, how does the home address agent find out the current care-of agent? *Beaconing* solves the first problem. Each base station periodically transmits a beacon, which is an identification packet transmitted on a well-known frequency. The beacon contains the ID of the base station, and the IP address of the corresponding care-of agent. Each mobile host listens to beacons to detect the best base station to use (depending on the signal strength of the beacon). It then registers itself with the care-of agent using a registration packet. The care-of agent, in turn, passes on the registration to the home address agent, which then knows which care-of agent to use for the mobile host. If the mobile host moves to a new care-of agent, it knows this from the new base station's beacon, which contains a new care-of-agent address. The mobile host sends a registration message to the new care-of agent and "unregisters" itself from the old care-of agent. Thus, the home address agent is aware that the mobile host is now with a new care-of agent. The old care-of agent forwards any packets it receives for the mobile host to the new care-of agent, until the home address agent becomes aware of the change.

Security is an important consideration in designing mobile networking protocols. Wireless broadcasts are easy to tap. Second, the home address agent has to implicitly trust the care-of agent for carrying packets to the mobile host. A malicious intruder could fake a message from any machine to the home address agent informing it that the intruder's machine was the care-of agent. If the home address agent does not authenticate its messages, the intruder's machine could receive all the packets meant for the mobile host.

To prevent this, the mobile host and the home address agent share a common secret, which the home address agent checks before sending packets to the care-of agent. This does not prevent the care-of agent from snooping on the packet, or even prevent a determined cracker from listening to the shared secret and then spoofing it, but adds a modicum of security to the exchange. Improving mobile security is an important area of current research.

A second open problem concerns the formation of loops when mobile hosts move from one care-of agent to another. This is illustrated in Example 11.20.

EXAMPLE 11.20

Recall that a care-of agent (COA) forwards packets to the new care-of agent until the home address agent is aware of the change. Suppose a mobile host moves from COA A to COA B (Figure 11.34). Then, A gets an unregister message from the mobile host asking it to redirect packets to B. If the mobile host moves back to A, the host tells B to redirect packets for it back to A. Now, if a duplicate of an old unregister message reaches A, it forwards messages for the mobile host to B, which forwards it again to A, forming a loop. Since IP does not detect or prevent duplicates, this might well happen! (Routers discard looping IP packets when their time-to-live field eventually drops to zero.)

A third major problem is that packets to the mobile host must always go through the home address agent, even if the packet is generated from a LAN attached to the local care-of agent. For example, if the mobile host is running a file transfer with a machine on the care-of agent's LAN, every packet from the corresponding host to the mobile host must still go all the way back to its home address agent, then return to the LAN,

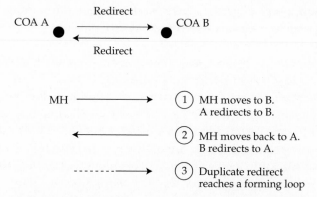

Figure 11.34: Looping in mobile routing. If a MH moves from COA A to COA B and back, and a redirection message is duplicated, a loop can form.

which is inefficient. Several schemes for eliminating the extra hops (called the *dog-leg*) from the corresponding host to the home address agent are under active study [Huitema 95].

11.14 Summary

In this chapter, we studied many aspects of routing in the Internet and the telephone network in detail. The hard problem in routing is summarizing volatile and voluminous global state to something that a router can use in making local decisions. This problem exists both in the Internet and in the telephone and ATM networks. However, in the latter two networks, switch controllers route calls, instead of packets.

We would like a routing protocol to be robust, minimize its use of memory in routers, choose optimal paths, and require the least overhead. We have several choices in designing such a protocol, including centralized or distributed routing, source-based or hop-by-hop routing, single or multiple-path routing, and static or dynamic routing. Different combinations make different trade-offs in their complexity and use of resources.

Telephone network routing differs from Internet routing in many ways, because telephone networks are much better connected and have more reliable links and switches. Moreover, they have a better idea of traffic characteristics. Telephone network routing boils down to choosing the order in which to try 2-hop paths in the network core. We studied several algorithms such as DNHR, TSMR, and RTNR. In all three algorithms, the fundamental problem is that choosing a route determines the load on a link, which in turn influences the routing. This is formalized in the notion of the Erlang fixed-point solution to the Erlang map.

The two fundamental ways to route packets in the Internet are to use distance-vector and link-state routing. Distance-vector routing is easy to implement, but suffers from problems such as counting to infinity. We can overcome these problems using techniques such as path-vector, source-tracing, and diffusion-update algorithms. Link-state routing allows each router to get its own copy of the global topology. We have to be careful in disseminating topology to avoid corruption of the individual copies of the topology. This is done with error detection techniques, as well as the lollipop sequence space and aging link-state packets to remove stale information. Once we have the topology, we can compute shortest paths using Dijkstra's algorithm.

Both link-state and distance-vector routing have their pros and cons, and neither seems uniformly superior. They are both common in the Internet.

Choosing the cost of a link is a fundamentally hard problem. The cost influences the shortest routes in the network, and these, in turn, affect the load on a link, and hence its cost (this is similar to the Erlang map in telephone networks). The network response map and the link metric map allow us to find cost metrics that guarantee convergence of routes and link costs.

In a large network, a router cannot store information about every other router. Instead, we divide the network into a hierarchy of levels, and each router knows only about other routers in its own level of the hierarchy. This reduces routing table sizes, though at the expense of suboptimal routing. Border routers participate in routing in more than one level, mediating exchange of information across levels to minimize the effects of hierarchical routing.

Many of the techniques used for point-to-point wide-area networks are not directly applicable to broadcast LANs, where broadcast and multicast are cheap. The Internet uses a set of special protocols in the local area to efficiently exploit these properties. These include router discovery and path redirection.

Multicast routing requires an entirely new set of protocols. Our goal is to connect one or more sources to one or more receivers with the shortest possible paths, the least control overhead, and the least possible state in the routers. Several approaches, such as flood-and-prune, core-based trees, and protocol-independent multicast, make different trade-offs in achieving this objective.

Besides choosing routes based on the shortest path, we would like to use other metrics to choose paths. This includes the time of day, the monetary cost, security at each intermediate point, or other administrative policies. Policy routing allows consistent choices to be made in dealing with multiple routing metrics. A variant of policy routing becomes important in networks where paths allow reservations, and we need to use crankback to choose a path with sufficient free resources.

In recent years, mobile telephones and mobile computers have become much more common. Routing protocols to deal with mobility assume the existence of a nonmobile "home" that handles routing on behalf of mobile hosts. Packets to the mobile pass through the home, which forwards it to the nearest wired access point. Packets from the mobile either pass through the home or cut through directly to the remote corresponding host. This description is valid for both the Internet and the telephone network.

Routing is a rich field for study, and we have only touched on some essentials. Moreover, many aspects, such as ATM routing, are still areas of active research. This chapter describes some of the basic ideas common to routing in the telephone and ATM networks, and the Internet. The bibliography provides pointers to many relevant papers and books that contain more detailed information.

Review questions

1. What is the trade-off made with source routing? With address aggregation?
2. Why does the telephone network core not use 3-hop paths?
3. What does each toll switch receive from the central DNHR controller?
4. What technique is used to avert metastability in telephone networks?
5. What is a distance vector?
6. When does a router's distance vector change?
7. What is a path vector?
8. How does split horizon prevent counting to infinity in some cases?
9. How many LSPs does a router create?

10. What is the LSP flooding rule?
11. How do we protect the LSP database from wrapped sequence numbers?
12. Why do we prefer the lollipop sequence space to aging?
13. What is the purpose of LSP database description records?
14. When is it reasonable to use hop-count metrics?
15. How does the restriction that a link cost can only change by half a hop control routing oscillations?
16. What is the network response map?
17. Why do we need hierarchical routing?
18. Why are Internet routing tables so large?
19. What are external and summary records?
20. What is the purpose of a designated router in OSPF?
21. What additional considerations must an exterior gateway protocol take into account, compared with an interior gateway protocol?
22. How does an endpoint on the Internet know that a packet's destination is on the local LAN?
23. How can an administrator use the preference indication in a router advertisement packet?
24. What is a multicast group?
25. How does an expanding-ring search work?
26. Why is multicasting more efficient than multiple unicasts?
27. How do IP hosts translate from a Class D address to a LAN multicast address?
28. What is the purpose of IGMP?
29. What is the rule in reverse-path forwarding?
30. What does pruning do?
31. Why does MOSPF require tie-breaking rules for equal-length paths?
32. What is the main problem with a core-based tree?
33. What is the danger in routing with multiple metrics?
34. Why do cellular calls always go through the home MTSO?
35. How does a mobile host know that it has a new care-of agent?
36. Why does Mobile-IP require tunneling?

Exercises

11.1. Suppose toll switch A wants to set up a call to toll switch B using RTNR and has three elements in its list of lightly loaded trunks. If the AB trunk is full, and the probability that any other trunk is full is 0.05, what is the probability that A cannot find a path to B?

11.2. In Figure 11.4: (a) What is D's initial distance vector? (b) What is the distance vector after it receives a vector from C? (c) What is its vector when it receives a vector from B?

11.3. In Figure 11.4, if D uses split horizon with poisonous reverse, what is the distance vector that B receives from D?

11.4. In Figure 11.4, if B reports path vectors to D, what is the path vector eventually computed by D? If BA goes down, how can B use this to avoid counting to infinity? What is the sequence of actions by which B starts routing to A through C?

11.5. In Figure 11.4, assume that link BA goes down, so that B routes to A through C. If B uses split horizon, it will report to C an infinite distance to A, since B uses C to reach A. Similarly, D also reports to C an infinite distance to A. Now, suppose the CA link goes down. (a) What distance to A will C report to B and D? (b) What is the distance to A that D reports to B? (c) What does B think the shortest path to C is? (d) What does B tell C about its distance to A? (e) What is C's route to A now? (f) What does C tell D? (g) When does this cycle end?

11.6. In Figure 11.11, use source tracing at A to find the path from A to F. If the shortest path to D changes to go through B, what does the source-tracing rule say about the shortest path to F?

11.7. A router using link-state routing receives LS packets with sequence numbers 4094, 4093, 3, −4096, −4093, and −4096. Assume we use the lollipop sequence space. (a) How many bits does the sequence number use? (b) Explain how this sequence could be received. (c) What actions should the router take?

11.8. Use Dijkstra's algorithm to compute shortest paths for the network in Figure 11.35.

11.9. What would happen if a router received an LSP from a router with the smallest possible sequence number in the lollipop sequence space such that its link cost is corrupted to zero?

11.10. Consider a two-router network with routers A and B. They are connected by two links in parallel, L1 and L2. Suppose the cost of each link is either low or high. If the cost is low, then all the traffic from A to B uses that link; if it is high, no traffic uses it. If the link is more than 50% utilized, it has a metric "high"; otherwise, its metric is "low." (a) Show the network response and metric maps. (b) Trace a path showing routing oscillations.

11.11. What are the external records emitted by router 6.0.0.0 in Figure 11.15?

11.12. What are the summary records emitted by router 6.0.0.0 in Figure 11.15?

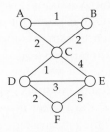

Figure 11.35: Figure for Exercise 11.8.

11.13. On the Internet, a router checks whether the destination is local by testing the destination address's network number with its *own* subnet mask. Prove that this will always work.

11.14. Suppose a network administrator adds a new router on a LAN. When do hosts first hear of its presence? What happens if the administrator simultaneously removes the old router (consider both alternatives for the relative preferences of the two routers)?

11.15. What is the drawback with expanding-ring search when a host is connected to links with a range of weights?

11.16. IGMP cleverly exploits LAN multicast to reduce the number of control messages. For example, if one host sends a group membership report, all the other hosts on the LAN can hear this and cancel their pending membership reports. How would you implement reliable multicast on a LAN that exploits the same technique? (Hint: Use NACKS.)

11.17. We can emulate a multipoint-to-multipoint multicast with a set of point-to-multipoint multicasts. However, this has two drawbacks, which we explore in this exercise. (a) What is the state needed at each router for each point-to-multipoint tree? How does this compare with the state needed for a multipoint-to-multipoint tree? (b) What happens in the point-to-multipoint case when a new sender wants to send packets to all the receivers? What happens in the multipoint-to-multipoint case?

11.18. Suppose a router obeyed the flooding rule that it forwarded an incoming packet to every interface (except the one it arrived on) if the packet was not a duplicate. In this exercise, we will study the cost of determining that a packet is a duplicate. (a) Assume that the routers do not see any part of the packet header except the destination address. The simplest way to know if a packet is duplicated is to store every packet, and comparing incoming packets with stored ones. If the mean packet length is 500 bytes, and a router receives 200 multicast packets per second, how much storage does the router consume every second? (b) If the router decides to discard packets that are more than 10 minutes old, how much storage does it need? (c) How many packets are stored on average? (d) If comparing entire packets takes 200 microseconds, how much time does it take to compare an incoming packet with every stored packet? (e) How does this compare with the interarrival time between multicast packets? (f) Suppose the router computes a 10-byte checksum for a packet, and stores checksums instead of packets, using the checksum to compare packets. If computing a checksum takes 200 microseconds, and comparing checksums takes 2 microseconds, what is the gain in space and time of this approach over storing entire packets? (g) Suppose packets carried sequence numbers visible to routers. What comparison must the router do to test if the packet is a duplicate (hint: use the lollipop sequence space)? (h) What if the multicast group has more than one sender?

11.19. What happens in DVMRP if packets are not periodically flooded?

11.20. How would you extend a core-based tree to allow multiple cores?

11.21. Suppose a HAA received a spoofed packet from a cracker saying that packets for an MH should be forwarded to the cracker's IP address. What precautions must the HAA take to ensure that it does not start forwarding packets to the cracker?

Chapter 12

Error Control

The end-to-end transfer of data from a transmitting application to a receiving application involves many steps, each subject to error. With adequate error control, we can be confident that the transmitted and received data are identical, although the communication occurred over a series of error-prone routers and links.

Errors can occur both at the bit and at the packet level. At the bit level, the most common error is the inversion of a 0 bit to a 1, or a 1 bit to a 0. We call this *bit corruption.* At the packet level, we see errors such as packet loss, duplication, or reordering. *Error control* is the process of detecting and correcting both bit and packet errors.

Bit-level error control usually involves adding redundancy to the transmitted data so that the receiver can detect bit errors. In some schemes, there is sufficient information for the receiver not only to detect errors, but also to correct most of them. At the packet level, we assume that bit-level error control can detect all bit errors. (Detectable but uncorrectable bit errors are treated as a packet loss.) Packet-level error control mechanisms detect and correct packet-level errors such as loss, duplication, and reordering.

We typically implement bit-level error control at the datalink layer of the protocol stack, and packet-level error control is typically found at the transport layer. Thus, bit-level error control is usually hop-by-hop, whereas packet-level error control is usually end-to-end. Generally speaking, we prefer hop-by-hop error control on links where the error rate is high (so-called *lossy links*) and end-to-end error control when entire path is more or less error free. However, there are many exceptions to this general rule.

In this chapter, we will study both bit-level and packet-level error control. We first study the causes of bit errors (Section 12.1) and bit-level error control (Section 12.2). Section 12.3 describes some causes for packet errors, and Section 12.4 describes mechanisms for packet-level error control.

12.1 Causes of bit errors

Information is transmitted on a link by varying the state of a signal, such as its voltage level, intensity, phase, or frequency. On a digital link, each signal state corresponds to one or more 0's and 1's—a signal that can take 2^n states represents n bits of information. To decipher a signal on a digital link, the receiver compares the received signal with a set of predefined references.

EXAMPLE 12.1

For concreteness, consider a digital link where a 0 voltage level represents a 0 bit, and a 5-volt level represents a 1. Here, the receiver compares the received voltage level with 0-V and 5-V references to determine whether it received a 0 or a 1. It can do so by using a simple rule such as the following: if the voltage level is more than 2.5 V, the received signal is a 1, else it is a 0.

If the transmission link were ideal, then the transmitted and received signal would be identical. However, in real life, every link is subject to noise and attenuation. For instance, in the link described in Example 12.1, a receiver may receive a voltage level of 3 V, which is greater than its comparison threshold of 2.5 V, although the transmitter transmitted a voltage of 0 V. This results in a bit inversion, causing a bit error. The greater the probability that the noise level exceeds the threshold, the more likely a bit error becomes.

We can quantify the noise on a link using the *signal-to-noise ratio* (*SNR*), which is:

$$\text{SNR (in dB)} = 10 \log ((\text{peak signal level}/\text{root-mean-square noise level})^2) \qquad (12.1)$$

The probability that a bit is received with an error depends primarily on the peak level of the signal and the signal-to-noise ratio. The SNR decreases with increasing link length. In practice, given a desired error probability and peak signal level, the transmission link is chosen to be short enough so that the SNR is sufficiently high. By introducing a repeater that detects a 0 or a 1 and regenerates the signal on its output (a *regenerative repeater*), we can make the error probability on a digital link as small as desired, subject to the cost of repeaters, and the noise introduced by the repeaters. For optical receivers, the main cause of errors is noise in the receiver itself.

We usually measure the error probability on a digital link in terms of the *bit error ratio* or BER, which is the ratio of the mean number of errors in any given interval to the total number of bits transmitted in that interval. Typical fiber-optic links have a bit error ratio in the range of $10^{-18}-10^{-14}$, but copper links can have a substantially higher bit error ratio, depending on shielding and the operating environment.

To design an efficient error control scheme, it is necessary to have a good model for the physical processes that cause bit errors in data transmission (the *error model*). The major causes of bit errors are Gaussian and non-Gaussian noise, loss of line synchronization, scramblers, protection switching, and, for cellular communication, handoffs and fading. We study each of these in turn in the following subsections.

12.1.1   Gaussian noise

A common assumption is that the noise amplitude is described by a Gaussian (normal) distribution. We call such noise *Gaussian noise.* Gaussian noise on a line leads to uncorrelated and sporadic bit errors.

12.1.2   Non-Gaussian noise

Non-Gaussian noise, which refers to noise that does not obey a Gaussian distribution, can lead to bursts of errors. Common sources of non-Gaussian noise are electrical impulses, such as lightning or electrical sparks. The causes of non-Gaussian noise are specific to each transmission line, so we have to build situation-specific error models for them.

12.1.3   Loss of synchronization

A third source of bit errors is loss of bit synchronization between the transmitter and the receiver [BC 92]. Receivers periodically sample the received analog waveform to extract digital information. They typically use the 0–1 and 1–0 transitions in the transmitter's signal as the input to a phase-locked loop to determine the transmitter's clock automatically. If there are too few transitions in the transmitted signal, then the phase-locked loop can drift, leading to a loss of bit synchronization. Thus, the receiver might sample a signal while it is rising or falling, leading to a burst of bit errors until synchronization is reestablished.

12.1.4   Scramblers

To prevent loss of synchronization, a transmitter must ensure that the transmitted signal has enough signal transitions per second to prevent clock drift at the receiver. If the information being handed to the transmitter from an upper layer contains too few bit transitions (if it is predominantly 0's or predominantly 1's), then the transmitter can introduce additional transitions by modifying the data, which the receiver must undo. The modification is usually done with a *scrambler,* a hardware device that "scrambles" information before it is transmitted. In a scrambler, data from a higher layer is serially

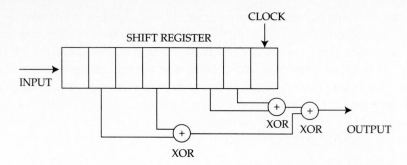

Figure 12.1: A scrambler. Bits enter the scrambler from the left, one per clock tick, and are shifted to the right. Taps from the shift register XOR selected bits to "scramble" them. At the receiver, a symmetric process restores the original bits. Scrambling introduces random 0–1 transitions in the transmitted bit-stream so that the receiver can synchronize and extract clock. It also results in error multiplication.

shifted, once per clock cycle, into a shift register (Figure 12.1). Several taps extract bits from different depths of the register and exclusive-OR them to produce an output bit. This introduces transitions in the output bit stream removed by a symmetric process at the receiver [BC92]. Note that scramblers are not foolproof. For every scrambler, there exists a sequence such that the output of the scrambler is all 0's or all 1's. If such a sequence should accidentally be transferred on a link, we could see a loss of bit synchronization.

Scramblers have an unfortunate property—if a received bit is in error, then the error is repeated as many times as there are taps, leading to a burst of errors with a span as large as the span of the taps. Thus, scramblers, while preventing loss of bit synchronization, simultaneously introduce the problem of *error multiplication*. The error model for a scrambled line takes error multiplication into account—the error probability for a bit error is computed from a Gaussian or non-Gaussian noise model, then assigned to an error burst corresponding to the span of the taps in the scrambler.

12.1.5 Protection switching

Telephone networks duplicate many key network components to provide reliable service. For example, at least two separate physical paths connect each switch to other switches. Within each switch, hardware components such as CPUs and buses are duplicated. In normal operation, only one of a pair of alternates is in operation. However, if a monitoring processor finds that the error rate in a component is above a threshold, then the system automatically cuts over to the "hot spare." We call this *protection switching*. Protection switching is a routine operation in telephone networks—a DS3 line might be switched as many as ten to twelve times a day (though the average is far less). Telephone companies prescribe the maximum duration of a protection switch as follows: a detection period of 10 ms, a switch time of 50 ms, and restore time of 20 ms. During the switch and restore time (but not during detection), incoming data is buffered, and so each protection switch can cause up to 10 ms of disruption on a high-speed line. Although protection switching is unnoticeable for analog voice calls, data sources see it as a burst of errors that lasts for as long as 10 ms. At high data rates, this is an appreciable length of time.

EXAMPLE 12.2

Assume a protection switch on a DS3 takes at most 10 ms to complete. What is the worst case error burst length?

Solution: A DS3 has a data rate of roughly 45 Mbps. Thus, the worst case error burst length is $45 * 10^6 * 10 * 10^{-3} = 450{,}000$ bits.

12.1.6 Handoffs and fading

Handoffs and fading can cause error bursts in cellular communication. Recall from Section 2.6.2 that in a handoff, a mobile unit is switched from one base station to another. It is common for some information from the mobile unit to be lost in this process. Again, although voice callers may not notice this, data sources (such as modems) can be badly hit. Typical handoffs last for about 150 ms during which time the received signal is almost completely in error. Handoff errors can be substantially reduced by making the new connection before the old one ends. However, this makes it necessary to overlap base-station ranges, which leads to less efficient spatial reuse of the radio spectrum. The error model for handoff depends on the details of the handoff algorithm and must be designed specifically for each situation.

If a mobile station does not receive a strong signal from a base station because of hills, buildings, or other obstacles, then its received signal is in error until the unit moves away from the obstacle. We call this loss of signal strength *fading,* and it causes long burst errors. There are two types of fading: *shadow fading,* which is due to macroscopic environmental conditions, and *short-term Rayleigh fading,* primarily due to vehicle movement. Detailed error models can be found in reference [Jakes 93].

12.2 Bit-error detection and correction

The basic idea in error coding is to add redundancy to the transmitted information to allow a receiver to detect or correct errors. The literature concerning error coding and coding theory is vast. In this book, we can only touch on some essentials and present an overview of the results. A much more detailed introduction to these techniques can be found in references [PW 72, Blahut 90].

There are two common kinds of error coding schemes—*block codes* and *convolutional codes*. In a block code, each block of k bits of data is encoded into n bits of information, so that the code contains $n - k$ bits of redundancy. We call the k bits the *data* bits, the encoded n bits the *codeword*, and the code an (n, k) code. For example, if we add 3 bits of redundancy to 5 bits of data, we obtain an 8-bit codeword using an $(8, 5)$ code. In this example, we can identify sets of 8 bits in the coded stream that each correspond to a set of 5 data bits. Unlike a block code, every coded bit in a convolutional code depends on a different set of data bits. Thus, the coded stream does not contain blocks of bits in direct correspondence to a block of data bits. In this section, we will first study block codes, moving from simple schemes to sophisticated ones. We will then study one example of a convolutional code.

12.2.1   Parity

A parity code is a $(k + 1, k)$ block code where 1 bit is added to each block of k data bits to make the total number of 1's in the $k + 1$-bit codeword even (or odd). The receiver counts the number of 1's in the codeword and checks if it is even (or odd). If the check fails, the codeword is in error.

EXAMPLE 12.3

Compute the even and odd parity codes for the string "101101."

Solution: The string contains four 1's, which is an even number of 1's. To obtain the even-parity codeword, we add a 0 to the end, so that the total number of 1's in the codeword is even. This gives us the even parity codeword as "1011010." For the odd-parity codeword, we must make the number of 1's in the codeword odd, so the codeword is "1011011."

Parity can detect only odd numbers of bit errors. If a codeword has an even number of bit errors, the number of 1's remains even (or odd), so a parity check incorrectly declares the codeword to be valid. For example, if the original codeword with even parity is "1011010," the same codeword with the first two bits in error, that is, "0111010," also has even parity. A second problem with parity is that if the parity check on a codeword fails, there is no indication of which bits are in error. Thus, we can use parity for error detection, but not for error correction.

The main advantage of using parity is that we can compute the parity of a string on-the-fly, with no additional storage and no added delay. However, because of its deficiencies, parity is used only when extremely few errors are expected, and a parity failure suggests a serious problem in the system.

12.2.2 Rectangular codes

In a rectangular code, we arrange data bits into an array and compute parity along each row and column. Thus, a single error shows up as a parity failure in one row and one column, allowing us to both detect and correct the error. This is an example of an *error-correcting* code.

EXAMPLE 12.4

Consider the string of data bits "101100 011100 001001 101000 001101 010100," which we arrange in an array with six rows and six columns, as shown below:

$$
\begin{array}{ccccccc}
1 & 0 & 1 & 1 & 0 & 0 & \mathit{1} \\
0 & 1 & 1 & 1 & 0 & 0 & \mathit{1} \\
0 & 0 & 1 & 0 & 0 & 1 & \mathit{0} \\
1 & 0 & 1 & 0 & 0 & 0 & \mathit{0} \\
0 & 0 & 1 & 1 & 0 & 1 & \mathit{1} \\
0 & 1 & 0 & 1 & 0 & 0 & \mathit{0} \\
\mathit{0} & \mathit{0} & \mathit{1} & \mathit{0} & \mathit{0} & \mathit{0} & \mathit{1}
\end{array}
$$

The values in italics are even parities over the rows and the columns. Each row of 7 bits constitutes a codeword, and all rows but the last contain both data bits and redundant information. If the second bit in the third row is corrupted from a 0 to a 1, then parity checks on both the second column and third row fail, pinpointing the location of the error.

If two errors occur in the same row or column, a rectangular code can only detect them, not correct them. For example, if 2 bits in row 1 are corrupted, then there are parity errors in the corresponding columns, so these errors are detected. However, since the parity check of every row still succeeds, we cannot isolate and correct these errors (see Exercise 12.4).

The advantage of a rectangular code is that it is easy to compute, and it can correct a single-bit error. However, before we can compute a rectangular code, we must accumulate at least one row of bits in memory. This introduces coding delay.

12.2.3 Hamming codes

We call the combination of a user's data bits and redundant information a *valid codeword*. An *errored codeword* is a valid codeword with one or more corrupted bits. A key idea in error coding is that we cannot detect an error if it corrupts a valid codeword so that the errored codeword is identical to another valid codeword. Thus, valid codewords must be "different" enough that errored codewords derived from them do not resemble other valid codewords. We quantify this intuition using the concept of *Hamming distance.*

The Hamming distance between two codewords is the minimum number of bit inversions required to transform one codeword into another. For example, the Hamming distance between "101101" and "011101" is 2. If all valid codewords are at least a Hamming distance h apart, at least h bit corruptions must occur before one valid codeword is transformed to another. Thus, with fewer corruptions, the resulting codeword is distinguishably an errored codeword, which means we can detect up to $h - 1$ errors.

EXAMPLE 12.5

Consider an error code where we represent 1 as 111, and 0 as 000. The only two valid codewords are 000 and 111, which are a Hamming distance 3 apart. A single-bit error in a valid codeword, say, 000, can result in errored codewords 100, 010, or 001. None of these is a valid codeword, so we know that an error has occurred. Moreover, all three errored codewords are a Hamming distance 1 from 000, and a Hamming distance 2 from 111. Thus, we can interpret them as corrupted versions of the codeword 000. In other words, a receiver receiving an errored codeword 010 can assume that the actual data bit was a 0, which automatically corrects the error.

If the valid codeword 000 is corrupted with two bit errors, the errored codewords possible are 110, 011, and 101. Since none of these is a valid codeword, we can detect two errors. However, these errored codewords are closer to the valid codeword 111 than to the valid codeword 000. Thus, if we try to correct the two bit errors, we will be mistaken. We should use this code for error correction only when the chance of two bit errors in the same codeword is smaller than our error threshold.

In general, if we want to *detect* up to E errors, then all valid codewords should be at least $E + 1$ distance apart from each other. If we want to *correct* up to E errors, the minimum distance should be at least $2E + 1$.

Besides coming up with the idea of a Hamming distance, Hamming studied the design of *perfect* parity codes. To motivate these codes, consider the problem of determining the least number of redundant bits necessary for a code that can correct one bit error. For codewords of length n, a single-bit error can happen in one of n ways, so each valid codeword can be transformed into one of n patterns. The redundant bits must indicate either no error occurred, or one of the n positions where the error occurred. For example, the codeword 010, of length 3, can be transformed by one bit error into three codewords: 110, 000, and 011. Thus, a single error-correcting code (which must identify the bit in error) must identify one of four possible patterns: 010, 110, 000, and 011. This requires at least 2 bits. In general, we need at least c redundant bits, where $c \geq \log_2(n + 1)$ *or*

$2^c \geq (n + 1)$. For a perfect code, c achieves its minimum. For example, if the codeword is 7 bits long ($n = 7$), then $c \geq 3$, and for a perfect code, $c = 3$.

We can construct a perfect parity code as follows. Consider an n-bit codeword written out as a series of bits $b_1, b_2, \ldots, b_n$. Let $b_1, b_2, b_4, \ldots b_{2^r}$ (i.e., bit positions corresponding to powers of 2) be parity bits, and the rest be data bits. For example, in the 7-bit codeword 1101001, counting from the left, the first, second, and fourth bits are parity bits, and the rest are data bits. Consider the data bits at position 5, 6, and 7. If we write these positions in binary, we get 101, 110, and 111. All three have a "1" in the high-order bit (which corresponds to 4). The rule for creating a perfect parity code is that the fourth bit in a codeword is a parity check on the data bits whose position, when written out in binary, has a 1 in the fours place. In general, a parity bit at position b_{2^l} checks all bits b_p whose bit positions p, when written out in base 2 representation, have a 1 in the lth position (where the LSB is counted as 0). Table 12.1 shows how to construct the perfect Hamming parity code for a (7, 4) code. Using these rules, we can compute the (7, 4) perfect Hamming code, which is shown in Table 12.2

A receiver computes the same parity checks as the transmitter. For example, suppose the 6th bit is received in error. From Table 12.1, we see that the bit in this position is checked by the parity bits at positions 4 and 2. Therefore, parity fails at the 2nd and 4th bit positions, and the sum of the two is 6. In general, if only one bit is in error, the parity check fails at one or more of the $b_1, b_2, b_4, \ldots b_{2^r}$ positions, and the bit in error is at the position corresponding to the sum of the errored parity positions. The set of positions of the errored parity bits is also called the *error syndrome*, because it pinpoints the error.

Hamming codes, like rectangular codes, are error correcting. However, they do not require storage. Moreover, they can be precomputed and stored in a table for quick lookup. Thus, they are suitable for simple hardware and software implementation. For these reasons, a Hamming perfect-parity code is widely used in the field.

Position	Binary	Comment	Data	Parity	Checks
1	001	1 in 1's place		*	All positions with 1 in 1's place, i.e., 1,3,5,7.
2	010	1 in 2's place		*	All positions with 1 in 2's place, i.e., 2,3,6,7.
3	011	1 in 2's and 1's place	*		
4	100	1 in 4's place		*	All positions with 1 in 4's place, i.e., 4,5,6,7.
5	101	1 in 4's and 1's place	*		
6	110	1 in 4's and 2's place	*		
7	111	1 in 4's, 2's, and 1's place	*		

Table 12.1 Rules for constructing a (7,4) Hamming code.

Data	Codeword	Data	Codeword
0000	*0000000*	1000	*1110000*
0001	*1101001*	1001	*0011001*
0010	*0101010*	1010	*1011010*
0011	*1000011*	1011	*0110011*
0100	*1001100*	1100	*0111100*
0101	*0100101*	1101	*1010101*
0110	*1100110*	1110	*0010110*
0111	*0001111*	1111	*1111111*

Table 12.2: A (7,4) Hamming code.

12.2.4 Interleaved codes

The coding techniques described so far are best suited to random, nonbursty bit errors. Error bursts introduce multiple bit errors within a codeword, which cannot be detected or corrected using parity, rectangular, or Hamming codes. The standard way to solve this problem is to use *interleaving* to convert burst errors to bit errors. In this technique, m consecutive codewords are written in a $n \times m$ matrix, then transmitted column-wise instead of row-wise. Thus, a burst error of up to m bits appears as a single-bit error in each of the m codewords. These single-bit errors can then be corrected with Hamming or other parity codes. Interleaved codes require buffering the input, and so add memory cost and delay.

EXAMPLE 12.6

Construct a four-way interleaved (7, 4) Hamming code for the bit sequence 1001 0000 1101 0110.

Solution: We first use Table 12.2 to convert the data bits to their corresponding 7-bit codewords. The (7, 4) codewords for the bit sequence are written in a 7×4 matrix below.

$$
\begin{array}{ccccccc}
0 & 0 & 1 & 1 & 0 & 0 & 1 \\
0 & 0 & 0 & 0 & 0 & 0 & 0 \\
1 & 0 & 1 & 0 & 1 & 0 & 1 \\
1 & 1 & 0 & 0 & 1 & 1 & 0 \\
\end{array}
$$

In an interleaved code, we transmit the bits column-wise. Thus, the transmitted sequence is 0011 0001 1010 1000 0011 0001 1010. We see that an error burst of up to 4 bits results in up to four single-bit errors (one in each row), which a Hamming code can correct.

12.2.5   Cyclic redundancy check

A *cyclic redundancy check* (*CRC*) is one of the most popular techniques for error detection. In this technique, we treat the entire string of data bits as a single number. We divide this number by a predefined constant, called the *generator* of the code, and append the remainder to the data string. The receiver performs the same division and compares the remainder with what was transmitted. If the data string was received without errors, then the remainders match. For example, suppose the string to be transmitted is "110011," which corresponds to decimal 51. If the generator is "110" (decimal 6), the remainder is decimal 3, or binary "011." We append "011" to the data string and send it to the receiver. If the receiver received everything correctly, it should come up with the same remainder. Intuitively, it is unlikely that a corruption in the data string will result in a number that has the same remainder as the original data. In this example, for the CRC to fail, the received string should also have a remainder of 3 when divided by 6, which is unlikely. This is the basic idea behind CRC.

A detailed explanation of CRC coding requires an understanding of Boolean algebra and polynomial arithmetic beyond the scope of this book. A good introduction can be found in reference [Stallings 88, p. 107]. Here, we will merely state some results important to the engineer. Before we do so, we will need some notation.

We represent a block of $(k + 1)$ bits by a polynomial of degree k in the dummy variable x, written as $a_k x^k + \ldots + a_1 x^1 + a_0 x^0$, where a_k is 0 if the bit in that position is 0 and 1 otherwise. For example, the string "10011" is represented by the polynomial $x^4 + x + 1$.

The effectiveness of a CRC code depends on the choice of the generator G, which, when written in polynomial form, is called the *generator polynomial G(x)*. It can be shown that a CRC detects the following:

- All single-bit errors
- Almost all double-bit errors, if $G(x)$ has a factor with at least three terms
- Any odd number of errors, if $G(x)$ has a factor $x + 1$
- All bursts of up to m errors, if $G(x)$ is of degree m
- Longer burst errors with probability $1 - 2^{-m}$, if bursts are randomly distributed

Thus, with a good choice of the generator polynomial, CRCs are a powerful mechanism for error detection (and rarely correction). Standard generator polynomials are prescribed by international standards bodies, depending on the expected error pattern. Common international standards are as follows:

$$
\begin{aligned}
\textit{CRC-10} \quad & 1 + x + x^4 + x^5 + x^9 + x^{10} \\
\textit{CRC-12} \quad & 1 + x + x^2 + x^3 + x^{11} + x^{12} \\
\textit{CRC-16} \quad & 1 + x^2 + x^{15} + x^{16} \\
\textit{CRC-32} \quad & 1 + x + x^2 + x^4 + x^5 + x^7 + x^8 \\
& + x^{10} + x^{11} + x^{12} + x^{16} + x^{22} \\
& + x^{23} + x^{26} + x^{32} \\
\textit{CRC-CCITT} \quad & 1 + x^5 + x^{12} + x^{16}
\end{aligned}
$$

CRC codes are popular because they can be efficiently implemented in hardware or software. A hardware implementation requires only a shift register and some XOR gates, uses no additional storage, and can compute the CRC on-the-fly [Stallings 88, p. 109]. An efficient software algorithm is to precompute the remainder for each possible data string of a certain length (say, 16 bits) and store the result in a lookup table. The algorithm looks up the remainder for each 16-bit chunk of the input and adds these, modulus 2, to a running sum. It can be shown that this is equivalent to computing the remainder over the entire string [Sarwate 88]. Thus, we can compute the CRC for an arbitrarily long input string on-the-fly in software, with only one lookup per block of input bits.

12.2.6 | BCH and Reed–Solomon codes

Bose–Chaudhuri–Hocquenghem (BCH) codes are CRC-like codes constructed over *blocks* of m bits, instead of over single bits. In other words, the alphabet of a BCH coder is not {0, 1}, as in CRC codes, but a set of 2^m symbols, where each symbol is a distinct m-bit binary string. BCH codes are robust to burst errors, since a burst of up to m errors results in at most two errors in the BCH alphabet (for errors that span two BCH symbols). BCH codes are also some of the best-known codes for correcting random errors. The details of BCH encoding are beyond the scope of this book, but can be found in books on error coding, such as references [Blahut 90] and [PW 72].

Reed–Solomon codes are a special case of BCH codes where the block size (that is, the number of data symbols + the number of redundant symbols) is 2^m, which is also the largest possible block size for a BCH code. It can be shown that a Reed–Solomon code that has $2t$ redundant bits can correct any combination of t or fewer errors. Reed–Solomon codes are one of the best block codes for dealing with multiple bursts of errors in a codeword—one variant can correct errors up to 1200 bytes long.

12.2.7 Convolutional codes

Recall that in a block code, bits in the ith coded block are independent of the bits in the other blocks. In a convolutional code, a coded bit depends on a range of data bits, and the range is different for each coded bit. This can sometimes give better error protection properties than a block coder.

Specifically, each coded bit is obtained by *convolving* the data bits with a convolution polynomial. If the convolution polynomial has degree m, then a coded bit depends on a neighborhood of $2m$ data bits.

Convolutional coders are appropriate when there is sufficient bandwidth, the noise distribution is stationary Gaussian, and the computation possible is tightly constrained. We will study convolutional coders in detail because they lead to some powerful error coding techniques that are rapidly growing in popularity and are used in important applications such as satellite transmission, high-speed modems, and cellular links.

Figure 12.2 is an example of a simple convolutional coder. Data enters from the right into a two-stage shift register. Each data bit results in three code bits, A, B, and C, and the output of the coder is the sequence ABC. The coder shown here has 2 bits of memory that store the input bits from the last two time steps. The system can be in one of four states, depending on the values of these bits. Each input to a convolutional coder causes a state transition and a corresponding output sequence. Thus, we can represent a convolutional coder by an equivalent finite-state machine, as shown in Figure 12.3. Another

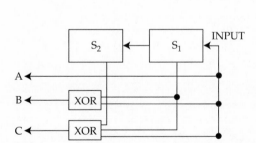

Figure 12.2: A simple convolutional coder. Data enters from the right and is stored in storage elements S1 and S2. Each input bit results in transmission of three output bits, A, B, and C.

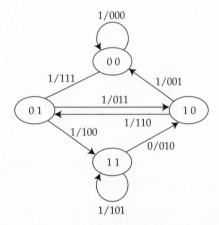

Figure 12.3: State diagram for the convolutional coder in Figure 12.2. The two storage elements S_2 and S_1 can be in one of four states. We represent each state by a 2-bit binary number, which corresponds to the states of S_2 and S_1. For example, state 01 means that S_2 is in state 0, and S_1 is in state 1. The output is shown by a 3-bit number, which corresponds to the outputs labeled A, B, and C, in Figure 12.2. Each input bit results in a new state and a corresponding output as shown.

Encoder state

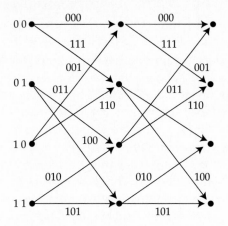

Figure 12.4: Trellis diagram for three transitions of the convolutional coder in Figure 12.2. Each circle represents a state. Transitions along upper arcs correspond to a 0 input and transitions along lower arcs correspond to a 1 input. Numbers along an arc represent the coded sequence output during that transition. An input sequence corresponds to a path in the trellis, and the corresponding output sequence can be read off from the numbers along the arcs.

representation is as a *trellis* (Figure 12.4). In a trellis, the upper line leading out from a state represents the transition on input 0, and the lower line the transition for input bit 1. The number on a line is the corresponding output. We can obtain the code for any input bit sequence by following a path from state to state in the trellis.

EXAMPLE 12.7

Compute the output of the convolutional coder in Figure 12.4 for an input 10 if the initial state is 00.

Solution: Starting from state 00 in Figure 12.4, we follow the lower arc (corresponding to an input of 1) to state 01. This results in an output of 111. On the next input, 0, we follow the upper arc to state 10, with an output of 011. Thus, the code for the sequence 10 is 111011. Note that the convolutional coder transforms 2 input bits to 6 output bits, of which 4 are redundant.

We can decode a convolutional code in many ways. A common technique, which we will study, is called *trellis* or *Viterbi* decoding. We assume that the encoder and the decoder are synchronized, so that the decoder knows which bits in the encoded sequence correspond to A, B, and C. The decoder tries to discover the sequence of states the encoder went through to generate the coded sequence. We call this sequence a *trajectory* in state space.

To see how this works, notice that in the trellis diagram, certain code sequences are prohibited in certain states. In other words, a receiver should not receive these sequences when it is that state. For example, in state 11, the code sequence 111 is prohibited. Thus, if the decoder sees a 111 when it knows that the encoder is in state 11, then at least one received bit must be corrupted. The only feasible bit sequences in state 11 are 101 and 010. If the original sequence was 101, the decoder's next state should be 11; otherwise, if the original sequence was 010, the next state should be 10. If the decoder decides to move to state 11, the received bit sequence (111) and the assumed (feasible) bit sequence (i.e., 101) differ by a Hamming distance 1; if it moves to a state 10, the corresponding distance is 2. The Viterbi decoder thus creates a set of *candidate* trajectories, all of which are feasible, but lead to different states and have corresponding *penalties* (which is the net Hamming distance between the feasible trajectory and the actual bit sequence received). Continuing with our example, the candidate trajectory leading to state 11 has a penalty 1, and the candidate leading to state 10 has a penalty 2. Without further information, the best choice for the decoder is to choose a trajectory with the minimum penalty, i.e., the trajectory leading to state 11.

Suppose the next 3 bits received are 001. We can now extend the two candidate trajectories another step and recompute their penalties. The candidate at 10 would go to state 00 with no additional penalty. The candidate at 11 does not have any obvious choice, since 001 is not a valid input in state 11. Thus, we split this trajectory into two candidates, one going to 11 with penalty $1 + 1 = 2$, and the other going to 10 with a penalty $1 + 2 = 3$. We now have the situation in Table 12.3.

Clearly, we can repeat this step on succeeding inputs to compute, for each input sequence, a set of candidate trajectories and their corresponding penalties. At the end of its operation, a Viterbi decoder declares the candidate trajectory with the minimum penalty as the most likely encoded sequence.

Notice that each infeasible codeword leads to two new elements in the set of feasible candidate trajectories. Thus, a coded sequence with k errors will result in at most 2^k can-

Trajectory	Penalty for first step	Penalty for second step	Total penalty
11−10−00	2	0	3
11−11−10	1	2	3
11−11−11	1	1	2

Table 12.3: Candidate trajectories in a convolutional coder.

didate trajectories in this set. Even if k is as small as 20, the decoder would need to consider approximately a million candidate trajectories for each input bit after the 20 errors, which is computationally infeasible. There is, however, a way to prune candidate trajectories, which makes the problem more manageable.

Suppose two trajectories reach the same state due to some input sequence. Then, their behavior for subsequent inputs is independent of the path taken to get to that state. Thus, if candidate trajectories A and B, with penalties $p(A)$ and $p(B)$, reach state S simultaneously, then their future behaviors will be identical after that point. Now, if $p(A) > p(B)$, the ultimate trajectory with prefix A would have a larger penalty than the ultimate trajectory with prefix B. If we prune A from the set of feasible trajectories, we will never have incorrectly ignored a viable solution. Because, in this example, there are only four states, at any step at most four candidates will remain after pruning. In general, if the encoder has m storage elements, the encoder and decoder will have 2^m states, and the decoder must consider no more than 2^m candidates at any given time. This result makes Viterbi decoding feasible.

Thus far, we have assumed that each input bit leads to three output bits, which leads to a coding efficiency (also called *code rate*) of only 33%. A simple generalization of the scheme is to shift k bits into $n - 1$ storage elements, then read n outputs, leading to an efficiency of k/n.

Our discussion has also assumed that a receiver can unambiguously decide whether an incoming bit is a 0 or a 1. Consider a scheme where the signal levels are $+5$ V and -5 V, and the decision threshold to decide whether a signal is a 0 or a 1 is 0 V. If the received voltage is $+0.01$ V, the receiver declares it a 0, and if the voltage is -0.01 V, the receiver declares it a 0. Thus, even a small change in the value of a received signal can result in a 0 bit being interpreted as a 1 and vice versa. An alternative decision mechanism, applicable to Viterbi decoding, is for the receiver to keep track not only of whether the incoming bit was declared a 0 or a 1, but also of the voltage level used to make this decision. Continuing with our example, the receiver stores ((1,0.01), (0, -0.01)) instead of "10." Now, when pruning candidate paths, penalties are decided not just as Hamming distances, but as the voltage difference between a feasible and errored path. This is a more effective decoding technique than Viterbi decoding with Hamming distance alone. The use of voltage levels instead of Hamming distances is also called *soft decision decoding*.

EXAMPLE 12.8

Compute the Hamming and soft distance between trajectories ((0, -5 V), (1, $+5$ V)) and ((0, -0.02 V), (1, $+0.4$ V)).

Solution: The Hamming distance is the distance between "01" and "01," which is 0. The soft distance between (0, -5), and (0, -0.02) is 4.98, and the soft distance between (1, 5) and (1, 0.4) is 4.6. Adding, we get a net soft distance of 9.58. Thus, although the transmitted and received sequences are identical from the perspective of Hamming distance, the soft distance tells us the true story, that we have little confidence in the received bit sequence.

An encoder that knows that the decoder is using soft decisions can use this fact to improve its performance. Instead of transmitting at voltage levels corresponding to only 0's and 1's, it can choose signal levels that maximize the probability that the receiver's soft decisions are correct. We call this type of coding *trellis* coding (not to be confused with trellis or Viterbi *decoding).* More details can be found in reference [Blahut 90].

12.2.8   Software coders

Most of the schemes we have studied thus far are meant to be implemented in hardware. Because software speeds are much slower than those of hardware, an efficient error-detection scheme implemented in software must use only the simplest of operations and must minimize the number of times it touches data. Moreover, in many instances, we may be willing to tolerate a higher degree of errors for speed of operation in the common (error-free) case. Thus, schemes such as rectangular coding or convolutional coding, which touch each data byte several times, are unsuitable for software implementation. We have already mentioned that CRCs can, however, be implemented relatively efficiently in software.

A common software error detection scheme, used extensively in the Internet protocol suite (for example, in IP, UDP, and TCP) is the *16-bit one's-complement* checksum [PHS 95, BBP 88]. Here, the data string is treated as a series of 16-bit words. The algorithm adds the words together, with end-around carry (that is, if an addition causes an overflow, we add 1 to the sum). The checksum is the one's complement of the sum. The receiver carries out the same computation, over both the data and the checksum. If the final sum is 0, then the data passes the checksum.

The 16-bit one's-complement checksum can catch all 1-bit errors in the data, and, if the data values are uniformly distributed, is expected to incorrectly validate corrupted data only about one time in 65,536. It is efficient, because it touches each 16-bit word only once, and, if the machine word is a multiple of 16 bits, only one or two additions per machine word of data.

12.3   Causes of packet errors

Bit-level and packet-level error control mechanisms are fundamentally different. Bit-level error control uses redundancy to detect, and possibly correct, bit errors. Packet-level error control uses bit-level or packet-level error detection to identify and discard packets in error (including those with uncorrectable bit errors), at the receiver. The receiver sends the sender either a *positive acknowledgment* (ack) for every packet correctly received, or a *negative acknowledgment* (nack) indicating which packets it did not receive. The sender uses these indications to decide which packets were lost, and retransmits them. Thus, in packet-level error control, error correction is usually based on retransmission, rather than redundancy. In this section, we study some causes for packet errors. Section 12.4 describes techniques for packet-level error control.

We can classify packets errors as (a) packet loss, (b) duplication, (c) insertion, and (d) reordering. We study these in turn.

12.3.1 Packet loss

Packet loss due to uncorrectable bit errors is common in wireless links, where loss rates as high as 40% have been measured in the field. The packet loss model for such links is roughly the same as for bit loss, which we discussed in Section 12.1.5.

In wired links, particularly fiber-optic links, undetectable bit errors are rare, and the dominant cause of errors is a temporary overload in switch and multiplexor buffers (i.e., congestion). The packet loss behavior of such a network is strongly dependent on its workload. For example, if most traffic sources are *smooth,* that is, the ratio of the standard deviation in the transmission rate to its mean is small, then overloads are uncommon and the packet loss rate is small. As the traffic becomes burstier, for the same network utilization, the loss rate increases, because transient overloads are more common. Networks that carry primarily voice and video data can expect to see fairly smooth data, so that, with reasonably small buffers, packet losses can be kept to a minimum. In data networks such as the Internet, burstiness is a fact of life, so every endpoint should expect to see, and deal with, packet loss.

We now summarize some facts about packet-loss behavior:

- For realistic workloads, packets are more likely to be lost as the network utilization increases [AMS 82, Bolot 93].

- If a switch or multiplexor drops a packet, it is more likely that consecutive packets arriving to the switch or multiplexor will also be dropped. Thus, there is a strong correlation between consecutive losses at a buffer. That is, packet losses are *bursty* [CKS 93].

- Packet losses decrease as the number of buffers available in the network increases. Under some simplifying assumptions, it can be shown that the probability of packet loss at a multiplexor decreases exponentially with the size of the buffer [AMS 82]. Recent measurements suggest, however, that these assumptions may not hold in practice. Thus, the dependence of the packet loss rate on buffer size in real networks is still a matter of debate.

- A low-bit rate (relative to the line speed), widely spaced periodic stream, such as a packetized-audio stream, sees essentially uncorrelated queue lengths and a context-independent packet loss probability at the overloaded network element. Thus, such a stream does not see bursty losses [Bolot 95].

- When measuring packet loss on the same path over the period of a day, measurements indicate a positive correlation between packet loss and metrics of end-to-end delay (such as its mean, minimum, and maximum) [Mukherjee 94].

12.3.2   Loss of fragmented data

Consider a switch or multiplexor that serves data in units of fixed-size cells. We will assume, as in ATM networks, that some of these cells represent portions of packets, and that if any cell in a packet is lost, the packet is in error. During overload, the incoming data rate is higher than the service rate, and if the overload is sustained for long enough, the data buffer at the switch or multiplexor will overflow, leading to cell loss. Suppose that fifty cells are lost during a particular loss event. If all fifty cells belong to the same packet, then the cell-loss event corresponds to a single packet loss. If the cells belong to fifty different packets, then the cell-loss event corresponds to fifty lost packets. Thus, a single cell-loss event may lead to many lost frames, a form of *error multiplication*. The degree of error multiplication depends on the arrival pattern of cells during a loss event, which is workload dependent. If overloads are caused by bursts from a single source, there may be no error multiplication. On the other hand, if many sources contribute to the overload, each of them could see a packet loss. Note that as the packet size increases, each cell loss proportionally decreases the error-free (or effective) throughput.

EXAMPLE 12.9

Assume that the cell loss rate in an ATM network is 10^{-5}, and a packet has a mean size of 100 cells. (a) What is the range of mean packet loss rates? (b) If a link serves 1000 cells/s, has a packet loss rate of 10^{-3}, and each loss recovery takes 1 s, what is the effective throughput of the link?

Solution: (a) The packet loss rate can be as low as (if all cells lost are from a single packet) and as high as 10^{-5} (if each cell lost is from a different packet). (b) Consider the time taken to serve x packets. First note that of these x packets, $x/1000$ will be lost, and it will take time $x/1000$ s to recover from these losses (assume that there are no losses during recovery). Since the link speed is 10 packets/s, the remaining $x - x/1000$ packets will take time $(x - x/1000) * 0.1$ s. Thus, the total time to send x packets is $x/1000 + (x - x/1000) * 0.1$ s, so that the effective throughput is 9.91 packets/s.

Romanow and Floyd [RF 94] studied the behavior of a TCP connection in an ATM network with cell losses. They showed that, for a fixed buffer size, as the packet size increases, the effective throughput decreases, since each cell loss event causes a larger and larger fraction of the successful cell transfers to be wasted. This can be prevented by having switches and multiplexors drop entire packets instead of cells. A clever way to do so is to mark a virtual circuit as being in the drop state whenever the buffer capacity exceeds a threshold. The switch drops cells arriving to a connection in the drop state until it sees a cell with the end-of-packet mark. At this point, the state of the circuit may revert to normal, or may persist in the drop state. In either case, switches mostly drop entire packets, without having to look through their queues. This variant of packet dropping, called *early packet discard,* substantially improves TCP performance over that of ATM networks and is further described in Section 9.7.2 [RF 94].

12.3.3 Packet duplication, insertion, and reordering

Retransmission is a common technique to compensate for packet loss. In this technique, the sender sends data, then waits for an *acknowledgment* (ack) of receipt. If it receives no answer for some time, it retransmits the packet. The packet, however, may have been correctly received, but its acknowledgment may have been delayed or lost. Thus, on retransmission, the receiver would receive a duplicate, out-of-sequence packet. This is the main cause for packet duplication and reordering in computer networks.

Packet reordering can also happen if packets belonging to the same stream follow different data paths from source to destination. For example, in the technique of *dispersity routing* [Maxemchuk 75], a source sends data to a destination along multiple paths to increase its bandwidth share in the network. Since different packets arrive at different times, the receiver sees reordered packets.

Packet insertion can happen when a packet's header is undetectably corrupted. For example, assume that two processes at a destination are expecting cells on VCIs 1 and 2. Suppose the VCI field in the header of a cell in VCI 2 is undetectably corrupted, so that the cell appears to be on VCI 1. Then, the entity waiting for a cell incorrectly receives this cell on VCI 1 at the destination, leading to a packet insertion error. Another mechanism for packet insertion is the arrival of a packet delayed beyond the close of its connection. For example, a packet on VCI 1 may be delayed in the network beyond the close of VCI 1. If a new connection at the receiver is also allocated VCI 1, it may incorrectly accept the delayed packet, leading to packet insertion.

12.4   Packet-error detection and correction

In the preceding section, we studied some causes for packet errors. In this section, we focus on mechanisms for packet-error detection and correction. We will assume that bit-error detection and correction mechanisms are simultaneously active, so that the information in a packet header used by a packet-level error-control mechanism is very unlikely to be corrupted.

We start with a description of sequence numbers, which are the first line of defense against packet loss, reordering, and insertion.

12.4.1 Sequence numbers

A sequence number in a packet's header indicates its unique position in the sequence of packets transmitted by a source. A sender labels each packet that has not been previously transmitted with a consecutive sequence number in its header. Sequence numbers help the receiver to detect packet loss, reordering, insertion, and duplication.

- Packet reordering and duplication are immediately obvious with sequence numbers.

- Packet loss shows up as a *gap* in the sequence numbers seen by the receiver. For example, assume a transmitter sends packets with sequence numbers $0, 1, 2, \ldots$. If the packet with sequence number 4 is lost, the receiver receives packets with sequence numbers 0, 1, 2, 3, 5, 6, etc., with a gap between sequence numbers 3 and 5.

- We can detect packet insertion if the sequence number of the misdelivered packet is very different from the sequence numbers of packets already on that connection. For example, if the last packet received on a connection has a sequence number 5, and the misdelivered packet has a sequence number of 41,232, the receiver can guess that the packet was misdelivered.

We will often use the abstraction of a *sequence number space,* which is the subset of the natural numbers that represents all possible sequence numbers in a packet header. If a sequence number is n bits long, the space is of size 2^n. When a sequence number reaches the largest number in this space, it *wraps around* to the smallest number in the space, typically 0. For example, if a sequence number is 3 bits long, the sequence number space is {0, 1, 2, 3, 4, 5, 6, 7}. When the sequence number reaches 7, the next sequence number wraps around to 0.

In the next two subsections, we will study two important considerations when using sequence numbers: choosing a sequence number length, and choosing an initial sequence number.

12.4.2 Sequence number size

Because sequence numbers take up header space, and every packet must have a header, it is important to minimize the number of bits devoted to a sequence number. How long should a sequence number be? The intuition here is that the sequence number should be long enough so that, taking sequence number wraparound into account, a sender can disambiguate acks even in the worst case. Our treatment is based on reference [Watson 81].

We define the following terms and symbols:

MPL or *maximum packet lifetime:* The maximum time a packet can exist in the network (also called, in TCP, *maximum segment lifetime,* or *MSL*) (in seconds)

T: The maximum time a sender waiting for an ack persists in retransmitting a packet (in seconds)

A: The maximum time a receiver can hold a packet before sending an ack (in seconds)

R: The maximum transmission rate of the sender (in packets/second)

Consider a packet with sequence number, say, 4, that is repeatedly lost by the network. The sender keeps retransmitting the packet until a time T after it first transmitted the packet. In the worst case, the receiver successfully receives the packet the final time it is retransmitted, at time $T + MPL$. The receiver may now dally for a time A before sending an ack, which takes at most an additional MPL time to reach the sender. The sender may have generated as many as $(2\,MPL + T + A)\,R$ more sequence numbers in that time, so if the sequence number space wraps around, another packet with sequence number 4 may be transmitted before the sender received the earlier ack. Thus, the arrival of an ack for packet 4 at the sender would be ambiguous. To remove this ambiguity, we must ensure that the sequence number is at least n bits long, where $2^n \geq (2\,MPL + T + A)\,R$. This is the desired lower bound on the sequence number size.

EXAMPLE 12.10

Assume that the MPL is 2 min, $T = 1$ min, $A = 500$ ms, and the source transmits no faster than 2 Mbps. What is the smallest possible sequence number size if the packet size is at least 40 bytes?

Solution: The largest possible number of packets that could be generated while some packet is still active is given by the expression $(2MPL + T + A)R$. We have:

$$MPL = 2 \text{ min} = 120 \text{ s}$$

$$T = 1 \text{ min} = 60 \text{ s}$$

$$A = 500 \text{ ms} = 0.5 \text{ s}$$

$$R = 2 \text{ Mbps} = 2^6/8 \text{ bytes/s} = 2^6/(40 * 8) \text{ packets/s}$$

Plugging this into the right hand side of the expression, we get its value to be $(2 * 120 + 60 + 0.5)\, 2^6/(40 * 8) = 1{,}878{,}125$. This corresponds to a minimum sequence number size of 21 bits, since $2^{20} = 1{,}048{,}576$, and $2^{21} = 2{,}097{,}152$.

Note that the lower bound on sequence number size requires a bound on MPL. Theoretically, we can ensure that a packet does not live in the network longer than a given MPL by placing a generation time in its header. Network elements can discard packets with a time stamp more than MPL old. This technique requires additional space in the packet header and additional computation at each hop, and so is not used in practice. Instead, the header typically contains a counter decremented by each intermediate network element. If a network element decrements the counter to zero, it discards the packet. Although this technique does not directly give us a bound on MPL, if we can estimate the worst-case delay at each network element, knowing the largest possible value of the counter, we can roughly bound MPL. This is sufficient for most engineering purposes. This technique is used in IP, and more details can be found in Section 15.3.2.

We can make the sequence number space much smaller if a source does not retransmit packets, because it only needs to be large enough to detect losses and reordering. Two factors, then, determine the minimum size of the sequence space. First, a single burst loss should not lead to a seamless wraparound in the sequence space; otherwise, a receiver would be unable to detect this burst loss. For example, if the sequence number is 3 bits long, the sequence space is of size 8, and a loss of 8 packets causes a wraparound. If a receiver received packet 2, did not receive packets with sequence numbers 3, 4, 5, 6, 7, 0, 1, 2, and then received packet 3, it would be unable to detect the packet loss. Thus, if we expect the longest possible burst length to be 8 packets, the sequence number should be at least 4 bits long. In general, if the largest possible burst loss is expected to be n packets, then the sequence number must be longer than $\log(n)$ bits. Second, a receiver must not mistake a reordered packet for a valid packet. If the largest possible reordering span is of length n, then a similar argument shows that the sequence number should be longer than $\log(n)$ bits. In practice, we choose the sequence number to be the larger of the two lower bounds. This, however, is usually much smaller than the sequence number required when retransmissions are possible.

In real life, a system designer may not be able to tightly bound the longest possible error burst or reordering span. The only recourse, then, is to design for the worst-case scenario, add a fudge factor, and hope for the best. With any luck, the network design will be obsolete before the worst-case scenario actually happens!

Sequence numbers can be used for error control at both the datalink and the transport layer. Datalink layers usually do not retransmit data, whereas transport layers usually do. Thus, we can use a smaller sequence number at the datalink layer than at the transport layer.

12.4.3   Dealing with packet insertion

Packet-switched networks may delay a packet for up to one MPL inside the network. We should somehow identify and reject a delayed packet arriving at a connection; otherwise, we will have a packet insertion error. One can completely avoid the problem by flushing every packet belonging to a connection on connection termination. This is easy if every layer in the network is connection oriented, so that the connection-teardown message propagates to every switch controller along the path. On receiving this message, each controller instructs its local switch to flush all packets belonging to that connection.

For connections layered over a connectionless network, however, there is no explicit connection termination message. Thus, we have to use more sophisticated schemes to solve the problem. We will study some of them next.

Before we begin, we need to know how connections are identified when a connection is established over a connectionless network. In most connectionless networks, packets exchanged between two connected processes carry a pair of numbers, called *port numbers*, identifying the connection endpoints (this is the case when TCP runs over IP). For example, process A on a machine with address 1.2.3 may be associated with port number 123, and process B on a machine with address 4.5.6 may be associated with port number 456. Then, a packet from the first process to the second carries the source address (1.2.3), the destination address (4.5.6), the source port number (123), and the destination port number (456). These four numbers uniquely identify a connection.

The insertion problem arises when a delayed packet from an old connection has the same set of four connection identifiers as a newer connection, whose sequence number is in the range used by the newer connection. Continuing with our example, suppose packets with sequence number 1, 2, and 3 are sent from process A on machine 1.2.3 to process B on machine 4.5.6. Assume that packets 2 and 3 are delayed in the network for one MPL, and, meanwhile, process B closes the connection (Figure 12.5). If (a) the same or other processes on these machines open a new connection, and (b) the machines reassign these processes the same port numbers, and (c) the receiving process in the new connection receives delayed packets 2 and 3 just after packet 1 of the new connection, then it may accept the delayed packets as part of the new connection.

One way to avoid the problem is to label each packet with an *incarnation number* that is unique for each connection between a pair of endpoints. Thus, packets from different connections can be distinguished by their incarnation numbers. This has the problem that each packet needs an additional field in the header, which reduces the bandwidth efficiency. Moreover, incarnation numbers need to be remembered across system crashes. Otherwise, machine 1.2.3 may crash and, on rebooting, reuse an incarnation number. This requires memory that can survive crashes. Such memory, called *stable storage,* is not

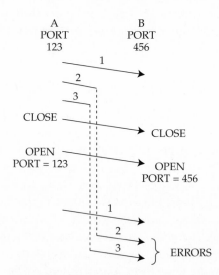

Figure 12.5: Problems with delayed packest for connections layered over connectionless networks. Packets 2 and 3 from the old connection cannot be distinguished from packets 2 and 3 of the new connection. Thus, B accepts the delayed packets as valid.

generally available, and it tends to be expensive. This scheme, therefore, is not popular in practice.

A second solution is to reassign a port number only after one MPL. Then, by the time a process can reuse a port number, all old packets would have been discarded. This requires an endpoint to remember the time at which it assigned every port number. If the set of possible port numbers is large, this takes storage, which can be expensive. Moreover, an argument similar to the one in the previous paragraph shows that the system must remember these times across crashes, which again requires expensive stable storage.

Unix-like systems, therefore, use a third scheme, where an end-system assigns port numbers to processes serially, starting from port number 1024. This makes it unlikely, but not impossible, that a newly opened connection will have the same port number as a recently closed one. One way the scheme can fail is when a process opens and closes connections so rapidly that the port numbers wrap around back to 1024 before the expiration of one MPL. To solve this problem, we ensure that successive connections initiated from the same endpoint use different initial sequence numbers by choosing the initial sequence number from a register that is incremented every clock tick. This guarantees that even if port numbers wrap around, connections that share the same port number choose different initial sequence numbers. Since the new connection's initial sequence number would be much larger than that of the delayed packet, this prevents packet insertion. The modified scheme, however, is still not foolproof! If the computer running process A crashes and reboots, it might reassign port 1024 to another process before the expiration of one MPL. Moreover, since the initial sequence number register is reset on a crash, the sequence numbers might still match.

There are several ways to avoid this problem. First, on a reboot, a machine could remember the port numbers and sequence numbers it used earlier. This again requires stable storage, which rules it out as a general solution. Second, we could prevent the clock from resetting on startup. This requires a battery backup for the clock, and we again rule it out for the same reasons. Third, and this is the solution used in practice, a rebooted computer can keep silent for one MPL. This flushes all the packets from the earlier connection from the network. So, even if a packet from a new connection has the same port number *and* the same sequence number as a potentially delayed packet, by the time the new connection is allowed to start, the delayed packet would have been discarded. This finally solves the problem.

Internet hosts usually use an MPL of 30 s to 2 min. Since a crashed computer takes around 2 min to reboot anyway, we expect all delayed packets to have been flushed by the time the computer restarts. If a computer reboots faster than one MPL, it should remain silent for the rest of the interval (though this is rarely done in practice!).

To sum up, the solution requires us (a) to assign ports serially, (b) to choose an initial sequence number from a clock, and (c) to ensure that a system remains silent for at least one MPL after a crash. When these three conditions are fulfilled, we can guarantee that no packet will be inserted into a conversation (unless, of course, the header is undetectably corrupted). This solution is mandated for all Internet-connected hosts.

12.4.4   Three-way handshake

After choosing an initial sequence number (ISN), as described in Section 12.4.3, a sender must inform its peer about the ISN it plans to use for the connection. The receiver stores this value in its expected sequence number (ESN) for that connection. If the connection is bidirectional (as in TCP), the receiver will, in turn, tell the sender the ISN it plans to use for the reverse connection. The ESN is necessary to distinguish packets from expired connections from packets from active connections, as discussed in Section 12.4.3.

A naive way to exchange ISNs is for the connection initiator to start the connection with a SYNchronization (SYN) packet containing its ISN. The connection acceptor replies with a SYN containing its choice of ISN. The ISNs are then stored in the ESN state of the connection initiator and connection acceptor. Note that the SYN packet itself is not protected against delayed packets because, when a SYN is received, the recipient does not know the expected sequence number. Thus, a delayed SYN can confuse the acceptor, as explained next (Figure 12.6).

Suppose processes A and B are trying to establish a full-duplex connection, and B is the connection acceptor in the "wait-for-SYN" state. Suppose a delayed SYN from A arrives at B. Since B has no way to tell that this is a delayed SYN, it accepts the ISN as valid. B then replies with its own SYN containing its choice of ISN. If, meanwhile, A has already launched its SYN, it might think that the SYN from B was in response to its latest SYN, and consider the connection open. However, B will reject A's second SYN as a duplicate and will choose an ESN from the earlier SYN. Thus, every subsequent packet from A has an incorrect sequence number and is rejected.

We can solve this problem by adding an extra step to the connection setup (Figure 12.7). In the first step, A sends B a SYN with its ISN, as before. In the second step, B picks an ISN and sends a SYN-ACK packet that contains B's ISN and an ack of A's ISN. In the third step, A acknowledges B's choice of ISN with an ACK packet carrying B's ISN.

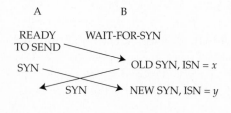

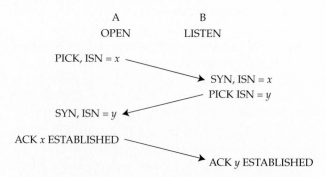

Figure 12.6: A simple two-way handshake is susceptible to errors from old SYN packets. An old SYN might be accepted by a receiver awaiting a connection request, so that the new (correct) SYN is incorrectly rejected.

Figure 12.7: Three-way handshake. In a three-way handshake, the initiator (A) sends the acceptor (B) a SYNchronize packet with its choice of ISN. B replies with a SYN-ACK that contains B's ISN and also acks A's ISN. If the SYN-ACK is valid, A replies with an ACK of B's SYN. B establishes a connection only when its SYN is correctly acked.

When the B receives this packet, both A and B know each other's correct ISN. It can be shown that a three-way handshake is the minimum required to achieve this happy situation.

Note that if a delayed SYN arrives at B, A gets a SYN-ACK that contains the old ISN. It can inform B to discard this connection with a RESET packet. In the same way, if A replies to B with an incorrect ACK packet, B can send A a RESET packet. On receiving a RESET packet, an endpoint replies with a RESET-ACK and drops the connection.

12.4.5 Dealing with system crashes

If a system crashes while it has open connections, then when it restarts, the remote end must not confuse packets from reestablished connections with packets from old connections. A connection where one endpoint has crashed, has closed the connection, or is otherwise unaware of the connection is called a *half-open* connection.

We use four techniques to deal with half-open connections. First, on booting up, an endpoint waits for all of its previously unacknowledged packets to die away, as described in Section 12.4.3. Second, also on booting up, an endpoint rejects all acks that arrive during a "quiet time." In the worst case, a sender may have sent a packet just before the endpoint crashed, which would take MPL to reach the receiver. The ack may return as late as $2 * MPL + A$ seconds later. By discarding all incoming packets for $2 * MPL + A$, the endpoint can protect itself from acknowledgments arriving to half-open connections. Third, an endpoint times out a connection if there has been no activity for some time, say, $2 * MPL$. Thus, if an endpoint reboots, all endpoints that are its connection peers automatically abort the connections. (If an endpoint wants to maintain a connection that would otherwise be timed out, it should periodically send a dummy "keep-alive" packet.) Fourth, and finally, endpoints actively detect and abort half-open connections. If an endpoint receives an unsolicited packet, that is, a packet on an unestablished connection, from a system that erroneously thinks a connection is still up, it should send back a RESET packet to abort the connection. This interlocked set of mechanisms allows us to provide error-free packet transmission despite system crashes and half-open connections.

12.4.6 Loss detection

Thus far, we have assumed that a lost packet is retransmitted by its sender. There are two ways in which a sender can find out that a loss has occurred. First, it can detect a loss with a *timeout*, and second, it can be told about the loss by the receiver using a *negative acknowledgment*. We study these two schemes next.

Timeouts

A sender can use timeouts to detect losses by setting a timer every time it sends a packet. If it does not receive an ack before the timer expires (i.e., times out), it guesses that the packet or its ack was lost and retransmits the packet. The tricky part is in choosing a timeout interval wisely, because a poor choice can degrade performance. If the timer interval is too small, variations in packet service time in the network trigger spurious timeouts, and if the timer interval is too large, a loss is corrected only after a long, annoying pause. We now study some techniques for choosing timer values.

The simplest way to set a timer is to choose a timer interval *a priori*. This works well if the system is well understood and the variation in packet-service times is small. Fixed timeouts are common in simple, special-purpose systems where these assurances can be made.

A better way to choose a timeout is to base it on past measurements of the round-trip time (RTT), which is the measured time interval between sending a packet and receiving an ack for it. If the receiver acknowledges every packet, and the sender does not receive an ack one RTT after it sent the packet, it can guess that the packet was lost. Thus, the timeout value should be on the order of one RTT. If the system has no variability, the timeout value can be exactly one RTT. However, most practical systems use a value somewhat larger than one RTT (usually twice the measured RTT) to deal with variations in packet-processing time and queuing delay.

As a sender sends a series of packets, it receives a series of acks, and thus accumulates a series of RTT measurements. Instead of using the last measured RTT to set the timer, it makes sense to *smooth* the series to eliminate random fluctuations (noise). A common technique for doing so is based on the *exponential averaging filter,* which we describe next.

If $r(k)$ represents the measured value of the RTT using the kth packet, and a is a tuning parameter in the range $[0,1]$, then the output of the filter is a smooth RTT estimate, $s(k)$, which is given by:

$$s(k) = as(k-1) + (1-a)\,r(k) \tag{12.2}$$

In other words, the estimate adds a fraction of the new RTT to itself, retaining a fraction a of past history. The closer a is to 1.0, the larger the weight placed on past history, with a correspondingly smaller dependence on recent measurements. Thus, if the RTTs vary quickly, choosing a small a allows the estimate to track the input quickly. Conversely, if RTTs vary slowly, choosing a large a allows the estimate to ignore most of the noise. Given this estimate, the timeout is chosen to be $bs(k)$, where b is a constant that reflects the variability in packet-processing time and queuing delay in the system. Typical values for b are 1.5 to 2, and for a are 0.6 to 0.9. (TCP recommends $a = 0.9$ and $b = 2$.)

An exponential averager is sensitive to the initial value if a is close to 1 and tracks the input closely if a is close to 0. Spikes in the input are smoothed out better if a is close to 1. Thus, the choice of a is critical. Static choices of a tend not to work well if the system dynamics change over time. Ways to adapt a dynamically as a function of the workload are presented in references [FKY 81, KK 92].

Time series	Initial 1, a 0.1	Initial 1, a 0.9	Initial 0.1, a 0.1	Initial 0.1, a 0.9
0.1	.190	.910	.100	.100
0.15	.154	.834	.145	.105
0.17	.164	.767	.167	.111
0.18	.178	.708	.169	.118
0.50	.467	.687	.467	.156
0.19	.217	.638	.217	.163
0.20	.201	.592	.201	.167
0.19	.191	.553	.191	.169

Table 12.4: The influence of a and the initial estimate on exponential averaging.

EXAMPLE 12.11

Compute the series of estimator values for initial values 0.1 and 1.0, with a 0.1 and 0.9 given the measured round-trip times to be 0.1, 0.15. 0.17, 0.18, 0.5, 0.19, 0.20, 0.19 (note the spike in the fifth input value to 0.5).

Solution: See Table 12.4. Note that (a) the effect of the initial value rapidly disappears when a is 0.1; (b) when a is 0.9, the spike to 0.5 is almost completely ignored; (c) if a is 0.9, choosing an initial value that is in the right range dramatically improves the estimator.

A better estimate for the timeout is based on the mean deviation in the RTT [Jacobson 88]. In this technique, we maintain an additional error term $e(k)$ and its smoothed estimate $m(k)$. These are computed as follows:

$$s(k) = (1 - a)r(k) + as(k - 1)$$
$$e(k) = |s(k) - r(k)|$$
$$m(k) = (1 - a)e(k) + am(k - 1)$$
$$timeout(k) = s(k) + bm(k)$$

(12.3)

The term m measures the mean deviation from the mean and is an estimate of the standard deviation in r. If the distribution of the RTTs is approximately Gaussian, we expect a packet to be processed with time $s + bm$, where different values of b give different confidence intervals. So, for example, if $b = 5$, we expect fewer than 1% of packets to be delayed beyond this timeout value.

Problems with choosing timer values

The previous paragraphs have presented some clever ways to choose timeout based on measuring RTTs. However, even the best timeout estimates have some intrinsic problems [Zhang 87]. For example, consider timeout values based on an exponential average of the round-trip times. First, it is not clear what the initial value for the timeout estimate s should be. This is particularly hard to deal with when a is large, so that the system converges slowly from the initial value of the estimate to the true RTT. Second, measuring the RTT is difficult in the presence of packet losses. When losses are few, every packet is acked, and a sender can correctly measure RTTs. However, when losses are bursty, as during congestion episodes, the variability in the RTTs is large. Moreover, if an ack acknowledges more than one packet, determining the packet from which the RTT should be measured is difficult. (One way to work around this, called *Karn's algorithm*, is to ignore *all* RTT measurements from retransmitted packets [KP 87].) Finally, even if we correctly determine the timeout, it is still not a good indicator of the system state. If a packet S is timed out, one of several things may have happened: S may be awaiting transmission at some link. It may have been correctly received, but its ack may have been lost. Or, finally, the network may actually have dropped it. The sender cannot choose among these situations solely from the timeout. Thus, timeouts should be used rarely, and if used, must be augmented with other information to disambiguate between possible system states.

Negative acknowledgments

One way to avoid timeouts entirely is for a sender to be informed by the receiver that a packet has been lost by means of a negative acknowledgment or *nack*. A receiver sends a nack when it detects a gap in the sequence of packets it receives. A nack contains a range of sequence numbers of packets that have been lost and must be retransmitted. On receiving a nack, the sender retransmits these packets.

The problem with nacks is that they are generated during loss events, which are typically caused by buffer overflow during congestion. In other words, they add to the network load precisely when it is already overloaded. Of course, nacks and packets travel in opposite directions, so packet congestion does not necessarily indicate that the reverse path is also congested. Nevertheless, the network is likely to be overloaded, and it seems somewhat risky to add to the load. A second problem with nacks is that if the nacks themselves are lost, then the receiver must retransmit them. This moves the time-out problem from the sender to the receiver, but does not solve the problem of determining what timeout value should be used. For these two reasons, many recent protocols prefer timeouts to nacks.

12.4.7   Retransmissions

Timeouts suggest that a packet was lost—the retransmission strategy decides *which* packets to retransmit on a loss. Moreover, some retransmission strategies can detect packet loss *without* a timeout. Two retransmission strategies are in common use: *go-back-n* and *selective retransmission.*

Go-back-n

Before studying go-back-n, we make a small diversion to understand the notion of an *error-control window,* which is the smallest contiguous subset of the sequence space that contains the sequence numbers of all the packets transmitted but not acknowledged. In other words, a sender does not know whether packets in its error-control window have been successfully received or have been lost. For example, if packets with sequence numbers 5–10 have been transmitted, and only sequence numbers 7 and 8 are known to be correctly received, the error-control window is of size 6 and spans the range 5–10.

It is often useful to limit the size of the error-control window, for reasons we will discuss shortly. For the moment, assume that we fix, in advance, the largest allowed size of the error-control window. When the sender sends a packet, the window expands by 1. Thus, the limit on the size of the error-control window eventually forces the source to stop. Each ack shrinks the window by 1, allowing a blocked sender to send another packet. Note that sending a packet and receiving an ack both shift the window one step forward in sequence space (Figure 12.8). Thus, we call this mechanism *sliding-window* error control.

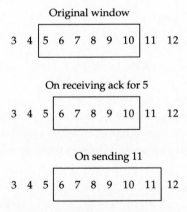

Figure 12.8: Sliding window. An error control window is the smallest subset of the sequence number space that spans across all packets sent but still unacknowledged. The window moves one step to the right on packet transmission or acknowledgment receipt. Thus, it "slides" to the right during the course of a transmission.

Returning to go-back-n, in this strategy, a timeout (or nack) causes the entire error-control window to be retransmitted. For example, a sender that has sequence numbers 5–10 in its error-control window would retransmit all six packets on a timeout. We can now see the reason to limit the size of the error-control window with go-back-n. The larger the error-control window, the more the sender has to retransmit on a time-out or nack. Thus, in go-back-n, we prefer to use the smallest feasible error-control window.

Besides its simplicity, go-back-n has several other advantages. First, it is conservative, because a single loss triggers a retransmission of every possible lost packet. Thus, it is suitable when losses are bursty. Second, the receiver's algorithm is also very simple: it accepts a packet if it is in sequence, and rejects it otherwise. Third, a receiver does not require any storage for out-of-order packets. However, go-back-n wastes bandwidth, because more packets are retransmitted than are strictly necessary. Moreover, if the original loss was due to buffer overload, the burst of packets triggered by go-back-n is likely to contribute to the overload, making it worse. Unless checked by other forces, this can lead to a state where the network carries only retransmissions, and thus makes no net progress! We call this *congestion collapse*.

Because of its waste of bandwidth, a sender using go-back-n can never fully use the link's capacity, unless there are no losses. We can compute the link utilization as a function of the packet loss probability and the error-control window size. Let the packet loss probability be p, and the window size be w. Then, with go-back-n, the maximum link efficiency (the percentage of the link bandwidth used by non-retransmitted packets) is:

$$\frac{1 - p}{1 - p + p^w} \tag{12.4}$$

[DJNS 93]. Note that, keeping the end-to-end propagation delay constant, w increases with link speed (because more packets will be outstanding when more packets can be transmitted in a given amount of time). Thus, the link efficiency *decreases* with link speed for a given probability of loss. For reasonable window sizes, the efficiency degrades rapidly for error rates larger than about 1 in 10,000.

EXAMPLE 12.12

Compute the maximum link efficiency with go-back-n when $p = 0.01$ and $w = 250$ packets. Recompute this when $p = 10^{-5}$.

Solution: For $p = 0.01$, the efficiency is bounded by $(1 - 0.01) / (1 - 0.01 + 0.01 * 250)$ = 0.283. For $p = 10^{-5}$, the efficiency bound improves to 0.997.

Selective retransmission

Selective retransmission is a more intelligent strategy than go-back-n. Here the sender uses additional information to decide which portion of its window is likely to have been lost. This information can come in many ways:

- Each ack from the receiver can carry a bit map of the current error-control window, marking the packets received. Thus, on a timeout, the sender need only retransmit packets that the receiver has not acknowledged. Continuing with our example, if the window is 6 packets, and packets 7 and 8 have been received, the ack for packet 8 might carry the bitmap 001100. On a timeout, if no further information is received, the sender can assume that packets 5, 6, 9, and 10 are lost and can retransmit them. This scheme requires the overhead of a bit map for every ack.

- To avoid the bit-map overhead, the receiver might periodically send a STATE packet with a bit map containing sequence numbers of all the packets that it has received in the recent past [CZL 87, Henderson 95, NRS 90]. The sender can use this information in much the same way as in the previous paragraph.

- The sender might do *fast retransmission* [Jacobson 90]. Assume that every ack carries the sequence number of the last in-sequence packet seen by the receiver (also called the *cumulative acknowledgment*). If the sender sees the ack sequence number repeated, this indicates either a packet loss or a reordering. For example, if the receiver received packets up to 5 in sequence, but then got packets 7, 8, and 9, then its acks would repeat the cumulative acknowledgment for 5, since this was the last packet received in proper sequence. When the sender receives the ack due to packet 7 with a repeated cumulative acknowledgment, it guesses that 6 was not received, either because it was lost, or because 6 was reordered, perhaps after 7. When the sender receives the ack due to packet 8, the same two possibilities hold, except that 6 must now be reordered after 8. If the cumulative sequence number repeats several times, the sender can guess with high probability that 6 was lost. The sender could use this information to retransmit 6. In general, the rule is that if a cumulative ack repeats several times, then the sender should retransmit the packet with a sequence number one larger than the cumulative ack. In connection-oriented networks, where packet reordering is very rare, even a single repeated cumulative ack is sufficient to trigger a retransmission. Note that this scheme does not require any timers. On the other hand, it does not work well if more than one packet was lost within an error-control window.

The advantage of selective retransmission is that a sender retransmits only the packets which were lost, thus conserving bandwidth. However, both the sender and the receiver need more complex error-control algorithms. Moreover, a receiver needs to buffer packets out of order, awaiting retransmission of a lost packet. As with go-back-n, selective retransmission works best with a limit on the size of the error-control window, since this limits the size of the buffer the receiver needs to reorder out-of-order packets. To see this, consider the situation where the error control window is of size 4, and the source has sent packets 5, 6, 7, and 8. The source cannot send packet 9 before it receives an ack for 5. Now, suppose that 5 is lost, but 6, 7, and 8 are correctly received. The receiver can either drop these packets, or hold on to them, awaiting 5. The source will eventually time out and retransmit 5. When the receiver receives 5, if it has saved 6, 7, and 8, it can pass packets 5–8 to the upper layer. Note that for this to work, the receiver may have to save all but one packet of the error-control window, which requires buffers. Thus, limiting the size of the error-control window reduces the number of buffers needed at the receiver.

SMART

A recent proposal, called SMART (Simple Method to Aid ReTransmissions), combines the benefits of selective retransmissions and go-back-n [KM 97]. In this scheme, each ack from a receiver carries two pieces of information: the last in-sequence packet received, and the sequence number of the packet that caused the ack to be sent. For example, if the receiver received packets 5, 7, 8, 10, it would send acks (5, 5), (5, 7), (5, 8), (5, 10), where the first element of the pair is the cumulative ack, and the second element is the sequence number of the packet initiating the ack. A sender can use this information to construct a bit map of the received packets, exactly as in the first selective retransmission scheme discussed above. However, we avoid the overhead of carrying a bit map in each ack.

When the sender sees a repeated cumulative acknowledgment, it does a fast retransmission, as discussed earlier. Continuing with our example, on receiving (5, 7), the sender immediately sends 6. When the sender gets (5, 8), it knows that 5 has been received, 6 has been retransmitted, 7 has been received, and so has 8. So, it takes no action. However, when it receives (5, 10), it notices that 9 has been neither retransmitted nor received; thus, it retransmits 9.

This scheme is not effective if retransmitted packets themselves are lost. To deal with that, the sender periodically inspects the last cumulative acknowledgment it received. If this value does not change for some time, the sender guesses that its retransmission of the cumulative acknowledgment+1 was lost, and retransmits it. In the worst case, on a timeout, the entire window is retransmitted, as in go-back-n, except that packets known to have been correctly received are not retransmitted. Thus, the scheme combines the efficiency of selective retransmission (but without its overhead) and the conservatism of go-back-n (but without its inefficiency). However, like selective retransmission, it requires a complicated algorithm and also buffers at the receiver.

12.4.8 Forward error correction

Unlike bit-level error control schemes, none of packet-level error control schemes we have discussed so far have used redundancy for error control. In fact, we can use redundancy for packet-level error control as well. This is called *forward error correction* (*FEC*).

For example, if all packets are the same size, and if every eighth packet is a parity check over the previous seven, the loss of any one of the eight packets can be corrected.

The advantage of forward error correction is that a receiver can recover from a packet loss without a retransmission. For real-time information, such as voice and video, the retransmission delay, which is at least as long as the round-trip time, is larger than can be ergonomically tolerated. Thus, FEC schemes are attractive for real-time data streams, and for links with long propagation delays, such as satellite links.

FEC has several disadvantages. First, error correction can substantially increase the load from a source. Because packet losses increase with load, FEC may actually cause more losses, degrading overall performance [Biersack 92]. Moreover, FEC is not effective when the packet losses are bursty, as is the case with high-speed networks [CKS 93]. Finally, FEC increases the delay in end-to-end transmission, because a receiver must wait for the entire FEC block to be received before it can process the packets in the block. However, if packets from a stream arrive spaced far enough apart that they are not affected by the bursty losses, and the error correction overhead is designed to be small, then FEC schemes might perform well [Bolot 93]. Although some standards for audio and video transmission require FEC, at least from the research perspective, it appears that the jury is still out on FEC schemes.

12.5 Summary

Data transmission in a network suffers from bit and packet errors. We distinguish between bit-level and packet-level error control, because they have different causes and different solutions. Both single-bit and multibit errors can be detected and corrected using schemes that add redundancy to the transmitted data, such as parity, Hamming codes, CRC, and convolutional codes. Packet errors include not only damage due to bit errors, but also losses, duplication, insertion, and reordering. Packet errors can be corrected with sequence numbers, timeouts, and retransmissions. Each of these techniques requires careful attention to details such as the choice of the initial sequence number, the choice of timer values, and determining which packets to retransmit. When properly done, error control allows us to reliably transport a packet across a series of unreliable links.

Table 12.5 summarizes the techniques described in this chapter.

Review Questions

1. What differentiates packet errors from bit errors?
2. What is SNR?
3. Why are scramblers needed in digital transmission lines?
4. What is protection switching?
5. What is an (n, k) block code?
6. What are even and odd parity?
7. Can a rectangular code correct two bit errors?

Bit errors	Causes (12.1)	Gaussian noise (12.1.1)
		Non-Gaussian noise (12.1.2)
		Loss of synchronization (12.1.3)
		Scramblers (12.1.4)
		Protection switching (12.1.5)
		Handoffs and fading (12.1.6)
	Detection and correction (12.2)	Parity (12.2.1)
		Rectangular codes (12.2.2)
		Hamming codes (12.2.3)
		Interleaved codes (12.2.4)
		CRC (12.2.5)
		BCH and Reed–Solomon (12.2.6)
		Convolutional codes (12.2.7)
		Software codes (12.2.8)
Packet errors	Causes (12.3)	Packet loss (12.3.1)
		Packet duplication, insertion, and reordering (12.3.3)
	Detection and correction (12.4)	Sequence numbers (12.4.1)
		Choosing the initial sequence number (12.4.3)
		Three-way handshake (12.4.4)
		Timeout (12.4.6)
		Retransmission (12.4.7)
		Forward error correction (12.4.8)

Table 12.5: Summary of techniques studied in Chapter 12.

8. What is the Hamming distance between two codewords?
9. What is a perfect code?
10. What is an error syndrome?
11. What is an interleaved code?
12. Express 1101 1011 as a polynomial.
13. What purposes does a sequence number serve?
14. What problem does a three-way handshake solve?
15. How do nacks work? What problem do they cause during congestion?
16. What is the go-back-n retransmission protocol?
17. Why should timeouts be avoided as far as possible?
18. What is forward error correction?

Exercises

12.1. If 0 V and 5 V represent 0 and 1, respectively, and the standard deviation of the noise is 0.3 V, compute the SNR in decibels.

12.2. What is the error multiplication introduced by a scrambler described by the polynomial $1 + x^{23}$?

12.3. Compute the even and odd parity for the hexadecimal string 0x CE11 FEED. Will parity succeed on 0x CE00 FEED?

12.4. Can a rectangular code detect three errors? Why or why not?

12.5. Compute the 4×4 even rectangular code for 0xCE11.

12.6. What is the percent redundancy in a 31-bit perfect codeword?

12.7. What is the smallest pairwise Hamming distance between the codewords 000, 011, 101, and 111?

12.8. In a (63, 57) perfect Hamming code, which bit positions are checked by bit 16?

12.9. Compute the error syndrome if codeword 000 0000 in a (7, 4) Hamming code is corrupted to 010 0000.

12.10. What is the largest burst error that can be detected by a five-way interleaved dual error detecting code?

12.11. What is the output of the convolutional coder in Figure 12.4 for an input 010110 if the initial state is 01?

12.12. Give the trajectories and penalties for a convolutional decoder starting from initial state 01 when its input is 011 111 111.

12.13. Generalize Example 12.9 to derive an expression for normalized effective throughput as a function of the frame size S, frame loss rate l, loss-recovery throughput ratio r, loss-recovery time t, and normal throughput T.

12.14. If the sequence number is 32 bits long (as in IP), $T \leq 1.5$ Mbps, $R = A = 500$ ms, what is the largest allowed MPL for a minimum packet size of 40 bytes?

12.15. Is a two-way handshake sufficient for termination?

12.16. If the sender has packets 10–15 outstanding, and the receiver sends a nack for 12, which packets would be retransmitted with go-back-n and selective-ack?

12.17. Compute the bound on maximum link efficiency with go-back-n with $p = 0.001$, $w = 10$, and $w = 1000$. What does this say about go-back-n's performance as a function of the window size?

12.18. What do acks contain when a SMART receiver gets acks for packets with sequence numbers 11, 12, 14, 15, 13, 17? What does the sender do in each case?

Chapter 13

Flow Control

Consider a server transferring a file to a client after fragmenting it into packets. The server faces the nontrivial problem of choosing the rate at which to inject these packets into the network. If it sends all the packets at once, it may send them faster than the network or the client can process them, leading to packet loss. Because the server must retransmit lost packets, it is better off sending packets at a rate that both the network and the client can handle. If, however, the server sends packets slower than the highest sustainable rate, transferring the file takes longer than necessary. Thus, the server should carefully choose its transmission rate to neither overflow nor underflow the network or the client.

Flow control refers to the set of techniques that enable a data source to match its transmission rate to the currently available service rate at a receiver and in the network. Besides this primary goal, a flow control mechanism should meet several other, sometimes mutually contradictory objectives. It should be *simple* to implement, use the *least possible network resources* (in terms of bandwidth and buffers at multiplexing points), and work effectively even when used by many sources (that is, *scale* well). If possible, each member of the ensemble of flow-controlled sources sharing a scarce resource should restrict its usage to its *fair* share. Finally, the ensemble of sources should be *stable*, which means, loosely speaking, that when the number of sources is fixed, the transmission rate of each source settles down to an equilibrium value. Stability also implies that, if a new source becomes active, existing active sources adjust their transmission rates so that, after a brief transient period, the system settles down to a new equilibrium. (A more technical explanation of stability requires a background in control theory and can be found in introductory texts such as reference [Ogata 90].)

This range of objectives allows for many interesting trade-offs. For example, we can trade simplicity for fairness, designing a scheme that is simple to implement, but does not guarantee a fair share to every source. Other, more complex trade-offs are also possible, and we will see many of them later in this chapter. The variety of choices available to the designer has led to many different flow-control schemes being proposed in the literature (practically every networking conference in the last decade has one or more papers on flow control!). Some schemes described in the literature are only paper proposals, whereas others have been implemented in real networks and are widely used. In general, the more widely used a flow-control algorithm, the better it has been studied, and the more it deals with implementation difficulties. In this chapter, we will study flow-control schemes that either illustrate an important control mechanism or are widely used, or both. We will also evaluate the pros and cons of these schemes, based on how well they satisfy the objectives just described.

We can implement flow control at the application, transport, network, or datalink layer of a protocol stack. The choice of layer depends on the situation at hand. The most common design is to place end-to-end flow control at the transport layer, and hop-by-hop (link-level) flow control in the datalink layer. However, other arrangements are possible and, depending on the situation, are just as correct. In this chapter, we will study the abstract flow control problem, without worrying too much about layering.

We mention in passing that flow control is often confused with congestion control. *Congestion* refers to a sustained overload of *intermediate* network elements. Thus, flow control is one mechanism for congestion control. We study other techniques for congestion control in Chapters 9 and 14.

This chapter is organized as follows. We present a model for flow control in Section 13.1, and a taxonomy of flow control schemes in Section 13.2. We can divide flow control techniques into three broad categories: *open loop, closed loop,* and *hybrid.* In Section 13.3, we study open-loop flow control, and in Section 13.4 we study closed-loop flow control. Finally, Section 13.5 discusses hybrid flow control. In each section, we study a handful of representative schemes that cover an illustrative range of flow-control techniques.

13.1   Model

We will study flow control in the context of a single *source* sending a stream of packets on a connection to a single *destination* or *sink,* over a path with many switches or routers. We assume that the sink acknowledges every packet. We model each network element, such as a switch, router, or multiplexing point, as a *server* that serves a certain number of packets from that connection per second. If the scheduling discipline is rate allocating, the *service rate* refers to the rate allocated to the connection (see Section 9.5.1). Otherwise, it is the instantaneous service rate available to the connection at that server. We call the slowest server along the path the *bottleneck* server. Low has shown that, for the purposes

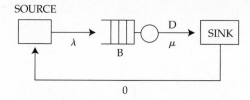

Figure 13.1: A reduced model for flow control. The source sends data at a rate λ. The single server has a rate μ equal to the slowest server along the path, and a buffer as large as the slowest server's buffer. The delay D is the sum of the delays on the data and acknowledgment path (this is also called the round-trip time).

of flow control, we can ignore all but the bottleneck server [Low 92]. Thus, the flow control model reduces to the one shown in Figure 13.1.[1]

We can view flow control as *rate-matching with delays*. The bottleneck server removes data from its buffer at a variable rate. The source must match this rate so that the buffer neither overflows nor underflows. The problem is that we know the bottleneck server's current drain rate only after a delay, and the new source rate takes effect only after another delay. The sum of these delays is the *round-trip time* (*RTT*), which is the time taken for a packet to traverse the path from the source to the sink and for its acknowledgment to return. (We can exclude the portion of the path from the bottleneck server to the sink if the bottleneck server directly informs the source of its current service rate.) The round-trip time is the fundamental time constant in all feedback flow-control mechanisms, because it is the minimum time required for a source to learn of the effect of its control actions.

Perhaps a more intuitive model of flow control is to imagine a tank of water from which water drains at a variable rate. A source must control its flow so that the tank neither overflows nor empties. If the source's control actions take effect immediately, the problem is straightforward, because the source can simply increase its flow whenever the tank is in danger of emptying, and decrease it when it nears an overflow. However, if the tank is situated, say, a hundred kilometers away, a change in the source's flow rate takes effect only after some time. Moreover, the source knows about the current water level only after a delay. The fundamental time constant in the system is the sum of the times taken for the source's changes to take effect, and for the source to learn of the effect of its change (the round-trip time).

Flow control is a variant of the classical control problem. In classical control, a controller is allowed to change its input to a black box and observe the corresponding output. Its aim is to choose an input as a function of the observed outputs, so that the system state conforms to some

---

[1]We do not study flow control for multicast connections, because this is a difficult open problem that is still an area of active research.

desired objective. The main difference in flow control is that the output of the system (the service rate of a connection) may depend not only on the actions of a particular source, but also on the actions of every *other* source sharing a resource with that connection. This coupling among sources makes flow control fundamentally hard, and not easily amenable to techniques from classical control theory.

13.2 Classification

We can classify flow control schemes into *open-loop, closed-loop,* and *hybrid* schemes. In *open-loop* flow control, a source describes its traffic to the network with a few parameters. During call establishment, the network reserves resources (such as bandwidth and buffers) corresponding to these parameters. During data transmission, if the source shapes its traffic to match its traffic's description, network overload, and thus congestion, is avoided. The difficult problem in open-loop flow control is choosing the right set of parameters to describe a source adequately. Once this is done, the actual flow control (or *regulation,* as it is usually called) is straightforward. We study open-loop flow control in Section 13.3.

In *closed-loop* schemes, a source dynamically adapts its flow to match its current share of network resources. As this share increases and decreases, a source should send faster or slower. There are many interesting and hard problems associated with closed-loop schemes. For example, how should the network inform a source that its service rate has changed? In an *explicit feedback* scheme, it explicitly conveys this information to the source. In an *implicit feedback* scheme, the source infers a change in its service rate by measuring its current performance. Once it receives this information, the source must decide how best to react to the current system state. This depends on its *flow-control strategy.* We study closed-loop flow control schemes in Section 13.4.

Finally, *hybrid* schemes combine aspects of open- and closed-loop flow control. For example, a source may reserve some minimum resources during call setup, but may be given a larger share if the network is idle. Thus, the source must do call setup, as in open-loop flow control, but also adapt to the network state, as in closed-loop flow control. We study such schemes in Section 13.5.

13.3 Open-loop flow control

In open-loop flow control, during call establishment, a source describes its behavior with a set of parameters called its *traffic descriptor* and negotiates bandwidth and buffer reservations with network elements along the path to its destination. The network operator prescribes the descriptor's parameters, and each source decides parameter values that best describe its traffic. During call setup, each network element examines this description and decides whether it can support the call. If it can, it forwards the setup request to the next element along the path. Otherwise, it negotiates the parameters down to an acceptable value, or blocks the call. In the data transmission phase, the source shapes its traffic to match its descriptor, and each network element schedules traffic from admitted calls to meet the bandwidth, delay, and loss guarantees it makes to them. The hard problems in open-loop flow control are (a) choosing a descriptor at a source, (b) choosing a scheduling discipline at intermediate network elements, and (c) admitting calls so that their performance objectives are met (*call admission control*). We study the choice of descriptors in Section 13.3.1, scheduling disciplines in Chapter 9, and call admission control in Chapter 14.

In open-loop flow control, a source has to capture its entire future behavior with a handful of parameters, because the network's admission-control algorithm uses these parameters to decide whether to admit the source or not. Thus, open-loop flow control works best when a source can describe its traffic well with a small number of parameters, and when it needs to obtain quality-of-service guarantees from the network. If either of these conditions fails to apply, the source is better off with closed-loop or hybrid flow control.

13.3.1   Traffic Descriptors

A traffic descriptor is a set of parameters that describes the behavior of a data source. Typically, it is a behavior *envelope*, that is, it describes the worst possible behavior of a source, rather than its exact behavior. A descriptor plays three roles besides describing source traffic. First, it forms the basis of a *traffic contract* between the source and the network: the source agrees not to violate the descriptor, and in turn, the network promises a particular *quality of service.* If a source violates its part of the contract, the network cannot guarantee it a performance bound. Second, the descriptor is the input to a *regulator,* a device through which a source can pass data before it enters the network. To ensure that the source never violates its traffic descriptor, a regulator delays traffic in a buffer when the source rate is higher than expected. Third, the descriptor is also the input to a *policer,* a device supplied by the network operator that ensures that the source meets its portion of the contract. A policer delays or drops source traffic that violates the descriptor. The regulator and policer are identical in the way they identify descriptor violations: the difference is that a regulator typically delays excess traffic, while a policer typically drops it.

A practical traffic descriptor must have these important properties [Verma 91]:

- *Representativity:* The descriptor must adequately represent the long-term behavior of the traffic, so that the network does not reserve too little or too much.

- *Verifiability:* The network must be able to verify that a source is obeying its promised traffic specification quickly, cheaply, and preferably in hardware.

- *Preservability:* The network may inadvertently modify source traffic behavior as it travels along its path. Thus, the amount of resources allocated to a channel may change along the path. The network must be able either to preserve the traffic characteristics along the path, or to calculate the resource requirements of the modified traffic stream.

- *Usability:* Sources should be able to describe their traffic easily, and network elements should be able to perform admission control with the descriptor easily.

Coming up with good traffic descriptors is difficult because of these conflicting requirements. For example, the series of times at which a source places data onto a connection is a representative, verifiable, and preservable traffic descriptor. However, this time series is potentially very long and, for interactive traffic sources, is unknown. Thus, the descriptor is unusable. In contrast, if we choose the source's peak rate as its descriptor, the descriptor is usable, preservable, and verifiable, but not representative, because resource reservation at the peak rate is wasteful if a source rarely generates data at this rate.

Several traffic descriptors have been proposed in the literature. They are roughly equivalent, though there are subtle differences in their ease of use and descriptive power [Rathgeb 91]. We study three common descriptors: peak rate, average rate, and linear bounded arrival process. For each descriptor, we also study the corresponding regulator.

13.3.2 Peak rate

The peak rate is the highest rate at which a source can ever generate data during a call. A trivial bound on the peak rate of a connection is just the speed of the source's access link, because this is the instantaneous peak rate of the source during actual packet transmission. With this definition, a source on a 10-Mbps Ethernet that generates one 100-byte packet per second can be said to have a peak rate of 10 Mbps! Although accurate, this definition is not satisfactory because it does not give a true picture of a source's traffic load. Instead, we measure the peak rate in one of two ways. For networks with fixed-size packets, the peak rate is the inverse of the closest spacing between the starting times of consecutive packets. For variable-sized packets, we must specify the peak rate along with a time window over which we measure this peak rate. Then, the peak rate bounds the total number of packets generated over all windows of the specified size.

EXAMPLE 13.1

(a) If all packets on a connection are 50 bytes long, and the closest packet spacing is 10 ms, what is the peak rate? (b) If the peak rate of a connection is 8 Mbps over *all* intervals of 15 ms, what is the largest amount of data that can be generated in 75 ms? (c) In 70 ms?

Solution: (a) The peak rate is 5000 bytes/s. (b) The largest amount allowed in 75 ms is 8 Mbps * 75 ms = 600,000 bits. (c) Since traffic is specified only over an interval of 15 ms, the worst-case amount of data generated in 70 ms is also 600,000 bits (for example, all the data could be generated in the first 5 ms of every consecutive 15-ms interval).

A peak-rate regulator consists of a buffer and a timer. For the moment, assume a fixed-size packet network. When the first packet in a call arrives at the buffer, the regulator forwards the packet and sets a timer for the earliest time it can send the next packet without violating the peak-rate bound, that is, the smallest interarrival time. It delays subsequently arriving packets in a data buffer until the timer expires. If the timer expires before the next packet arrives, it restarts the timer on packet arrival, and the incoming packet is forwarded without delay. The generalization of this scheme to networks with variable-sized packets is left as an exercise to the reader.

The peak-rate descriptor is easy to compute and police, but it can be a very loose bound, because it is an *extremal* bound. That is, a single outlier can change this descriptor. For example, consider a data stream where a source generates one fixed-size data packet exactly once a second. It has a peak rate of 1 packet per second. However, even if one packet in the stream "slips" and is sent, say, 10 ms after an earlier packet, the peak rate increases to 100 times its previous value! Peak-rate descriptors are useful only if the traffic sources are very smooth, or if a simple design is more important than efficiency.

13.3.3   Average rate

The key problem with the peak rate is that it is subject to outliers. The motivation behind average-rate descriptors is that averaging the transmission rate over a period of time reduces the effect of outliers. Researchers have proposed two types of average-rate mechanisms. Both mechanisms use two parameters, t and a, defined as follows:

$$t = \text{time window over which the rate is measured}$$
$$a = \text{the number of bits that can be sent in a window of time } t$$

(13.1)

In the *jumping-window* descriptor, a source claims that over consecutive windows of length t seconds, no more than a bits of data will be transmitted. The term "jumping window" refers to the fact that a new time interval starts immediately after the end of the earlier one. The jumping-window descriptor is sensitive to the choice of the starting time of the first window.

In the *moving-window* scheme, the time window moves continuously, so that the source claims that over *all* windows of length t seconds, no more than a bits of data will be injected into the network. The moving-window scheme (also called the (r, T) model in reference [Golestani 90]) removes the dependency on the starting time of the first window. It also enforces a tighter bound on spikes in the input traffic.

An average-rate regulator is identical to a variable-packet-size peak-rate regulator, because both restrict the maximum amount of information that can be transmitted in a given interval of time. For a jumping-window descriptor, at time 0, a counter is initialized to 0 and is incremented by the packet size of each departing packet. Every t seconds, the counter is reset to 0. When a packet arrives, the regulator computes whether sending the packet would result in too much data being sent in the current window. This test reduces to testing whether the sum of the current counter value and the current packet size is larger or smaller than *a*. Depending on the result, the regulator either forwards the packet immediately or buffers it until the next time window.

In one technique for building a moving-window descriptor, besides the counter described earlier, the regulator stores the departure time and packet size of every departing packet. The test for delaying or forwarding a packet is the same as before. In addition, *t* seconds after a packet departs, the counter is decremented by its size. Thus, the counter reflects the number of bits sent in the past *t* seconds. If the regulator decides to delay a packet, it can determine the earliest time it can transmit the packet by examining the list of packet departure times. This technique is not used in practice because it requires the regulator to store a lot of information, which is hard to do at high speed. A second technique for building a moving-window regulator, which is the one used in practice, is the leaky-bucket regulator described in the next subsection (13.3.4).

EXAMPLE 13.2

An average-rate descriptor is specified with $a = 100$ Kbytes, $t = 1$ s. Packet arrival times and sizes are (0.2 s, 20 Kbytes), (0.25 s, 40 Kbytes), (0.5 s, 20 Kbytes), (0.6 s, 20 Kbytes), (0.8 s, 10 Kbytes), (1.0 s, 30 Kbytes), (1.7 s, 30 Kbytes), (1.9 s, 30 Kbytes). What are the departure times with the jumping-window and moving-window regulators?

Solution: With a jumping window, the packet arriving at time 0.8 s is delayed to the second window. With a moving window, the packet arriving at time 0.8 s is delayed to time 1.0. The packet arriving at time 1.0 is delayed until a time x such that no more than 100 Kbytes have been sent in the interval $[x - t, x]$, i.e., 1.25 s. At this time, the effects of the first two packets are erased and the packet arriving at time 1.0 can be sent. For both regulators, the last two packets depart as soon as they arrive, because the jumping-window counter is not exceeded, and by time 1.7, the moving-window counter is 40 Kbytes.

13.3.4 Linear bounded arrival processes

Linear bounded arrival processes, or *LBAPs,* are a popular class of source descriptors [Cruz 87]. An LBAP-constrained source bounds the number of bits it transmits in any interval of length *t* by a linear function of *t*. We characterize this linear function by two parameters, σ and ρ, so that:

$$\text{Number of bits transmitted in any interval of length } t \leq \rho t + \sigma \qquad (13.2)$$

ρ corresponds roughly to the long-term average rate *allocated* by the network to the source (which may be substantially larger than the source's true average rate), and σ the longest burst a source may send, given the choice of ρ, while still obeying the LBAP descriptor. In other words, assuming for the moment that ρ is the source's average rate, an LBAP characterizes a source that has an intrinsic long-term average rate ρ, but can sometimes deviate from this rate, as specified by σ. Since an LBAP is a generalization of the average-rate descriptor, it is also insensitive to outliers.

A variant of an LBAP descriptor uses four parameters (and therefore is less general than an LBAP) [FV 90]. The parameters are as follows:

$$
\begin{aligned}
S &= \text{The largest possible packet size} \\
Xmin &= \text{The smallest interval between the starting time of two} \\
&\quad \text{consecutive packets (the peak rate is defined to be } S/Xmin) \\
I &= \text{The averaging interval} \\
Xave &= \text{The mean interval between two consecutive packets (the average} \\
&\quad \text{rate over all intervals of length } I \text{ is at most } S/Xave)
\end{aligned}
\tag{13.3}
$$

This characterization has an additional limit on the peak rate, so that the rate at which the source generates a burst is limited. Moreover, unlike the basic LBAP descriptor, it models burstiness at the level of a packet, because it explicitly constrains the largest packet size. The inclusion of the $Xmin$–$Xave$–I–S model in the class of LBAP descriptors can be seen by noticing that the largest number of bits that the source can send in an interval of length t in the $Xmin$–$Xave$–I–S model is bounded by:

$$
\left(\frac{t}{I} + 2 \right) \left\lceil \frac{I}{Xave} \right\rceil S
\tag{13.4}
$$

because $(t/I + 2)$ bounds the number of intervals of length I that can be spanned by an interval of time t, and in each such interval, the source can transmit at most $\lceil I/Xave \rceil S$ bits. This is a linear function of t.

A *leaky-bucket regulator* regulates an LBAP descriptor [Turner 86]. Intuitively, the regulator collects *tokens* in a bucket, which fills up at a steady drip rate. Each token is permission for the source to send a certain number of bits into the network. When a packet arrives at the regulator, the regulator sends the packet if the bucket has enough tokens. Otherwise, the packet waits either until the bucket has enough tokens or until the packet is discarded. If the bucket is already full of tokens, incoming tokens overflow and are not available to future packets. Thus, at any time, the largest burst a source can send into the network is roughly proportional to the size of the leaky bucket.

More formally, a leaky bucket accumulates fixed-size tokens in a token bucket and transmits a packet only if the sum of the token sizes in the bucket adds up to the packet's size (Figure 13.2). On a packet departure, the regulator removes tokens corresponding to the packet size from the token bucket. The regulator periodically adds tokens to the bucket (at a rate ρ). However, the bucket overflows if the number of tokens crosses some

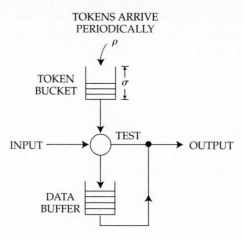

Figure 13.2: Leaky bucket regulator. A leaky-bucket regulator shapes incoming traffic to conform to a linear bounded arrival process. Packets are transmitted only when there are sufficient tokens available in the token bucket. Tokens are periodically placed in the token bucket and are removed on packet departure. If the token bucket overflows, excess tokens are discarded. The largest burst is bounded roughly by the token bucket size, and the bound on the average service rate is the token arrival rate.

threshold, called its *depth, σ*. A leaky bucket limits the size of a transmitted burst to a little more than the bucket's depth (since tokens may arrive while the bucket's worth of packets are being transmitted), and over the long term, the rate at which packets depart the regulator is limited by the rate at which tokens are added to the bucket. The regulator delays a packet if it does not have sufficient tokens for transmission. Typically, we initialize the bucket to be full.

EXAMPLE 13.3

Tokens of size 100 bytes are added to a leaky-bucket regulator of capacity 500 bytes twice a second. (a) What is the average rate, peak rate, and largest burst size of the regulated traffic stream? (b) Can this regulator handle a packet of size 700 bytes? (c) If a packet of size 400 bytes arrives when the bucket contains tokens worth 200 bytes, and there are no other packets awaiting service, what is the least and most delay it could have before transmission?

Solution: (a) The average rate is 200 bytes/s = 1.6 Kbps. The largest burst size is 500 bytes. The peak rate is unbounded, because a burst of up to 500 bytes can be transmitted arbitrarily fast. (b) No, because the packet will never have enough tokens to be transmitted. (c) If the packet arrives just before the arrival of a token, it need wait for only a little over 0.5 s; if it arrives just after the token, it has to wait for 1 s.

A leaky bucket can be used both as a peak-rate and a moving-window average rate regulator, because they are both special cases of an LBAP. If the token replenishment interval corresponds to the peak rate, and the token bucket size is set to one token, then the leaky bucket is a peak-rate regulator. Similarly, setting the token-bucket limit to one token and replenishing the bucket at the average rate makes it a moving-window average rate regulator. (In both cases, with variable-sized packets, we have to be careful that the token is at least as large as the largest packet.)

In a common variant of the leaky-bucket regulator, the token bucket is augmented with a peak-rate regulator, so that packet bursts arrive into the network no faster than this peak rate. This allows us to control the average rate, the peak rate, and the largest burst from a source.

Note that a leaky bucket regulator has both a token bucket and a data buffer (if it did not have a data buffer, it would be a policer). Packets that arrive to the regulator that cannot be sent immediately are delayed in the data buffer. Intuitively, the larger the token bucket, the smaller the data buffer need be, because an arriving packet uses a token and departs the regulator, instead of being delayed in the data buffer. In fact, Berger and Whitt have shown that the performance of a leaky bucket with a data buffer and a token bucket (in terms of the packet loss rate from the regulator) depends only on the *sum* of the token-bucket size and the data-buffer size [BW 92]. In other words, confirming our intuition, a larger token bucket size *exactly* offsets a smaller data buffer.

Choosing LBAP parameters

Given an intrinsically limited traffic source, such as a stored compressed video, we would like to come up with an LBAP descriptor for the source that is minimal in the sense that no other descriptor has both a smaller σ and a smaller ρ. If a source must pay for the resources it consumes, a minimal descriptor is likely to have the smallest price. Unfortunately, the minimal LBAP descriptor for a source is not unique. Given the size of the data buffer at the regulator and the maximum loss allowed at the regulator, each choice of the token arrival rate has a corresponding minimum burst size so that the loss parameter is met. To see this, consider a source that has some intrinsic peak rate P and average rate A measured over a long interval. If the token arrival rate ρ is less than or equal to A, then the regulator buffer grows without bound, and σ must be infinite if we want to avoid packet loss. If $\rho > P$, then there are always tokens on hand when a packet arrives, and σ can be as small as one maximal-sized packet (Figure 13.3). As we increase ρ in the range $[A, P]$, the minimum σ needed to meet the loss bound decreases. Any ρ and its corresponding σ is an equivalent minimal descriptor of the source. The set of all (σ, ρ) pairs that form the minimal LBAP descriptors for a source are described by the (σ, ρ) curve for the source.

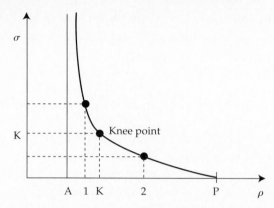

Figure 13.3: Typical (σ, ρ) curve. This curve shows the knee point K. If the token rate ρ is slightly smaller than at K (point 1), σ is much larger. Similarly, if σ is slightly smaller than at K, there is a rapid increase in ρ (point 2). Thus, it is best to choose K as the descriptor for the source.

For arbitrary sources, there is no easy way to pick the appropriate (σ, ρ) pair that describes it "best." However, for many common sources, the (σ, ρ) curve has a distinct "knee," which makes the choice of parameters straightforward. A knee in the (σ, ρ) curve indicates that for descriptors that are slightly away from the knee, either the σ or the ρ parameter rapidly increases. Thus, the optimal choice of the parameters is the value at the knee (Figure 13.3).

LBAP descriptors are popular in practice and also in academic papers, because they are usable, verifiable, and, to some extent, preservable. They correctly model the fact that even a "smooth" source may have periods in which it is bursty. However, they do not accurately represent sources that have occasional very large bursts. For such sources, if the regulator delay is to be small, and the loss probability low, the σ parameter has to be chosen to be fairly large so that the burst is drained away into the network. Unfortunately, this makes the network more expensive, because it has to size internal buffers to be large enough to handle large bursts. A better solution is to renegotiate the LBAP descriptor just before the burst (if the occurrence of a burst can be predicted, or is already known, as with stored video), so that we increase the drain rate to handle the burst, then decrease it back to the long-term average rate [GKT 95]. If a burst lasts long enough, we can start renegotiation *after* detecting the start of the burst. However, this does not perform as well, because the regulator's data buffer fills while the renegotiation procedure, which can take more than one round-trip time, is going on. Dynamic renegotiation of traffic descriptors is still an area of active research (see Section 14.7).

13.4   Closed-loop flow control

In open-loop flow control, a source specifies a traffic descriptor during call establishment, and, during data transfer, ensures that its traffic meets this description. Even if the network load changes while the call is in progress, an admitted source need not change its descriptor or its traffic, because each network element reserves sufficient resources to meet the source's performance requirements.

In closed-loop flow control, we assume that network elements do not reserve sufficient resources for the call, either because they do not support resource reservation, or because they overbook resources to get additional statistical multiplexing gain. In Chapter 9, we studied how a network element can use a scheduling discipline to dynamically allocate transmission rates to an ensemble of feedback flow-controlled sources. Given such an allocation, the aim of closed-loop flow control is to adjust a source's transmission rate dynamically, in response to feedback signals, so that the ensemble of sources does not overload the network. If closed-loop flow control is ineffective, sources either suffer excessive packet loss or underutilize network resources.

Taxonomy of closed-loop flow-control schemes

In general, a traffic source must control its transmission rate not only in response to the receiver's state, but also in response to the network state. The *first generation* of flow-control protocols did not explicitly consider network state; they simply matched the source rate to the service rate at the destination (Table 13.1). The three important protocols in this generation, which we will study in Sections 13.4.1–13.4.3, are *on–off, stop-and-wait*, and *static-window* flow control.

The second generation of protocols changes the source rate in response to both the sink state and the network state. We can categorize these protocols in three complementary ways:

- *Implicit versus explicit state measurement:* With explicit measurement, a network element uses an explicit control message to communicate the current sustainable data rate to every source. In an implicit measurement scheme, a source uses performance measurements to dynamically infer its share of network bandwidth. Explicit schemes can control a source's rate more precisely than implicit schemes, because a source has better information. On the other hand, they require both a communication and a computation overhead. Ideally, we would like a scheme that has as little overhead as an implicit scheme, but performs nearly as well as an explicit scheme (also see the discussion in Section 6.3.11).

First generation (match sending rate to destination service rate)	On–off (13.4.1)		
	Stop-and-wait (13.4.2)		
	Static window (13.4.3)		
Second generation (match sending rate to destination and network service rate)	State measurement	Choice of control	Point of control
	Explicit	Dynamic window	End-to-end
	Implicit	Dynamic rate	Hop-by-hop

Table 13.1: Taxonomy of closed-loop flow-control schemes.

- *Dynamic window versus dynamic rate:* We define the error-control window to be the number of packets sent from a source, but yet to be acknowledged. Because the source must stop after it has a window's worth of packets in flight (see Section 12.4.7 for more details), by limiting the error-control window size, we automatically limit the source's transmission rate. Thus, we can use the error-control window for flow control. To distinguish between these distinct uses of a window, we will call the window used for flow control the *flow-control window* or the *transmission window*. In an *adaptive-window* scheme, we indirectly control a source's transmission rate by modifying its transmission window. In an *adaptive-rate* scheme, we directly control the source rate. Every time a source sends a packet, it sets a timer with a timeout value equal to the inverse of the current transmission rate, and transmits the next packet when the timer expires.

  A dynamic-window scheme has the disadvantage that the window is used for both error control and rate control. This coupling is often problematic. For example, if a receiver has only a few buffers to hold out-of-order packets, and error control is based on selective retransmission, the error-control window must be small. Unfortunately, this limits the maximum transmission rate from the source. We comment on some other disadvantages of window-based flow control at the end of Section 13.4.5, after we have more context for these comments.

  Window-based control has two main advantages over rate-based flow control. First, it is easier to implement, because it does not require a fine-grained timer, which can be expensive in some systems. Second, a window automatically limits the damage a source can inflict on a network. After transmitting a window's worth of packets, a source stops. With rate-based flow control, a source may continue to send packets into the network if it fails to receive rate-throttling information. Thus, we must carefully engineer rate-based flow control to be robust to packet loss and corruption.

- *Hop-by-hop versus end-to-end control:* We can automatically make a first-generation flow-control scheme responsive to network state (in addition to receiver state) by implementing it between every adjacent pair of network elements. For example, stop-and-wait becomes a second-generation flow control scheme if we use it not just between a source and a sink, but also between every pair of adjacent routers. This change typically improves performance: the control delay is smaller, and each element only needs to react to a change in the next element, which is typically more effective than responding to changes in all elements along the path. Besides, by limiting the buffer buildup at each element, a hop-by-hop scheme more evenly distributes buffer usage. Hop-by-hop schemes, however, make the network elements more complicated. Moreover, unless hop-by-hop control is done per-connection, it can be unfair [MK 92].

Because these design elements are complementary, we can come up with eight possible combinations. Note that there are no implicit hop-by-hop closed-loop flow control

	Explicit		Implicit	
	Dynamic window	Dynamic rate	Dynamic window	Dynamic rate
End-to-end	■ DECbit (13.4.4)	■ ATM Forum EERC (13.4.9)	■ TCP-Tahoe and TCP-Reno (13.4.5) ■ TCP-Vegas (13.4.6)	■ NETBLT (13.4.7) ■ Packet-pair (13.4.8)
Hop-by-hop	■ Credit-based (13.4.11)	■ Mishra/Kanakia (13.4.10)		

Table 13.2: Representative closed-loop flow-control schemes.

schemes. An implicit scheme tries to minimize the work done within the network by guessing the available service rate in the network. A hop-by-hop scheme requires a considerable amount of work to be done at each switch, so the additional overhead for explicit control is small. Thus, hop-by-hop schemes tend to use explicit control.

In Sections 13.4.4–13.4.11 we will study representatives of each combination as shown in Table 13.2. Table 13.5 in Section 13.4.12 is a summary of these schemes and a road map.

Of these schemes, we will study the DECbit, TCP, and ATM Forum EERC schemes in more detail than the others for two reasons. First, they are widely implemented on a variety of platforms. Second, the ideas in these schemes form the basis of many other schemes that are in the literature, but are not covered here.

13.4.1   On–off

In *on–off* flow control, the receiver sends the transmitter an *On* signal when it can receive data, and an *Off* signal when it can accept no more data. The transmitter sends as fast as it can when it is in the On state, and is idle when it is in the Off state.

Evaluation

On–off control is effective when the delay between the receiver and the sender is small. It works poorly when the propagation delay between the sender and receiver is large, because the receiver needs to buffer all the data that arrive before the Off signal takes effect. If the Off packet is delayed or lost, the receiver continues to receive data at the source's peak rate, leading to potential buffer overflow and loss. Moreover, intermediate network elements are subjected to abrupt data bursts from the sources, making packet loss in the network more likely.

On–off control is primarily used over short serial lines or LANs, where propagation delays are small and packet losses are rare. It is the basis for the XON/XOFF protocol used to control serial input–output devices such as printers and mice.

13.4.2 Stop-and-wait

In the stop-and-wait protocol, one of the earliest attempts at flow control, a source sends a single packet and waits for an acknowledgment before sending the next packet. If it receives no acknowledgment for some time, it times out and retransmits the packet.

Stop-and-wait simultaneously provides error control and flow control. It provides error control because if a packet is lost, the source repeatedly retransmits it until the receiver acknowledges it. It provides flow control because the sender waits for an acknowledgment before sending a packet. Thus, stop-and-wait forces the sender to slow down to a rate slower than can be supported at the receiver.

Evaluation

Stop-and-wait is useful in networks where the propagation delay is small, but is inefficient otherwise (see Figure 13.4). In the figure, each vertical line corresponds to a network element. Time increases along the vertical axis. We represent a packet transmission as a parallelogram: the slope of the parallelogram represents the link delay, and the width is inversely proportional to the transmission rate of the link (thus, the width is also proportional to the time a packet spends on a link). It is clear from the figure that a source must wait for one round-trip time to elapse after it sends a packet before it can send the next one. Thus, the best possible throughput is one packet per round-trip time. This decreases rapidly as the propagation delay, relative to the packet transmission time, increases.

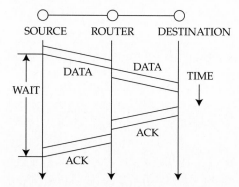

Figure 13.4: Stop-and-wait protocol. Each parallelogram corresponds to a packet, and each vertical line to a network element. Time increases down the vertical axis. The source sends a packet, then waits for it to be acknowledged before sending the next packet. Thus, it has to wait for one round-trip time before proceeding, which limits the maximum achievable throughput.

EXAMPLE 13.4

What is the peak throughput achievable by a source employing stop-and-wait flow control when the maximum packet size is 1000 bytes, and the network spans (a) 10km, (b) 5000 km?

Solution: Assuming a direct fiber-optic line between endpoints, the speed-of-light propagation delay is $1/(0.7 * 3 * 10^5)$ s/km, since the speed of light in fiber is approximately $0.7c$, where c (the speed of light in vacuum) $= 3 * 10^5$ km/s. This works out to 4.76 μs/km. For the purposes of this example, we will ignore the effects of queuing and switching delays. (a) For a 10 km line, the round-trip delay is thus $2 * 47.6$ μs $= 95.2$ μs. The maximum possible throughput is thus 1 packet/RTT $= 1000 * 8$ bits/95.2 μs $= 84.03$ Mbps. (b) Since the link is 500 times longer, the maximum speed goes down by a factor of 500 to 84.03/500 Mbps $= 0.168$ Mbps.

13.4.3 Static window

Stop-and-wait flow control has a peak throughput of one packet per round-trip time (RTT). This is inefficient if the propagation delay, and thus the RTT, is large. In static-window flow control, we allow a source to send up to w packets before it stops and waits for an acknowledgment. In other words, we have:

$$\text{Transmission window} = w \tag{13.5}$$

When a source that has w packets outstanding receives an ack, we allow it to transmit another packet, because the left edge of the sliding window slides one step forward. It takes at least one round-trip time for the source to receive an ack for a packet. In this time, it could have sent at most w packets. Thus, its maximum achievable throughput is w/RTT packets/s, a factor of w better than stop-and-wait. Figure 13.5 illustrates a source allowed to have three packets outstanding at any time, i.e., has a window of size three. Thus, its throughput is almost triple that of a corresponding stop-and-wait source.

How large should w be? Let:

$$\text{Bottleneck service rate along the path} = \mu \text{ packets/s} \tag{13.6}$$

$$\text{Round-trip time} = R \text{ s}$$

The source's sending rate is at most w/R packets/second. If this is to keep the bottleneck fully utilized, we must have:

$$w/R \geq \mu \Rightarrow w \geq R\mu \tag{13.7}$$

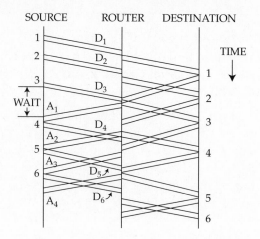

Figure 13.5: Static-window flow control. A source is allowed to send more than one packet before it must wait for an acknowledgment. Here, the source has a window of three, so it transmits three packets before it waits for an acknowledgment. This triples the throughput compared to that of a corresponding stop-and-wait source.

If this is an equality, that is, $w = R\mu$, the source transmits packets exactly as fast as the bottleneck can handle them, and the flow control is optimal. If $w < R\mu$, then the bottleneck is idle for part of the round-trip time, and if $w > R\mu$,

$$\text{Number of packets buffered at the bottleneck} = w - R\mu \qquad (13.8)$$

Because of the importance of the value $R\mu$, we call it the *bandwidth-delay product* or the *optimal window size.*

EXAMPLE 13.5

Compute the optimal window size when packet size is 53 bytes, the RTT is 60 ms, and bottleneck bandwidth is (a) 1.5 Mbps (the standard T1 trunk speed), (b) 155 Mbps (the standard OC-3 trunk speed).

Solution: (a) The bottleneck rate in packets/sec is 1.5 Mbps/53 ∗ 8 bits/packet = 3537.7 pkts/s. Thus, the optimal window is 3537.7 ∗ 0.06 = 212.3 packets. (b) Similarly, at OC3 rates, the bottleneck rate is 365,566 pkts/s, and the optimal window is 21,933 packets.

Evaluation

The problem with static-window flow control is that the optimal window size depends on the bottleneck service rate and the round-trip time. However, not only do the bottleneck rate and the round-trip time differ from connection to connection, but they also vary with time even for the same connection. Choosing a single static window size suitable for all connections is therefore impossible. Unfortunately, a poor choice of w can lead to severe performance problems. If w is too small, a source may have data to send, and the bottleneck may have spare capacity, but the window size prevents the source from using the available capacity. If w is too large, from Equation 13.8, $w - R\mu$ packets are buffered at the bottleneck; if the bottleneck does not have sufficient buffering, packets may be lost. We avoid these problems in the second generation of flow-control protocols by dynamically varying a connection's window size to be always close to the current optimal.

13.4.4 DECbit flow control

Explicit	Dynamic window	End-to-end
Implicit	Dynamic rate	Hop-by-hop

The key idea behind the DECbit scheme [RJ88, RJ90] is that every packet header carries a bit that can be set by an intermediate network element that is experiencing congestion (i.e., a sustained queue buildup). The receiver copies the bit from a data packet to its acknowledgment, and sends the acknowledgment back to the source (Figure 13.6). The source modifies its transmission-window size based on the series of bits it receives in the

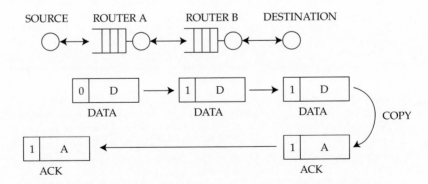

Figure 13.6: DECbit flow control. Packets carry a congestion-indication bit that is set by an intermediate router if the router detects persistent queuing, and the packet's source is sending faster than its fair-share rate. Bits are copied from packets on to their acknowledgments, and the source uses the sequence of bits to adjust its transmission window size.

acknowledgment headers as follows: The source increases its windows until it starts building queues at the bottleneck server (because its window size is larger than the optimal window size), causing that server to set bits on the source's packets. When this happens, the source reduces its window size, and bits are no longer set. In equilibrium, therefore, the source-window size oscillates around the optimal window size. If the propagation delay R or the bottleneck service rate μ changes, the source-window size adapts to this change and oscillates about a new optimal point. Note that the scheme does not require any particular scheduling discipline at multiplexing points. In our discussion, we assume, as the authors did, that this is first-come-first-served. We now study the scheme in more detail.

The important elements in the DECbit scheme are (a) when bits get set, and for which connections, and (b) how these bits are interpreted by the source. We examine these two issues in turn.

Router actions

In the DECbit scheme, each network element monitors packet arrivals from each source to compute its bandwidth *demand* (a measure of the bandwidth the source is using) and the *mean aggregate queue length* (the mean length of the queue shared by all the sources). Monitoring these values may be expensive in practice, in which case a source may choose to use the nonselective DECbit scheme described at the end of this subsection. The network element computes source demands and queue lengths as averages over *queue regeneration cycles* (Figure 13.7). A queue regeneration cycle has a *busy* and an *idle* component. The busy period starts when the queue size goes from zero to one (we count the packet being transmitted as part of the queue) and ends when the queue size goes back to zero. Thus, during the busy period, the queue always has data to send. The idle period spans the time when the queue is idle; it ends when the next busy period starts. A source's demand is the mean number of packets it transmits during the current (partial) and pre-

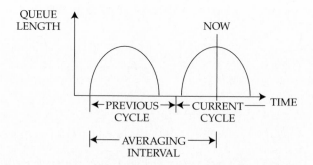

Figure 13.7: Regeneration periods. A regeneration period begins when a queue goes from 0 to 1, and ends when the next period begins. In the DECbit scheme, routers measure quantities averaged since the beginning of the previous regeneration period.

vious regeneration cycles. The network element similarly computes the aggregate mean queue length over the current and previous regeneration cycles.

Measuring source demands and the mean queue length over regeneration cycles may seem, at first, to introduce unnecessary complexity. Notice, however, that the two metrics, by definition, must be computed over *some* time interval. The choice, then, is only of how long this interval should be. The measurement interval should represent a balance between sensitivity to the current system state (which argues for short measurement intervals) and stability in the measurement, to prevent the control mechanism from reacting to a transient burst of packet arrivals (which argues for longer measurement intervals). Experiments show that averages computed over regeneration cycles provide a good balance between the two objectives [RJ 90].

Although a server could compute averages over the immediately past complete regeneration cycle, and use these to set bits until the end of the current cycle, this does not work well if the current regeneration cycle is long and measures during the past cycle are outdated. The source avoids this by measuring demands and queue lengths over the immediately past and current (partial) regeneration cycle, so that as the current regeneration period increases in length, its contribution to the system performance measures becomes increasingly important.

A server takes control actions if the measured mean queue length crosses one of two thresholds. The first threshold is set to 1.0. If the mean queue length exceeds this value, the server always has at least one packet in service, so that it is 100% utilized, and in danger of being swamped by the sources. Thus, it sets bits on packets from sources whose demand is larger than their *max–min fair share,* as defined in Section 9.2.2. This causes them to reduce their window size, and thus their rate, relieving the load on the server. The second threshold is set to 2.0. If the mean queue length exceeds this value, not only is the server 100% utilized, but its efforts at setting bits have not decreased the queue size. The server therefore goes into panic mode and sets bits on *all* packets. The idea is that the server should rarely enter this state, and if it does, it should get out of it as soon as possible, irrespective of fairness.

Source actions

A source keeps track of the bits it receives in the ack headers and uses this to dynamically adapt its flow control window. Notice that once a source changes its window size, it takes one RTT before this change propagates to every server along the path. For the control to be stable, the source should measure the network state for an additional RTT before it changes its window size again. Thus, a source should change its window once every *two* RTTs. Specifically, if, after changing the window size, the previous window size is p and the current window size is w, the source should wait till it receives $w + p$ acknowledgments, then examine the bits in the last w acks. It is recommended that a source reduce its window size if more than 50% of the bits are 1, and otherwise increase its window size. The control mechanism, however, is insensitive to this choice of threshold [RJ 90].

The window change policy is *additive increase multiplicative decrease (AIMD)*. When the window increases, it increases by an additive factor, but when it decreases, it decreases by a multiplicative factor. Chiu and Jain have shown that this behavior leads to a stable system [CJ 89]. Intuitively, the source increases its transmission rate cautiously (additively), but decreases it rapidly (multiplicatively). The recommended additive increase value is 1, and the recommended multiplicative decrease factor is 0.875. The justification for these choices can be found in references [RJ 90, CJ 89].

Nonselective DECbit

In the scheme we have studied thus far, the router must compute a demand per source, which is expensive in terms of both storage and computation. In an alternative scheme, called *nonselective DECbit*, the router measures only the mean aggregate queue length, which does not need per-source storage and therefore is less expensive. In this scheme, if the mean queue length exceeds 1.0, then the server sets bits on all packets. This reduces the aggregate queue length rapidly, but can be unfair to sources that have their bits set although their demand is less than their fair share. It is also unfair to connections that have longer RTTs, because they take longer to recover from a rapid window decrease. Source actions for the selective DECbit and nonselective DECbit scheme are identical.

Evaluation

The DECbit scheme has several useful properties. It requires only one additional bit in the packet header and does not require per-connection queuing at servers. Endpoints can implement the scheme in software, without additional hardware support. Moreover, many simulations, and experience in the field, have shown that the control is stable [RJ 90]. Figure 13.8 shows the behavior of the scheme in a simple scenario (from [RJ 90]).

However, the DECbit scheme has two serious flaws. First, it assumes that the endpoints are cooperative. If a source chooses to ignore the bits it receives in its acks, it can drive the server to the panic state, so that all other sources sharing the server are affected [DKS 89]. Thus, a single malicious or misbehaving source can affect the performance of all other sources. As we saw in Chapter 9, to control misbehaving or malicious sources, a network must provide either per-connection queuing, or per-connection policing using a traffic descriptor.

The second problem with DECbit is that it has a very conservative window increase policy. If the initial window size is 5 and the optimal window size is 200, the source will take 390 RTTs to reach this value, because the window increases by only 1 every two RTTs. If a source does not have much data to send, it finishes its transmission before reaching its optimal window size! Thus, DECbit performs poorly in networks where the bandwidth–delay product is large, which is expected to be the case for future wide-area networks.

EXAMPLE 13.6

If the RTT is 60 ms, which corresponds to a cross-continental path, the service rate available to a source is 5 Mbps, and its mean packet size is 500 bytes, its optimal

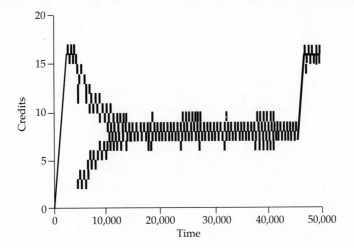

Figure 13.8: Window sizes (in packets) versus time (in simulation units) for two DECbit sources. Source 1 starts at time 0 and increases its window linearly until the bottleneck queue builds up. Subsequently, the window size oscillates around the optimal value. When a second source starts up, source 1 reduces its window size, and at equilibrium, both sources share the bottleneck bandwidth evenly, because they both have the same window size. (From [RJ 90].)

window is $5^6 * 60^{-3} = 300{,}000$ bits $= 300{,}000/4000 = 75$ packets. Thus, the source takes 150 RTTs $= 150 * 60^{-3} = 9$ s to reach its optimal window size. If its transfer size is smaller than about 5 Mbytes, it would complete its transmission before reaching this value.

13.4.5 TCP flow control

Explicit	Dynamic window	End-to-end
Implicit	Dynamic rate	Hop-by-hop

The flow-control scheme in TCP, designed by Jacobson and Karels, is similar to the DECbit scheme, but differs in one important detail [Jacobson 88]. Instead of receiving explicit congestion information from network elements, a source dynamically adjusts its flow control window in response to *implicit* signals of network overload. Specifically, a source increases its window size until it detects a packet loss. At this point, the source reduces the window size, and the cycle repeats (Figure 13.9).

A source starts with a window of size 1 and increases it exponentially until the window size reaches a threshold, and linearly after that. We maintain the current window

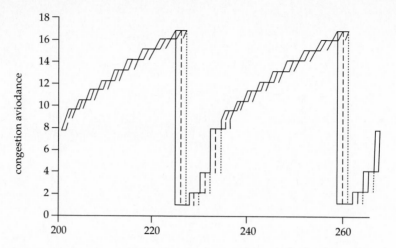

Figure 13.9: Behavior of three TCP-Tahoe sources. Three sources start simultaneously, and the figure shows the evolution of their window sizes. Each source increases its window linearly in the congestion-avoidance stage. When the queue fills up, all three sources see one loss, and all of them drop their window size to 1. The window increases first exponentially, then linearly, till each source loses one packet each, and the cycle repeats. (From [ZSC 91].)

size in a floating-point number, the integral part of which is the window size (this is explained further in Example 13.7). In the exponential (or *slow-start*) phase, a source increases its window by 1 every time it receives an ack. If every packet is acked, this doubles the window size every RTT (in practice, some receivers send only one ack for every two packets, halving the increase rate). In the linear (or *congestion-avoidance*) phase, the source increases its window by $1/\lfloor current\_window \rfloor$ every time it receives an ack. This increases the window by 1 every RTT. A threshold variable called the *slow-start threshold* or *ssthresh* controls the transition from the exponential to the linear phase. The source initializes this variable to half the initial window size, and, on detecting a loss, resets it to half the current window size.

There are two widely used variants of TCP. The *Tahoe* version detects losses using timeouts. On a timeout, it decreases its flow control window to 1, sets *ssthresh* to half the current window size, and enters slow start. The window thus rises exponentially to half its previous value, then continues with a linear increase. The *Reno* version detects losses using both timeouts and the receipt of three acks with the same cumulative sequence number (the *fast retransmit* scheme explained in Section 12.4.7). On a timeout, a TCP Reno source behaves in the same way as a TCP Tahoe source. However, on a fast retransmit, it decreases both *ssthresh* and its flow-control window to half its previous value. At this point, since the flow-control window is already as large as *ssthresh*, the source goes directly into the linear increase phase, skipping the exponential increase phase. Moreover, after a fast retransmit, the source is allowed to send one packet for each duplicate cumulative ack received, even if this causes it to exceed the flow-control window size (this is called *fast recovery*). The intuition is that each cumulative ack, even if duplicate, signals the availability of network resources. By "inflating" the actual window beyond the nominal window, a source can exploit this capacity. This window inflation ceases when a source receives the first nonduplicate cumulative ack, indicating that the retransmission succeeded.

EXAMPLE 13.7

Let us trace the evolution of the window size of a source that is transmitting data over a connection with RTT 1. Assume that its initial value for *ssthresh* is 5, and the largest allowed flow control window is 10. We will also assume that the bandwidth–delay product on the connection is 4 (that is, the bottleneck service rate is 4 packets/second), and the bottleneck has a buffer size of 4 packets.

In the first RTT, the source sends packet 1 at time 0 and receives an ack at time 1. At the end of the first RTT, the source increases its window by 1 for this ack, doubling its window to 2. Thus, at time 1, it sends packets 2 and 3. As each ack arrives, the window increases by 1, so that at the end of the second RTT, the window is 4.

In the third RTT, the source sends packet 4, 5, 6, 7. At the end of the third RTT, when the ack for 4 arrives, the window increases to 5 and reaches the slow-start threshold. Thus, the acks for 5, 6, 7, which arrive during the fourth RTT, each contributes $\frac{1}{5}$ to the window size, and when the ack for 7 is received, the window reaches 5.6 (only the integer portion is used for flow control).

In the fourth RTT, five packets can be outstanding, and the source transmits 8, 9, 10, 11, 12. When the source receives the ack for 9, during the fifth RTT, the window finally increases to 6, and acks for 10, 11, and 12 each contribute $\frac{1}{6}$ to the window. Thus, at the end of the fifth RTT, the window reaches 6.5. In the absence of losses, the window increases slowly until it reaches nine packets during the eighth RTT. Of these, four are "in the pipeline," because the bandwidth delay product is 4. Four more can be buffered in the bottleneck buffer. Thus, one packet is lost at the bottleneck (the packet with sequence number 42). This causes the receiver to repeat the cumulative acknowledgment on packets sent during the ninth RTT, triggering a fast retransmission.

At the start of the ninth RTT, the source has nine packets outstanding and has a window size of 9.333. During the ninth RTT, the source receives acks for packets 34–41, which increases its window, at the end of the ninth RTT, to 10.2. Thus, the source, during the 9th RTT, sends ten packets, 43–52. The last ack received during the ninth RTT is the ack for 41, which was the last packet sent before a packet loss.

In the tenth RTT, the source receives acks for packets sent in the ninth RTT. The acks for packets 43–52 all carry the same cumulative ack number, that is, 41 (these acks increase the window from 10.2 to 10.5). On the third such duplicate, the source invokes fast retransmission (see Section 12.4.7) and retransmits 42. (Meanwhile, when it got the acks for 43 and 44, it transmitted 53 and 54.) In both TCP-Tahoe and TCP-Reno, fast retransmission causes the source to set its *ssthresh* value to $\lfloor 10.5/2 \rfloor = 5$. TCP-Reno sets its window size to $10.5/2 = 5.25$ and enters the linear increase phase. Thus, in the tenth RTT, a TCP-Reno source has five packets outstanding: 42 and 53–56. In TCP-Tahoe, the window drops to 1. It cannot send any more packets after 42. Thus, in the tenth RTT, a TCP-Tahoe source has three packets outstanding: 53, 54, and 42. In two round-trip times, the window comes back to 4, and the source reenters the linear increase phase.

The table below illustrates the behavior of TCP-Reno.

RTT #	Window range during RTT	Packets sent in this RTT	ssthresh	Peak buffer size
1	1–2	1	5	0
2	2–4	2, 3	5	0
3	4–5	4–7	5	0
4	5–5.6	8–12	5	1
5	5.6–6.5	13–18	5	2
6	6.5–7.428	19–25	5	3
7	7.428–8.375	26–33	5	4
8	8.375–9.333	34–42	5	4/drop
9	9.333–10.2	43–52	5	4/drop
10	10.2–10.5/5.25	42, 53–56	5	1

This example is somewhat artificial, because it uses packet sequence numbers rather than TCP's segment ranges, and because the RTT is always 1, without any variation during the connection. Many real-life traces of TCP in action, with copious explanations, can be found in reference [Stevens 94].

The TCP-Tahoe and TCP-Reno flow-control algorithms have motivations similar to the DECbit algorithm we studied in Section 13.4.4. Both use dynamic-window flow control. In either case, a source uses a conservative window-increase policy (exponential and then additive in TCP, additive in DECbit), and a multiplicative decrease policy. We know that an additive-increase, multiplicative-decrease policy is stable, unlike variations such as additive increase, additive decrease, or multiplicative increase, additive decrease, so this coincidence is not surprising [CJ 89]. The main difference between the algorithms is that the TCP-Tahoe and -Reno algorithms do not require explicit information about the current congestion status from the network. They view the network as a black box, which they probe by increasing the transmission-window size and looking for packet loss. In contrast, with DECbit, the network explicitly communicates information about queue buildups to the sources. A second difference is that the two TCP algorithms do not filter information at the source, for example, by treating multiple packet losses over a time interval as an indication of congestion, instead of a single packet loss. This is because they operate the network close to overload, and unless they cut back the window size immediately after detecting a loss, the network is in danger of sustained overload.

Evaluation

TCP flow-control algorithms are effective over a wide range of bandwidths, and because of their popularity, there is considerable experience in understanding their performance

bottleneck buffer. The source does not change its window if this number lies in a range α to β, where these are user-selected low and high watermarks. Otherwise, the source adjusts the transmission window so that in the next RTT the expected number of packets in the buffer reaches this value.

Evaluation

TCP-Vegas has been simulated and tested in the field [BP 95, ADLY 95]. Current experience shows that it performs better than TCP-Tahoe or -Reno. A serious concern is whether TCP-Vegas connections sharing a link with TCP-Reno connections gain better performance at the expense of TCP-Reno. Small-scale simulations and experiments indicate that this is probably not the case. Given the popularity of TCP, incremental improvements in its performance are worth the effort. TCP-Vegas, though not an ideal flow-control scheme, is a step in the right direction.

13.4.7   NETBLT

Explicit	Dynamic window	End-to-end
Implicit	Dynamic rate	Hop-by-hop

NETBLT was the first widely known *rate-based flow-control* protocol [CLZ 88]. Dynamic-window flow-control schemes control the transmission rate by adjusting the size of the transmission window. Thus, the window is used both for error control and flow control. In contrast, in rate-based flow control, the transmission rate does not depend on a flow-control window. Consequently, losses and retransmissions, which modify the error-control window, do not directly affect the rate at which data is transmitted into the network. This decoupling of error and flow control considerably simplifies both components.

A NETBLT source divides application data into several *buffers,* where each buffer consists of some number of packets. The source and destination negotiate a transfer rate for each buffer. The rate is expressed as a burst size and a burst rate, so that a source needs to control the rate only at the granularity of a burst. Data packets are placed in a transmission queue drained at the negotiated rate. If packets are lost, retransmitted packets are also placed in the same transmission queue so that the source transmission rate is limited to the negotiated rate independent of the loss behavior. This is unlike TCP, where a packet loss causes a decrease in the source transmission rate.

In the original NETBLT scheme, the source and the destination negotiate a transfer rate independent of the capacity available in the network. If the negotiated rate is too high, however, this leads to persistent packet loss. To solve this problem, in the revised version of the protocol, when a source transmits data at a rate r, it explicitly informs the receiver about this rate, and the receiver measures the rate r' at which it receives data. If $r' < r$, then the largest rate the network can support must be smaller than r. Thus, the source multiplicatively reduces its rate to βr, where $\beta < 1$. On the other hand, if $r' = r$, the source additively increases its rate to $r + \alpha$.

Evaluation

NETBLT's main contribution to flow control is in its separation of flow and error control. The original design ignored bottlenecks in the network, and the revised algorithm adapts only slowly to changing capacity in the bottleneck, because a source takes control decisions only once for each buffer's worth of packets. Thus, the algorithm tends to either overflow or underflow the bottleneck buffer. Nevertheless, rate-based flow control, an idea first embodied in NETBLT, is a rich and interesting area for research. When carefully implemented, rate-based flow control has the potential to provide a complete solution to the flow-control problem.

13.4.8 Packet-pair

Explicit	Dynamic window	End-to-end
Implicit	Dynamic rate	Hop-by-hop

Packet-pair flow control improves on NETBLT's performance by better estimating the bottleneck capacity in the network [Keshav 91, Keshav 97]. Moreover, it *predicts* the future service rate in the network and *corrects* for incorrect past predictions. These allow it to maintain a certain number of packets in the bottleneck queue precisely (its *setpoint*) despite variations in the bottleneck service rate.

Unlike other flow-control schemes, packet-pair explicitly assumes that all the bottlenecks in the networks serve packets in round-robin order. Thus, when two packets belonging to the same connection enter a server back-to-back, an interval that is inversely proportional to the connection's service rate at the bottleneck separates them when they leave (Figure 13.10). Note that the separation is largest at the bottleneck server. Thus, if the receiver measures the packet separation (or if the source measures the acknowledgment separation), the receiver (or source) can directly determine the bottleneck service rate. A packet-pair source sends *all* packets as pairs (except if the source only has a single packet to send). Thus, a source can update its estimate of the bottleneck service rate with every pair of acks it receives. If the bottleneck service rate changes with time, the source automatically detects and adapts to the change.

Assume, for the moment, that all packets are the same size. Let $\mu(k)$ be the bottleneck service rate detected by the kth ack pair. Packet-pair does *exponential averaging* of the time series $\mu(1), \mu(2), \ldots \mu(k)$ to predict $\hat{\mu}(k + 1)$ (see a description in Section 12.4.6), so that

$$\hat{\mu}(k + 1) = \alpha * \hat{\mu}(k) + (1 - \alpha) * \mu(k), \qquad 0 < \alpha < 1 \qquad (13.10)$$

The averaging factor, α, is altered dynamically to simultaneously eliminate spikes in the measured $\mu(k)$ and quickly latch on to "long-term" changes [KK 92].

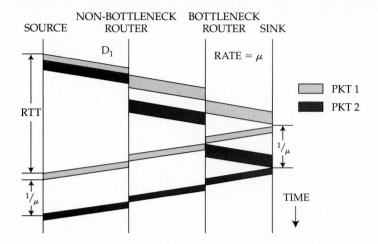

Figure 13.10: Packet pair. The source sends two packets back-to-back, and they are separated at every server because of cross traffic. If the servers obey a round-robin-like discipline, the largest separation of the pair measures the bottleneck service rate for this source. The packet separation is reflected in the inter-ack spacing, which can be measured at the source.

Given the round-trip propagation delay R and the number of packets outstanding (that is, transmitted, but not acknowledged) S, packet-pair estimates X, the number of packets in the bottleneck buffer, as:

$$X = S - R\,\hat{\mu}(k + 1), \tag{13.11}$$

because of the S packets, $R\hat{\mu}(k + 1)$ are "in the pipe," so the rest must be in the bottleneck buffer. If the setpoint is B, then the source adjusts the actual transmission rate so that it reaches the setpoint in approximately one round-trip time. Thus, the transmission rate $\lambda(k + 1)$ is given by:

$$\lambda(k + 1) = \hat{\mu}(k + 1) + (B - X)/R \tag{13.12}$$

It can be shown both analytically and through simulation that this choice of λ results in a control system that is stable and does not oscillate [Keshav 91, ABB 93]. In practice, λ is updated using this equation on the arrival of each ack pair. When a source sends a pair of packets, it uses the latest value of λ to set a timer for the next pair of packets.

The hard part in packet-pair is in computing the number of outstanding packets, S, accurately in the presence of packet losses. If a source does not decrement S to account for lost packets, the estimate for X is too large, and thus λ is too small, leading to underutilization of the bottleneck. Fortunately, we can reliably estimate S using the SMART algorithm presented in Section 12.4.7. Simulations show that by carefully accounting for packet and ack losses, packet-pair, with SMART, works extremely well even with loss rates as high as 10% [KM 97].

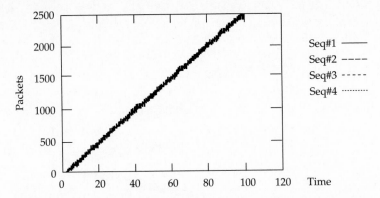

Figure 13.11: Packet-pair performance. The figure shows the sequence-number trace of four sources sharing a bottleneck. All four sources get an equal share of the bandwidth and make progress at nearly equal rates. None of the sources experiences a pause in transmission due to a timeout. This behavior is nearly the best possible. (From [Keshav 97].)

Evaluation

Exhaustive simulations show that packet-pair flow control is stable in a variety of scenarios. For example, Figure 13.11 (from [Keshav 97]) plots the sequence number versus time for four packet-pair sources that share a common bottleneck server. We see that all four sources make progress at equal rates. Moreover, there are no pauses due to timeouts and retransmissions. Indeed, this is the best performance that one can expect. It has been shown that for many scenarios, packet-pair's performance is nearly as good as an (unimplementable) optimal flow-control scheme that assumes that network elements have infinite buffers [KKM 93, Keshav 97]. Packet-pair scales well with network size and does not require any explicit information from network elements. Thus, it is a good choice for flow control in networks of round-robin servers.

Unfortunately, most current networks do not provide round-robin-like servers (though the situation is rapidly changing). In such networks, a scheme such as the EERC scheme described in Section 13.4.9 can be used to explicitly convey rate and buffer size information to an endpoint. If one or both quantities are available, a source can plug them into the equations given earlier.

13.4.9   ATM Forum end-to-end rate-control scheme

Explicit	Dynamic window	End-to-end
Implicit	Dynamic rate	Hop-by-hop

The ATM Forum has adopted an explicit *end-to-end rate-based flow-control* (*EERC*) scheme, similar to the DECbit explicit end-to-end dynamic *window* flow-control scheme we studied in Section 13.4.4, for controlling *available bit-rate* (*ABR*) traffic (see Section 14.4.3)

[BF 95]. In this scheme, each source periodically sends a *resource management* (*RM*) cell with a request for an allocation of a particular transmission rate in the next time interval. Each network element (or server) computes a rate allocation per-source according to the max–min fairness criterion described in Section 13.4.4. It writes this rate in the RM cell, which carries it back to the source. At the source, the rate in the RM cell is used to dynamically modify its transmission rate. The scheme therefore is similar to the DECbit scheme, except that a bottlenecked server is allowed to return more information to the sender, and the sender uses this to adapt a rate rather than a window.

We begin a detailed description of this scheme with a table of acronyms (Table 13.3), which the ATM Forum liberally uses in its documents. Starred acronyms refer to fields negotiated at the time of call establishment.

Acronym	Expansion	Explanation
RM cell	Resource management cell	A probe cell periodically sent by a source that returns with the currently available service rate.
NRM	Number of resource management cells	A source sends an RM cell every NRM data cells.
ER	Explicit rate	A field in the RM cell that initially carries the rate a source requests and is modified by intermediate network elements.
ACR	Allowed cell rate	The rate at which the source actually transmits.
PCR*	Peak cell rate	The highest rate at which a source can ever transmit.
ICR*	Initial cell rate	The initial rate at which a source transmits.
MCR*	Minimum cell rate	The minimum transmission rate. A source is guaranteed to have a rate of at least MCR always available.
RIF*	Rate increase factor	An increase factor used for additive increase. If there is no congestion, a source increases its rate by RIF times PCR.
RDF*	Rate decrease factor	A decrease factor used for multiplicative decrease in the allowed cell rate.
EFCI or EFCN bit	Explicit forward congestion indication or notification bit	A bit in the header of every cell that can be set by a congested network element.
CI bit	Congestion indication bit	A bit in an RM cell (instead of a cell header) that carries the value of the EFCI field from the destination to the source.

Table 13.3: Acronyms used in the ATM Forum end-to-end rate-control scheme. Starred acronyms refer to fields negotiated at the time of call establishment.

A source interleaves its data cells with RM cells by transmitting one RM cell for every *NRM* data cells, where NRM is a parameter to the scheme and is usually around 32. The RM cell contains an *explicit rate (ER)*, which is the rate at which the source would like to send in the immediate future. When a network element receives an RM cell, it computes the source's bandwidth share in some fashion (not defined in the standard), and if this share is smaller than the source's demanded rate (ER), it reduces the value of the ER field. A bit in the RM cell selects either network elements in the forward (source-to-destination) direction or elements in the backward (destination-to-source) direction. A network element modifies the ER only if it is on the appropriate path. As the RM cell traverses the duplex virtual circuit from the source to the destination and back to the source, each selected network element decreases the ER value in the RM cell to the smallest allocated share along the path. Thus, a source discovers its allocated bandwidth share, in the forward or backward direction, one round-trip time after injecting an RM cell.

The ATM Forum does not specify how a network element computes a bandwidth share. This freedom allows manufacturers to introduce innovative and efficient algorithms into their products while still being standard-compatible and interoperable with other manufacturers' equipment. The ATM Forum does recommend a source *reference behavior* to respond to RM cells. Most sources will probably obey the reference behavior, to which we now turn our attention.

During call setup, the network guarantees a source that its ACR will never be smaller than the *minimum cell rate (MCR)*. A source informs the network that its transmission rate will never be larger than some *peak cell rate (PCR)*. Moreover, immediately after call setup, the network allows the source to send data at a rate called the *initial cell rate (ICR)*.

At any given time, a source sends data into the network at a rate called the *allowed cell rate (ACR)*. We thus define the intercell spacing between any two cells to be 1/ACR. Every RM cell returns with a new value of ER. A source changes its ACR in response to the ER field in a received RM cell as follows:

$$
\begin{aligned}
&\text{If } ER > ACR, \\
&\qquad \text{then } ACR = ACR + RIF * PCR \\
&\text{If } ER \le ACR, \\
&\qquad \text{then } ACR = ER
\end{aligned}
\tag{13.13}
$$

If the ER is larger than the ACR, the ACR is increased by the product of the *peak cell rate (PCR)* (negotiated at call establishment) and the *rate increase factor (RIF)*. This is the additive increase step corresponding to DECbit's additive increase of its transmission window. If ER is smaller than ACR, then the ACR is reduced to ER.

The EERC scheme is designed to interoperate with network elements that are not sophisticated enough to process RM cells. Instead, when such elements are congested, they set a bit in the standard ATM cell header called the *explicit forward congestion indication (EFCI)* bit. Thus, the destination of a virtual circuit passing through a congested network element receives a stream of cells with the EFCI bit set. When a source sends an RM cell, the destination, when returning the cell to the source, copies the value of the last

EFCI bit it received into the *congestion indication (CI)* bit in the RM cell. Thus, when an RM cell returns, it carries not only an explicit rate, but also the latest value of the EFCI bit. The source uses this to adjust its transmission rate (ACR) as follows:

If (CI bit is 0)
　　　　If ER > ACR,
　　　　　　then ACR = ACR + RIF * PCR
　　　　If ER ≤ ACR,
　　　　　　then ACR = ER   (13.14)
If (CI bit is 1)
　　　　ACR = ACR (1 − RDF)
　　　　If ER ≤ ACR,
　　　　　　then ACR = ER

If the CI bit is not set, the source behaves exactly as before. If the CI bit is 1, then the source does a multiplicative decrease of its ACR. If this is still greater than the ER, it reduces its rate to the ER value. Since the scheme considers both ER and the CI bit, it allows interoperability between network elements that provide only EFCI bits and network elements that provide the full RM cell functionality.

There are two additional details. First, what if a source does not use its allocated rate? We do not want it to start after a while and use a rate allocated to it a long time ago, when the network was less utilized, and the ACR much higher. Thus, the EERC has the notion of "use it or lose it." If a source is idle for 500 ms (or a higher value that can be negotiated during call establishment), its ACR is reset back to the initial cell rate (ICR). Thus, a source awakening after a long idle period injects traffic into the network no faster than ICR. One round-trip time after waking up, it can use the information in the first RM cell to update its ACR to the currently sustainable rate in the network.

Second, what if an outage causes no RM cells to return to a source? We do not want the source to keep pumping information into a black hole! Thus, the source keeps track of whether it receives an RM cell back. If it does not receive any RM cells for a prescribed interval, it decreases its sending rate by a multiplicative factor. Thus, when a link goes down, all affected sources eventually stop transmission. This makes the flow control scheme more robust.

Evaluation

The EERC scheme has been studied in many scenarios. It has been shown to be responsive, stable, and capable of sharing bandwidth fairly among competing sources (assuming that network elements mark RM cells with this fair share). The scheme improves on DECbit in several ways. The RM cell potentially allows sources to know their exact bandwidth share, instead of having to guess it from the DECbits (at the expense of using much more bandwidth). The scheme also allows switches that only support EFCI bits to interoperate with fully functional switches. Finally, by allowing sources to start with an MCR or ICR value, the scheme eliminates the extremely conservative slow start of DECbit.

However, the scheme has several problems. First, the source interleaves RM cells with the data cells. Thus, every switch must contain special data paths to pull out the RM cell, modify it, and reinject it into the data stream. This is complicated, particularly at high speeds, leading to a higher cost for source and server hardware.

Second, at every source, the arrival of an RM cell updates its sending rate. At high speeds, this updating can only be done in complex hardware. This has its own problems, because tracing and repairing algorithmic bugs embedded in hardware is hard. Moreover, improvements in the scheme require a hardware change at every endpoint, stifling innovation.

Third, in the current standard, the network expects sources to space cells exactly 1/ACR seconds apart. If an endpoint has several connections simultaneously open, then it must schedule cells on each of these connections at a different ACR. Again, at high speeds, this can be done only in complicated hardware.

Fourth, to be interoperable with network elements that do not support RM cells, the scheme does not directly use the explicit rate as the current sending rate. Instead, if the CI bit is not set, when the explicit rate is larger than the current rate, the current sending rate is increased by an additive step. If the step size is too small, a source takes a long time to use newly available resources, wasting them. If it is too large, on a path where no congested network element processes RM cells, a source oscillates between the congested and uncongested state, with a potential for congestive cell loss. Thus, interoperability comes only at a cost.

Finally, a server must compute the resource share of each source based on the source's demand. The demand either can be estimated by direct measurement, as in the DECbit scheme, or can be read from the ER field in the RM cell. Either course of action has its problems. If a server must estimate source demand by observation, then it must maintain information about the number of cells transmitted on each VC, and may need to keep track of regeneration periods as in the DECbit scheme. As with DECbit, this can be hard to do at high speeds. If the source demand is read from the ER field of the RM cell, the switch must be sure that a source cannot send at a rate different from the one claimed in the RM cell. This means that the source must be policed at the edge of the network, or trusted hardware at every endpoint must enforce the ACR. Clearly, both alternatives lead to additional complexity in the system, and thus an added cost. These problems mean that although the EERC scheme has some desirable properties, it is complex and forces a hardware-oriented solution to flow control.

13.4.10 Mishra/Kanakia hop-by-hop scheme

Explicit	Dynamic window	End-to-end
Implicit	Dynamic rate	Hop-by-hop

All the schemes we have studied thus far have been implemented end-to-end. We now consider two flow-control schemes implemented not only at the endpoints, but also at every intermediate hop. In general, the performance gain of a hop-by-hop scheme depends on the ratio of the largest hop delay to the overall end-to-end delay. The larger this ratio, the smaller the gain in performance. For connections that span a LAN, the largest hop delay is usually a small fraction of the end-to-end delay, since all hops have roughly the same propagation delay. For connections that span WANs, a wide-area hop may contribute to a significant fraction of the end-to-end delay. In this situation, the performance of a hop-by-hop scheme degrades to that of a comparable end-to-end scheme.

The Mishra/Kanakia flow-control scheme [MK 92] is a rate-based flow-control scheme similar to packet-pair flow control, but implemented at each hop along a connection's path. Neighboring network elements periodically exchange explicit resource management packets that contain the buffer occupancy and actual service rate of every connection traversing that path. For a particular simplex connection, we can order network elements as *upstream* or *downstream* of each other, depending on whether they precede or follow each other in the connection's path. Every network element periodically samples a sending rate and buffer occupancy for each connection passing through it, and sends this information to that connection's neighboring upstream element (Figure 13.12). The upstream element uses this information to control its sending rate, and to update the information it sends *its* upstream element. Thus, when an intermediate queuing point gets overloaded, its upstream network element throttles each connection sharing the queue, and this throttling propagates upstream until every affected source also reduces its rate. Mishra and Kanakia have shown using simulations that with well-chosen control parameters, a source controls its transmission rate to match the current bottleneck rate within a couple of round-trip times from the onset of congestion.

We now study the mechanics of rate control in a simplified version of the MK scheme. Each network element receives a series of per-connection buffer-length and ser-

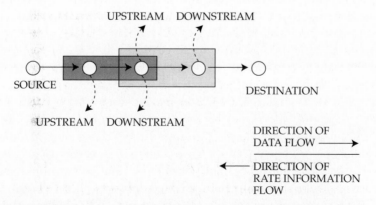

Figure 13.12: Data and control flow in the MK scheme. Data flows downstream. Each downstream network element periodically sends information about the data rate and buffer occupancy of each connection to the corresponding upstream neighbor.

vice-rate updates from its downstream element. Let the buffer length in update k be $x(k)$ and the downstream service rate, which is the number of packets the downstream element sent in the previous update interval, be $\mu(k)$. Let the buffer setpoint at the downstream element be B, and the round-trip propagation delay along the hop be R_{hop}. Then, the source estimates $\nu(k + 1)$, the future sending rate at the downstream node, using an exponential average, as:

$$\nu(k + 1) = \alpha\nu(k) + (1 - \alpha)\mu(k) \tag{13.15}$$

The future buffer occupancy at the downstream node, $y(k + 1)$, is computed as:

$$y(k + 1) = x(k) + (\lambda(k - 1) + \lambda(k)) - (\nu(k - 1) + \nu(k)) \tag{13.16}$$

We compute the sending rate during the $(k + 1)$th interval, $\lambda(k + 1)$, as:

$$\lambda(k + 1) = \nu(k + 1) + (\beta / R_{hop})(B - y(k + 1)) \tag{13.17}$$

The first term on the right-hand side of Equation 13.17 is the estimated service rate. The second term is a correction factor to account for the existing buffer size. Note the close relationship between Equations 13.15 and 13.17 and packet-pair's Equations 13.10 and 13.12. In the MK scheme, $\beta(0 \leq \beta \leq 1)$ is a damping factor that controls the time taken by the system to reach its desired value. The MK scheme and packet-pair were independently developed, but both use the same control equation, which represents a one-step-ahead predictive control system.

The scheme described here has one control action taken per feedback. In the extended version of this scheme, if the upstream network element receives many feedback packets in one time interval R_{hop}, it averages their values, and still takes control action only once per interval R_{hop}. We leave it as an exercise to the reader to modify the preceding equations so that a source appropriately averages the feedback information (see also reference [MK 92]).

Evaluation

Because of the close relationship between the packet-pair and MK control equations, their behavior is similar. The MK scheme, however, always performs better because the delay in its control loop is smaller than that of packet-pair. Moreover, unlike packet-pair, the MK controller does not require round-robin scheduling. Simulations show that on the same set of benchmark scenarios, the MK scheme usually performs within 5% of an (unimplementable) optimal scheme (which assumes infinite buffering at servers), whereas packet-pair usually performs within 10% of optimal [KKM 93].

The main problem with the MK scheme, as with any hop-by-hop scheme, is that because network elements must control every connection, they are more complex, and thus more expensive. Moreover, the network must implement the scheme at *every* network element, which makes it unsuitable for heterogeneous networks. The rate information packets add to the network traffic, though this is insignificant for high-speed networks. Given network elements with sufficient power, and the ability to implement the scheme at every node, the MK scheme is a nearly optimal solution for flow control.

13.4.11 Credit-based scheme

Explicit	Dynamic window	End-to-end
Implicit	Dynamic rate	Hop-by-hop

A recent proposal for hop-by-hop flow control in ATM networks is based on a per-connection per-link flow control window [KC 93, KBC 94, KM 95]. The key idea is that a per-hop window restricts a connection's rate in much the same way as in the MK scheme. Moreover, by restricting a source to its window, and reserving a window's worth of buffers at the downstream network element, we eliminate congestive losses. Table 13.4 helps navigate the description of the scheme.

The two components of the hop-by-hop dynamic window scheme are (a) the techniques used to enforce the per-connection window, and (b) the algorithm used to dynamically recompute the window size. Enforcing the window is as follows: A downstream network element, D, allocates B cell buffers to each connection arriving from an

Acronym	Expansion	Explanation
D	Downstream network element	
U	Upstream network element	
CB(U)	Credit balance at upstream network element	The number of cells the upstream element is allowed to send before receiving a credit update.
C(U)	Counter at upstream network element	Counts the number of cells sent from the upstream element.
C(D)	Counter at downstream network element	Counts the number of cells sent from the downstream element.
B	Buffer at downstream network element	Allocated to each connection from each upstream network element.
CUP	Credit update packet	A cell sent from a downstream element to an upstream element informing it of how many more cells it can send before it must stop.

Table 13.4: Acronyms used in the credit-based scheme.

upstream node, U. U and D both maintain per-connection counters $C(U)$ and $C(D)$. $C(U)$ counts the number of cells transmitted from U, and $C(D)$ the number of cells transmitted from D. U also maintains a *credit balance* $CB(U)$, and transmits data only if $CB(U)$ is positive. U decrements $CB(U)$ every time it sends a packet. Now, $C(U) - C(D)$ measures the number of packets that are either in transit between U and D, or in D's buffers. Thus, U can send up to $B - (C(U) - C(D))$ packets without overflowing D's buffer. D periodically sends U a *credit update packet* that contains the current value of $C(D)$ and B. When U gets this packet, it updates $CB(U)$ to $B - (C(U) - C(D))$. We call this the *credit update protocol*.

EXAMPLE 13.8

Suppose the upstream counter for a particular connection was 100, and the corresponding downstream counter was 25. Then, the upstream element has sent 75 more cells than the downstream element. Where could these cells be? Some of them are in transit between the upstream and the downstream elements, and the others must be in the downstream element's buffers. Suppose the downstream element has space for 200 cells. If it tells the upstream element that (a) it sent only 25 cells on the connection, and (b) it has space for 200, then the upstream element, from its counter, knows that the buffer contains at most 75 cells, and so has space for 125 more. It therefore sets its credit balance to $200 - 75 = 125$. If it never sends a cell when the credit balance is zero, it can be sure that none of its cells will be lost to a buffer overflow.

The second component of the scheme is the adaptation of the buffer allocation at a downstream node to control the rate of each incident connection. The scheme assumes that a fair scheduling algorithm allocates service rates to the connections queued at the network element. The goal of the buffer adaptation is to ensure that the throughput constraint on a connection is always the allocated service rate, rather than the flow-control window. We can ensure this if switches have sufficient buffering, and if each connection is allocated a window at least as large as the largest possible bandwidth–delay product on that link. However, this may require many buffers and can be expensive. Thus, the credit-based scheme reallocates the window size in proportion to the source's actual service rate.

Each network element maintains counts T and $V(i)$ defined as:

$$T = \text{total number of cells forwarded along a link at any time} \tag{13.18}$$

$$V(i) = \text{per-connection count of the cells forwarded along connection } i$$

The ratio $V(i)/T$ thus measures connection i's link share. The aim of the buffer-reallocation protocol is to allocate buffers to connections in proportion to their link share. This is done iteratively, and connections move exponentially rapidly toward their fair-share allocations. Specifically, if:

$$M = \text{the total buffer size}$$

$$Q = \text{total queue occupancy} \tag{13.19}$$

$$N = \text{number of connections sharing the switch,}$$
$$\text{each of whom is guaranteed at least one cell worth of buffering,}$$

then the buffer allocation for connection i is given by:

$$B(i) = (V(i)/T)(M/2 - Q - N) \tag{13.20}$$

Kung and Morris [KM 95] have shown that this update equation guarantees (a) no cell loss, and (b) exponential ramp-up to the fair share, if:

$$M > 4RTT\mu + 2N, \quad \text{and}$$

$$Q < \left(\frac{2}{3}\right)RTT\mu,$$

where

$$RTT = \text{the largest round-trip propagation delay on the incoming links} \tag{13.21}$$

$$\mu = \text{the line speed of the outgoing link}$$

If RTT is large, that is, if the link spans a wide area, this may require substantial buffering. To deal with this problem, Kung et al. have proposed that the downstream buffers be statistically shared [KBC 94]. Of course, this introduces the possibility of packet loss. Ozveren et al. [OSV 94] have proposed an algorithm that allows efficient sharing of a small number of downstream buffers while still avoiding packet loss. We can also reduce the buffer size if we carefully account for packets in transit in the analysis [GVSS 96].

Evaluation

A hop-by-hop dynamic-window scheme separates error control and flow control: the hop-by-hop flow-control window does not affect the end-to-end error-control window. Thus, we use the window size purely for flow control and buffer control at downstream network elements. This separation of error and flow control is desirable.

The main advantage of the credit-based scheme is that it guarantees zero loss despite the traffic arrival pattern of a source, if it stays within its credit balance. Moreover, the scheme introduces little additional complexity in the end-system host adaptor. Finally, since a credit-based scheme buffers packets from sources at the bottleneck, if any source is idle, even for a moment, packets from other sources are available for transmission, so we do not waste the bottleneck bandwidth. Extensive simulations show that the scheme is responsive to network transients, robust, and efficient in using network bandwidth [KM 95]. When combined with a fair scheduling algorithm, it gives connections the ability to share bandwidth fairly and to quickly take up any slack in the bottleneck line.

The main disadvantage of the scheme is that it complicates switches. Each switch not only must maintain per-connection statistics, but also must do per-connection credit-based flow control. This is possible only in hardware, which has the problems we noted in Section 13.4.10. Moreover, the scheme requires a substantial number of buffers per switch, increasing its cost. For these reasons, the ATM Forum decided to abandon the credit-based scheme in favor of the rate-based approach discussed in Section 13.4.10. Nevertheless, there are strong arguments for using credit-based schemes in the local area, and rate-based schemes in the wide area [RN 95]. This would combine the responsiveness of credit-based schemes with the reduced switch complexity of rate-based schemes.

13.4.12 Comparison of closed-loop schemes

In this section, we have studied several closed-loop flow-control schemes. Starting with the simplest schemes, such as on–off and stop-and-wait, we examined incrementally more complex schemes. The increasing complexity reflects the deeper understanding of flow control that the past decade of research has produced. With the many choices for flow control, a natural question is to ask which scheme is the "best." Unfortunately, there is no simple answer to this question. Each scheme makes different assumptions about its environment of operation; comparing schemes that make different assumptions is like comparing apples with oranges. As described in Chapter 6, the "best" scheme depends on the environment of operation and the constraints on the system. Given the binding constraints in effect, a designer must choose a flow-control scheme that best matches the situation.

For example, Fraser argues that a static window scheme is sufficient if the scheduling discipline is round-robin-like and we can give every router sufficient buffering [Fraser 83, Fraser 91]. Given the current price of memory and technology trends in the cost of memory and the capacity of wide-area trunks, he claims that giving every connection a maximal-sized window (the speed of the fastest trunk in the network multiplied by the largest possible delay) is affordable, and avoids the complexity of dynamic window schemes. However, his proposal requires admission control for every call and round-robin queuing, and switches must have enough memory to ensure an acceptably low blocking rate even at peak call-arrival rates. These complications drive up the cost of the switch compared to, say that of an FCFS datagram switch assumed by TCP-Vegas. If switch cost is a constraint, a reasonable trade-off might be to make the buffer management mechanism more complex, such as by using the credit-based scheme, or the end-point control more sophisticated, as with TCP-Vegas, because this substantially reduces the memory cost. The point is that we do not really have the "best" solution; we only have a range of solutions that make different trade-offs among complexity, cost, and performance.

We now make some general observations about the trade-offs made by the various schemes:

- Flow control is easier if servers implement fair-share (round-robin like) scheduling. Otherwise, either all the endpoints must be cooperative, or their allocated rate must be policed. Unfortunately, all three options have their own problems: (a) Fair-share scheduling requires per-connection state at the switches, making them more complex. (b) We cannot assume cooperation in a public network, though it is reasonable in a private network. (c) Policing requires more hardware at the network edge, adding to the cost.

- Explicit schemes perform better and are more robust than implicit schemes. However, they not only put a greater traffic load on the network, but also require more complex switches. Unless carefully designed, this increased load may make them less likely than implicit schemes to scale to large networks.

- Hop-by-hop schemes are more responsive to rapid changes in bottleneck utilization, but add complexity to intermediate network elements.

- Separating error control and flow control is a good idea, because changes in the error-control window should not necessarily affect flow control. However, if the only indication of congestion is a lost packet, this is hard to do.

- Rate-based schemes are intrinsically unstable, because sources continue to send even if the rate update packets are lost (unless, as in the EERC scheme, sources reduce their rate automatically lacking feedback). Credit-based schemes are intrinsically stable. However, rate-based schemes typically require less complexity and fewer buffers at the switches.

In a given situation, these trade-offs must be kept in mind when choosing a flow control scheme.

For quick reference, Table 13.5 summarizes the closed-loop schemes we have studied.

Key	
E/H	End-to-end or hop-by-hop control
W/R	Dynamic window or dynamic rate
I/E	Implicit or explicit detection of network state

Name	E/ H	W/ R	I/ E	Summary	Advantages	Disadvantages
On–Off	E	R	—	Receiver controls whether a sender sends at the peak rate or not at all.	Easy to implement.	Works only when the RTT is small and the receiver has many buffers. Intermediate switches are heavily loaded.
Stop-and-wait	E	W	—	Source does not send a packet until the receiver acknowledges the previous one.	Easy to implement. Requires only one buffer at the receiver.	When RTT is large, the bottleneck is underutilized.
Static window	E	W	—	Source can keep more than one packet outstanding.	If the service rate and round trip do not change, and the window size is correctly chosen, this scheme is optimal.	Hard to choose the window size a priori. Bad choice leads to either packet loss or poor bottleneck utilization.
DECbit [RJ 88, RJ 90]	E	W	E	Switches set a bit in the packet header when congested, causing cooperating sources to reduce their window size using an AIMD policy.	Uses only one bit in the packet header. Effective when bandwidth–delay product is small. Endpoint algorithm can be implemented in software. Does not assume fairshare scheduling at switches. Minimal buffering needed at switches.	Assumes cooperative sources. Startup is too conservative in environments with large bandwidth–delay products. Routers need to compute fair shares explicitly. Nonselective version discriminates against connections with long RTTs.

Table 13.5: Comparison of closed-loop flow-control schemes.

Name	E/ H	W/ R	I/ E	Summary	Advantages	Disadvantages
TCP-Tahoe and TCP-Reno [Jacobson 88, Stevens 94]	E	W	I	In the absence of loss, sources increase their window size; on a loss, the size is reduced using an AIMD policy.	Effective over a wide range of bandwidth–delay products. Works with FCFS scheduling. Well understood in the literature. Extensively tested in the field. Implemented completely in software.	Assumes cooperative sources. Sensitive to non-congestive losses. Keeps buffer close to full. Performs poorly if bottleneck has less than approximately $RTT\mu/3$ buffers.
TCP-Vegas [BP 95]	E	W	I	Congestion avoidance by adjusting window size as a function of the expected and measured throughput.	Same advantages as TCP. Usually performs better than TCP-Tahoe or TCP-Reno.	Less well understood and tested than TCP-Tahoe or TCP-Reno.
NETBLT [CLZ 88]	E	R	I	Source and destination negotiate a transfer rate once per RTT. If receiving rate is smaller than sending rate, the rate is decreased; otherwise, it is increased.	First scheme to separate error and flow control. Works well over uncongested networks.	Not studied in any detail. Ignores bottlenecks in the network.
Packet-pair [Keshav 91, Keshav 97]	E	R	I	Source sends all data as pairs. The gap in ack spacing is used to measure the bottleneck rate. This rate is fed into a one-step-ahead predictive flow control.	Provably stable. Requires no support from switch other than round-robin-like service at bottleneck points. Can be implemented in software. Requires less than one bandwidth–delay product worth of buffers at the bottleneck.	Assumes round-robin-like scheduling at the bottleneck.

Table 13.5: Continued.

Name	E/H	W/R	I/E	Summary	Advantages	Disadvantages
ATM Forum end-to-end scheme [BF 95]	E	R	E	Source periodically injects a resource management cell into its cell stream. Switches write the sustainable fair share into this cell, which is carried back to the source.	Works well over a wide range of bandwidth–delay products. Sources know the exact fair share. Allows room for innovation in source flow-control algorithms. Interoperates with DECbit switches. Does not require fair-share scheduling. Switches do not need per-connection state. Does not assume cooperative sources.	Interleaved RM cells mix the data and control paths. Only feasible in hardware at the endpoints. Endpoints are complex. Fair-share computation is explicit and can be expensive. Source rate needs to be policed.
Mishra/ Kanakia [MK 92]	H	R	E	Switches control the rate per-connection per-link to prevent overflow at the next switch and fully use link. Switches exchange rate and buffer occupancy information that is plugged into a one-step-ahead predictive flow control.	Performs nearly optimally. Rapid reaction to changes. Requires very little buffering in switches. Does not require fair-share scheduling at switches. Can be implemented in software at endpoints.	Makes switches complex. Control messages take up bandwidth.
Credit-based Scheme [KC 93, KBC 94, KM 95]	H	W	E	Switches adjust per-connection window per-link to ensure no loss at downstream switch and full utilization of bottleneck link.	Rapid reaction to available capacity at the bottleneck link. No assumptions about source behavior.	Assumes fair scheduling at switches, and per-connection queuing. Requires about $4\ \mathrm{RTT}\mu$ worth of buffers at each switch.

Table 13.5: Continued.

13.5   **Hybrid flow control**

In open-loop flow control, a source reserves capacity according to its expected traffic, whereas in closed-loop flow control, the source must adapt to changing network conditions. In hybrid control, a source reserves some minimum capacity, but may obtain more if other sources are inactive. We have already seen an example of hybrid control in the ATM Forum EERC scheme, where the network guarantees a source a minimum cell rate, but the source may get an allowed cell rate that could be larger. Thus, the source must go through admission control during the call-setup phase, during which every switch must test whether the minimum cell rate is available. Subsequently, sources adjust their demand in response to the bandwidth available in the network. We can also modify other closed-loop schemes to perform hybrid control.

Hybrid control schemes not only inherit the problems of open-loop and closed-loop control, but also introduce some new ones. As in open-loop control, a source must find descriptors for its traffic that satisfy the criteria in Section 13.3. However, note that source descriptors in hybrid control can be looser than in open-loop control, because its descriptor does not limit a source. In other words, a source that asks for too little may not notice it, because the actual capacity available to it is likely to be much greater. Hybrid controlled sources must obey all appropriate closed-loop control mechanisms, and thus hybrid control inherits all the problems and constraints of closed-loop control discussed in Section 13.4.

A new problem introduced by hybrid control is that of *resource partitioning* at switches [GF 95]. Recall that a network operator can choose to have some or all of the network resources (bandwidth and buffers) available for reservation by open-loop control sources. With a hybrid flow-control scheme, the operator must decide what fraction of the resource can be reserved, and what fraction should be contended for. Clearly, if too large a fraction is reserved, then, during congestion, purely closed-loop controlled sources would get very little bandwidth. On the other hand, if too small a fraction is reserved, only a few hybrid-controlled sources can be admitted. Appropriate partitioning depends on the pricing policy for hybrid and closed-loop flow-controlled sources and is still an open research area.

Despite these problems, hybrid control has a strong advantage: a guaranteed minimum resource allocation to an admitted call, even when the network is overloaded. Thus, a hybrid-controlled source, once admitted, knows that even in the worst case, it has some minimum bandwidth guaranteed to it, and in the average case, it will obtain substantially more bandwidth. This is a desirable property for applications that involve voice and video transfer, because they must have at least a minimum bandwidth to provide utility to users. For example, if an application can provide degraded, but acceptable, voice transfer at 8 Kbps, and can provide excellent voice quality at 16 Kbps, then it might ask for a minimum cell rate of 4 Kbps, but contend for, and obtain, a higher rate on average. In the presence of congestion (which we presume is a rare event), the application can still provide utility to its users. If it did not have this minimum guaranteed rate, congestion would cause the application to become unusable.

To sum up, hybrid control has one main advantage, that is, the ability to guarantee a minimum service rate to admitted calls even in the worst case, and all the problems of open-loop and closed-loop flow control. Nevertheless, this advantage seems worth the trouble, and it is likely that future networks will provide some form of hybrid flow control.

13.6   Summary

Like error control, flow control can be performed at many layers of the protocol stack. This chapter describes a set of flow-control techniques that we can apply in a variety of situations. We studied the three forms of flow control: open-loop, closed-loop, and hybrid. We examined some problems in open-loop control, particularly in choosing appropriate flow descriptors. We also studied several closed-loop schemes that use (a) implicit or explicit rate measurements, (b) hop-by-hop or end-to-end control, and (c) dynamic-window or dynamic-rate control. These schemes make widely varying assumptions about their environment of operation, and thus are not directly comparable. Table 13.5 is a summary of these schemes. Finally, we looked at some problems and advantages with hybrid flow control.

Review Questions

1. What is the bottleneck rate in the equivalent reduced flow model?
2. What is the flow-control problem?
3. What are the three types of flow-control schemes?
4. What is a traffic descriptor, and what purposes does it serve?
5. What are regulators and policers? How do they differ?
6. What is a jumping-window regulator?
7. What is an LBAP?
8. What parameters control the performance of a Leaky Bucket regulator?
9. What is a (σ, ρ) curve, and how does it help in selecting a traffic descriptor?
10. What information is conveyed in an explicit state-measurement packet?
11. Can the on–off scheme be implemented hop-by-hop?
12. When does a stop-and-wait scheme have poor performance?
13. What is the optimal choice for a static-window size?
14. When does a DECbit router set bits, and on which sources?
15. When does a DECbit source reduce its window, and by how much?
16. How long is a queue regeneration cycle?
17. What are the two problems with the nonselective DECbit algorithm?
18. What does the *ssthresh* value in TCP-Tahoe determine?
19. To what value does TCP-Reno reduce its window size on a timeout?
20. How does TCP-Vegas determine how many packets are in the bottleneck buffer?
21. What are the MCR and ICR values in the ATM Forum EERC scheme?

22. What is an RM cell?
23. How does the packet-pair source measure the bottleneck service rate?
24. What is a *setpoint* in the packet-pair and MK schemes?
25. What information does a credit-update packet contain?
26. Why are rate-based schemes intrinsically unstable?
27. What is the resource partitioning problem with hybrid control?
28. What is the main advantage of hybrid control?

Exercises

13.1. A source is on an Ethernet with a propagation delay of 100 μs and a service rate of 10 Mbps. This is connected to a T1 line via a router with propagation delay 30 ms. The destination is connected via a symmetric arrangement. Assuming 1-ms service times at the routers, what are the equivalent delay and service rates for a reduced-flow model that describes this path?

13.2. If the peak rate of a connection is 1.5 Mbps, and the packet size is fixed at 53 bytes, how close in time can two packets be?

13.3. A hypothetical source is cell-smooth with an intercell spacing of 0.1 ms, except that once every second, it emits two cells instead of one. If the service rate is exactly 10,000 cells/s, what is the queuing delay at the peak-rate regulator 1 h after the source starts? Suggest two ways this delay can be eliminated.

13.4. Give an example to show that the jumping window-descriptor is sensitive to the choice of the starting time of the first window.

13.5. Packets arrive to a moving-window regulator as follows: (40 bytes, 0.1 s), (20 bytes, 0.2 s), (40 bytes, 0.5 s), (60 bytes, 0.7 s). If the regulator has a constraint of 100 bytes over 1-s intervals, what is the output stream?

13.6. If a token is 200 bytes long, the token bucket is 1Kbytes, and tokens arrive at the rate of 1 every second, what is the least and most delay suffered by a packet of size 800 bytes if it arrives when the token bucket has 100 bytes in it?

13.7. If a DECbit source has bits set on all its packets when it reaches a window size of 16, and none before, what is the range in which the window size oscillates? If the RTT is 1, and the optimal window size is 16, what is the utilization of the bottleneck line (assuming this is the only source) when the source has a window size of w? Use this to compute the mean utilization of the bottleneck if it only carries this single source.

13.8. If a TCP-Tahoe source has a packet loss when its window size is 16, what is the range in which its window size oscillates? If the RTT is 1, and the optimal window size is 16, what is the utilization of the bottleneck link when the source has a window size w? Use this to compute the mean utilization of the bottleneck if it only carries a single source.

13.9. Is it possible in the ATM Forum EERC scheme for the CI bit to be set to 1, but the ER field to be larger than the source's ACR? What action does a source take when this happens?

13.10. Consider a packet-pair source that has an RTT measurement of 1.0 s, a predicted service rate of 10 packets/s, 20 packets outstanding, and a setpoint of 5 packets. What will be its transmission rate? What will be its transmission rate if it has 100 packets outstanding?

13.11. In the credit-based scheme, let $C(U)$ be 100 and $C(D)$ be 60. What is the largest number of packets buffered in D? If D has 100 cell buffers, of which 20 are occupied by 10 active connections, and a connection's share of D's link is 0.2, what is the connection's new buffer share?

Chapter 14

Traffic Management

14.1 Introduction

Imagine a busy executive participating in a videoconference with other executives around the world. As the conference proceeds, she whips out a personal digital assistant, scrawls a note, and mails it to her colleague. Another participant brings up a spreadsheet that they edit together. While the meeting is in progress, an important telephone call interrupts one of the participants. At the end of the meeting, a video transcript of the proceedings is saved in the company archives. A librarian edits the transcript to create a meeting summary that is placed on the company Web site. Later, absentees use this summary to find out what went on in the meeting.

This scenario, though largely a fantasy in 1996, might be commonplace a decade from now. To make it happen, the participants must have access to a multimedia network that supports voice and video transport for videoconferencing, low end-to-end delays for telephony, reliable data transport for email, and bulk data transport for copying and editing the transcript. How can a network provider efficiently build such a network? How can it make sure that the network's services are available on demand, and that users are satisfied with the service they receive? How can the operator reduce the cost of providing service so that its services are competitively priced, yet profits are maximized? These are the broad questions that we will study in this chapter.

Traffic management is the set of policies and mechanisms that allow a network to efficiently satisfy a diverse range of service requests. The two fundamental aspects of traffic management, *diversity* in user requirements and *efficiency* in satisfying them, act at cross purposes, creating a tension that has led to a rich set of mechanisms. We have already studied some of these mechanisms, such as scheduling and flow control, in Chapters 9 and 13. In this chapter, we will tie together these concepts to form a unified framework for traffic management.

Traffic management subsumes many ideas traditionally classified under *congestion control*. We say that a resource is congested when it is overloaded, so that a user experiences performance degradation. Congestion-control policies either restrict access to the resource or scale back user demand dynamically so that the overload situation disappears. Since an overload results in a loss of network efficiency, we can view congestion control as one aspect of traffic management. Traffic management is more general because it includes other mechanisms, such as scheduling and signaling, that are unrelated to congestion control.

We begin with an economic framework for traffic management in Section 14.2. To manage traffic, we need to understand traffic behavior (Section 14.3) and user behavior (Section 14.4). We introduce the notion of multiple time scales of management in Section 14.5. Subsequent sections deal with some mechanisms for traffic management, such as signaling, admission control, and capacity planning, in more detail. Finally, Section 14.12 summarizes the chapter.

14.2   An economic framework for traffic management

An economic formulation of the traffic management problem gives some useful insight. We model each network customer as having a *utility function u* that translates from a given *quality of service* or *QoS* (such as the bandwidth associated with a call[1] or the mean delay of packets sent during a call) to a degree of satisfaction, or *utility*. The greater the satisfaction, the greater the utility function of that quality of service. A user's utility function is known only to the user, and we will assume that *rational* users take actions that maximize their utility function. This modeling of user behavior, which is fundamental to the economic model, is general enough to capture a wide range of service requests, as the following example shows.

EXAMPLE 14.1

Suppose a particular user wants to transfer a file as soon as possible. We can model this with the utility function $u(t) = S - \alpha t$, where t is the time to transfer the file, S is the utility derived when the file transfer is infinitely fast, and α is the rate at which the utility declines as a function of time. Thus, as the file transfer takes longer and longer, the user's utility from the transfer linearly decreases. Note that when

---

[1] We use the term "call" to loosely refer to an association between a sender of data and its receiver. In an ATM network or a telephone network, a call is the same as a virtual circuit, or a physical circuit, respectively. On the Internet, with a connection-oriented transport layer such as TCP, a call is delimited by an explicit connection open and close. With a connectionless transport layer protocol such as UDP, a call is delimited by "long" idle times. (This definition is imprecise, but about the best we can do for connectionless networks!)

$t > S/\alpha$, the utility becomes negative. This reflects the fact that if the file transfer takes too long, the user feels that he or she is worse off than if the transfer had never been initiated. (Presumably this is because the file is delayed too long and the user has to pay for the transfer anyway!)

Suppose a user is participating in a videoconference. Then, to preserve inter-activity, he or she may want *every* packet to arrive at the receiver before a deadline. Otherwise, the packet is too late and cannot be used to present an audio or video signal. We can model this user's requirements by:

$$u(t) = \text{if } (t < D)$$

$$\text{then } S$$

$$\text{else } -\beta$$

Here, t is the end-to-end delay experienced by a packet, D is the delay deadline, S is the satisfaction from a packet that meets the deadline, and $-\beta$ is the cost of missing a deadline. The penalty reflects the fact that the user has to pay for the packet even though it cannot be used.

A more sophisticated utility function measures not just the delay, but also the *probability* that a packet meets a certain delay or loss bound. For example, the utility function $u(\epsilon) = S(1 - \epsilon)$, where ϵ is the packet loss probability, reflects the fact that a user derives satisfaction S when no packets are lost, and as the probability of loss increases, the utility decreases. This loss probability here is an a priori loss probability: it might be advertised by the network provider and used by the user to choose a particular provider.

The key idea is that the utility function completely captures the user's requirements. Once we know a user's utility function, we know exactly how much he or she values a higher bandwidth over a lower delay, or lower loss rate over a lower price. This allows us to engineer a network to satisfy these requirements best. In other words, utility functions give us the vocabulary to talk about the diversity of performance requirements that we expect future applications to have.

How useful are utility functions?

Although an economic formulation of the traffic-management problem requires us to model users as having utility functions, do users really have such functions that they can express mathematically? Economists assume that even if users cannot come up with a mathematical formula, they can still express preferences for one set of resources (or one degree of performance) over another. These preferences can then be codified as a utility function. What is less clear is whether user utility functions have the "nice" mathematical properties that economists want. Perhaps the best way to think about utility functions is that they allow us to come up with a mathematical formulation of the traffic-management problem that gives some insight. Although practical economic algorithms may never be feasible, policies and mechanisms based on these insights are still relevant.

14.2.1 Economic principles of traffic management

We will assume for the purposes of our discussion that a user knows his or her own utility function and tells it to the network. Given a set of user utility functions, it is desirable for the network provider to implement policies and mechanisms that try to optimize some metric on the ensemble of utility functions, such as maximizing their sum, while minimizing the cost of network infrastructure (this is often called *social welfare maximization*). The solution to this problem leads to three general principles for traffic management [Shenker 95]:

- The network should try to match its menu of service qualities to user requirements. Service menus that are more closely aligned with user requirements are more efficient. Intuitively, the more loosely a service menu matches user requirements, the more resources a network has to expend to achieve the same level of user utility. Thus, when building an integrated-services network, we should first determine the demands that will be placed on it.

- Building a single network that provides heterogeneous qualities of service is better than building separate networks for different qualities of service. For example, building a network that carries both voice and data is better than building separate networks for voice and data. Intuitively, this is because with an integrated network, the capacity not used by a voice call is available to carry data traffic, and vice versa. With separate networks, unused capacity lies idle.

- For typical utility functions, if network utilization remains the same, the sum of user utility functions increases more than linearly with an increase in network capacity. Thus, one way to increase overall user utility is to increase network capacity. Intuitively, the larger the network, the smaller the effect of statistical fluctuations. Thus, individual users experience fewer fluctuations in their service, making their use of the network more pleasant. This is a consequence of the law of large numbers.

EXAMPLE 14.2

This example is based on a similar one in reference [Shenker 95]. Consider a network consisting of a single switch with users A and B with utility functions $u(d) =$

$4 - d$ and $v(d) = 8 - 2d$, respectively, where d is the mean packet delay. B is more sensitive to delay, because its utility falls off more steeply with an increase in delay. Recall from Chapter 9 that the conservation law states that if $\rho()$ denotes a user's transmission rate, and the sum of these transmission rates is fixed, then for all delay allocations $d(A)$ and $d(B)$,

$$\rho(A)d(A) + \rho(B)d(B) = \text{constant}$$

Assume $\rho(A) = \rho(B) = 0.4$. Suppose a network does not distinguish between service qualities for the two users, so that $d(A) = d(B) = d$. Then, $0.4\, d + 0.4\, d = \text{constant} = C$. Thus, $d = C/0.8 = 1.25\, C$. The user utilities are $4 - 1.25C$ and $8 - 2(1.25C)$, so that their sum is $12 - 3.75C$.

Now, suppose the network can give a smaller delay to B and a larger one to A, through an appropriate choice of scheduling discipline. If the delay to B is $0.5C$, (which is smaller than its earlier delay of $1.25C$), then A's delay, from the conservation law, must be $(C - 0.5C * 0.4)/0.4 = 2.0C$. Thus, the sum of utilities is $4 - 2.0C + 8 - 2(0.5C) = 12 - 3C$. Clearly, this is larger than $12 - 3.75C$ for all $C > 0$. Thus, by giving higher priority to users that want lower delay, the network can increase its utility. Of course, in the process, A's utility decreases from $4 - 1.25C$ to $4 - 2C$. So, an overall increase in utility does not necessarily benefit all users. This trade-off between individual and global optimality must be made by the network operator. If the operator gives priority to B's traffic, it may compensate A for its higher delay by giving it a lower price, so that its overall utility (including its price) does not decrease.

Example 14.2 shows that the network operator, by aligning its service menu with user needs, can increase overall user utility. However, it can also increase overall user utility merely by increasing network capacity, which decreases the network's utilization and therefore its mean packet delays. To take a concrete example, suppose users of an online service complain about their response time when using interactive applications. The operator can either introduce mechanisms to give a higher priority and a lower delay to traffic from interactive applications, or increase capacity, decreasing delays to *all* applications. Both approaches will fix the problem, and the operator should choose the cheaper solution. This is a classic choice between "big and dumb" and "small and smart." How should the network operator choose between these alternatives?

When resources are scarce, then no matter how efficiently a network operator manages the network, user utility will still be low. However, once the network capacity increases beyond a minimum, one can argue that implementing intelligent traffic management is more effective than increasing capacity. As a case in point, consider a hypothetical network that provides the same quality of service (synchronous, 64-Kbps circuits with minimal jitter and delay) to all its users. Suppose some users wanted to send data at 1 Mbps instead. One solution would be to give *all* users a 1-Mbps connection, of which most use only a 64-Kbps portion. A more efficient solution is for the network to provide heterogeneous QoS, where some users get 64 Kbps, and others get 1 Mbps. Similarly, consider another hypothetical network where no user gets a guarantee on bandwidth or delay. If some users wanted to get a guarantee of at least 8 Kbps (measured over some interval) for their calls, one solution would be to increase capacity so that *all* calls get more than 8 Kbps. The alternative, to reserve bandwidth only for these calls, usually proves more efficient, and thus is cheaper.

The choice between overprovisioning ("big and dumb") and intelligent traffic management ("small and smart") is still a matter of much debate. Some people feel that network operators should concentrate on increasing the bandwidth available to all users, and the rising tide will raise all ships. Although it is still too early to pass judgment, the ultimate decision depends on whether it will prove cheaper to build intelligent traffic management schemes, or use the same money to increase the raw capacity of the network. In this chapter, we will assume that intelligent traffic-management schemes are desirable and worth studying.

The call

The argument between the two camps led me to write this ditty, sung to the tune of Pink Floyd's "The Wall."

> We don't need no reservation
> We don't need ad-mission control
> All applications must be adaptive
> The Net works just fine, so leave it alone
> Hey! Professor! Leave the Net alone!
>
> We don't need no traffic management
> Overprovision bandwidth for all
> The only true god is TCP/IP
> The Net isn't broken, so leave it alone
> Hey! Professor! Leave the Net alone!
>
> All we want is just flat rate pricing for all

14.2.2 | Pricing

In this subsection, we will briefly study the problem of network pricing, that is, how much a public network should charge for its services. This area is fraught with complications, as the following example shows.

Consider a network with a fixed capacity, where increased usage causes every user's individual utility to decrease (for example, with increased usage, every user's mean delay might increase, thus decreasing his or her utility). If we charge users a flat fee for access, then, under some general assumptions, it can be shown that a few bandwidth hogs, who are insensitive to delays, dominate the network and displace delay-sensitive users [MV 95]. Intuitively, with a flat fee, there is no incentive for a user to limit his or her use of the network. Thus, users who are sensitive to delay cede the network to users who are insensitive to delay. Another way to view this is to observe that the network is congested from the perspective of delay-sensitive users, but not from the perspective of delay-insensitive users, biasing the network to support only delay-insensitive users. This is probably not desirable for the network provider, because it loses revenue from delay-sensitive users.

To avoid this situation, a network operator could use *congestion pricing,* where the operator charges a user according to the *disutility* his or her traffic causes to other users. Thus, if a user sends a lot of traffic when the network is already loaded, causing delays and packet losses to other users, it is charged heavily for the discomfort it causes. If it sends the same load at an off-peak time when the network is underloaded, then because it causes almost no discomfort to other users, its price is low. With this scheme, the eventual equilibrium is optimal in the sense that it not only maximizes the network operator's revenue, but also each user's utility [MV 95]. Congestion fees discourage excessive network usage when the network is loaded, thus making the network usable by delay-sensitive users.

However, congestion pricing in the simple form just stated requires the network provider to know every user's utility function, something a network provider has no way to directly determine. To begin with, users may not even know what traffic their application might generate, much less their utility function. Even if users knew these things, and had some way of informing a network of their utility function, they could lie. Thus, a simple-minded approach to congestion pricing, which, unfortunately, is the only kind of approach amenable to analysis, cannot be used in a network setting right away. We can only use the insights gained from the analysis when developing pricing schemes.

Here is another example of a complication we run into with network pricing. Suppose we claim that a network provider can infer users' utilities from their willingness to pay for services. The idea is that the more utility a user obtains from using the network, the higher the price he or she is willing to pay. Thus, the network could charge different prices for different services, and users' willingness to pay this price would reveal their utility functions. However, when we use this principle with congestion pricing, we run into a chicken-and-egg problem. The network operator chooses a price depending on each user's inferred utility function (which allows it to determine the disutility caused by each user) and the inferred utility function itself depends on the price! If we are not careful, this can lead to a situation where the price charged from each user oscillates wildly over time.

Despite these complications, the key point is that by setting a price for usage, the network can *control* user demand, at least broadly, thus modifying the traffic load on the system. Therefore, pricing can be used as a tool for traffic management. This is still an area of ongoing research.

14.3   Traffic models

To effectively manage traffic, a network provider must know not only the requirements of individual applications and organizations, but also their "typical" behavior. For example, an Internet service provider must guess at how long a "typical" user uses a modem line, so that modem pools have sufficient modems to keep the probability of a blocked call low. A *traffic model* summarizes the expected behavior of an application or an aggregate of applications.

Traffic models fall into two broad categories. Some models are obtained by detailed traffic measurements of thousands or millions of connections over days or years. Others are chosen because they are amenable to mathematical analysis. Unfortunately, only a few models are both empirically obtained and mathematically tractable.

In this section, we outline the state of the art in traffic modeling. As new applications become popular, these models are likely to change.

14.3.1   Telephone traffic models

Telephone companies rarely publish detailed traffic measurements and consider them sensitive, proprietary information. However, two characteristics of calls are well known:

- How calls are placed (*call arrival model*)
- How long a call lasts (*call holding-time model*)

Call arrival model

Numerous call arrival measurements show that calls arrive at a switch as a *Poisson process*, that is, the interarrival time between calls is drawn from an *exponential* distribution. If X represents the time between the arrival of two calls, then $P(X > x)$, that is, the probability that the interarrival time is longer than x, is given by $e^{-x/\lambda}$, where λ is the mean interarrival time. An interesting property of this process is that it is *memoryless:* the fact that a certain time has elapsed since the last arrival gives us no information about how much longer we must wait before the next call arrives. A more detailed description of the Poisson model and its interpretation can be found in books on probability and statistics, such as references [Bulmer 79, Billingsley 95, Shiryaev 96].

Call holding-time model

Call holding times in telephone networks have traditionally been modeled as drawn from an exponential distribution. That is, the probability that a call lasts longer than a given length x decreases exponentially with x. However, recent studies have shown call holding times to be *heavy-tailed* [DMRW 94] (Figure 14.1). Intuitively, this means that many calls last for very long times. More precisely, if T represents the call holding time, and $c(t)$ is defined to be a slowly varying function of t when t is large, the probability that the call is held longer than t is given by:

$$P(T > t) = c(t)t^{-\alpha} \text{ as } t \rightarrow \infty, 1 < \alpha < 2 \tag{14.1}$$

As Figure 14.1 shows, a heavy-tailed distribution has a significantly higher probability mass at large values of t than an exponential distribution.

14.3.2   Internet traffic models

A few common applications—FTP, telnet, email, and WWW—account for almost all the traffic on the Internet. Thus, modeling these applications is important [DJCME

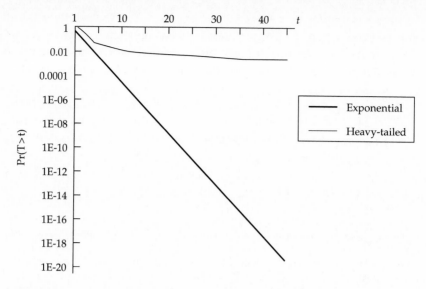

Figure 14.1: Exponential versus heavy-tailed distribution. The exponential distribution has a mean of 1, and the heavy-tailed distribution is $t^{-1.5}$. Note that for large t, the heavy-tailed distribution has much larger values than the exponential distribution.

92]. We can characterize an application on the Internet with a combination of four parameters:

- The distribution of arrival times between application invocations
- The duration of a connection
- The number of bytes transferred during the connection
- The interarrival times of packets within a connection

Unfortunately, there is little consensus on models for these parameters. For example, some studies indicate that the interarrival times between telnet and FTP sessions are best modeled by an exponential distribution [PF 94], whereas others find a good fit with a generalization of the exponential distribution called the *Weibull* distribution [Feldmann 95]. The only effective method to model applications may be to build an empirical distribution for application parameters from exhaustive measurements without trying to fit the measurements to any statistical model [DJCME 92]. Even here, one has to be careful to eliminate biases in the measurement due to protocol idiosyncrasies.

However, two features of individual connections are clearly important. First, traffic in a local-area network differs from traffic carried over wide areas. More bandwidth is available locally, local connections are free, and the connectivity is more stable. This encourages very long connection holding times, with high peak data rates. In contrast, in the wide area, connection durations tend to be shorter with fewer data bytes transferred.

The second important feature is that parameters such as the amount of data carried in the connection, burst length, idle time, and connection duration are often heavy-tailed [PF 94, GW 95, Feldmann 95]. So, for example, a *few* FTP connections dominate a link at any given time, and a *few* telnet connections last for very long times. This is analogous to the call holding times measured in telephone networks. The implication is that if these few connections are well behaved (that is, use appropriate traffic-management policies), the network will be well managed. Heavy-tailedness in burst durations is a strong motivation for parameter renegotiation (see Section 14.7).

The aggregation of heavy-tailed sources leads to *long-range-dependent* traffic [WTSW 95]. With aggregated Poisson traffic, bursts do not last very long, and traffic parameters from widely separated times are likely to have no correlation. In contrast, in a long-range-dependent stream, very long bursts are likely, and traffic parameters from widely separated times may still be correlated. Aggregate traffic on the Internet, both in the local area and in the wide area, has been found to be long-range-dependent [PF 94, WTSW 95]. This implies that network elements can be subject to long bursts of traffic even when multiplexing hundreds or thousands of sources. Therefore, traffic management policies must be aware of the possibility of such bursts and take corrective action. In particular, capacity-planning algorithms, which operate at a time scale of weeks or longer, should consider long-term burstiness when assigning capacities to network elements [PF 94]. Measurement-based admission control schemes, which we will study in Section 14.9.6, are also affected.

Traffic measurement and modeling is an ongoing process. As new applications become popular, the aggregate traffic stream is affected. For example, the first version of the HTTP protocol used for WWW access opened one TCP connection for each image in a home page. As WWW browsers became popular, the number of TCP connection requests surged, changing the aggregate traffic measurements. Thus, our understanding of traffic, poor as it is, must keep pace with changing network usage.

The long-range dependence "revolution"

Individual connection parameters such as call interarrival times, call holding times, and the number of bytes transferred in a call have traditionally been modeled as Poisson processes for three reasons. First, Poisson processes are amenable to rigorous analysis using queuing theory. Second, lacking measurements, a Poisson model is as good as any. Third, the Poisson process is the limiting distribution of many random point processes (this is also called the *Poisson limit theorem* [Billingsley 95]).

Recent measurements of real networks show Poisson modeling to be woefully inadequate [PF 94]. Not only are many individual connection parameters heavy-tailed, but aggregate traffic exhibits long-range dependence. This suggests that connection parameters should be modeled as *self-similar* processes instead of Poisson processes [WTSW 95]. The implications of these ideas are still the subject of much debate [GB 96, HL 96, RE 96]. Some researchers argue that self-similarity is interesting, but of marginal consequence. Others doubt the validity of the measurements or their representativeness. However, a growing number of researchers believe that future network designers must factor in self-similar traffic into their designs [GB 96, PF 94]. We have yet to see the practical implications of this "revolution," but it is likely to play an increasingly important role in designing traffic-management algorithms of the future.

14.4 Traffic classes

We saw in Section 14.2 that networks that provide heterogeneous qualities of service (or *integrated service networks*) are likely to cost less than networks that provide a single quality of service. In this section, we study the expected service requirements, corresponding to utility functions, of applications in integrated services networks. Instead of studying the service requirements for individual applications, we find it convenient to place applications in *traffic classes* that represent the shared requirements of a set of widely used applications [Garrett 94]. Traffic classes also represent the types of service provided by the network. Because these correspond to application requirements, in the rest of the chapter, we will not distinguish between application classes and service classes, calling both "traffic classes."

14.4.1 Guaranteed-service and best-effort applications

We partition applications into two fundamental classes, depending on whether they require a performance guarantee from the network. The difference between *guaranteed service* and *best-effort service* is like flying with a reservation and flying standby. With a reservation, an airline guarantees that with high probability, you will get a seat on the airplane. The airline thus guarantees you bandwidth (one seat), a nominal delay (which may be affected by weather conditions), and a loss probability (that the flight is over-booked, and you are "bumped"). On the other hand, if you travel standby, you may fly or you may not. The trade-off is that flying standby is cheaper, and, if you have time to spare, you may not care about the uncertainty.

An integrated service network guarantees traffic from a *guaranteed-service (GS)* application a particular quality of service, if its traffic obeys a given traffic descriptor (see Section 13.3.1 for a discussion of traffic descriptors). Typical guaranteed-service applications include audioconferencing, telephony, videoconferencing, remote sensing, video-on-demand, interactive multiplayer games, distance learning, and collaborative environments. With these applications, users derive utility from the network only if the network bounds the delay and provides a minimum amount of bandwidth. The utility function for a guaranteed-service application penalizes traffic that does not meet its service requirement, which is typically described by parameters for three orthogonal quantities: *bandwidth, delay,* and *loss.*

- Typical bandwidth parameters are the minimum bandwidth and the sustained bandwidth.
- Typical delay parameters are the mean delay, the worst-case delay, the 99-percentile delay, and the delay jitter.
- Typical loss parameters are the loss probability and a bound on the maximum number of packets lost over every consecutive set of packets transmitted.

We describe these performance parameters in more detail in Section 9.2.3.

An integrated-services network does not guarantee *best-effort (BE)* applications a service quality. The network undertakes to deliver BE packets only when bandwidth is available, and packets may be dropped at any time. Typical best-effort applications are the ones found on the Internet today, such as file transfer, name service, email, network news, and the World Wide Web. These applications are willing to adapt to whatever quality of service is available. The utility function for a best-effort application does not degrade significantly with a drop in service quality. More precisely, unlike a guaranteed-service application, a best-effort application derives utility from the network even if its packets suffer large delays, or it receives only a small bandwidth allocation from the network.

Guaranteed-service and best-effort applications also differ in the *degree of synchrony* between the endpoints. We define this to be the time scale at which the peer applications or their users interact with each other. With *synchronous* or *interactive* applications, the endpoints interact with each other on the time scale of a round-trip-time propagation delay. For example, with a telephone call, a user's actions (such as replying to a question) depend on the actions of his or her peer (such as asking a question) about a round-trip-time ago. Synchronous applications require the network to guarantee them a bandwidth and delay bound. Thus, they naturally are guaranteed-service applications. With *bounded-asynchronous* or *noninteractive* applications, the sender and receiver interact with each other on the time scale of a few minutes to a few days. Traffic from bounded-asynchronous applications can be delayed in the network if necessary, or even dropped, because the delay from retransmitting lost information does not affect user utility. Thus, these applications fall naturally into the best-effort class. In other words, the separation between guaranteed-service and best-effort applications also partitions applications based on their inherent degree of synchrony and interactivity.

A third way to look at the GS–BE dichotomy is based on an application's sensitivity to time and delay. GS applications are also called *real-time* applications, because their utility depends on the real (as opposed to virtual) time. BE applications are also called *elastic* applications, because they can elastically adapt to changes in network quality of service. Many applications on the Internet (as of 1996), such as FTP, telnet, and interactive chat, are elastic applications. They perform well if sufficient resources are available, but automatically scale back when resources become scarce. Although WWW is currently supported on a best-effort network, it would probably do a lot better if at least some Web sites could be accessed using guaranteed-service connections. In this sense, the Web is an application of the future trapped in a network of the past!

14.4.2 Traffic subclasses

We can further subdivide guaranteed-service and best-effort applications based on their relative sensitivity to bandwidth and delay. The two standardization bodies involved in setting standards for integrated services networks are the *ATM Forum,* which is a commercial association of ATM equipment manufacturers and researchers, and the *Internet Engineering Task Force* or *IETF,* which is the Internet's standardization body. Both bodies have proposed a tentative classification of guaranteed-service and best-effort applications into subclasses. The ATM Forum classifies applications based on their *bandwidth* sensitivity, and the IETF based on sensitivity to *delay* [Garrett 94, CWSA 95] (Table 14.1). Keep in mind, though, that what follows is a snapshot of the standardization efforts as of late 1995. It is possible, and even likely, that as we learn more about engineering integrated services networks, these classifications will change.

14.4.3 ATM Forum subclasses

The ATM Forum subdivides the guaranteed-service class into *constant bit-rate (CBR)* and *variable bit-rate (VBR)* subclasses. A CBR application generates a constant cell-smooth traffic stream (that is, with the same spacing among all transmitted cells) and expects that the receiver will receive the stream with a small delay jitter, also called *cell delay variation.* CBR applications model applications on the current circuit-switched telephone network and are implicitly assumed to require a minimal-delay, low-delay-jitter service. CBR service thus models telephone service, with the bonus that a stream can reserve bandwidth at an arbitrary rate, not just a multiple of 64 Kbps.

	Guaranteed service *(synchronous, interactive, real-time)*		Best effort *(bounded-asynchronous, noninteractive, elastic)*		
Bandwidth sensitivity *(ATM Forum)*	Constant bit-rate (CBR)	Variable bit-rate (VBR)	Available bit-rate (ABR)	Unspecified bit-rate (UBR)	
Delay sensitivity *(IETF)*	Intolerant (guaranteed service)	Tolerant (controlled load service)	Interactive burst	Interactive bulk	Asynchronous bulk

Table 14.1: Traffic subclasses according to the IETF and the ATM Forum.

Variable bit-rate

The VBR subclass models applications that generate traffic in bursts, rather than in a smooth stream. A VBR source is modeled as having an intrinsic long-term bit rate (called its *sustained cell rate*), with occasional bursts (of limited length) at a rate as high as a specified peak rate. A VBR application expects that the network will carry its bursty stream with minimal delay. However, since VBR sources are likely to be multiplexed together to obtain statistical multiplexing gain (see Section 4.4), we implicitly assume that VBR applications can tolerate higher delays and higher delay variations than can CBR sources. VBR applications can specify a worst-case end-to-end delay, a worst-case delay jitter, and a worst-case loss fraction. Typical applications in the VBR class are those sending compressed video streams (such as video-on-demand) where the bit rate varies with the degree of achievable compression.

Constant bandwidth versus constant quality

Variable bit-rate service was principally designed for carrying compressed video traffic [VPV 88]. Video streams need to be compressed because uncompressed streams take up too much bandwidth (up to 270 Mbps per stream, depending on the picture size and resolution). Moreover, they can be compressed by a factor of 30 to 100 with a fairly small loss of resolution.

We can compress video streams in one of two ways. With constant-bit-rate compression, the output of the compression engine (also called a *video coder*) is constant bit-rate, but variable quality. Specifically, scenes with a lot of motion or flashing colors take up much more bandwidth than other scenes. To preserve a constant bandwidth, the coder must degrade the spatial or temporal resolution of such scenes. We can avoid this by coding at a constant quality, but a variable bit-rate. With such coders, scenes with more visual information take up more bandwidth than others. Compressed video with a constant bit-rate is suitable for CBR service, and compressed video with a variable bit-rate is suitable for VBR service.

Most video coders available in 1996 are constant-bit-rate coders, because variable-bit-rate service is not widely available. These coders generate traffic at 64 Kbps (to fit in a single telephone circuit) or at multiples of 64 Kbps, such as 384 Kbps. The next generation of coders, based on the *Moving Pictures Expert Group* or *MPEG* video coding standard, are likely to be variable-bit-rate coders. These coders will probably use variable-bit-rate service from future integrated services networks.

Unspecified bit-rate and available bit-rate

The ATM Forum divides best-effort services into two subclasses. The *unspecified bit-rate* or *UBR* class comes closest in spirit to the current service on the Internet. A UBR source neither specifies nor receives a bandwidth, delay, or loss guarantee. It is assumed to be able to deal with fluctuations in these parameters by using techniques such as forward error-correction or application-level flow control. In contrast, *available bit-rate (ABR)* service guarantees a zero-loss rate if sources obey the dynamically varying traffic management signals from the network. The network uses *resource management cells* (Section 13.4.9) to inform an ABR source about the currently available bandwidth at the bottleneck in its path. If the source obeys these signals, it is guaranteed zero loss. However, the network does not need to guarantee a delay or mean bandwidth bound (sometimes, the network may guarantee a minimum bandwidth). The difference between an ABR application and a UBR application is that an ABR application is willing to listen to resource management signals to obtain a zero loss bound. An ABR application differs from a VBR application in that a VBR application need not alter its behavior in response to network signals: sufficient resources are reserved for the source that its performance bounds are met. In contrast, an ABR application is guaranteed only a zero *loss* bound, and it must follow the network's orders to obtain this bound. A network provider will presumably compensate for this inconvenience by charging a lower price for ABR service than for VBR service. Common Internet applications such as FTP, WWW, and telnet are likely to be the initial applications using UBR/ABR service.

14.4.4 IETF subclasses

Guaranteed-service applications

The IETF divides the guaranteed-service class into *tolerant* and *intolerant* subclasses based on an application's sensitivity to delay [SCZ 93, BCS 94]. A tolerant application requires a nominal mean delay, but is tolerant of "occasional" lapses from this mean. In other words, its utility function does not degrade much if some of its packets get a large delay. An example of a tolerant application is an interactive-voice application that is willing to drop packets delayed significantly beyond the mean. The IETF does not quantify how often the delay bound can be violated or by how much, since this requires extensive source characterization, which is difficult to achieve in real life.

In contrast, *intolerant* applications require a worst-case delay bound and cannot tolerate a delay larger than the bound (in other words, its utility function degrades significantly if packets are delayed beyond the bound). An example of an intolerant application is a multiparticipant interactive game, where user satisfaction derives from a small response time. Both tolerant and intolerant applications implicitly require either a constant or variable bit-rate bandwidth guarantee. Both implicitly require a guarantee of low loss, though the IETF proposals do not address this issue.

The network serves tolerant applications with *controlled-load* service. With this service, during call establishment, the user informs the network of its expected traffic pattern. The network (using an unspecified admission control algorithm) denies a call if it will appreciably degrade the service quality of existing calls. The precise specifications for controlled-load service are still being defined. Intolerant applications are served with *guaranteed service,* which is nearly identical to VBR service in ATM networks.

Best-effort applications

The IETF divides best-effort applications into three subclasses, based on their delay sensitivity. The *interactive burst* subclass models applications such as paging and messaging. These applications require bounded asynchronous service, where the bound is fairly tight (at least at human time scales). The second class of service is the *interactive bulk* class, such as file transfer, where a human being may be waiting for the transfer to complete. The network should give such applications a lower delay than traffic from the *asynchronous bulk* class, which are truly asynchronous. An example of an application in the asynchronous bulk subclass is Usenet (Internet news).

14.4.5 Some notable points

Three points about providing heterogeneous qualities of service are worth noting.

- Current networks provide only a limited service menu. The Internet gives all applications a single best-effort quality of service. The telephone network essentially provides only voice-quality calls, though users can also purchase multiples of a single voice call (for example, as a DS1 or DS3 circuit). Recently, specialized packet-switched networks called *frame-relay* networks have been built mainly for interconnecting geographically separated LANs. Frame-relay service does allow LAN administrators to ask for a sustained rate and a peak rate, similar to the ATM Forum VBR specification. However, all applications on the wide-area link share this specification. Thus, it is a step in the right direction, but still far removed from the capabilities we expect from a full-scale integrated service network.

- We have focused here on *application* requirements. Besides these, both the IETF and the ATM Forum recognize the need for meeting *organizational* quality-of-service requirements. For example, if several organizations share a wide-area link, they may want to partition the link into prespecified bandwidth shares when they overload the link. If organizations A and B each pay for half the cost of a link, they may want to ensure that when both have traffic to send, the link sends equal amounts from A and B, and when one is inactive, the other gets the excess capacity. This link-sharing agreement constrains the set of applications that can be admitted on the link from each organization. It also constrains the service order among packets from the two organizations. We will study these interactions in Section 14.6.

- We have concentrated on numerically expressed quality-of-service parameters for three performance metrics: delay, bandwidth, and loss. Users may be sensitive to other qualities of service that we have not considered here. Examples are media synchronization (such as voice synchronization with video), security, availability, freedom from billing errors, and privacy of billing records. Although we recognize the need for providing quality of service along these dimensions, they are orthogonal to the performance metrics described above. Moreover, many of these have been extensively studied and implemented in the current telephone network and the Internet. Therefore, we will not study them in this book.

14.5   Time scales of traffic management

Let us return to our busy executive participating in a videoconference and examine some steps the network must take to meet the service requirements of her voice and video traffic. Video (depending on how we code it) may require nearly a hundred times more bandwidth than voice, but voice is more sensitive to delay. Therefore, the network must be made aware of the bandwidth requirements of both streams and told that if a queue builds up, link schedulers should give voice packets priority over video packets. The videoconferencing application communicates with the network using *signaling*, which is done just once, when the call is set up. Traffic-management mechanisms operating at this time scale, by choosing an appropriate route through the network, and by reserving sufficient resources at each multiplexing point, ensure that the voice and video transferred during the call meet their bandwidth and delay requirements. After call setup, while the conference is going on, the network must make scheduling decisions at a much faster time scale. Moreover, if the video application is required to obey a traffic descriptor, it may need to regulate traffic at this time scale. Thus, to provide a videoconferencing service, the network must provide traffic management not only at the time scale of a session, but also at a very fast time scale corresponding to packet scheduling. Traffic-management mechanisms operating at multiple time scales cooperate to serve traffic efficiently and maximize the utility delivered by the network.

Table 14.2 outlines the five time scales at which we must control a network, the mechanisms at each time scale, and whether these mechanisms operate in the network, at the endpoints, or both [Keshav 91]. We have already studied some of these mechanisms (shaded in the table) in earlier chapters. In the rest of the chapter we will study the remaining mechanisms in more detail. Bear in mind that at each time scale, the network operator seeks to carry out the same optimization: to maximize overall user satisfaction at least cost.

14.5.1   Less than one round-trip time

One round-trip time (RTT) is the smallest time between sending a message and getting a response from the network or destination. Depending on the network diameter, this can be anywhere from hundreds of microseconds to hundreds of milliseconds. The main idea is that at this time scale, because the source cannot adapt to network conditions, all control is open-loop. The mechanisms that operate at this time scale are *scheduling, traffic regulation and policing,* and *forward error correction*. This time scale is also called the *cell-level* time scale.

Time scale	Mechanism	Network	Endpoint	Reference
Less than one round-trip time (cell level)	Scheduling and buffer management	X	X	Section 14.6
	Regulation and policing	X	X	Section 13.3
	Routing (datagram networks)	X	X	Chapter 11
	Error detection and correction	X	X	Chapter 7
One or more round-trip times (burst level)	Feedback flow control	X	X	Section 13.4
	Retransmission		X	Section 12.4.7
	Renegotiation	X	X	Section 14.7
Session (call level)	Signaling	X	X	Section 14.8
	Admission control	X		Section 14.9
	Service pricing	X		Section 14.2.2
	Routing (connection-oriented networks)	X		Chapter 11
Day	Peak-load pricing	X		Section 14.10
Weeks or longer	Capacity planning	X		Section 14.11

Table 14.2: Time scales of control, and the mechanisms at these time scales.

14.5.2 One or more round-trip times

At the multiple RTTs time scale, endpoints can *react* to changes in the network, thus allowing them to scale their load in response to network state dynamically. The mechanisms operating at this time scale for best-effort sources are *feedback flow control* and *retransmission*. Because it takes at least one RTT for a source to inform every scheduler along the path about its traffic descriptor and service requirement, the multiple RTT time scale is the shortest time-scale at which applications in the guaranteed-service class can *renegotiate* their traffic and service descriptors. This is also called the *burst-level* time scale.

14.5.3 Session

The session or call-level time scale is the time over which applications establish, use, and tear down an end-to-end connection. Guaranteed-service applications declare their traffic descriptors and resource requirements using the *signaling* mechanism at this time scale. To meet these requirements, the network must do *admission control*, allowing some calls and denying others. In connection-oriented networks, *routing* is done at this time scale. *Service pricing*, which limits call volumes, also operates at this time scale. Connectionless networks do not make a distinction between the multiple-RTT and session time scales.

14.5.4 Day

A strong diurnal cycle, based on the working day, dominates network usage. Usage peaks during working hours, with a dip during lunchtime, and slacks off as night progresses. A network provider can use *peak-load pricing* to shift part of the peak load to off-peak hours, thus decreasing the peak load.

14.5.5 Weeks or longer

Over a longer time scale, the network provider can dynamically adapt network topology to match traffic demands. Since link and switch provisioning takes time and can be expensive, these changes are carried out in the weeks-to-months time scale.

14.6 Scheduling

What scheduling discipline must we use to simultaneously satisfy the performance requirements of guaranteed-service and best-effort applications? We have seen in Chapter 9 that scheduling disciplines such as weighted fair queuing and rate-controlled static priority scheduling allow individual connections to obtain guarantees on bandwidth, delay, and delay jitter. Thus, packets from guaranteed-service sources should be scheduled according to one of these disciplines. These sources should reserve enough resources (such as a service weight for WFQ) to meet their performance requirements. In contrast, packets from best-effort sources should receive fair service, as described in Chapter 9.

We can meet the performance bounds of both GS and BE connections by implementing a scheduler with multiple priority levels, where the highest priority level is devoted to packets from GS connections, and the lower levels to packets from BE connections. Because packets from GS connections have higher priority than packets from BE connections, BE traffic interferes minimally with GS traffic. Similarly, we can give delay-sensitive BE applications lower delays by scheduling them at a higher priority level than delay-insensitive BE applications. Although a connection assigned to a higher-priority BE level is not guaranteed an absolute delay bound, it gets a smaller delay than lower-priority BE connections.

14.6.1 Hierarchical link sharing

We mentioned earlier that scheduling should meet not only individual, but also organizational performance requirements. Although we could use the disciplines in Chapter 9, aggregating connections from the same organization, this does not completely capture the semantics of sharing. In this section, we will study scheduling to meet organizational performance requirements.

Note that a conflict between individual and organizational performance requirements is possible, in that a packet might need to be given a low delay to meet its delay bound, but the connection on which the packet arrived might have already used its bandwidth quota. If the scheduler delays the packet, the organizational performance requirement is met, but the individual performance requirement is not. If the scheduler sends the packet before its deadline, the opposite holds true. In general, a network operator that provides both individual and organizational performance bounds should specify their precedence.

We now sketch a scheduling architecture for meeting organizational link-sharing requirements, based on reference [FJ 95]. The principal idea behind link sharing is the *a priori* hierarchical partitioning of a link's bandwidth among organizations, traffic classes, or protocol families. An example of a one-level partition is a link shared between guaranteed-service and best-effort connections, where, during an overload, the network guarantees best-effort applications at least 20% of the link (Figure 14.2a). Suppose constant-bit-rate connections are further guaranteed that they can reserve at least 30% of the link capacity, and variable-bit-rate connections are guaranteed at least 50% of link capacity. This corresponds to a two-level partition, where we have subdivided the 80% share allocated to the GS class into shares for two subclasses (Figure 14.2b). Similarly, we can partition a link share allocated to an organization into shares for traffic classes within the organization, for subclasses within a class, and finally for individual applications or protocol types within a subclass. This results in a multilevel hierarchical partition of the link (Figure 14.2c).

Given a link partition, the scheduler monitors the bandwidth usage of each entity allocated a link share and ensures that it uses no more than its share. A bandwidth-sharing entity represents either a single connection or an aggregation of connections, such as all connections originating from a particular corporation. If an entity uses more than its share, we call it *overlimit*. A scheduler can delay or drop traffic from an overlimit entity (the *overlimit action*). If it delays overlimit packets, they must be queued separately and marked eligible to be sent at a future time. This time is chosen such that, by delaying packets from an overlimit connection until this time, the overlimit class's bandwidth consumption returns below its limit. An overlimit entity can also borrow bandwidth from its parent if the parent is under its limit. Finally, if an entity is using less bandwidth than its share, the scheduler may distribute the excess to overlimit entities in proportion to their original allocations. Reference [FJ 95] describes a simple mechanism that implements these requirements. Further refinements using a hierarchical version of weighted fair queuing are described in reference [BZ 96].

The nature of the interaction between link sharing and packet scheduling is still a matter of debate [FJ 95, SCZ 93]. The disagreement is about which set of requirements is more important: application or organizational. Depending on the answer, the scheduler may choose to delay a packet, because it comes from an organization that has already exceeded its share of link capacity, or choose to give it immediate service, because it

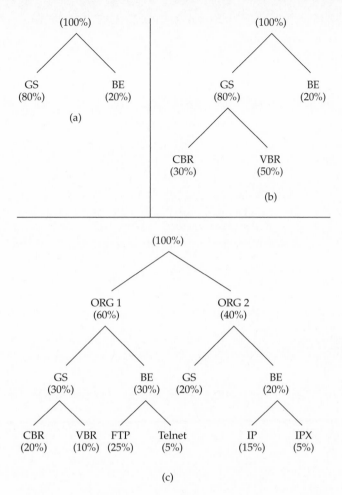

Figure 14.2: Example of a link partition. (a) A link partitioned between guaranteed-service and best-effort applications. (b) The guaranteed-service share further partitioned among constant-bit-rate (CBR) and variable-bit-rate (VBR) classes. (c) How the link may be partitioned among two organizations, which in turn partition them as in (b).

comes from an application that requires very low end-to-end delays. Of course, with a sufficiently clever admission control algorithm and policing, we can ensure that a GS packet that conforms to a given traffic descriptor will never exceed the application's link share. The question is whether such admission control algorithms are at all feasible.

Putting link sharing and the scheduling considerations for GS and BE traffic together, we get the scheduling architecture shown in Figure 14.3 [SCZ 93]. We assume that individual application requirements are given preference over link-sharing requirements (or, equivalently, an admission-control algorithm ensures that admitted GS calls do not violate the link-sharing constraint). Thus, the highest priority level corresponds to the

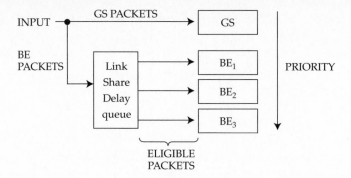

Figure 14.3: One possible way to reconcile link sharing and scheduling. Packets arrive from the left, and if they belong to guaranteed-service applications, are scheduled immediately by an appropriate guaranteed-service scheduling algorithm. If they are from a best-effort connection, they are delayed or dropped if they belong to an overlimit entity. Delayed best-effort packets enter a lower-priority service level.

GS class. Lower priority levels correspond to the three BE subclasses, where BE service is contingent on meeting link-sharing constraints. The scheduler first checks whether any GS packets are awaiting service (and, if the discipline is non-work-conserving, whether they are eligible). If any eligible GS packets exist, the scheduler transmits them. The scheduler also marks BE packets to be eligible for service or not, depending on the link-sharing algorithm. If any eligible BE packets exist, the scheduler serves them in order of their priority. The scheduler repeats this algorithm after each packet service, allowing it to simultaneously satisfy GS, BE, and link-sharing requirements.

14.7   Renegotiation

Recall that a guaranteed-service connection must specify its traffic descriptor at the time of connection establishment. However, in the real world, it is often impossible to *a priori* determine satisfactory traffic descriptors. Consider an application that digitizes input from a camera and sends it over a network. It is easy to bound the peak rate of the application loosely, but if it compresses the data, its sustained bit rate (average rate) depends on how often the camera moves and the scenes it captures. The application designer or application user can only guess the expected average rate of the application. If this guess is too high, then the user pays an unnecessarily high fee for its service, because the network must reserve resources for at least the user's declared average rate. If the guess is too low, the policer drops excess traffic, so that the received quality degrades. Thus, for interactive compressed video applications, which are expected to be common in future networks, a one-shot traffic descriptor makes little sense.

Sometimes, finding an adequate descriptor is hard even if we know the entire source behavior in advance. Consider, for example, an application that plays stored compressed video. Experimental evidence suggests that compressed video applications exhibit burstiness at multiple time scales and that bursts can last as long as 10 s [GKT 95]. Let us see how a single long burst influences the choice of a source's leaky-bucket descriptor. If the burst is at a peak rate, P, and has a burst size B, then two leaky-bucket descriptors that capture the traffic behavior, and allow for zero loss at the regulator, are $(0, P)$ and (B, A), where A is the long-term average rate. The first descriptor needs zero buffering in the network and in the regulator. However, the connection gets no *temporal* statistical multiplexing gain, because the network reserves resources for this connection at its peak rate (see Section 6.3.1 for more description of temporal statistical multiplexing gain). The second descriptor allows the largest possible temporal statistical multiplexing gain, but allows bursts of size B into the network. Since B can be as large as 15 Mbytes for typical movies, this imposes a substantial burden on the network. Of course, we can choose an intermediate descriptor with a drain rate intermediate between P and A, and a corresponding bucket size. However, because of the sustained peak phenomenon, token rates even slightly smaller than P lead to large bucket sizes. To see this, note that if ρ is the drain rate and T the burst duration, the bucket size needed is roughly $(P - \rho)T$. Thus, as T increases, even small differences are magnified. The conclusion is that for sources with sustained peaks, a one-shot leaky-bucket descriptor is inadequate.

We can solve these problems if we allow the application to renegotiate its traffic descriptor. If a source can renegotiate its traffic descriptor at the beginning and end of every burst, its effective reserved rate is identical to its long-term average rate. However, this imposes a heavy signaling load on the network. Keeping worst-case delay and loss rate fixed, as the renegotiation frequency decreases (and the mean renegotiation interval increases), the effective reserved rate moves farther away from the average rate and approaches the source's peak rate. It has been shown that with a mean renegotiation interval of roughly 10 s, sources that exhibit burstiness at multiple time scales need only reserve 5% more bandwidth than their long-term average rate [GKT 95]. With stored traffic, the series of renegotiation points and renegotiation values can be precomputed. Even for online interactive traffic, the application can observe past behavior and use this to predict future behavior. It has been shown that simple predictors can predict average rates (over time scales of approximately 1 s) quite well [CLG 95]. Thus, renegotiation does not pose a severe burden on applications. It does increase the network signaling load, and a user must trade off between renegotiation frequency and the degree to which the effective reserved rate approaches the true long-term average rate.

14.7.1   Fast buffer reservation

Renegotiation for each burst, when carrying data traffic, is also called *fast buffer reservation* [BT 92]. In this scheme, before a source transmits a burst, it sends a *fast reservation* request to the network. This request is handled by special-purpose hardware that reserves buffers at each switch along the path. If the reservation succeeds, the source is allowed to send a burst, with the knowledge that no data will be lost. At the end of the burst, the source releases the reservation. The scheme has the advantage that a source does not have to reserve buffers for the entire duration of a call. Thus, it gains efficiency in multiplexing buffers in the same way as renegotiating traffic descriptors efficiently multiplexes bandwidth.

Renegotiation is not free. A source that reserves bandwidth at its peak rate (or buffers for its longest possible burst), knows that it *always* has bandwidth (buffers) available. On the other hand, a renegotiation for an increased bandwidth (more buffers) may fail. Thus, the price for increased efficiency of a renegotiated system is the possibility of renegotiation failure. On a failure, an application retains its existing reservation so it must adapt itself to conform to the existing reservation and try again. The network provider should admit renegotiable calls only if it has a reasonably high expectation that future renegotiations will succeed. We will discuss this in Section 14.9.

14.8 Signaling

Signaling is the process by which an endpoint requests the network to set up, tear down, or renegotiate a call. One can think of it as the mechanism that informs the network of a source's utility function, so that the network can take steps to maximize a user's utility. Two distinct mechanisms are involved in signaling: one that carries signaling messages reliably between signaling entities (which corresponds to the first six layers of the OSI stack), and another that interprets the messages (which corresponds to an application). Separating these mechanisms allows them to evolve independently, so that we can make the message semantics arbitrarily complicated without changing the method by which a signaling message is carried within the network. We will first study the semantics of signaling, then study some implementations in Sections 14.8.3 and 14.8.4.

14.8.1 Signaling semantics

We show the basic steps in source-initiated signaling in Figure 14.4 (we will study receiver-initiated signaling in Section 14.8.5). If the appropriate communication paths exist, a source sends a SETUP message to the first switch controller along the path. The controller acknowledges the SETUP message with a SETUP-ACK message, allowing hop-by-hop error recovery from lost or corrupted signaling messages at the application level. If the call is for a GS application, the switch controller tentatively reserves sufficient resources for the call. If sufficient resources are not available, the switch controller rejects the call (this is called *admission control*, and we will study it in more detail in Section 14.9). If the call can be accepted, the switch controller forwards it to the next controller along the path. When the signaling message reaches the destination, the destination can choose to either accept or reject the call. This response is carried in the SETUP-RESPONSE message back to the source. As the SETUP-RESPONSE propagates

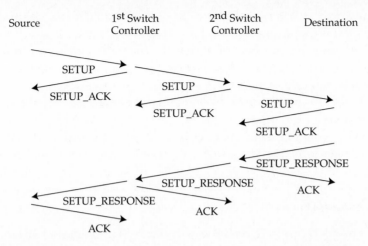

Figure 14.4: Typical source-initiated signaling exchange. The source initiates signaling with a SETUP request, which propagates to the receiver. Each intermediate switch-controller acknowledges the message with a SETUP_ACK message. The receiver either accepts or denies the call using a SETUP_RESPONSE message, which returns to the source.

back, if the call is accepted, the switch controllers along the path confirm the resources reserved for the call, and, in an ATM network, set up the switching table to recognize the VCI allocated to the call. Otherwise, they free the tentatively allocated resources. Thus, the network informs the source whether the call setup completed or not one round-trip time from the time it initiated the call.

Note that the setup message can reserve resources and set up switching tables in one of two ways. In *simplex* setup, switch controllers make reservations only in the source-to-destination direction. In *duplex* setup, switch controllers make reservations in both directions. The ATM Forum signaling standard specifies duplex signaling (except for point-to-multipoint connections), and the IETF signaling standard specifies simplex signaling.

This simple signaling model is the basis for signaling in both the telephone network and ATM networks. The model is greatly enhanced in the telephone network to provide services such as three-way calling, conference bridging, and 800-number service. Similarly, it has been enhanced in ATM networks to allow sophisticated admission-control policies. As we will see shortly, this basic model does not scale well when dealing with multipoint multicast, so the proposed IETF integrated-services signaling model differs from this basic model in several important ways.

14.8.2 Resource translation

An interesting problem in resource reservation is translating a global resource requirement to a set of local requirements. Consider an application that would like to get an end-to-end delay bound of 100 ms. Suppose that the end-to-end propagation delay is

25 ms. Then, the intermediate switches must somehow share a part of the remaining 75 ms. One simple approach is for each switch controller to allocate as many resources as possible in the forward pass, and to write the allocated resources in the signaling message as it propagates through the network. The destination compares the performance achievable with the best possible resource allocation with the requested bound, and if part of the performance budget is still available, distributes it among the switch controllers. In the reverse pass, the resources at each controller are *relaxed* so that the application gets a performance bound close to what it requested. Of course, if the best possible performance is worse than the bound, the destination rejects the call.

EXAMPLE 14.3

Consider a connection that wants an end-to-end delay of 100 ms over a path with propagation delay 25 ms, where the connection passes through two switches, and both switches implement WFQ scheduling. Suppose the connection's leaky-bucket descriptor is (100 Kbytes, 1 Mbps), all link speeds are 45 Mbps, and the largest packet size is 8 Kbytes. Assume also that the available capacity at the first switch is 20 Mbps, and at the second switch is 40 Mbps. Then, we know from Equation 9.14 that the end-to-end delay is given by (100 Kbytes) $/ g + 2 * 8$ Kbytes $/ g + 2 * 8$ Kbytes $/ 45$ Mbps, where g is the smaller of the allocated bandwidths at the two switches. When the signaling message reaches the first switch controller, the best value for g it can get is 20 Mbps, and this value is written on the signaling message. The second switch controller, similarly, can allocate at most 40 Mbps and appends this value to the message. The destination, using the smaller of the two values, can compute the best achievable worst-case delay bound as 50.4 ms. Since a delay bound of 75 ms is acceptable, the receiver computes the necessary bandwidth as 13.17 Mbps. This value is written on the SETUP-RESPONSE packet, and on the reverse pass, both switch controllers relax their reservation to 13.17 Mbps. Note that while the forward pass is going on, no other connection can be accepted, which is a serious problem with this approach. We can avoid this problem by limiting the resources for which any single connection is eligible. Of course, this may result in denying admission to some connections that might otherwise be admitted.

Although this approach to resource translation has the advantage of simplicity, it has some severe problems, noted in the example just given. Resource translation is an area where we still need research into good heuristics or optimal algorithms.

14.8.3 Signaling in the telephone network

Signaling System No. 7 (SS7) is the signaling system used in the international telephone network [MS 90]. Recall from Section 2.5 that in the telephone network, signaling is carried on a separate overlay network called the *Common Channel Interoffice Signaling (CCIS)* network. The CCIS network is logically distinct from the circuit-switch network used for carrying voice calls. In fact, it is a connectionless packet-switched data network that carries messages using the SS7 protocol stack.

The SS7 protocol stack is based loosely on the ISO layering model. Its lower layers (the transport subsystem) provide reliability and message routing, and the application layer is responsible for interpreting signaling messages. Packet routers in SS7 are called *signaling transfer points*, or STPs. Switch controllers receive signaling messages from STPs on the CCIS network, and interpret them to set up circuits on the circuit-switched voice network. We will study the SS7 protocol stack in more detail in Section 15.2.4.

14.8.4 Signaling in ATM networks

The current standard for ATM signaling, called *Q.2931*, is a variant of SS7, with a source-initiated call setup as just described. Q.2931 is part of the interface specification between an ATM user and the network standardized by the ATM Forum, known as the *User Network Interface* or *UNI*. This interface is still under development, and the latest version of the specification, UNI 4.0, is being finalized at the time of this writing. However, the concepts underlying UNI 4.0 and Q.2931 are similar to those in SS7 and in RSVP, which we discuss in Section 14.8.5.

The ATM transport subsystem provides the same functionality as in SS7, though using a different protocol structure. The ATM signaling application is layered over the *Service-Specific Connection-Oriented Protocol (SSCOP)* transport protocol, which provides flow and error control using static windows, sequence numbers, and negative acknowledgments [Henderson 95]. SSCOP is layered over *AAL5* (see Section 15.4.4 for details).

The Q.2931 standard defines the semantics of applications running on the ATM signaling stack. These applications are expected to provide telephony services by subsuming the functionality of SS7 applications. They will also provide B-ISDN services, which have yet to be fully defined. However, one significant difference between SS7 applications and ATM applications is that the resources reserved for an ATM network call depend on the connection class and required quality of service. In contrast, nearly all calls handled by an SS7 application have the same bandwidth. We will study this further when dealing with admission control in Section 14.9.

14.8.5 IETF signaling: RSVP

The IETF has adopted the *Resource reSerVation Protocol (RSVP)* [ZDEZ 93] as its signaling standard.[2] RSVP's designers had the freedom to design their protocol from scratch, because the Internet does not widely support a connection-oriented network layer or

---

[2] Actually, the Internet supports other signaling standards as well. Prominent among these are the *Stream Transport* protocol, usually referred to by its initials, *ST*, and its successors *ST 2* and *ST2+* [DB 95]. However, these are not currently in favor, because they do not support multipoint-to-multipoint multicast nearly as well as RSVP.

resource reservation. The main motivation for RSVP is to allow efficient support for establishing *multipoint multicast* connections. Because this is critical to understanding RSVP, we will digress briefly to discuss the implications of this service.

In traditional *unicast*, a single source communicates with a single destination. This is the case, for example, with a telephone call. In a unicast, the signaling message must traverse a path from a source to the destination and back (Figure 14.5a). In a *multicast*, a source communicates with more than one destination. An example of a multicast application is stock-market quote distribution. In naive multicast signaling, a signaling message traverses a path from a source to every destination and back (Figure 14.5b). In a more intelligent implementation, the setup message from the source is duplicated on each link on a path to a receiver, and the responses are merged. Thus, the setup message travels twice over every link of a *spanning tree*, that is, a tree that is rooted at the source, with a leaf at every receiver (Figure 14.5c). A multipoint multicast service is an extension of multicast service, where a set of users forms a *multicast group*. Any member of the group may send messages to every other member of the group and is guaranteed to have adequate resources for its transmission. The IETF believes that applications based on guaranteed-service multicast groups (such as videoconferencing) will become important in the future Internet. Therefore, it believes it necessary to develop efficient signaling mechanisms to establish and maintain multipoint multicast connections.

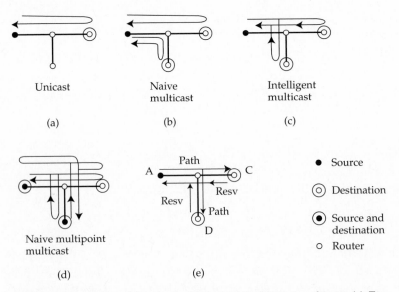

Figure 14.5: Signaling styles for multicast and multipoint multicast. (a) Traditional unicast. (b) How (a) might be extended naively for multicast. (c) The two messages used in (b) are merged so that the messages travel each link only twice. Even this is not sufficient for multipoint multicast, as is shown in (d). (e) The RSVP technique, explained in the text.

A naive way to set up a multipoint multicast connection would be for each source to send a setup message over a spanning tree rooted at that source to every receiver (Figure 14.5d). This has many disadvantages. Suppose that the receivers in the multicast group are heterogeneous, so that they absorb data at different rates. If a source is to initiate the multicast reservation, it must know not only the identity of every member, but also the resources that must be reserved on each member's behalf. This poses a heavy burden on the source, especially for large groups. Second, since sources establish the point-to-multipoint multicast independently, they cannot easily share resources. So, even if only one source in the group is active at any point, reservations will be made for all of them. These disadvantages become worse if the multicast group can be large, with frequently changing membership, and receivers frequently joining and leaving multicast groups (similar to channel surfing on a television set).

Mechanism

RSVP solves these problems by using two important mechanisms. First, receivers initiate signaling, instead of senders. Second, resource reservation state is associated with a multicast group, rather than with a connection. To see these mechanisms in action, consider source A that initiates a multicast group that is eventually joined by sources C and D, as shown in Figure 14.5e. In the first step, source A sends a PATH message that is multicast along a spanning tree to all receivers in the multicast group (in this case, C and D). The PATH message creates an entry in each intermediate router that allows it to determine the next hop toward the source. For example, in Figure 14.5e, when router B gets a PATH message from A, it remembers that link A–B is the next hop to forward messages back to A. Note that the PATH message does not set up reservations: reservations are initiated by a receiver. Note also that every router that might ever receive a resource reservation must receive the PATH message to deal with future reservations correctly.

When C wants to receive data from the multicast group, it sends an RESV message to its nearest router, B. The RESV message contains the amount of resources C would like to reserve for messages from the multicast group traversing the link B–C. This allows C to choose what it wants to receive, instead of leaving this decision to the source. When B gets the RESV message, it reserves resources on that link, and forwards the message to A. A then reserves resources on A–B. Thus, in response to C's RESV message, sufficient resources are reserved on the entire path from A to C.

When D wants to join the multicast group, it sends an RESV message to B. B reserves resources on the B–D link, but need not forward the reservation to A, because resources have already been reserved for the group on the A–B link. However, if D's reservation request is larger than C's, then D's request is forwarded to A so that A can increase the reservation on the A–B link. The rule is that a receiver's RESV message is forwarded only if the reservation request is larger than the reservation already held for its multicast group. Thus, RSVP avoids the overhead of forwarding RESV messages by associating reservation state with a multicast group, rather than with a connection.

Filters

Notice that in Figure 14.5e when D sends an RESV message to B, B reserves resources for the *group* on the B–D link. Therefore, if C also becomes a transmitter in the group, the reservation on link B–D is shared by packets from both A and C. For some applications, this type of link sharing is acceptable. For example, consider an audioconference where only one speaker can be active at a time. In this situation, the reservation on B–D is shared by A and C as they take turns to speak. For other applications, this sharing may not be desirable. D may want to have a separate reservation for packets from A and packets from C. RSVP supports this by associating *filters* with each outgoing link and multicast connection. Packets that satisfy the filter specification use the associated reserved resources. With a *fixed* filter, a receiver chooses to receive data from a single source or a single type of data from any source. With a *dynamic* filter, a receiver can dynamically choose which source uses the reservation on the link. With *no* filter, the receiver agrees to receive packets from all senders in the group. Continuing with our example, if D wants to receive only packets from A on the B–D link, it uses a fixed filter set to A. B then filters out C's packets on the B–D link. If D wants to choose between A's and C's packets on-the-fly, it uses a dynamic filter. By tuning this filter, it selects the source that can use the reservation on B–D. This permits channel surfing, as desired.

Soft state

Switch controllers implementing RSVP store reservations using *soft state,* that is, state that is periodically refreshed (also see Section 6.3.10). To understand why this is necessary, consider the consequences of a link failure in an ATM network. On a link failure, all calls using that link are canceled, because VCIs have only local significance. If an application wants to continue the conversation, it must reestablish the call. Thus, a link failure is catastrophic and requires intervention from an endpoint. In contrast, with RSVP, PATH and RESV messages are periodically refreshed by each source and destination. If a link goes down and the routing topology changes, new PATH and RESV messages traverse routes on the new topology. This reserves resources for the multicast group without intervention by the endpoints (assuming that resources are available on the new spanning tree corresponding to the multicast group). Therefore, if all goes well, RSVP can gracefully work around link and switch failures.

Problems

Though RSVP addresses many important issues in efficiently establishing multipoint multicast connections, it still has some unresolved problems. For example, a receiver who thinks that a group has two cooperative senders might choose to have no filter for a link reservation, sharing the resources between the two sources. Now, if a third, non-cooperative sender joined the group, the receiver would experience poor performance on the link until it realized that an intruder had joined the group and appropriately modified its filter. The problem really is that since RSVP merges RESV and PATH messages to gain efficiency, it inevitably loses some information (such as the fact that a new sender joined the group) that might potentially be of interest to group members. These and other problems are areas of active research interest.

Why is signaling hard?

Signaling is often the most complex component of a computer network. For example, each switch controller in the AT&T telephone network requires millions of lines of signaling code. (Bugs in this code were the cause of large-scale service outages in the early 1990s.) There are many reasons for this complexity [Kalmanek 95]. One is that signaling is necessary for providing complex network services, such as conference bridging, calling collect, and accounting. Even a simple function such as call forwarding requires interaction between many signaling entities, each of which must implement complex, asynchronous state machines. The richer the set of services (or *features*), the more complex the associated signaling.

A deeper problem concerns *feature interaction*. Consider a call-screening service, which allows a user to decide not to accept calls from certain numbers. If a user decides to use both call forwarding and call screening, the call-forwarding element must check with the call-screening element whether the call should be forwarded or not. Perhaps the user may want some calls to be screened, but only if they are not forwarded. Interactions of this sort complicate signaling.

A third reason for complexity is that signaling has strict requirements on *performance* and *reliability*. Fast call completion requires that the signaling entity take the minimum amount of time in completing its processing. Because signaling is essential to the operation of the network, it must be robust to link and switch failures. A large fraction of signaling code deals with unlikely error situations that must still be tested for and handled.

Finally, signaling software evolves as the network provider adds services and new pricing plans. Teams of hundreds of programmers update signaling software daily. This means that the software should be *extensible* and *maintainable*.

14.9 Admission control

The signaling network carries signaling messages and makes resource reservations. However, before a switch controller can make these reservations, the *admission-control* algorithm checks whether admitting the call would reduce the service quality of existing calls, or whether the incoming call's quality-of-service requirements cannot be met. This decision depends on the choice of scheduling disciplines and the set of services provided by the network. If either of these conditions holds, the call is either delayed until resources are available, or rejected. Admission control plays a crucial role in ensuring that a network meets its quality-of-service requirements. In this section, we will study some basic algorithms for admission control: a more detailed exposition can be found in the references cited in the text.

14.9.1 CBR admission control

Admission control for CBR calls is simple because a CBR call i can be described by a single number: its rate, $\rho(i)$ (since CBR traffic is defined to be smooth at the cell level, we do not need to specify the interval over which the rate is measured). If a link has capacity C and has an admitted load L, then a new call i can be admitted if and only if $L + e(i) \leq C$. If a CBR call also has a delay requirement, and the link scheduler can provide delay bounds (for example, with an RCSP scheduler), the call may fail the admission control test if the best delay bound available from the scheduler is worse than the call's delay requirement. A call that fails the admission control test is either rerouted, delayed till the link becomes available, or denied. A switch controller that denies calls instead of delaying them is said to implement a *loss system*.

14.9.2 Best-effort admission control

Connections requiring either best-effort service or a guarantee of *relative* service quality are never rejected because of lack of bandwidth or buffer space (they may only be rejected, for example, because a switch may have run out of VCIs) . Each switch controller, on admitting the call, should choose an appropriate service priority level depending on the call's relative service priority. If best-effort calls desire some minimum bandwidth, then the controller performs a CBR-style admission control test on the desired minimum, as the next example shows.

EXAMPLE 14.4

Consider a scheduler that has three best-effort priority levels, roughly corresponding to email, FTP, and Usenet. (a) How many Usenet connections can be admitted, if they require no minimum bandwidth? (b) Can each email connection be guaranteed a bandwidth of at least 100 Kbps?

Solution: (a) We can admit as many Usenet connections as we want, because they are best-effort. (b) We can guarantee email connections a minimum bandwidth if the highest best-effort priority level is guaranteed some minimum bandwidth, and we assign email connections to this priority level. (We can also allocate bandwidth shares to priority levels using the link-sharing techniques in Section 14.6.) If this minimum is m, then each email connection is guaranteed 100 Kbps if the number of email connections is restricted to $\lfloor m / 100 \text{ Kbps} \rfloor$.

14.9.3   VBR admission control

Unlike CBR calls, which send data at an even rate, VBR calls send data in bursts, so that their peak rate (during a burst) differs from their average rate. Admission control for VBR calls is hard because VBR calls are inherently *bursty*. That is, they have periods where they send data at a rate that can be much greater than the average rate. The principal insight in VBR admission control is that as a link's capacity increases and it carries more and more connections, the probability that all the sources simultaneously send a burst into the link becomes small. Thus, if the number of sources is large, a burst from one source is likely to coincide with an idle period from another. So, in this regime, the admission-control algorithm can admit a call as if it were sending a CBR stream with a rate close to its long-term average. This considerably simplifies the admission-control algorithm, but can result in delay bound violations due to statistical fluctuations. Thus, by characterizing the behavior of an ensemble of bursty sources, we can make statistical delay guarantees to each source. Note that this approach works well only when the number of sources is "large." We will examine this point in more detail in Section 14.9.5. Before we do that, we study a simple but inefficient way to admit VBR traffic.

14.9.4   VBR admission control: Peak rate

The easiest admission-control algorithm for VBR calls is to treat them as CBR calls with a rate set to their peak rate (*peak-rate allocation*). Thus, the switch controller reserves enough resources to deal with a call even if it has no idle time between bursts. Clearly, this is correct, though potentially conservative. The next example quantifies the loss of efficiency from peak-rate allocation.

EXAMPLE 14.5

A link of capacity 155 Mbps serves sources that have a peak rate of 15.5 Mbps and a peak-to-average ratio r. How many calls can be admitted with peak-rate and average-rate allocation?

Solution: With peak-rate allocation, no more than $155/15.5 = 10$ sources can be admitted. With average-rate allocation, the bandwidth reserved for a source is $15.5 / r$. Thus, we may admit $155/ (15.5 / r) = 10r$ calls.[3] Typical compressed video sources have a peak-to-average ratio of 4.0 to 5.0, and typical data calls have a peak-to-average ratio of 500–1000. Thus, the loss of efficiency by using peak-rate allocation is potentially large.

---

[3] Assuming 100% link utilization. In practice, engineers usually add a "fudge factor" to allow for unforeseen circumstances, and rarely run a link at higher than 90% utilization.

A second problem with peak-rate allocation is that because of scheduling jitter, after a connection passes through a few schedulers its peak rate may increase. This effect is hard to capture analytically, and a careful engineer must add a fudge factor to allow for variations in the connection's peak rate.

14.9.5 VBR admission control: Worst-case

Another simple approach, which is less conservative than peak-rate allocation, is to use the results of Chapter 9 to allocate resources so that a connection meets its performance guarantees even in the worst case. This avoids making statistical assumptions about other sources. For example, if the scheduler implements WFQ, we can allocate sufficient bandwidth at each switch so that the worst-case delay along the path is bounded, and sufficient buffers so that no packets are lost. This would simultaneously meet the bandwidth, delay, and loss bounds. See Example 14.3 for more details.

As with peak-rate allocation, worst-case admission control has the potential to underutilize the network. The intuition is that the worst case rarely happens, so reserving capacity for the worst case wastes resources. On the other hand, the source gets a guarantee that the delay bound will never be exceeded.

14.9.6 VBR admission control with statistical guarantees

In real life, where equipment failures and rerouting may lead to unforeseen delays, the utility of a "worst-case" delay is debatable, because this only covers queuing delays. There may be a substantial performance gain (in the number of admitted calls) if each call is willing to tolerate a small probability that the network will not meet its performance bound. This subsection and the next study algorithms for admission control with statistical performance guarantees.

Before we begin, note that statistical or probabilistic performance bounds imply that the admission-control algorithm knows something about the statistical behavior of the sources. We usually assume that the sources contending for shared resources are independent. In other words, if a source is sending a burst of data, it does not affect the likelihood that another source is also sending a burst. A direct consequence of this independence assumption is that the likelihood that n sources are *simultaneously* bursting drops as n grows large (this insight is formalized in the *law of large numbers*). Thus, if the link has capacity for n bursts, it can choose to admit $N > n$ connections while keeping the probability that the link is overloaded sufficiently small.

EXAMPLE 14.6

Consider an ensemble of ten identical sources, each of which is on with probability 0.1, and when on, has a transmission rate of 1.0. What is the probability that they overflow a shared link of capacity 8?

Solution: If the sources are independent, the probability that any n are on is given by

$$\binom{10}{n} (0.1^n) (0.9^{10-n})$$

(because we can choose any n from 10, and of these we would like exactly n to be on and the rest to be off). This allows us to compute Figure 14.6. If the link has capacity 8, the probability that it will be overloaded is smaller than 10^{-6}. Note that with peak-rate allocation, we would need a link of capacity 10. By allowing a very small probability of overflow, we can reduce resource requirements by 20%.

The general mathematical technique to quantitatively bound this overflow probability is called the theory of large deviations [SW 95]. This theory, although beyond the scope of this book, provides one insight that we will find useful: When the number of multiplexed sources is small, an admission-control algorithm should treat a source as if it sends data at its peak rate. This guarantees zero loss and very small queuing delays. As the number of sources increases, the admission-control algorithm should assign smaller and smaller bandwidths to a source, and when the number of sources is infinite, the algorithm may assign a source its average rate.

Equivalent or effective bandwidth

We now turn our attention to the concept of *equivalent bandwidth,* which is fundamental to providing connections with statistical performance guarantees. Consider a connection that sends data into a buffer of size B drained at a constant rate e. Assume that the packets on the connection are infinitely small, so that we can ignore packet boundaries, and the packet stream

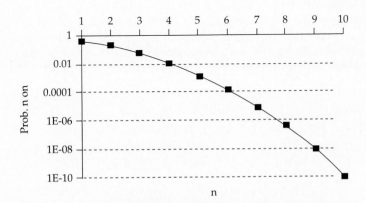

Figure 14.6: Figure for Example 14.6. Probability that n sources out of 10 are simultaneously active, if they are uncorrelated, and each source has a 0.1 probability of being active. Note that the probability decreases exponentially with n.

resembles a *fluid*. The fluid approximation is valid when link capacities are large and packet sizes are small, as in ATM networks. Given fluid arrivals, the worst-case delay at the buffer is B/e (this is the delay when the buffer is full—data packets arriving when the buffer is full are dropped). The *equivalent bandwidth* of the connection, then, is the value of e such that the probability of a buffer overflow is smaller than the call's cell loss bound, ϵ [GAN 91, GG 92]. By appropriately choosing e, we can simultaneously meet a connection's bandwidth, delay, and loss bounds. Moreover, the equivalent bandwidth of an ensemble of calls is a simple function of each call's equivalent bandwidth. Thus, the equivalent bandwidth of a call allows easy testing for admission control.

The key problem with using the equivalent bandwidth model is determining the equivalent bandwidth of an arbitrary source. We will study three representative approaches. We note here that all three approaches make strong assumptions about source behavior, not all of which have been verified in practice. Although it would be satisfying to claim that we can compute the equivalent bandwidth of an arbitrary source, it may be too early to do so. Nevertheless, the approach is promising and is worth studying, if only as a way to get a taste for an analytical approach to engineering networks.

The first approach, described in reference [Roberts 92], assumes fluid sources and zero buffering in the switches (so that two simultaneously active sources would cause data loss). If the cell loss ratio is to be smaller than 10^{-9}, each source has a peak rate P and mean rate m, and the sources are to be multiplexed on a link with capacity C, then a *heuristic* to estimate the equivalent bandwidth, e, of a source is:

$$e = 1.2m + 60m(P - m) / C \tag{14.2}$$

The intuition is that even with infinite link capacity, the equivalent capacity of a source is 1.2 times its mean rate (this is probably an overestimate for large C). The second term increases a source's equivalent bandwidth in proportion to the gap between its mean and peak rates, which corresponds to its burstiness. This is mitigated, however, by the link capacity: the greater the link capacity, the smaller the effect of a source's burstiness. The coefficients are insensitive to the assumed cell loss ratio of 10^{-9}. The expression also assumes that all sources require the same low cell-loss ratio.

The second approach takes switch buffers into account, which makes the analysis more complicated [GH 91]. In this approach, we assume that sources are either on for an exponentially distributed length of time with mean length $1/\mu$, when their rate is the peak rate P, or off for an exponentially distributed interval of length $1/\lambda$, when the rate is 0. If we know the leaky-bucket parameters for the source, so that ρ is the buffer drain rate and σ is the token bucket size, then λ and μ are given by:

$$\mu = (P - \rho) / \sigma$$
$$\lambda = P/\sigma \tag{14.3}$$

Let sources thus characterized share a single buffer of size B and require an acceptable cell loss ratio of ϵ. Then, we define $\xi = (\log \epsilon)/B$, and the equivalent bandwidth of the source, e, is given by:

$$e(\xi) = \frac{\xi P + \lambda + \mu - \sqrt{(\xi P + \mu - \lambda)^2 + 4\lambda\mu}}{2\xi} \tag{14.4}$$

The problem with this approach is that it is pessimistic when the buffer size is small. Moreover, it is valid only for asymptotically large link capacities.

The third approach solves the equivalent bandwidth problem in three steps [GG 92]. In the first step, we compute the equivalent bandwidth for an on–off source (that is, a source that is either on and sending data at the peak rate, or off). Assume that we already know for connection i:

peak rate P_i

mean rate m_i

average on-time (burst-time) b_i

Also assume that all connections sharing a link require the same loss probability ϵ. Finally, assume that the admission test is being conducted at a switch that has allocated B_i buffers to the connection. These are strong assumptions, because to know these parameters, we may have to measure the connection for a very long time, which is impossible for interactive sources.

If these parameters are known or can be measured, the probability that the source is on, ρ_i, is given by m_i/P_i. Define:

$$\gamma_i = ln(1 \ / \ \epsilon)b_i(1 \ - \ \rho_i)P_i.$$

Then, the equivalent bandwidth of an ensemble of N connections is given by the following set of equations:

$$\alpha = \sqrt{-2ln\epsilon \ - \ ln2\pi}$$
$$\sigma_i = \sqrt{m_i(P_i \ - \ m_i)}$$
$$\hat{c}_i = P_i\left(\frac{\gamma_i \ - \ B_i \ + \ \sqrt{[\gamma_i \ - \ B_i]^2 \ + \ 4B_i\gamma_i\rho_i}}{2\gamma_i}\right)$$
$$e(N) = min\left(\sum_{i=1}^{N}(m_i \ + \ \alpha\sigma_i), \ \sum_{i=1}^{N} \hat{c}_i\right)$$

(14.5)

The first equation gives a correction factor α. The second equation is the standard deviation of an on–off source. The third equation is the equivalent bandwidth of a source assuming that all sources are simultaneously on (that is, assuming zero statistical multiplexing gain): it is the peak rate multiplied by another correction term. The fourth equation gives the equivalent bandwidth of the ensemble as the smaller of two terms. The first term is the equivalent capacity computed as if the number of connections is very large: therefore, it is the sum of the mean rates with a correction factor that grows larger the more stringent the loss bound, and the larger the standard deviation of the sum. The second term applies when the number of connections is small, and assumes no statistical multiplexing gain. Note that the expression gives the equivalent bandwidth of the ensemble, but not the equivalent bandwidth of a single connection in the ensemble.

In the second step, we compute the leaky-bucket parameters to describe an on–off source optimally. The key idea here is to choose leaky-bucket values that minimally delay data at the regulator or policer, without violating the loss probabilities at the links. Note that we cannot set the drain rate to a fraction of the equivalent bandwidth, that is, $e(N) \ / \ N$, because N changes with time. Instead, we first compute N^*, the number of homogeneous connections with the given descriptors P, m, and b that can be supported on a link. If N^* is larger than some threshold, we call the source "multiplexable" and set its drain rate to $C \ / \ N^*$, where C is the smallest available link bandwidth along the path. Otherwise, we fall back on the conservative assumption and set the drain rate to $\hat{c}_i$. We choose the token bucket size M to be large enough so that the probability that a packet arrives when the token bucket is empty is smaller than some threshold ξ. It can be shown that this corresponds to:

$$M = \left[\frac{b(1 - \rho)\gamma(P - \gamma)}{(\gamma - \rho P)} \ln\left(\frac{(\gamma - \rho P) + \rho\xi(P - \gamma)}{\xi\gamma(1 - \rho)} \right) \right] \tag{14.6}$$

In the third step, we use heuristics to model an arbitrary source with an equivalent on–off source by measuring its actual behavior at a leaky-bucket regulator. If we can measure a source "long enough," we can directly estimate P and m, its peak and mean rates. Computing b is harder. One way to measure it would be to measure burst lengths directly, then compute their average. Instead, it can be shown that if the token bucket size is M, and the probability that a source packet arrives when the token bucket is empty is ξ, then a good estimate for the mean burst length b is obtained by inverting Equation 14.6:

$$b = \left[\frac{(1 - \rho)\gamma(P - \gamma)}{M(\gamma - \rho P)} \ln\left(\frac{(\gamma - \rho P) + \rho\xi(P - \gamma)}{\xi\gamma(1 - \rho)} \right) \right]^{-1} \tag{14.7}$$

Thus, with the three steps just outlined, we can model an arbitrary source with an on–off source (step 3), and then compute not only the leaky-bucket regulator for the source (step 2), but also its equivalent bandwidth (step 1), which tells us whether the source can be admitted. Experimental results with a variety of sources show that the approach works for a variety of sources. However, this approach makes many simplifying assumptions that may not always be valid. There is an extensive literature that expands on these ideas to remove these assumptions, often at the cost of added complexity (for example, see [EMW 95] and the references therein).

14.9.7 Measurement-based admission control

Measurement-based admission control allows us to deal with traffic sources that do not describe themselves, either because they choose not to or because their traffic descriptors change unpredictably with time—for example, because of renegotiations. The idea is to admit calls based on a nominal description, but then to measure actual source behavior to automatically construct an appropriate descriptor. The next example is based on a scheme described in more detail in reference [JDSZ 95].

EXAMPLE 14.7

Consider a network where sources describe themselves with a peak rate, average rate, and token bucket size. We assume that sources are confident that they will never exceed their peak rate (or sufficiently overestimate it). They may be less sure of their other parameters. Switch controllers measure the current *average* load due to an ensemble of sources by measuring the number of packet arrivals over a fixed time interval t. When a new call arrives, the switch controller admits the call if the sum of the measured load over the past t seconds and the new call's peak rate is less than the link capacity. The idea is that even if the new call sends data at its peak rate, it will still not oversubscribe the system. On the other hand, if it sends data at a slower rate, its actual load on the system, which is expected to be less than its peak rate, will be reflected in new load measurements. Thus, the admission-control algorithm will admit more calls than admission at the peak rate.

The danger with measurement-based admission control is that it assumes that past measurements of the system are a good indication of future behavior. If this is not true, for example, because of long-range dependency in the aggregated traffic, then the controller might admit too many or too few calls. The hope is that with enough calls, a switch's load will change only very slowly compared with the number of calls arriving and leaving the network. Thus, even if the controller admits too many calls, it can simply deny admission to future calls, so that as some calls leave, the remaining calls receive adequate service quality.

Measurement-based admission control is particularly well suited for the controlled-load service model. Recall that in this service model, the network guarantees a connection a nominal delay bound, but the connection's packets may still suffer deviations from this bound. A simple generalization of Example 14.7 allows us to compute the expected worst-case delay bound for a connection when the measured current load is known [JDSZ 95]. If the connections behave similarly in the future, the delay bound will continue to hold. Because controlled-load service applications are willing to tolerate some packets with excessive delays, the measurement-based admission control algorithm can make some errors without aggravating customers.

Measurement-based admission control is also necessary when sources can renegotiate their resource allocation. When a source sets up a call, it may not know its future renegotiations. Thus, the admission-control algorithm must guess, based on past behavior, whether or not to admit the call. This leads naturally to a measurement-based scheme, which is outlined in reference [GKT 95].

14.10 Peak-load pricing

Traffic exhibits strong cyclical behavior at the time scale of a day and at the time scale of a week [Mukherjee 94]. In fact, operators at AT&T's Network Operation Center look for traffic anomalies simply by overlaying traffic measured a week earlier over the current measurement. During the day, traffic peaks from 9 to 5, reflecting the working day. There is typically a drop at lunchtime and dinnertime. However, it picks up again around 11 P.M., when telephone rates become lower, thus allowing users to save on tolls. This shifted peak is the result of *peak-load pricing*, which is a traffic management mechanism operating at the time scale of a day. Peak-load pricing shifts some user demand from the peak time to off-peak times, decreasing the peak load. It is equally applicable to time scales of a week or more.

We can divide resources into those that we can store, such as cars and crude oil, and those that we must either consume immediately upon production or lose forever, such as airline seats, hotel rooms, and bandwidth. It is in the best interests of the provider of a nonstorable resource to ensure that the resource is always used at full capacity. It is

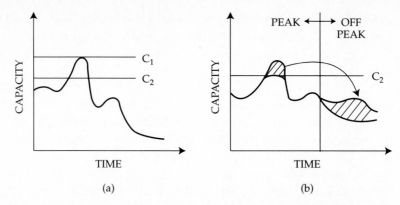

Figure 14.7: Peak-load pricing. (a) Typical aggregate traffic demand curve as a function of time. If a network is built with capacity C1, then users are always satisfied, but the network is often idle. With a capacity C2, the network is happier, but the users are dissatisfied when the overall load increases beyond C2. (b) We shift some demand to off-peak times by making capacity more expensive during peak times. This results in a more even network usage, making both users and the network provider happier.

also in the best interests of the provider to ensure that the resource is not overloaded, since this makes customers unhappy. These two goals are contradictory. To see this, consider the situation shown in Figure 14.7a. We see that the user demand is high during a peak, and much lower later in the day. If the network provider provides resource C1, then customers are always happy, but the network is idle most of the time. On the other hand, if the network provides resource C2, the network is happier (because the network is less idle), but customers are less happy.

With peak-load pricing, the network charges more during peak hours, and less during off-peak hours. Some customers cannot wait until the off-peak hours, and they thus pay more. However, some customers can wait, and their demand is shifted to off-peak hours (Figure 14.7b). Thus, peak-load pricing allows the network provider to deliver more utility to its customers (because overloading is reduced), despite a reduced capacity C2. With peak-load pricing, what should the peak and off-peak prices be? A considerable body of literature deals with this topic (see, for example, [BL 76] and [Pressman 70]). The consensus is that off-peak users should pay only for operational costs plus the profit, whereas peak users should additionally pay for capital depreciation and capacity expansion costs.

EXAMPLE 14.8

Suppose a network experiences peak demand 100 (in some units) and off-peak demand 10. Suppose the prices during both intervals were 1 unit. Then, the network's total revenue would be 110. Suppose the network's capacity were C. We can denote the user's utility by (−total price − overload) = −110 − (100 − C). The network's utility is the revenue minus the idleness in the system, which is just 110 − (C − off-peak load). If C = 100, the user's utility is −110, and the network's utility is 110 − 90 = 20. If C = 60, the user's utility is −150, and the network's utility is 60. Thus, the network operator's increased happiness comes at the cost of increasing the customer's unhappiness.

   Now, suppose the network decreases the off peak price to 0.2, thus causing the peak load to decrease to 60, and the off-peak load to increase to 50. The total revenue becomes 60 ∗ 1 + 50 ∗ 0.2 = 70. We might expect this to decrease the network's happiness, because it is lower than the earlier revenue of 110. However, because the peak demand has decreased, the network can decrease the capacity to 60. With C = 60, the user's utility becomes −70, which is better than before, and the network's utility is 70 − 10 = 60, which is the same utility as earlier. Thus, peak-load pricing increases the user's utility without changing the network's utility. If the network operator wanted to, the network could slightly increase the off-peak price, increasing its utility, while still making it worth the user's while to spread its load.

A simple generalization of the scheme to multiple pricing intervals can even out the demand through the day. This would allow the network provider to build the least possible capacity for the anticipated demand. However, customers have a hard time keeping track of more than two or three prices. In the future, with the introduction of intelligent endpoints, sophisticated peak-load pricing schemes may become more popular.

14.11 Capacity planning

If a resource is overloaded, users suffer packet loss and delay, thus lowering the utility they gain from the network. As we have seen, at short time scales, some of this disutility can be avoided by careful resource management using scheduling, admission control, and the like. However, in the face of persistent shortages, even the best admission control algorithm can only deny some users admission so that the rest receive a reasonable quality of service. The only solution to persistent overcrowding is to increase network capacity. Installing new trunks and switches takes weeks or longer. Thus, the traffic-management techniques that deal with persistent overload (or, conversely, persistently high call-blocking) operate at this time scale. These techniques are often studied under the heading of *capacity planning*.

   Unfortunately, in practice, capacity planning tends to be a matter of trial and error rather than systematic design. This is because many assumptions and requirements for a theoretically well-founded solution do not hold in the field. In this section, we will study the steps in capacity planning, noting where the problems arise in practice. We will then focus on one well-known technique for capacity planning in telephone networks.

14.11.1 Steps in capacity planning

The first step in capacity planning is to measure or estimate user demand (see Section 14.3 for more details on workload modeling). If a network is already in place, we can instrument switch controllers to build a *traffic matrix,* that is, a matrix of the call load from every source to every destination. Since traffic varies during a day, the matrix typically represents the load during the peak traffic hour of the day (the *busy hour*).[4] If a network does not already exist, we must estimate the traffic matrix from the expected user population and their expected usage patterns. The results of capacity planning are as incorrect as these estimates. One can imagine the potential for error when designers have to guess the load from adding, say, a hundred new sites to a network over a year. In the face of this uncertainty, many network providers opt simply to build a skeleton network, adding new resources as congestion points arise (which is the trial-and-error method noted earlier).

Given a traffic matrix, the second step is to decide a topology to connect sources to destinations through switches. Often, geographical or administrative concerns constrain topologies. For example, switches may need to be placed in secure areas on company premises. Moreover, to deal with link or switch failures, providers may want to ensure that there are at least two (or three) paths between every source–destination pair (this is called *two-* or *three-connectivity*). There are many well-known techniques to construct a topology subject to these constraints, which is the domain of *graph theory* (see, for example, reference [Grossman 90]).

After constructing the topology, we need to assign a capacity to each link and compute routes between endpoints. This step is perhaps the most complex, because the two are closely linked. To see this, note that if we allocate a link a higher capacity, more routes pass through it, justifying the allocation. Similarly, if we give a link a lower capacity, routes shun it, so that its load is lower, justifying the lower allocation! Since routing adapts to the capacity allocation, there is no easy way to pick a set of routes and a set of capacities simultaneously. One heuristic is to choose capacities assuming that links are always up, and that routing is static, so that we know the load on each link. We can then study how much bandwidth we must allocate to the link to meet user demands. We study this problem in the context of the telephone network in the next subsection.

14.11.2 Capacity allocation in telephone networks

Given an anticipated call volume on a link, where all calls have the same bandwidth requirement, how should we size a link to meet some bound on call-blocking probability? Conversely, given excessive call blocking, how much additional capacity is required to bring the call-blocking probability back within bound? Erlang answered these questions in pioneering work in 1917 [Bellamy 91, Chapter 10]. He computed the

---

[4]The busy hour may be different on different source–destination pairs, so the overall busy hour traffic matrix may never be achieved in practice!

call-blocking probability given a *call load* (the mean number of calls present in the system over some interval) and the link capacity. In his honor, we measure call loads in *erlangs*. One erlang equals an average of one call present on the link at any given time.

EXAMPLE 14.9

Consider a link with capacity 10 calls. Let call 1 start at time 0 and last 4 s, call 2 start at time 2 and last 6 s, and call 3 start at time 6 and last 4 s. What is the call load in the interval [0,10]?

Solution: In the interval the total call volume is 14 call seconds: 4 from call 1, plus 6 from call 2, plus 4 from call 3. Dividing by the interval length = 10 s, we get the call load to be 1.4 erlangs. The link capacity is 10 erlangs, so its mean utilization is 14%.

Two quantities characterize the call load:

Average call arrival rate $= \lambda$ (calls/s)
Average call holding time $= m$ (s/call).

Then,

Call load in erlangs $= A = \lambda m$

When a link is in equilibrium, we expect it to be carrying A calls.

Erlang-B formula with infinite sources

We say that a switch controller implements a loss system if it drops calls it cannot accept. If the population of users generating calls is infinite, the time between call arrivals is drawn from an exponential distribution, and the switch controller implements a loss system, then Erlang's loss formula (also called the Erlang-B formula) computes the call blocking probability as a function of the link capacity and the call load. Let:

Number of channels a link can carry $= N$
Blocking probability $= B$

Then,

$$B = \frac{A^N}{N \sum_{i=0}^{N} \dfrac{A^i}{i!}} \tag{14.8}$$

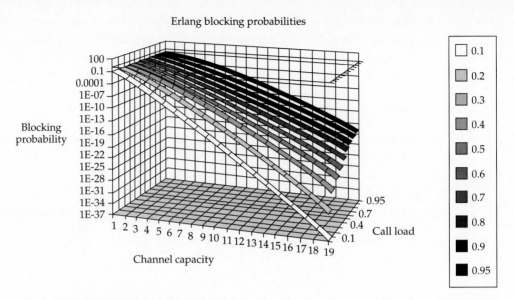

Figure 14.8: Erlang blocking probabilities as a function of the call load and the channel capacity. Note that as the channel capacity increases, the blocking probability decreases exponentially for the same call load.

Curves of B versus A and N, such as the one shown in Figure 14.8, can be found in telephone company engineering manuals and allow us to compute N, given A and B.

EXAMPLE 14.10

Suppose a link has capacity 5 calls, and has a mean load of 3 erlangs. What is the probability that an incoming call will be blocked?

Solution: $N = 5$, and $A = 3$. Plugging into Equation 14.8, we get $B = 0.11$.

In Equation 14.8, notice that when A is fixed and N increases by 1, the numerator increases by a factor of A, but the denominator increases at least by a factor of $N + 1$. Thus, for $N > A$ and a fixed call load, as the link capacity N increases, the blocking probability exponentially decreases. Equivalently, for a given B, as N increases, the allowable call load increases. In practical terms, this means that it is more efficient to have a single large trunk carry a large number of calls than to distribute the calls to several smaller trunks. Another way to interpret this result is that as the number of calls being multiplexed grows large, spatial multiplexing allows us to reduce the trunk capacity without affecting the call-blocking probability. This is another manifestation of the law of large numbers we saw earlier in Section 14.9.5.

Note also from Figure 14.8 that when the channel capacity is large, a small change in the fractional call load results in an order-of-magnitude increase in the call-blocking probability. The reason is that a large channel is more efficient in its use of bandwidth, and thus more sensitive to small changes in the load. Because we can only roughly estimate the call load in practice, it pays to be cautious when using the Erlang-B formula when the channel capacity is large.

Finite number of sources

We have assumed thus far that there are an infinite number of sources. We now consider the case where the number of sources is finite and denoted by M. As before, let m represent the mean holding time of a call. We distinguish between two quantities: the intrinsic activity factor of a source, ρ, and the idle source call initiation rate, λ'. The first quantity represents the load originating from a source if all calls are accepted. The second quantity represents the rate at which an idle source initiates a call (in call attempts per minute), if the switch controller can block some calls. If ρ is known, then we can derive λ' from the equation:

$$\lambda' m = \frac{\rho}{1 - \rho(1 - B)} \tag{14.9}$$

where B is the blocking probability and is given by Erlang's formula:

$$B = \frac{\binom{M-1}{N} (\lambda' m)^N}{\sum_{i=0}^{N} \binom{M-1}{i} (\lambda' m)^i} \tag{14.10}$$

Note that λ' depends on B, and B in turn depends on λ'. Therefore, the only way to determine the blocking probability with finite sources is to guess a value for B or λ', then iterate to reach a fixed point (see Exercise 14.14). Computing the blocking probability is much easier when the number of sources is infinite. Since the blocking probability with infinite sources is always larger than with finite sources, assuming infinite sources allows us to get a quick-and-dirty approximation to the call-blocking probability. In practice, this approximation works rather well, because the number of sources, M, is anywhere from a hundred to a few million.

Variations on Erlang's formula

We have assumed that calls arriving at a full link are dropped immediately. If these calls instead are held and retried when the system becomes less full, then the dynamics of the system changes. This leads to a variation of the Erlang-B formula that is discussed in reference [Bellamy 91]. Another variation is to allow sources to immediately retry calls that were denied. Teletraffic engineers choose an appropriate variation depending on the accuracy required from the model.

Network blocking probability

Erlang's formula gives us the blocking probability for a single link. These blocking probabilities must be composed to compute the blocking probability along a path. If we assume that each link in the network is independent of all other links, then the probability of a call being blocked is given by $1 - \Pi_{i=1}^{n} (1 - B(i))$, where the ith link along the path has a blocking probability of $B(i)$. The analysis gets complicated if calls can choose from multiple routes, where each route has its own blocking probability. The mathematical treatment of call rerouting and its effect on call blocking is complex, and can be found in references [BF 77, Kelly 91].

14.11.3 Complications in capacity planning

Given the call load, network topology, and a routing strategy, a network operator can use Erlang's formula and some heuristics to size the network's links to meet a call-blocking requirement. However, if we make the problem less constrained, allowing call characteristics, topology, routing, and link capacities to change, capacity planning becomes very hard. In the general problem, given a traffic matrix, call mix, and a call-blocking requirement, a network provider must choose a network topology, link capacities, and a routing strategy to meet this requirement. Very little is known about simultaneously meeting these criteria, because they are interlinked in complicated ways. For example, the choice of topology is dictated not only by call-blocking requirements, but also by survivability requirements in the case of link or switch failure. Similarly, if routing is dynamically modified depending on the network load, *a priori* computation of call blocking may not make sense, because the network may route calls along paths in unanticipated patterns. Thus, the area of traffic management at slow time scales is a rich area for future research.

Capacity planning on the Internet

Capacity planning on the Internet is mostly a matter of trial and error. However, a few rules of thumb help administrators size network capacity. Informal measurements indicate that the sustained bandwidth required to support the average Internet user in 1996 is on the order of 50 Kbps. A service provider should thus plan on an allocation of 100 Kbps per active user, incorporating a fudge factor of 2 and leaving some breathing room for increased usage. Measurements also show that during the busy hour, which is around 11 A.M., about 40% of potential users are active. Thus, a campus with 2500 potential users would have about 1000 active users during the busy hour and should have an internal network capable of sustaining a load of about 100 Mbps. This is feasible using a Fast Ethernet or FDDI backbone.

Regional and backbone Internet service providers size their network knowing that the load entering their network is limited by the capacity of the access link. By charging more for a higher-speed access link, a provider can limit the traffic entering its network. For example, UUnet, one of the world's largest Internet service providers, charged, in early 1996, around $1500/month for T1 access, and up to $50,000/month for T3 access. This restricts T3 access to a few large customers.

Something like 10% of the traffic generated by a campus leaves it. So, a 2500-person campus should have an external link capacity of around 10 Mbps. In practice, because of its prohibitive cost, the external link from a campus is often undersized. For example, typical 2500-person campuses use a 1.5-Mbps T1 link, and typical 25,000-person campuses, which need a 100-Mbps external link, use a 45-Mbps T3 link.

Because traffic from many access links must share a regional trunk, such a trunk usually has several times the capacity of an access link. Consequently, most of the queuing on the Internet happens on the campus router immediately preceding the access link. For example, most regional networks in the United States in 1996 have installed a T3 backbone and price access lines such that all but a handful of customers access them at T1 speeds. This gives them a comfortable speedup factor of 30. Customers with a Fast Ethernet backbone accessing the provider over a T1 see most of their packets queued at their egress router, where there is a 100:1.5 speed mismatch. As larger campuses upgrade to 45-Mbps access links, the backbone will migrate to OC3 speeds (though this gives a speedup of only around 4). This will probably introduce queuing within the network, requiring additional buffering in regional network routers.

14.12 Summary

Traffic management allows a network to give users the most utility with the available resources. The two orthogonal axes of traffic management are *multiple traffic classes* and *multiple time scales*. A simple economic model suggests that it is in a network's best interests to provide service classes that match user requirements, some of which have been anticipated and classified by the IETF and the ATM Forum. Based on application behavior, we can broadly divide them into guaranteed-service and best-effort applications, with finer subdivisions reflecting varying sensitivities to bandwidth and delay. This is the multiple traffic class axis.

In addition, we must also deal with traffic management policies and mechanisms at five time scales of control: (a) less than one round-trip time, (b) one or more round-trip times, (c) session, (d) day, and (e) weeks or longer. This is the multiple time-scale axis.

This chapter brings together traffic-management schemes discussed in earlier chapters with six other mechanisms—link sharing, renegotiation, signaling, admission control, peak-load pricing, and capacity planning—in an overall architecture presented in Table 14.2. This architecture provides the context for studying the many open problems in this area.

Review Questions

1. What are the two requirements for traffic management?
2. What does a utility function measure?
3. What is the key idea in congestion pricing?
4. What are the Guaranteed Service subclasses according to the ATM Forum?
5. What principle does the IETF use to divide the GS class?
6. What are the five time scales for traffic management?
7. What is the trade-off made in renegotiation?
8. Why are signaling messages acked?
9. Why do receivers initiate reservations in RSVP?
10. When does a router forward an RESV message?
11. Why is VBR admission control hard?
12. Is peak-rate allocation reasonable for data traffic?
13. What is peak-load pricing?
14. What is one erlang?
15. Is it better to build a single large trunk to carry a call load of 100 erlangs or to build two trunks of half the capacity with a call load of 50 erlangs each?
16. What is a simple way to approximate the call-blocking probability with a finite number of sources?

Exercises

14.1. User A has a utility function $10 - 4d$, and user B a utility function $5 - d$, where d is the mean packet delay. Which user is more sensitive to delay? If an increase in the traffic from user A increases the mean delay for both A and B by 4 units, what is the increase in the disutility for B? What is the increase in disutility if B's utility function is $5 - 2d$? With congestion pricing, what extra price must A pay in each case?

14.2. Traffic on a connection can arrive at a peak rate of 10 Mbps and can be served as slow as 8 Mbps. If the worst-case queuing delay is 10 ms, what is the buffer size needed for zero loss?

14.3. A compressed video source occasionally sends a burst at its peak rate of 4.5 Mbps for 10 s. Its long-term average rate is 1.5 Mbps. What token bucket size must it use to have zero loss if the regulator has a zero-size data buffer, and the buffer drain rate is 1.8 Mbps? Recompute this value assuming a drain rate of

4 Mbps. If the regulator has a 64-Kbyte buffer, how do these values change? Assume that bursts do not overlap.

14.4. Suppose an RCSP scheduler has delay levels of 100 ms, 400 ms, and 1 s. Using the resource translation scheme of Example 14.3, what is the delay level tentatively allocated to new calls? What is the best possible queuing delay over a path with three switches? If a source wants an end-to-end delay of 900 ms, and the utilizations at the switches are 10%, 40%, and 20%, what might be a reasonable way to partition the excess delay?

14.5. In Figure 14.5e, assume that B has received a PATH message from A for multicast group G. Suppose B subsequently receives a PATH message from C. What action should B take? What should B do when an RESV arrives from D for G?

14.6. Assume that a link is shared by five identical sources, each with a peak rate of 4.5 Mbps, and an average rate of 1.5 Mbps. What is the probability that a particular source is on? What is the probability that exactly three sources are on? If the link has a capacity of 3 Mbps and zero buffers, what is the overflow probability?

14.7. Use the heuristic in Equation 14.2 to compute the equivalent bandwidth of a source that has a peak rate of 4.5 Mbps and a mean rate of 1.5 Mbps and sends data to a link of capacity 45 Mbps. Recompute the equivalent bandwidth when the link capacity is 622 Mbps.

14.8. If the source in Exercise 14.7 has a token bucket of size 64 Kbytes, and the link buffer is 4 Mbytes, use Equation 14.3 to compute the equivalent bandwidth for a 10^{-6} loss probability. Recompute the bandwidth when the buffer is of size 500 Kbytes.

14.9. With the same source as in Exercise 14.8, and a mean burst length of 64 Kbytes, compute the equivalent bandwidth for a single source using a link buffer of size 4 Mbytes (use Equation 14.5).

14.10. In Example 14.8, suppose the network charged 0.4 during off times and 1 during peak times. If the off-peak load remains at 50, and the peak load remains at 60, what are the user and network utilities?

14.11. Calls arrive to a PBX from a sufficiently large number of customers at the rate of 3 calls per minute. A typical call is held for 3.5 minutes. What is the call load in erlangs?

14.12. In Exercise 14.11, suppose the PBX has the capacity to carry 15 calls. What is the call-blocking probability?

14.13. Suppose the number of customers is known to be 30, and each customer has an intrinsic load-generation rate of 0.1 calls a minute. What is the call-blocking probability?

Section 3

Practice

Chapter 15:

Common Protocols

15.1 Introduction

We began our study of computer network engineering with an overview of the telephone network, the Internet, and ATM networks, then explored issues such as error control, flow control, scheduling, and switching in greater detail. Our discussion emphasized general principles rather than details of specific protocols, because specific protocols are ephemeral, but the principles underlying them are enduring. Moreover, any real-life protocol must draw on a wide range of concepts. For example, the Internet's TCP protocol provides not only error control, but also flow control, sequencing, and a form of traffic management. Without a detailed study of these topics, merely examining the fields in the TCP header adds little insight. Thus, we have deferred a detailed discussion of real-life protocols to the end, where we can better understand the motivations and trade-offs in their design.

In this chapter, we will use the principles discussed in earlier chapters to dissect some common protocols. Our goal is to provide enough intuition to allow readers to decipher the standards documents describing these protocols (which are their most detailed descriptions). Keep in mind that the protocols discussed in this chapter are chosen because of their widespread use. Many others are not as popular, but are designed just as well, if not better! (Protocols defined by a committee, even if widely used, are notoriously clunky.) The case studies in this chapter serve as a guide to analyzing these other protocols.

The next three sections examine examples of some important protocols in the telephone network, in the Internet, and in ATM networks. Section 15.2 describes telephone network protocols, with an emphasis on datalink-layer protocols. Section 15.3 studies four important protocols in the Internet: IP, ICMP, TCP, and HTTP. Section 15.4 examines protocols in the ATM stack, focusing mainly on the different ATM Adaptation Layers. Finally, Section 15.5 is an overview of techniques used for carrying IP traffic in ATM networks.

15.2 Telephone network protocols

This section surveys some common protocols in the telephone network. We start with a description of the telephone network protocol stack in Section 15.2.1. Section 15.2.2 deals with the traditional (asynchronous) digital transmission hierarchy, and Section 15.2.3 describes its replacement, which is called SONET in the United States and SDH by the International Telecommunications Union. Finally, Section 15.2.4 is a description of MTP, which is a protocol used to control the telephone network.

15.2.1 Protocol stack

We show a typical telephone network protocol stack in Table 15.1. We show the control and data stacks (also called the control and data *planes*) separately. The control plane is used for call establishment and network management, and the data plane moves 8-bit samples generated at a constant bit rate. The data plane has only the physical, datalink, and application layers. The application layer consists of telephony and telephony-like applications such as fax and modems. The control plane is essentially the Signaling System 7 stack we will study in Section 15.2.4.

	Data plane	Control plane (SS7)
Application	Voice/fax	ASE/ISDN-UP
		TCAP
Session		
Transport		
Network		SCCP/MTP-3
Datalink	SONET/P.H.	MTP-2
Physical	Many	MTP-1

Table 15.1: Telephone network protocol stack. In the data plane, applications directly use the datalink layer. In the control plane, Application Service Elements (ASEs) use the services of a datagram-oriented protocol stack (SS7) described in Section 14.8.3.

15.2.2   The traditional digital transmission hierarchy

Telephone companies find it economical to multiplex long-distance calls onto high-speed trunks, because this reduces the number of physical long-distance trunks needed in the network. If each multiplexed trunk were able to carry a different number of calls, each trunk would need specialized equipment running at its own transmission rate, which is not cost effective. International standards bodies have therefore decreed a few standard multiplexed rates that form the *digital transmission hierarchy* [Bellamy 91].

The base level in the hierarchy is the equivalent of a single digitized voice call that requires a bandwidth of 64 Kbps. Higher levels of the hierarchy carry more calls over higher-speed trunks. The transmission hierarchy differs from region to region: we show the hierarchies in the United States (also used in Japan) and those in Europe in Table 15.2.

We say that a system is *plesiochronous* (which means "almost synchronous") if each component generates data at nominally the same bit rate, but these bit rates may vary within a tightly controlled tolerance. Traditionally, telephone networks are plesiochronous (with one exception, to which we will return shortly), because this only requires each component to have a good-quality clock, and components do not need to synchronize with each other explicitly. However, a plesiochronous network suffers from some serious problems, described in the next few paragraphs.

Consider a multiplexor that multiplexes two 1-Mbps input streams or *tributaries* to form a single 2-Mbps output stream. If both tributaries are exactly 1 Mbps, then the output can be just the bitwise (or bytewise) interleaving of each stream. If, however, one tributary runs at 1.001 Mbps, and the other at 0.999 Mbps, the output occasionally contains more bits from the first tributary than the second. A multiplexor that naively interleaves bits from each source must therefore occasionally drop bits from the first source. Otherwise, to avoid bit loss, the output stream must somehow distinguish between bits arriving from different tributaries. This would be easy if the bits from each stream

Multiplexing level	United States and Japan			Europe		
	Name	# calls	Rate (Mbps)	Name	# calls	Rate (Mbps)
1	DS1	24	1.544	CEPT1	30	2.048
2[1]	DS2	96	6.312	CEPT2	120	8.448
3	DS3	672	44.736	CEPT3	480	34.368
4[2]	DS4	4032	274.176	CEPT4	1920	139.264

[1] Used in Japan, but not the United States.
[2] Obsolete, and used only in a few rare instances.

Table 15.2: Traditional digital transmission hierarchy in United States, Japan, and Europe.

arrived as packets and we could examine a packet header to determine its origin. This is not possible in the circuit-switched telephone network, so it is done using a process called *justification* or *bit stuffing*.

Justification

The basic idea in justification is that the multiplexed output runs slightly faster than the sum of the tributaries. We call the excess the *overhead.* For example, a multiplexor that multiplexes sixteen 1-Mbps streams might produce an output stream at a rate of 16.25 Mbps, where the overhead has a bit rate of 0.25 Mbps. The output stream therefore consists of data or *payload* bits, interspersed with periodic *overhead* bits (Figure 15.1). The payload and the overhead together form an output *frame.* When a tributary runs a little faster, it steals one bit from the overhead bits, and other overhead bits are used to identify the tributary currently using the overhead.

The allocation for each tributary at the output is always slightly slower than the slowest possible input bit rate, so that the output never underflows. For example, if the input can send between 205 and 207 bits per output frame, the output allocates 205 bits. Whenever the input sends more than 205 bits, it uses some overhead bits. Consequently, data from a tributary appears not only in the payload, but also in the overhead bits. To extract all the data from a single tributary, we need to parse the entire frame.

> The allocation of overhead bits in a frame, and the precise positioning of the bits in the frame, is different at different levels of the digital transmission hierarchy. The principles used, however, are the same [Bellamy 91]. First, if an overhead bit is used, this fact is redundantly specified. Usually, each time a tributary uses an overhead bit, the remaining overhead bits repeat the tributary number three times. Second, the overhead is dispersed throughout the frame, to make it less sensitive to burst errors. Finally, the output frames are always fixed length, with the overhead bits padding out any variations in the inputs. We show an example of a plesiochronous frame in Figure 15.2, which outlines the structure of a DS3 frame composed from seven DS2 frames.

We mentioned earlier that there is one exception to plesiochrony in the telephone network. The exception is that master–slave synchronization is used at the lowest level of the digital hierarchy, when twenty-four (or thirty) calls are *byte interleaved* to form a mul-

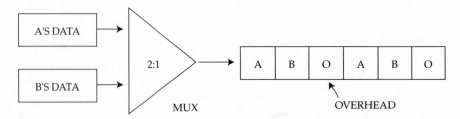

Figure 15.1: Justification. When multiplexing plesiochronous streams, a multiplexor inserts overhead bits in the output, which accommodates a stream that occasionally runs faster than it ought.

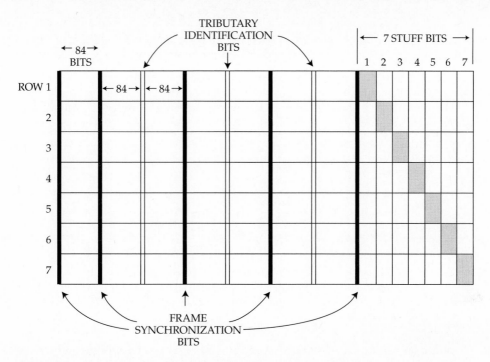

Figure 15.2: DS3 frame format. A DS3 frame bit-interleaves seven DS2 frames. Every 85th bit is an overhead bit, except that the last seven bits in every row are all stuff bits. The frame format allows a tributary that is slightly faster than the others to occasionally place overflow bits in the stuff bits. In the figure, if the third, fifth, and seventh overhead bits in the ith row are all 1, then the ith stuff bit in that row carries overflow information from tributory i. The first, second, fourth, sixth, and eighth overhead bits in each row (marked with a dark vertical line) are used primarily for frame synchronization.

tiplexed DS1 (or CEPT1) frame. This is because a DS1 frame typically consists of twenty-four analog voice inputs that are digitized using the same clock. Higher multiplexed levels are created by *bit-interleaving* each tributary stream. Since the lowest level is synchronous, single voice calls can be picked out from a DS1 frame. However, once the DS1 frame is multiplexed into a DS2 or higher, individual voice calls, or indeed individual DS1s, cannot be isolated without fully demultiplexing the input stream.

Problems with plesiochrony

Plesiochronous networks have three significant problems [BC 92]. First, each part of the world has its own digital transmission hierarchy. Thus, connecting calls internationally requires expensive interface equipment. Second, we saw that the process of justification spreads data from a tributary all over the output frame. Thus, extracting data from a single tributary is hard. This makes it hard to build an *add–drop multiplexor* (see Section 8.2.1 for a description of such a multiplexor). Finally, for the same reason, it is hard to build switches that switch bundles of voice calls instead of individual calls. Every telephone switch in the plesiochronous hierarchy must demultiplex down to the level

Multiplexing level	Data rate (Mbps)	U.S. name	European name
1	51.84	OC-1	(not defined)
2	155.52	OC-3	STM-1
3	466.56	OC-9	STM-3
4	622.08	OC-12	STM-4
5	933.12	OC-18	STM-6
6	1244.16	OC-24	STM-8
8	1866.24	OC-36	STM-12
9	2488.32	OC-48	STM-16
10	9953.28	OC-192	STM-64

Table 15.3: SONET multiplexing hierarchy. Note that the United States and Europe use the same hierarchy speeds, except that the lowest U.S. level is not defined in Europe. There are also minor differences in the framing structure.

of a DS0 before it can switch voice calls. This makes telephone switches unnecessarily expensive.

15.2.3   SONET/SDH

The problems with plesiochrony described earlier disappear if all the tributaries entering a multiplexor are precisely synchronized. Because synchronous tributaries need no justification, they occupy a fixed portion of the multiplexed frame, and thus can easily be extracted. In theory, in a synchronous network, even a single voice call can be extracted from a multiplexed trunk containing many calls. This is the basis of the *Synchronous Optical NETwork (SONET)* standard.[1] Unfortunately, in practice, small deviations from synchrony, and the need to accommodate plesiochronous streams from existing networks, mean that SONET needs a way to justify streams anyway. We will study SONET justification later in this section.

Synchronous hierarchy

SONET defines a multiplexing hierarchy in much the same way as does the plesiochronous digital hierarchy. The allowed link speeds in SONET are shown in Table 15.3. A link at a higher speed is formed by byte-interleaving data from lower speed links. Note that the higher-speed trunks are *exact* multiples of the speeds of lower-speed trunks. This is because the higher-speed trunks do not contain additional justification overhead: they run off a common clock source.

---

[1]This is the U.S. standard. A nearly identical standard called the *Synchronous Digital Hierarchy* or *SDH* is used in Europe.

SONET frame structure

SONET defines multiple frame types, where each type corresponds to a particular link speed (and, therefore, a particular level in the *synchronous transmission hierarchy*). Because SONET is synchronous, higher-level frames are formed simply by byte-interleaving the lowest-level (OC-1) frame. Therefore, we need to study the structure of only the OC-1 frame. (In contrast, each level of the plesiochronous digital hierarchy defines its own frame structure.)

An OC-1 frame consists of 810 bytes, arranged in 9 rows and 90 columns (Figure 15.3) [Bellamy 91, p. 406]. A switch or multiplexor sends each frame in exactly 125 μs, so that each byte in the payload of a frame corresponds to one 64-Kbps call. The first three col-

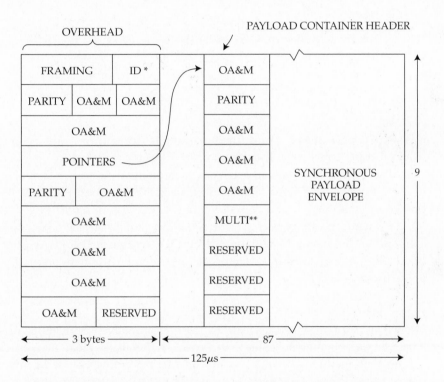

* ID = IDENTIFIES THE OC-1 NUMBER (1 . . N) IN AN OC-N FRAME

** MULTI = INDICATES THAT PAYLOAD SPANS MULTIPLE PAYLOAD ENVELOPES

Figure 15.3: OC-1 frame format. An OC-1 frame has 9 rows and 90 columns. Each frame is sent in 125 μs, so that each payload byte in each row corresponds to one 64-Kbps call. The first three columns contain mostly Operations, Administration, and Maintenance (OA&M) overhead. They also contain a pointer to the start of the synchronous payload envelope (which has its own header) in the data stream. In general, the payload envelope spans multiple OC-1 frames. An OC-N frame consists of N byte-interleaved OC-1 frames.

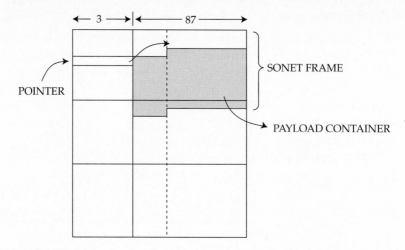

Figure 15.4: SONET payload envelope. In general, a payload envelope can span multiple OC-1 frames. A pointer in the header points to the start of the payload envelope in the frame. This allows us to locate the envelope even after justification.

umns are overhead bytes, and the remaining 87 contain (mostly) byte-interleaved data from multiple tributaries. Data from each tributary is placed in a *payload container,* also called the *synchronous payload envelope.* Each payload container has its own descriptive header. Usually, the payload spans multiple SONET frames (Figure 15.4). The overhead portion of a SONET frame contains many *Operations, Administration, and Maintenance (OA&M)* fields, parity bytes for error detection, and a pointer to the start of the payload container in the frame. Note that since an OC-*N* frame is just a byte-interleaved version of the OC-1 frame, each OC-*N* frame has *N* payload containers pointed to by *N* pointers in the frame overhead.

SONET justification

The use of pointers simplifies justification of nominally synchronous SONET streams. If a tributary sends slightly faster than expected, then its payload arrives in a time slightly shorter than the time taken to transmit its corresponding payload container. The multiplexor uses 1 byte of the overhead to send payload information, thus *decreasing* the time needed to send the payload container and increasing its effective rate. This moves the next container a little backward, and the pointers are adjusted accordingly (Figure 15.5). A symmetric operation is performed when a tributary is slightly slower. The key point is that with pointer adjustment, even when a tributary is justified, it can still be located within the SONET frame, making it possible to build a simpler add–drop multiplexor.

SONET rings

SONET technology is gradually being introduced into the U.S. telephone system. Because this requires overhauling the transmission infrastructure, telephone companies

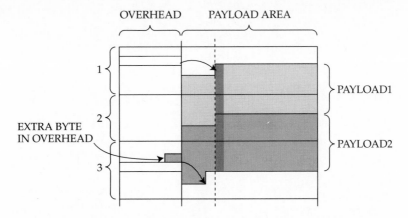

Figure 15.5: SONET justification. We show the case when a stream sends slightly faster than it ought. By sending one of the stream's bytes in the overhead portion of the frame, the duration spanned by the stream's data is made shorter, giving it a temporarily higher service rate.

have taken this opportunity to increase the fault tolerance of the telephone system. Instead of installing SONET links as point-to-point replacements for DS3 trunks, add–drop multiplexors in central offices and backbone switches are connected in a dual ring with SONET links, similar to the dual-ring topology described in Section 7.5.4. Thus, if a link breaks, service is restored almost immediately (within 50 ms) by placing the ring in "wrap" mode.

Backward compatibility

An important goal for SONET is to be able to carry existing traffic from both the European and U.S. plesiochronous digital hierarchy. This is accomplished by defining *virtual containers* to hold data from, for example, one DS3 or one CEPT 4 frame. SONET treats this data as if it arrived from a synchronous line. Slippages between a DS3 and an OC-1 frame are corrected using the justification mechanism just described. In this way, SONET links at OC-3 and higher are completely compatible with both U.S. and European hierarchies. Of course, if a European multiplexor receives a SONET frame containing a DS3 frame, it still needs to convert this to CEPT frames. However, as the world eventually converges to an all-synchronous network, the need for this conversion will eventually disappear.

SONET prescribes not only a multiplexing hierarchy, but also optical standards (how to represent 0's and 1's) at each link speed. It also has a great deal to say about procedures for OA&M. These details can be found in the SONET standard [ANSI 88]. More details on justification, framing, and SONET headers can be found in [Bellamy 91, BC 92].

15.2.4 Signaling System 7

The plesiochronous digital hierarchy and SONET standards describe the *data transport* protocols in the telephone network. *Network control,* including call establishment, routing, and enhanced services, is accomplished using the SS7 protocol stack (Table 15.4).

OSI layer name	SS7 layer name	Functionality	Example Internet protocol
Application	Application Service Element (ASE)	Application-level functionality, such as interpreting signaling messages	FTP
	Transaction Capabilities Application Part (TCAP)	Allows a system to invoke procedure calls on remote machines	RPC
Transport	Signaling Connection Control Part (SCCP)	Connections, sequence numbering, segmentation and reassembly, window flow control	TCP
Network	Message Transfer Part-3 (MTP-3)	Routing	IP
Datalink	Message Transfer Part-2 (MTP-2)	Framing, link-level error detection, and retransmission	Ethernet
Physical	Message Transfer Part-1 (MTP-1)	Physical bit transfer, usually on a T1 circuit	Ethernet

Table 15.4: Details of the SS7 protocol stack

Note that the digital transmission hierarchy and SS7 represent a separation of data and control.

Protocol layers in SS7 are called *Parts*. The SS7 transport subsystem consists of the *Message Transfer Part (MTP)* and the *Signaling Connection Control Part (SCCP)*. The overall responsibility of MTP is to reliably transfer signaling messages from a source to a destination over the signaling network, compensating for link and router failures. MTP is partitioned into MTP Level 1, MTP Level 2, and MTP Level 3, corresponding to the physical, datalink, and network layers, respectively.

- *MTP Level 1* is a physical link, typically a standard T1 voice circuit devoted to signaling.

- *MTP Level 2* provides message framing on a link, CRC-16 error detection, per-link go-back-n error correction, and static-window flow control. If too many errors are detected on a link, or the receiver withholds acknowledgments for too long, the link is declared down, and SS7 routing at MTP Level 3 is informed about this change.

- *MTP Level 3* is responsible for datagram routing. SS7 identifies endpoints with 24-bit addresses called point codes. When a signaling message is received at an

STP, MTP-3 at the STP uses the destination point code and a routing table to forward the message on the correct outgoing link. MTP Level 3 also updates routing tables when a link goes down or comes up. SCCP, which corresponds to the transport layer, sits above MTP 3. Note that MTP provides only datagram, that is, connectionless, service.

- SCCP optionally provides connections layered over MTP's datagrams. It also provides sequence numbering, segmentation and reassembly, and window flow control.

One of the main applications in SS7 is the *Telephone User Part (TUP)*, which is responsible for setting up voice calls. The TUP interprets dialed digits to route calls, reserves resources for calls, maintains accounting information, and provides services such as three-way calling and 800-number service. In modern telephone networks, the TUP has been replaced by the *Integrated Services Digital Network—User Part (ISDN-UP)*, which subsumes TUP functionality and additionally provides 64-Kbps data channels. All telephone carriers in North America use ISDN-UP in their SS7 networks. ISDN-UP uses both SCCP (when the higher-level functionality is needed) and MTP-3 (when performance is critical). The Q.931 standard defines ISDN-UP semantics (that is, the signaling messages it understands, and the actions it takes on receipt of each signaling message), which are outlined in Section 14.8.1.

Another application layer that uses SCCP is the *Transaction Capabilities Application Part*, which provides remote procedure calls (allowing an application to invoke a procedure on a remote switch controller). TCAP thus makes it easier to develop distributed applications, which are called *Application Service Elements* or ASEs in SS7 jargon. An example of an ASE is the *Operations, Maintenance and Administration Part-ASE (OMAP-ASE)*, which provides network management. OMAP-ASE allows network managers to ping a remote destination, trace routes to see if they are up, or retrieve status information from remote switch controllers.

SS7 forms the basis not only for signaling, but also for creating enhanced services, as the next example shows.

EXAMPLE 15.1

Consider a call-forwarding service, where a user can ask for incoming calls to be forwarded to another phone number. When a user wants to register a remote location for call forwarding, he or she dials a special phone number that connects that user to a call-forwarding ASE. This ASE authenticates the user, then picks up the dialed digits and stores them in a special database. When a call arrives at the central office serving the user's telephone, ISDN-UP, which is responsible for call setup, checks the database to see if call forwarding is active. If so, the call is rerouted to the forwarding number. Thus, call-forwarding service requires cooperation among

ISDN-UP, the call-forwarding ASE, and a database ASE that stores the forwarding number. SS7 provides the services necessary for communication and coordination between these entities.

MTP frame details

This section examines the mapping between the services provided by the SS7 network layer and the MTP header (Figure 15.6) [MS 90]. This roughly corresponds to a combination of the IP and datalink headers on the Internet (the SCCP header provides addi-

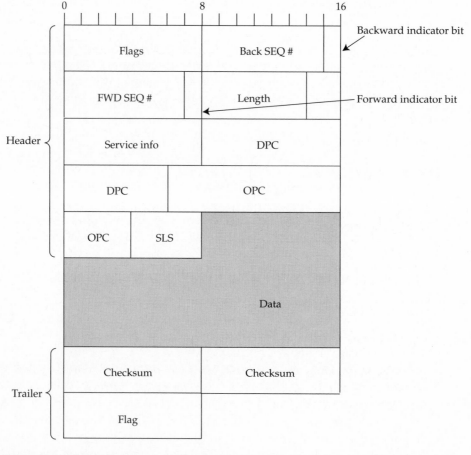

Figure 15.6: MTP packet format. MTP provides not only link framing (using the flag bits in the header and trailer), but also datagram transport, error control, flow control, and a way to spread packets over multiple routes. We can make out this functionality by carefully examining the fields in the MTP packet header and trailer.

tional network-layer functionality, not presented here). Recall that MTP layers 1–3 provide link-layer framing, error detection, and retransmission, as well as end-to-end routing.

The first byte, FLAG, allows the packet to be framed on the link, so that the destination knows that the succeeding bits belong to a valid packet and are not just random bits on the wire. The next 2 bytes are the sequence numbers used for window-based error control (see Section 12.4.7). The length field detects a partial frame and is also used for error control. The service-info field allows demultiplexing, that is, the receiver knows which of several receiving entities at a given destination should be given the data for further processing. This allows multiple senders and receivers to exist on a single endpoint.

The destination point code and origination point code (DPC and OPC) are the source and destination addresses. The DPC is used for routing the packet to the destination, and the OPC allows the destination to determine to whom to reply. SS7 routers maintain multiple routes between a source and destination. Each SLS value selects one of the possibly many routes to a destination. By choosing different SLS values, a source can balance its load in the network among many paths. This has some of the flavor of a source route, but without the total flexibility allowed by source routing. The checksum field provides error detection. Finally, the FLAG field ends the packet on the link.

Thus, we see that the fields in the MTP packet embody the services provided by MTP: link-level framing, error control, and routing. Of course, the fields alone do not tell us *how* the sequence numbers are used, or the route computation algorithm. Nevertheless, they provide a quick summary of the services provided by MTP. Usually, we can quickly determine what a protocol does by looking at the fields in its protocol header; this is a technique we will use frequently in this chapter.

MTP layering

MTP combines the functions traditionally assigned to datalink, network, and transport layers. One lesson to draw from this is that real-world protocols do not necessarily follow the OSI model. Designers have considerable freedom in assigning functionality to protocol layers as they deem best.

The reason for this discrepancy is simple: MTP was designed before the OSI layering model was developed. Because of the lack of clear layering in SS7, it is hard to introduce new services and protocols at the lower layers. One reason telephone companies want to migrate to ATM is that the ATM protocol stack layer boundaries are more crisply architected, and thus much more amenable to modification, than the MTP "stack."

15.3 Internet protocols

In this section, we will study some representative protocols in the Internet. We begin with Section 15.3.1, which presents an overview of the control and data planes in the

Internet. IP is the workhorse of the Internet, and every Internet protocol must be layered, at some point, over IP. In Section 15.3.2, we will study IP in some detail. Section 15.3.3 describes ICMP, which is a control plane protocol that works hand-in-hand with IP. Section 15.3.4 is devoted to TCP, which provides end-to-end reliable service. Finally, Section 15.3.5 describes HTTP, which is the basis for the World Wide Web.

Interestingly, the Internet and telephone data planes are complementary to each other. This is not accidental: much of the Internet is still carried over telephone lines. Thus, the Internet stack provides functionality that is not already provided by the telephone network.

Internet link technologies

We can divide Internet link technologies into roughly three categories: those used within a campus, those used in the wide area, and those used to access the Internet from home.

Within a campus, Internet packets are carried over LANs. A popular solution is to place 10BaseT Ethernet hubs in a wiring closet in each hallway and attach desktop machines with twisted-pair wire drops. The hubs are typically interconnected with either 10BaseT Ethernet or 100-Mbps Fast Ethernet. Each building on a campus usually has a high-capacity router that links the building to similar routers in other buildings (several smaller buildings may share such a router). These routers are connected with FDDI, Copper-FDDI, or ATM. Thus, Internet connectivity on a campus is provided by a mixture of Ethernet, FDDI, and ATM. For example, each building on the Cornell University campus provides desktop Internet access using 10BaseT Ethernet hubs. These hubs are connected within a building using 10BaseT Ethernet. Each building has a router. Groups of about ten routers are connected with an FDDI ring, and a backbone FDDI ring interconnects one router in each such ring.

Wide-area links (anything longer than about 5 kilometers) almost always use the telephone network infrastructure. A common approach is to lease a point-to-point T1 or T3 line to connect two wide-area routers, such as a campus router and a router belonging to an Internet service provider. As SONET enters the telephone infrastructure, leased OC3 links are gradually becoming available. As an aside, it is worth noting that leased links are not cheap. A T3 link costs roughly $1000 per mile per year, so that a T3 link from San Francisco to New York, a distance of around 2500 miles, costs about $2.5 million/year. OC3 is expected to be substantially more expensive!

A second solution for wide-area connectivity is *frame relay*. A frame-relay network is a connection-oriented packet-switched network that supports variable packet sizes and, currently, only permanent virtual circuits (see Section 4.1.4). Since all connections in a frame-relay network are permanent, there is no overhead in signaling or admission control, making the network easier to build and maintain than an ATM network. The main service available from a frame-relay network is a virtual link (corresponding to a permanent virtual circuit) that is guaranteed a minimum bandwidth called the *committed information rate (CIR)*. A frame-relay access point encapsulates incoming packets in a frame-relay header (which contains the VCI, here called the *datalink channel identifier* or *DLCI*). These packets are switched to the destination along the preestablished path. At the destination, the packet is decapsulated and delivered to the customer. The actual technology used for providing frame-relay service is not specified and usually is ATM. Since a frame-relay PVC can have an arbitrary bandwidth, and users are charged only for the bandwidth they use, a frame-relay link proves to be much cheaper than a leased line. Moreover, frame-relay allows the single leased line between the frame-relay access point on a campus and the frame-relay network to be multiplexed among several PVCs, so that a campus needs only one leased line for several virtual links. These benefits make frame relay very attractive, and frame-relay service is growing enormously in popularity.

Home access to the Internet is traditionally through modems. These are restricted to 56 Kbps because of the way voice is sampled during analog-to-digital conversion. Somewhat higher bandwidth to the home, at a substantially higher cost, can be obtained using ISDN lines. These provide up to 128 Kbps of bandwidth. However, several new technologies for high-speed Internet access are on the anvil. Several local telephone companies are poised to offer *asymmetric digital subscriber link (ADSL)* modems, which offer 6 Mbps to the home and 1.5 Mbps from the home. However, these modems can only be used for homes within about 18,000 feet of the central office. In areas where the cable TV operator has installed two-way cable, homes can access the Internet at speeds of about 10 Mbps. Although this sounds attractive, upgrading the cable plant to make it two-way is expensive. Besides, it is estimated that, as of late 1996, less than 7% of the homes in the United States could use this technology. In the interim, a promising solution is to use the telephone network to provide the return path, with the cable TV plant providing only one-way access. This gives users a peak access rate of about 1.5 Mbps. No matter which technology wins, it seems certain that by 2001, a substantial portion of American homes will be able to access the Internet at speeds greater than 56 Kbps.

Technologies in all three areas are evolving rapidly, and the picture may well change in the next couple of years. However, the general features of Internet transmission technologies, to wit, LANs within campuses, virtual links between campuses, and relatively low speed to the home, are likely to remain with us for the foreseeable future.

15.3.1   Internet protocol stack

Though the Internet protocol stack has only a few protocols defined at the network and transport layers, it has many more at the application layer. Table 15.5 shows a typical

	Data plane	Control plane
Application	Web browser	
	HTTP	RSVP/OSPF
Session	Sockets/streams	
Transport	TCP/UDP	
Network	IP	IP/ICMP
Datalink	Many	Many
Physical	Many	Many

Table 15.5: Internet Protocol Stack. In the data plane, we choose HTTP and two standard Web browsers as example applications. These are layered over the TCP and UDP transport-layer protocols and the IP network-layer protocol. In the control plane, RSVP and OSPF run over "raw" IP. RSVP provides connection setup, and OSPF is used for intradomain routing. The ICMP control protocol is layered over IP, but provides control functions at the network layer.

Internet protocol stack, where we have chosen the *Hypertext Transfer Protocol (HTTP)* as an example application-level protocol. The main protocols in the data plane are *Internet Protocol (IP)*, *Transmission Control Protocol (TCP)*, and *User Datagram Protocol (UDP)*, which provide network- and transport-layer services. The Internet's network layer is not connection oriented, so the Internet does not need a signaling protocol like SS7 in the control plane. However, the future integrated-services Internet will use the *Resource Reservation Protocol (RSVP)* described in Section 14.8.5. Moreover, the Internet's routing protocols, such as BGP and OSPF (described in Section 11.9) can legitimately be considered to be control-plane protocols, since they are not involved in data transfer. Thus, in the control plane, we show RSVP and OSPF as representatives of resource reservation and routing protocols.

15.3.2 IP

The *Internet Protocol* provides two network-layer services in the Internet. First, it provides every endpoint with an IP address. Second, packets injected into the Internet from an arbitrary endpoint are forwarded to the destination whose IP address is in the packet's header. When forwarding packets, IP hides the details of link-level technologies from the endpoints and provides the abstraction of an *unreliable, best-effort, end-to-end* link.

- By *unreliable*, we mean that IP does not guarantee that a packet will reach its destination.

- By *best-effort*, we mean that IP does not guarantee packets a quality of service (see Section 14.4.1). However, if a packet is too large to be carried by a particular

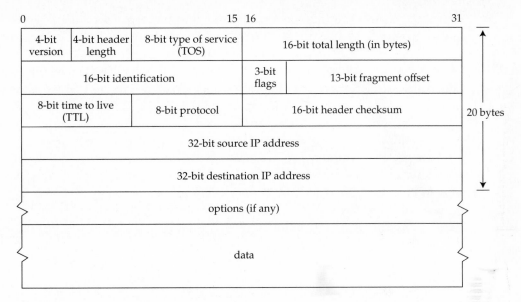

Figure 15.7: IP header. IP provides unreliable datagram service, but supports segmentation and reassembly. The meaning of each field is explained in the text.

datalink-layer protocol, IP will fragment the packet and reassemble it at its destination.

- Finally, by *end-to-end*, we mean that IP carries a packet from the source to the destination by consulting routing tables established by an independent routing protocol[2] (see Chapter 11).

Because the Internet does not specify a physical- or datalink-layer standard, we can layer IP over practically any physical- and datalink-layer technology, such as Ethernet (CSMA/CD), FDDI (token ring), wide-area telephone trunks (SONET or PDH), wireless links (CSMA/CA), satellite links (ALOHA), and other networking technologies such as X.25 and ISDN. This allows the Internet to interconnect networks built with widely varying technologies, and allows network managers to upgrade the underlying technology without affecting higher-level protocols and applications. This is an important reason for the Internet's popularity.

We can understand IP's functionality by studying the IP header (Figure 15.7) [Postel 81]. The first field is the *version number*, which allows the network to upgrade to newer versions of IP. The current version is 4, so the IP version described here is also called IPv4. This field is used to allow the next version of IP, called IPv6, to coexist with IPv4. The next field is the length of the header in 4-byte words (this automatically con-

---

[2]We emphasize again that the routing tables are computed by specialized routing protocols in the control plane, such as RIP, EGP, BGP and OSPF. IP merely uses these routing tables to forward data packets.

strains the header length to be a multiple of 4 bytes). Since the field is 4 bits long, the longest header length is $2^4 - 1 = 15$ words or 60 bytes long. The IP header has a fixed mandatory part (20 bytes) and a set of options (up to an additional 40 bytes). The header length field allows a router or endpoint to distinguish between header and data bytes. Moreover, if the packet has no options (header length is 5 words), which is the common case, the packet can be processed at high speed using special-purpose hardware. This is a common trick in high-performance IP routers.

The third field, *type of service,* or TOS, allows endpoints to choose a quality of service for their packets. Endpoints can request a path with low delay, high throughput, high reliability, or low monetary cost. If multiple routing metrics and non-FIFO scheduling were uniformly implemented in the Internet, this field would make sense. As this is not the case, this field is usually ignored both when routing and when scheduling.

The fourth field, *length,* is the length of the datagram in bytes. It is 16 bits long, so the longest IP packet is (64 Kbytes $-$ 1) = 65,535 bytes long.

Fragmentation

The fifth field, *ID,* uniquely identifies an IP packet among those that have a given source and destination address. Some link technologies limit the packet size. For example, Ethernet does not allow packets larger than 1500 bytes. If a router receives an IP packet that is too large for the next hop, IP allows the router to fragment the packet into smaller packets. The destination then uses the ID field to reconstruct the original packet.

The next 3-bit field, *flags,* also supports fragmentation. Only 2 of the 3 bits are significant. One of them is the "More Fragments" flag. If this flag is 1, the destination knows that this packet is not the last fragment in the packet. It therefore places the fragment in a queue, waiting for a fragment with the "More Fragments" flag set to 0. When this fragment arrives, IP reconstructs the original packet and hands it to the designated upper layer. What happens if the last fragment never arrives? The remaining fragments will occupy space in the buffer, denying access to incoming packets. Eventually, as the destination accumulates partial packets in its buffers, it can accept no more packets, because it runs out of buffer space! To avoid this situation, the destination must periodically toss out partial packets that have overstayed their welcome.

The other flag is the "Don't Fragment" flag. If this is set, a router that gets a packet that is too large for the next hop must discard the packet. It also sends a *control message* using the *Internet Control Message Protocol (ICMP)* to the source, telling it that the packet was too large. A source that receives this message should reduce its packet size and retransmit the packet, if necessary.

Mogul and Kent have argued that IP fragmentation is a bad idea [MK 87], because it adds to a router's work and introduces complexity at the endpoint (which must reassemble fragments and clean out incomplete packets). Besides, even if a single fragment is lost, the entire packet must be discarded. Finally, excessive fragmentation can lead to *reassembly lockup.* In this situation, a destination's buffers are full of partial packets, so it cannot accept any more fragments. Thus, none of its existing partial packets can be completed, and the destination must waste time waiting for some or all of the partial fragments eventually to be tossed out. To avoid fragmentation, Mogul and Kent recommend using the "Don't Fragment" flag to *discover* the largest packet size allowed on a particular path (in IP jargon, this is called the *maximum transmission unit*, or *MTU*). A source implementing *path MTU discovery* sends a large packet with the "Don't Fragment" flag set. If it receives an ICMP error message, it tries again with a smaller size. Eventually, it finds the largest packet size that the path can support. This strategy avoids fragmentation, but relies on routers properly returning ICMP error messages.

The *fragment offset* field is also required for supporting fragmentation and reassembly. This field tells the destination which part of the original packet, described by a byte offset and length, is contained in the current fragment.

TTL

The *time-to-live (TTL)* field serves many purposes. Recall from Section 12.4.2 that to correctly choose initial sequence numbers, we must know the longest time a packet can be delayed in the network. The TTL field was originally supposed to have been decremented once every second. A router or destination that decremented a packet's TTL field to zero discarded it. Thus, a source could control how many seconds a packet lived in the network, allowing it to correctly choose initial sequence numbers. Also, in the case of a routing loop, the TTL field would eventually kill off the packet.

Current implementations decrement the TTL field each time a packet is forwarded, instead of once every second. As before, when the TTL field reaches zero, the packet is discarded. This is not quite right, because a router may take substantially less (or more) than one second to forward a packet. Thus, a source cannot strictly bound a packet's maximum lifetime. Nevertheless, even this use of the TTL field protects against looping packets in case of transient routing loops, which can form with both distance-vector and link-state routing (see Sections 11.5 and 11.6). Besides, if the delay at a router is <1 s, which is usually true, the TTL is an upper bound on the packet's lifetime. Thus, the engineering decision to decrement the TTL once per hop is reasonable, and substantially decreases the cost of implementing IP.

We can exploit the TTL field to determine the route from a source to a destination. This technique depends on the fact that when a router decrements a packet's TTL to zero, it is supposed to send an ICMP "timer-expired" message to the source. A source that wants to find its path to a destination first sets the TTL to 1 and sends it to the destination. This evokes an error from the first router along the path. The source then sets the field to 2 and tries again, thus telling it the second router in the path. Continuing in this fashion, the source can find the entire path. This technique is used in the *traceroute* utility.

The TTL field is also used to clean up fragments at the destination. Once every second, a destination decrements the TTL of every fragment that has not yet been reassembled. If the TTL reaches 0, the destination removes the fragment from its buffers.

Finally, we can use the TTL field for an *expanding-ring search*, as described in Section 11.11.2.

Remaining fields

The *protocol* field tells IP to which upper layer protocol it should pass the packet. This is typically TCP or UDP. The set of protocol numbers for "well-known" protocols is specified in RFC 1700 [RP 94].

The *header-checksum* field protects against corruption in the packet header. IP does not checksum data. The checksum is a 16-bit one's complement of the header, which is easy to implement in software and reasonably effective in practice [BBP 88, Rijsinghani 94].

The next two fields, *source* and *destination IP address,* are used to route packets to the destination and for the destination to reply to the source. These are required in any datagram network (without a source address, the destination would not be able to reply to the source).

Options

The last set of fields, the *option* fields, allow further expansion of the IP header for special purposes. (This is an example of good protocol design: the protocol has "hooks" to allow future options to be added as necessary.) Five sets of options are commonly used:

- *Security and handling options* are mainly used in the military portion of the Internet [Kent 91].

- When the *record route* option is set, each router along the path stores its 4-byte IP address in the header's option field. Since the header length field is 4 bits long and counts the number of 4-byte words, the longest IP header is 15 words or 60 bytes. The mandatory portion of the header is 20 bytes, so this option only works for up to 9 routers (3 bytes are used to identify the option as the record route option).

- When the *time stamp* option is set, each router along the path adds its own IP address and a time stamp to the packet header.

- The *loose source routing* option allows a source to specify a set of routers that *must* be traversed in reaching the destination (Section 11.3).

- Finally, the *strict source routing* option allows a source to choose the entire path to reach the destination.

Two points about options are worth noting. First, they are not universally implemented in the Internet. Thus, a source cannot count on routers obeying an option field. Second, they are not the common case, so most routers in the field take much longer to process IP packets with options than IP packets without options. This interferes, for example, with measuring processing times with the time-stamp option.

Further details about the IP header can be found in reference [Stevens 94].

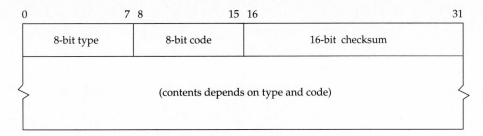

Figure 15.8: ICMP packet header.

15.3.3 ICMP

We mentioned earlier that the *Internet Control Message Protocol* carries error messages from the network to an IP source. The ICMP header, shown in Figure 15.8, contains only *type, code,* and *checksum* fields [Postel 81a]. The type and code fields encode the error message. The following are some important error messages:

- *Destination unreachable:* Sent by a router to a source when it cannot find a route.

- *Source quench:* Informs a source that it is sending data too fast, and should reduce its rate (see Section 13.4).

- *Redirect:* Informs a source to use another router for reaching a particular destination (see Section 11.10).

- *Router advertisement:* Advertises the presence of a router on a broadcast LAN (see Section 11.10).

- *Time exceeded:* A router has decremented a packet's TTL to zero. Used by *traceroute* (see Section 15.3.2).

- *Fragmentation needed but "Don't-Fragment" bit set:* Used by path-MTU discovery (see Section 15.3.2).

Notice that ICMP is closely tied to IP (though it is layered above IP, and therefore is carried in the data portion of an IP datagram). Thus, one can think of ICMP as the extension of IP for carrying error messages.

ICMP sits directly over IP, and ICMP messages, if lost, are not retransmitted. A source cannot count on receiving an ICMP message and must operate correctly even if it receives none. Similarly, the network cannot assume that sources receive or obey ICMP control messages and must be robust to loss of all ICMP messages.

15.3.4 TCP

The *Transmission Control Protocol* [Postel 81b] provides a multiplexed, duplex, connection-oriented, reliable, flow-controlled, byte-stream service.

- By *multiplexed,* we mean that many applications can share access to a single TCP layer, and the sending and receiving TCP layers coordinate actions to correctly route packets to the desired destination.

- By *duplex,* we mean that both ends of a TCP connection can simultaneously read and write packets.

- By *connection-oriented,* we mean that TCP does connection establishment before data transfer, to establish initial sequence numbers for data transfer in each direction (see Section 12.4.3).

- By *reliable,* we mean that TCP uses timeouts and retransmissions to ensure that a destination receives a transmitted packet (see Section 12.4.6).

- By *flow-controlled,* we mean that a TCP source uses feedback flow control to adjust its transmission rate to the rate currently supportable in the network (see Section 13.4.6).

- Finally, by *byte-stream,* we mean that TCP provides the abstraction of carrying bytes in sequence from source to destination, ignoring message boundaries. A source may send two messages of length 50 and 100 bytes, but the destination receives an undifferentiated set of 150 bytes, which it can read in as many messages as it wants.

These aspects of TCP can be seen from the TCP packet header, shown in Figure 15.9.

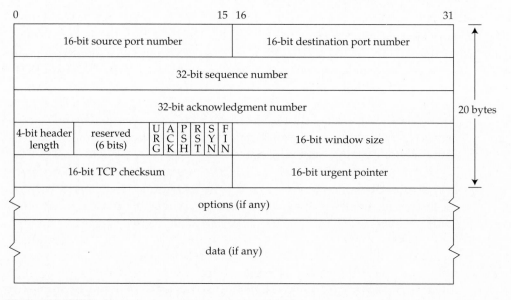

Figure 15.9: TCP header.

Port numbers

The first two fields in the TCP header are the source and destination *port numbers*. A single interface, identified by a single IP address, may carry data from many different applications (think of a server that replies to simultaneous requests from many clients). To differentiate between these applications sharing the same IP address, each is assigned a different port number by the operating system. The destination port number therefore identifies the application program that should receive the incoming TCP packet. The source port number allows the application to reply to the sender. The four quantities—the source IP address, source port number, destination IP address, and destination port number—uniquely identify a TCP connection.

Some port numbers are "well known" in the sense that end-systems always assign them to certain common applications [RP 94]. For example, the telnet remote login application uses port 23, the Simple Mail Transfer Protocol uses port 25, and the Hypertext Transfer Protocol uses port 80. In Unix, all port numbers below 1024 are reserved for trusted applications, and cannot be used by user programs. The /etc /services file in most Unix systems describes well-known port numbers.

Sequence and acknowledgment number

The 32-bit TCP sequence number is the *byte* offset of the start of the packet from the initial sequence number used in the stream. For example, if the initial sequence number is 120, a packet with sequence number 153 and length 14 has the 14 bytes from 33 to 46. (TCP does not carry a length field, because this is available from the IP header.) The acknowledgment number uses the same format as the sequence number and is a *cumulative* acknowledgment used for providing reliable transmission, as described in Section 12.4. In TCP, the acknowledgment number is the next byte that the receiver expects and indicates that the receiver has correctly received all bytes with a smaller sequence number (allowing for wraparound).

Header length

We need the header length field because the TCP header is variable length and, like the IP header, may contain several option fields.

Flags

The TCP header has six flag bits. The first bit, URG, indicates that the *urgent pointer,* discussed later, is valid. The ACK bit indicates that the acknowledgment field contains valid information, that is, the packet contains a piggybacked acknowledgment. The PSH (*push*) bit requests the receiver to hand the packet to the application program as soon as possible. The RST bit resets the receiver during a three-way handshake (see Section 12.4.4). The SYN and FIN bits are also used during a three-way handshake.

Window size

The window size field allows a receiver to control how much data the sender is allowed to send before it must wait for an acknowledgment (i.e., it is an upper bound on the *flow-control window*). It is usually set to the size of the buffer at the receiver that holds out-of-order packets. The last byte the sender may send is the acknowledgment sequence number added to the window size. Since a 16-bit field describes this size, the largest possible flow-control window size is 64 Kbytes − 1, which may be too small for a long-delay, high-bandwidth connection (see Section 13.4.3). In this case, the window size can be *scaled.* When a sender wants to use window scaling, during the three-way handshake, an option in its SYN packet proposes that window sizes be interpreted as the most significant bits of a larger window size. If the receiver agrees, then both sides can use a much larger window size. For example, if the endpoints agree to treat the window as the MSB of a 20-bit window (by shifting the window size 4 positions to the left before interpreting it), the effective largest window size increases to 1 Mbyte.

The window size depends on the amount of buffer space left in the receiver. If the receive buffer is full (perhaps the application did not read any data from the buffer), then the receiver sets the window size to zero, preventing the sender from sending any more data. The sender periodically sends a 1-byte packet, checking to see whether the window size has increased. This is called *sender persistence,* and the timer used to send a probe packet is called the *persist timer.*

Sometimes a TCP sender and receiver can get into a situation where the receiver advertises only small windows, and the sender sends only small packets. For example, the sender may initially send many packets, until the receiver buffer fills, and the receiver advertises a zero-size window. The application may then read a few bytes from the receive buffer, so that the persist probe returns a small window size, and the sender sends a small packet. If the receiving application only reads data in small chunks, the sender will then be forced to send data in small packets, incurring a substantial overhead for the TCP and IP headers. This is called the *silly-window syndrome* [Stevens 94, pp. 325–330]. A receiver can avoid this syndrome by advertising a zero window until it has enough free buffers to advertise a reasonably large window. A sender can also help avoid this syndrome by holding off packet transmission until it has a sufficiently large window size.

Checksum

The TCP checksum is computed not only over the TCP header, but also over the data in the packet. Thus, the TCP checksum protects against corruption in the data packet. The checksum itself is the same as the IP checksum, that is, the one's complement of the sum of all words in the TCP header and the data in the packet. It is reasonably good in practice and can be efficiently implemented [BBP 88, MK 90, Rijsinghani 94]. Computing the TCP checksum is often the most time-consuming part of the TCP protocol, because it needs to touch every data byte once. Some experimental host adaptors peek into the IP packet to see if it is a TCP packet, and, if so, compute the TCP checksum in hardware [EWLBCD 94]. This considerably improves TCP throughput.

Urgent pointer

This points to the last byte in the packet that contains "urgent" data. Bytes from the start of the packet to the byte pointed to by the urgent pointer are considered urgent. TCP, however, does not define what actions the receiver must take on receiving such information. Presumably, the receiving operating system should pass this data to the application as soon as it can. Different implementations take different actions when receiving urgent data, which can be confusing. A more detailed explanation of the use of urgent pointers can be found in reference [Stevens 94, pp. 292–296].

Options

The most common option is the choice of the *maximum segment size (MSS)*. In TCP jargon, each packet is called a *segment,* and the MSS is the largest segment a sender may send. If a receiver wants to control the MSS of the sender, it advertises it in the option field during the three-way handshake. Other options are described in more detail in reference [Stevens 94].

15.3.5   HTTP

The Internet does not specify a session- or presentation-layer protocol. Instead, the session layer is usually provided by the host operating system. The two common session layers are *sockets* [LMKQ 89] and *streams* [Ritchie 84].

We focus on the *Hypertext Transfer Protocol (HTTP)* as an example of a common application-layer protocol on the Internet [BFF 95, FFBGM 96]. To the less technically minded, HTTP, or, more precisely, its use in the World Wide Web, is nearly synonymous with the Internet! Thus, it is worthy of more careful study.

HTTP is a *request–response* protocol. Servers are passive entities that reply to client requests. Much of the complexity in the World Wide Web is in the client's browser software. A browser needs to decide when and where to send a request, and how to interpret the response (for example, uncompressing and displaying graphics, or playing a sound file). Since HTTP is layered over TCP, it uses the error-control, flow-control, and in-sequence ordering features of TCP. HTTP merely provides a way to represent queries and replies. Indeed, it has more in common with a word-processing program than with a classical network protocol such as TCP or IP.

An important concept in HTTP is the notion of a Universal Resource Locator (URL) [Berners-Lee 94]. A URL is ". . . a way to encapsulate a name in any registered name space, and label it with the name space, producing a member of the universal set [of URLs]" [Berners-Lee 94]. An example URL is `http://www.aw.com/`, where `http` is the name space, and `www.aw.com` is a path in this name space that, by convention, refers to the directory associated with the HTTP protocol on the machine named `www.aw.com`. Similarly, in the URL `mailto:skeshav@cs.cornell.edu`, `mailto` is the namespace, and `skeshav@cs.cornell.edu` is a name in this name space that corresponds to an address to which email can be sent. Loosely speaking, a URL is a way to refer to an arbitrary resource on a server, such as a file or a service, so that it can be accessed by a client. URLs are always of the form ⟨name_space⟩:⟨path⟩, where both the name space and the path use 7-bit ASCII characters. The ⟨path⟩ is name-space specific, except that certain characters such as "%" and "#" are disallowed. This allows the URL space to be extensible (the entire set of names in a name space can be added to HTTP simply by registering a new name space with it), complete (any name space can be encapsulated), and printable.

EXAMPLE 15.2

Suppose we wanted to refer to postal addresses using URLs. All we need do is to define a name space, say, `postal`. Then, a postal address such as "700 Mountain Avenue, Murray Hill, NJ 07974" might be represented by the URL `postal:700 Mountain Avenue/Murray Hill/NJ 07974`.

An HTTP request is a *GET, HEAD,* or *POST* request. The GET request is of the form *GET request URL,* followed by zero or more modifiers on subsequent lines. Modifiers include restrictions such as "If-Modified-Since" and "Authorization." The former allows a client to retrieve a resource only if it has been modified since a given date. The latter allows the server to authenticate the client. The *HEAD* request is identical to a GET, except that the server returns only a short "header" (which we will look at next), instead of the actual resource. A client uses it to test the validity of a link. Finally, a *POST* request of the form *POST URL ⟨blank line⟩ body* allows a client to give the server some information (in the body) to post to some location in the server, which might correspond to a form or a bulletin board.

An HTTP response is of the form *status line ⟨line break⟩ headers ⟨line break⟩ ⟨blank line⟩ ⟨body⟩.* The status line describes the server's version of HTTP and contains some standard response codes. The headers modify the response, for example, with an "Expires" field, which indicates how long the information is valid. The actual text of the response is in the body field. Much of the complexity in the protocol is in coming up with clean ways to describe the multiplicity of data formats and encoding conventions found in the real world. More details on HTTP requests and responses can be found in reference [BFF 95].

15.3.6 RSVP

The primary signaling protocol in the control plane on the Internet is the *Resource reSerVation Protocol* (RSVP) [ZDEZ 93, BZBHJ 96]. Unlike TCP or IP, which use a single simple header format, the complex operations in RSVP (see Section 14.8.5) require many different protocol headers and protocol interactions. Details of RSVP are still being worked out at the time of this writing (1996). Internet routing protocols, which are also in the control plane, are described in Section 11.9.

15.4 ATM network protocols

Like the telephone network, an ATM network separates the data and control planes. Control-plane protocols are used to establish connections, also called virtual channels (VCs), and data-plane protocols are used to carry cells on these connections. As with the telephone network, current ATM networks define protocols only at the lower layers of the data plane. It is still a matter of considerable debate whether ATM data-plane protocols can be thought of as defining network-layer protocols, or whether they only provide a datalink-layer interface (see the next box for more details).

In this section, we will study some typical ATM protocols in the data plane. Section 15.4.1 is an overview of the protocol stack, and Section 15.4.2 describes the ATM layer. The ATM adaptation layer (AAL) in its several forms is described in Section 15.4.3. Finally, in Section 15.4.4 we study the SSCOP protocol used in the ATM control plane. Higher-level control-plane protocols, such as UNI and PNNI, are still being finalized at the time of this writing.

15.4.1 Protocol stack

ATM networks distinguish between the data and control planes (Table 15.6). The data plane defines only the physical, datalink, and network layers. The physical layer, as with other technologies, is diverse, ranging from twisted-pair copper wire to radio-frequency wireless, as well as the more common optical fiber. (It is a common fallacy to assume that ATM networks are defined only for, or require, optical fiber.)

We will discuss the datalink and network layers of the data plane, corresponding to the *ATM layer,* and the *ATM adaptation layer.* In the control plane, we will discuss the

	Data plane	Control plane
Application		UNI/PNNI
Application		Q.2931
Session		
Transport		SSCOP
Network	AAL1–5	S-AAL (AAL5)
Datalink	ATM	ATM
Physical	Many	Many

Table 15.6: ATM protocol stack. In the data plane, ATM standards currently define only up to the network layer. In the control plane, SSCOP provides reliable, flow-controlled transport, and Q.2931 is used for connection establishment. The semantics of the User–Network Interface (UNI) and Network–Network Interface (NNI) are defined in the application level of the control plane.

SSCOP transport layer. We will not study the details of the Q.2931 signaling protocol, which is outlined in Section 14.8.1. More details on ATM protocols can be found in reference [HHS 94].

15.4.2 ATM

The ATM layer provides connection-oriented, in-sequence, unreliable, quality-of-service assured cell transport.

- By *connection-oriented,* we mean that an ATM connection must be established before cells can be sent on the connection.

- By *in-sequence,* we mean that an ATM network guarantees that cells within a virtual channel will never be reordered.

- By *unreliable,* we mean that the network does not guarantee that cells from a transmitter will arrive at the receiver, or that they will arrive without errors.

- By *quality-of-service assured,* we mean that the network gives cells in a virtual circuit (also called *virtual channel* or *VC*) a quality-of-service guarantee corresponding to the traffic class associated with that VC at each intermediate switch and multiplexor (see Section 14.4.1).

We show the ATM cell format in Figure 15.10. Note that the ITU-T actually defines two cell formats, one at the *User–Network Interface (UNI),* and the other at the *Network–Network Interface (NNI).* The UNI is the interface an ATM network presents to the user. It consists of the signaling protocol that the user uses to set up a QoS-assured circuit, and

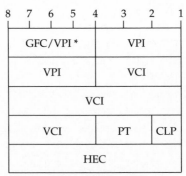

*GFC in UNI and VPI in NNI

Figure 15.10: ATM cell format. Note that the formats at the User–Network Interface (UNI) and Network–Network Interface (NNI) are different.

the format of the cells crossing the boundary. The NNI is the interface between two network elements within the ATM network. The NNI deals with issues of signaling and data transfer, as well as routing, operations, administration, and management. The NNI is still being designed at the time of this writing.

To return to the cell formats at the UNI and the NNI, we see that the only difference is that the first field, *generic flow control*, has been added to the second field (*virtual path identifier* or *VPI*) to make the second field longer. The idea is that GFC is a local matter between the network and an attached interface. Thus, the GFC field is not necessary within the network. Here, it is better used as part of the VPI. This will become clearer when we discuss each field in detail, next.

GFC

The 4-bit *generic flow control* field is meant for local flow control between the network access point (typically a switch belonging to the network provider) and one or more attached endpoints. If the endpoint is directly connected to a switch, the GFC field can be used to slow the endpoint's transmission rate (presumably by sending cells with appropriate GFC values from the switch to the endpoint). If more than one endpoint shares a common medium (such as a wireless link) in accessing the network, the GFC field can be used for multiple access. The ITU-T does not specify any particular use of the GFC field, and it is currently (1996) ignored by almost every manufacturer. In this case, the field is simply set to 0000.

As the GFC is not relevant inside the network (flow control here uses RM cells, as discussed in Section 13.4.9), the 4-bit GFC field is reused for the VPI inside the network.

VPI

A virtual path refers to a set of virtual channels that share the same path in the network. We can think of the virtual path identifier (VPI) as the high-order bits of the virtual channel identifier (VCI). The idea is that switches can save on the size of their translation table if they store per-path state instead of per-VC state. Specifically, all virtual channels in the same virtual path share a single entry in the translation table and use a single resource reservation at each switch along the path.

The advantage of a virtual path is that once it is set up, individual virtual channels do not need any signaling: the path already exists, and cells on the virtual channel can simply be forwarded without waiting for call setup. Moreover, this dramatically reduces the signaling overhead. On the other hand, if we size a virtual path for a certain number of virtual channels, we waste resources when fewer channels share it. Besides, to reduce signaling overhead, we need to pre-establish virtual paths to every likely destination. Thus, virtual paths are likely to prove too expensive other than in significantly over-provisioned networks, or ones whose traffic patterns are quite predictable. Dynamic renegotiation of VP capacity might be a promising middle ground that trades off some signaling overhead for a possibly large reduction in the resource overhead [Pendara-kis 96].

VCI

The 16-bit *virtual channel identifier* is the standard ATM VCI, as discussed in Section 4.1.4. The current standard reserves VCIs 0–15 for special purposes. For example, VCI 1 is reserved for *metasignaling*, that is, negotiating which VCI to use for signaling, and what quality of service the signaling VC should have. Similarly, VCIs 3 and 4 are reserved for maintenance, for example, to check the error rate on a link, or to report alarm conditions. Other reserved VCIs can be found in reference [HHS 94].

PT

The 3-bit *payload type* field identifies the cell type. The high-order bit selects between cells containing user data and those containing management information. If the high-order bit is 0, then the second bit is used to signal congestion, as described in Section 13.4.9, and the third bit is used to mark the end of an AAL5 frame (discussed next). If the high-order bit is 1, then the payload types are as follows: 100 and 101: reserved for link management, 110: resource management cell (see Section 13.4.9), and 111: reserved for future use.

CLP

The *cell loss priority (CLP)* bit is used in two contexts. A source can use it to mark cells that are lower priority than others. For example, if a source encodes an image with a *hierarchical encoder*, that is, one that encodes pictures with a base and an enhancement layer, it can mark the base layer cells with CLP = 0, and the enhancement layer with CLP = 1. If the network gets congested, it should drop enhancement-layer cells rather than base-layer cells.

The CLP bit can also mark cells that fail a traffic policing test (see Section 13.3). This allows the network to preferentially drop packets that would otherwise have been dropped at the policer. Thus, if a source that violates a policing function is lucky, its cells will make it to the other end. Otherwise, a congested multiplexor drops these excess cells without affecting well-behaved users.

HEC

The *header error check (HEC)* field is the CRC over the fields in the header, excluding the HEC itself, exclusively ORed with the bit string 01010101 (see Section 12.2.5). The CRC is defined by the polynomial $x^8 + x^2 + x + 1$.

15.4.3 ATM adaptation layers

The ATM adaptation layer (AAL) adds functionality to the ATM layer to make it more suitable for higher layers and applications. The diversity in application requirements have resulted in the development of four different AALs, which we discuss next.

AAL design philosophy

ATM adaptation layers (AALs) were originally meant to provide the interface between an application and the underlying ATM network. ITU-T's original design was that an application would sit directly above an AAL. Thus, the AAL would have to provide all the mechanisms to provide the quality-of-service guarantees described in Section 14.4.1. For example, an AAL supporting variable-bit-rate service would need to provide traffic shaping to ensure that the source traffic was leaky-bucket constrained. Similarly, an AAL supporting constant-bit-rate service would need to monitor the incoming traffic stream to eliminate any jitter along the path.

This design philosophy leads to a rather complicated AAL functionality, because it incorporates presentation, error, and flow-control functions that we would normally perform at higher layers. With the evolution of ATM architecture, AAL functionality has gradually been reduced, with many functions moved out to higher layers of the protocol stack. This movement is most evident when we compare the functionality of AAL1, which was one of the first AALs to be defined, with that of AAL5, which came last. It is possible that future ATM networks will use only AAL5, with the other AALs withering away into historical curiosities.

AAL1

AAL1 is meant to carry constant-bit-rate (CBR) traffic. The AAL1 layer at the transmitter expects to receive precisely spaced cells from an application, and the AAL1 layer at the receiver ensures that its higher layer receives these cells precisely at the right time. AAL1 detects cell corruption and loss and provides time synchronization between the transmitter and the receiver. The idea is that replacing a plesiochronous or synchronous circuit with an AAL1 virtual channel should require no change at the endpoints.

The AAL1 cell format is shown in Figure 15.11. AAL1 uses the first data bit in the 48-byte payload to carry a 1-bit time-stamp indicator, a 3-bit sequence number, a 3-bit CRC, and a 1-bit parity. Consecutive time-stamp bits encode the difference between the sender's clock and a common reference, allowing the receiver to synchronize to the send-

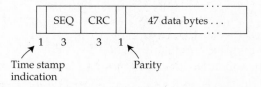

Figure 15.11: AAL1 frame format. An AAL1 frame is one cell long and adds a 1-byte header in the ATM cell data area.

er's clock. The CRC and parity protect the sequence number, allowing single-bit correction and multiple-bit error detection. The sequence number, in turn, allows the receiver to detect small loss bursts.

An AAL1 connection is associated with a constant bit rate. The receiver buffers data in a playout buffer to correct for jitter in the network, then plays data out at the specified rate. It may also insert dummy information if it detects a cell loss. Finally, AAL1 supports forward error correction of the payload bytes using a Reed–Solomon code (see Section 12.2.6). This combination of payload encoding, which really ought to be a higher-layer function, and AAL-level framing reflects the AAL design philosophy of providing all application services in a single adaptation layer.

AAL2

AAL2 has not been defined at the time of this writing, and it is debatable whether it will ever be defined, because its expected functionality can be supported over AAL3/4 and AAL5.

AAL3/4

AAL3/4 combines the specifications for AAL3 and AAL4. Originally, it was thought that different AALs would be needed for connection-oriented and connectionless variable-bit-rate traffic. Eventually these requirements merged to form a single AAL3/4 specification.

AAL3/4 carries packets (also called frames) that are smaller than 64 Kbytes, with detection of corrupted, out-of-sequence, and lost packets. Moreover, it allows multiple endpoints to share a single VCI, which is important for implementing multipoint-to-multipoint ATM multicast (see Section 14.4). Since the packet handed to AAL3/4 (also called a *protocol data unit* or *PDU*) may be larger than 48 bytes, AAL3/4 must *segment* the PDU into ATM cells, then *reassemble* it at the receiver.

AAL3/4 modifies data from an upper layer in two steps. It first adds a header and a trailer to form what we will call an *encapsulated protocol data unit (EPDU)*.[3] It then segments this EPDU into ATM cells, where each ATM cell, in turn, has a header and a trailer (Figure 15.12).

We first study the header and trailer in the EPDU (Figure 15.13). The EPDU header has three fields, the *common part indicator (CPI)*, the *beginning tag (Btag)*, and the *Buffer allocation size (BASize)*.

- The CPI is used to interpret the rest of the fields in the EPDU (it is like the version number in the IP header). Currently, the only defined CPI is 0.

- The Btag field (which matches the *ending tag* in the EPDU trailer) allows the destination to match up the beginning and the end of the EPDU.

---

[3]ITU-T and the ATM Forum refer to this as the *Common Part Convergence Sublayer-Protocol Data Unit* or *CPCS-PDU*, which is quite a mouthful. We will use EPDU instead.

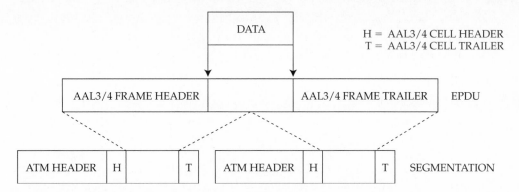

Figure 15.12: AAL3/4 segmentation. User data is encapsulated with a header and trailer to form an encapsulated protocol data unit (EPDU), which is then segmented into multiple ATM cells, each with its own header and trailer inside the ATM cell data area.

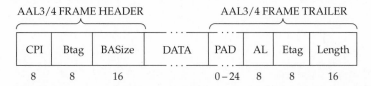

Figure 15.13: AAL3/4 encapsulated PDU.

- The BASize field, which is a hint about the size of the EPDU, allows the receiver to allocate a buffer of the appropriate size even before it receives all the cells in the EPDU. Sources may choose to ignore this field.

The EPDU trailer has four fields, the *pad, alignment, ending tag (Etag),* and *length* fields.

- The pad is used to align the EPDU data field to a 32-bit boundary.

- The alignment (AL) field is used to fill the EPDU trailer to 32 bits (i.e., the bits are set to 0, and the corresponding bandwidth is wasted).

- The Etag field (which matches the Btag field in the header) allows the receiver to match the EPDU header and trailer.

- The length field is the true length of the EPDU payload field (as opposed to the BASize field, which is only a hint). It allows the receiver to detect whether some cells in the EPDU were lost.

Besides the per-packet EPDU header and trailer, AAL3/4 specifies a *per-cell* header and trailer that use 4 bytes of the 48 in the ATM cell payload (Figure 15.14). The header has a 2-bit *type,* a 4-bit *sequence number,* and a 10-bit *multiplexing identifier (MID).* The type identifies the cell as the first or last cell in the EPDU (10 or 01), a cell in the middle (00), or a

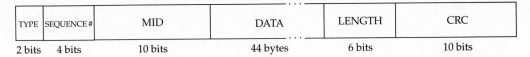

Figure 15.14: AAL3/4 cell format. AAL3/4 provides per-cell CRC. The MID field allows multiple endpoints to share a single VCI, which is useful in multipoint-to-multipoint multicast.

single-cell EPDU (11). The sequence number allows the receiver to detect lost cells in the EPDU. As with AAL1, the small sequence-number space is only effective for small error bursts. Finally, the MID field allows the receiver to distinguish among as many as 1024 transmitters sharing a single VCI. If the VCI is set up as multipoint-to-multipoint multicast VCI (Section 14.4), this allows all senders to share a single VCI, making it much easier to add new senders and receivers to the multicast tree (the alternative is to ask each new sender to set up a point-to-multipoint VCI with every receiver). However, this limits the number of senders on the shared VCI to 1024.[4]

The AAL3/4 ATM cell trailer has a 6-bit length field and a 10-bit CRC. The length field indicates the number of valid data bytes in the ATM cell. The CRC protects the AAL3/4 headers, the length field, and the payload in each cell (but not the 5-byte ATM header).

AAL5

AAL3/4 provides error detection, segmentation, and reassembly, but only at the cost of considerable overhead. Not only must we suffer the overhead of an EPDU header and trailer per PDU, each *cell* gives up 4 of its 48 bytes for a header and trailer. Part of the reason for this inefficiency is that because of strict layering, the ATM layer does not know of the existence of the ATM adaptation layer. Thus, when segmenting a PDU into cells, the AAL layer must place enough information in each cell for the receiver to reassemble the original PDU. With this constraint, each cell must contain at least the *type* field in its payload, indicating its position in the PDU.

If, however, we violate layering a little, we can make significant gains in performance. (This is a trade-off between performance and cleanliness in design.) The idea is to use 1 bit in the ATM header to mark the end of a PDU. Then, a receiver simply buffers cells on a VCI, waiting for a cell with the bit set to 1. When this happens, it hands the PDU to the AAL, which can then check for errors in the EPDU (Figure 15.15). The first cell following is assumed to be the start of the next PDU. We also move all the other per-cell fields to the EPDU overhead, and collapse the EPDU header and trailer into a single trailer. This results in the AAL5 trailer shown in Figure 15.16.

The 8–55-byte trailer consists of a *pad,* a *user-to-user* field *(UU),* a *common part indicator (CPI),* a *length,* and a *CRC.*

---

[4]Of course, without the MID field, only one endpoint may share a VC.

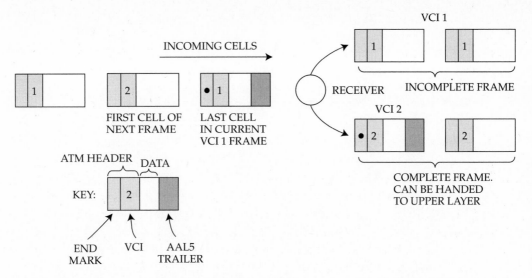

Figure 15.15: AAL5 reassembly. AAL5 segments on EPDU into cells as in AAL 3/4. Each cell carries, in its header, an indication whether it is the last cell in the EPDU. A receiver stores cells from each VCI in a separate queue, and when it sees a cell with the last-cell indication set, hands the complete frame to the upper layer for processing.

DATA	PAD	UU	CPI	LENGTH	CRC
< 64 KBYTES	0–47 BYTES	8	8	16	32

Figure 15.16: AAL5 EPDU format.

- *Pad:* Extracting the AAL5 trailer is easier if it is always in a fixed position in the last cell. We can guarantee that the trailer bytes are always the last 8 bytes of the last cell by using up to 47 bytes of padding (in the worst case, the second-to-last cell has 7 bytes of padding, and the last cell has 40 bytes of padding).

- *User-to-user (UU):* The UU field (whose use is currently unspecified) allows a higher-layer protocol at the transmitter to send some information to the receiver *opaquely,* that is, without being examined by the AAL5 layer. It can be used as a hook to provide innovative services in the future.

- *CPI:* The CPI field is a type field, as in AAL3/4, and, as in AAL3/4, must be set to 0.

- *Length:* The length field is the length of the PDU in the EPDU. It allows a receiver to detect lost cells.

- *CRC:* The CRC is a 32-bit CRC over the entire EPDU, including all the data bytes. It uses the CRC-32 polynomial described in Section 12.2.5. As with TCP, this CRC computation is the most expensive part in implementing AAL5 and is usually performed in hardware.

AAL5 versus AAL3/4

Do we need both AAL5 and AAL3/4? Both provide segmentation, reassembly, and detection of lost cells. AAL3/4 is arguably more robust, because it checksums data in each cell, whereas AAL5 has only one checksum for the entire EPDU. Moreover, AAL3/4 allows multipoint-to-multipoint connections using the MID field. On the other hand, AAL5 has far smaller header and trailer overhead. Besides, the 32-bit AAL5 checksum is more robust to scrambler errors than the 10-bit AAL3/4 checksum. Recent work [GR 96] shows that with a small change to current ATM switches, even AAL5 can support multipoint-to-multipoint connections. Each switch queues cells on such a connection until it sees the end-of-PDU bit, then releases them back to back on the VCI, thus preventing interleaving of PDUs on the VCI. Consequently, most manufacturers preferentially support AAL5, and it is likely that AAL3/4 will reach vestigial status in the future.

Is AAL a network layer or a datalink layer?

There is considerable debate about whether the ATM adaptation layer is a network or a datalink layer. The ITU-T, which is the last word on ATM standards, does not say anything about the matter. Many experts, especially those in the IP world, feel that AAL is a datalink-layer protocol because it does not provide addressing and routing the way IP does. Moreover, unlike IP, AAL cannot be layered over arbitrary link-layer technologies. Thus, these experts claim that AALs should not be considered a "true" network layer, like IP.

Despite these claims, just like IP, AAL does provide end-to-end connectivity. Besides, the view of a transport layer situated above AAL is similar to that of a transport layer over IP. Although it is true that AAL does not provide routing or addressing, these functions are conveniently moved to the control plane, which has its own advantages. Thus, a reasonable view, and one that we adopt in this book, is that AAL is the equivalent of the ISO network layer.

15.4.4 SSCOP

We now turn our attention from the data plane to the control plane. Signaling protocols usually rely on an underlying reliable transport layer to deal with error control and flow control. The ATM data plane, however, does not provide a reliable transport service. Thus, we need to layer the signaling protocol over the *Service-Specific Connection-Oriented Protocol (SSCOP)*, which, in turn, sits above AAL5 (also called *Signaling AAL* or *S-AAL* in this context) in the control plane (see Table 15.6) [MS 90].

Type	Intended traffic type	Comments
1	Constant bit rate, particularly voice calls	Meant primarily as a substitute for a voice circuit
2	—	Not defined
3/4	Variable bit rate and best-effort data	Allows multicast, but has per-cell overhead
5	Data traffic	Harder to implememt multicast, but much more efficient than AAL3/4

Table 15.7: The four AAL types currently specified, and their features.

SSCOP provides functionality similar to TCP—that is, reliable transport using timeouts and retransmissions, flow control, and error control—but uses different mechanisms [Henderson 95]. The key goal in SSCOP is to minimize the control overhead, since it was originally designed to operate over 64-Kbps voice channels. A secondary goal is to avoid the use of timeouts to the extent possible (this has the benefits discussed in Section 12.4.6).

The four basic packet types in SSCOP are *Sequenced Data (SD), POLL, STAT,* and *USTAT.* A transmitter sends SD packets to a receiver that have the usual type, length, sequence number, data, and checksum fields. A receiver does not explicitly acknowledge packets. Instead, the sender periodically sends (either once every N packets, or once every T seconds) a POLL packet inquiring about receiver state. The receiver replies with a STAT message that tells the sender which packets were correctly received, the largest sequence number packet the sender may transmit, and the next sequence number the receiver expects. The first field allows the sender to decide exactly which packets were lost, and the last two fields correspond to the window size and cumulative acknowledgment fields in TCP. The sender uses the STAT message to adjust its window size, and then retransmits lost packets, giving them higher priority than newly generated packets. Thus, the POLL/STAT mechanism allows the sender to recover from losses without using a per-packet timeout. Besides, the control overhead is minimal, because acknowledgments (STATs) are generated only once for a group of packets, instead of per-packet. However, on a packet loss, the recovery time obviously depends on the choice of the POLL timer. With infrequent polling, the control overhead is minimized, but the recovery time is also large.

SSCOP uses another mechanism to avoid large recovery times even when the poll interval is large. The receiver monitors the sequence numbers of arriving packets, and on detecting a loss, which shows up as a gap in the sequence space, sends a USTAT or unsolicited STAT packet to the sender. The USTAT packet has the same format as a STAT packet, except that it is not in response to a POLL. It is, therefore, functionally equivalent to a nack and suffers from the same problems (see Section 12.4.6).

SSCOP uses a static-window type flow control (see Section 13.4.3). Its performance therefore depends on the choice of the window size. If the window size is larger than the product of the available bandwidth and the sum of the round-trip time and the poll timer (which is the time the sender has to wait before it can get acknowledgments), then performance is good. Performance severely degrades with a smaller window size or high packet-loss rates [Henderson 95].

15.5   IP-over-ATM

Though IP networks are the most common packet-switched networks, ATM networks are rapidly being installed in both research and commercial environments. Thus, it is becoming increasingly important to interconnect IP and ATM networks. The easiest way to do so is for IP to treat ATM as a link-level technology (like Ethernet or FDDI), ignoring the routing and quality-of-service aspects of ATM. We call this approach IP-over-ATM. This is still an area of active research, and universally accepted solutions are still to come. In this section, we will look at some basic ideas in building IP-over-ATM networks. Further information can be found in references [Armitage 95a, SJ95].

15.5.1   IP encapsulation in AAL5

Carrying IP over ATM requires us to: (a) encapsulate IP datagrams in AAL5 frames, and (b) translate from an IP destination address to an ATM destination address. The easiest way to encapsulate IP in AAL5 is to put the IP datagram in the data portion of an AAL5 frame. This works well if the ATM network is used only for establishing application-to-application virtual circuits, where all the AAL5 frames carried on the virtual circuit encapsulate IP datagrams. In real life, a single virtual circuit may interconnect two LANs and carry not only IP, but also other protocols such as IPX and Appletalk. Therefore, it becomes necessary to add a multiplexing header to decide what kind of packet is being encapsulated. Instead of just using 1 or 2 bytes, which would allow 256- or 64-K protocols, the IETF decided to use *8* bytes for the encapsulation header to make it compatible with the IEEE 802 LAN header [Heinanen 93]. (Decision making by committee is often suboptimal.) The multiplexing header for an IP packet is defined to be 0x AA AA 03 00 00 00 08 00, where the first 3 bytes state that the encapsulated packet is not an ISO-compatible packet, and the next 3 bytes indicate that the protocol type is carried in the last 2 bytes (Figure 15.17). So, we are down to 64-K protocol types after all!

The IETF requires an encapsulation layer to be interposed between the IP layer and the AAL5 layer. This layer adds the 8-byte header on the transmit side, and, on the receive side, forwards a received packet to the protocol handler specified in the last 2 bytes of the encapsulation header.

15.5.2   Classical[5] IP-over-ATM

The second problem in carrying IP over ATM is to translate from an IP address to an ATM address. Recall that IP uses the IPv4 4-byte address, and ATM endpoints are addressed by variable-length NSAPs. How should we translate from one to the other? One solution is to use something like the Address Resolution Protocol (ARP) that trans-

---

[5]Though not in the style of Beethoven and Bach. The Internet is evolving so fast that the "classical" version is the one developed all of twenty-five years ago!

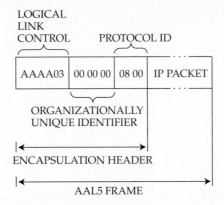

Figure 15.17: IP encapsulation over AAL5. An 8-byte header prepends the IP packet, of which the last 2 bytes indicate that the carried packet is an IP packet. The first 6 bytes are similar to an IEEE 802 LAN address.

lates from an IP address to a datalink MAC address. We cannot use ARP directly, because ARP assumes that the LAN supports broadcast, whereas an ATM LAN is a *nonbroadcast multiple access (NBMA)* LAN. A straightforward alternative is to designate one of the ATM hosts as an *ARP server* (Figure 15.18) [Laubach 94].

An ARP server contains an authoritative translation from an IP address to an ATM address for every member of the LAN. When an ATM host wants to send an IP packet to

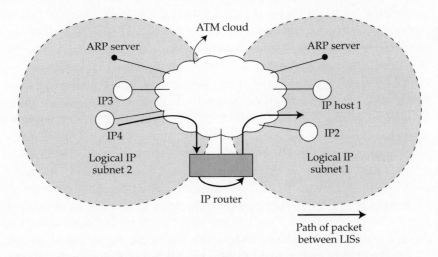

Figure 15.18: Classical IP-over-ATM. We partition IP hosts on the ATM network into logical IP subnets (LISs). An ARP server translates IP addresses within an LIS to ATM NSAPs. IP routers provide connectivity between LISs.

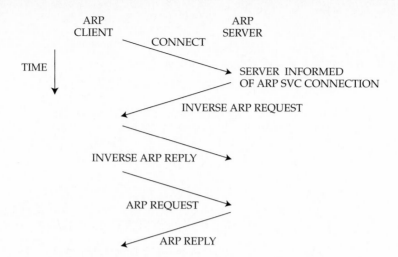

Figure 15.19: ATM ARP. When a host makes an ARP request to the server, the server first finds out the host's IP and NSAP addresses, then answers the ARP query.

another host on the same LAN, it sends a query to the ARP server with its own ATM address and the IP address it wants to resolve. The ARP server replies with a message containing the translation. Actually, what happens is that when a host establishes a connection to an ARP server (using ATM signaling), the ARP server preemptively sends an *inverse ARP* query to the host that initiated the connection (Figure 15.19). The reply to the inverse ARP reply contains the translation from the host's IP address to the host's ATM address. The server stores this reply, then eventually fields the query from the host. This allows the ARP server to automatically build up a translation table at the expense of doubling the number of messages required for address resolution.

Consider an ATM network with thousands of hosts, where each host also supports IP. If they were all in the same IP subnet, a broadcast to the subnet, which is commonly used in Internet protocols such as ARP, IGMP, and DHCP, would reach all the hosts in the network, generating a lot of traffic. To prevent this, in the classical IP-over-ATM model, we partition the larger ATM network into a set of IP subnets, called *logical IP subnets* or *LISs* (Figure 15.18). Then, broadcasts from a host only reach the other hosts on the same LIS. Unfortunately, with this partitioning, a host has no way to know that it has a direct ATM path to another host on a different LIS. To send a packet to a host on another LIS, the host must first set up a VC to an IP router attached to more than one LIS. The router accepts the packet and uses IP routing to decide the destination of the packet. If the packet is destined to another LIS on the same ATM network, it opens a VC to the destination (which may be another router) and forwards the packet. If the IP packet's destination is not reachable using ATM, the packet is forwarded using normal IP routing.

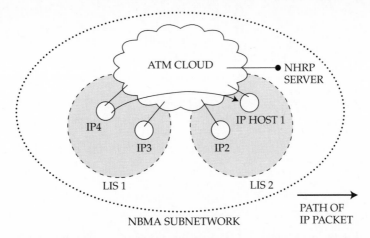

Figure 15.20: Next-Hop Routing Protocol (NHRP). NHRP allows an IP host to determine the ATM address of a destination even if the destination is not in the host's LIS. NHRP servers coordinate among themselves to provide IP-address-to-ATM-address translations, and to determine the best next-hop IP address.

15.5.3 Next-Hop Routing Protocol

We just noted that in Classical IP, a host must always use an IP router to reach other LISs. We remove this restriction with the *Next-Hop Routing Protocol (NHRP)* (Figure 15.20). A *next-hop server (NHS)* that implements NHRP stores IP-to-ATM translations for all hosts in the ATM cloud that choose to register with it. These hosts are considered part of a logical grouping called the *nonbroadcast multiple access (NBMA) subnetwork,* which is similar to an LIS. An NHS can forward requests for address resolution for nonlocal addresses to other NH servers in a manner reminiscent of the Domain Name System (Section 10.8). If the NH server can resolve an IP address, then the destination is guaranteed to be contactable over an all-ATM path. Thus, the resolved name is handed to signaling for connection establishment. Since the connection bypasses IP routing to reach the destination, we also call this *cut-through* routing. If the resolution fails, then the packet is forwarded to the local IP router for transmission through the normal channel. If the local NBMA subnetwork contains more than one router, the NHS can determine which of these is the best choice for the next hop. The details of how an NH server decides which other NH server to contact for resolving an IP address are still being finalized, as of 1996, and are available from reference [KPCL 96].

15.5.4 Multicast address resolution server

Although an ARP server resolves an IP address to an ATM address, it does not work for Class D (multicast) IP addresses, which actually correspond to a multicast group. We saw in Section 11.11.5 that in a LAN, a Class D address corresponds to some number of

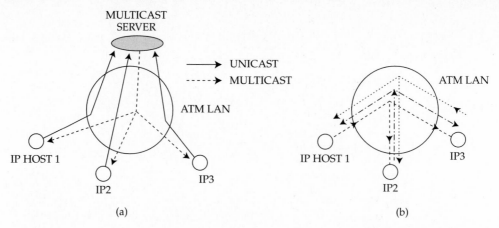

Figure 15.21: Two ways to carry IP multicast packets in an ATM LAN. (a) Hosts send the IP packet to a multicast server, that uses an ATM point-to-multipoint VC to disseminate the packet. (b) Each host maintains its own point-to-multipoint virtual circuit.

receivers, who program their host-interface to capture packets from a MAC address that is directly derived from the Class D IP address. Thus, if the LAN allows broadcast, the LAN multicast is trivial.

Because ATM is a nonbroadcast technology, LAN multicast is somewhat harder to accomplish. We must translate the Class D address to a set of ATM addresses, where this set may change over time. Thus, the dissemination of the current translation must be an active process. The problem is made more complex because we can implement multicast in an ATM LAN in one of two ways (Figure 15.21). Both techniques exploit the capabilities of an ATM switch to set up a point-to-multipoint ATM connection, that is, a virtual circuit that sends cells from a single source to multiple destinations (see Section 8.6). In one technique, a Class D address is associated with a *multicast server* that coordinates the multicast. The server is similar to the core in a core-based tree. Senders send multicast packets to the server, which maintains a single multicast connection to every receiver and copies the packet to receivers. In the second way to implement multicast, each sender maintains a separate multicast connection to every receiver in the group. This emulates a multipoint-to-multipoint connection with a set of point-to-multipoint connections.

In both solutions, either the multicast server or a source needs to translate a Class D address to a set of ATM addresses. This is provided by a *multicast address resolution server (MARS)* (Figure 15.22) [Armitage 95b]. A MARS is an extension of an ARP server, and, like an ARP server, operates only within a single LIS. However, unlike an ARP server, the MARS maintains a point-to-multipoint ATM connection to every ATM destination in the LIS. This connection, called the *cluster control VC,* is used to update the mapping from a Class D address to a set of ATM addresses as receivers join or leave the multicast group. Multicast servers, or sources that listen to control packets on the cluster control VC, use it to adjust the set of receivers to which they send packets. The MARS scheme includes

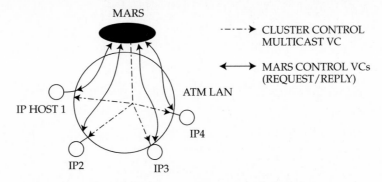

Figure 15.22: Multicast address resolution server (MARS). A MARS translates an IP multicast address to a set of ATM addresses. Since hosts may dynamically join and leave the multicast group, group members receive updates on group membership information using a multicast cluster control virtual circuit.

many other optimizations to minimize control traffic and extensions to provide finer control on address resolution. These can be found in reference [Armitage 95b].

15.5.5 LAN emulation

IP-over-ATM allows a host to send an IP packet to any destination on the ATM LAN or elsewhere by translating from an IP address to an ATM address using an ARP server. If we restrict the destination to be in the same LAN (either another host or a router), as in classical IP-over-ATM, then the translation need not be done below the IP layer, but can be done below the MAC layer. This not only allows "legacy" hosts to use the large bandwidth available from an ATM LAN, but has the added advantage that the translation is not IP specific and can be used to carry other protocols (such as Appletalk, which is used to connect computers from Apple Corp.) over ATM with no extra work. The idea is to insert an extra layer, called the *LAN emulation client (LEC),* between the datalink (MAC) layer and AAL5, as shown in Figure 15.23 [TELMP 95]. When the LEC layer receives a packet formatted with a MAC address, it first tests to see if the MAC address is unicast or multicast. If it is multicast, the packet is sent to a *broadcast server,* which sends a copy of the packet to every host on the LAN. Otherwise, it checks a local ARP cache to see if it has a translation from the MAC address to an existing switched virtual circuit (SVC). If no SVC exists, the LEC sends an ARP message to a *LAN emulation server (LES)* requesting it to resolve the address. The LES is configured (either manually or otherwise) with the translation from every MAC address on the LAN to ATM addresses. The ARP response to the LEC thus contains an ATM address that the LEC can then use to set up an SVC. (Note that this requires a LANE endpoint to implement ATM signaling.) Thus, the LEC and LES allow arbitrary network-layer protocols to use an ATM network with no modification in their operation. This makes it easy to replace Ethernet or FDDI with ATM at

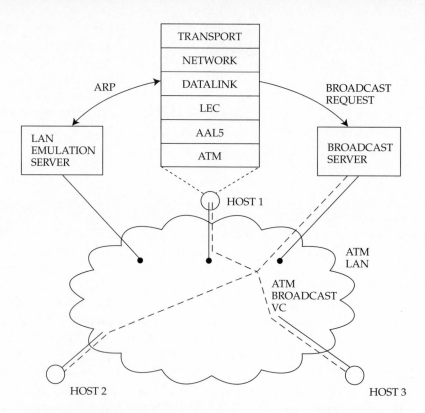

Figure 15.23: ATM LAN emulation (LANE). We insert a LANE client layer (LEC) below the datalink layer. A LANE client translates a MAC address to an ATM address using the LANE server. Packets with multicast MAC addresses are handed to the broadcast server. LANE requires only minor modifications at the endpoints and does not depend on the network-layer protocol.

the LAN level. On the other hand, as with IP-over-ATM, the quality-of-service guarantees available from the ATM network are unused: all traffic is carried as Undefined Bit-Rate. Work on LAN emulation was still in progress as of early 1996, and the final standards were expected later in the year.

15.5.6 Cells in Frame

Although LANE allows easy migration from a legacy LAN to an ATM infrastructure, it requires endpoints to install expensive ATM host adaptor cards.[6] This problem is eliminated with the Cells in Frame (CIF) proposal [Brim 96]. A CIF endpoint reuses existing Ethernet cards (which are cheap and already available on most hosts), in conjunction with a multiplexing device called a CIF-Attachment Device (CIF-AD), to obtain ATM service. A CIF-AD has several Ethernet cards and an ATM card. It shares the cost of the

---

[6]In 1996, a typical Ethernet card cost about $50, and a typical ATM card about $750.

ATM card among several users by converting data between Ethernet encapsulation and ATM encapsulation.

The main idea in CIF is to encapsulate groups of ATM cells in an Ethernet frame between a CIF endpoint and a CIF-AD. A CIF endpoint requires only an Ethernet host adaptor. From the perspective of an ATM protocol stack at the endpoint, the Ethernet host adaptor is made to look exactly like an ATM host adaptor. We first examine a simplified implementation of CIF, assuming that the CIF endpoint communicates using AAL5 frames.

Consider the transmission of an AAL5 frame from a CIF endpoint into an ATM network. The ATM protocol stack creates an AAL5 encapsulated PDU or frame (see Section 15.4.3), optionally leaving the CRC field blank to be filled in by the CIF-AD. A CIF *shim* between the ATM stack and the Ethernet device driver encapsulates the AAL5 frame with a CIF header. The header contains, among other things, the ATM cell header that should be carried by cells corresponding to that EPDU. Thus, the CIF-AD knows the VCI for every Ethernet frame it receives. Since an AAL5 frame can be as large as 64 Kbytes, but an Ethernet frame cannot exceed 1500 bytes, the shim may need to fragment the AAL5 frame into multiple Ethernet frames. The CIF header contains the AAL5 end-of-frame bit to allow frame reassembly. Data checksums on the Ethernet segment are provided only by the Ethernet header and are not part of the CIF header.

At the CIF-AD, Ethernet frames are received by the Ethernet driver and handed to a CIF protocol handler, which reassembles them into an AAL5 frame and hands it to an ATM device driver. This driver, along with the ATM host adaptor card, fragments the frame into ATM cells, attaching the ATM cell header carried in the CIF header. Thus, an AAL5 frame generated by the ATM protocol stack at a CIF endpoint enters the ATM network in the same way it would if the endpoint had an ATM host adaptor.

In the other direction, ATM cells arriving at the host adaptor on a CIF-AD are reassembled by the driver or host adaptor into AAL5 frames. These frames are given to the CIF protocol handler at the CIF-AD, which fragments the AAL5 frame if necessary, adds a CIF header, and hands fragments to the Ethernet device driver. At an endpoint, the shim strips the CIF header, reassembles AAL5 frames if needed, and hands the AAL5 frame to the ATM protocol stack for further processing.

Besides cost, a second advantage of CIF over LANE is that applications at a LANE endpoint cannot request a lower bound on bandwidth or an upper bound on delay from the ATM network. This is a problem if we would like an ATM network to carry voice calls. In contrast, native-ATM applications at a CIF endpoint can obtain an application-to-application quality-of-service guarantee [AKS 96]. However, this requires that the Ethernet connection between a CIF endpoint and the CIF-AD be point-to-point and non-shared, as is the case with Ethernet variants such as 10BaseT.

We have assumed that the CIF-AD reassembles an entire AAL5 frame before handing it to the ATM network. The CIF standard allows this, but to reduce reassembly latency, the CIF-AD can forward an Ethernet frame into the ATM network before it sees the last fragment of the AAL5 frame. In this case, however, if it is responsible for the AAL5 CRC, it must keep track of the partial CRC, inserting the CRC in the AAL5 trailer in the last cell. Symmetrically, the CIF-AD may send a part of an AAL5 frame to an endpoint. In this case, the endpoint cannot be sure of the correctness of the frame until it receives the length and CRC fields in the last cell of the AAL5 frame.

The CIF standard has several details not covered here. For example, a single Ethernet frame is allowed to carry data from many AAL5 frames. CIF also allows AALs other than AAL5. Finally, CIF allows endpoints to discover attachment devices and negotiate services, such as CRC generation, at discovery time. These details can be found in reference [Brim 96].

15.5.7 The holding-time problem

When a host implementing classical IP-over-ATM or LAN emulation gets a packet, it looks up the IP address and checks whether it has an open connection corresponding to that address. If so, it forwards the packet, encapsulating it in AAL5. How long should the host keep the connection open? From the principle of locality, if a packet arrives on a connection, it is likely that more packets will arrive on the same connection. Thus, it makes sense to hold the connection for a while, instead of closing it immediately after sending the packet. This allows future packets to avoid the call-setup latency. On the other hand, if the host has to pay for each second or minute it holds the connection open, keeping an idle connection open wastes money. Thus, the choice of a holding time depends on the expected arrival time of future packets, and the "cost" of delaying packets relative to that of holding an idle connection. Several heuristics for this problem have been studied; one of the best is to maintain an interarrival-time histogram for packets on the connection. With this histogram, we can compute a nearly optimal connection holding time. Details of the problem and its solution can be found in reference [KLPRS 95].

15.6 Summary

This chapter presents an overview of the protocols used in three example networks—telephone networks, the Internet, and ATM networks—and the details of a few selected protocols. We also studied some standard techniques for efficient protocol implementation.

We began with a description of the data and control planes in a typical telephone network. A telephone network provides essentially only the datalink and physical layers in the data plane. We studied datalink-layer framing formats in the plesiochronous and synchronous digital transmission hierarchies. The primary design problem in both hierarchies is in designing a multiplexed framing format that can adapt to small differences in input rates. We also studied the control plane, which uses the SS7 protocol stack for call setup, network management, and network maintenance.

The Internet's workhorse protocol is IP, a network-layer protocol that provides endpoints with the abstraction of an unreliable, best-effort, end-to-end link using the mechanisms of addressing, routing, and fragmentation. We studied IP's services by examining its packets header in great detail. IP works hand-in-hand with ICMP, the Internet Control

Message Protocol, which returns error messages and network status information to endpoints. In the data plane, TCP is layered over IP, and it provides an upper layer with the abstraction of a reliable, best-effort, flow-controlled, end-to-end link. These functions are evident from a detailed analysis of the TCP header. Finally, we studied the HTTP protocol, which is layered over TCP and is the protocol underlying the World Wide Web.

Our third set of protocols is from the ATM world. Here, as in the telephone network, the emphasis is on network- and datalink-layer protocols. The ATM layer provides the abstraction of an end-to-end, unreliable, QoS-enabled virtual channel. It uses fixed-size cells and an associated control-plane protocol for call establishment. In the data plane, several ATM Adaptation Layers provide applications with services such as error detection and segmentation and reassembly.

Although ATM networks are intended to provide a complete end-to-end solution for data services, by necessity, they must interwork with existing IP networks. Unfortunately, many of the design decisions (such as the choice of addressing, routing, and quality-of-service provisions) in IP and ATM networks are incompatible. This has given rise to an entire class of protocols that bridge the gap between IP and ATM. Important among these are classical IP-over-ATM and NHRP, which translate from IP addresses to ATM NSAPs. The MARS protocol allows ATM networks to resolve IP multicast addresses and map IP multicast to ATM multicast. Finally, LANE and CIF allow legacy LAN hosts to migrate to an ATM LAN.

Review questions

1. What is the difference between the data plane and the control plane?
2. What is the digital transmission hierarchy?
3. What is a plesiochronous system?
4. What is justification, and why does a telephone multiplexor need to justify input streams?
5. Why does an ATM network not deal with justification?
6. Why are higher-level SONET stream rates exact multiples of lower-level SONET stream rates?
7. How many rows and columns are there in an OC-1 frame? In an OC-3 frame?
8. What is a synchronous payload envelope in SONET?
9. Why does SONET use pointers in its header to point to a synchronous payload envelope?
10. What are the OPC and DPC fields in an MTP packet used for?
11. What are the two primary services provided by IP?
12. What is the size of the longest IP header?
13. What happens if IP fragments a packet, and one of the packets gets lost?
14. How does path-MTU discovery work?
15. How does traceroute work?
16. What is the largest number of routers that can be recorded in an IP packet when the record-route option is on?

17. Can a source count on receiving ICMP error messages when an error occurs?
18. What is the purpose of a TCP port number?
19. How does TCP window scaling work?
20. Why does TCP require a persist timer?
21. How can HTTP encapsulate an arbitrary set of names?
22. What does an HTTP POST request do?
23. What is a virtual path?
24. What is metasignaling?
25. How does a policer use an ATM CLP bit?
26. How many bytes of the ATM payload does the AAL1 header use?
27. What kind of traffic is expected to use AAL1?
28. What are the Btag and Etag fields in the AAL3/4 header used for?
29. What is the purpose of the MID field in the AAL3/4 header?
30. Why does AAL5 violate layering?
31. Why is AAL5 more efficient than AAL3/4?
32. What is the purpose of the AAL5 pad field?
33. In SSCOP, how does a sender detect a packet loss?
34. What is the key parameter in SSCOP?
35. How do hosts on different LISs on the same ATM network communicate using classical IP-over-ATM?
36. What is the role of a MARS server?
37. How does LAN emulation handle LAN multicast packets?
38. What is the function of a CIF-AD?

Chapter 16

Protocol Implementation

16.1 Introduction

To engineer computer networks, we must understand not only protocols and protocol stacks, but also their implementation in real systems. Although the details of implementing a protocol in a given operating system, such as Unix or MS-DOS, are often system specific, good protocol implementations in all environments share certain common features. In this chapter, we will focus on some standard frameworks for efficient protocol implementation, then discuss some rules of thumb for building efficient implementations. Other guidelines, in a more general context, can be found in Section 6.3.

16.2 Factors affecting protocol stack performance

A protocol stack's performance depends mainly on: (a) the *structure* of the stack, and (b) the cost of certain common OS functions such as context-switching and interrupt-processing [Clark 82]. By "structure," we mean how the functions of the stack, such as error control, flow control, and device management, are partitioned between user space and the kernel space. Experience shows that careless partitioning of functions between user and kernel space causes frequent context switches, which leads to poor performance.

"Structure" also refers to the degree to which an implementation separates the processing carried out by each layer. Combining the processing performed by several layers can considerably improve overall performance, but violates the layering principle (therefore, changes in one layer could require changes in other layers). Unfortunately, this means that an implementor has to make a ". . . delicate trade-off between good structure and good performance" [Clark 82].

The second factor affecting protocol performance is the cost of common OS functions such as process scheduling, memory allocation and management, and interrupt handling. Any protocol implementation must, at some level, use the basic resource-sharing mechanisms provided by the operating system. If these are poorly designed or have poor performance, protocol stack performance will also be poor. For example, consider what happens when a packet arrives for an application waiting for it in user space. The packet first generates an interrupt, invoking the interrupt handler. Suppose the interrupt handler does all the protocol processing and hands the packet to the user. The OS must still do at least a data copy (or a page remap) to get the data into user space, and a context switch from the kernel context to the user context. Measurements in a variety of systems indicate that the interrupt, copy, and context switch overheads are at least as expensive as protocol processing [KP 93]! Thus, protocol performance depends critically on the implementation environment—in particular, on the latency in accessing memory and the memory bandwidth. The implementation environment is platform specific, so despite its importance, in the rest of the chapter we will focus mainly on the effect of protocol *structure* on performance.

16.3   Common protocol stack structures

Many techniques for protocol stack implementation have been explored in the literature. We will outline some standard approaches, referring the reader to research papers for more details.

We categorize techniques for protocol implementation along two orthogonal axes (Table 16.1). The first axis is the way in which protocol functions are partitioned between the application process in user space and in the kernel (a survey of these choices can be found in reference [TNML 93]). The second axis is the choice of interface between protocol layers. Along the first axis, we identify three cases: (a) monolithic implementation in kernel space, (b) monolithic implementation in user space, and (c) per-process implementation in user space. Along the second axis, the three interface strategies are

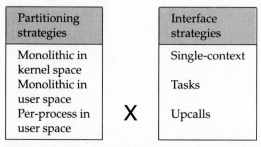

Partitioning strategies		Interface strategies
Monolithic in kernel space		Single-context
Monolithic in user space	X	Tasks
Per-process in user space		Upcalls

Table 16.1: Techniques for protocol implementation lie along two orthogonal axes described in the text.

(a) single-context, (b) tasks, and (c) upcalls. A suitable choice of partitioning and interface strategies generates most of the implementations described in the literature. We will study choices along each axis in the next two subsections.

16.4   Partitioning strategies

The basic question in partitioning protocol functionality is to choose how much functionality should be in (untrusted) user space and how much in (trusted) kernel space. Clearly, user applications belong in user space, and the lowest level of device access (such as the interrupt service routine) belongs in the kernel. However, the remaining services of a protocol stack, such as error control, flow control, and in-sequence delivery, can reside in either user or kernel space. In choosing where to implement a particular service, we have to balance *software engineering considerations* (how hard is it to write, test, and maintain the code?), *customizability* (how easy is it to allow protocols to exploit application characteristics or support application requirements?), *security* (how hard is it for a user to harm another user?), and *performance* (how fast does it go?). The complexity of this multi-way tradeoff is reflected in the wide variety of implementations proposed in the literature. We will study three basic choices in this section.

16.4.1   Monolithic implementation in kernel

The simplest, and most common, implementation choice is to place all but the application layer in the kernel (Figure 16.1). This has the greatest security and potentially the best performance. On the other hand, it is hard to write and debug kernel code, making

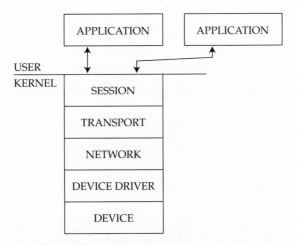

Figure 16.1: Monolithic protocol stack in kernel. Applications in user space share access to the stack in the kernel. The stack is efficient, but hard to customize and maintain.

it hard to customize the stack for each application. This is the approach taken in most Unix-like operating systems, and also non-Unix systems such as OS/2 and Windows NT.

16.4.2 Monolithic implementation in user space

Some flexibility and customizability in developing and maintaining the protocol stack can be achieved by moving all but the lowest layer of functionality to a trusted user-level *server* process (Figure 16.2). This process manages host adaptors either directly or by interacting with a proxy in the kernel. Applications make read and write calls to the server process, instead of to the kernel. This approach is used in the Mach operating system, where the UX process implements the TCP/IP protocol stack. It is also used in Windows 3.1, where the WINSOCK Dynamic Linked Library provides a single access point to the network.

This approach is not only secure, but also desirable from the view of software development. However, its performance can be poor, because every read or write access requires *two* context switches: from the application context to the server context, and from the server context to the kernel. Second, if the CPU scheduler does not give the server process special preference, delays in scheduling the server process harm the performance of every process accessing the network. Third, because the implementation is monolithic, it may be as hard to customize as a monolithic implementation in the kernel. Some flexibility in the implementation can be achieved by partitioning the single monolithic server into a server process per protocol stack, with demultiplexing in the kernel.

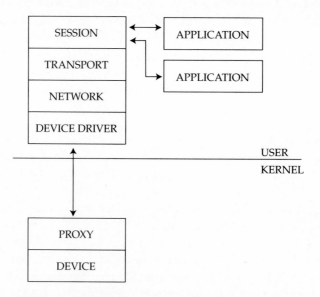

Figure 16.2: Monolithic protocol stack in user space. The move to user space makes the stack easier to maintain and customize. However, the performance is poor, because every data access involves two context switches.

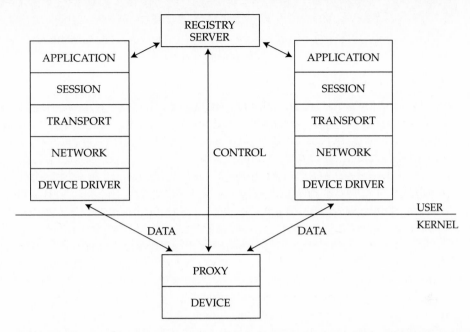

Figure 16.3: Per-application protocol stack. Each application is bound to an instance of the protocol stack (usually in a library). The registry server prevents applications from accessing each other's data. This approach has problems if the application is not multithreaded.

On a packet arrival, a *filter* function decides which user-level server process should get the packet, thus allowing considerable freedom in adding new application-specific protocols. This strategy was used in the *Packet Filter* [MRA 87]. Though it makes the protocol stack much easier to customize, it still has the performance overhead of multiple context switches.

16.4.3 Per-process implementation in user space

We can avoid the problems with associating a server with each protocol stack if the stack is implemented as a library linked to an application (Figure 16.3). This has performance comparable to an in-kernel implementation and the best customizability. Moreover, because the library is in user space, implementation is easy (except for the caveat below). Thus, this satisfies all the criteria except that of security: because the protocol stack library allows any application to access the device, malicious applications can harm others, for example, by deleting their packets from the device queue. We can avoid this using two techniques. First, we can restrict the operations that a library can perform on the device [DPD 94]. Second, we can partition device resources among registered applications, authenticating accesses to each partition [TNML 93, EWLBCD 94, VBBV 95]. This requires a trusted *registry server* that sets up device resources on an application's behalf. However, because this server is not on the data path, we achieve security without giving up on performance [TNML 93].

The per-process library strategy has two further disadvantages. First, since the entire protocol stack is linked to each application, the binary image of an application can be quite large. This can be avoided by using shared libraries. Second, if the application is not multithreaded,[1] protocol semantics may require applications to be partitioned into two processes [EM 95]. For example, TCP allows an application to exit after its last write, and TCP timeouts and retransmissions will ensure that the last write succeeds. However, if we implement TCP as a procedure call linked to an application, then when the application exits, so does TCP. Thus, if the data in the last write is lost and cannot be retransmitted, the implementation violates TCP semantics! We can avoid this by running TCP as a separate thread in the application process, so that even if the thread implementing the application terminates, the TCP thread is still active and able to retransmit packets. If the operating system does not support threads, or the application is not structured to use threads, then we must run TCP as a separate child process that continues even after the termination of its parent. Unfortunately, this introduces context switching and locking overheads, which can prove expensive. Nevertheless, with careful implementation, it has been shown that a user-level implementation has nearly the same performance as a monolithic in-kernel implementation [EM 95].

Are user-space implementations necessarily slower?

Protocol implementation lore says that user-space implementation is always slower and less secure than kernel implementation. This is true when the protocol stack is implemented in a server process, so that each send and receive operation involves two context switches and at least two data copies. Recent work shows that carefully designed user-space implementations are just as fast as in-kernel implementations. Moreover, by linking the protocol stack to an application, we avoid both data copies and context switches (since the application directly writes to the device, it need never enter the kernel!). We also gain in customizability and protocol development cost. Thus, user space implementation, following the pioneering work in references [TNML 93, EM 95, VBBV 95], is likely to be increasingly common in future networks.

16.4.4 Summary

Table 16.2 summarizes the pros and cons of each approach.

---

[1] A "multithreaded" application has multiple threads of execution that share a common address space. This allows some threads to be blocked waiting for I/O while others are active. The process terminates when all the threads become inactive.

Technique	Customizability	Performance	Security	Protocol development cost
In-kernel monolithic	Poor	Good	Good	Expensive
User-space monolithic	Poor	Poor	Good	Reasonable
Per-protocol stack server in user space	Good	Poor	Good	Low
Per-process, per-protocol-stack library	Excellent	Good, with careful design	Good	Low, assuming multithreaded applications

Table 16.2: Comparison of protocol stack partitioning techniques.

16.5   Interface among protocol layers

After partitioning protocol stack functionality using one of the strategies described in the previous section, we have to decide how to interface the layers *within* the protocol stack. The three common techniques for doing so are:

- Single context
- Tasks
- Upcalls

16.5.1   Single context

In this approach, protocol layers share a single uninterrupted thread of execution (Figure 16.4). On a write from an application, the network and transport layers add their protocol headers, and the packet is deposited in a datalink layer buffer awaiting transmission by the card. We must ensure that only one write is in progress at any time by locking access to the stack when a write is in progress. On packet arrival, the device interrupts the datalink layer (in the device driver), which strips the datalink layer header and calls the network layer (either in kernel or user space). This strips the network layer header and calls the transport layer. This, in turn, does transport-layer processing (as discussed in Section 16.6), and queues the packet for a read from the user.

Only one packet is processed at any given time, so shared data structures need not be locked, and code need not be reentrant. Besides, because packets are not copied between layers, implementations following this model are usually quite efficient. This approach also has the least possible latency. However, to ensure that only one packet is being processed at a time, the stack must mask interrupts when it is processing a packet. If the device cannot buffer the packets that arrive while it is waiting for the interrupt to

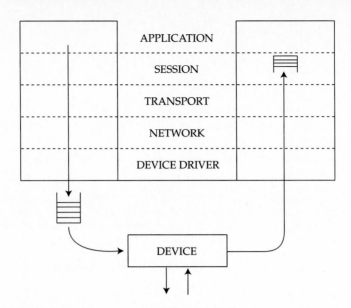

Figure 16.4: Layers implemented as a single context. Writes from the application make their way through the entire stack and are deposited in the device buffer. Similarly, on a receive interrupt, protocol processing occurs in a single context before being deposited in a buffer.

be unmasked, packets may be lost. Moreover, we cannot give some packets priority over others during protocol processing, because there are no preemption points in the execution path.

16.5.2 Tasks

The task model is an innovative approach to interfacing protocol layers that was probably first used in the MIT C-Gateway (Figure 16.5). The idea is to write each layer as a *task*, which is just a procedure called from a central *task scheduler* with a pointer to a data buffer containing a packet. Each task is therefore associated with a single packet that it processes before returning from the function call. Tasks can continue packet processing by calling another task, or can ask to reschedule themselves after a timeout. For example, when a user wants to send data, the write system call simply copies the user's packet into the shared buffer and schedules a transport-layer send task. When the task scheduler calls this task, it does send-side transport layer processing and schedules a network layer task for that packet, if flow control allows it. Otherwise, it simply returns: it will be scheduled by the transport-layer receive task when the flow-control window opens because of an acknowledgment. Similarly, the network-layer send task picks up the packet and adds a network-layer header, scheduling a datalink-layer send task to be executed later.

Because each task does a limited amount of work, the task scheduler has the freedom to schedule high-priority tasks without waiting too long for a lower-priority task to com-

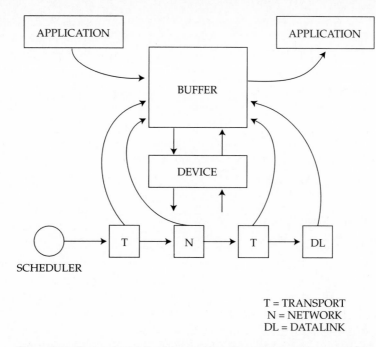

T = TRANSPORT
N = NETWORK
DL = DATALINK

Figure 16.5: Protocol stack implementation using tasks. A task is a procedure call from a task scheduler, which is handed a pointer to a packet in a shared buffer and carries out protocol actions corresponding to one layer. The task scheduler can prioritize among tasks and provides a single execution context.

plete [AKS 96]. Note that at any time, more than one packet may be present in the protocol stack, and that each packet is shepherded though the stack by a sequence of tasks that mutually schedule each other.

A task-based implementation has several advantages. First, it allows the stack to provide quality-of-service guarantees while carrying out protocol processing, because every task is individually scheduled by a single task scheduler. For example, a high-priority packet would reach user space much more rapidly than a lower-priority packet. Second, tasks can be written and debugged in isolation. Third, we can add new protocols simply by adding more tasks to the pool of available tasks. Fourth, the scheduler can guarantee fair access to CPU and memory, and it provides a single point of management and control. Fifth, in the task model, there is a single buffer that holds both incoming and outgoing packets. Tasks simply pass each other pointers to packets in this buffer. This eliminates all data copies (except, perhaps, to copy packets to and from the physical device). Finally, because tasks are procedure calls, calling a task is as fast as a procedure call.

The main problem with the task model is that all tasks must cooperate. We cannot preempt a malicious or misbehaved task, so it can hold up the working of the entire stack. However, this is not a problem in most implementations, where adding a task to the stack would probably require administrative approval. A second problem is that tasks must be nonblocking. A task that might block on some operation must reschedule itself instead of waiting for the operation to complete. Since we can easily implement timers within the task scheduler, this does not pose a problem in practice. Finally, a task-based approach has a higher latency than the single-context model, because a scheduler may need to intervene several times before a packet makes its way through the entire stack. This problem can be alleviated to some extent by defining "super-tasks" that do the same processing as in the single-context model. We can assign low-latency packets to these super-tasks, which provide low latency, while higher-latency packets can be handled by the regular set of tasks.

16.5.3   Upcall architecture

The key idea in an upcall architecture is to associate a thread per packet. When an application makes a write call or a packet arrives at the host interface, the protocol stack spawns a new thread and associates it with the packet (Figure 16.6). The thread is responsible for *all* the layers of protocol processing. Higher-priority packets can be handled by giving higher priority to the thread associated with them.

To implement the upcall architecture, each layer registers send and receive *entry points* with the layer below it. When a layer wants to hand a packet to, or receive a packet from, the higher layer, it makes a procedure call (an *upcall*) on the preregistered entry point [Clark 85, HP 91]. Because the procedure calls execute in the same context as the caller, a single task shepherds a packet through the stack.

For example, consider the set of actions on the receive side. When an endpoint boots up, the network layer tells the datalink layer which network-layer function to call when a packet arrives. The transport layer similarly registers an entry point with the network layer. When a packet arrives at the datalink layer, the kernel spawns a new thread that initially executes datalink-layer functionality. To invoke the network layer, the thread simply executes the associated upcall. This, in turn, eventually calls the transport-layer function. Thus, the sequence of upcalls allows the thread to carry the packet through the protocol stack. Note that upcalls allow us to avoid context switches in moving from layer to layer.

The advantage of the upcall model is that, as in the task model, no data is copied between layers. Moreover, as in the task model, multiple sends and receives can be active simultaneously. The problem with the upcall approach is that if two threads share a common resource, they must use locks to prevent inconsistent accesses. In contrast, because all tasks execute in the same context (the context of the task scheduler), they do not need locks on shared data structures. Second, the upcall architecture makes it hard to add new protocols to the stack. To add a new protocol layer, not only must the layer register a new entry point with its lower layer, but every existing upper layer must also register an entry point with the new protocol (Figure 16.7). In contrast, with the task model, adding new protocols is easier, because existing layers do not need to explicitly register entry points with the new protocol.

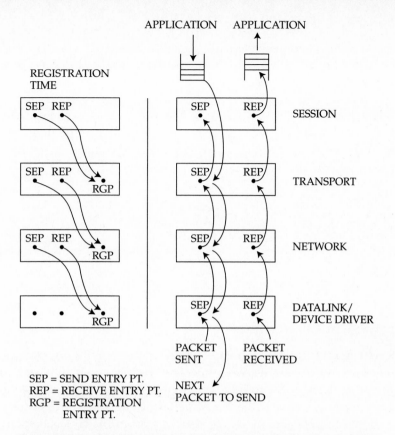

Figure 16.6: Implementing a protocol stack using upcalls. During registration, each layer registers its send and receive entry points with a lower layer's registration entry point. When a packet has been sent, the upcall chain is used to retrieve the next packet. When a packet is received, the upcall chain processes the packet and deposits it in the application buffer.

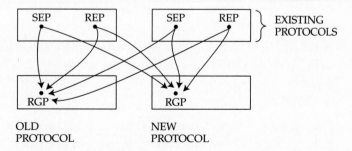

Figure 16.7: Problem with including a new protocol layer with an upcall architecture. We need to register the entry points of every upper layer with the new protocol layer.

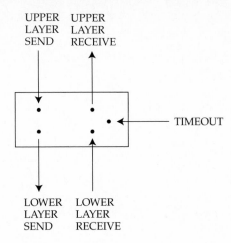

Figure 16.8: Entry points to a protocol layer. A protocol layer usually supports at least five entry points.

16.6 Protocol implementation

We now move from discussing the implementation of the entire stack, and the interfaces between protocols, to describing how to implement a single layer in the stack. Most network protocols have the five interfaces shown in Figure 16.8. These interfaces correspond to *asynchronous* events, in the sense that they can happen at any time. A good framework for protocol implementation is to structure protocol code as responses to each of these events. As an example, let us consider the work done to handle each of the five events in a transport layer protocol, such as TCP or SSCOP:

- *Upper-layer send:* The normal action on a write from the upper layer is to add a protocol header or trailer for error control (such as a sequence number and a checksum) and forward the packet to the lower layer. The transport layer may not be able to forward a packet immediately if, for example, the flow control window does not permit it. Therefore, it must buffer such packets, releasing them later.

- *Upper-layer receive:* On an upper-layer read, the transport layer delivers any data received from the network layer. If the transport layer supports in-sequence delivery, it may not be able to deliver packets in its buffers if they are out of sequence.

- *Lower-layer send:* This corresponds to a request for data from the network layer. If the transport layer has data to send, and open or closed-loop flow control permits, it appends protocol headers or trailers for error-control and hands it to the network layer. If the transport layer has packets from several connections awaiting service, it must schedule access to the network layer using one of the disciplines discussed in Section 9.4. If the transport layer supports reliable service, it also starts a timer (see Section 12.4.6).

- *Lower-layer receive:* The lower (network) layer writes to the transport layer when it receives a packet from the network interface. The transport layer must process the incoming packet, which could be either a data packet or an acknowledgment (such as a STAT in SSCOP).

    If it is a data packet, the transport layer checks for errors such as corrupted data or a gap in the receive sequence space. The packet may need to be acknowledged, in which case the acknowledgment must be added to one of the queues waiting for a lower-layer read. If the packet is uncorrupted, it is placed in a queue awaiting an upper-layer read.

    If it is an acknowledgment packet, the transport layer needs to adjust its flow-control window (perhaps it has increased). It can discard buffers holding packets that it has delivered. The acknowledgment may also trigger a fast retransmission (see Section 12.4.7).

- *Timeout:* A timeout is usually associated with an identifier that allows the transport layer to determine who set the timer, and thus what actions to take. For example, if the timer was set at the time of sending a packet, then on a timeout the appropriate packet is retransmitted. Similarly, if the timer was a TCP-style persist timer, on a timeout the transport layer sends a 1-byte probe to see if its window changed.

The point of this example is that all the actions of a transport layer or, usually, any protocol layer can conveniently be structured as responses to one of the five basic asynchronous actions. It is a good idea, when implementing a protocol, to classify all protocol actions according to the events that invoke them.

16.7   Some rules of thumb

In this section, we will study some rules for building high-performance protocol implementations (a good reference for more details is [PH 95]). Let us start with some simple arithmetic. If we want to build a protocol stack that can send 500-byte packets with a throughput of 10 Kbps, we need to send a packet every 400 ms; for 100 Kbps, every 40 ms; for 1 Mbps, every 4 ms; and for 100 Mbps, every 40 μs. At higher speeds, we have very little time to deal with operating-system and protocol-processing overheads. To achieve higher and higher performance, we must take greater care to avoid inefficiencies in protocol implementation. To understand this point clearly, consider the cost of some common operations in a typical endpoint, such as a 66-MHz Intel 486 microprocessor running the Free BSD operating system, again assuming 500-byte packets (see [KP 93] for costs on a DECstation platform):

User-to-kernel context switch	~40 μs
Copying the packet	~25 μs

Checksum in software	~40 μs
Scheduling delays	~150 μs (depends on workload)
Interrupt handling	~10–50 μs (depends on the bus)
Protocol processing	~15–100 μs (depends on protocol complexity)

To send a packet, we need at least one context switch, one copy, and one pass through the protocol-processing software. This requires at least 80 μs, immediately limiting us to a throughput of around 50 Mbps! If the protocol stack wastes any time at all, we cannot meet even this target. How can we optimize an implementation to squeeze out every ounce of performance from the protocol stack? Although each implementation environment lends itself to its own set of cunning optimizations,[2] some of these are common to all environments and are discussed next.

Optimize for the common case

This is probably one of the soundest rules in system design [Clark 82, WM 87]. The idea is to measure a system and identify common actions, then make sure that the common case takes the least possible time. For example, suppose measurements indicate that getting a kernel buffer using the `malloc()` system call takes 20 μs. Since we must make this call for every packet transmission and receipt, we can save time by preallocating kernel buffers that are separately managed by a customized memory manager. When properly executed, this trick can reduce memory allocation time to a few microseconds.

When we implement network protocols, the common case is error-free data flow with in-sequence generation and receipt of packets [CJRS 89]. By optimizing protocols for this case, we can gain substantial improvements in performance—for example, by precomputing send and receive headers.

Be aware of bottlenecks

In Chapter 6, we studied the fundamental resource constraints and some trade-off techniques. A good technique for system design is to ask the question "What is the bottleneck? How can I trade off a nonbottlenecked resource to ease the bottleneck?" As we saw in Chapter 6, by achieving a balanced pipeline, we can maximize performance.

Fine-tune inner loops

Often a small part of the code contributes to most of the overhead (the innermost loop of the program is the most common candidate). Spend the most effort in getting this tuned to run fast. The rest of the system does not matter as much. Perhaps the inner loop can be unrolled or recoded in assembly language. Every instruction counts!

Choose good data structures

The choice of a data structure can dramatically affect performance [Clark 82]. It is usually a good idea to take special care in designing data structures to store headers, buffers, and

---

[2]See reference [Mogul 93] for an excellent description of Internet-specific optimizations.

timers. For example, a data structure holding a header should allow easy access to all the fields in the header. It should also allow the header to be easily extended (by a lower layer) or trimmed (by an upper layer). The buffer data structure should allow buffers to be shared by multiple entities, with copy-on-write (a copy of the buffer is made only when an entity writes on it). The timer data structure should allow timers to be set and cleared quickly. Detecting that a timeout has occurred should be easy. A good data structure for a timer is a *hashed timing wheel,* which is a variant of the *calendar queue* data structure described in Section 9.3.2 [VL 87, CV 95].

Beware of touching data!

One of the worst mistakes in implementing a protocol is to copy a packet more times than strictly necessary. Moreover, an implementor should make every effort to avoid touching data bytes more than once. With careful design, unavoidable data-touching overheads can be combined, perhaps at the expense of layering. A good example is to checksum a packet as it is copied into or out of the protocol stack. Because both the copy and the checksum touch every data byte, combining them in the same loop saves much time (although it may violate layering) [CT 90].

Minimize packets sent

Packet reception and, to a lesser extent, packet transmission cost network and endpoint resources. Thus, an implementor should try to minimize the number of packets sent. One useful technique is to *piggyback* information on packets that are already being sent to a particular destination. For example, on a duplex connection, the receiver can piggyback acknowledgments in data packets being transferred in the reverse direction. Another example of waste of network resources is in HTTP, which opens a new TCP connection for each embedded file (such as a picture). Since each TCP connection costs at least three packets in overhead (for the SYN, SYN-ACK, and FIN packets), HTTP can be substantially improved by retrieving multiple images over a single TCP connection [Mogul 95]. (This also allows the flow control window to grow beyond one or two packets, improving connection efficiency.)

Send the largest packets possible

The larger the packet, the smaller the overhead wasted on headers. Thus, an application that wants to be efficient should send the largest packets it can. Of course, it may be constrained by the largest packet size that a protocol (such as IP) or a link technology (such as Ethernet) can accept. Nevertheless, within these constraints, large packets are more efficient than small ones.

Cache hints

Caches exploit locality (see Section 6.3). Thus, if some actions seem to have locality, caching information about them can often improve performance. For example, measurements indicate that a protocol control block, if recently used, is very likely to be used again in the near future. By caching recently used protocol control blocks, an endpoint can save the time spent in searching for the control.

Use hardware when possible

In many situations, it is worth developing custom hardware to speed up common, computing-intensive operations. For example, many modern host-adaptor boards compute the TCP checksum in hardware, so that the software portion of TCP never needs to touch data bytes at all. This use of hardware substantially speeds up performance. Modern programmable hardware, such as field-programmable gate arrays, offers high computational speed with much of the flexibility of software.

Exploit application properties

When possible, exploit application features to make clever trade-offs. For example, the most common use of HTTP is to retrieve a Web page, then follow one of the links on the page. If we want to reduce the latency in following this link, we can start retrieving all the links on the page even before the user clicks on anything. This way, if some link is followed, the data is already there. This technique trades off bandwidth for reduced delay (and is commonly called *prefetch*).

To sum up, high-performance protocol implementations require us to intelligently use the entire available capacity of the underlying hardware. We can do so by using one of the techniques described in this section.

16.8 Summary

In this chapter, we surveyed some approaches for protocol implementation. We essentially have to solve three problems: how to partition the stack between the user and kernel space, how to implement the interfaces between the layers, and how to implement each individual layer. We studied several alternatives for each approach, concluding that a user-space implementation with a task-based interface between layers seems to be the best choice in terms of software development, customizability, and security.

Review questions

1. What are the two factors influencing the performance of a protocol stack?
2. What are the three common partitioning strategies?
3. What are the three common interface strategies?
4. What are the problems with a monolithic implementation in kernel space?
5. What is the main drawback of a monolithic implementation in user space?
6. What is the purpose of a registry server?
7. Can some packets be given priority over others when layers are implemented in a single context?
8. What does a task scheduler do?
9. In an upcall architecture, what is the role of a thread?
10. What are the five actions to which a protocol layer must respond?

References

References for Chapter 1: Atoms, Bits, and Networks

[BK 95] D. Burstein and D. Kline. Road Warriors: Dreams and Nightmares along the Information Highway. *Dutton,* 1995.

> A fascinating introduction to the realities of the digital revolution. The revolution will bring not only technological opportunities, but jarring societal changes that the authors think ought to be the subject of conscious social policy.

[Penzias 89] A. A. Penzias. Ideas and Information: Managing in a High-Tech World. *W.W. Norton,* 1989.

> Penzias, formerly Vice President of Bell Labs, talks informally about the impact of computers and communications on corporations and society. An interesting look at how computers affect the nuts-and-bolts operation of corporations.

[Negroponte 95] N. Negroponte. Being Digital. *Alfred A. Knopf,* 1995.

> A visionary exploration of what it means to live in a digital world. Negroponte is a sage of the digital era, and every page of this book is insightful.

References for Chapter 2: The Telephone Network: Concepts, History, and Challenges

[Bellamy 91] J. Bellamy. Digital Telephony, Second Edition. *John Wiley and Sons,* 1991.

> A lucid description of telephone network design and operation, with details on some recent advances such as SONET.

[Blahut 90] R. E. Blahut. Digital Transmission of Information. *Addison-Wesley,* 1990.

> Standard reference on error coding.

[Boettinger 77] H. M. Boettinger. Telephone Book: Bell, Watson, Vail and American Life, 1876–1976. *Riverwood,* 1977.

> A fascinating coffee-table book with lots of pictures of the telephone network in its early days. A great way to spend a rainy day!

[BS 82] Bell Telephone Laboratories. Engineering and Operations in the Bell System. *Bell Telephone Laboratories*, 1982.

> Prepared in anticipation of divestiture by Members of the Technical Staff of the undivided Bell Laboratories, this is an exhaustive description of *everything* in the Bell System, as it existed in 1980. It is the ultimate introduction to the telephone system.

[Noll 86] A. M. Noll. Introduction to Telephones and Telephone Systems. *Artech House*, 1986.

> Crisp and clear high-level introduction to telephone networks.

[PN 90] J. R. Pierce and A. M. Noll, Signals: The Science of Telecommunications. *Scientific American Library*, 1990.

> A fascinating introduction to basic concepts in telecommunications, including coding, modulation, switching, and multiplexing.

References for Chapter 3: The Internet: Concepts, History, and Challenges

[BK 95] D. Burstein and D. Kline. Road Warriors: Dreams and Nightmares along the Information Highway. *Dutton*, 1995.

> A fascinating introduction to the realities of the digital revolution. The revolution will bring not only technological opportunities, but jarring societal changes that the authors think ought to be the subject of conscious social policy.

[Clark 88] D. D. Clark. The Design Philosophy of the DARPA Internet Protocols. *Proceedings of ACM SIGCOMM '88*, August 1988, pp. 106–114.

> Describes the reasoning behind the design of TCP and IP. Anecdotes about the early days.

[LR 93] D. C. Lynch and M. T. Rose (eds.). Internet System Handbook. *Addison-Wesley*, 1993.

> Comprehensive, though slightly dated, outline of Internet technology. Excellent surveys on routing, performance tuning, and network management, and an historical overview.

[MV 95] H. MacKie-Mason and H. R. Varian. Pricing Congestible Network Resources. *IEEE Journal on Selected Areas in Communication*, Vol. 13, No. 7, September 1995, pp. 1141–1149.

> Shows the impact of flat-rate and congestion pricing on network behavior.

[SRC 84] J. H. Saltzer, D. P. Reed, and D. D. Clark. End-to-End Arguments in System Design. *ACM Transactions on Computer Systems*, Vol. 2, No. 4, November 1984, pp. 277–288.

> Classic paper describing the need for the "end-to-end principle" and giving examples of its application.

[Zimmerman 80] H. Zimmerman. OSI Reference Model—The ISO Model of Architecture for Open Systems Interconnection. *IEEE Transactions on Communications*, Vol. 28, No. 4, April 1980, pp. 425–432.

   Formal introduction to concepts of ISO protocol layering.

References for Chapter 4: ATM Networks: Concepts, History, and Challenges

[Fraser 74] A. G. Fraser. Spider—An Experimental Data Communications System. *Proceedings of IEEE Conference on Communications,* June 1974.

   Describes an early ATDM system that uses virtual circuits and fixed-size cells.

[Fraser 83] A. G. Fraser. Towards a Universal Data Transport System. *IEEE Journal on Selected Areas in Communication,* Vol. 1, No. 5, November 1983.

   Describes Datakit, a follow-on to Spider that had much better error and flow control.

[Fraser 93] A. G. Fraser. Early Experiments with Asynchronous Time Division Networks. *IEEE Network,* January 1993, pp. 12–26.

   A survey of early work, with historical anecdotes.

[HTK 64] T. Hasegawa, Y. Tezuka, and Y. Kasahara. Digital Data Dynamic Transmission Systems. *IEEE Transactions on Communication Technology,* 1964.

   Early paper on asynchronous time-division multiplexing.

[KTNH 61] Y. Kasahara, Y. Tezuka, S. Nakanishi, and T. Hasegawa. On an Asynchronous Time Multiplexing Communication System. *Joint Convention Record Institutes Related with Electrical Engineering,* Kansai Branch, Pt. 19, October 1961, pp. 292 (in Japanese).

   Early paper describing the concept of packet headers for efficient use of a transmission link.

[Marcus 69] M. G. Marcus. The Design and Analysis of a New Type of Time-Division Switching System. *M.Sc. Thesis,* MIT, June 1969.

   An early ATM switch design.

[Stallings 88] W. Stallings. Data and Computer Communication, Second Edition. *Macmillan,* 1988.

   Standard textbook on computer networking.

References for Chapter 5: Protocol Layering

[Clark 82] D. D. Clark. Modularity and Efficiency in Protocol Implementation. *RFC 817,* July 1982.

   Classic reference on protocol implementation strategies.

[DZ 83] J. Day and H. Zimmerman. The OSI Reference Model. *Proceedings of the IEEE,* Vol. 71, No. 12, December 1983.

      Outline of the OSI reference model.

[EC 83] W. Emmons and H. Chandler. OSI Session Layer Services and Protocols. *Proceedings of the IEEE,* Vol. 71, No. 12, December 1983.

[Stallings 88] W. Stallings. Data and Computer Communication, Second Edition. *Macmillan,* 1988.

      Standard textbook on computer networking.

[Zimmerman 80] H. Zimmerman. OSI Reference Model—The ISO Model of Architecture for Open Systems Interconnection. *IEEE Transactions on Communications,* Vol. 28, No. 4, April 1980, pp. 425–432.

      Formal introduction to concepts of ISO protocol layering.

References for Chapter 6: System Design

[Ferrari 78] D. Ferrari. Computer Systems Performance Evaluation. *Prentice Hall,* 1978.

      Classic text on performance evaluation.

[FJMZL 95] S. Floyd, V. Jacobson, S. McCanne, L. Zhang, and C. Liu. A Reliable Multicast Framework for Lightweight Session and Application Level Framing. *Proceedings of ACM SIGCOMM '95,* September 1995.

      Describes several uses of randomization for scalable reliable multicast.

[Jain 91] R. Jain. The Art of Computer Systems Performance Analysis: Techniques for Experimental Design, Measurement, Simulation, and Modeling. *Wiley,* 1991.

[Kaplan 92] A. E. Kaplan. A History of the COSNIX Operating System: Assembly Language Unix 1971 to July 1991. *USENIX Winter 1992 Technical Conference,* San Francisco, January 1992, pp. 429–434.

      A blow-by-blow account of how an early Unix system was tuned to reduce response time for interactive jobs, while allowing access to large disk-resident databases.

[PH 95] D. Patterson and J. Hennesey. Computer Organization and Design: The Hardware/Software Interface. *Morgan Kaufman,* 1995.

      Standard introductory text on computer architecture.

[SG 94] A. Silberschatz and P. Galvin. Operating Systems Concepts, Fourth Edition. *Addison-Wesley,* 1994.

      Standard introductory text on operating systems.

[Tanenbaum 92] A. Tanenbaum. Modern Operating Systems. *Prentice Hall,* 1992.

      Standard introductory text on operating systems.

References for Chapter 7: Multiple Access

[Abramson 70] N. Abramson. The ALOHA System—Another Alternative for Computer Commmunications. *Proceedings of Fall Joint Computer Conference,* 1970.
> The original description of the influential ALOHA protocol.

[Abramson 94] N. Abramson. Multiple Access in Wireless Digital Networks. *Proceedings of the IEEE,* Vol. 82, No. 9, September 1994.
> Argues that CDMA requires only a single code and shows how to extend ALOHA to obtain the same benefits as CDMA.

[AnyLAN FAQ 96] AnyLAN FAQ. `http://www.io.com/~richardr/vg/`, 1996.
> Introduction to 100VG AnyLAN, with links to products and other related technologies.

[AnyLAN 96] AnyLAN tutorial. `http://www.iol.unh.edu/training/vganylan/teach/intro.html`, 1996.

[BDSZ 94] V. Bhargavan, A. Demers, S. Shenker, and L. Zhang. MACAW: A Media Access Protocol for Wireless LANs. *Proceedings of ACM SIGCOMM '94,* London, September 1994.
> Discusses problems with MACA, and some solutions.

[Binder 75] R. Binder. A Dynamic Packet Switching System for Satellite Broadcast Channels. *Proceedings of the ICC,* 1975.
> Describes a variant of R-ALOHA.

[Cox 96] D. Cox. Wireless Communication Networks. *Tutorial Notes, IEEE INFOCOM '96,* March 1996.
> A practitioner's view of wireless communication.

[CRWOH 73] W. Crowther, R. Rettberg, D. Walden, S. Orenstein, and F. Heart. A System for Broadcast Communication: Reservation ALOHA. *Proceedings of the Sixth Hawaii International System Science Conference,* 1973.
> Early description of Reservation ALOHA.

[DN 96] A. DeSimone and S. Nanda. Wireless Data: Systems, Standards, Services. *Journal of Wireless Networks,* Vol. 1, February 1996, special issue on recent advances in wireless networking technology.
> Tutorial on IEEE 802.11, CDPD, and reliable transport over wireless networks.

[Ethernet FAQ 96] Ethernet FAQ. `http://toolbox.rutgers.edu/~qman/techsupport/ethernetfaq.html`, 1996.

[FAG 95] David D. Falconer, F. Adachi, and B. Gudmundson. Time Division Multiple Access Methods for Wireless Personal Communications. *IEEE Communications Magazine,* January 1995, pp. 50–57.
> Tutorial on TDMA.

[FDDI FAQ 96] FDDI FAQ. `http://sholeh.nswc.navy.mil/x3t12/FDDIFAQ.html`, 1996.
    Frequently asked questions about FDDI (and their answers).

[Hayes 84] J. F. Hayes. Modeling and Analysis of Computer Communications Networks. *Plenum Publishing Corporation*, 1984.

[Jain 94] R. Jain. FDDI Handbook: High-Speed Networking Using Fiber and Other Media. *Addison-Wesley*, 1994.

[Johnson 96] H.W. Johnson. Fast Ethernet—Dawn of a New Network. *Prentice Hall*, 1996.

[Karn 90] P. Karn. MACA—A New Channel Access Method for Packet Radio. *Proceedings of ARRL/CRRL Amateur Radio 9th Computer Networking Conference*, September 1990.
    Insightful description of MACA.

[Kleinrock 75] L. Kleinrock. Queueing Systems, Vol. 1 and Vol. 2. *Wiley-Interscience*, 1975.
    Classic textbook on queueing theory.

[Lam 80] S. S. Lam. Packet Broadcast Networks—A Performance Analysis of the R-ALOHA Protocol. *IEEE Transactions on Computers*, July 1980.

[MB 76] R. Metcalfe and D. R. Boggs. Ethernet: Distributed Packet Switching for Local Computer Networks. *Communications of the ACM*, July 1976.
    Classic paper describing Ethernet design and implementation.

[Metricom 96] Metricom Ricochet Home Page. `http://www.metricom.com/ricochet/product.html`, 1996.
    Describes the Metricom packet-radio product.

[PF 94] V. Paxson and S. Floyd. Wide-Area Traffic: The Failure of Poisson Modeling. *Proceedings of ACM SIGCOMM '94*, London, September 1994.
    Uses measurements to claim that Poisson models do not adequately describe real traffic.

[PGH 95] J. E. Padgett, C. G. Gunther, and T. Hattori. Overview of Wireless Personal Communications. *IEEE Communications Magazine*, January 1995.

[PL 95] K. Pahlavan and A. H. Levesque. Wireless Information Networks. *John Wiley and Sons*, New York, 1995.
    Textbook devoted to wireless communication networks. Detailed description and a solid mathematical approach.

[Roberts 75] L. Roberts. ALOHA Packet System with and without Slots and Capture. *Computer Communication Review*, April 1975.
    Describes Roberts's scheme for R-ALOHA.

[Sklar 88] B. Sklar. Digital Communications—Principles and Applications. *Prentice Hall*, 1988.

[Stallings 88] W. Stallings. Data and Computer Communications, Second Edition. *Macmillan Publishing*, 1988.
>   Textbook on data communications.

[Switched Ethernet FAQ 96] `http://www.xedia.com/FAQ.html`, 1996.

[TK 75] F. A. Tobagi and L. Kleinrock. Packet Switching in Radio Channels, Part II: The Hidden-Terminal Problem in Carrier Sense Multiple Access and the Busy-Tone Solution. *IEEE Transactions on Communication*, Vol. 23, 1975, pp. 1417–1453.
>   Describes need for BTMA, the solution, and its analysis.

[Viterbi 95] A. J. Viterbi. CDMA: Principles of Spread Spectrum Communication. *Addison-Wesley*, 1995.
>   CDMA, as described by one of its inventors and a practitioner.

References for Chapter 8: Switching

[AD 89] H. Ahmadi and W. E. Denzel. A Survey of Modern High-Performance Switching Techniques. *IEEE Journal on Selected Areas in Communication*, Vol. 7, No. 9, September 1989, pp. 1091–1103.
>   An excellent survey of third-generation switching fabrics.

[AOST 93] T. E. Anderson, S. S. Owicki, J. B. Saxe, and C. P. Thacker. High Speed Switch Scheduling for Local Area Networks. *ACM Transactions on Computer Systems*, Vol. 11, No. 4, November 1993, pp. 319–352.
>   Describes the Parallel Iterated Match algorithm for arbitration in input-queued switches.

[Batcher 68] K. E. Batcher. Sorting Networks and Their Application. *Proceedings of the Spring Joint Computer Conference*, AFIPS, 1968, pp. 307–314.
>   Classic paper on sorting and merging networks.

[Bellamy 91] J. Bellamy. Digital Telephony. *John Wiley and Sons*, 1991.
>   Excellent introduction to telephony.

[Clos 53] C. Clos. A Study of Non-Blocking Switching Networks. *Bell System Technical Journal*, Vol. 32, No. 3, March 1953, pp. 406–424.
>   Early paper on conditions that a nonblocking circuit switch should satisfy.

[CT 92] F. M. Chiussi and F. A. Tobagi. A Hybrid Shared-Memory/Space-Division Architecture for Large Fast Packet Switches. *Proceedings of SUPERCOMM ICC'92*, June 1992.
>   A critique of problems with Banyan switches, and a proposal for a new switch fabric.

[DJ 81] D. M. Dias and J. R. Jump. Analysis and Simulation of Buffered Delta Networks. *IEEE Transactions on Computers*, Vol. 30, No. 10, October 1981, pp. 273–282.
>   Proposes and analyzes variants of Banyan networks where switching fabric elements have buffers.

[DLV 89] J. J. Deegan, G. W. R. Luderer, and A. K. Vaidya. Fast Packet Technology for Future Switches. *AT&T Technical Journal,* March–April 1989, pp. 36–50.

> A survey of packet-switching technology.

[Duncanson 95] J. Duncanson. The Technology of Inverse Multiplexing. *Available from* http://www.ascend.com.au/techdocs/articles/imux/imux.html, 1995.

[Fraser 83] A. G. Fraser. Towards a Universal Data Transport System. *IEEE Journal on Selected Areas in Communication,* Vol. 1, No. 5, November 1983, pp. 803–816.

> Describes the Datakit network, and in particular, the design of the second-generation Datakit switch.

[GCM 87] I. S. Gopal, I. Cidon, and H. Meleis. Paris: An Approach to Integrated Private Networks. *Proceedings of ICC '87,* June 1987, pp. 764–773.

> Describes the PARIS ring-based second-generation packet switch.

[GHMSL 91] J. N. Giacopelli, J. J. Hickey, W. S. Marcus, W. D. Sincoskie, and M. Littlewood. Sunshine: A High-Performance Self-Routing Broadband Packet Switch Architecture. *IEEE Journal on Selected Areas in Communication,* Vol. 9, No. 8, October 1991, pp. 1289–1298.

> Overview of the Sunshine Batcher-Banyan switch.

[GL 73] L. R. Goke and G. J. Lipovski. Banyan Networks for Partitioning Multiprocessor Systems. *Proceedings of the 1st Annual International Symposium on Computer Architecture,* December 1973, pp. 21–28.

> The paper that first described Banyan switching fabrics.

[HA 87] J. Y. Hui and E. A. Arthurs. A Broadband Packet Switch for Integrated Transport. *IEEE Journal on Selected Areas in Communication,* Vol. 5, October 1987, pp. 1264–1273.

> Proposes a scheme to avoid contention in Banyan switches by preceding a packet by a probe that determines whether a collision is possible.

[HK 84] A. K. Huang and S. Knauer. Starlite: A Wideband Digital Switch. *Proceedings of GLOBECOM '84,* Atlanta, December 1984, pp. 121–125.

> Describes an early Batcher–Banyan switch with recirculation.

[HK 88] M. G. Hluchyj and M. J. Karol. Queueing in Space-Division Packet Switching. *Proceedings of IEEE INFOCOM '88,* New Orleans, March 1988, pp. 334–343.

> A study of buffer-placement strategies in third-generation switches.

[Jacob 90] A. R. Jacob. A Survey of Fast Packet Switches. *ACM SIGCOMM Computer Communication Review,* Vol. 20, No. 1, January 1990, pp. 54–64.

> A survey of third-generation switches.

[Jenq 83] Y. C. Jenq. Performance Analysis of a Packet Switch Based on a Single-Buffered Banyan Network. *IEEE Journal on Selected Areas in Communication,* Vol. 1, December 1983, pp. 1014–1021.

> Analyzes the theoretical limits on the performance of Banyan switches with buffers in switching-fabric elements.

[Kanakia 94] H. Kanakia. Datapath Switch. *AT&T Bell Laboratories Internal Technical Memorandum,* 1994.
> Describes the shared-memory Datapath switch-on-a-chip.

[KHM 87] M. J. Karol, M. G. Hluchyj, and S. P. Morgan. Input versus Output Queueing on a Space-Division Switch, *IEEE Transactions on Communications,* December 1987, pp. 1347–1356.
> Classic paper proving that if traffic is uniformly distributed to all output ports, a single shared queue at the input leads to head-of-line blocking and a maximum achievable throughput of 58%.

[Lee 88] T. T. Lee. Nonblocking Copy Networks for Multicast Packet Switching. *IEEE Journal on Selected Areas in Communications,* Vol. 9, No. 9, December 1988, pp. 1455–1467.
> Describes copy networks used in multicast switches.

[LPR 96] C. Lund, S. Phillips, and N. Reingold. Fair Prioritized Scheduling in an Input-Buffered Switch. *Proceedings of Broadband '96,* Montreal, April 1996.
> Describes a modification to the parallel iterated matching algorithm in input-queued switches that allows an input-queued switch to emulate a multipriority round-robin discipline at an output-queued switch.

[Marcus 69] M. G. Marcus. The Design and Analysis of a New Type of Time-Division Switching System. *M.Sc. Thesis,* MIT, June 1969.
> An early ATM switch design that introduces buffers at crosspoints.

[MAW 96] N. McKeown, V. Anantharam, and J. Walrand. Achieving 100% Throughput in an Input-Queued Switch. *Proceedings of IEEE INFOCOM'96,* San Francisco, March 1996.
> A theoretical analysis of arbitration strategies in input-queued switches.

[McKeown 95] N. McKeown. Scheduling Algorithms for Input-Queued Cell Switches. *Ph.D. Thesis,* University of California at Berkeley, May 1995.
> A survey of techniques for input-queued switches and an analysis of the SLIP approach to arbitration.

[NL 96] P. Newman and T. Lyon. Flow Labeled IP: A Connectionless Approach to ATM. *Proceedings of IEEE INFOCOM'96,* March 1996.
> Describes a second-generation switch where a flow of IP-over-ATM packets automatically sets up a call in an ATM switch.

[OSMKM 90] Y. Oie, T. Suda, M. Murata, D. Kolson, and H. Miyahara. Survey of Switching Techniques in High-Speed Networks and Their Performance. *Proceedings of IEEE INFOCOM '90,* June 1990, pp. 1242–1251.
> A survey of third-generation switches.

[Perlman 92] R. Perlman. Interconnections: Bridges and Routers. *Addison-Wesley,* 1992.
> An excellent description of an engineering approach to designing and building routers and bridges.

[Scorpio 95] Scorpio Inc. Description of the Scorpio ATM Switch. *Available from* `http://www.scorpio.com`, 1995.

    This site has a detailed description of the Scorpio buffered crossbar switch.

[TKC 91] F. A. Tobagi, T. Kwok, and F. Chiussi. Architecture, Performance, and Implementation of a Tandem Banyan Fast Packet Switch. *IEEE Journal on Selected Areas in Communication*, Vol. 9, October 1991, pp. 1173–1193.

    Proposes and analyzes the Tandem Banyan switch, where several banyan fabrics are linked in tandem to reduce blocking.

[Tobagi 90] F. A. Tobagi. Fast Packet Switching Architectures for Broadband Integrated Services Digital Networks. *Proceedings of IEEE*, Vol. 78, No. 1, November 1990, pp. 133–167.

    A survey of third-generation packet switches.

[Turner 85] J. S. Turner. Design of Integrated Services Packet Network. *Proceedings of 9th ACM Data Communication Symposium*, September 1985, pp. 124–133.

    Describes an early buffered Banyan switch design and its role in providing both voice and data service.

[Turner 88] J. S. Turner. Design of a Broadcast Packet Switched Network. *IEEE Transactions on Communications*, Vol. 36, June 1988, pp. 734–743.

    Describes an early buffered Banyan switch design that allows muticast and broadcast.

[TW 83] J. S. Turner and L. F. Wyatt. A Packet Network Architecture for Integrated Services. *Proceedings of GLOBECOMM '83*, San Diego, Nov. 1993, pp. 2.1.1–2.1.6.

    Early description of a buffered Banyan switch design.

[Vries 90] R. J. F. de Vries. Gauss: A Simple High Performance Switch Architecture for ATM. *Proceedings of ACM SIGCOMM '90*, September 1990, pp. 126–134.

    Describes the Gauss switch, which is based on output queueing and a variation of the knockout principle.

[YHA 87] Y. S. Yeh, M. G. Hluchyj, and A. S. Acampora. The Knockout Switch: A Simple, Modular Architecture for High-Performance Packet Switching. *IEEE Journal on Selected Areas in Communication*, Vol. 5, October 1987, pp. 1426–1435.

    Describes the knockout principle and a switch based on this principle.

References for Chapter 9: Scheduling

[BG 92] D. Bertsekas and R. Gallager. Data Networks, Second Edition. *Prentice Hall*, 1992.

    Classic textbook on computer networking from a formal, algorithmic perspective.

[BK 93] A. Banerjea and S. Keshav. Queueing Delays in Rate-Controlled Networks. *Proceedings of IEEE INFOCOM '93*, San Francisco, 1993.

    Gives an algorithm to compute the worst-case delay over a network of rate-controlled servers, taking internal burstiness into account.

[Brown 88] R. Brown. Calendar Queues: A Fast 0(1) Priority Queue Implementation for the Simulation Event Set Problem. *Communications of the ACM*, Vol. 31, No. 10, October 1988.

>   Describes the design and evaluation of a calendar queue.

[BZ 96] J. C. R. Bennet and H. Zhang. WF^{2}Q: Worst-Case Fair Weighted Fair Queueing. *Proceedings of IEEE INFOCOM '96*, San Francisco, 1996.

>   Describes WF^{2}Q and proves that the service received under this discipline is no more than one packet ahead or behind GPS.

[CR 96] A. Charny and K. K. Ramakrishnan. Time Scale Analysis of Explicit Rate Allocation in ATM Networks. *Proceedings of IEEE INFOCOM '96*, March 1996.

>   Derives a minimum bound on the time taken for a distributed computation of a globally max–min fair allocation. Shows that in order to avoid overloading switches, each source must adapt its rate only after a delay.

[CSZ 92] D. D. Clark, S. Shenker, and L. Zhang. Supporting Real-Time Applications in an Integrated Services Packet Network: Architecture and Mechanism. *Proceedings of ACM SIGCOMM '92*, Baltimore, August 1992.

>   Presents a framework for real-time service on the Internet. Describes predictive service, FIFO+, and the concepts of sharing and isolation.

[DH 90] J. Davin and A. Heybey. A Simulation Study of Fair Queueing and Policy Enforcement. *Computer Communication Review*, Vol. 20, No, 5, October 1990, pp. 23–29.

>   Studies how WFQ can be used to implement isolation policies. Proposes self-clocking, though without proving that it is a valid emulation of GPS.

[DKS 89] A. Demers, S. Keshav, and S. Shenker. Design and Analysis of a Fair Queueing Algorithm. *Proceedings of ACM SIGCOMM '89*, Austin, September 1989.

>   Presents GPS and WFQ. Simulations show that it is effective in protecting well-behaved sources from misbehaving ones.

[FJ 93] S. Floyd and V. Jacobson. Random Early Detection Gateways for Congestion Avoidance. *IEEE/ACM Transactions on Networking*, August 1993.

>   Presents the RED policy. Simulations show its effectiveness and compare it with drop-from-tail.

[FV 90] D. Ferrari and D. Verma. A Scheme for Real-Time Channel Establishment in Wide-Area Networks. *IEEE Journal on Selected Areas in Communication*, Vol. 8, No. 3, April 1990, pp. 368–379.

>   Proposes Delay-EDD and a framework for providing end-to-end delay and bandwidth bounds using a combination of resource reservation and admission control. Describes deterministic and statistical performance bounds.

[GGPS 96] L. Georgiadis, R. Guerin, V. Peris, and K. N. Sivarajan. Efficient Network QoS Provisioning Based on Per-Node Traffic Shaping. *Proceedings of IEEE INFOCOM '96*, March 1996.

Shows that with proper choice of regulators, end-to-end delay bounds with rate-controlled disciplines are the same as or better than with GPS emulations.

[GLV 95] P. Goyal, S. Lam, and H. Vin. Determining End-to-End Delay Bounds in Heterogeneous Networks. *Proceedings of Fifth International Workshop on Network and Operating System Support for Digital Audio and Video,* Durham, NH, April 1995, pp. 287–298.

Proposes a unified framework for determining end-to-end delays over networks of GPS-emulation schedulers.

[GM 92] A. G. Greenberg and A. N. Madras. How Fair Is Fair Queueing? *Journal of the ACM,* Vol. 3, No. 39, 1992.

Proves a one-sided absolute fairness bound for WFQ.

[Golestani 90a] S. Jamaloddin Golestani. Congestion-Free Transmission of Real-Time Traffic in Packet Networks. *Proceedings of IEEE INFOCOM '90,* San Francisco, June 1990, pp. 527–542.

Presents the stop-and-go discipline and proves delay and delay-jitter bounds.

[Golestani 90b] S. Jamaloddin Golestani. A Stop-and-Go Queueing Framework for Congestion Management. *Proceedings of ACM SIGCOMM '90,* Philadelphia, September 1990, pp. 8–18.

Extends stop-and-go to allow multiple frame times.

[Golestani 94] S. Jamaloddin Golestani. A Self-Clocked Fair Queueing Scheme for Broadband Applications. *Proceedings of IEEE INFOCOM '94,* Toronto, June 1994, pp. 636–646.

Presents and analyzes the SCFQ disciplines. Proposes the relative fairness bound as a metric of how well a discipline emulates GPS.

[GV 95] P. Goyal and H. Vin. Generalized Guaranteed Rate Scheduling Algorithms: A Framework. *Technical Report TR-95-30,* University of Texas, Austin, September 1995.

Presents a framework for computing end-to-end delay bounds for GPS-emulations and Delay-EDD. Extends the bounds in [GLV 95] for the case when every packet on a connection can be served with a different service rate, and when packets are fragmented and reassembled within the network.

[GVC 96] P. Goyal, H. Vin, and H. Chen. Start-Time Fair Queueing: A Scheduling Algorithm for Integrated Services Packet Switching Networks. *Proceedings of ACM SIGCOMM '96,* August 1996.

Describes a variant of self-clocked fair queueing called start-time fair queueing. Shows that the discipline is fair, provides throughput and delay bounds, and is easy to implement.

[Hashem 89] E. Hashem. Analysis of Random Drop for Gateway Congestion Control. *Technical Report LCS/TR-465,* Laboratory for Computer Science, Massachusetts Institute of Technology, Cambridge, MA, 1989.

Compares early-random-drop, random-drop, and drop-from-tail drop policies.

[HLP 91b] J. Hyman, A. Lazar, and G. Pacifici. Real-time Scheduling with Quality of Service Constraints. *IEEE Journal on Selected Areas in Communication,* Vol. 9, No. 9, September 1991.

> Introduces the notion of a schedulable region and shows its importance in system stability.

[Keshav 91] S. Keshav. On the Efficient Implementation of Fair Queueing. *Journal of Internetworking Research and Experience,* Vol. 2, No. 3, September 1991.

> Presents and compares several techniques for efficiently implementing WFQ.

[KKK 90] C. R. Kalmanek, H. Kanakia, and S. Keshav. Rate Controlled Servers for Very High-Speed Networks. *Proceedings of Globecom '90,* San Diego, December 1990, pp. 300.3.1–300.3.9.

> Describes HRR scheduling and two fast implementations of the discipline. Simulations evaluate its effectiveness.

[Kleinrock 75] L. Kleinrock. Queueing Systems, Volume 2: Computer Applications. *Wiley Interscience,* 1975.

> Classic textbook on queueing theory.

[LNO 95] T. V. Lakshman, A. Neidhardt, and T. J. Ott. The Drop from Front Strategy in TCP and in TCP over ATM. *Proceedings of IEEE INFOCOM '96.*

> Evaluates the performance of drop-from-head drop policy and shows that this reduces the time taken for a source to detect a loss.

[Nagle 87] J. Nagle. On Packet Switches with Infinite Storage. *IEEE Transactions on Communications,* Vol. 35, No. 4, April 1987, pp. 435–438.

> Shows that even with infinite storage, if packets have a time-to-live, there can still be significant packet loss. Proposes round-robin scheduling to give a source an incentive to reduce its flow rate when the network is congested.

[Parekh 92] A. K. Parekh. A Generalized Processor Sharing Approach to Flow Control in Integrated Services Networks. *Ph.D. Dissertation, issued as Technical Report LIDS-TH-2089,* Massachusetts Institute of Technology, Cambridge, MA 02139, February 1992.

> Analysis of end-to-end delay bounds with networks of WFQ schedulers.

[Partridge 91] C. Partridge. Isochronous Applications Do Not Require Jitter-Controlled Networks. *RFC 1257,* September 1991.

> Lays out the case against the need for delay-jitter control in integrated services networks.

[PG 93] A. K. Parekh and R. G. Gallager. A Generalized Processor Sharing Approach to Flow Control in Integrated Services Networks—The Single Node Case. *IEEE/ACM Transactions on Networking,* June 1993, pp. 344–357.

> Single-hop delay bounds for a WFQ scheduler.

[PG 94] A. K. Parekh and R. G. Gallager. A Generalized Processor Sharing Approach to Flow Control in Integrated Services Networks—The Multiple Node Case. *IEEE/ACM Transactions on Networking*, April 1994, pp. 137–150.
>
> Analysis of end-to-end delay bounds with networks of WFQ schedulers.

[Restrick 94] R.C. Restrick. Personal communication, 1994.

[RF 94] A. Romanow and S. Floyd. The Dynamics of TCP Traffic over ATM Networks. *Proceedings of ACM SIGCOMM '94*, September 1994.
>
> Shows that when TCP/IP packets are carried as AAL5 frames, cell losses are multiplied. Shows that this effect is reduced with random early drop.

[Shenker 90] S. Shenker. A Theoretical Analysis of Feedback Flow Control. *Proceedings of ACM SIGCOMM '90*, Philadelphia, September 1990, pp. 156–165.
>
> Analyzes the fairness, stability, and time-scale invariance of scheduling disciplines when used in conjunction with an ensemble of feedback-flow-controlled sources.

[SV 95b] M. Shreedhar and G. Varghese. Efficient Fair Queueing Using Deficit Round Robin. *Proceedings of ACM SIGCOMM '95*, Boston, September 1995.
>
> Describes DRR and evaluates its effectiveness.

[SV 96] S. Stiliadis and A. Verma. Latency-Rate Servers: A General Model for Analysis of Traffic Scheduling Algorithms. *Proceedings of IEEE INFOCOM '96*, 1996.
>
> Describes latency-rate servers, which emulate GPS, and computes end-to-end delay bounds for networks of LR servers.

[VZF 91] D. Verma, H. Zhang, and D. Ferrari. Guaranteeing Delay Jitter Bounds in Packet Switching Networks. *Proceedings of Tricomm '91*, Chapel Hill, NC, April 1991.
>
> Describes J-EDD and evaluates its effectiveness.

[ZF 93] H. Zhang and D. Ferrari. Rate-Controlled Static Priority Queueing. *Proceedings of IEEE INFOCOM '93*, San Francisco, 1993 pp. 227–236.
>
> Proposes RCSP and presents theorems to compute delay and delay-jitter bounds with networks of RCSP servers.

[ZF 94] H. Zhang and D. Ferrari. Rate-Controlled Service Disciplines. *Journal of High Speed Networking*, Vol. 3, No. 4, 1994, pp. 389–412.
>
> Generalizes RCSP to RC schedulers and proves some theorems about their properties.

[Zhang 89] L. Zhang. A New Architecture for Packet Switching Network Protocols. *Technical Report MIT/LCS/TR-455*, Laboratory for Computer Science, Massachusetts Institute of Technology, Cambridge MA, August 1989.
>
> Proposes and analyzes the Virtual Clock discipline. Proposes end-to-end quality of service for flows, which are like connections. Also studies large-scale oscillations with networks of TCP sources.

[Zhang 90] L. Zhang. Virtual Clock: A New Traffic Control Algorithm for Packet Switching Networks. *Proceedings of ACM SIGCOMM '90*, Philadelphia, September 1990.
   A shorter description and analysis of the Virtual Clock algorithm.

[Zhang 95] H. Zhang. Service Disciplines for Guaranteed Performance Service in Packet-Switching Networks. *Proceedings of IEEE*, October 1995.
   A survey of scheduling disciplines and their performance bounds.

[ZK 91] H. Zhang and S. Keshav. Comparison of Rate-Based Service Disciplines. *Proceedings of ACM SIGCOMM '91*, Zurich, 1991.
   Compares Delay-EDD, WFQ, Virtual Clock, Jitter-EDD, HRR, and SnG for cell-smooth input traffic.

References for Chapter 10: Naming and Addressing

[DH 96] S. Deering and R. Hinden. IP Version 6 Addressing Architecture. *RFC-1884*, January 1996.
   The authoritative reference for IP version 6 addressing.

[Droms 93] R. Droms. Dynamic Host Configuration Protocol. *RFC-1531*, October 1993.
   Describes the design, features, and details of the DHCP protocol.

[Huitema 94] C. Huitema. The H Ratio for Address Assignment Efficiency. *RFC-1715*, November 1994.
   Computes the number of IPv6 addresses per square meter of the earth's surface.

[ISO 93] ISO/IEC Information Processing Systems—Data Communications: Network Service Definition. International Standard 8348, *ISO/IEC JTC 1*, Switzerland, 1993.
   International standard describing NSAPs.

[ITU-E.164] Recommendation E.164/I.331—Numbering Plan for the ISDN Era. *International Teletraffic Union, available from* http://www.itu.ch/.
   International standard describing telephone numbers.

[Laubach 94] M. Laubach. Classical IP and ARP over ATM. *RFC 1577*, January 1994.

[LR 95] T. Li and Y. Rekhter. An Architecture for IPv6 Unicast Address Allocation. *RFC-1887*, December 1995.
   A proposed architecture for unicast address allocation that describes how to use additional levels of hierarchy in the address, and how to encode topological hints to reduce routing overheads.

[MD 88] P. Mockapetris and K. J. Dunlap. Development of the Domain Name System. *Proceedings of ACM SIGCOMM '88*, Stanford, August 1988.
   Excellent description of the design and operation of the Domain Name System.

[Mockapetris 87] P. Mockapetris. Domain Names—Implementation and Specification. *RFC-1035*, November 1987.

[Partridge 86] C. Partridge. Mail Routing and the Domain System. *RFC 794*, January 1986.
> Describes how MX records work.

[Plummer 82] D. C. Plummer. An Ethernet Address Resolution Protocol. *RFC-826*, November 1982.
> Describes ARP.

References for Chapter 11: Routing

[Akinpelu 84] J. M. Akinpelu. The Overload Performance of Engineered Networks with Non-Hierarchical Routing. *AT&T Technical Journal*, Vol. 63, No. 7, September 1984, pp. 1261–1281.
> Shows the existence of metastability in DNHR and the need for trunk reservation.

[BE 90] L. Breslau and D. Estrin. Design of Inter-Administrative Domain Routing Protocols. *Proceedings of ACM SIGCOMM '90*, Philadelphia, September 1990.
> Overview of issues in designing policy routing protocols between autonomous systems.

[Bellman 57] R. E. Bellman. Dynamic Programming. *Princeton University Press*, 1957.
> Classic text with first description of distance-vector routing.

[BFC 93] A. Ballardie, P. Francis, and J. Crowcroft. Core Based Trees (CBT): An Architecture for Scalable Inter-Domain Multicast Routing. *Proceedings of ACM SIGCOMM '93*, San Francisco, August 1993.

[Braden 89] R. Braden. Requirements for Internet Hosts—Communication Layers. *RFC 1122*, 1989.
> Exhaustive list of requirements that hosts attached to the Internet ought to obey.

[Clark 89] D. D. Clark. Policy Routing in Internet Protocols. *RFC-1102*, May 1989.
> Early paper on policy routing.

[CRKG 89] C. Cheng, R. Riley, S. Kumar, and J. J. Garcia-Luna-Aceves. A Loop-Free Extended Bellman–Ford Routing Protocol without Bouncing Effect. *Proceedings of ACM SIGCOMM '89*, Austin, September 1989.
> One of the two papers on source tracing.

[Deering 91a] S. Deering. Multicast Routing in a Datagram Internetwork. *Ph.D. Thesis, Stanford University*, 1991.
> Classic Ph.D. thesis that lays out the basic ideas in Internet multicast.

[Deering 91b] S. Deering. ICMP Router Discovery Messages. *RFC-1256*, September 1991.

[DEFJLW 94] S. Deering, D. Estrin, D. Farinacci, V. Jacobson, C.-G. Lue, and L. Wei. An Architecture for Wide-Area Multicast Routing. *Proceedings of ACM SIGCOMM '94,* London, September 1994.
> Describes the PIM approach to IP multicast.

[Dijkstra 59] E. W. Dijkstra. A Note on Two Problems in Connection with Graphs. *Numerical Mathematics,* October 1959.
> Presents the famous algorithm for computing shortest paths in graphs.

[DM 78] Y. Dalal and R. Metcalfe. Reverse Path Forwarding of Broadcast Packets. *Communications of the ACM,* Vol. 21, December 1978, pp. 1040–1048.
> First description of reverse path forwarding for flooding.

[Estrin 89] D. Estrin. Policy Requirements for Inter-Administrative Domain Routing. *RFC-1125,* November 1989.

[FF 62] L. R. Ford and D. R. Fulkerson. Flows in Networks. *Princeton University Press,* Princeton, NJ, 1962.
> Another classic paper on distance-vector routing.

[Garcia-Luna-Aceves 89] J. J. Garcia-Luna-Aceves. A Unified Approach to Loop-Free Routing Using Distance Vectors or Link States. *Proceedings of ACM SIGCOMM '89,* Austin, September 1989.
> Describes DUAL loop-free distance-vector routing.

[Girard 90] A. Girard. Routing and Dimensioning in Circuit-Switched Networks. *Addison-Wesley,* 1990.
> A good introduction to the area.

[Halpern 96] J. M. Halpern. The Architecture and Status of PNNI. `http://www.vivid.newbridge.com/documents/Joel.html`, 1996.
> A concise and informative description of PNNI routing.

[Hedrick 88] C. Hedrick. Routing Information Protocol. *RFC 1058,* June 1988.

[Huitema 95] C. Huitema. Routing in the Internet. *Prentice Hall,* 1995.
> Excellent description of Internet routing protocols.

[Kelly 88] F. P. Kelly. Routing in Circuit-Switched Networks: Optimization, Shadow Prices, and Decentralization. *Advances in Applied Probability,* Vol. 20, 1988.
> Describes how to compute and use shadow prices for routing in telephone networks.

[Kelly 91] F. P. Kelly. Loss Networks. *The Annals of Applied Probability,* 1991, pp. 319–378.
> Exhaustive survey of recent research in routing in telephone networks.

[KZ 89] A. Khanna and J. Zinky. The Revised ARPANET Routing Metric. *Proceedings of ACM SIGCOMM'89,* August 1989.
> Describes problems with the older routing metric and the hop-normalized cost

used to correct these problems. Introduces the metric map and the network response map to study the dynamics of routing.

[LHH 95] W. C. Lee, M. G. Hluchyj, and P. A. Humblet. Routing Subject to QoS Constraints in Integrated Communication Networks. *IEEE Networks Magazine,* Vol. 9, No. 4, July/August 1995.

[ME 90] N. Maxemchuk and M. El Zarki. Routing and Flow Control in High-Speed Wide-Area Networks. *Proceedings of IEEE,* Vol. 78, No. 1, January 1990.
> Broad survey of the field.

[Moy 91] J. Moy. OSPF Version 2. *RFC-1247,* July 1991.

[Moy 94] J. Moy. Multicast Extensions to OSPF. *RFC-1584,* March 1994.

[Perlman 83] R. Perlman. Fault-Tolerant Broadcast of Routing Information. *Computer Networks,* Vol. 7, 1983, pp. 395–405.
> Classic paper on how to keep LSP databases sane and consistent.

[Perlman 92] R. Perlman. Interconnections: Bridges and Routers. *Addison-Wesley,* 1992.
> Introductory text on routing. Covers routing in ISO networks.

[RF 89] B. Rajagopalan and M. Faiman. A New Responsive Distributed Shortest-Path Routing Algorithm. *Proceedings of ACM SIGCOMM '89,* Austin, September 1989.
> One of the two papers on source tracing.

[RL 95] Y. Rekhter and T. Li. A Border Gateway Protocol-4. *RFC-1771,* March 1995.

[Rosen 82] E. Rosen. Exterior Gateway Protocol. *RFC-827,* October 1982.

[Tsuchiya 91] P. F. Tsuchiya. Efficient and Robust Policy Routing Using Multiple Hierarchical Addresses. *Proceedings of ACM SIGCOMM '91,* Zurich, September 1991.
> Describes a clever scheme for provider selection.

[WPD 88] D. Waitzman, C. Partridge, and S. Deering. Distance Vector Multicast Routing Protocol. *RFC-1075,* November 1988.
> Standard reference for DVMRP.

References for Chapter 12: Error Control

[AMS 82] D. Anick, D. Mitra, and M. M. Sondhi. Stochastic Theory of Data-Handling System with Multiple Sources. *Bell System Technical Journal,* Vol. 61, No. 8, 1982, pp. 1871–1894.
> This classic paper introduced fluid flow models and asymptotic analysis to study buffer sizing in multiplexors.

[BBP 88] R. Braden, D. A. Borman, and C. Partridge. Computing the Internet Checksum. *RFC 1071,* September 1988.
> Tricks and advice in implementing the IP checksum (this checksum is also used in UDP and TCP).

[BC 92] C. C. Bissell and D. A. Chapman. Digital Signal Transmission. *Cambridge University Press*, 1992.
> A technical introduction to digital transmission at the senior undergraduate level. Excellent treatment of telephone transmission and communication system design.

[BH 90] A. Bhargava and M. Hluchyj. Frame Losses Due to Buffer Overflows in Fast Packet Networks. *Proceedings of IEEE INFOCOM '90,* June 1990, pp. 132–139.
> Models frame loss as a function of cell loss in framed networks.

[Biersack 92] E. Biersack. Performance Evaluation of Forward Error Correction in ATM Networks. *Proceedings of ACM SIGCOMM '92,* Baltimore, 1992.
> Raises questions about the effectiveness of forward error correction, because of the additional load it generates.

[Blahut 90] R. E. Blahut. Digital Transmission of Information. *Addison-Wesley,* 1990.

[Bolot 93] J.-C. Bolot. End-to-End Delay and Loss Behavior in the Internet. *Proceedings of ACM SIGCOMM '93,* San Francisco, 1993.
> Presents models for packet loss in the Internet based on periodic "ping"s.

[Bolot 95] J.-C. Bolot. Analysis of Audio Packet Loss in the Internet. *Proceedings of Workshop on Networks and Operating Systems Support for Digital Audio and Video,* April 1995, pp. 163–174.
> Presents a model for audio packet loss; shows that FEC is effective for audio on the Internet.

[CKS 93] I. Cidon, A. Khamisy, and M. Sidi. Analysis of Packet Loss Processes in High-Speed Networks. *IEEE Trans. On Information Theory,* Vol 39, No. 1, January 1993.
> Shows that losses are bursty, and that ignoring burstiness causes significant errors in analysis.

[CZL 87] D. D. Clark, L. Zhang, and M. Lambert. NETBLT: A High Throughput Transport Protocol. *Proceedings of ACM SIGCOMM '87,* 1987.
> Overview of the NETBLT protocol, an early rate-based protocol that did selective acks on blocks.

[DJNS 93] B. T. Doshi, P. K. Johri, A. N. Netravali, and K. K. Sabnani. Error and Flow Control Performance of a High Speed Protocol. *IEEE Transactions on Communications,* Vol. 41, May 1993, pp. 707–720.
> Analyzes the periodic state exchange protocol, comparing it with go-back-n and a form of selective ack.

[FKY 81] T. R. Fortesque, L. Kershenbaum, and B. Ydstie. Implementation of Self-Tuning Regulators with Variable Forgetting Factors. *Automatica,* Vol. 17, No. 6, 1981, pp. 831–835.
> Describes exponential averagers with dynamically varying decay factors.

[Henderson 95] T. R Henderson. Design Principles and Performance Analysis of SSCOP: A New ATM Adaptation Layer Protocol. *ACM Computer Communication Review,* Vol. 25, No. 2, April 1995.

> Describes *Service Specific Connection-Oriented Protocol,* a transport protocol used in ATM signaling.

[Jacobson 88] V. Jacobson. Congestion Avoidance and Control. *Proceedings of ACM SIGCOMM '88,* Stanford, 1988.

> Classic paper on congestion-avoidance strategies in TCP.

[Jacobson 90] V. Jacobson. Modified TCP Congestion Avoidance Algorithm. *End-to-end mailing list,* April 1990. Available from `ftp://ftp.isi.edu/end2end/end2end-interest-1990.mail`.

> Describes the fast-retransmit algorithm in TCP.

[Jakes 93] W. C. Jakes (ed.). Microwave Mobile Communications. *IEEE Press,* 1993.

> A classic text and standard reference on all aspects of cellular communications.

[KK 92] P. S. Khedkar and S. Keshav. Fuzzy Prediction of Timeseries. *Proceedings of IEEE Conference on Fuzzy Systems, FUZZ-IEEE,* March 1992.

> Uses fuzzy logic to identify a system and decide an appropriate exponential decay factor.

[KM 97] S. Keshav and S. P. Morgan. SMART: Performance with Overload and Random Losses. *Proceedings of IEEE INFOCOM '97,* April 1997.

> Describes SMART retransmission, and how it works with packet-pair.

[KP 87] P. Karn and C. Partridge. Improving Round-Trip Time Estimate in Reliable Transport Protocols. *Proceedings of ACM SIGCOMM '87,* 1987.

> Details of Karn's algorithm to deal with estimating the round-trip time when packets have been retransmitted.

[Maxemchuk 75] N. F. Maxemchuck. Dispersity Routing in Store and Forward Networks. *Ph.D. Thesis,* University of Pennsylvania, May 1975.

> Proposes the idea that a source can increase throughput and decrease loss probability by distributing data over several alternative paths simultaneously.

[Mukherjee 94] A. Mukherjee. On the Dynamics and Significance of Low Frequency Components of Internet Load. *Journal of Internetworking: Research and Experience,* Vol. 5, 1994, pp. 163–205.

> An exhaustive measurement and modeling of Internet delay, loss, and reordering over long time periods.

[NRS 90] A. Netravali, W. D. Roome, and K. K. Sabnani. Design and Implementation of a High Speed Protocol. *IEEE Transactions on Communications,* Vol. 38, 1990, pp. 2010–2024.

> Describes a transport protocol that introduces the idea of explicit periodic state exchange.

[PHS 95] C. Partridge, J. Hughes, and J. Stone. Performance of Checksums and CRCs over Real Data. *Proceedings of ACM SIGCOMM '95,* Cambridge, 1995.

[PW 72] W. W. Peterson and E. J. Welden. Error Correcting Codes. *John Wiley and Sons,* 1972.
> Standard reference on error-correcting codes.

[RF 94] A. Romanow and S. Floyd. Dynamics of TCP Traffic over ATM Networks. *Proceedings of ACM SIGCOMM '94,* London, 1994.
> Studies the effect of error multiplication on TCP throughput in ATM networks.

[Sarwate 88] D. Sarwate. Computation of Cyclic Redundancy Checks via Table Look-up. *Communications of the ACM,* August 1988, pp. 1008–1013.
> Presents a simple algorithm for fast CRC computation.

[SD 78] C. Sunshine and Y. Dalal. Connection Management in Transport Protocols. *Computer Networks,* Vol. 2, No. 6, 1978, pp. 454–473.
> Classic reference on connection management, with analysis of connection establishment and termination in connectionless networks.

[Stallings 88] W. Stallings. Data and Computer Communication, Second Edition. *Macmillan,* 1988.
> Standard textbook on computer networking.

[Watson 81] R. Watson. Timer-Based Mechanisms in Reliable Transport Protocol Connection Management. *Computer Networks* 5, North-Holland, Amsterdam, 1981, pp. 47–56.
> Describes implicit relationships that must hold in connection management protocols for reliable connection establishment and termination.

[Zhang 87] L. Zhang. Why TCP Timers Don't Work Well. *Proceedings of ACM SIGCOMM '87,* 1987.
> A critique of timer mechanisms in general, with conclusions about why timers are needed, and when they should be used.

References for Chapter 13: Flow Control

[ABB 93] E. Altman, F. Baccelli, and J.-C Bolot. Discrete-Time Analysis of Adaptive Rate Control Algorithms. *Proceedings of 5th International Conference on Data Communications,* Raleigh, NC, October 1993, pp. 121–140.
> Analyzes the one-step-ahead predictive control scheme used in the MK and packet-pair schemes and shows that they are stable even when taking the non-linearity at the endpoints of the control into account. Also proves that flow-control schemes that ignore the queue length are unstable.

[ADLY 95] J. S. Ahn, P. B. Danzig, Z. Liu, and L. Yan. Experience with TCP Vegas: Emulation and Experiment. *Proceedings of ACM SIGCOMM '95,* Boston, August 1995.
> An emulation and simulation study of TCP-Vegas, which confirms its effectiveness both in simulations and over the Internet.

[BF 95] F. Bonomi and K. Fendick. The Rate-Based Flow Control Framework for the Available Bit Rate ATM Service. *IEEE Network Magazine,* March/April 1995, pp. 25–39.
An overview of the process leading to the ATM Forum's decision to adopt rate-based flow control, and a detailed description of the adopted scheme.

[BP 95] L. S. Brakmo and L. L. Peterson. TCP Vegas: End to End Congestion Avoidance on a Global Internet. *IEEE Journal on Selected Areas in Communication,* Vol. 13, No. 8, October 1995, pp. 1465–1480.
Describes the TCP-Vegas scheme and evaluates its performance.

[BW 92] A. W. Berger and W. Whitt. The Impact of a Job Buffer in a Token-Bank Rate-Control Throttle. *Stochastic Models,* Vol. 8, 1992, pp. 685–717.
Proves that the parameter important in a leaky bucket is the sum of the data buffer and the token bucket.

[CJ 89] D.-M Chiu and R. Jain, Analysis of Increase and Decrease Algorithms for Congestion Avoidance in Computer Networks. *Computer Networks and ISDN Systems,* Vol. 17, 1989, pp. 1–14.
A control-theoretic analysis that shows that additive-increase–multiplicative-decrease is the only stable control algorithm for dynamic window flow control.

[CLZ 88] D. D. Clark, M. L. Lambert, and L. Zhang. NETBLT: A High Throughput Transport Protocol. *Proceedings of ACM SIGCOMM '88,* Stanford, August 1988.
Describes the insights that went into the design of NETBLT and gives an overview of its operation.

[Cruz 87] R. L. Cruz. A Calculus for Network Delay and a Note on Topologies of Interconnection Networks. *Ph.D. Thesis,* University of Illinois, issued as Report UILU-ENG-87-2246, July 1987.
The first analysis of the worst-case end-to-end delay suffered by a leaky-bucket controlled source. Introduces LBAP-constrained sources.

[DKS 89] A. Demers, S. Keshav, and S. Shenker. Analysis and Simulation of a Fair Queueing Algorithm. *Proceedings of ACM SIGCOMM '89,* Austin, August 1989.
Describes the fair queueing algorithm and evaluates its effectiveness in many simulated scenarios. Early comparison of DECbit and JK algorithms.

[Floyd 91] S. Floyd. Connections with Multiple Congested Gateways in Packet-Switched Networks, Part 1: One-Way Traffic. *ACM Computer Communications Review,* Vol. 21, No. 5, October 1991, pp. 30–47.
A detailed simulation study of TCP performance in a multihop congested network.

[Fraser 83] A. G. Fraser. Towards a Universal Data Transport System. *IEEE Journal on Selected Areas in Communication,* Vol. 1, No. 5, November 1983, pp. 803–816.
Describes the motivations for, and design of, the Datakit network.

[Fraser 91] A. G. Fraser. Designing a Public Data Network. *IEEE Communications Magazine,* October 1991, pp. 31–35.
> Describes technology trends and requirements for building a public data network.

[FV 90] D. Ferrari and D. C. Verma. A Scheme for Real-Time Channel Establishment in Wide-Area Networks. *IEEE Journal on Selected Areas in Communications,* Vol. 8, No. 3, April 1990, pp. 368–379.
> Classic paper describing a scheme for providing real-time performance guarantees to connections by using a combination of resource reservation, admission control, and intelligent packet scheduling.

[GF 95] A. Gupta and D. Ferrari. Resource Partitioning for Multi-Party Real-Time Communication. *IEEE/ACM Transactions on Networking,* October 1995.
> Describes issues and algorithms in partitioning a resource among services such as real-time and best-effort communication.

[GKT 95] M. Grossglauser, S. Keshav, and D. Tse. RCBR: A Simple and Efficient Service for Multiple Time-Scale Traffic, *Proceedings of ACM SIGCOMM '95,* Boston, September 1995.
> Proposes renegotiated constant-bit-rate service as a viable alternative for providing service to video streams that show slow-time-scale variations in the traffic rate.

[Golestani 90] S. J. Golestani. A Stop-and-Go Queueing Framework for Congestion Management. *Proceedings of ACM SIGCOMM '90,* Philadephia, September 1990.
> Proposes the (r,T) moving-average descriptor for traffic, as part of the stop-and-go congestion management framework.

[GVSS 96] P. Goyal, H. Vin, C. Shen, and P. Shenoy. A Reliable, Adaptive Network Protocol for Video Transport. *Proceedings of INFOCOM '96,* San Francisco, 1996.
> Improves on Kung and Chapman's buffer and delay bounds by a detailed analysis of the credit update protocol and by estimating the future bandwidth requirements of each connection.   .

[HKM 91] E. L. Hahne, C. R. Kalmanek, and S. P. Morgan. Fairness and Congestion Control on a Large ATM Data Network with Dynamically Adjustable Windows. *13th International Teletraffic Congress,* Copenhagen, June 1991.
> Description and evaluation of the DAWM scheme.

[Hoe 96] J. C. Hoe. Improving the Start-up Behavior of a Congestion Control Scheme for TCP. *Proceedings of ACM SIGCOMM '96,* Stanford, August 1996.
> Improves TCP performance by better estimating initial parameters and dealing better with multiple losses.

[Jacobson 88] V. Jacobson. Congestion Avoidance and Control. *Proceedings of ACM SIGCOMM '88,* Stanford, August 1988.

Classic paper describing the modifications to TCP subsequently called TCP-Tahoe.

[KBC 94] H. T. Kung, T. Blackwell, and A. Chapman. Credit-Based Flow Control for ATM Networks: Credit Update Protocol, Adaptive Credit Allocation, and Statistical Multiplexing. *Proceedings of ACM SIGCOMM '94*, London, September 1994, pp. 101–114.

Studies the credit update protocol's behavior in many scenarios. Proposes overbooking of buffers at the downstream switch to cut down on buffer requirements.

[KC 93], H. T. Kung and A. Chapman. The Flow-Controlled Virtual Channels Proposal for ATM Networks. *Proceedings of 1993 International Conference on Network Protocols,* San Francisco, 1993, pp. 116–127.

The first description of the hop-by-hop credit-based scheme.

[Keshav 91] S. Keshav. A Control-Theoretic Approach to Flow Control. *Proceedings of ACM SIGCOMM '91,* Zurich, September 1991.

Proposes packet-pair flow control and uses control theory to analyze its performance.

[Keshav 97] S. Keshav. Packet-pair Flow Control. *IEEE/ACM Transactions on Networking,* to appear, 1997.

A detailed description and performance analysis of packet-pair flow control.

[KK 92] P. S. Khedkar and S. Keshav. Fuzzy Prediction of Timeseries. *Proceedings of IEEE Conference on Fuzzy Systems, FUZZ-IEEE,* March 1992.

Uses fuzzy logic to identify a system and decide an appropriate exponential decay factor.

[KKM 93] H. R. Kanakia, S. Keshav, and P. P. Mishra. A Comparision of Congestion Control Schemes. *Proceedings of Fourth Annual Workshop on Very High Speed Networks,* Baltimore, Maryland, March 1993.

Compares the performance of several popular closed-loop flow control schemes on a benchmark of ten test scenarios.

[KM 95] H. T. Kung and R. Morris. Credit-Based Flow Control for ATM Networks. *IEEE Network Magazine,* March/April 1995, pp. 40–48.

An overview of the credit-based scheme.

[KM 97] S. Keshav and S. P. Morgan. SMART: Performance with Overload and Random Losses. *Proceedings of IEEE INFOCOM '97,* April 1997.

Describes SMART retransmission, and how it works with packet-pair.

[LM 95] T. V. Lakshman and U. Madhow. Performance Analysis of Window-Based Flow Control Using TCP/IP: the Effect of High Bandwidth–Delay Products and Random Loss. *IFIP Transactions C-26, High Performance Networking V,* North-Holland, 1994, pp. 135–150.

Detailed analysis of TCP-Tahoe and TCP-Reno behavior with and without random losses.

[Low 92] S. Low. Traffic Management of ATM Networks: Service Provisioning, Routing, and Traffic Shaping, *Ph.D. Thesis*, U.C. Berkeley, 1992.
> Proves the basic theorems on bottleneck behavior and flow control.

[MK 92] P. P. Mishra and H. R. Kanakia. A Hop-by-Hop Rate-based Congestion Control Scheme. *Proceedings of ACM SIGCOMM '92*, Baltimore, August 1992.
> Describes the MK scheme.

[Mogul 93] J. C. Mogul. IP Network Performance. In Internet System Handbook (D. C. Lynch and M. T. Rose, eds.). *Addison-Wesley*, 1993, pp. 575–675.
> Hints in improving TCP/IP performance for Internet administrators.

[Ogata 90] K. Ogata. Modern Control Engineering. *Prentice Hall*, 1990.
> Standard text on control theory for engineers.

[OSV 94] C. Ozveren, R. Simcoe, and G. Varghese. Reliable and Efficient Hop-by-Hop Control. *Proceedings of ACM SIGCOMM '94*, London, September 1994, pp. 89–100.
> Improves on the credit-based scheme by efficient sharing of downstream buffers while still avoiding loss.

[Rathgeb 91] E. Rathgeb. Modeling and Performance Comparison of Policing Mechanisms for ATM Networks. *IEEE Journal on Selected Areas in Communications*, Vol. 9, No. 3, April 1991, pp. 325–334.
> Compares several traffic-policing schemes.

[RJ 88] K. K. Ramakrishnan and R. Jain. A Binary Feedback Scheme for Congestion Avoidance in Computer Networks with a Connectionless Network Layer. *Proceedings of ACM SIGCOMM '88*, Stanford, August 1988, pp. 303–313.
> First description of the DECbit scheme.

[RJ 90] K. K. Ramakrishnan and R. Jain. A Binary Feedback Scheme for Congestion Avoidance in Computer Networks. *ACM Transactions on Computer Systems*, Vol. 8, No. 2, 1990, pp. 158–181.
> Detailed description of the DECbit scheme and its performance.

[RN 95] K. K. Ramakrishnan and P. Newman. Integration of Rate and Credit Schemes for ATM Flow Control. *IEEE Network Magazine*, March/April 1995, pp. 49–56.
> Compares the relative merits of credit- and rate-based flow control, and proposes three ways in which we might combine them.

[Stevens 94] W. R. Stevens. TCP/IP Illustrated, Vol. 1. *Addison-Wesley*, 1994.
> Comprehensive description of Internet protocols and TCP/IP as implemented in 4.4 BSD Unix.

[SZC 90] S. Shenker, L. Zhang, and D. D. Clark. Some Observations on the Dynamics of a Congestion Control Algorithm. *ACM Computer Communication Review*, 20(4), October 1990, pp. 30–39.
> Simulation study of TCP's behavior with elementary analysis.

[Turner 86] J. Turner. New Directions in Communications (or Which Way to the Information Age?). *IEEE Communications Magazine*, Vol. 25, No. 10, pp. 8–15, October 1986.
> A road map for research in high-speed networks. This paper is famous mostly for introducing the concept of a leaky bucket.

[Verma 91] D. Verma. Guaranteed Performance Communication in High Speed Networks. *Ph.D. Thesis*, U.C. Berkeley, issued as Technical Report UCB/CSD 91/663.
> A thorough study of issues in open-loop flow control. Proposes jitter-control schemes with traffic reshapers and separation of rate control from delay management.

[ZSC 91] L. Zhang, S. Shenker, and D. D. Clark. Observations on the Dynamics of a Congestion Control Algorithm: The Effects of Two-Way Traffic. *ACM SIGCOMM '91*, Zurich, 1991.
> Simulation study of TCP in the presence of two-way traffic. Describes the ACK-compression phenomenon.

References for Chapter 14: Traffic Management

[BCS 94] R. Braden, D. Clark, and S. Shenker. Integrated Services in the Internet Architecture: An Overview. *RFC 1633*, available from `ftp://ds.internic.net`, 1994.
> Reviews the IETF service model.

[Bellamy 91] J. Bellamy. Digital Telephony, Second Edition. *John Wiley and Sons*, 1991.
> A detailed introduction to telephone networking.

[BF 77] P. R. Boorstyn and H. Frank. Large-Scale Network Topological Optimization. *IEEE Transactions on Communications*, January 1977, pp. 29–47.
> Studies how to optimize topology given a traffic matrix and call blocking requirement.

[Billingsley 95] P. Billingsley. Probability and Measure. Third Edition. *John Wiley & Sons*, 1995.
> Advanced textbook on probability.

[BL 76] E. Bailey and E. Lindenberg. Peak Load Pricing Principles: Past and Present. In New Dimensions in Public Utility Pricing, MSU Public Utilities Studies, 1976.
> Introduction to peak-load pricing.

[BT 92] P. E. Boyer and D. P. Tranchier. A Reservation Principle with Applications to ATM Traffic. *Computer Networks and ISDN Systems*, Vol. 24, 1992, pp. 321–334.
> Discusses the fast-reservation procotol for BE traffic.

[Bulmer 79] M. G. Bulmer. Principles of Statistics. *Dover Publications*, 1979.
> An elementary introduction to statistics, with historical anecdotes.

[BZ 96] J. C. R. Bennett and H. Zhang. Hierarchical Packet Fair Queueing Algorithms. *Proceedings of ACM SIGCOMM '96*, Stanford, August 1996.

Describe practical algorithms that simultaneously support guaranteed real-time service, rate-adaptive best-effort, and controlled link sharing.

[CLG 95] S. Chong, S. Q. Li, and J. Ghosh. Predictive Dynamic Bandwidth Allocation for Efficient Transport of Real-Time Video over ATM. *IEEE Journal on Selected Areas in Communication,* Vol. 13, No. 1, January 1995, pp. 12–23.

Describes techniques to predict compressed video traffic online to allow renegotiation.

[CWSA 95] J. Crowcroft, Z. Wang, A. Smith, and J. Adams. A Rough Comparison of the IETF and ATM Service Models. *IEEE Network Magazine,* Vol. 9, No, 6, November/December 1995.

[DB 95] L. Delgrossi and L. Berger (eds.). Internet Stream Protocol Version 2 (ST2) Protocol Specification—Version ST2+, RFC 1819, August 1995.

[DJCME 92] P. Danzig, S. Jamin, R. Caceres, D. Mitzel, and D. Estrin. An Empirical Workload Model for Driving Wide-Area TCP/IP Network Simulations. *Journal on Internetworking: Research and Experience,* Vol. 3, No. 1, 1992, pp. 1–26.

[DMRW 94] D. Duffy, A. McIntosh, M. Rosenstein, and W. Willinger. Statistical Analysis of CCSN/SSN Traffic Data from Working CCS Subnetworks. *IEEE Journal on Selected Areas in Communication,* Vol. 12, No, 3, April 1994, pp. 544–551.

[EMW 95] A. Elwalid, D. Mitra, and R. H. Wentworth. A New Approach for Allocating Buffers and Bandwidth to Heterogeneous, Regulated Traffic in an ATM Node. *IEEE Journal on Selected Areas in Communication,* Vol. 13, No. 6, August 1995, pp. 1115–1127.

Extends the notion of equivalent bandwidth and shows that some sources are more multiplexable than others.

[Feldmann 95] A. Feldmann. On-line Call Admission for High-Speed Networks. *Ph.D. Thesis,* issued by School of Computer Science, Carnegie Mellon University as Technical Report CMU-CS-95-20, Pittsburgh, PA 15213, 1995.

A theoretical study of call-admission strategies, backed up by empirical studies of traffic behavior.

[FJ 95] S. Floyd and V. Jacobson. Link-Sharing and Resource Management Models for Packet Networks. *IEEE Transactions on Networking,* Vol. 3, No. 4., August 1995.

Describes link sharing.

[GAN 91] R. Guerin, H. Ahmadi, and M. Nagshineh. Equivalent Capacity and Its Application to Bandwidth Allocation in High-Speed Networks. *IEEE Journal on Selected Areas in Communication,* Vol. 9, No. 7, September 1991, pp. 968–981.

Seminal paper on using equivalent bandwidth for admission control.

[Garrett 94] M. W. Garrett. ATM Service Architecture: From Applications to Scheduling, *ATM Forum Contribution 94–0846 TM SWG,* September 1994, available from `ftp://thumper.bellcore.com/pub/mwg/ATM-Forum.qos.mwg`.

Overview of the ATM Forum service model.

[GB 96] M. Grossglauser and J. Bolot. On the Relevance of Long-Range Dependence in Network Traffic. *Proceedings of ACM SIGCOMM '96,* September 1996.
> Argues that with finite buffers and phenomena involving short time scales, long-range dependence may not affect performance.

[GG 92] R. Guerin and L. Gun. A Unified Approach to Bandwidth Allocation and Access Control in Fast Packet-Switched Networks. *Proceedings of IEEE INFOCOM '92.*
> Shows how to estimate the burst parameters for a source, and the corresponding leaky-bucket regulator.

[GH 91] R. J. Gibbens and P. J Hunt. Effective Bandwidths for Multi-Type UAS Channel. *Queueing Systems,* Vol. 29, No. 10, October 1991, pp. 17–28.
> Computes equivalent bandwidth for a call when sharing a buffer with other calls.

[GKT 95] M. Grossglauser, S. Keshav, and D. Tse. RCBR: A Simple and Efficient Service for Multiple Time-Scale Traffic. *Proceedings of ACM SIGCOMM '95,* Boston, September 1995.
> Proposes renegotiated constant-bit-rate service as a viable alternative to provide service to video streams that show slow-time-scale variations in the traffic rate.

[Grossman 90] J. W. Grossman. Discrete Mathematics: An Introduction to Concepts, Methods, and Applications. *Macmillan,* 1990.
> Introductory textbook.

[GW 94] M. Garrett and W. Willinger. Analysis, Modeling, and Generation of Self-Similar VBR Video Traffic. *Proceedings of ACM SIGCOMM '94,* London, September 1994.

[Henderson 95] T. R. Henderson. Design Principles and Performance Analysis of SSCOP: A New ATM Adaptation Layer Protocol. *ACM Computer Communication Review,* Vol. 25, No. 2, April 1995.
> Describes *Service Specific Connection-Oriented Protocol,* a transport protocol used in ATM signaling.

[HL 96] D. P. Heyman and T. V. Lakshman. What Are the Implications of Long-Range Dependence for VBR Video Traffic Engineering? *IEEE/ACM Transactions on Networking,* Vol. 4, June 1996.

[JDSZ 95] S. Jamin, P. B. Danzig, S. Shenker, and L. Zhang. A Measurement-Based Admission Control Algorithm for Integrated Services Packet Networks. *Proceedings of ACM SIGCOMM '95,* Boston, September 1995.
> Proposes measurement-based admission control for predictive service.

[Kalmanek 95] C.R. Kalmanek. Why Is Signaling Hard? *Proceedings of Workshop on Open Signaling,* Columbia University, October 1995.

[Kelly 91] F. P. Kelly. Loss Networks. *The Annals of Applied Probability,* 1991, pp. 319–378.
> Exhaustive survey of recent research in routing in telephone networks.

[Keshav 91] S. Keshav. Congestion Control in Computer Networks. *Ph.D. Thesis,* U.C. Berkeley, issued as UCB Technical Report 91/469, August 1991.

[MS 90] A. Modarressi and R. A. Skoog. Signaling System No. 7: A Tutorial. *IEEE Communications Magazine,* July 1990, pp. 19–34.
    A crisp summary of the SS7 protocol stack.

[Mukherjee 94] A. Mukherjee. On the Dynamics and Significance of Low Frequency Components of Internet Load. *Journal of Internetworking: Research and Experience,* Vol. 5, 1994, pp. 163–205.
    A detailed examination of Internet behavior on the time scale of a day.

[MV 95] H. MacKie-Mason and H. R. Varian. Pricing Congestible Network Resources. *IEEE Journal on Selected Areas in Communication,* Vol. 13, No. 7, September 1995, pp. 1141–1149.
    Shows the impact of flat-rate and congestion pricing on network behavior.

[PF 94] V. Paxson and S. Floyd. Wide-Area Traffic: The Failure of Poisson Modeling. *Proceedings of ACM SIGCOMM '94,* London, September 1994.
    Uses measurements to claim that Poisson models do not adequately describe real traffic.

[Pressman 70] I. Pressman. A Mathematical Formulation of the Peak Load Pricing Problem. *Bell Journal of Economics and Management Science,* Vol. 1, Autumn 1970, pp. 304–326.

[RE 96] B. K. Ryu and A. Elwalid. The Importance of Long-Range Dependence of VBR Video Traffic in ATM Traffic Engineering: Myths and Realities. *Proceedings of ACM SIGCOMM'96,* September 1996.

[Roberts 92] J. W. Roberts, ed. Performance Evaluation and Design of Multiservice Networks. COST 224 Final Report, Commission of the European Communities, Brussels, 1992.
    An analytical view of integrated services network design.

[SCZ 93] S. Shenker, D. Clark, and L. Zhang. A Scheduling Service Model and a Scheduling Architecture for an Integrated Services Packet Network. *Working Paper, Xerox PARC,* August 1993.
    An early description of the service architecture that is being adopted by the IETF.

[Shenker 95] S. Shenker. Service Models and Pricing Policies for an Integrated Services Internet. In Public Access to the Internet (Brian Kahin and James Keller, Eds.). *Prentice-Hall,* 1995.
    Uses simple economic models to formulate economic principles for traffic management.

[Shiryaev 96] A. N. Shiryaev. Probability, *Springer Verlag,* 1996.
    Graduate textbook on probability.

[SW 95] A. Shwartz and A. Weiss. Large Deviations for Performance Analysis: Queues, Communications, and Computing. *Chapman & Hall,* New York, 1995.

> A textbook that describes this powerful technique for queueing analysis.

[VPV 88] W. Verbiest, L. Pinnoo, and B. Voeten. The Impact of the ATM Concept on Video Coding. *IEEE Journal on Selected Areas in Communication,* December 1988, pp. 1623–1632.

> Describes how to carry variable-bit-rate compressed traffic with ATM services.

[WTSW 95] W. Willinger, M.S. Taqqu, R. Sherman, and D.V. Wilson. Self-Similarity through High-Variability: Statistical Analysis and Ethernet LAN Traffic at the Source Level. *Proceedings of ACM SIGCOMM'95,* Boston, September 1995.

> Proposes the superposition of heavy-tailed arrival processes as the mechanism giving rise to long-range dependence and self-similarity in aggregated traffic.

[ZDEZ 93] L. Zhang, S. Deering, D. Estrin, S. Shenker, and D. Zappala. RSVP: A New Resource ReSerVation Protocol. *IEEE Network Magazine,* Vol. 7, No. 5, September 1993, pp. 8–19.

> A description of the first version of the RSVP protocol. A formal description of the latest version is available online.

References for Chapter 15: Common Protocols

[AKS 96] R. Ahuja, S. Keshav, and H. Saran. Design, Implementation and Performance Measurement of a Native-Mode ATM Transport Protocol. *IEEE/ACM Transactions on Networking,* August 1996.

> Describes the design and implementation of a task-based in-kernel transport layer that exploits AAL5 functionality in hardware to deliver high performance on cheap personal computers.

[ANSI 88] American National Standards Institute. ANSI T1.105-1988 American National Standard for Telecommunications, Digital Hierarchy-Optical Interface Rates and Formats Specifications, 1988.

> SONET standard.

[Armitage 95a] G. J. Armitage. Multicast and Multiprotocol Support for ATM-based Internets, *ACM SIGCOMM Computer Communication Review,* Vol. 25, No. 2, April 1995.

> Excellent tutorial on several approaches for carrying IP traffic over ATM networks.

[Armitage 95b] G. J. Armitage. Support for Multicast over UNI3.1-based ATM Networks, *Internet Draft ⟨draft-ietf-ipatm-ipmc-04.txt⟩,* February 1995.

> Describes the MARS approach to IP multicast support in ATM LANs.

[BBP 88] R. Braden, D. A. Borman, and C. Partridge. Computing the Internet Checksum. *RFC 1071,* September 1988.

Tricks and advice in implementing the IP checksum (this checksum is also used in UDP and TCP).

[BC 92] C. C. Bissell and D. A. Chapman. Digital Signal Transmission. *Cambridge University Press*, 1992.

Excellent reference on the physical and datalink layers in telecommunication networks.

[Bellamy 91] J. Bellamy. Digital Telephony. *John Wiley and Sons*, New York, 1991.

A good introduction to telephone network engineering.

[Berners-Lee 94] T. Berners-Lee. Universal Resource Identifiers in WWW: A Unifying Syntax for the Expression of Names and Addresses of Objects on the Network as Used in the World Wide Web. *RFC 1630*, June 1994.

Formal definition of URIs and URLs.

[BFF 95] T. Berners-Lee, Roy T. Fielding, and H. Frystyk Nielsen. Hypertext Transfer Protocol, Version 1.0, Draft 5. `http://www.w3.org/hypertext/WWW/Protocols/Overview.html`, 1995.

[BMM 94] T. Berners-Lee, L. Masinter, and M. McCahill. Uniform Resource Locators (URL), *RFC 1738*, December 1994.

[Brim 96] S. Brim (Ed.). Cells in Frames, Version 1.0: Specification, Analysis, and Discussion. `http://www.cif.cornell.edu`, October 1996.

Rationale and specification of the Cells in Frame proposal.

[BZBHJ 96] R. Braden, L. Zhang, S. Berson, S. Herzog, and S. Jamin. Resource ReSerVation Protocol (RSVP)—Version 1, Functional Specification. *Internet draft available from* `http://www.apocalypse.org:80/cgi-bin/mfs/04/draft-ietf-rsvp-spec-11.txt`, March 1996.

Work in progress that describes the RSVP signaling protocol.

[EWLBCD 94] A. Edwards, G. Watson, J. Lumley, D. Banks, C. Calamvokis, and C. Dalton. User-Space Protocols Deliver High Performance to Applications on a Low-Cost Gb/s LAN. *Proceedings of ACM SIGCOMM'94*, London, September 1994.

[FFBGM 96] R. T. Fielding, H. Frystyk Nielsen, T. Berners-Lee, J. Gettys, and J. Mogul. Hypertext Transfer Protocol, Version 1.1, Draft 2. `http://www.w3.org/hypertext/WWW/Protocols/Overview.html`, April 1996.

[GR 96] M. Grossglauser and K. K. Ramakrishnan. SEAM: Scalable and Efficient ATM Multipoint-to-Multipoint Multicasting. *Proceedings of NOSSDAV '96*, April 1996.

Describes a technique for efficient multipoint-to-multipoint multicast of AAL5 frames.

[Heinanen 93] J. Heinanen. Multiprotocol Encapsulation over ATM Adaptation Layer 5. *RFC 1483*, July 1993.

Describes how to encapsulate layer-3 protocols over AAL5, including IP.

[Henderson 95] T. R. Henderson. Design Principles and Performance Analysis of SSCOP: A New ATM Adaptation Layer Protocol. *ACM Computer Communication Review,* Vol. 25, No. 2, April 1995.
>   Describes the SSCOP transport protocol used in ATM signaling.

[HHS 94] R. Handel, M. N. Huber, and S. Schroder. ATM Networks: Concepts, Protocols and Applications. *Addison-Wesley,* 1994.
>   Introduction to ATM standards.

[Kent 91] S. T. Kent. U.S. Department of Defense Security Options for the Internet Protocol. *RFC 1108,* November 1991.

[KLPRS 95] S. Keshav, C. Lund, S. Phillips, N. Reingold, and H. Saran. An Empirical Evaluation of Virtual Circuit Holding Time Policies for IP-over-ATM Networks. *IEEE Journal on Selected Areas in Communication,* October 1995.
>   A description, analysis, and experimental study of several holding-time heuristics.

[KPCL 96] D. Katz, D. Piscitello, Bruce Cole, and James V. Luciani. NBMA Next Hop Resolution Protocol (NHRP). *Internet Draft <draft-ietf-rolc-nhrp-07.txt,>* January 96.

[Laubach 94] M. Laubach. Classical IP and ARP over ATM. *RFC 1577,* January 1994.

[LMKQ 89] S. J. Leffler, M. K. McKusick, M. J. Karels, and J. S. Quarterman. The Design and Implementation of the 4.3BSD UNIX Operating System. *Addison-Wesley,* 1989.

[MK 87] C. A. Kent and J. C. Mogul. Fragmentation Considered Harmful. *Proceedings of ACM SIGCOMM '87,* 1987.
>   An influential and insightful criticism of IP fragmentation.

[MK 90] T. Mallory and A. Kullberg. Incremental Updating of the Internet Checksum. *RFC 1141,* January 1990.
>   A trick that allows IP routers to recompute the header checksum (required because the TTL changes) without touching every byte of the header.

[MS 90] A. R. Modarressi and R. A. Skoog. Signaling System No. 7: A Tutorial. *IEEE Communications Magazine,* July 1990.
>   A crisp summary of the SS7 protocol stack.

[Pendarakis 96] D. Pendarakis. On the Tradeoff between Transport and Signaling in Broadband Network. *Ph.D. thesis, Columbia University,* April 1996.
>   Analyzes the trade-offs between signaling overhead and resource wastage in ATM networks with virtual paths.

[Postel 81] J. B. Postel. Internet Protocol. *RFC 791,* September 1981.

[Postel 81a] J. B. Postel. Internet Control Message Protocol. *RFC 792,* September 1981.

[Postel 81b] J. B. Postel. Transmission Control Protocol. *RFC 793,* September 1981.

[Rijsinghani 94] A. Rijsinghani. Computation of the Internet Checksum via Incremental Update. *RFC 1624,* 1994.

[Ritchie 84] D. Ritchie. A Stream Input–Output System. *AT&T Bell Laboratories Technical Journal,* Vol. 63, No. 8, 1984, pp. 1897–1910.
      Classic reference on streams.

[RP 94] J. Reynolds and J. Postel. Assigned Numbers. *RFC 1700,* October 1994.
      The standard set of protocol numbers, and port numbers assigned to services, in the Internet.

[SJ 95] K.-Y. Siu and R. Jain. A Brief Overview of ATM: Protocol Layers, LAN Emulation, and Traffic Management. *ACM SIGCOMM Computer Communication Review,* Vol. 25, No. 2, April 1995.

[Stevens 94] W. R. Stevens. TCP/IP Illustrated, Vol. 1. *Addison-Wesley,* 1994.
      Comprehensive description of Internet protocols and TCP/IP as implemented in 4.4 BSD Unix.

[TELMP 95] H. Truong, W. Ellington, J. Le Boudec, A. Meier, and J. Pace. LAN Emulation on an ATM Network. *IEEE Communications Magazine,* Vol. 33, No. 5, May 1995, pp. 70–85.
      Overview of LANE.

[ZDEZ 93] L. Zhang, S. Deering, D. Estrin, S. Shenker, and D. Zappala. RSVP: A New Resource ReSerVation Protocol. *IEEE Network Magazine,* Vol. 7, No. 5, September 1993, pp. 8–19.
      A tutorial on RSVP.

References for Chapter 16: Protocol Implementation

[AKS 96] R. Ahuja, S. Keshav, and H. Saran. Design, Implementation and Performance Measurement of a Native-Mode ATM Transport Protocol. *IEEE/ACM Transactions on Networking,* August 1996.
      Describes the design and implementation of a task-based in-kernel transport layer that exploits AAL5 functionality in hardware to deliver high performance on cheap personal computers.

[CJRS 89] D. D. Clark, V. Jacobson, J. Romkey, and H. Salwen. An Analysis of TCP Processing Overhead. *IEEE Communications Magazine,* June 1989, pp 23–29.
      Insightful analysis into why TCP processing can be slow, and how to make it fast.

[Clark 82] D. D. Clark. Modularity and Efficiency in Procotocol Implementation. *RFC 817,* July 1982.
      Classic reference on protocol implementation strategies.

[Clark 85] D. D. Clark. The Structuring of Systems Using Upcalls. *Proceedings of 10th ACM Symposium on Operating Systems Principles,* December 1985, pp. 171–180.
> Describes upcall architecture.

[CT 90] D. D. Clark and D. L. Tennenhouse. Architectural Considerations for a New Generation of Protocols. *Proceedings of ACM SIGCOMM'90,* Philadelphia, September 1990, p. 200–208.
> Proposes controlled coalescing of protocol layers to improve performance.

[CV 95] A. M. Costello and G. Varghese. Redesigning the BSD Callout and Timer Facilities. Techical Report WUCS-95-23, Washington University, November 1995, available from `http://siesta.cs.wustl.edu/~amc/research/timer/`.
> Details of implementing timing wheels in the BSD operating system.

[DPD 94] P. Druschel, L. L. Peterson, and B. S. Davie. Experiences with a High-Speed Network Adaptor: A Software Perspective. *Proceedings of ACM SIGCOMM'94,* London, September 1994.
> Describes performance tuning for high-performance host adaptors and application device channels.

[EM 95] A. Edwards and S. Muir. Experiences Implementing a High-Performance TCP in User-Space. *Proceedings of ACM SIGCOMM '95,* Cambridge, September 1995, pp. 196–205.

[EWLBCD 94] A. Edwards, G. Watson, J. Lumley, D. Banks, C. Calamvokis, and C. Dalton. User-Space Protocols Deliver High Performance to Applications on a Low-Cost Gb/s LAN. *Proceedings of ACM SIGCOMM'94,* London, September 1994.

[HP 91] N. Hutchinson and L. Peterson. The x-Kernel: An Architecture for Implementing Network Protocols. *IEEE Transactions on Software Engineering,* Vol. 17, No. 1, January 1991, pp. 64–76.
> Describes a threads-based approach to protocol implementation.

[KP 93] J. Kay and J. Pasquale. The Importance of Non-Data-Touching Processing Overheads in TCP/IP. *Proceedings of ACM SIGCOMM'93,* San Francisco, September 1993, pp. 259–269.

[Mogul 93] J. Mogul. IP Network Performance. *In* Internet System Handbook (D. C. Lynch and M. T. Rose, Eds.). *Addison-Wesley,* 1993.
> An exhaustive survey of techniques for measuring and improving IP performance.

[Mogul 95] J. Mogul. The Case for Persistent-Connection HTTP. *Proceedings of ACM SIGCOMM'95,* Cambridge, September 1995, pp. 299–313.
> An analysis to show how HTTP wastes resources by opening a TCP connection per embedded object, and how to fix it.

[MRA 87] J. Mogul, R. F. Rashid, and M. J. Acetta. The Packet Filter: An Efficient Mechanism for User-Level Network Code. *Proceedings of 11th ACM Symposium on Operating Systems Principles,* November 1987, pp. 39–51.

> Describes the packet-filter approach, where packets are demultiplexed in the kernel and handed directly to applications.

[PH 95] D. Patterson and J. Hennesey. Computer Organization and Design: The Hardware/Software Interface. *Morgan Kaufman,* 1995.

> Standard introductory text on computer architecture.

[TNML 93] C. A. Thekkath, T. D. Nguyen, E. Moy, and E. D. Lazowska. Implementing Network Protocols at User Level. *Proceedings of ACM SIGCOMM'93,* San Francisco, September 1993.

> Pioneering work on user-level protocol implementation.

[VBBV 95] T. von Eicken, A. Basu, V. Buch, and W. Vogels. U-Net: A User-Level Network Interface for Parallel and Distributed Computing. *Proceedings of ACM Symposium on Operating Systems Principles,* December 1995.

> A high-performance user-level protocol implementation that emphasizes low-latency communication.

[VL 87] G. Varghese and T. Lauck. Hashed and Hierarchical Timing Wheels: Data Structures for the Efficient Implementation of a Timer Facility. *Proceedings of 11th ACM Symposium on Operating Systems Principles,* November 1987, pp. 25–38.

[WM 87] R. Watson and S. Mamrak. Gaining Efficiency in Transport Services by Appropriate Design and Implementation Choices. *ACM Transactions on Computer Systems,* Vol. 5, No. 2, 1987, pp. 97–120.

> Classic reference on protocol implementation techniques.

Glossary

The number at the end of each definition is the section in the text that provides a context for the term. Italicized words in definitions are further defined in the glossary.

(n,k) code: A block code where k bits of input data are converted to an n-bit *codeword*. [12.2]

μ-law: A particular choice of *quantization levels* used in the United States and Japan. [2.3.2]

100VG AnyLAN: A variant of Ethernet where the transmission speed is 100 Mbps, and stations are connected with a point-to-point link to a hub that explicitly synchronizes data transmission. [7.5.2]

A-law: A particular choice of *quantization levels* used outside the United States and Japan. [2.3.2]

AAL: See *ATM Adaptation Layer.*

ABR source: See *Available-bit-rate source.*

Absolute fairness bound: A bound on the difference in the amount of service received by a *backlogged* connection and the same connection when using *GPS*, over any time interval. [9.4.4]

ACR: See *Allocated cell rate.*

Add–drop multiplexor: A hardware device that allows some streams to be removed from a multiplexed stream, and replaced with other streams. [8.2.1]

Address: An easily-parsed, usually fixed-length descriptor for an endpoint. [10.1]

Addressing: The process of assigning unique *addresses* to endpoints. [10.1]

Addressing authority: An entity responsible for allocating *addresses* in a network. [10.2]

Address Resolution Protocol: A protocol that allows a host on a broadcast LAN to translate from an IP address to a datalink-layer address for the host adaptor with that IP address. [10.10]

AFI: See *Authority and format indicator.*

Allocated cell rate: The current sending rate of a source in the *EERC* scheme. [13.4.9]

ALOHA: A *multiple-access* scheme, used primarily in satellite networks, where a station that wants to send data just does so, without regard to other transmissions. [7.5.5]

Amdahl's law: The execution time after improving a system is given by:

Execution time after improvement =

(Execution time affected by improvement / Amount of improvement)

+ Execution time unaffected [6.3.5]

Anycast address: A type of multicast address in IP v6. A packet sent to an anycast address is sent to *one* of the interfaces associated with that address. [10.6.5]

Application service element: An application in the *SS7* protocol stack. [15.2.4]

Arbiter: A device that decides which set of packets should next access a *switching fabric* in an *input-queued switch.* [8.5.1]

Area code: The part of a telephone number that identifies a level in the telephone network hierarchy. [2.1]

ARP: See *Address Resolution Protocol.*

ARP server: A server that resolves IP addresses to ATM addresses. [15.5.2]

ASE: See *Application service element.*

Asynchronous time-division multiplexing: The idea of attaching a header to a voice sample to allow a recipient to distinguish between sources without being in exact synchrony with the sender. [4.1.1]

Asynchronous Transfer Mode: A *virtual-circuit* oriented, *packet-switched* networking technology, where information is carried in fixed-size *cells.* [4]

ATDM: See *Asynchronous time-division multiplexing.*

ATM: See *Asynchronous Transfer Mode.*

ATM cell: A fixed sized (53-byte) packet used in ATM networks. [4.2]

ATM Adaptation Layer: A layer that sits directly above the ATM layer and provides services such as segmentation and reassembly, loss detection, and jitter elimination. [15.4.3]

ATM Forum: An industry group that proposes interoperability standards for ATM equipment manufacturers. [4.6]

Authoritative server: A server that has the authoritative translation from a particular name to a particular address in the *Domain Name System.* [10.8]

Authority and format indicator: A field in an *NSAP address* that indicates the *addressing authority* delegated by the International Standards Organization to hand out parts of the address space. [10.7]

Autonomous system: A set of routers and end-systems that are administered by a single authority. [11.8.3]

Available-bit-rate source: A traffic source that adapts its cell generation rate to the rate the network can support. [14.4.3]

Average rate: The asymptotic rate at which a source transmits measured over increasingly longer time periods. [13.3.3]

Backlogged connection: A connection that has a packet-awaiting service in *GPS.* [9.4.1]

Balance circuit: An electrical circuit that partly eliminates *sidetone.* [2.2.2]

Balanced system: A system where all resources are simultaneously bottlenecked. [6.3]

Bandwidth: A measure of the information-carrying capacity of a link (the "width" of the information "pipe"). [2.3.1]

Banyan network: A type of *switching fabric* used in third-generation packet switches. [8.4.4]

Base station: A *station* in a *cell* that coordinates access to the wired network by *mobiles.* [2.6]

Batcher–Banyan network: A *switching fabric* consisting of a *Batcher network,* a *perfect shuffle network,* and a *Banyan network.* [8.4.6]

Batcher network: A form of *sorting network.* [8.4.5]

Batching: A technique to trade off response time for throughput by collecting a batch of tasks, then executing them all at once. This is efficient if task overhead increases sublinearly with the number of tasks. [6.3.3]

BCH code: See *Bose–Chaudhuri–Hocquenghem* code.

Beacon: A periodic signal sent by a *base station* to allow *mobiles* to determine the base station with the strongest signal. [2.6.1]

BER: See *Bit-error ratio.*

Best-effort application: An application that does not need a performance bound from the network. [9.1.1, 14.4.1]

Best-effort service: A service where the network only transports data, but does not guarantee *performance bounds* on its service. [9.1.1, 14.4.1]

BGP: See *Border Gateway Protocol.*

Binding: The process of translating from an abstraction to its current instance. [6.3.7]

Binding constraint: The most constrained resource in a system. [6.3]

BISDN: See *Broadband ISDN.*

Bit corruption: The conversion of a bit from a 0 to a 1 or vice versa, because of an error. [12]

Bit-error rate: See *Bit-error ratio.*

Bit-error ratio: The ratio of the mean number of errors in any given interval to the total number of bits in that interval. [12.1]

Black hole: Where misrouted packets go. [11.2]

Block code: A code where each block of input data is transformed into a longer *codeword.* [12.2]

Border gateway: A *router* that participates in both an *exterior gateway protocol* and an *interior gateway protocol.* [11.8.3]

Border Gateway Protocol: A *path-vector* protocol used as an *exterior gateway protocol* on the Internet. [11.9.4]

Bose–Chaudhuri–Hocquenghem code: A *CRC*-like code where the alphabet is a block of bits, instead of {0,1}. [12.2.6]

Bottleneck server: The slowest server on the path from a source to a destination for a particular *connection.* [13.1]

Bridge: A switch that works at the datalink layer. [8.3]

Broadband ISDN: Similar to *ISDN,* except that the data rates can be much higher (>1.5 Mbs). [4.6]

BTMA: See *Busy-tone multiple access.*

Bursty packet loss: The observation that packet losses in a multiplexor buffer occur in bursts (i.e., closely spaced in time), rather than evenly spread out in time. [12.3.1]

Busy-tone multiple access: A form of *CSMA* where a receiver places a busy tone on an auxiliary channel to indicate to potential transmitters that the medium is busy. This solves the *exposed terminal* and *hidden terminal* problems. [7.5.3]

Call arrival model: A model that describes how calls are placed. [14.3.1]

Call establishment: See *Call Setup.*

Call holding-time model: A model that describes how long a call lasts. [14.3.1]

Call setup: The process of establishing a *connection* between a source and a destination. [4.1.4]

Capacity: The maximum information flow possible over a link, given its noise characteristics. [2.3.1]

Capacity planning: The set of techniques used to manage a network over the time scale of a few weeks or longer. [14.11]

Capture: The situation in a radio link where a signal from one of the transmitting *stations* is much higher than the signal from other transmitters at a particular receiver, so that the receiver receives only the high-power signal. [7.2.2]

Care-of agent: The wired computer "nearest" to a *mobile host* that accepts and forwards packets on behalf of the mobile host. [11.13.2]

Carrier-sense multiple access: A set of *multiple-access* schemes where stations check whether the carrier is active before sending data, in order to avoid *collisions* with other packets. [7.5.2]

CBR source: See *Constant-bit-rate* source.

CBT: See *Core-based tree.*

CCIS: See *Common Channel Interoffice Signaling network.*

CCITT: An international telecommunications standardization body now subsumed by the *International Telecommunications Union.* CCITT is now called ITU-T. [4]

CDMA: See *Code-division multiple access.*

CDPD: See *Cellular Digital Packet Data.*

Cell: A geographical area that is assigned a particular set of frequencies for use in replacing the *local loop.* [2.6]

Cell: A fixed-size *packet,* usually used in the context of an *ATM* network. [4.2]

Cell loss priority: A bit in the ATM header that indicates to the network whether a packet should be preferentially dropped. [15.4.2]

Cells in Frame: A method by which hosts with Ethernet adaptors can attach through a *Cells in Frame Attachment Device* to an ATM network. [15.5.6]

Cells in Frame Attachment Device: A multiplexor that converts data in Ethernet frames to ATM format and vice versa. [15.5.6]

Cellular Digital Packet Data: A *packet-mode* overlay over the *EAMPS circuit-mode* cellular telephony service in the United States. [7.4.1]

Centralized multiple-access scheme: A scheme where a master controls which slave can next access a shared medium. [7.2.1]

Centralized routing: A form of routing where a central administrative authority installs routes at all *routers.* [11.3]

Central office: A telephone company office in the local area of a telephone subscriber that provides telephone service. [2.1]

CH: See *corresponding host.*

CIDR: See *Classless interdomain routing.*

CIF: See *Cells in Frame.*

CIF-AD: See *Cells in Frame Attachment Device.*

Circuit: A data path from a source to a destination that is much like an electrical circuit, with signals flowing simultaneously in both directions. [2.1]

Circuit-mode transfer: The transfer of a steady stream of information from a *station* in a *multiple-access scheme.* [7.2.1]

Circuit switch: A switch that switches a voice sample based on the time at which it arrives to the switch. [8.1.1]

Class A address: An Internet address that has 7 bits for the network number and 24 bits for the host number. The first bit of a Class A address is 0. [3.3.1]

Class B address: An Internet address that has 14 bits for the network number and 16 bits for the host number. The first 2 bits of a Class B address are 10. [3.3.1]

Class C address: An Internet address that has 21 bits for the network number and 8 bits for the host number. The first 3 bits of a Class C address are 110. [3.3.1]

Class D address: An Internet address that is reserved for multicast group addresses. The first 4 bits of a Class D address are 1110. [3.3.1, 11.11.1]

Classless interdomain routing: A technique that allows multiple network numbers to be aggregated together to form a single logical network number, for the sake of aggregation in routing tables. [10.6.3]

Closed-loop flow control: A form of *flow control* where a source's transmission rate depends on the congestion state of the network. [13.2]

CLP: See *Cell loss priority.*

CO: See *Central office.*

COA: See *Care-of agent.*

Coaxial cable: A cable consisting of a signal wire encased in an insulator surrounded by a wire-mesh carrying ground. [2.3.3]

Code-division multiple access: A technology where stations sharing a medium are separated both in time and in space simultaneously. [7.3.3]

Codeword: The block of bits that is the output of a block code. [12.2]

Collision: A situation in a *multiple access* scheme where two packets are simultaneously sent on the medium, so that neither is correctly received. [7.1]

Common Channel Interoffice Signaling network: A datagram network interconnecting *switch controllers* in the telephone network to control and manage the network. [2.5.2]

Congestion-avoidance phase: A phase in TCP flow control where the *flow-control window* size increases linearly with time. [13.4.5]

Congestion pricing: A form of pricing where a user's fee depends on the disutility the user's traffic causes other users. [14.2.2]

Conservation law: A law that roughly states that the weighted sum of queuing delays at a *server,* where weights represent mean arrival rates, is independent of the *scheduling discipline.* [9.1.1]

Constant-bit-rate source: A traffic source that generates cells that are equally spaced. [14.4.3]

Constrained resource: A resource that is scarce and whose availability determines overall system performance. [6.1.1]

Continuous media: Media such as audio and video that, when digitized, generate a continuous stream of packets. [9.2.3]

Controlled flooding: A form of *flooding* where a node forwards nonduplicate incoming packets on all but the incoming interface. [11.6.1]

Convolutional code: A code where each coded bit is obtained by the discrete convolution of a particular polynomial with a subset of the input string. [12.2.7]

Copy network: A component of a *switching fabric* that makes multiple copies of a single input packet for broadcast or multicast. [8.6.1]

Core-based tree: A technique for multicast routing where all multicast packets sent on a *multicast group* are sent through a special router called a core. [11.11.9]

Corresponding host: The host that a *mobile host* is communicating with. [11.13.2]

Count-to-infinity: A problem with *distance-vector routing* where, on a link failure, one or more nodes increase the cost to an unreachable destination incrementally to infinity, instead of directly detecting the problem. [11.5.2]

Crankback: The process by which, at the time of call establishment, a *switch controller* tries several alternative paths, in order to find one that can provide an adequate quality of service. [11.4.2, 11.12.3]

CRC: See *Cyclic redundancy checksum.*

Crossbar: A simple switch where inputs arrive along rows of a matrix, and outputs are connected to columns. Data is switched by activating the cross point connecting a particular row to a particular column. [8.2.4]

CSMA: See *Carrier-sense multiple access.*

CSMA/CA: A form of *CSMA* used in wireless LANs where a station that wants to send data and senses a busy medium waits until the end of the transmission, and then an additional time called the interframe spacing. [7.5.2]

CSMA/CD: *CSMA*/Collision Detect, a variant of *CSMA* where a station not only checks for other stations before transmission, but, during transmission, detects whether *collisions* occurred. [7.5.2]

Cumulative acknowledgment: An acknowledgment carrying the sequence number of the last in-sequence packet received by a receiver. [12.4.7]

Cyclic redundancy checksum: A common form of error detection where we treat the data string as a single number, divide it by a *generator,* and use the remainder as the checksum. [12.2.5]

Datagram: A *packet* that carries the destination address in its header. [4.1.3]

Datalink-layer address: The address of an end-system used by the datalink layer. [5.5.2]

Data plane: The *protocol stack* responsible for data transfer. [5.5.3]

DECbit flow control: A technique for *flow control* where *congested* network elements set a bit carried in each packet header, and sources use this information to decrease their *flow-control window* size. [13.4.4]

Default address: The address to which a *router* forwards packets whose destination address cannot be found in the *routing table.* [3.4.2]

Default route: The next hop for packets whose destination address cannot be found in the routing table. [11.10.1]

Degree of parallelism: The mean number of concurrent activities in a system. [6.2.1]

Delay jitter: The difference between the smallest and the largest delay received by any two packets in a connection. [9.2.3]

Delay-jitter regulator: A *regulator* that shapes traffic to remove *delay jitter* introduced at the previous switch. [9.4.2]

Demultiplexor: A hardware device that splits a *multiplexed* stream into its constituent streams. [8.2.1]

Designated router: A router participating in *OSPF* that acts on behalf of its peers on a broadcast LAN. [11.9.2]

Deterministic routing: The opposite of *stochastic routing.* With deterministic routing, a *router* always picks the same next hop for a given destination. [11.3]

Digital Network Architecture: Internet-style proprietary packet network developed by Digital Electronics Corporation. [3.6.2]

Digital signaling transmission hierarchy: The set of allowed multiplexing levels in the United States. [2.3.2]

Digital transmission hierarchy: The set of multiplexed rates allowed in the telephone network. [15.2.2]

Dijkstra's algorithm: An algorithm to compute the shortest path from a node to every other node in the network. [11.6.2]

Distance vector: An array of distances from a given node to every other node in the network. [11.5]

Distance-Vector Multicast Routing Protocol: A *distance-vector* protocol used to compute shortest paths between routers on the *MBONE.* [11.11.8]

Distance-vector routing: A *routing protocol* where the shortest-path computation is based on periodic exchange of *distance vectors.* [11.5]

Distributed routing: A form of routing where *routers* cooperate using a distributed *routing protocol* to create mutually consistent *routing tables.* [11.3]

Distributed Update Algorithm: A technique to assure loop-free routing tables where a router freezes its routing table when a change happens, and propagates the change to every other affected router before unfreezing its table again. [11.5.2]

Distribution: A function that maps a value *x* to the probability that a *random variable* takes this value. [14.3.1]

DNA: See *Digital Network Architecture.*

DNHR: See *Dynamic Non-Hierarchical Routing.*

DNS: See *Domain Name System.*

Dogleg routing: A problem in mobile IP where a *mobile host* talking to a "nearby" computer must still route packets through its remote *home address agent.* [11.13.2]

Domain: A portion of the *name space.* [10.3]

Domain Name System: A distributed set of servers in the Internet that translate from a *name* to an *address.* [10.8]

Downlink: The directional link from a master to a slave in a *centralized multiple-access scheme.* [7.2.1]

DS hierarchy: See *Digital Signal hierarchy.*

DS/CDMA: A form of *CDMA* where a station replaces each bit of transmitted data with a set of bits called the *codeword.* [7.3.3]

DUAL: See *Distributed Update Algorithm.*

DVMRP: See *Distance Vector Multicast Routing Protocol.*

Dynamic Nonhierarchical routing: A routing algorithm used in the *telephone network core* which assigns each *toll switch* a primary route and an ordered set of alternative routes, depending on the time of the day. [11.4.2]

Dynamic-rate flow control: A form of *flow control* where a source's transmission rate is directly controlled by adjusting the time interval between its packet transmissions. [13.4]

Dynamic routing: See *State-dependent routing.*

Dynamic-window flow control: A form of *flow control* where a source's transmission rate is controlled by adjusting its *flow-control window.* [13.4]

EAMPS: Extended Advanced Mobile Phone Service; the analog *FDD/FDMA* cellular phone service used in the United States and Japan. [7.4.1]

Earliest-due-date scheduling: A *scheduling discipline* that serves packets in order of their deadlines. [9.5.3]

Early packet discard: A buffer drop policy where an ATM multiplexor drops entire packets instead of individual cells by marking a *virtual circuit* as being in a "drop" state when the buffer occupancy crosses a threshold. Cells arriving to a virtual circuit in this state are dropped until a cell carrying an end-of-packet marker is seen. [12.3.2]

Echo cancellation circuit: An active circuit that eliminates annoying echoes due to *sidetone* in long-haul trunks. [2.2.2]

EDD: See *Earliest-due-date* scheduling.

EERC: A technique for *dynamic-rate flow control* proposed by the *ATM Forum* which uses explicit rate information carried in *Resource Management cells* to adjust a source's transmission rate. [13.4.9]

EGP: See *Exterior Gateway Protocol.*

Elasticity buffer: A buffer at the receiver in a *playback application* that eliminates *delay jitter.* [9.2.3]

Encapsulated Protocol Data Unit: A packet to which an *AAL* has added a header, trailer, or both. [15.4.3]

End-System Identifier: The number of a host using *NSAP addresses.* [10.7]

EPDU: See *Encapsulated Protocol Data Unit.*

Erlang: A load of one call for one unit of time. [14.11.2]

Erlang fixed point: The fixed-point solution for the *Erlang map.* The coupled equations reach mutually consistent solutions at the fixed point. [11.4.2]

Erlang formula: A formula that relates the call-blocking probability to the link capacity and the mean activity time of a source. [14.11.2]

Erlang map: The set of coupled equations that describe the dependency between the routing protocol and the load on a link. [11.4.2]

Error control: The process of detecting and correcting bit and packet errors. [12]

Error-control window: The smallest contiguous subset of the *sequence space* that contains the sequence numbers of all the packets that have been transmitted but not acknowledged. [12.4.7]

Error-correcting code: A code which allows one or more bit errors to be corrected. [12.2]

Errored codeword: A *codeword* with one or more corrupted bits. [12.2.3]

Error multiplication: The process by which a single error is multiplied to many. [12.1.4, 12.3.2]

Error syndrome: The set of parity checks that fail because of a bit error in a *perfect-parity* code. The failed checks identify the bit in error. [12.2.3]

ESI: See *End-System Identifier.*

Exchange: A *switch* in a *central office* that provides local switching to end-systems. [2.1]

Expanding-ring search: A form of resource discovery using *multicast.* [11.11.2]

Exponential averaging filter: A way to smooth a time series of values to reduce the effect of observation noise. [12.4.6]

Exponential distribution: A *distribution* where the probability that a *random variable* takes a value larger than x is given by $e^{-x/\lambda}$, where λ is the mean of the distribution. [14.3.1]

Exposed terminal problem: A problem in wireless LANs where a well-sited station can hear transmissions even from nonlocal networks, so that it thinks the medium is busy even when it is not. [7.5.3]

Exterior Gateway Protocol: A distance-vector *routing* protocol used as an exterior gateway protocol between *autonomous systems* in the Internet. [11.8.3, 11.9.3]

External record: A record in the *LSP database* that describes the cost to a router at a higher level in the routing hierarchy. [11.8.2]

Facility switch: See *transit switch.*

Fading: The loss of signal strength at a mobile station due to obstructions, interference, or movement. [7.2.2, 12.1.6]

Fast Ethernet: A variant of Ethernet where the transmission speed is 100 Mbps. [7.5.2]

Fast retransmission: A retransmission technique where the sender treats a repeated *cumulative acknowledgment* as an indication of packet loss and retransmits the lost packet. [12.4.7]

FDD: See *Frequency-division duplex.*

FDDI: A LAN based on *token-ring* technology, where the LAN consists of dual counter-rotating rings. [7.5.4]

FDMA: See *Frequency-division multiple access.*

Feature interaction: The problem where two signaling features specify inconsistent outcomes for the same actions. [14.8.5]

FEC: See *Forward error correction.*

FH/CDMA: A form of *CDMA* where a station hops from one frequency to another in a predetermined schedule during its transmission. [7.3.3]

Filter: A function specified using *RSVP* that selects certain packets for forwarding on each link. [14.8.5]

Finish number: The *service tag* used in WFQ. [9.4.4]

Flood-and-prune: An approach to IP *multicast* where a source periodically floods a network with its packets, and all receivers who do not want to be part of the *multicast group* can *prune* their membership. [11.11.6]

Flooding: A method of propagating information where a node copies an incoming packet to every output line. [11.6.1]

Flow control: The set of techniques that enable a data source to match its transmission rate to the currently available service rate at a receiver and in the network. [13]

Flow-control window: The largest number of packets a source may have outstanding without receiving an acknowledgment. This is similar to the *error-control window,* except that it is used for *flow control* rather than *error control.* [13.4]

Forward error correction: An error-control technique where a sender sends redundant packets of information to compensate for lost packets. [12.4.8]

FPODA: Fixed priority-oriented demand assignment, a centralized scheme for *packet-mode multiple access* in satellite environments. [7.4.3]

Frame relay network: A connection-oriented packet-switched network that supports *permanent virtual circuits* and variable packet sizes. [15.3]

Framing: The technique used to distinguish between data and idle bits on a link. [5.5.2]

Frequency-division duplex: A *full-duplex* channel where different directions use different frequencies. [7.3.4]

Frequency-division multiple access: A technology where stations sharing a medium use separate frequencies. [7.3.1]

Full duplex: A connection in which data simultaneously flows in both directions. [2.1]

Generalized processor sharing: An ideal scheduling discipline that results in a max–min fair allocation of resources. [9.4.1]

Generator polynomial: A polynomial representing a binary string that is used in a *cyclic redundancy checksum.* [12.2.5]

Generic flow control: A field in the ATM header, whose use has not been currently specified. [15.4.2]

GFC: See *Generic flow control.*

Go-back-n: A retransmission technique where the sender, on detecting a packet loss, retransmits the entire *error-control window.* [12.4.7]

GPS: See *Generalized processor sharing.*

GSM: Global System for Mobile Communication, the *FDD/TDMA* digital cellular phone service used primarily in Europe. [7.4.1]

Guaranteed-service application: An application that requires a *performance bound* for traffic served on its connection. [9.11, 14.4.1]

HAA: See *Home address agent.*

Half-open connection: A connection that is thought to be open by one endpoint, but not the other. [12.4.5]

Hamming distance: The minimum number of bit inversions required to transform one codeword to another. [12.2.3]

Handoff: The technique by which a *mobile* changes its associated *base station* when it moves. [2.6.2]

Head-of-line blocking: The phenomenon in an *input-queued switch* with a single shared queue at each input where a packet destined to an free output must wait because the packet at the head of the queue is *output blocked.* [8.5.1]

Heavy-tailed distribution: A distribution that has a more probability mass in its tail than an *exponential distribution.* [14.3.1]

Hidden terminal problem: A problem in radio links where a *station* can be heard only by a subset of other *stations* in its listening area. [7.2.2]

Hierarchical link sharing: A technique for sharing a link between organizations. [14.6.1]

Home address agent: The wired computer that is the "home" associated with a *mobile host.* The home address agent coordinates access to the mobile host. [11.13.2]

Hop-by-hop routing: A form of routing where the next hop for a packet is decided by each router, rather than by the source. [11.3]

Hop-count metric: A metric where each hop has a unit cost. [11.7.1]

Host adaptor card: See *Host interface card.*

Host-interface card: A hardware device that connects a computer to a network. [3.3]

Host number: See *Interface number.*

HTTP: See *Hypertext Transfer Protocol.*

Hybrid circuit: Another term for a *balance circuit.* [2.2.2]

Hybrid flow control: A form of flow control that borrows elements from both *open-loop* and *closed-loop* flow control. [13.2]

Hypertext Transfer Protocol: The request–response protocol underlying the World Wide Web. [15.3.5]

ICMP: See *Internet Control Message Protocol.*

IDI: See *Initial Domain Identifier.*

IETF: See *Internet Engineering Task Force.*

IGMP: See *Internet Group Management Protocol.*

Incarnation number: A number in the header of every packet that is unique for each connection between a pair of hosts. [12.4.3]

Indirection: A technique to delay *binding* by storing the current translation from an abstraction to an instance in a well-known location. [6.3.7]

Initial Domain Identifier: A *domain*-specific code, allocated by an *addressing authority*, that uniquely identifies that domain for the purposes of generating a unique *NSAP* address. [10.7]

Input-queued switch: A *switch* that has most of its buffers at the input. [8.5.1]

Integrated Service: The idea of using the same network to provide a diverse range of services such as voice, video, and data. [4.5, 14.4]

Integrated Services Digital Network: A technology that integrates voice and data over the telephone network by providing telephone subscribers with one or two 64-Kbps digital data channels in addition to a voice channel. [4.6]

Integrated Services Digital Network–User Part: An application in *SS7* that is responsible for setting up voice calls. It replaces the *TUP.* [15.2.4]

Interface number: The low-order part of an IP address. [3.3]

Interior gateway protocol: A *routing protocol* within an *autonomous system.* [11.8.3]

Internally nonblocking switch: A *circuit switch* in which no sample is blocked waiting for an output line, as long as the output line is available. [8.2.2]

International Organization for Standards: An international standards body that publishes a set of standards for data networking, including the *Open System Interconnect* (OSI) architecture. [3.6.2, 5.4]

International Telecommunications Union: International standards body dealing with telecommunications. Subsumes the standards body formerly called *CCITT.* [4]

Internet Control Message Protocol: A protocol in the control plane of the Internet protocol stack that allows routers to send error messages, network status, and warnings to endpoints. [15.3.3]

Internet Engineering Task Force: An organization responsible for creating standards and technologies for the Internet. [3.6.2]

Internet Group Management Protocol: A protocol that allows a router to discover which hosts on its LAN are interested in participating in which *multicast groups.* [11.11.5]

Internet Protocol: The protocol used to format packets in the Internet. It provides routing and reassembly. [15.3.2]

Intersymbol interference: Interference between successive signals on a link. [2.3.1]

Intolerant source: A source that cannot tolerate occasional deviations from its performance bound. [14.4.4]

Inverse multiplexor: A hardware device that splits a higher-rate stream into several lower-rate streams that are carried on separate connections. The inverse multiplexor also reassembles lower rate connections to reconstitute the original stream. [8.2.1]

IP: See *Internet Protocol.*

Iridium: A system proposed by Motorola Corporation that consists of 66 satellites in low-Earth orbits. [2.3.3]

IS-95: Interim Standard-95, the U.S. standard for *CDMA* digital cellular telephony. [7.4.1]

ISDN: See *Integrated Services Digital Network.*

ISDN-UP: See *Integrated Services Digital Network–User Part.*

ISM bands: The Industrial, Scientific, and Medical bands of the electromagnetic spectrum designated by the Federal Communications Commission in the United States for unlicensed communication. [7.2.2]

ISO: See *International Organization for Standards.*

ITU: See *International Telecommunications Union.*

Jumping-window descriptor: A *traffic descriptor* where a source claims that it never transmits more than a certain number of bits over consecutive windows of a certain length of time. [13.3.3]

Justification: The process by which a multiplexor adjusts the output stream to account for small variations in the bit rate of an input stream. [15.2.2]

Karn's algorithm: A technique where a transmitter ignores the *round-trip time* measured by acks that acknowledge retransmitted packets. [12.4.6]

Knockout principle: The principle that fewer than N packets will simultaneously arrive to the same output of an $N{\times}N$ switch most of the time. [8.5.2]

LANE: See *LAN emulation.*

LAN emulation: A way to carry non-ATM packets encapsulated in AAL5 by resolving datalink-layer addresses to ATM addresses, to which a virtual circuit can then be opened. [15.5.5]

LAN Emulation Client: A client in *LANE* that makes requests for datalink-layer address resolution. [15.5.5]

LAN Emulation Server: A server in *LANE* that resolves a datalink layer address to an ATM address. [15.5.5]

Layering: The use of the services provided by a protocol by another (higher layer) protocol. [5.1]

Layering violation: A situation where a layer uses knowledge of the implementation details of another layer in its own operation. [5.3]

LBAP: See *Linear bounded arrival process.*

Leaky-bucket regulator: A *regulator* that regulates an LBAP *traffic descriptor* by periodically accumulating credits in a finite "bucket" and preventing a packet from being transmitted unless it has sufficient credits. [13.3.4]

LEC: See *LAN Emulation Client,* or *Local exchange carrier.*

LES: See *LAN Emulation Server.*

Line switch: A switch that is connected directly to endpoints. [8.2.2]

Linear bounded arrival process: A process is a linear bounded arrival process if there exists a linear function of time, $f(t)$, such that the number of bits generated by the process in any interval of time, t, is bounded by $f(t)$. [13.3.4]

Link-state packet: A packet used in *link-state routing* that contains the cost of a link between two routers. [11.6]

Link-state routing: A protocol for computing *routing tables* where a router floods the network with *link-state packets* that contain its distance to each of its neighbors. [11.6]

LIS: See *Logical IP Subnet.*

LLC: See *Logical Link Control.*

Local area network: A network that spans a small ($<$10 km) geographical area.

Local exchange carrier: In the United States, a company that provides local telephone service and access to long-distance telephone service. [11.4]

Locality: The principle that if the system accessed some data at a given time, it is likely that it will access the same or "nearby" data "soon." [6.3.4]

Local loop: The pair of wires from a telephone endpoint to the *central office.* [2.1]

Logical IP Subnet: A portion of an ATM network such that all the hosts have IP addresses in the same subnet. [15.5.2]

Logical link control: The sublayer of the datalink layer responsible for framing packets. [5.5.2]

Lollipop sequence space: A special form of the sequence space that has a linear and a circular portion. In the linear portion, sequence numbers are uniquely ordered, and in the circular space, no two sequence numbers are greater or lesser than each other. [11.6.1]

Long-range-dependent traffic: Traffic such that bursts last for very long times. [14.3.2]

Loose source route: A form of routing where a source specifies the subset of *routers* that the packet must pass through, and the path may include routers not in the loose source route. [11.3]

LSP: See *Link-state packet.*

LSP database: A collection of *LSPs* stored in each router that allows it to compute shortest paths to every destination. [11.6.1]

MAC: See *Medium Access Control.*

MACA: See *Multiple Access Collision Avoidance.*

MARS: See *Multicast Address Resolution Server.*

Maximum packet lifetime: The longest time a packet can exist within a network before it is discarded. [12.4.2]

Maximum Segment Size: The largest packet size allowed in TCP. [15.3.4]

Max–min fair share: A type of resource allocation that maximizes the minimum resource allocated to a user whose resource demand is not met. [9.2.2]

MBONE: The Internet's Multicast Backbone, which is a set of routers that are capable of IP *multicast.* [11.11.18]

Medium access control: The sublayer of the datalink layer responsible for arbitrating access to a shared medium, and for filtering packets at a datalink-level receiver. [5.5.2]

Memoryless process: A process such that its past history does not influence its future behavior. [14.3.1]

Merging network: A component of a *switching fabric* that merges two lists of sorted packets at its inputs to create a longer sorted list at its output. [8.4.5]

Message Transfer Part: The datalink and network layer protocols in *SS7.* [15.2.4]

Meta-data: Something that describes data, usually the header in a *packet.* [3.2.1]

Metasignaling: The process by which an ATM network established a *virtual circuit* subsequently used for signaling. [15.4.2]

Metastability (in telephone networks): The situation where the *telephone network core* carries all traffic on two-hop paths, even though rearranging paths would allow most or all calls to be carried on one-hop paths. [11.4.2]

Metric map: A function that translates from the measured load on a link to its cost metric. [11.7.1]

MH: See *Mobile host.*

MID: See *Multiplexing identifier.*

Mips: Million instructions per second. A metric of computation power. [6.2.3]

Mobile host: The term used to refer to an IP endpoint that can move from one subnetwork to another. [11.13.2]

Mobile telephone switching office: A *central office* that provides transmission facilities to mobile telephones. [11.13.1]

MOSPF: See *Multicast Open Systems Shorted Path First routing.*

Moving-window descriptor: A *traffic descriptor* where a source claims that it never transmits more than a certain number of bits over *all* windows of a certain length of time. [13.3.3]

MPL: See *Maximum packet lifetime.*

MSS: See *Maximum Segment Size.*

MTP: See *Message Transfer Part.*

MTSO: See *Mobile telephone switching office.*

Multicast: The process by which a packet from a source is delivered to more than one destination. [11.11]

Multicast Address Resolution Server: A server that dynamically resolves an IP multicast address to an ATM multicast virtual circuit. [15.5.4]

Multicast group: A set of senders and receivers such that every receiver receives a packet from every sender. [11.11]

Multicast Open Systems Shorted Path First routing: An extension to *OSPF* to allow it to handle *multicast* routing. [11.11.8]

Multilevel priority with exhaustive service: A scheduling discipline in which packets from a particular priority level are served only if there are no packets awaiting service in any higher service level. [9.4.1]

Multipath interference: Interference caused at a receiver due to the same signal arriving over paths with different delays. [7.2.2]

Multiple access collision avoidance: An alternative to *BTMA* where stations exchange explicit request-to-send and clear-to-send messages to coordinate access to a shared medium. [7.5.3]

Multiple-access problem: The problem of coordinating access to a shared medium. [7.1]

Multiple-path routing: A form of routing where a *router* maintains multiple alternative next hops for each destination. [11.3]

Multiplexing: Sharing a single resource among many users. [6.3.1]

Multiplexing identifier: A field in the header of an AAL3/4 cell that identifies the endpoint that generated the cell on that virtual circuit. [15.4.3]

Multiplexor: A device that shares a resource, such as a transmission line, among many users. [8.2.1]

Multipoint-to-multipoint multicast: A type of *multicast* where more than one sender uses the same routing state to send packets to more than one receiver. [11.11]

Multistage crossbar: A *crossbar* which is broken up into several smaller crossbars in tandem. [8.2.4]

MX records: Records stored in a name server in the *Domain Name System* that translate from a destination name to the IP address of a system that will accept mail on behalf of that destination. [10.8]

Name: A human-understandable unique descriptor for an endpoint. [10.1]

Name space: The set of all possible *names*. [10.3]

Naming: The process of assigning unique *names* to endpoints. [10.1]

NBMA: See *Nonbroadcast multiple access.*

Near–far problem: See *Capture.*

NETBLT: A technique for *dynamic-rate flow control* in which receivers inform a source if the rate at which they receive packets is less the rate at which the source sent them, thus causing the source to reduce its transmission rate. [13.4.7]

Network–Network Interface: The set of protocols defining the interface between two network elements (usually *switch controllers*) in an ATM network. [15.4.2]

Network number: The high-order part of an IP address. [3.3]

Network response map: A function that translates from a cost metric to the load on the link that is due to a routing protocol that uses this metric. [11.7.1]

Network Service Access Point: The point at which the transport layer accesses the network layer. [5.5.3]

Network Service Access Point address: The address of an endpoint according to the International Standards Organization. [10.7]

Next-Hop Routing Protocol: A way to implement IP over ATM that does not require an IP router to intervene in carrying packets between *LISs.* [15.5.3]

NHRP: See *Next-Hop Routing Protocol.*

NNI: See *Network–Network Interface.*

Nonbroadcast multiple access: Refers to local area networks that do not support broadcast, such as ATM. [15.5.2]

Non persistent CSMA: A form of *CSMA* in which a station that wants to send data and senses a busy medium sets a timer and checks the medium again only when the timer expires. [7.5.2]

Non-work-conserving scheduler: A *scheduler* that may be idle even if its *service queue* is not empty. [9.4.2]

NSAP: See *Network Service Access Point.*

NSAP address: See *Network Service Access Point* address.

OC-1 frame: The frame format at the lowest level of the *SONET* hierarchy. [15.2.3]

On–off: A *flow-control protocol* where a receiver sends *on* and *off* messages to the sender. When the sender is *on,* it sends *packets* as fast as it can. When it is *off,* it sends nothing. [13.4.1]

Open-loop flow control: A form of *flow control* where a source's transmission rate is independent of the congestion state of the network. [13.2]

Open protocol: A protocol whose details are publicly available, and changes to which are managed by an organization whose membership and transactions are open to the public. [5.4]

Open Shortest Path First routing protocol: A *link-state routing* protocol used as an *interior gateway protocol* on the Internet. [11.9.2]

Open system: A system implementing a set of *open protocols.* [5.4]

Open System Interconnect: An international standard that describes a particular choice of *layering,* and a particular choice of *protocols* that carry out the services at each layer. [5.4]

Optical amplification: A technique to amplify an optical signal without converting it to electronic form. [2.3.1]

OSI: See *Open System Interconnect.*

OSI protocol architecture: A particular set of protocols that implement the *OSI service architecture.* [5.4]

OSI reference model: Formally defines what is meant by a layer, a service, a service access point, name, etc. These concepts provide the building blocks for defining a seven-layer model for communication. [5.4]

OSI service architecture: Describes the services provided by each layer of the protocol stack standardized by the *ISO.* [5.4]

OSPF: See *Open Shortest Path First routing protocol.*

Output blocking: The phenomenon where two packets or samples arrive for the same destination simultaneously, and only one can be forwarded. [8.2.2]

Output-queued switch: A switch that has most of its buffers at its output queues. [8.5.2]

Outstanding (packet): A packet that has been sent, but not acknowledged. [13.4]

Packet: A combination of information (data) and a description of this information (metadata or header). A packet is self-descriptive, unlike a voice sample. [3.2.1]

Packet filter: A piece of code in kernel space that demultiplexes incoming packets and hands them to the appropriate application in user space. [16.4.2]

Packet-mode multiple access: See *Packet-mode transfer.*

Packet-mode transfer: The transfer of a bursty stream of information from a *station* in a multiple-access scheme. [7.2.1]

Packet-pair: A technique for *dynamic-rate flow control* where a source estimates the bandwidth available to it by sending all data in the form of pairs of packets and measuring the interacknowledgment spacing. [13.4.8]

Packet switch: A switch that examines a packet header to determine the packet's destination. [8.1.1]

Packet switching: A form of *switching* using *packets* to carry information. [4.1.2]

Parallel iterated matching: An algorithm for an *arbiter* in an *input-queued switch* that uses randomization to evenly share access to the output trunks. [8.5.1]

Path vector: A solution to the *count-to-infinity* problem where each element in a *distance vector* is annotated with the path used to compute that element. [11.5.2]

Payload: The information carried in a *packet.* [3.2.1]

PBX: See *Private branch exchange.*

PDAMA: Packet-demand assignment multiple access, a centralized scheme for *packet-mode multiple access* in satellite environments. [7.4.3]

PDU: See *Protocol data unit.*

Peak-load pricing: A technique where the price at peak and off-peak times is different, to force some traffic from peak times to off-peak times. [14.10]

Peak rate: The highest rate at which a source can ever generate data during a call. [13.3.2]

Peak-rate admission: An *admission-control* algorithm that reserves capacity for a *VBR* connection at its peak rate. [14.9.4]

Peer entity: One of the parties involved in communication. [5.1]

Perfect parity code: A code that has the minimum number of redundant bits to perform error correction. [12.2.3]

Perfect-shuffle network: A *switching fabric* that rearranges its inputs in a particular way. [8.4.4]

Performance metric: A quantitative measure of some aspect of a system's performance. [6.1.1]

Permanent virtual circuit: A *virtual circuit* whose associated translation-table entries are hardwired, to avoid *signaling* overhead. [4.1.4]

Persistent CSMA: A form of *CSMA* where a station that wants to send data and senses a busy medium waits for the medium to become idle. [7.5.2]

PIM: See *Protocol-independent multicast.*

Pipeline: A set of processors that each execute one subtask in a set of *serially dependent* subtasks, passing on the remaining work to the processor that executes the next subtask. [6.3.2]

Plain old telephone service: Standard telephony using either analog or 64-Kbps digital lines to each subscriber. [2]

Playback application: An application that receives and plays back a *continuous media* stream. [9.2.3]

Plesiochronous system: A system where each component has nearly the same clock rate. [15.2.2]

Point-to-multipoint multicast: A type of *multicast* where a single sender sends packets to more than one receiver. [11.11] (See also *Multipoint-to-multipoint multicast.*)

Poisson process: A set of events such that the mean time between events is drawn from an *exponential distribution.* [14.2.1]

Policer: A device supplied by the network operator that ensures that a source meets its portion of the *traffic contract.* See also *regulator.* [13.3.1]

Polling: A *multiple-access* technique where a master checks whether each slave has data to send, and, if it does, gives it a chance to use the medium. [7.4.2]

Port number: A numerical identifier that distinguishes between multiple applications sharing access to a TCP implementation at an endpoint. [12.4.3, 15.3.4]

POTS: See *Plain old telephone service.*

p-Persistent CSMA: A form of *Persistent CSMA* where a station that wants to send data and sends a busy medium waits for the medium to become idle, then sends a packet with probability *p*. [7.5.2]

Predictive service: A service where the network hints at, but does not guarantee, the performance bounds a connection will receive. [14.4.4]

Prefix indication: A tag associated with an IP address, when using *CIDR,* that allows us to determine the network number. [10.6.3]

Private branch exchange: A small switch on a customer's premises used for on-premises switching and multiplexing. [8.2.3]

Probing: A form of *polling* where sets of stations are polled simultaneously to minimize the time wasted on polling idle stations. [7.4.2]

Protection: The ability of a scheduling discipline to protect well-behaved connections traffic from that of misbehaving connections. [9.2.2]

Protection switching: The process by which a system cuts from a subsystem whose error rate is above a threshold to a redundant backup. [12.1.5]

Protocol: A set of rules and formats that govern the communication between *peer entities*. [5.1]

Protocol data unit: The packets used by a layer for providing service. [5.1]

Protocol-independent multicast: A technique for IP *multicast* that uses a combination of *core-based trees* and *flood-and-prune,* depending on the density or sparsity of a network's interconnections. [11.11.10]

Protocol layering: A form of protocol dependency where the higher-layer protocol uses the lower-layer protocol as a step in its execution. [5.1]

Protocol stack: A *layered* set of protocols that work together to implement a complex service. [5.1]

Provider selection: A form of *source routing* where a host can select a network provider that provides all, or almost all, of the transmission facilities in reaching a destination. [11.12.2]

Pruning: A technique to reduce the cost of a *multicast,* where routers not interested in getting packets from a *multicast group* excise themselves from the group. [11.11.7]

PVC: See *Permanent virtual circuit.*

Q.2931: The signaling protocol used in *ATM* networks. [14.8.4]

Q.931: The signaling protocol used in *SS7.* [15.2.4]

Quantization levels: The set of amplitude thresholds against which a voice signal is compared when digitizing it. [2.3.2]

Queue regeneration cycle: A cycle consisting of a busy and an idle period in which the queue occupancy goes from idle, to busy, to idle again. [13.4.4]

Queuing delay: The time a service request spends waiting for a *server.* [9.1]

Random early detection: A packet-drop strategy that drops packets even before a queue fills, with a certain loss probability that is a function of the mean queue length. [9.7.3]

Random variable: A number associated with the outcome of a situation involving an element of chance.

Rate-jitter regulator: A *regulator* that shapes incoming traffic to match a given rate descriptor. [9.4.2]

Rational user: A user who acts to maximize his or her *utility function.* [14.2]

Real-time application: An application whose *utility* is closely linked to the delay or delay jitter in receiving a packet. [14.4.1]

Real-time network routing: A form of routing in the *telephone network core* where each *toll switch* monitors the loading of every outgoing trunk and uses the list of lightly loaded trunks to compute the best set of alternative routes. [11.4.4]

Rearrangably nonblocking switch: A *circuit switch* which is *internally nonblocking* if existing circuits can be rearranged. [8.2.4]

RED: See *Random early detection.*

Regenerative repeater: A device that detects and repeats a signal, thus improving its *signal-to-noise ratio.* [2.1, 8.3]

Registry server: A server in user space that manages contention between multiple applications for a shared resource. [16.4.3]

Regulator: A device that ensures that the source never violates its *traffic descriptor*. [13.3.1]

Relative fairness bound: A bound on the difference in the amount of service received by two *backlogged* connections over any time interval. [9.4.4]

Rendezvous point: A router in *PIM* that coordinates the way in which members join and leave the *multicast group*. [11.11.10]

Repeater: See *regenerative repeater*.

Request for Comments: Internet document to disseminate information, usually about Internet standards. [3.6.2]

Reservation-ALOHA: A class of schemes similar to *ALOHA* where a station dynamically reserves a slot in the shared transmission schedule. [7.5.5]

Reservation Protocol: The signaling protocol proposed for use on the Internet. [14.8.5]

Resource constraint: A limitation on a resource such as time, bandwidth, or computing power that a design must obey. [6.1.1]

Resource Management cell: A special *ATM cell* that carries rate information in the *EERC* scheme for *ABR* traffic. [13.4.9]

Response time: The mean time to complete a task. [6.2.1]

Reverse-path forwarding: A technique for managing *multicast* where a router forwards an incoming packet from source S on if it arrived on the interface that the router uses as its shortest path to S. [11.11.6]

RFC: See *Request for Comments*.

RIP: See *Routing Information Protocol*.

Roll-call polling: A form of polling where stations are checked in turn. [7.4.2]

Round-trip time: The time between sending a packet and receiving its acknowledgment. [12.4.6, 13.1]

Router: A specialized computer that examines *datagram* headers to forward them to their next-hop destination. [8.1.1]

Router discovery: The process by which an endpoint discovers which routers are accessible to it on its broadcast LAN. [11.10.1]

Routing: The process of finding a path from a source to every destination in the network. [11.1]

Routing Information Protocol: A *distance-vector protocol* used as an *interior gateway protocol* on the Internet. [11.9.1]

Routing protocol: A protocol that creates *routing tables* in *routers* and *switch controllers*. [11.1]

Routing table: A table at each switch or router that indicates the next hop for each destination in the network. [11.1]

RSVP: See *Reservation Protocol*.

RTNR: See *Real-time network routing*.

RTT: See *Round-trip time*.

Sample switching: The process of switching samples using a *circuit switch*. [8.2]

SAP: See *Service access point*.

SCCP: See *Signaling Connection Control Part.*

SCFQ: See *Self-clocked fair queuing.*

Schedulable region: A region that identifies all combinations of connections such that if this combination of connections is accepted at a scheduler, their performance bounds are met. [9.2.4]

Schedule: The order in which a server permits access to a shared resource. [2.4, 6.3.1]

Scheduler: An entity that schedules access to a multiplexed resource. [9.1]

Scheduling discipline: An algorithm that decides the order in which a *server* serves requests in a *service queue.* [9.1]

Scrambler: A device that introduces additional transitions in a transmitted signal, so that the receiver can more easily extract the transmission clock. [12.1.4]

SDH: Synchronous Digital Hierarchy. The European name for *SONET.* [15.2.3]

SDU: See *Service data unit.*

Selective retransmission: A retransmission technique where the sender retransmits only those packets that are lost. [12.4.7]

Self-clocked fair queuing: A variant of *WFQ.* [9.4.5]

Self-routing switch fabric: A *switch fabric* where appropriately tagged packets make their way from any input to the correct output without centralized control. [8.3.5, 8.4]

Sender persistence: A technique used by a TCP transmitter to periodically probe a receiver that has previously advertised a zero-size flow control window in an acknowledgment. [15.3.4]

Sequence number space: The subset of the natural numbers that represents all possible sequence numbers in a packet header. [12.4.1]

Serially dependent tasks: Tasks A and B are serially dependent if B can execute only after A completes execution. [6.3.2]

Server: An entity that controls access to a shared resource. [6.3.1]

Service access point: The interface between the higher and lower protocol layers involved in *layering.* [5.1]

Service data unit: The packets handed to a layer by an upper layer. [5.1]

Service queue: A queue of requests waiting for access to a *server.* [9.1]

Service-Specific Connection-Oriented Protocol.: The transport layer used for reliable, flow-controlled communication in the control plane of an ATM network. [14.8.4, 15.5.4]

Service tag: A tag on a packet that indicates the order in which it is served. [9.3.4]

Shadow price: A fictitious price charged by a link, depending on its load. If the price of a path is greater than the expected revenue from a call, the call should be rejected. [11.4.2]

Shannon capacity: See *Capacity.*

Shared memory switch: A switch where input and output queues share the same memory. [8.5.3]

Sidetone: The fraction of the transmitted signal that can be heard in the colocated receiver. [2.2.2]

Signaling: The communication between an end-system and the network that allows them to exchange information, for example, a request to set up a *circuit* or *virtual circuit.* [2.5]

Signaling Connection Control Part: The transport-layer protocol in *SS7.* [15.2.4]

Signaling System 7: The signaling system used in the *CCIS* network by telephone companies. [15.2.4]

Signal-to-noise ratio: 10 log ((peak signal level/root-mean-square noise level)^2). [12.1]

Signal Transfer Point: A *router* in *SS7* terminology. [15.2.4]

Silly-window syndrome: A condition where a TCP transmitter sends only small packets. [15.3.4]

Single-path routing: A form of routing where a *router* maintains only one next hop for each destination. [11.3]

Slotted-ALOHA: A version of *ALOHA* where the starting time of a transmission must coincide with a periodic time signal. [7.5.5]

Slow start: A phase in TCP flow control where the *flow-control window* size increases exponentially with time. [13.4.5]

Slow-start threshold: The *flow-control window* size, in TCP, which triggers a change from the *slow-start* phase to the *congestion-avoidance phase.* [13.4.5]

SMART: A retransmission technique where an acknowledgment carries not only the *cumulative ack,* but also the sequence number of the packet that initiated the acknowledgment. This allows the sender to retransmit only packets that were lost, in the common case, without using timeouts. [12.4.7]

SNA: See *Systems Network Architecture.*

SNR: See *signal-to-noise ratio.*

Soft decision decoding: A form of *trellis decoding* where the distance between a feasible and infeasible trajectory is measured using analog signal levels, instead of the *Hamming distance.* [12.2.7]

Soft state: State that is automatically removed after a time period, unless explicitly renewed. [6.3.10]

SONET: Synchronous Optical NETwork. A *digital transmission hierarchy* where all streams share the same clock base, so that multiplexed streams are exact multiples of the rates of the inputs. [15.2.3]

Sorting network: A component of a *switching fabric* whose outputs are sorted according to the tags on the packets at its inputs. [8.4.5]

Source routing: A form of routing where the entire path of a packet is placed in its header by the source. [11.3]

Source tracing: A technique to implicitly determine the path used to compute every element of a *distance vector.* [11.5.2]

Space-division switching: A form of switching where samples in the *switch* are on separate data circuits. [2.4]

Spatial statistical multiplexing gain: The decrease in resource usage obtained by exploiting statistical knowledge about the number of active users in the population. By sizing a resource proportional to the mean number of active users (instead of sizing to the size of the entire population), we can decrease resource usage. [6.3.1]

Split horizon with poisonous reverse: A variant of *split horizon* where, if a router A has a path to C via B, it tells B that it has an infinite cost to C. [11.5.2]

Split horizon: A solution to the *count-to-infinity* problem where a router never advertises a cost of a destination to a neighbor N, if N is the next hop to that destination. [11.5.2]

SS7: See *Signaling System 7.*

SSCOP: See *Service-Specific Connection-Oriented Protocol.*

ssthresh: See *Slow-start threshold.*

Stable storage: Memory that retains its contents even if a computer crashes. [12.4.3]

Stage: A processor in a *pipeline.* [6.3.2]

Starvation: A situation where a lower-priority level never gets served because a higher-priority level always has work. [9.4.1]

STAT: A message type in *SSCOP* that informs a sender of the packets received correctly by a receiver. [15.4.4]

State-dependent routing: A form of routing where the choice of a route depends on the current (measured) network state. [11.3]

State-independent routing: A form of routing where the choice of a route does not depend on the current state. [11.3]

Static routing: See *State-independent routing.*

Static-window flow control: A form of *flow control* where a source has a fixed number of *packets outstanding.* [13.4.3]

Station: A participant in a multiple-access scheme. [7.1]

Station management: The administrative functions performed in a *token ring* to make the ring robust to failures such as loss of a *token,* a failed link, or a failed station. [7.5.4]

Statistical multiplexing: The use of statistical knowledge about a system to reduce its resource usage. The gain from such knowledge is called statistical multiplexing gain. The two types of statistical multiplexing gain are *spatial statistical multiplexing gain* and *temporal statistical multiplexing gain.* [6.3.1]

Stochastic routing: A form of routing where a *router* randomly picks the next hop from one of several alternatives. [11.3]

Stop-and-wait: A *flow control protocol* where a source only has a single *packet* outstanding (sent but not acknowledged). [13.4.2]

Store-and-forward: A form of *switching* where a packet can be stored at a switching point for an essentially arbitrary time before it is forwarded to a destination. In contrast, in the telephone network, a voice sample cannot be stored, since the destination of the sample is encoded in the time at which it arrives at a switch. [3.2.2]

STP: See *Signal Transfer Point.*

Subnet mask: A mask that partitions an *IP* address into a network number and a host number. [10.6]

Subnetting: The division of a single IP network into smaller networks to allow finer-grained partitioning of the Internet address space and smaller *routing tables* within a network. [10.6.2]

Summary record: A record in the *LSP database* that describes the cost to a router at a lower level in the routing hierarchy. [11.8.2]

SVC: See *Switched virtual circuit.*

Switch: A piece of hardware that transfers information from an input to an output. [2.4]

Switch controller: A special-purpose computer that controls a switch to set up and tear down *circuits.* [2.4]

Switched Ethernet: A variant of Ethernet where stations are connected to a hub with a point-to-point link, eliminating *collisions.* [7.5.2]

Switched virtual circuit: A *virtual circuit* that is established for the duration of a call, then torn down. An SVC requires *signaling.* [4.1.4]

Switch fabric: A hardware device that interconnects the inputs and outputs in a circuit or packet switch. [8.1, 8.4]

Switching: The act of transferring data arriving at any input of a *switch* to a specific output. [2.4]

Switching-fabric element: A component of a *switch fabric* that is replicated many times over and interconnected in various ways to form *self-routing* switching fabrics. [8.4.3]

Switching schedule: The order in which a *crossbar* rearranges its connections so as to connect different inputs to different outputs at every step in the schedule. [8.4.1]

Switching system: A combination of a *switch* and a *switch controller* that provides both *sample switching* and *call establishment.* [8.1.1]

Synchronous payload envelope: The portion of a *SONET* frame that contains data. Pointers in the frame header point to the start of the synchronous payload envelope in the frame. [15.2.3]

Synchronous transfer mode: A form of link sharing where the identity of a connection is determined by the time at which a sample from that connection arrives at a switch or multiplexor. [4.1.1]

Systems Network Architecture: Internet-style proprietary packet network developed by IBM. [3.6.2]

Target token rotation time: A number used in FDDI to provide a form of *guaranteed service.* A station limits the number of packets it sends to ensure that the token rotates past it within the selected *TTRT* value. [7.5.4]

Task: A procedure that performs protocol actions corresponding to one layer on one packet. [16.5.2]

Task scheduler: An entity that schedules *tasks.* [16.5.2]

TCP: See *Transmission Control Protocol.*

TCP-Reno: The version of TCP implemented in the Reno release of BSD Unix. [13.4.5]

TCP-Tahoe: The version of TCP implemented in the Tahoe release of BSD Unix. [13.4.5]

TCP-Vegas: A technique for *flow control* that improves on *TCP-Reno* by actively estimating the available bandwidth and buffer occupancy in the network. [13.4.6]

TDD: See *Time-division duplex.*

TDMA: See *Time-division multiple access.*

Telephone network core: The set of *toll switches* in the telephone network. [11.4]

Telephone User Part: An application in *SS7* that is responsible for setting up voice calls. [15.2.4]

Temporal statistical multiplexing gain: The gain in efficiency by serving data streams at a rate less than their peak rate. This gain is possible only when the peak rate differs from the average rate, and comes at the expense of either added delay or the possibility of packet loss. [4.4, 6.3.1]

Three-way handshake: A mechanism to allow peer endpoints to reliably exchange initial sequence numbers. [12.4.4]

Throughput: The number of tasks completed in a unit time. [6.2.1]

Time-division duplex: A *full-duplex* channel where different directions use different time slots. [7.3.4]

Time-division multiple access: A technology where stations sharing a medium use separate time slots. [7.3.2]

Time-division multiplexing: A technique of sharing a resource where contenders share the resource over time. [2.4]

Time-division switching: A form of switching where samples in the *switch* share data circuits, but are separated in time. [2.4]

Time-to-live: A field in the *IP* packet header that is decremented by 1 at each hop in the Internet. [15.3.2]

Token: A specially formatted packet that gives a station a right to transmit packets in a *token ring.* [7.5.4]

Token bus: A form of LAN where *tokens* are exchanged over a bus instead of a ring. [7.5.4]

Token ring: A form of LAN where a special packet called a *token* is used to coordinate access to the shared medium. [7.5.4]

Tolerant source: A source that can tolerate occasional deviations from its performance bound. [14.4.4]

Toll switch: A *circuit switch* that provides access to the long-distance telephone network. [11.4]

Top-level domain: The *domain* at the highest level in a hierarchical *name space.* [10.3]

Total internal reflection: The physical phenomenon where light entering a medium with low refractive index from a medium with high refractive index is completely reflected back into the medium with high refractive index when the angle of incidence is small. [2.3.3]

Traceroute: A way to determine the route from a source to a destination in the Internet by exploiting the *ICMP* protocol. [15.3.2]

Traffic class: A parametrization of the shared requirements of a set of widely-used applications. [14.4]

Traffic contract: A contract between a source and the network. The source agrees not to violate a *traffic descriptor,* and the network agrees to provide a guarantee on performance. [13.3.1]

Traffic descriptor: A set of parameters that describe a source's traffic (for open-loop flow control). [13.3.1]

Traffic management: The set of policies and mechanisms that allow a network to satisfy a wide range of service requests as efficiently as possible. [14.1]

Traffic matrix: A matrix describing the average load between every source-destination pair. [14.11.1]

Traffic model: A mathematical model that summarizes the typical behavior of a user. [14.3]

Transit switch: A switch that connected to multiplexed trunks, rather than individual subscribers. [8.2.2]

Translation table: A table in a virtual circuit switch that gives the output interface and new VCI for each input interface and incoming VCI. [4.1.4]

Transmission Control Protocol: The protocol used in the Internet to provide reliable, flow-controlled, in-sequence, end-to-end connections. [15.3.3]

Trellis decoding: A form of decoding used with a *convolutional code.* [12.2.7]

Trie: A data structure optimized for looking up routing tables. [8.3.3]

Trunk status map routing: A form of routing in the *telephone network core* where the set of alternate routes is centrally computed based on real-time measurements of the trunk loads. [11.4.3]

TSMR: See *Trunk status map routing.*

TTL: See *Time-to-live.*

TTRT: See *Target token rotation time.*

Tunneling: A process by which two routers on the *MBONE* can encapsulate IP within IP to establish a virtual link over a set of non-multicast routers. [11.11.8]

TUP: See *Telephone User Part.*

UBR source: See *Unspecified-bit-rate source.*

Unconstrained resource: A resource that is freely available, and so does not affect system performance. [6.1.1]

UNI: See *User–Network Interface.*

Universal Resource Locator: A way to encapsulate a name in any registered name space to produce an object that can be referred to using *HTTP.* [15.3.5]

Unspecified-bit-rate source: A traffic source whose cell generation rate is unspecified. [14.4.3]

Upcall: A procedure call made by a procedure implementing a lower layer to a procedure implementing an upper layer, indicating either the completion of packet transmission or the arrival of a packet. [16.5.3]

Uplink: The directional link from a slave to a master in a *centralized multiple-access scheme.* [7.2.1]

Urgent pointer: A pointer in the TCP header that points to the start of data in the packet that the receiver should hand immediately to an application. [15.3.4]

URL: See *Universal Resource Locator.*

User–Network Interface: The set of protocols defining the interface between a user and an ATM network, according to the *ATM Forum.* [14.8.4, 15.4.2]

USTAT: (Unsolicited STAT) A message type in *SSCOP* that a receiver sends to the transmitter when it receives a packet out of sequence. [15.4.4]

Utility function: A function that describes the degree of satisfaction a user receives from a set of goods or services. [14.2]

UTP: Unshielded twisted pair. A type of wire commonly used for Ethernet and telephony. [2.3.3]

Valid codeword: A *codeword* formed from data bits and redundant information that is uncorrupted. [12.2.3]

Variable-bit-rate source: A traffic source that generates cells *burstily,* sending more cells in certain intervals of time than others. [14.4.3]

VBR source: See *Variable-bit-rate source.*

VCI: See *Virtual channel identifier.*

Virtual channel identifier: A short numerical identifier carried in a packet header that is associated with a particular path from a source to a destination during *call setup.* [4.1.2, 4.1.4]

Virtual circuit: A technique for *packet switching* where short identifiers in the header (also called virtual circuit identifiers) identify the destination of a *packet.* [4.1.4]

Virtual container: A *synchronous payload envelope* that holds data from *plesiochronous* frames. [15.2.3]

Virtualization: A technique that combines *multiplexing* with *indirection* to allow an entity to refer to a virtual resource exactly as it would a physical resource. [6.3.8]

Virtual path: A preestablished set of *virtual circuits* that share the same high-order bits in their identifiers and the same path in the network. [4.1.4, 15.4.2]

Viterbi decoding: See *Trellis decoding.*

Weighted fair queuing: A discipline that emulates *GPS.* [9.4.4]

WFQ: See *Weighted fair queuing.*

Window of vulnerability: The time during which, in *ALOHA,* a packet from a station can be corrupted by a packet from another station. [7.5.5]

Window scaling: A technique that allows TCP endpoints to negotiate a flow-control window larger than 64 Kbytes. [15.3.4]

Winsock: A implementation of the Internet protocol standards that allows applications in the Microsoft Windows operating system to access the Internet. [5.2]

Work-conserving scheduler: A *scheduler* that is idle only if its *service queue* is empty. [9.4.2]

Answers to Review Questions and Selected Exercises

Chapter 7: Answers to review questions

1. Replace a broadcast medium with a point-to-point medium.
2. The ratio of the propagation delay to the transmission time for a single packet.
3. When sources have a steady stream of data for transmission.
4. The Industrial, Scientific, and Medical bands in the electromagnetic spectrum allocated by the FCC in the United States for unlicensed data communication.
5. A receiver can hear transmission from two stations, but they cannot hear each other.
6. The number of non-retransmitted packets carried across a link in a given time period.
7. Goodput, mean delay, and stability.
8. Since the spectrum is crowded, this increases capacity by spatial reuse of frequencies.
9. Prefer to use TDMA, since to give double the bandwidth, you give twice the number of slots. With FDMA, the station has to transmit on two frequencies, and the receiver has to receive on both frequencies simultaneously.
10. Because the transmitter's frequency band is a function of time.
11. One bit of a direct-sequence code in CDMA.
12. When a station is near the border of a cell, both its current base station and the base station of the cell it is moving to send it the same information, using the same CDMA code. Thus, when the station moves cells, it does not notice a break in reception (a "soft" handoff).
13. Because it needs a large contiguous frequency band.
14. Analog FDD/FDMA.
15. Digital FDD/TDMA.
16. Because it uses capacity unused by analog voice in EAMPS. As the voice load fluctuates, the available capacity varies.
17. In polling, each station is asked in turn whether it has data to send. In probing, groups of stations are simultaneously asked the question, thus quickly eliminating large groups of inactive stations.

18. Reservation messages are smaller, and collisions of reservation messages waste less bandwidth.

19. They all sense the medium to see if it is idle before sending a packet.

20. With nonpersistent CSMA, a source that senses that the medium is busy waits for a random time and tries again. With p-persistent CSMA, a source continuously senses a busy medium till it becomes idle, then sends a packet with probability p.

21. After the kth consecutive collision, each colliding station waits for a random time chosen from the interval $[0, 2^k * \text{max\_propagation\_delay}]$.

22. To ensure that all colliding stations agree that a collision has happened.

23. Situations where collisions cannot be immediately detected because the transmitter overpowers a colocated receiver.

24. A.

25. A terminal that defers to transmissions from remote transmitters, even when it need not, because of its exposed location.

26. To notify potential transmitters that the receiver is busy.

27. Pause for a sufficient time to allow a CTS to return to the sender without a collision.

28. Since the RTSs will collide, they will not get a CTS. They should try again, using a binary exponential backoff.

29. Operation of the two rings as a single double-length ring—caused by a hardware fault.

30. The ring becomes idle, and the monitor eventually regenerates the token.

31. Send a packet without regard to anyone else, then see if it got through. If it did not, time out and try again.

32. In S-ALOHA, time is divided into fixed-length slots, and a station may transmit only on a slot boundary. S-ALOHA requires stations to acquire and maintain time synchronization. Moreover, if their data does not fill a time slot, the rest of the slot is wasted.

33. Bandwidth hogs oust the rest, and one-slot packet-mode transfers have severe overhead.

Chapter 7: Answers to exercises

7.2. Yes. We first divide the medium using a base technology such as FDMA, TDMA, or CDMA. Some fraction of the channel is assigned to circuit-mode access, and the remaining to packet-mode access. For example, with EAMPS, some frequencies could be assigned by the base station for voice channels. The other channels could be used for packet-mode access using MACAW.

7.4. A speaker says the same sentence in several pitches simultaneously. The receiver listens to all the pitches, and uses bits and pieces from all the pitches to decipher's the sender's message.

7.6. Polling a station that has no data to send takes time $R + 2l/b$ ($2l$ because of the poll and poll reply message). On average, Np stations have data to send. Thus, polling the remaining $N - Np$ stations takes time $(N - Np)(R + 2l/b)$. The Np stations take time $R + Np((l + L)/b)$ to send their data ($R/2$ to get the poll message, $R/2$ to send the data). Thus, the total time for a poll is $(N - Np)(R + 2l/b)$ $+ Np(R + (l + L)/b)$, of which only Np $(R/2 + L/b)$ is spent on actually carrying data. Thus, the goodput is $Np(R/2 + L/b)/((N - Np)(R + 2l/b) + Np(R +(l + L)/b))$. Plugging in the values, we get a peak goodput of 0.0054. Thus, the overhead for polling takes 99.5% of the time! With $p = 0.9$, the goodput rises to 0.049, which means the overhead is still over 95%. This is mainly because of the large value of R compared to L/b, that is, a large a. Thus, a lot of time is wasted in propagating packets and poll messages.

7.9. Reduced goodput and increased delay for stability.

7.10. Making implicit information (that the receiver is busy) explicit (by sending a CTS).

7.11. Suppose both stations collide on their first RTS. One of them, say, A, will pick a lower random timeout value than the other—call it B. So, A goes next, and sends a steady stream of packets to the receiver. At some point B times out and sends an RTS. This will collide with A's packet. A will choose a random backoff interval in the range [0,1], whereas B, which is seeing its second consecutive collision, will choose a random backoff interval in the range [0,2]. It is likely that B will choose the longer timeout, and that A will resume its transmission. In the next collision, A chooses a timeout in the range [0,1], but B choose a timeout in the range [0,4]. Again, it is more likely to lose. Eventually, B gets shut out, while A gets the entire link bandwidth.

7.13. The sum of the synchronous allocations may not exceed TTRT. If a station uses up the entire TTRT for non-real-time data, successive stations can still send real-time data for TTRT more seconds. Thus, the real rotation time would become as large as 2 TTRT. However, in the next rotation time, no station could send any non-real-time data, so that the rotation time would return to its target.

7.15. This is a matter of taste. I would pick ALOHA, because of its simplicity. But, just to be safe, I would allow a cutover to R-ALOHA (Roberts) in the face of persistent collisions and a switch back to ALOHA if most minislot reservations are idle. This allows us to get the best of both worlds, with a little work for monitoring the collision rate. Since all stations must cut over at the same time, we also need to introduce a protocol that coordinates the cutover from R-ALOHA to ALOHA and vice versa.

Chapter 8: Answers to review questions

1. Share transmission lines.
2. Translates a packet header to an output port.

3. Because an input can be directed to any one of a number of output trunks, all of which are heading to the same destination.

4. One.

5. By rearranging the time slots associated with a sample.

6. No path from input to output though the output is idle.

7. No.

8. Yes.

9. Yes.

10. Yes.

11. 128; 64 at the inputs, and 64 at the outputs.

12. TSI at the input can delay a sample until crossbar is available.

13. TS fabric blocks if the crossbar is not available during the time slot that the sample must be sent on at the output. A TST switch blocks only if the crossbar is not available at all to reach the output trunk during any slot of the incoming frame.

14. A computer with multiple line cards.

15. CPU speed.

16. Efficiently find best match.

17. The shared bus or ring.

18. At the front-end processors. It can be input queuing, output queuing, or both.

19. It provides multiple simultaneous paths between input and output front-end processors.

20. Yes, if it has input buffers.

21. No, because the equivalent of a schedule is downloaded to the outputs at call setup time.

22. No.

23. Yes.

24. Colliding packets are misrouted and tagged. Tagged packets enter another Banyan; untagged packets are sent to the output.

25. A packet at the head of a FIFO input queue that cannot reach an output blocks packets behind it in the queue that are eligible for service. The solution is to queue per-output at each input.

26. Picking the most inputs that do not share an output port.

27. The component that arbitrates access to the output queues.

28. The output queue.

29. Memory access time.

30. At the output port.

Chapter 8: Answers to exercises

8.1. First, let us determine the formula to compute the number of lines. If there are n users, the first needs a line to $(n - 1)$ others, the second needs a line to $(n - 2)$

others etc. Thus, the total number of lines is $(n - 1) + (n - 2) + \ldots + 1$. This is just the sum from 1 to $n - 1$, which is $n(n - 1)/2$. Plugging in 5, we get the number of lines to be 10. For $n = 50$, the answer is 1225.

8.3. A T1 runs at 1.544 Mbps, so 8 bits last 5.18 μs. On a 44.736-Mbps DS3, a sample lasts 0.178 μs.

8.5. (a) First multiplex the trunks, then hand them to a TSI, then demultiplex them. (b) A sample time on the multiplexed trunk lasts 8bits/(1024 $*$ 1.544 Mbps) = 5.07 ns. So the switch should be able to read a sample into memory in 5.07 ns. (c) With the crossbar, we multiplex the 1024 trunks into 16 groups, each with 64 trunks. Thus, the access time for a memory on the multiplexed trunk should be 16 $*$ 5.07 = 81.12 ns. (d) The controller must find a path from a given slot on a given input trunk to any slot on a given output trunk. It first scans the crossbar schedule to find a time when it can get to the output trunk. Then, it uses an input TSI to swap the incoming time slot to the chosen time slot. (e) If the output is immediately demultiplexed, then the controller must find a path from a given input trunk and time slot to a given output trunk and output time slot. Given the output time slot, we have to ensure that the crossbar is available for that output trunk on that time slot. We then have to use the input TSI to swap a sample onto that time slot. With a TST switch, any available crossbar slot can be used to get the sample to the correct output trunk, and the output TSI can be used to reswap the sample's time slot. Thus, the blocking probability decreases with a TST switch.

8.6. The formula for the packet-switching bandwidth is $(s * 8 * 1{,}000{,}000)/((20s/4) + n) * 0.00752 + i)$, where s is the packet size in bytes, n is the non-data-touching overhead in cycles, and i is the interrupt processing time in microseconds. Plugging in the values, we get the answers as (a) 158.1 Mbps, (b) 135.4 Mbps, (c) 14 Mbps. (d) Clearly, there is not much gain in decreasing non-data-touching overheads. Reducing the interrupt processing time gains us nearly 20% increase in throughput, so this should be a priority. Smaller packet sizes drastically reduce throughput—the packet switch would have rather low performance were it routing ATM cells, with an interrupt per cell. With an interrupt per packet, the switching speed increases from 14 Mbps to 132 Mbps, a factor of 9!

8.8. (a) Packets entering one of the processors would be placed on a bus, and one or more of the other processors would be asked to load the packet. At the output processor, the packet would be routed to one of the output trunks. (b) Since each processor is capable of 132 Mbps, the bus can support up to seven processors. (c) If more processors are attached, we would have output blocking. The processors would then need input queuing. (d) We are restricted to 58% of the throughput, i.e., 580 Mbps.

8.10. In the best case, the throughput is 64 $*$ 132 Mbps = 8.45 Gbps. With FIFO input queuing, the throughput reduces to 58%, that is, 4.9 Gbps. In the worst case, all the traffic uses the same output, so that the speed is reduced to 132 Mbps.

8.12. Consider the eight outputs of the first stage. Each of the upper outputs has to go to the one input of the upper 4×4 Banyan, and each of the lower has to go to an input at the lower 4×4 Banyan. The first output has four choices, the second, third, etc., so that we can choose the first in one of $4 \times 3 \times 2 = 24$ ways. For each, we can choose one of 24 ways to connect to the lower 4×4 fabric, giving us $24 \times 24 = 576$ ways to connect the first stage to the second stage. Within a 4×4 fabric, there are, clearly, 4 choices. Since there are two 4×4 fabrics, this gives us 16 ways to choose their interconnection. Thus, the total number of equivalent 8×8 Banyans is $576 \times 16 = 9216$. Actually, this ignores the ways to permute the inputs. Since any input can go to any of the ports at the first stage, we actually have $8 \times 7 \times \ldots \times 1$ possible permutations $= 40,320$. If we allow these as well, we get a total of 371 million possible equivalent fabrics!

8.15. A cell arrives at each input every 2.73 μs. We can store a 53-byte cell in 14 cycles, taking 1.12 μs. Thus, the largest switch we can build is $2.73/1.12 = 2 \times 2$. With cell-wide access, N can be as large as $2.73/0.08 = 34 \times 34$. If outputs need to run at only $0.4N$ times the input speeds, we get a 2.4 speedup. Thus, with 4-byte-wide access, we can build a 6x6 switch, and with cell-wide access, an 85×85 switch.

Chapter 9: Answers to review questions

1. Resolve contention for access to a shared resource.
2. At the input queue, if the switch fabric is the bottleneck, but usually at the output queue.
3. A connection can obtain a lower mean delay only at the expense of another connection.
4. Because it is run every time a packet is served at the output trunk.
5. The misbehavior of a connection should not affect the performance of other connections.
6. Fairness refers to the shares allocated to the connections. Protection implies that the shares (which may not be fair) are obeyed.
7. It is the difference between the largest and smallest delay received by packets on a connection. The delay jitter determines the size of the elasticity buffer at the receiver for playback applications.
8. It increases the possible statistical multiplexing gain.
9. It is the set of connections that can be simultaneously served without violating their performance bounds.
10. (a) The number of priority levels; (b) whether each level is work-conserving or non-work-conserving; (c) the degree to which individual connections are aggregated in determining their service order; and (d) service order within a level.
11. That a lower-priority connection will starve.
12. To regulate traffic so that downstream switches see a well-behaved traffic stream.

13. A delay-jitter regulator fully reconstructs the traffic stream by accounting for delays at the previous switch. A rate-jitter regulator partially reconstructs traffic and only examines the departure times of previous packets at the local switch.

14. To delay events or packets until they are eligible to be executed.

15. Events are rounded off to the size of a clock tick, possibly leading to reordering.

16. When the connections being aggregated would like to share the jitter among themselves.

17. FCFS and GPS.

18. No, this is true only for GPS scheduling.

19. Bandwidth is allocated in proportion to mean packet size, which is unfair.

20. The worst-case WRR delay is a function of the frame time, whereas the worst-case WFQ delay is independent of the frame time.

21. If the largest finish number of a packet either in its queue or last served from its queue is larger than the current round number.

22. The round number depends on the number of active connections, which, in turn, depends on the round number. Thus, the round number at a given time must be computed by guessing a value, iteratively deleting inactive connections, then recomputing the round number. In the worst case, this takes time proportional to the number of active connections.

23. If the source is leaky-bucket bounded by parameters (σ, ρ), and each server along the path allocates the connection a bandwidth of at least ρ, the worst-case end-to-end queuing delay is σ/ρ. If the source is not leaky-bucket bounded, the worst-case delay is not known.

24. The largest excess service one connection receives compared to another.

25. It is the finish number of the packet currently in service.

26. It is the number of bits served per-round from each connection. It should be at least as large as the largest possible packet size for the scheduler's operations to take a constant time per packet.

27. Because it specifies two parameters per connection. The bandwidth parameter is used to implicitly regulate the bandwidth (via the finish number computation), and the delay bound is used to compute the EDD deadline.

28. By reconstructing traffic with a DJ regulator at every hop, jitter at the previous scheduler is removed.

29. Yes, if the regulators shape incoming traffic to a leaky bucket.

30. (a) Degree of aggregation, (b) choice of drop priorities, (c) early or overloaded drop, and (d) drop position.

31. (a) Multilayer coders are harder to build. (b) Hard to determine how much bandwidth should be reserved. (c) Receiver has to deal with losses and jitters on multiple streams.

32. To send a message to the endpoint that queues are getting full, and it should reduce its flow rate.

33. Sources are able to detect a loss sooner.

Chapter 9: Answers to exercises

9.2. The peak rate is valid over 100 ms, so over 500 ms, 5 Mbits of data could arrive and would all need to be buffered. Thus, the buffer needs to be 5 Mbits = 625 Kbytes.

9.4. At 16 Mbps, 2 Kbytes = 16 Kbit packets should be separated by 1 ms. Thus, the 5th packet would become eligible at time 5.001 s.

9.5. The scheduler can maintain pointers for the current, next, and all other years in three separate data structures. The scheduler serves events from the current year. The "next" year is asynchronously updated from the "future" data structure whenever the scheduler has time. At the end of the year, the next year and current year are interchanged. (Solution due to H. Zhang.)

9.8. Since the finish numbers are 100 and 200, the service order is A, then B. (a) The real completion times are 1 s and 3 s. (b) At real time 1 s, the round number is $100/2 = 50$, and at real time 3 s, the round number is 200. (c) In [0,200] the round number increases at the rate of $\frac{1}{2}$, so at real time 1.5 s, it is 75. The packet from A has a size of 10, so its finish number is max $(75,100) + 10 = 110$. Note that the packet from B, with a finish number of 200, is already in service at real time 1.5 s, so even though the second packet from A has a smaller finish number, it will be served after the packet from B. This is the bounded unfairness property of FQ.

9.9. (a) The weighted finish numbers for connections A and B are $100/2 = 50$ and $200/5 = 40$, respectively. Thus, the packet from B is served before the packet from A. The packet from B completes service at real time 2.0 s, and the packet from A at real time 3.0 s. (b) The round number initially has slope $1/(5 + 2) = \frac{1}{7}$. The packet from B completes at real time 2 s, so the round number at that time is $200/7 = 28.57$. The slope will remain at $\frac{1}{7}$ until the round number reaches 40, which happens at time 2.8 s, since $100 * 2.8/7 = 40$. In [2.8 s, 3.0 s], the round number increase with slope $\frac{1}{2}$, so at time 3 s, it reaches 50. (c) We first need to compute the round number at time 1.5. From (b), we know that both connections are active at that time, so the round number at that time is $150/7 = 21.42$. The finish number for the packet is max $(21.42,50) + 10/2 = 55$.

9.11. The first two packets obtain finish numbers 10 and 15. At time 9, the packet with finish number 10 is in service, so the incoming packet gets a finish number of $10 + 5 = 15$. At time 17, the packet with finish number is in service, so the incoming packet gets a finish number of $15 + 10 = 25$.

9.13. Packets in the burst will receive deadlines as if they had been sent at the negotiated rate. If sufficient bandwidth is available, then despite these deadlines, the packets could still be sent with little delay. However, if this is not the case, the packets are buffered awaiting their turn. If the source has adequate buffers to hold the burst, then it suffers no loss; otherwise, it could lose packets.

Chapter 10: Answers to review questions

1. Names are usually variable length and human understandable, while addresses are usually fixed length and meant for easy parsing by computers. Both identify an endpoint.

2. Virtual-circuit switches (actually, the switch controllers) need to look up a routing table only during connection establishment. Packets are forwarded based on their VCI. Datagram routers need to look up a routing table on every packet arrival.

3. The top-level domain is the highest domain in the naming system. The name server for this domain should be replicated, since every noncached name must be resolved by first querying this name server. If this server becomes unavailable, the system cannot translate any noncached name.

4. To allow global uniqueness, and to allow aggregation in routing tables.

5. Four: national, area, exchange, and subscriber.

6. No.

7. Yes.

8. 16 bytes.

9. The network number.

10. 6 bytes; 3 bytes.

11. To prevent catastrophic failure if the root server goes down.

12. Translates from network-layer address to datalink-layer address. An ARP cache temporarily stores ARP replies.

Chapter 10: Answers to exercises

10.1. (a) To change an endpoint's address without changing its name, the administrator should inform the name-resolution service of the change in the name-to-address translation. If the new address is not a part of the current network number, then the local router should be instructed to advertise reachability to that address. (b) To change a name without changing the address, both the new and old authoritative servers for that name should be informed. All applications that use the old name should also be informed (there is no automatic way do this). (c) If the endpoint moves to a new location, the changes depend on whether the endpoint retains its name or address. If it retains neither, then the only change is in informing the name service of the creation of a new endpoint and the deletion of the old. If it retains only the name (the address changes), the old authoritative server must be told of the new address. If it retains only the address (the name changes), the new authoritative server must be told of the address. If local routers do not advertise that address, they should be instructed to do so. If the endpoint retains both the name and the address, the name-resolution service is unchanged, but the router entries may need to change, depending on whether the old routing advertisement for that address is still valid or not.

10.4. Since we use 20 bits in the prefix, the remaining 12 bits must be used for the address, giving us 4096 addresses. These start at 205.12.192.0, so they must go up to 205.12.207.255.

10.5. It would make most sense to give each university control over one part of the *edu* domain. However, we have now run out of levels in the name space. Thus, each university must set up mechanisms to ensure that all names within its domain are unique. Perhaps a name administrator might be hired to accept and process applications for machine names! Since DNS allows arbitrary-depth names, the university can dispense with the name administrator by devolving naming authority all the way down to end users who name machines.

10.7. ARP translates from a network-layer address to a datalink-layer address. In the telephone network, all links are point-to-point. We do not need a datalink-layer address to identify an endpoint (as is needed in a broadcast link). Thus, we do not need to translate to a datalink-layer address, nor do we need the equivalent of ARP.

Chapter 11: Answers to review questions

1. Increased header size, more overhead in exchanging routers, and inability to reroute for complete control over the path of packet. Smaller routing table size for nonoptimal routes.

2. Because in an N-element core, there are $N - 1$ two-hop alternative paths, and one of these is almost always available.

3. For each time period, an ordered list of alternative routes.

4. Trunk reservation for primary routes.

5. A list of distances from a router to every other router in the network.

6. If its cost to a neighbor decreases, or if the arrival of a distance vector results in a shorter route to some destination.

7. A distance vector annotated with the path taken to compute each distance.

8. A router R tells its neighbor N that its distance to destination D is infinity if R's shortest path to N passes through D. This prevents counting to infinity for cycles of length 2, because N will never use R for routing to D.

9. One each for each real or virtual link to which it is attached.

10. Copy an arriving LSP to all interfaces other than the one it arrived on, unless it is a duplicate, corrupted, or older than some LSP already in the database.

11. Use large sequence numbers, and treat a numerically smaller sequence number as larger if the difference between the smaller and the larger sequence number is larger than half the size of the sequence number space.

12. Faster startup.

13. Recovery from network partition.

14. In a homogeneous network with uniformly distributed load.

15. This prevents a link from changing from high-load to low-load rapidly, dampening oscillations.

16. A function that maps the load on a link as a function of the link's reported metric, keeping the overall network load constant.

17. To reduce the size of routing tables and the time taken to compute routes.

18. Because the Internet only allows address aggregation at the level of networks, and the number of networks is rapidly increasing because of exhaustion of the Class B space.

19. An external record tells a router which routers its border gateway can reach, and at what cost. A summary record tells a border router which routers inside some other border router's network it can reach, and at what cost.

20. To reduce the number of LSPs required to describe interconnections between routers on a broadcast LAN.

21. Choosing a set of trusted peers, enforcing constraints on which routes are advertised, checking for authorization of routing packets.

22. Destination AND subnet mask = my_address AND subnet mask.

23. To designate primary and backup routers for a LAN.

24. An association of senders and receivers tied together by a group identifier; packets from any sender are received by every receiver.

25. The source sets the IP time to live (TTL) to 1 hop and multicasts it to a provider group address. If no one replies, the source increases the TTL and tries again, repeating this step as many times as necessary.

26. Only one copy of a packet is ever sent on a link.

27. The lower 23 bits of the class D address form the lower 23 bits of the LAN multicast address (the higher bits are ignored by other host-adaptors on the LAN).

28. To discover whether any host on a LAN is interested in listening to a particular multicast group.

29. Forward packets from source S to all interfaces (other than the one on which the packet arrived), if the interface on which the packet arrived is the shortest-path interface to S.

30. Eliminate forwarding on links that lead to routers with no listening hosts.

31. Since there is no unique shortest-path for reverse-path forwarding, if tie-breaking rules are not used, either no packet will be forwarded, or packets will be unnecessarily forwarded on both interfaces.

32. Single point of failure (also traffic concentration).

33. Unless all routers use the same metrics in determining the shortest path, loops may form.

34. To allow easy access to billing and accounting. Also, the system design is simple, because the home MTSO acts as a central coordination point in dealing with all the cellular phones assigned to it.

35. From the periodic beacons broadcast by each base station.

36. To transfer a packet from the HAA to the COA without having intermediate routers send it right back to the HAA.

Chapter 11: Answers to exercises

11.1. The probability that the primary path, AB, is available is .95. To this, we must add the probability that a lightly loaded two-hop path exists. For no lightly loaded two-hop path to exist, all members of A's lightly loaded set must be simultaneously overloaded. This has probability 0.05^3. Thus, the probability that at least one of them is not overloaded is $1 - 0.05^3$. Thus, the overall probability of finding a lightly loaded path is $0.95 + 0.05 * (1 - 0.05^3) = 0.99999375$. This shows that with RTNR, even if individual trunks have a 5% blocking probability, the rich topology dramatically lowers the overall blocking probability.

11.4. D's path vector is ($\langle A, 2, D\text{-}B\text{-}A \rangle$, $\langle B, 1, D\text{-}B \rangle$, $\langle C, 2, D\text{-}B\text{-}C \rangle$, $\langle D, 0, - \rangle$). This allows D to determine the entire path to A, B, and C. If BA goes down, when B receives D's path vector, it sees that D's path to A is through B, so it will not use D to reach A. When BA goes down, B reports an infinite cost to C, which realizes that AC is a shorter path. When B receives a path vector from C with the AC cost of 4, it realizes it has a nonlooping path through C to reach A with cost 5. It therefore starts routing to A through C.

11.6. At A, from F's table entry, A knows that the last router on the path is E. From E's entry, it knows that the last router is D. From D's entry, it knows that D is directly connected. Therefore, the path is A–D–E–F. Since F is reached through E, if the shortest path to E is through B, so must the shortest path to F be.

11.7. (a) The sequence number spans from -4086 to $+4095$, so it requires 13 bits. (b,c) The first packet's sequence number is near the end of the circular space. The second packet is an old duplicate and should be ignored. The third packet's sequence number wraps around to 3 (intermediate packets are presumably lost). The fourth packet has the unique smallest sequence number, indicating that the router rebooted. So, it replaces the LSP with sequence number 3. The fifth packet replaces the packet with sequence number -4096, since it is larger than -4096 and in the linear part of the space. The last packet indicates that the router rebooted again and went back to the start of the sequence space. The router receiving these packets should inform the rebooting router, if it is a neighbor, to update its sequence number to 4 both times it receives the packet with sequence number -4096.

11.10. See Figure on page 637.

11.12. $\langle 6.1.*, 2 \rangle$, $\langle 6.2.*, 3 \rangle$, $\langle 6.3.*, 1 \rangle$, $\langle 6.4.*, 2 \rangle$.

11.13. First, we know that every endpoint in a network uses the same subnet mask. Now, either the destination D is in the same network, or it is not. If it is, then it has the same subnet mask as the source S, and the test works. If D is not in the same network, it may have a different-length subnet mask. Suppose the D's subnet mask is longer, which means D's network number has more bits. D's network number masked with S's subnet mask *must* differ from the S's network number, because S's network owns every address that has S's network number as a prefix.

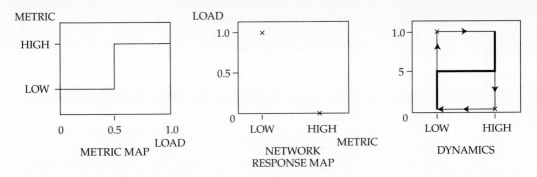

Figure for the solution to Exercise 11.10. The metric map is obvious. The network response map has only two points, since the load varies discontinuously with the metric. The resulting oscillation is shown in the routing dynamics.

Thus, the test with S's subnet mask will succeed. The last case is when D is in a different network, and D's network mask is shorter. Arguing as before, we see that D's network number cannot be a prefix for S's network number. Therefore, if we use S's (longer) subnet mask, we will certainly detect that D is remote.

11.16. The sender sends packets with sequence numbers. If a receiver detects a skipped sequence number, it sets a timer to send a nack. If no one else sends a nack before the timer expires, the nack is multicast to everyone. The sender re-multicasts the packet, and receivers who already got the packet discard the duplicate. With properly chosen timers, only one of the recipients sends a nack, and, in the common case, no acks are needed. This technique is used in the Internet's *wb* whiteboard tool.

11.17. (a) With point-to-multipoint, a router needs to keep a list of outgoing interface *per source,* since the point-to-multipoint tree is identified only by a source. With multipoint-to-multipoint, the router keeps only one such list *per group.* (b) With multipoint-to-multipoint, the sender simply sends to the group address. With point-to-multipoint, the sender has to establish a multicast tree to all the existing members before it can send anything.

11.18. (a) 100,000 bytes/s. (b) 60 Mbytes. (c) 12,000. (d) 2.4 s. (e) 480 times the interarrival time! (f) Gain in space = 500/10 = 50. Gain in time = 2.4 s/(200 + 12,000 * 2) μs = 99.17. (g) The packet is newer (should be flooded) if its sequence number is greater than the last sequence number seen on that group. (h) Senders must make sure that they use consecutive sequence numbers: impossible in practice.

11.19. A host that has pruned the source and wants to rejoin will never be able to do so.

11.21. Forwarding requests must be authenticated using a shared secret between the HAA and the MH. If the MH-to-HAA path can be tapped (for example, on the air) then MH should use a challenge–response protocol to authenticate the MH.

Chapter 12: Answers to review questions

1. Bit errors cause a bit to flip from a "1" to a "0" or vice versa. Packet errors can be due to packet loss, damage, duplication, or reordering.
2. It is the ratio of signal power to noise power.
3. To allow sufficient 0–1 transitions so that the phase-locked loop at the receiver can extract the transmission clock.
4. Switching from one physical transmission facility to another due to errors on the transmission line.
5. It is a code where $n-k$ bits of redundancy are added to a block of k bits of data to create an n-bit codeword.
6. An even parity bit makes the total number of "1" bits in a codeword even, and odd parity bit makes the total number odd.
7. No.
8. The smallest number of bit inversions necessary to transform one codeword to the other.
9. It is the code that has the smallest amount of redundancy in order to correct one bit error.
10. The set of positions of the errored parity bits in the codeword that point to the errored bit in the codeword.
11. In an interleaved code, the transmitter interleaves bits from several codewords on the transmission line.
12. $x^7 + x^6 + x^4 + x^3 + x + 1$.
13. It detects losses, duplication, and reordering.
14. Prevents acceptor from accepting delayed SYNs.
15. The receiver sends a nack to a sender when it suspects that a packet has been lost. During congestion, nacks can add to the load, since congestion causes bursts of packet losses.
16. Retransmit the entire outstanding window on detection of a loss.
17. Timeouts do not give sufficient information about the state of the system. The timed out packet could be delayed or lost, or its ack could be lost, even though it was successfully received.
18. Sending redundant packets to compensate for packet loss.

Chapter 12: Answers to exercises

12.1. SNR(dB) = $10 \log 5 * 5/0.3 * 0.3 = 24.4$ dB.
12.2. Since this polynomial has two terms and depth 24, there will be two bit errors spaced 24 bits apart.
12.4. Not always. For example, a rectangular cannot distinguish between bit errors in the (0,0), (1,0), and (0,1) positions and a single bit error in the (1,1) position.
12.6. A 31-bit perfect codeword must have 5 redundant bits (since $2^5 = 31 + 1$), so that the percent redundancy is $5/31 * 100 = 16.12\%$.

12.8. 16–31 and 48–63.

12.10. $5 * 2 = 10$.

12.12. The possible trajectories are 01–10–00–01, penalty 2; 01–10–00–00, penalty 5; 01–10–01–10, penalty 2; 01–10–01–11, penalty 3; 01–11–10–00, penalty 7; 01–11–10–01, penalty 6; 01–11–11–10, penalty 6; 01–11–11–11, penalty 5.

12.13. Since x frames will be served in time $(xlt + (x - xl)/T)$, the normalized through-put is $1/(1 - 1 + ltT)$. Notice that as the line speed (T) increases, the effective throughput decreases!

12.15. Yes, because the ESN field at the receiver allows it to discard delayed termination messages.

12.17. The bounds, for $w = 10, 100$ are 0.990, 0.499. As the window grows, go-back-n performs worse.

12.18. The acks are (11,11), (12,12), (12,14), (12,15), (15,13), (15,17). On receiving (12,14), the sender retransmits 13, and on receiving (15,17), it retransmits 16. There are no other retransmissions.

Chapter 13: Answers to review questions

1. The rate of the slowest server.

2. To send at a rate so that the bottleneck server's buffers neither overflow nor underflow.

3. Open-loop, closed-loop, and hybrid.

4. It bounds the worst-case traffic from a source. Contract, regulation, and policing.

5. A regulator is at the source and ensures that the source traffic meets its descriptor. A policer is at the network access point and performs the same function. The difference is that a regulator typically buffers excess traffic, whereas a policer typically drops it.

6. A regulator that ensures that the source rate measured over adjacent time windows is bounded.

7. A linear bounded arrival process; a process whose data rate is constrained by a linear function of t for every interval of time t.

8. The service rate and the sum of the token and data buffers.

9. It is the curve that represents the set of minimal equivalent leaky-bucket descriptors for a source. The best choice for a descriptor is at the knee, if that exists, and is uniquely defined.

10. The bottleneck service rate and, optionally, the current buffer occupancy of a source at the bottleneck server. In the DECbit scheme, only a single bit is carried, and this is set if the queue is overloaded.

11. Yes. Adjacent switches send on and off signals as and when their queues are empty or full.

12. When the bandwidth–delay product is much larger than one packet.

13. It must be exactly the product of the round-trip propagation delay and the bottleneck service rate, where both these quantities are assumed to be fixed.

14. When the mean aggregate queue length is more than 1, and on those sources whose demand exceeds their fair share.

15. If the current window size is w, and the previous window size is p, the source waits to receive $w + p$ acks, and if more than 50% of the bits have been set on the previous w packets, it reduces its window by a factor of 0.875.

16. It starts when a queue goes from idle to busy, and ends the next time this transition occurs.

17. An allocation such every source gets no more than its demand, and all sources whose demand is not met get an equal share of the resource.

18. Unfairness to sources who have a small demand but still have bits set, and to sources with longer RTTs.

19. The window size at which the increase rate changes from exponential increase to linear increase.

20. To 1. It reduces the window to half its previous value on a fast retransmission.

21. As the product of RTT and (expected_throughput − actual_throughput), where these quantities are measured over an entire RTT.

22. These are the Initial Cell Rate and the Minimum Cell Rate.

23. It is a Resource Management cell, and it carries explicit rate information from the bottleneck back to the source.

24. As the inverse of the inter-ack spacing at the source.

25. The target number of packets that the source would like to maintain in the bottleneck buffers.

26. The count of forwarded packets and the allocated buffer at the downstream network element.

27. Because a source will keep sending packets even if the rate-control information is delayed or lost.

28. Deciding what fraction of the bottleneck bandwidth can be reserved, and what fraction must be contended for.

29. Even in the worst case, a source is guaranteed some minimum resources.

Chapter 13: Answers to exercises

13.1. The total delay is $2 * (2 * 100^{-6}$ (2 ethernets) $+ 2 * 1^{-3}$ (2 routers) $+ 30^{-3}$ (link)) $=$ 64.4 ms, which is the delay in the reduced equivalent model. The bottleneck bandwidth is 1.5 Mbps, which is the service rate of the server in the reduced model.

13.3. The regulator accumulates one cell a second, so in 1 hour, it will add a queuing delay of 3600 cells. Two ways to eliminate this are: (a) choose a larger service rate, and (b) choose an LBAP descriptor with a burst size of two cells.

13.4. Consider a source that sends two cells back-to-back when it starts up, then one cell a second. If the starting window ends between the first two packets, then the source is bounded by one cell per second. If the starting window includes both the initial cells, the source is bounded by two cells per second.

13.6. If the packet arrives just before a token, it must wait for seven more tokens, which will take 7 s. If it arrives just after, it must wait 8 seconds.

13.7. The range is $[16*0.875, 16] = [14,16]$. The utilization is $w/16$ when the window is w. Thus, the mean utilization is $\frac{1}{3}$ (14/16 + 15/16 + 1) = 93.75%.

13.10. The source estimates the number of packets in the bottleneck as 20 pkts − 10 pkts/s ∗ 1 s = 10 pkts. Since the setpoint is 5, the transmission rate is 1.0 pkts/s − (10 − 5) pkts/10 s = 0.5 pkts/s. If 100 packets are outstanding, the transmission rate will be −8.5 pkts/s, which is impossible. The source instead idles for 9 s, so that at the end of this time, the setpoint is reached.

13.11. The largest number is 100 − 60 = 40. Plugging in the values into Equation 13.20, we get the new allocation to be (100/2 − 20 − 10) ∗ 0.2 = 4.

Chapter 14: Answers to review questions

1. Service diversity and efficiency.
2. The degree of user satisfaction from goods or services.
3. Users pay according to the disutility they cause other users.
4. Constant-bit-rate and variable-bit-rate.
5. Sensitivity to delay bound violation.
6. Less than one RTT, multiple RTTs, session, day, weeks, or longer.
7. Efficiency for signaling load; risk of not getting an increase when asked for.
8. To allow the signaling application to recover from lost messages.
9. To allow heterogeneous receivers, be scalable, and prevent interruption of service.
10. When the reservation exceeds the reservation for that group on an upstream link.
11. Sources are bursty, and the admission control algorithm has to determine the probability of receiving simultaneous bursts.
12. No, because data traffic is very bursty, and peak-rate allocation will lead to highly underutilized links.
13. Charging more when the network demand is higher.
14. A unit to measure call load. One erlang equals an average of one call present in the system at all times.
15. It is better to build a larger trunk.
16. Assume infinite sources and use the Erlang-B formula.

Chapter 14: Answers to exercises

14.2. The queue can build up at most at 10 − 8 = 2 Mbps. Thus, over 10 ms, it can grow at most 2500 bytes, which is also the buffer size required for zero loss.

14.3. The burst size is 4.5 Mbps $*$ 10 = 45 Mbits = 5.625 Mbytes. If the drain rate is 1.8 Mbps, then the effective rate at which the regulator buffer builds up is 2.7 Mbps. Over 10 s, the buffer would become 3.375 Mbytes. If the buffer is of size 0, then the token bucket must be 3.375 Mbytes. With a 64-Kbyte buffer, the bucket must be 3.311 Mbytes. With a 4-Mbps drain rate, the effective buffer length at the end of the burst is 5 Mbits = 625 Kbytes. With no buffer, the token bucket must be 625 Kbytes. With a 64-Kbyte buffer, we need 561 bytes.

14.6. The probability that a source is on is $\frac{2}{3}$. The probability that three sources are on is $4!/(3! * 1!) (1/3)^3 (\frac{2}{3})^1 = 0.099$. The probability that all four are on is $(\frac{1}{3})^4 = 0.012$. Thus, if the link has capacity 3 Mbps, the probability of overflow is P(3 on) + P (4 on) = 0.11.

14.7. We have P = 4.5 Mbps, m = 1.5 Mbps, and C = 45 Mbps. Plugging into Equation 14.2, we get e = 7.8 Mbps. Note that this is actually larger than the source's peak rate! When C = 622 Mbps, e = 2.23 Mbps, which is more reasonable. Thus, the heuristic is useful only with fairly large link capacities.

14.9. We get $\gamma = 2.172 * 10^{13}$, $\alpha = 4.60$, $\sigma = 2.29 * 10^6$. Thus, C $\cong$ P = 4.5 Mbps. This gives e = min (12.03 Mbps, 4.5 Mbps) = 4.5 Mbps. Thus, with a single source, the equivalent bandwidth is the peak rate.

14.11. The call arrival rate is 3 and the holding time is 3.5, so the load is 3 $*$ 3.5 = 10.5 erlangs.

14.13. We have M = 30 and N = 15. Also, $\rho = \frac{1}{3}$. Let us guess B = 0.01. Then, $\lambda'm$ = 0.490. From Equation 14.7, this gives us B = 0.016. Replacing this in Equation 14.9, we get $\lambda'm$ = 0.44. We plug this into Equation 14.10 to get B = 0.0089. Iterating in this fashion (it is very useful to have a spreadsheet handy), we get convergence for $\lambda'm$ = 0.4955 and B = 0.0178. Comparing with Exercise 14.12, we see that the infinite-source assumption gives us, for the same load, a blocking probability estimate of 0.047, which is 2.6 times too high.

Chapter 15: Answers to review questions

1. Data-plane protocols move data, but control-plane protocols control the network, for example, to set up and tear down connections.
2. The set of multiplexed speeds allowed in the telephone network.
3. A system where each component has nearly the same clock speed.
4. The process of combining bits from input streams of slightly different rates by adding overhead bits in the multiplexed output. A telephone networks needs to do this because any real network is plesiochronous.
5. Cell headers allow us to easily distinguish between bits from each tributary without elaborate justification strategies.
6. Because the network is synchronous, and the higher levels do not need additional overhead bits.
7. Eight rows and 80 columns; 8 rows and 240 columns.

8. The part of the SONET frame that contains data.
9. To allow a multiplexor to find the start of the envelope even after justification.
10. The destination point code is used to route the packet to its destination. The origin point code allows the destination to determine the originator of the packet.
11. Addressing and packet forwarding.
12. 60 bytes.
13. The remaining fragments are eventually discarded by the destination.
14. The source sends successively smaller packets with the "don't fragment" flag set, repeating until it does not get an error.
15. The source sends packets with successively larger TTLs, starting from 1, determining the route from the ICMP error messages.
16. 9.
17. No.
18. To distinguish between applications sharing access to a single TCP implementation.
19. If the sender and receiver negotiate to scale windows during the three-way handshake, the window size field in subsequent packets is interpreted as the higher-order bits of a longer window-size field.
20. To periodically check if the receiver can accept more bytes after the sender receives a zero-size window in an acknowledgment.
21. By prepending the name with the name of the name space.
22. Deliver some data in the payload of the packet from the client to the server.
23. A set of virtual circuits that share the same higher-order bits and flow along the same path.
24. The protocol used to choose a VCI for signaling.
25. It sets the bit on packets that fail the policing test. The network preferentially drops packets with the CLP bit set.
26. 1.
27. Constant-bit-rate voice calls.
28. To match the header and trailer of an AAL3/4 frame.
29. To distinguish between multiple senders who share the same AAL3/4 VCI.
30. Because the end-of-frame bit is logically at the AAL level, but is carried in the ATM header.
31. No overhead per cell.
32. To align the trailer with the end of the last cell in the AAL5 frame.
33. It either gets an USTAT from the receiver, or detects a hole in the STAT reply to its POLL.
34. The interval between polls.
35. Through a router attached to both LISs.
36. To translate from an IP multicast address to a set of ATM NSAPs reached by that multicast address.

37. Through a broadcast server that has a multicast VC to every host.
38. To take data in Ethernet frames and put them on an ATM network, and vice versa.

Chapter 16: Answers to review questions

1. Its structure, and the cost of operations such as memory access and interrupt processing in the operating system.
2. Monolithic in kernel space, monolithic in user space, and per-process in user space.
3. Single-context, tasks, and upcalls.
4. Hard to write and debug kernel code. Hard to customize stack per-application.
5. An extra context switch per read and write.
6. To manage access to a network device on behalf of an application.
7. No, because there are no preemption points.
8. Schedule access to tasks, where each task carries out a set of operations corresponding to one layer on one packet.
9. To perform protocol processing associated with all the layers for a single packet.
10. Upper-layer read and write, lower-layer read and write, and timeout.

Index